The Dynamic Dominion

Realignment and the Rise of Virginia's Republican Party Since 1945

Frank B. Atkinson

GEORGE MASON UNIVERSITY PRESS
FAIRFAX, VIRGINIA

Distributed by arrangement with
National Book Network

4720 Boston Way
Lanham, MD 20706

3 Henrietta Street
London WC2E 8LU England

Library of Congress Cataloging-in-Publication Data
Atkinson, Frank B.
The Dynamic Dominion : Realignment and the
Rise of Virginia's Republican Party since 1945
/ Frank B. Atkinson.
p. cm.
Includes bibliographical references and index.
1. Virginia—Politics and government—1951-
2. Republican Party (Va.)—History—20th century.
3. Virginia—Politics and government—20th century.
I. Title.
F231.A88   1991
324.275504—dc20   91-30509 CIP

ISBN 0-913969-39-7 (cloth : alk. paper)

 The paper used in this publication meets the minimum requirements of
American National Standard for Information Sciences—Permanence
of Paper for Printed Library Materials, ANSI Z39.48–1984.

*This book is dedicated
to the memory of my parents,*

*PAUL TULANE ATKINSON, JR.
1920 – 1988*

and

*MARGARET WHITTLE ATKINSON
1926 – 1978,*

*who through their faith, love, and example
taught me all of the truly important things.*

Acknowledgements

A book should not take twelve years to write—at least, not this one. But, since political perspectives tend to mellow with age, perhaps the lengthy effort to bring this project to fruition will have some incidental benefits. Certainly the project's longevity created opportunities for contributions by many persons other than the author, and to each of those persons I owe much. Though there is the inevitable risk of omission, I would be remiss if I did not attempt in these pages to identify the many who have provided assistance and encouragement to me in the course of work spanning more than a decade.

When, in 1979, I initially undertook to chronicle Virginia's partisan realignment and to describe the emergence of the Republican Party as a competitive force in the state, my immediate purpose was to fulfill academic requirements as an undergraduate student with a political science major at the University of Richmond. My "independent" study was supervised by two excellent and accomplished professors there—Thomas R. Morris and John T. Whelan—and by a third scholar of Virginia politics, the inimitable Professor Larry J. Sabato of the University of Virginia, who was then visiting the Richmond campus weekly to teach his perennially popular "Campaigns and Elections" course. Each of them critiqued my original manuscript, assigned it a mark, and sent me on my way. Their attention could have ceased there, but did not. Rather, to these three teachers, advisers, and friends goes much of the responsibility for the eventual publication of this book. All three encouraged me to continue my work on the project with an eye toward eventual publication. And all three provided me with invaluable advice, insights, and other assistance at every juncture thereafter. I am greatly indebted to each of them.

Also in this category of scholarly mentors is J. Harvie Wilkinson III, under whom I studied at the University of Virginia School of Law, and with whom I enjoyed a very satisfying professional association in the Department of Justice during the Reagan administration. Well before embarking upon and achieving distinction in his current pursuit as a federal appeals court jurist, Jay Wilkinson left his indelible mark on Virginia politics as the author of *Harry Byrd and the Changing Face of Virginia Politics, 1945-1966* (University Press of Virginia, 1968). Indeed, any serious student of modern Virginia politics will inevitably lean heavily on Wilkinson's superb work, as I have done in these pages. When that book was published in 1968, it was the most detailed overview of Virginia politics in many years. This book represents the first attempt since then to provide a similarly comprehensive description of the state's postwar political evolution. To the extent this attempt succeeds, Jay Wilkinson deserves a significant measure of the credit. Not only did his work provide an indispensable foundation, but his example and encouragement motivated me to see the project through to completion despite the frequent pull of competing professional and political obligations.

Assistance with an undertaking of this magnitude comes in many forms, of course. And, with the notable exception of my immediate family, no one has contributed more in the form of forbearance than two professional colleagues whom I hold in exceedingly high esteem: Robert H. Patterson, Jr., and Anne Marie Whittemore. The McGuire Woods Battle & Boothe law firm and various of its partners and employees have assisted my efforts in myriad ways, but I am especially indebted to Bob Patterson and Anne Whittemore of that firm, both for their selfless indulgence of my occasional detours from the practice of law, and for their unflagging support of this particular endeavor. Another McGuire Woods colleague and friend, Richard Cullen, also has my appreciation for lending his time and talents to this project in a variety of ways.

The list of persons who have contributed materially to this undertaking is long. But among these, the early and continuous support provided by Richard, Jas, and Marc Short of Virginia Beach has been especially important. The Shorts' enthusiasm for this project stemmed chiefly from their own fervent commitment to the governmental principles espoused by some of the central figures in this book, but I am grateful for the confidence they placed in me as the story teller. I am also particularly appreciative of the assistance provided at key junctures by Lawrence Lewis, Jr., George N. McMath, J. Marshall Coleman, Robert B. Atkinson, M. Boyd Marcus, Jr., Elizabeth J. Davis, and Thomas J. Bliley, Jr.

Through the years, an unusually large number of persons reviewed drafts or portions of drafts of the manuscript that has become this book. Of those who examined the completed manuscript, none was more painstaking nor more helpful than David Bovenizer, a friend and dedicated scholar who lent both his historical insight and his enormous editorial talents to the improvement of this work. James Latimer, who was for many years the chief political reporter for the *Richmond Times-Dispatch*, and who continues to make major contributions to the literature on Virginia politics, reviewed more than one draft and provided numerous invaluable suggestions. I am grateful to those gentlemen for their assistance, and also for the time, effort, and contributions of the following readers: Henry N. Butler, John G. Colligan, Jr., Kirk Cox, Todd Culbertson, Wyatt B. Durrette, Jr., Margie R. Fisher, R. Jefferson Garnett, Robert Holland, Donald C. Harrison, John T. ("Til") Hazel, Jr., Donald W. Huffman, William H. Hurd, Steven Johnson, Paul J. Larkin, Robert Lauterberg, Ross Mackenzie, James McClellan, Hugh Mulligan, David W. Robertson, Jeff E. Schapiro, Jeffrey L. Schlagenhauf, W. Roy Smith, Todd A. Stottlemyer, and Michael E. Thomas.

This book would not have been possible without clerical and technical assistance rendered by a number of highly skilled and exceedingly patient persons, who variously deciphered drafts, transcribed interviews, made computers work, provided proofreading and indexing services, and performed other essential tasks. To Helen Whitley, Shirley Mays, Ann Peters, Margie Mullen, Margaret W. A. Rosen, Patricia J. Heflebower, Mary Shea

Sutherland, Beverly Dean, Kathryn R. Foy, Nancy Arnett, Debbie Stikes, and Deborah Thornton, I extend my heartfelt thanks. I also wish to acknowledge the professional assistance provided by several colleagues—Mary Dalton Baril, John W. Burke, III, and Robert C. Carlson. Finally, Mark Carroll, James Fisher, and Isabelle Gibb of the George Mason University Press were a delight to work with throughout the process of preparing this manuscript for publication.

More than 100 persons consented to be interviewed for this book—some provided multiple interviews—and, of these, several merit special mention. Though the untimely death of Richard D. Obenshain in 1978 deprived me of his unique insights during the course of my study, I was assisted immensely by his widow, Helen, who spent numerous hours recalling for me the details of the Obenshains' political endeavors. Similarly, Senator Harry F. Byrd, Jr., shared recollections of his own political experiences and those of his larger-than-life father. Several federal judges took time from their hectic schedules to reminisce about their earlier political days, and two, since deceased, provided especially entertaining and illuminating commentary: Ted Dalton and Dortch Warriner. Former Governors Mills Godwin, Linwood Holton, and the late John Dalton each indulged the imposition of multiple interview sessions, with each session consuming a considerable amount of time. While serving as governor, Chuck Robb took several hours from his demanding schedule to share his opinions and observations, as did Senator John Warner. A pivotal figure in Virginia politics during the 1960s and 1970s, Henry Howell, also provided lengthy, enlightening, and typically colorful commentary. To them and the many others whose recollections and insights have enriched this book, I am most appreciative.

Two persons who have studied the history of the Virginia Republican Party deserve special recognition for their indirect but highly important contributions to this book. First, George L. Vogt's 1978 dissertation at the University of Virginia, entitled *The Development of Virginia's Republican Party*, contains a wealth of information, particularly on the lean, early years of the Virginia GOP. Those disappointed by this book's failure to treat in greater depth the state GOP's development from the aftermath of Reconstruction through 1945 should turn to Vogt's meticulously researched and well-written work. Second, the historical research conducted by Deborah Wood under the auspices of the Republican Party of Virginia in 1979-1980 included a series of very informative interviews that supplemented my own. In addition, my research was facilitated throughout the 1980s by cooperation from the leadership and archive staff of the Republican Party of Virginia.

There are, of course, many others—too numerous to mention by name—who have contributed in direct and indirect ways to my understanding of the substantive material that comprises this book. As an observer of and participant in many of the events described herein, at least since the mid-1970s, I have come to understand something of the inner workings of

Virginia politics, and much of Parts Five, Six, and Seven of this book is drawn from my experiences and observations. As a result, there are many whose contributions to this book can never be reconstructed, let alone recorded in this space. However, two individuals were instrumental in providing opportunities for me to learn about Virginia politics first-hand at an unusually early age, and it is difficult to imagine how I might have come to write this book without those opportunities. To these two dedicated public servants—the late Congressman J. Kenneth Robinson of Frederick County and the late Senator Paul W. Manns of Bowling Green—I wish to pay tribute.

Finally, but most important, is a public expression of gratitude to my wonderfully supportive family. This book is dedicated to the memory of the two people who are most responsible for whatever contribution it may ultimately represent—my devoted parents. For an appreciation of history and a love of learning, I have also had the benefit during my lifetime of two extraordinary examples in my grandmother, Esther Thomas Atkinson, and my great uncle, the late Robert L. Whittle. Each of my siblings, Paul T. Atkinson, III, Margaret W. A. Rosen, and Robert B. Atkinson, has taken a personal interest in this project and has assisted it in significant and tangible ways. Young sons Robert and Paul each supplied inspiration, albeit obliviously. Most of all, there is my wife, Diane, without whose steadfast support, continual sacrifice, and uplifting spirit this book would have remained an elusive hope.

Frank B. Atkinson
Hanover, Virginia
April 9, 1991

Table of Contents

"The greatness of this party, the reason we've been stacked here to the rafters with this enthusiasm, is because of our commitment to the great, historic, fundamental principles of Virginia. Thousands of Virginians are here today because of that commitment of our party. And thousands and thousands more are waiting around the state of Virginia for this campaign to take to them the message of the principles and the strengths that the Republican Party offers to this state, and also offers for constructive leadership to the United States of America."

Richard D. Obenshain
Accepting the U.S. Senate Nomination
Virginia Republican Convention
June 3, 1978

Introduction
A Heritage of Leadership

When Dick Obenshain gazed out across the sea of delegates who had just nominated him as the Republican candidate for the United States Senate, it must have been a very proud moment. There they were—nearly 9,000 Virginians—assembled for the 1978 Republican state convention, the largest political convention in the history of the nation, perhaps the world. In his short lifetime, the Republican Party of Virginia had abandoned the proverbial telephone booth as its meeting place and had occupied Richmond's mammoth coliseum, where its enthusiastic faithful had been stacked to the rafters. Virtually dormant for more than a half-century, the GOP in three decades had become the seemingly dominant force in Virginia politics. It had been an amazing feat, and one for which Obenshain was due no small amount of credit.

A dozen years before that 1978 apogee, scarcely a person could have imagined it. And, a dozen years thereafter, it seemed almost as implausible again. The surging wave of Republicanism crashed onto the Virginia political beaches in 1980 as Ronald Reagan was arriving in Washington, and then receded, leaving in its wake a more-or-less level partisan landscape. Democrats rebounded during the 1980s in statewide races; Republicans simultaneously made significant strides toward competitiveness at the state legislative and local levels; and, after nearly a half-century of transition and tumult, Virginia politics settled into something resembling routine.

This is the story of the rise of the Republican Party as a competitive force in Virginia politics. It is the story of the Commonwealth's evolution from a one-party Democratic state—a conservative Camelot under the deft domination of Harry F. Byrd, Sr.—to a two-party competitive system under no party's and no person's thumb. Central in this drama is the sweeping political realignment that brought the Virginia parties largely into accord philosophically with their counterparts at the national level. Though this transformation was dramatic, it nevertheless was incomplete. Hence, this book also describes the failure of Virginia's Republicans and conservative independents to convert their fleeting electoral successes into a dominant, durable political organization capable of staving off a Democratic resurgence. In all of these respects, this story is part of a larger regional and national saga: the long postbellum march from Southern ostracism to Southern prominence in American politics. And, it is part of a much grander Virginia story: the remarkable, four-century-old experiment in enlightened self-governance that is the Old Dominion.

Surrounded by so many monuments to history as to make the extraordinary seem commonplace, Virginians need to be reminded occasionally that no state in the nation has a heritage of political leadership like theirs. The gifted generation—the Virginia-born freedom fighters and founding fathers of the late eighteenth century—took the ideas of independence and constitutional self-rule and forged a free nation. When North and South collided in the convulsion of a horrendous civil war, Virginians cast their lot with the Confederacy and proceeded to lead her through battle. Recovered eventually from the ravages of war and reconstruction, the politically cohesive South came to dominate the Congress in the twentieth century, and Virginia's Senator Byrd and his venerable lieutenants—at one point, with a combined congressional seniority among them of more than a century—chaired the key committees. From there, the Virginians endeavored with mixed success to impede developments they perceived—sometimes rightly, sometimes not—as detrimental to the national interest: the creation of a federal welfare state, the civil rights movement, the accumulation of a large federal debt, and the growth of central government power at the expense of state prerogatives. More recently, Virginia has been a political trend-setter for the nation. The conservative Virginia Republican successes of the 1970s presaged the Reagan Revolution, and the resurgence by moderate Virginia Democrats in the 1980s has provided the national Democratic Party with a formula for possible renewal.

What is it about Virginia? When Guy Friddell, one of the Commonwealth's most thoughtful sons, first posed that rhetorical question in 1966 and then set about supplying the answer in a delightful book,[1] the post-Second World War period of political dynamism in the Commonwealth was already well underway. Though many through the years had sensed Virginia's uniqueness, few were able to put it into words. Virginia was of the Mother Country, of the new Nation, of the old South. But, more than any of these, Virginia was of itself. It was a distinctive culture; a state of mind; a set of values and principles; a sense of the permanent coexisting often uneasily with the present, and casting a hopeful yet wary eye upon the future. In measuring the importance of things, Virginians tended to look inward rather than to the opinions of others— though some undiscerning critics saw in this introspection little more than a preoccupation with glories long past. Possessing all the frailties and deficiencies that are the unhappy lot of human kind, Virginia was at her best when she was looking inward, or backward, to remind herself of the important things—the enduring principles—so as to have a surer guide through the perils and opportunities of the moment.

The essential question left after the 45 years of political transition chronicled in this book is still Friddell's, but with this twist: How much of Virginia's fundamental character remains after these years of rapid change? The reader will find in these pages ample evidence of both constancy and change in Virginia politics. The parties have changed immensely; the dominant political philosophy, less so. The Commonwealth has been transformed socially and economically; the nature and extent of the cultural change is less apparent. After years of resistance to national trends, Virginia in recent years has found

---

[1]Guy Friddell, *What Is It About Virginia?* (Richmond: The Dietz Press, Inc., 1966).

itself in the national vanguard; yet, on whose terms this accommodation has been struck may be fairly debated. It is at least puzzling that, in a time when the names of Jefferson and Reagan are invoked with admiration and even reverence by freedom-seeking patriots abroad, and when tenets of personal liberty, free enterprise, limited government, freedom of conscience, and democratic self-rule are on the march in parts of the world long under the heel of a hostile ideology, Virginians seem more uncertain than ever about the proper application, and even the relevance, of these principles in their own political processes.

The immediate object of this book is to contribute to a better understanding of contemporary Virginia politics. The ultimate object is to enhance Virginians' appreciation of their political traditions and the values that undergird those traditions. As the reader walks through the minutiae of Virginia campaigns and elections found in these pages, it is to be hoped that he or she will bear in mind that politics is but a process, not an end in itself. Whether the process has been employed for good or ill can be judged only by reference to the policies and principles promoted through it. Who won and who lost are far less important than how and why, and electoral outcomes are insignificant except as they bear upon governmental performance. At the end of the day, what really matters is how well government serves the interests of the citizenry. And the only sure measure of that service is the proximity of governmental policy to the intersection of citizens' highest ideals and maximum freedom.

Part One

The Byrd Organization's Loosening Grip

1945 - 1953

Chapter 1

Harry Byrd's Virginia

"Of all of the American states, Virginia can lay claim to the most thorough control by an oligarchy. Political power has been closely held by a small group of leaders who, themselves and their predecessors, have subverted democratic institutions and deprived most Virginians of a voice in their government . . . . It is a political museum piece."[1]

V. O. Key, Jr., 1949

Election Day, November 6, 1945, no doubt was a day of great importance to many Virginians. These, after all, were exciting and promising times. With the tumultuous period of world war rapidly receding into the past, thousands of young men recently back from the battlefields of Europe and the Pacific were reassembling their lives. Families with loved ones lost in distant places could now take pride in the victory as well as the sacrifice, and move on. In Virginia, as elsewhere in the nation, young and old—but especially the young— brimmed with a new confidence and hope for the future. A great enemy had been vanquished, an evil menace removed, and if such a feat could be accomplished on a global scale, certainly major deeds could also be achieved by industrious individuals pursuing dreams of a better life at home in a free land.

So it was that most Virginians were occupied on election day in 1945, not with things political but with more personal and parochial matters long neglected. Of course, even without such interests, relatively few Virginians would have voted in the elections for governor, lieutenant governor, and attorney general in 1945. That was just their way. Between 1925 and 1945, the successful candidates in gubernatorial elections never needed more than 12 percent of the votes of Virginia's adult population to win elections. It was a phenomenon that surely would have puzzled the founders of the republic, particularly those who hailed from the Old Dominion and prided themselves on her unique contribution to American self-governance.

The reasons for the nonparticipation were not mysterious. Part of the explanation lay in Virginia's near perpetual state of electioneering, a consequence of the Commonwealth's practice of holding state elections in odd-numbered years rather than simultaneously with national elections in

---

[1] V.O. Key, Jr., *Southern Politics in State and Nation* (New York: Alfred A. Knopf, Inc., 1949), p. 19.

even-numbered years. With some election held every year, the novelty of political activity wore off quickly for most Virginians.

More pertinent in explaining voter apathy, however, was the predictability of election outcomes in Virginia. Without a viable state Republican Party, two-party competition was virtually nonexistent in the half-century before the Second World War. There was some competition, though seldom much suspense, within the Virginia Democratic Party as various mavericks and malcontents occasionally challenged the chosen candidate of the party leadership in primary elections. But Virginians usually knew who would win statewide elections before the polls opened, and they responded by investing their time in more productive pursuits.

At least as numerous as those who would not vote in Virginia were those who could not vote because state law—or those enforcing it—disqualified them. There were poll taxes, literacy tests, and frequent discriminatory application of registration procedures by local registrars. These measures had been in place since 1902, when a revised state constitution was promulgated for the explicit purpose of disfranchising black voters. The 1902 revisions caused black voter registration in the Commonwealth to plummet immediately by more than 86 percent, and it also provided a mechanism for the more gradual exclusion of Republicans and other white voters who refused to support the candidates of the dominant Democratic faction. With the assistance of these devices, the Democratic Party leadership in Virginia succeeded in restricting the size and controlling the general composition of the state's electorate, thereby ensuring one-party domination of the state's political processes.

As had been the case for two decades, the Democratic Party in Virginia in 1945 was governed, managed, and led by U.S. Senator Harry Flood Byrd. If Virginia was "a political museum piece,"[2] as V.O. Key, Jr., wrote in 1949, Senator Byrd was both sculptor and curator. So complete was his control and so pervasive his influence that observers seldom referred to the Democratic Party (or Virginia's government, for that matter) as anything other than the "Byrd organization," unless they employed the slightly more disparaging "Byrd machine" label. Staunchly conservative in his political views, steadfast in his devotion to Virginia, honest, seemingly tireless, always engaging and personable, Harry Byrd was respected and revered by Virginians like no other. His organization's domination of state politics was the result of several factors, including the restricted electorate, the organization's system for imposing discipline on its members, and Byrd's steady administrative hand. But it owed its preeminent position as much, perhaps, to the intense personal popularity and close philosophical compatibility that Harry Byrd enjoyed among a clear majority of the state's politically aware citizens.

Byrd was not the first leader of the dominant Democratic organization in Virginia. With the subsidence of Reconstruction-era turmoil, Senator Thomas

---

[2]Ibid.

Staples Martin emerged in the late nineteenth century as the Democratic chieftain, and until his death in 1919, the "Martin organization" controlled Virginia's government. Byrd became governor in 1925—at age 38, he was one of the youngest since Thomas Jefferson—and his successful tenure earned him broad popularity among Virginia's voters.

Byrd's gubernatorial administration was a decidedly progressive one by Virginia standards. The young and energetic chief executive tackled some of the state's most vexing problems, including its convoluted tax system, a confused and inefficient state government bureaucracy, pressing conservation needs, and state responsibility for road construction. Byrd's proudest achievements, however, were financial. During his administration, the state's $1.25 million deficit was replaced by a surplus twice that size, and Virginia embarked on a constitutionally mandated policy against state bonded indebtedness. For the young man from Winchester who had left high school at age 15 to rescue his father's debt-ridden weekly newspaper, there was but one way for Virginia to go, and that was to "pay as you go."

If Byrd was much admired by Virginia voters for his accomplishments as governor, he was doubly respected by political associates for his uncanny political skill. "[N]obody in the world ever loved politics like Harry loved politics," commented former Governor Colgate W. Darden, Jr. "He loved the organizing, loved working on it. . . . Nobody would do the work as he would. He had a powerful constitution. He'd work on it morning, noon and night."[3] When, in 1929, Byrd successfully backed John Garland Pollard to succeed him as governor against the wishes of influential U.S. Senator Claude Swanson, there was no longer any doubt about who was in charge of the Democratic organization in Virginia. Byrd went to the U.S. Senate in 1933, and from there for 32 years he ruled the powerful organization that bore his name.

Though the Byrd organization surpassed even some of the Northern big city political machines in terms of power and longevity, its structure was a loose one. Notwithstanding his progressive tenure as governor, Byrd's political philosophy was distinctly conservative, and it became even more so with the passage of years. Because he was in tune philosophically and culturally with the relatively small number of conservative-minded Virginians who comprised the state's electorate, Senator Byrd usually was able to lead by consensus. When, however, the senator made his wishes known in any of the discreet ways in which his orders were issued, those orders were followed. The general appearance of consensus within the organization was more than illusion, less than reality. As one historian has written, "The Word sometimes came down from Richmond—or Berryville (Byrd's home)—and it was heeded, but only because Richmond and Berryville spent a considerable amount of time and effort in finding out how the constituency in Gloucester

---

[3]Conversations with James Latimer, "Living History Makers," WCVE-TV, 1975.

Courthouse, Accomack, Amelia, Warrenton, and Strasburg felt about these things."[4]

The commonality of background and viewpoint among those active in the organization and their constituents allowed Byrd and his lieutenants to employ self-effacing descriptions of Virginia's political order, to shroud the organization in mystery, and sometimes even virtually to deny its existence. Probably the most famous of those descriptions was offered by one of the stalwart Byrd organization governors, John S. Battle:

> As for this so-called iniquitous [Byrd] machine, it is nothing more nor less than a loosely knit group of Virginians . . . who usually think alike, who are interested in the welfare of the Commonwealth, who are supremely interested in giving Virginia good government and good public servants, and they usually act together.[5]

In addition to the very real philosophical kinship among the organization adherents, however, those men "usually act[ed] together" because there was in place a formidable array of carrots and sticks designed to ensure fealty to the organization.

The organization's roots were in the courthouses, especially in the rural areas of the state, where it controlled the key constitutional offices in most counties. Circuit court judges elected by the General Assembly had broad authority to appoint persons to other important county posts. "The key to the Byrd organization," commented 1961 GOP gubernatorial nominee H. Clyde Pearson,

> was the circuit court judges, . . . because the only way a circuit court judge could be appointed was to have the proper support [in the Byrd-dominated legislature] in Richmond. The circuit court judges controlled all of the operation of the system on the local level—the electoral system, the welfare system, the school boards and educational system. The circuit judges ran the whole county through these various boards. [The judge] was the appointive power, and invariably that resulted in the appointment of those people who were friendly to the Byrd organization in that county. And if you were not a part of the Byrd organization in that county, you had no participation whatsoever. You could never get on the school board or the welfare board no matter how much competency or expertise you had in that field.[6]

Democrats, of course, vigorously defended the integrity and fairness of the state's judiciary. James Latimer, a veteran political reporter for the *Richmond Times-Dispatch*, offered this objective view: "Some circuit judges are in politics up to their ears, some only up to their navels, and others seem a bit detached.

[4]Louis D. Rubin, Jr., *Virginia: A History* (New York: W. W. Norton and Company, 1977), p. 211.

[5]*Richmond Times-Dispatch*, May 24, 1979, quoted in Peter R. Henriques, *John S. Battle and Virginia Politics: 1948–1953*, Unpublished Dissertation, University of Virginia, 1971, p. 82.

[6]H. Clyde Pearson interview, June 17, 1980.

None is venal or corrupt, and most are not overtly partisan. It cannot be avoided, however, that the judges are part of the political power structure."[7]

Another controversial aspect of the organization's power structure was the State Compensation Board, which was empowered to fix salaries and expenses for those locally elected courthouse officials whose responsibilities included certain state governmental functions. The board was chaired for many years by the man widely regarded as Senator Byrd's chief lieutenant, E. R. ("Ebbie") Combs. Organization critics commonly charged that the board set salaries in such a manner as to reward political obedience and punish misbehavior. It was seldom, however, that Combs had to use his power of the purse strings overtly. The mere existence of that power provided a strong impetus for local officials to toe the organization line.

The Byrd organization's various devices for perpetuating its hegemony guaranteed that Virginia, like the other Southern states, would remain dominated completely by the Democratic Party. But the similarities between Virginia and her Southern sisters more or less ended there. The absence of two-party competition in the other states of the South gave rise to multiple factions within the Democratic parties in those states, and the result was a volatile political climate in which particularly forceful or appealing personalities often carried the day. As V. O. Key, Jr., pointed out in his highly acclaimed 1949 study of Southern politics, the colorful and charismatic demagogues who frequently won election in the South under this system typically owed no allegiance to a political party and had no platform or program to implement. By contrast, Virginia's Byrd organization was clearly dominant and seldom was confronted with serious challenges from opposing factions. Key noted that the organization's "high command permits, and even survives because of a degree of 'democracy' within the organization on candidacies. . . . Loyal organization men, that is, men who have not differed with Senator Byrd, may compete for the support of local leaders for statewide office."[8] Only after the senator's preference was made known and his "nod" was given to the chosen candidate did the carefully circumscribed competition necessarily come to an end. Once the chosen candidate was elected, a measure of accountability—to Senator Byrd and the organization—was present that typically did not exist in other Southern states.

The system gave Virginia competent and steady, if often unimaginative, government. Key offered this insightful description of the type of leaders the organization normally would give the Commonwealth:

> The practical monopoly that the organization enjoys in public affairs brings into its fold most of the able men of political ambition, who must conform to the machine mold. . . . [T]o succeed in politics a person must enjoy a relatively high social status commanding at least a measure of

---

[7]James Latimer, *Virginia Politics 1950-1960*, Unpublished Manuscript, 1961, p. 115.
[8]Key, p. 23.

respect. In a word, politics in Virginia is reserved for those who can qualify as gentlemen. Rabble-rousing and Negro-baiting capacities, which in Georgia or Mississippi would be a great political asset, simply mark a person as one not to the manner born. . . .

In essence, Virginia is governed by a well-disciplined and ably managed oligarchy of not many more than a thousand professional politicians, which enjoys the enthusiastic and almost undivided support of the business community and of the well-to-do generally. . . .[9]

Reflecting Senator Byrd's priorities, the organization prided itself on frugality, and it maintained low levels of spending on public services for years. Frugality as a virtue was second only to honesty; Senator Byrd insisted upon complete integrity from those in his organization. "The slightest deviation from that," explained former Governor Albertis S. Harrison, Jr., "and you were on Senator Byrd's list."[10] It was no small matter that during a time when many state and local governments around the country were riddled with corruption, Virginia under Byrd rule was largely graft-free. The price Virginians paid for this kind of government was an exceedingly low level of political participation. Of the 11 states of the South, Virginia at mid-century ranked last in average turnout in gubernatorial primaries.

With the entrenched Democratic organization calling all the shots, there was little reason to be a Republican in Harry Byrd's Virginia. The primary election contests within the Democratic Party were tantamount to election.[11] One wishing to have a voice in the selection of Virginia's leaders, to the extent that was possible, voted in the Democratic primary. The November election was, in the words of one prominent political reporter, only a "constitutional formality."[12] For ambitious young men the path to political as well as professional success was marked clearly. "The officeholders were Democrats," explained reporter Melville "Buster" Carico, "and it was said that any young lawyer who wanted to amount to anything would go into the Democratic Party, [especially] if he wanted to be a judge."[13] Locally, the Byrd organization was less like a political party than a social club to which all the right people belonged. As *The Washington Post* once observed, "The young lawyer knows that the road to political success begins not on the hustings but at the circuit court judge's Christmas party and he is apt to do nothing disloyal enough to endanger his invitation. . . . Acceptance into local Organization cliques always

---

[9]Ibid., p. 26.

[10]J. Harvie Wilkinson III, *Harry Byrd and the Changing Face of Virginia Politics, 1945–1966* (Charlottesville: The University Press of Virginia, 1968), p. 30. Wilkinson also was a law professor, editorial page editor of *The Virginian-Pilot,* GOP congressional candidate, and Justice Department official during the Reagan administration. In 1983, he became a federal appeals judge.

[11]See Larry J. Sabato, *The Democratic Party Primary in Virginia: Tantamount to Election No Longer* (Charlottesville: The University Press of Virginia, 1977).

[12]Melville Carico interview, June 16, 1980.

[13]Ibid.

carried a measure of social as well as political approval and a community's social elite in many cases was indistinguishable from its political leadership."[14]

If personal ambition pulled young Virginians toward the Democratic Party, political conviction did little to stem the tide. Those of a conservative bent seldom found anything objectionable in the Byrd organization's tending of state affairs, and, though many Virginians harbored grave doubts about the wisdom of Franklin Roosevelt's New Deal as America neared mid-century, their conservative views on national issues were shared and expressed in Washington by Senator Byrd. Moreover, the Republican Party had considerable baggage unattractive to tradition-conscious, conservative Virginians. It was the party of Reconstruction, Radicalism, black rule, corruption and big business—images the organization stalwarts seldom missed an opportunity to emphasize. At the other end of the spectrum, those with a more liberal perspective discovered philosophical kinsmen, though relatively few in number, within the Democratic Party's anti-organization faction. Though they occasionally found themselves in agreement with some Republicans on some state issues, liberals focused their efforts on the Democratic primaries where they had at least a remote prospect of success.

Throughout most of Virginia, there simply were no people who called themselves "Republicans." In 1946, young Dortch Warriner of Brunswick County went to Richmond to serve as a page in the state Senate. A future Virginia GOP leader, Warriner had grown up in a Democratic family "not knowing any Republicans—not knowing how you would even tell a Republican if you saw one."[15] Once in Richmond, however, he met several, including a state senator by the name of Ted Dalton, who quite unexpectedly "seemed to be like everybody else, only more attractive than the general run." Dalton, like the handful of other GOP partisans in the General Assembly, hailed from the Virginia highlands. It was a standard joke that if you wanted to join up with the Republicans in the Old Dominion, you should head for the hills.

---

[14]*The Washington Post*, July 18, 1965, quoted in Wilkinson, *Harry Byrd*, p. 35.
[15]D. Dortch Warriner interview, October 26, 1979, and August 30, 1984.

Chapter 2

Mountain-Valley Republicanism

"Yo hav fald to rechister."[16]

A registrar's letter notifying a Republican
that he had failed the literacy test.

In the first half of the twentieth century, the majority of Republicans in Virginia, as in the rest of the South, were highlanders. Though insurgents typically take to the hills for their protection, the geographical base of the Virginia Republican Party had more to do with historical developments than tactical exigencies.

In the western third of Virginia, in communities nestled beneath the peaks of the Blue Ridge and especially in the ruggedly mountainous areas to the south and west of Roanoke, there lived a breed quite apart from the Virginians of the Piedmont, Tidewater, and Southside. They were the descendants of pioneers, independent-minded folk for whom the wilderness to the west held more promise than the plantation life to the east. Some were descended from the Pennsylvania Dutch settlers that moved south and populated the Shenandoah Valley. From the earliest days, when Roanoke was a French and Indian War outpost and the mountain and valley inhabitants performed the unenviable task of serving as a buffer against the savage threat to the west, these people had a view of life altogether different from their genteel brethren in eastern Virginia.

It was the War Between the States, however, that drew the dividing line between east and west so sharply that it would have political relevance through the twentieth century. As the slavery debate raged, the Virginia highlanders had little economic stake in the outcome and little sympathy for the plight of the wealthy planters on the other side of the Blue Ridge. When the issue came down to one of secession, many of the mountaineers wanted to remain in the Union, and they bitterly resented being dragged into the war. The hostility was returned by the lowlanders who saw their way of life ended and their means of livelihood denied them, first by the ravages of an unsuccessful war and then by the scourge of a Radical Republican Reconstruction. Of course, the mountain

---

[16]Interview with Glen Williams conducted by Deborah L. Wood for the Republican Party of Virginia, June 23, 1979. Summaries of this and other interviews conducted by Ms. Wood are on file at the Republican Party of Virginia Archives.

inhabitants were far from unanimous in their views of the war. It was in the highlands that the tragedy of neighbor against neighbor and brother against brother often was played out. The allegiances forged during this time—the Unionists with the Republicans and the Secessionists with the Democrats— would prove tenaciously important and often central to politics in the region for years to come.

Outside of southwest Virginia, most Republicans chose their party affiliation because of the promise of patronage. Before the onset of the Great Depression and the lengthy reign of President Franklin Roosevelt, the prospect of a federal appointment during a national Republican administration drew some to the GOP. "The party structure," explained Roanoke newspaperman Buster Carico, "was honeycombed all over the state with people who just wanted to be on the [Republican] committee in case something happened and they might get a postmastership or some [other federal job]".[17] Somewhat ironically, however, patronage actually acted to stymie rather than facilitate Republican growth. With a limited number of federal posts available, patronage-preoccupied Republicans saw little to be gained and much to be lost from building the party. It was in their interest to keep local GOP committees small and inactive—to support Republican candidates in presidential elections and otherwise to refrain from political activity that might attract unwanted attention or converts.

The Republicans of southwest Virginia's Ninth Congressional District controlled the Virginia Republican Party during most of the first half of the twentieth century. A political wheeler-and-dealer of the first rank, C. Bascom Slemp, was elected state GOP chairman in 1905 and congressman from the Ninth District in 1908, and he and his allies proceeded to dominate state Republican affairs for decades.[18] Slemp immersed himself in national GOP politics, and, except for matters of patronage, showed little interest in the progress of Republicanism in Virginia. He confined his party-building efforts largely to his own Ninth District and spent much of his time fending off challenges to his leadership by Republican partisans scattered throughout eastern Virginia.

Chief among Slemp's rivals in the east as mid-century approached were two devout conservatives—Henry A. Wise of Accomack and Fred W. McWane of Lynchburg. Both men professed indignation at Slemp's crafty political manipulations and faulted him for a lack of ideological conviction as well. In challenging Slemp's leadership, their stated aim was to "emancipate . . . our party from the malevolent control of the Ninth district and . . . build up a party east of the Blue Ridge."[19] As historian George L. Vogt noted in his detailed

---

[17]Carico interview.

[18]Slemp served in Congress until 1923.

[19]George L. Vogt, *The Development of Virginia's Republican Party*, Unpublished Dissertation, University of Virginia, 1978, p. 60.

study of the early Virginia Republican Party, McWane and Wise sought to wrest control of the GOP so as "to guarantee its conservatism in the hopes of luring away Byrd Democrats and perhaps Byrd himself."[20] A factional division within the Virginia Republican Party that would persist throughout the century already was very much in evidence. The division, at least superficially, was geographical. But underlying it were profound differences in background (going back to the civil war and even before), in political philosophy, and in the approach to strengthening the GOP in the Old Dominion. Whether and how to achieve a realignment of Virginia's political parties in order to make them correspond philosophically with their national counterparts already was a matter of dispute among Republicans.

The admirers of Harry Byrd were numerous within the limited Republican circles of eastern Virginia and the northern Shenandoah Valley. Conservative Republicans shared Byrd's hostility toward the New Deal, increases in federal spending, and the national Democrats' welfare-state agenda. Henry Wise, who won election as Republican national committeeman from Virginia in 1936, referred to the senior senator as "one of the very few in either party who entertains very nearly my own views concerning national affairs."[21] He and McWane endeavored for years, energetically but unsuccessfully, to forge a bipartisan conservative alliance in the state. The problem was that Republicans wielded little leverage in bargaining with the Byrd men, and what leverage they had they failed to use.

State Republicans generally could be counted on to vote in Democratic primaries for the more conservative candidate, who inevitably also would happen to be the choice of the Byrd organization. "The Republican Party, by and large, was the insurance policy for the Byrd organization," explained Carico. "Byrd catered to the handful of Republicans in case he ever needed them."[22] The attention that the senator lavished on his Republican friends was usually enough to satisfy them, and they typically lacked the numbers to extract anything significant from Byrd in return for their support. For his part, the adroit senator was careful to keep his distance from the Republicans. An open arrangement with the GOP—any evidence that Byrd was giving help to the Republicans as well as receiving help from them—would send shock waves through the organization. Byrd could hardly demand party loyalty down through Democratic ranks and then flout the rule himself.[23]

The greatest obstacle to any alignment of like-minded Republicans and Democrats was the Byrd organization's self-serving use, and frequent abuse, of the state's election machinery. Republican platforms seldom took issue much with the Byrd organization's stewardship of state government. There

---

[20]Ibid.
[21]Wise to McWane, March 1, 1958, McWane Papers, quoted in Vogt, p. 177.
[22]Carico interview.
[23]For a detailed discussion of Byrd's relationship with the GOP, see Vogt, pp. 176–187.

was an occasional GOP call for more state spending on this or that, but angry
rhetoric spewed forth when Republicans commented on the organization's
harsh but effective devices for perpetuating political control—the poll tax,
discriminatory voter registration practices, the absent voters law, and even
outright fraud.

Nowhere was the resentment more bitter nor the determination to fight
back more keen than among the Republicans of southwest Virginia. There,
during much of the first half of the twentieth century, real two-party competition did exist at the local level, and thus abusive election practices were more
than merely insulting. Often they were the decisive factor in election outcomes. In the Ninth District, aptly nicknamed the "Fighting Ninth," party
loyalty ran deep and so, too, did partisan antagonisms. The stakes were high,
the rules were loose, the players were serious-minded and tough, and the competition was fierce.

William C. Wampler, a Republican who experienced firsthand the travails
of southwest Virginia politics as a congressional candidate there in the '50s,
noted that absentee voting procedures were a particularly effective device for
aiding candidates favored by county registrars. Well before the Second World
War, and continuing in some counties into the 1960s, it was common practice
for local election officials to scour the countryside securing the absentee
ballots of eligible voters who were unlikely to come to the polls on election
day. The "black satchel brigade," consisting of the registrar, a notary public, an
electoral board member, and a sack of applications and ballots, could
effectively bring the entire election machinery to the homes of sympathetic
voters.[24] Even more egregious was the practice of voting dead or fictitious
persons by absentee ballot. County registrars simply sent ballot applications to
fictitious addresses and then, alone or with help, forged signatures on the
applications and marked the ballots. Throughout the period it was not
uncommon for 25 percent of the vote in county elections to be cast by absentee
ballot. "In the Ninth District, abuses of the absent voters law were wholesale,"
commented Wampler, but Republicans "had virtue thrust upon them" because
the election machinery was controlled in almost all instances by the
Democrats.[25]

Bolder, less imaginative types of election fraud such as vote-stealing and
vote-buying also occurred with some frequency in southwest Virginia. The
Democrats—Byrd organization stalwarts in some counties and anti-organization politicos in others—were best situated to steal elections because of their
control of county offices. But Republicans for years countered the tactics as
best they could. Vote-buying, for example, was in many places an accepted
practice regarded by both parties as essential in order to have any realistic
prospect of electoral success. Even when fraudulent voting was uncovered,

---

[24]See Vogt, pp. 76–85; Wilkinson, *Harry Byrd*, pp. 223–225.
[25]William C. Wampler interview, February 22, 1984.

legal challenges were rare and difficult to win, particularly for Republicans. To overturn an election through a federal lawsuit, the plaintiff had to implicate the candidate in a conspiracy to violate civil rights. Violations of state election laws were easier to prove, but objective proof did not necessarily guarantee Republican litigants success before the Democratic appointees who manned the state's judiciary.

The registration process, of course, provided other opportunities for partisan chicanery. The blank paper registration form was used widely in the years before the Second World War. Would-be registrants were required to write out from memory specified portions of Virginia statutes. While the writings of those friendly to the Byrd organization were seldom found wanting, the forms submitted by others, particularly blacks and Republicans, were scrutinized meticulously. Many hours were spent by Republicans drilling their supporters in the Virginia Code sections "much like one would teach part of the Catechism."[26]

Similar in effect to the blank registration form were discriminatory applications of the "literacy" requirements in the election laws. In order to register, Republicans, blacks, and other recognizable organization foes were required to answer all manner of impertinent and obscure questions that supposedly indicated whether the applicant had an adequate understanding of the state's election laws. One registrar demanded to know how many people signed the Declaration of Independence; another required the registrant to identify the counties in the 27th judicial district.[27] The possibilities were endless, of course, and the practice infuriated Republicans, particularly since the registrars themselves often were not the most learned sort. Jonesville Republican Glen Williams, later a United States district judge, recalled one college graduate who was notified of his rejection by a postcard which read, "Yo hav fald to rechister."[28] Another young man who recently had been discharged from the service was denied registration because he incorrectly recited a provision of the state constitution. "I got a card from this registrar, who probably had not completed the sixth grade, stating that I had failed to pass the test," recalled Clyde Pearson. "He denied me the right to vote that year, and with that I became bitter about the whole system and became more active."[29] A decade and a half later, Pearson was the GOP nominee for governor.

Though absentee voting abuses persisted for a time and sporadic instances of election fraud continued to occur, most of the more offensive of these practices had been abandoned by 1945; however, the cornerstone of the Byrd organization's structure of electoral controls—the poll tax—remained firmly in

---

[26]Ibid.

[27]See Andrew Buni, *The Negro in Virginia Politics, 1902-1965* (Charlottesville: The University Press of Virginia, 1967), pp. 124-126.

[28]Interview with Glen Williams conducted by Ms. Wood for the Republican Party of Virginia.

[29]Pearson interview.

place. When applied fairly and uniformly, the poll tax had the effect of sharply reducing the size of the electorate. Moreover, it, too, was subject to abuse for partisan advantage. The Virginia statute required, as a prerequisite to voter registration, payment of the $1.50 tax for each of the three years preceding the election in which one wished to participate. In addition, the payment could be made no later than six months before the election. Not only was the cost an impediment for some and a disincentive for others, but the requirement that payment be made six months in advance frustrated many of the forgetful. Others who paid the tax arrived at the polls on election day only to find that their failure to retain the poll tax payment receipt many months before would prevent them from voting.

While Byrd organization leaders vigorously defended the poll tax and the literacy test as non-discriminatory devices designed to ensure an informed electorate and thus good government, criticism of the restrictive measures mounted in the years before, during, and after the Second World War. Active in the poll tax repeal effort, though working largely independent of each other, were the state Republicans, the National Association for the Advancement of Colored People (NAACP), and various black voter organizations, and the moderate-liberal Democratic foes of the Byrd organization.[30] Much of the impetus for repeal came from exposure of poll tax abuses. Illegal bloc payments of the taxes by both political parties and both factions of the Democratic Party were commonplace for years, especially in the Fighting Ninth. Democratic partisans enjoyed a distinct advantage over Republicans, however, because most county treasurers were Democrats.

For the Byrd organization, which prided itself on giving the Commonwealth honest government, the routine election frauds in the Ninth District were a source of embarrassment from which it continuously was trying to distance itself. Yet, the organization's complicity was undeniable. Key figures in the high command, chief among them the powerful E. R. Combs, hailed from the Southwest where they undoubtedly played more than a passive role in the local political trench warfare. Any lingering uncertainty about their active involvement was dispelled by George Vogt's exhaustive study, which revealed correspondence between local Democratic officials and their high-ranking organization allies in which fraudulent practices were discussed directly.[31] "The refusal of the Democratic organization over a period of generations to do anything to stop these absentee-voter and poll-tax frauds is something which has never been satisfactorily explained," wrote Virginius Dabney in 1971. "Political morality in Virginia is of so high an order in other respects that this long-continued lapse is the more disturbing."[32]

---

[30]For a detailed discussion of the poll tax and efforts to obtain its repeal, see Buni, pp. 124–136.

[31]Vogt, pp. 79–83. The correspondence, located in the papers of E. R. Combs, concerned election practices in Russell County in southwest Virginia. See also Vogt, p. 99.

[32]Virginius Dabney, *Virginia: The New Dominion* (New York: Doubleday and Company, 1971), p. 516.

Though both Republicans and blacks suffered politically from the Byrd organization's restrictive and discriminatory electoral system, the two groups were unable and apparently unwilling to forge an anti-Byrd coalition. Quite to the contrary, the first half of the twentieth century saw blacks in Virginia generally move away from their traditional post-Reconstruction Republican home. This was principally because the Virginia GOP—like the national Republican Party under President Herbert Hoover—excluded blacks from participation in party processes in an effort to shed the lingering stigma of Reconstruction among Southern whites. This "lily-white" strategy adopted for a time by the GOP reflected no greater hostility toward blacks than the treatment accorded them by the Byrd Democrats, but at the national level the Roosevelt-led Democratic Party and its platform seemed responsive to black aspirations.

Voting in gradually increasing numbers despite the organization's electoral restrictions, black Virginians found ready allies in the liberal-leaning anti-Byrd faction of the state Democratic Party. The alignment, in fact, seemed rather natural. Except for their shared objections to the state's election procedures, blacks in the Old Dominion had little in common politically with the right-of-center state Republicans. Though statewide GOP candidates frequently adopted a slightly more generous approach to state spending than did the Byrd Democrats, progress-minded blacks tended to focus their efforts on the Democratic primary contests where they could frequently support Byrd foes with whom they shared common ground on national as well as state issues.

Virginia Republicans did not accept passively their adverse political situation in the Old Dominion; instead, they made matters markedly worse by fighting bitterly among themselves almost continuously. The warfare between the feuding Slemp and Wise-McWane factions subsided in the '30s only to be reignited in 1944 by an especially acrimonious fight over the party chairmanship between I. Randolph Dovel of Luray and Ted Dalton of Radford. Dovel prevailed by a margin of 12 delegate votes out of nearly 2,000 cast, but subsequent charges of fraud set off a fierce power struggle that would continue until Dovel's resignation under fire less than three years later.[33] Unable to compete effectively with the Democrats, state Republicans seemed determined to stay in fighting form by battling each other.

The plight of the Virginia GOP was thus acute in November 1945, as the select few that comprised Virginia's restricted electorate prepared to go to the polls to anoint another "Byrd Democrat" as governor. Faction-ridden, preoccupied with patronage, geographically isolated, socially shunned, beset by fraud from without and dissension from within, largely abandoned by blacks, and deprived of their natural constituency by a Democratic machine and leader revered by the many conservatives in the Commonwealth,

---

[33]The period of intense factional infighting in the Virginia GOP is described in Vogt, pp. 117–135.

Republicans could be forgiven for being a little short on optimism. They had not elected a governor, lieutenant governor, or attorney general in the twentieth century. They had never popularly elected a United States senator. Of the state's nine members of the House of Representatives, none were Republicans. Of the 140 members of the General Assembly, the GOP could claim only four—two in the House of Delegates and two in the State Senate.[34] And, nationally, Republicans had not won a presidential election in almost two decades. If there was a bright side, it was that few Republicans in Virginia stayed awake at night worrying that a misjudgment on their part might wreck the ship of state or that a mistake by them might have consequences. They were out of power—as completely out of power, in fact, as a political party could be without being extinct.[35]

---

[34]In 1944–1945, GOP representation in the General Assembly was at its lowest level in the twentieth century. During the 1920s and 1930s, Republicans averaged five delegates and two senators.

[35]Republicans did, however, have an impact from the federal bench. Among the Virginia GOP leaders who become federal judges between 1945 and 1990 were: Ted Dalton of Radford; Walter Hoffman of Norfolk; J. Calvitt Clarke, Jr. of Richmond; Glen Williams of Jonesville; H. Emory Widener of Bristol; D. Dortch Warriner of Emporia; James C. Turk of Radford; and J. Harvie Wilkinson III of Charlottesville.

Chapter 3

Tuck, "Trumanism," and the 1948 Miscue

"The only sane and constructive course is to hold the anchor of our fundamental faith, remain in the house of our fathers, even though the roof leaks and there may be bats in the belfry, rats in the pantry, a cockroach waltz in the kitchen and skunks in the parlor.

"If we are to preserve the two-party system, which is indispensable under our form of government, we must do our housecleaning and fight our battles within....

"We cannot take our inheritance and depart into a far country. Where shall we go and to what shall we return?"[36]

J. Lindsay Almond, Jr., 1948

William Munford Tuck was not a typical organization candidate for governor. He was colorful, jovial, and to some—including Senator Byrd—he seemed a bit rough around the edges. The rotund and gregarious Tuck had wanted to run for governor in 1941, but he deferred when Senator Byrd signalled his preference for Second District Congressman Colgate W. Darden, Jr. Determined not to be sidetracked again in 1945, Lieutenant Governor Tuck took the unusual step of announcing his candidacy for governor without first securing the "nod" from Senator Byrd. Though initially reluctant, Byrd eventually acquiesced in Tuck's candidacy after being lobbied by Governor Darden and by E. R. Combs.

"Bill" Tuck was from Halifax County in the heart of Southside Virginia, and that was significant. More than any part of the state, the southern tier of rural counties stretching from the foothills of Campbell County to the fertile flatlands of Nansemond (now Suffolk) was a bastion of Byrd organization strength. It was this area of Virginia, sparsely populated with white farmers and a high proportion of poor blacks, that voted most heavily in favor of the 1902 constitutional convention that disfranchised most blacks and gave the Democratic organization near-absolute control of Virginia's government. In later years, Senator Byrd's dedication to an agrarian Virginia and his rigidly conservative views, particularly on racial matters, won him the fierce devotion of Southside whites. "If Byrd's word was law throughout most of Virginia,"

---

[36]Ben Beagle and Ozzie Osborne, *J. Lindsay Almond: Virginia's Reluctant Rebel* (Roanoke: Full Court Press, Inc., 1984), pp. 50–51.

wrote J. Harvie Wilkinson III in his seminal study of the Byrd organization, "it was nothing short of gospel throughout the Southside."[37] It was from that region that the organization would draw much of its top echelon in the years after the Second World War.

In the fall campaign, Tuck faced Republican State Senator S. Floyd Landreth of Galax. The match-up was most uneven, of course, though Landreth gave up little to Tuck in the categories of personality and girth. Landreth was a relaxed and affable lawyer-banker who took his politics seriously but generally avoided confrontation and strident rhetoric. He had been propelled into the limelight in 1912 when, at age 27, he successfully prosecuted members of the Allen gang for the infamous courtroom shootings in Carroll County. In 1944, he went to the Senate of Virginia where he was well regarded on both sides of the aisle.

The match-up was uneven, though, because it pitted Landreth, the standard-bearer of a largely moribund Republican Party, against the vast power and resources of the Byrd organization. Though Landreth campaigned statewide (something previous GOP nominees for governor had not bothered to do), he had no illusions about the outcome. He even went so far as to discourage supporters from wasting their money by contributing to his campaign. Nevertheless, Landreth's active stumping and his calls for increased funding for state schools and hospitals broadened the GOP's appeal beyond its western enclaves. Tuck won decisively, but Landreth polled nearly a third of the statewide vote, almost twice the share garnered by the GOP gubernatorial nominee four years earlier.[38] The improvement was most notable in the state's urban areas, which had begun to grow rapidly during the war years.

Virginia politics under Governor Tuck proved unusually lively and entertaining. The new chief executive was more flamboyant and less circumspect rhetorically than most of his organization predecessors, but Senator Byrd and his lieutenants found little cause for complaint about his adherence to conservative dogma or his vigilance in safeguarding the organization's interests. From the outset of his administration, the central theme of the Tuck tenure was hostility to organized labor. In his first message to the General Assembly, the new governor denounced public employee unions, and the legislators responded by declaring public employee collective bargaining to be contrary to the public policy of Virginia. When employees of the Virginia Electric and Power Company threatened a strike in the spring of 1946, Tuck declared that a state of emergency existed, mobilized the unorganized state militia, and threatened to induct 1,600 of the utility's employees. The next year he convened a special session of the General Assembly and secured passage of

---

[37]Wilkinson, *Harry Byrd*, p. 9.

[38]The vote totals were: Tuck (D) – 112,355 (66.6%); Landreth (R) – 52,386 (31.0%); Howard Carwile (I) – 4,023 (2.4%). Ralph Eisenberg, *Virginia Votes 1924-1968* (Charlottesville: The University Press of Virginia, 1971), p. 144.

two additional measures: one permitting state seizure of strike-plagued utilities, and another outlawing compulsory union membership (the "Right to Work Law").

The governor's labor-baiting came at a politically propitious time. Across the nation a rash of postwar strikes had caused the organized labor movement's popularity to plummet. President Truman in 1946 vetoed legislation designed to curb union power, and that move, in combination with concessions made by the administration in order to end a United Mine Workers strike, brought the new President widespread criticism. November saw Republicans capture control of both houses of Congress for the first time in 16 years. In Virginia, however, it was the Byrd organization that reaped the harvest of anti-union sentiment. Senator Byrd and the state's conservative Democratic congressmen spent much of their re-election campaigns in 1946 pillorying organized labor; Eighth District Congressman Howard W. Smith, for example, assailed the Congress of Industrial Organizations' political action committee ("CIO-PAC") as a "new swarm of carpetbaggers who are invading the Southern states [and] are impregnated with communism."[39] All of the Byrd candidates posted easy wins in November, including Congressman A. Willis Robertson, who prevailed in a special senatorial election occasioned by the death of U.S. Senator Carter Glass in May 1946.[40]

If there was cause for optimism among Virginia Republicans in the outcomes of the initial postwar election contests, it was not apparent. But the impending presidential election in 1948 held more promise. State GOP partisans spent much of 1947 getting their house in order for what they correctly anticipated to be a serious effort by the national Republican ticket to carry Virginia the following year. In an unusual turn for the faction-ridden party, a new state chairman, Robert H. Woods of Pearisburg, was installed without opposition. And the Virginia Republicans for the first time opened a state party headquarters in Richmond and hired a full-time executive director.[41] With electoral success a real prospect for the first time in many years, the Virginia GOP suddenly began to resemble a viable political organization.

The ever-widening gulf between Senator Byrd and the national Democratic Party was the principal reason for the Republicans' high hopes. Byrd supported Franklin Roosevelt for President in 1932, but he quickly became disenchanted as the new President repudiated the conservative thrust of his 1932 platform and embarked on a broad new social agenda. When Roosevelt's

---

[39]James Randolph Roebuck, Jr., *Virginia in the Election of 1948*, Unpublished Thesis, University of Virginia, 1969, p. 7.

[40]The vote totals in the regular Senate election were: Byrd (D) – 163,960 (64.8%); Lester S. Parsons of Norfolk (R) – 77,005 (30.5%). In the special Senate election, the totals were: Robertson (D) – 169,680 (68.2%); Robert H. Woods of Pearisburg (R) – 72,253 (29.0%). Eisenberg, *Virginia Votes*, pp. 152, 156.

[41]For a detailed description of developments within the state Republican Party in the mid-1940s, see Vogt, pp. 148–156.

ill-fated "court-packing" plan was advanced in 1937, Byrd and other Southern Democrats joined with Republicans to defeat it, thereby giving birth to the conservative coalition that would remain a formidable force within the Congress for decades. It was President Truman, however, who most infuriated Byrd.

Like most of his Southern colleagues, the Virginia senator initially greeted Harry Truman's ascension to the Presidency in April 1945 with favor. Truman, after all, was the son of a Confederate soldier, and his Missouri accent fueled the feeling among Southerners that one of their own finally was in charge. In fact, Truman owed his spot on the national ticket in 1944 to Southern party leaders who had insisted that Roosevelt jettison liberal Vice President Henry Wallace as the price for their continued support. From the new President, Byrd and his colleagues had expected leadership in moving their party back to the center. They did not get it.

By early 1948, Truman seemed to be moving resolutely in the opposite direction. In an apparent attempt to breathe new life into FDR's New Deal coalition, the President proposed a variety of liberal initiatives in his State of the Union message. Three weeks later he sent to the Congress a special message on civil rights that called for a number of specific measures long promoted by black voter groups and civil rights advocates. The proposals included creation of both a civil rights division in the Department of Justice and a separate commission on civil rights, prohibition of racial discrimination in interstate transportation facilities, voting rights protections, and suffrage and home rule for the District of Columbia. The President's initiative brought a sharp and swift denunciation from Virginia's senior senator. "[T]aken in their entirety," declared Byrd, "[the Truman civil rights proposals] constitute a mass invasion of states' rights never before even suggested, much less recommended, by any previous President."[42]

The senator's disdain for Truman was surpassed, perhaps, only by that of Governor Tuck. On February 25, 1948, the governor went before the General Assembly to denounce the Truman civil rights program and to propose a measure of his own for dealing with the President. The Tuck "ballot bill"[43] would keep the names of all presidential candidates off of the November ballot in Virginia. Instead, only the parties would be listed, and party committees would be authorized to instruct the electors, before *or after* the election, as to the presidential candidate for whom they should vote. The obvious aim of the measure was to keep Truman from getting Virginia's electoral votes by permitting the election of a Byrd-dominated slate of Democratic electors not bound to back Truman. In Washington, Senator Byrd took to the floor to strongly endorse the Tuck bill and to commend it to his Southern colleagues.

---

[42]Henriques, pp. 54–55.
[43]It also was known as the Tuck "Anti-Truman" Bill. See Latimer, p. 28.

At home, however, the proposal met sudden, strong, and somewhat surprising opposition. Normally supportive of the Byrd organization, the influential conservative editors of Richmond's two daily newspapers, Dr. Douglas Southall Freeman of the *News Leader* and Virginius Dabney of the *Times-Dispatch*, cautioned against an overreaction to the Truman civil rights measures and condemned the Tuck ballot bill. "Mistake it not for an instant . . .," warned Freeman, "[W]e of the South may win this campaign, but if we stand stubbornly on the defensive and do nothing to meet those Negro demands that are based on reason and justice, we shall lose the final contest."[42] Dabney's assault on the ballot bill was even sharper:

> If Virginia and the South want to show their resentment against President Truman, let them fight him openly in the Democratic National Convention. If he is nominated despite it, let the South go Republican, if it thinks the issues of states' rights and civil rights are that important. . . . But neither Virginians, nor any other Southerners, ought to be willing to abdicate their responsibilities as citizens by giving to a small group of politicians the right to decide after November for whom Virginia's electoral votes will be cast.[43]

With Republican lawmakers gleefully joining in the chorus of criticism, the organization men in the legislature resolved to push the bill through in some form, if only to allow the governor to save face. As finally written, the ballot bill permitted state party conventions, not committees, to substitute new electors after the national conventions chose their nominees, but no later than 60 days *before* the general election.

Though thrown off balance somewhat by the ballot bill furor, the Byrd leadership in Virginia remained firm in its opposition to Truman as the time for the national convention neared. But who would the Virginia Democrats support? One of the key players, Harry F. Byrd, Jr., recalled how the matter was decided at the party's 1948 state convention in Richmond:

> There was a good bit of Truman support in the convention, and throughout the state for that matter, but the leadership did not favor the re-election of Truman, and they were looking around for a candidate around whom the state convention might rally. So when the convention recessed to give the resolutions committee an opportunity to meet to consider the problem of what resolutions should be recommended to the convention by way of endorsing a presidential candidate, Senator Byrd, Sr., asked me to see Governor Tuck, who was chairman of the resolutions committee, and ask him to hold up or delay the meeting some. And then Senator Byrd, Sr., asked me to join him, and the two of us took a long walk.
>
> The convention was held at the Mosque. We walked around those adjoining blocks for about 30 minutes trying to determine who Virginia

---

[42]*The Richmond News Leader*, March 6, 1948, quoted in Roebuck, p. 28.

[43]*Richmond Times-Dispatch*, February 27, 1948, quoted in Roebuck, p. 22.

should endorse for President. Senator Byrd, Sr., sought my reaction as to what the thinking of my colleagues in the Virginia legislature (Byrd, Jr., was then a state senator) might be to endorsing General [Dwight D.] Eisenhower. My first question was, "Is he a Democrat or a Republican?" Senator Byrd, Sr., said he didn't really know what he was; he didn't think he had any political background. . . . But he was quite impressed with General Eisenhower, had seen him on a number of occasions, and was impressed with him as an individual, with his potential as a public official, and with his judgment and his character.

So at the end of about 30 minutes, Senator Byrd, Sr., . . . suggested that I suggest to Governor Tuck that he suggest to the committee that the committee recommend to the convention that it endorse General Eisenhower—which it did.[46]

Virginia was not alone in promoting the popular war hero as an alternative to Truman; prominent liberals and conservatives in the North as well as the South encouraged him to run. When Eisenhower firmly declined to enter the race, however, the anti-Truman effort lost most of its steam.

At the Democratic National Convention, Truman was re-nominated, and Virginia's votes went in protest to conservative Senator Richard Russell of Georgia. The administration, which had been soft-pedaling its civil rights program for months, failed narrowly in its effort to prevent a liberal civil rights plank championed by then-Minneapolis Mayor Hubert Humphrey from being inserted in the party platform. A few days later, Southern Democrats met in Birmingham, Alabama, and under the "States' Rights Party" banner nominated their own ticket headed by then-Governor Strom Thurmond of South Carolina. Virginia's Democratic leadership was notable by virtue of its absence at the "Dixiecrat" conclave in Birmingham. As the campaign proceeded in the fall, however, Governor Tuck unmistakably signalled his preference for the South Carolina governor. And when Thurmond stumped through the state in early October, he was hosted in Charlottesville by former Governor Colgate Darden and then introduced to a Richmond rally by Governor Tuck. Among those in attendance at the Thurmond event in Richmond was Mrs. Harry F. Byrd, Sr.

While some of the Byrd organization leaders were abandoning their party's incumbent President, Truman also was suffering defections from usually Democratic black leaders in Virginia. Many blacks questioned the sincerity of the President's support for civil rights. He had proposed sweeping legislation in the winter only to permit it to languish in the spring in the face of political fallout in the South. Then at the national convention his operatives had fought the platform plank so strongly preferred by blacks and liberals. The black-owned *Norfolk Journal and Guide* aired its distrust of the President. "When and if it becomes expedient," the newspaper commented, "Mr.

---

[44]Harry F. Byrd, Jr., interview, March 12, 1984.

Truman could just as ruthlessly trade away the interests of the Negro for the support of some other group which he felt more important."[47] Though President Truman probably garnered a slim majority of the black vote in the state, many black Virginians backed Republican nominee Thomas E. Dewey, whose public comments on racial matters and moderate record as New York's governor had considerable appeal to them.[48]

Responsibility for the Truman campaign in Virginia fell largely by default to the anti-Byrd faction of the Democratic Party. Delegate Robert Whitehead of Nelson County, an eloquent and widely respected organization foe, organized the "Straight Democratic Ticket Committee" and took to the campaign trail in Truman's behalf. The Byrd organization leadership was far from united in opposition to Truman, however. While Senator Byrd and most of his lieutenants simply refused to make any public comment on the presidential race, Senator Willis Robertson and all of the Democratic congressional candidates endorsed the President. The colorful attorney general of Virginia, J. Lindsay Almond, Jr., campaigned energetically for Truman, and he offered this answer to the conservative Democrats' dilemma:

The only sane and constructive course is to hold the anchor of our fundamental faith, remain in the house of our fathers, even though the roof leaks and there may be bats in the belfry, rats in the pantry, a cockroach waltz in the kitchen and skunks in the parlor.

If we are to preserve the two-party system, which is indispensable under our form of government, we must do our housecleaning and fight our battles within. . . .

We cannot take our inheritance and depart into a far country. Where shall we go and to what shall we return?[49]

Somewhat ironically, it was Attorney General Almond, the Democratic loyalist, who issued a legal opinion in 1948 that eased the way for Democrats to abandon their party's nominee in presidential elections and remain able to participate in the statewide Democratic primary elections that followed a year later. The problem had first arisen in 1928, when Virginians, over then-Governor Harry Byrd's objections, gave the state's electoral votes to Republican Herbert Hoover. Under state law, a voter was not eligible to participate in the Democratic primary unless he could declare both that he had voted for the party's nominees in the last election and would do so in the next. With many conservative Virginia Democrats having declined in 1928 to support their party's Catholic nominee, Al Smith, the organization needed a way for them to return to the fold in the 1929 Democratic primary. Attorney General John R. Saunders readily obliged, opining that presidential electors were not party "nominees" within the meaning of the loyalty requirement;

---

[47]*Norfolk Journal and Guide*, October 30, 1948, quoted in Buni, p. 159.
[48]Buni, pp. 158–160.
[49]Beagle and Osborne, pp. 50–51.

therefore, those who had voted for the Hoover electors remained Democrats in good standing. In 1948, Attorney General Almond reaffirmed and bolstered Saunders' interpretation. It would prove to be a critically important ruling in succeeding years as Virginians, taking their cue from Senator Byrd's "golden silence,"[50] repeatedly would place the Commonwealth in the Republican column in presidential elections.

The GOP victories would have to wait, however. To the surprise of almost everyone, Harry Truman defeated Governor Dewey and won a full term as President on November 2, 1948. Almost as great a shock was the race's outcome in the Old Dominion, where the underdog Truman scored a plurality victory. For Virginia's senior senator, the result hardly could have been less satisfying. "Though Senator Byrd learned in time to keep golden silence with great finesse," wrote J. Harvie Wilkinson III, "the presidential politics of the Byrd organization in 1948 were full of blunders."[51] First, it was the ballot bill episode; then, the conflicting signals emanating from various Byrd lieutenants in the fall campaign. The election returns revealed the cruelest cut of all: Truman had been helped immensely—perhaps decisively —by the Thurmond third-party effort, an effort assisted decisively in Virginia by the vehemently anti-Truman Governor Tuck. Thurmond polled more than 40,000 votes, the bulk of them from conservative Southside Virginia (Tuck's home base), while Truman's statewide margin over the second-place Dewey was less than 30,000 votes.[52]

Though it was the usually sure-handed Byrd men who fumbled the ball in 1948, it was the long-suffering Republicans who lost a contest they had seemed almost certain to win. They were bitterly disappointed. True enough, New York's Dewey was hardly the kind of conservative Republican who could be expected to fare well in the South. But he was clearly in the political mainstream, and, against the much-maligned Truman, who had earned the enmity of the state's most popular political leaders, victory had seemed assured. The state GOP had weathered a tough nomination battle: the Virginia delegation to the 1948 Republican National Convention split 10–10 between Dewey and Senator Robert Taft of Ohio on the first ballot before closing ranks behind Dewey after Taft's withdrawal. After the convention, the party had pulled together to wage its most vigorous campaign in many years. Its reward was yet another defeat.

Even more demoralizing for Virginia Republicans was the outcome of the congressional races. No one much expected the Senate race rematch between

---

[50]A comment by Senator Byrd during the 1960 election resulted in the "golden silence" label being applied to his quadrennial policy of withholding his support from the Democratic Party's presidential nominees, a policy which he followed from 1948 until his retirement in 1965. See *infra* p. 113.

[51]Wilkinson, *Harry Byrd*, p. 79.

[52]The vote totals in Virginia were: Truman (D) – 200,786 (47.9%); Dewey (R) – 172,070 (41.0%); Thurmond (States' Rights) – 43,393 (10.4%); Vice President Henry Wallace (Progressive) – 2,047 votes (0.5%). Eisenberg, *Virginia Votes*, p. 164.

incumbent Willis Robertson and party chief Robert Woods to turn out very differently from their 1946 special election contest, and indeed the results were nearly identical. Robertson won a full term in the Senate with almost two-thirds of the statewide vote.[53] But there were high hopes for the GOP in a number of House of Representatives contests where credible Republican candidates were fielded and Dewey coattails were anticipated. In the Tidewater Second, Richmond-area Third, Southwest Virginia Ninth, and northern Virginia Eighth districts, Republicans nominated youthful and attractive contenders who made spirited bids, but all fell short. The most remarkable showing was Republican Tyrell Krum's razor-thin, 5,000-vote loss to powerful Eighth District incumbent Howard W. Smith, one of the most senior Democrats in Congress. The most disappointing was Republican T. Eugene Worrell's narrow defeat at the hands of Democrat Thomas Fugate in the contest to succeed retiring Ninth District Congressman John W. Flannagan. Worrell, a strong campaigner from Bristol, had been expected to win, but lost by about 3,000 votes in a race in which some 9,000 absentee ballots were filed.

Though the Republican contenders were unsuccessful in 1948, the number and seriousness of the GOP challenges were signs of the competitiveness to come. The 1948 elections also were important for the experience and encouragement they gave to a new generation of Republicans who were just getting their feet wet in politics. It was during his involvement in Worrell's campaign that a 22-year-old student named William Wampler discovered his own political ambitions and launched the career that would make him the dominant figure in a Republican resurgence in southwest Virginia. In northern Virginia, a pair of young civic leaders, Joel Broyhill and Lee Potter, volunteered to assist the Dewey campaign and were appalled to discover the lack of precinct-level Republican activity. The two future Virginia GOP leaders resolved to do something to energize the Arlington Republican Party "as soon as this fiasco's over,"[54] and their efforts eventually would do much to transform the region into a GOP stronghold.

The 1948 competition also occasioned the revitalization of the state Young Republican federation, which had foundered during the war years. Young Republican Chairman P. L. Hockman of Winchester and the GOP's national committeewoman, Emily W. Logan, achieved unprecedented success in organizing Young Republican (YR) clubs and YR women's clubs around the state. The groups provided an important new source of volunteer manpower for voter canvassing and registration drives, and their youthful enthusiasm enlivened GOP gatherings. In the faces of these young Republicans, Ted Dalton wrote to Henry Wise, was "the look for a new era in the political life of

---

[53]The vote totals for the major-party candidates were: Robertson (D) – 253,865 (65.6%); Woods (R) – 119,366 (30.8%). Eisenberg, *Virginia Votes*, p. 168.

[54]Interview with I. Lee Potter conducted by Deborah L. Wood for the Republican Party of Virginia, July 26, 1979.

Virginia."[55] The Young Republican federation would become the recruiting, training, and testing ground for young activists who were destined to be the growing party's future candidates and leaders.

For years, one of the Virginia GOP's greatest drawbacks had been its lack of youthful talent. Young, energetic party organizers and politicos who could work their way up the ladder of elective office were few and far between in Republican ranks. Most such persons had been drawn to the Democratic Party by its vastly greater prospects for advancement. But that was now beginning to change. Virginia was growing and becoming more diverse demographically and economically. The war years had changed outlooks and broadened perspectives. Issues of war and peace, capitalism versus socialism, and the expansion of communism—national issues—were now at the fore. There was a restiveness among the young, and restiveness was what a comfortable old order like the Byrd organization needed least.

---

[55]Vogt, p. 179.

Chapter 4

1949: Thunder on the Left

"The [Byrd machine leaders] are incapable of building a free society because deep in their hearts they do not believe in a free society. They have no real faith in the future of our way of life or of this Republic. They profoundly distrust the judgment of the people. For them the show is over and the curtain is being rung down. They are time–servers—waiting for the sands to run out—half-heartedly fighting a rear guard action for a cause that has lost its meaning. . . . This is why they must go."[56]

Francis Pickens Miller, 1949

Virginia had become a very different place during the Second World War, and the change became increasingly apparent after the great conflict ended. For one thing, the slow population growth that the Commonwealth had experienced before the war gave way to a new rapid-growth trend in the 1940s. The state's population increased nearly 24 percent during the decade; the principal reason was the war-related expansion of federal government activities in the Old Dominion. Especially in the cluster of cities around Hampton Roads and in the Washington, D.C., area, new military installations and burgeoning federal agencies brought a wave of federal employees into the state. Suburban northern Virginia's population jumped by more than 126 percent between 1940 and 1950, and the Richmond and Roanoke metropolitan areas also experienced significant rises in population. The beginning of a business and industrial growth pattern that would flower fully in the state in the next two decades was already evident as the 1940s drew to a close. Together, the urbanization and industrialization trends would change the face of Virginia and its politics.

Growth of this sort did not bode well for the Byrd organization, which had its base in rural, agricultural Virginia. With new industries and federal installations came a diverse mix of people from points outside Virginia—more blue-collar workers, often with populist or liberal inclinations; more management personnel, typically with Republican tendencies; and more suburbanites expecting better public services than the Byrd organization had been willing to provide. The organization's refusal to recognize and adapt to the changes, especially the growing urban demands for services, soon would become a

---

[56]Francis Pickens Miller, *Man from the Valley* (Chapel Hill: University of North Carolina Press, 1971), pp. 175–178.

dominant theme in the state's political contests, as Republicans and anti-organization Democrats alike sought to give voice to, and reap the political harvest from, the increasing metropolitan dissension.

As much as anything, however, Virginia attitudes were changed by the Second World War—not so much by the war itself, but by the exposure of its younger generation to a horizon broader than that of the Old Dominion. Charles McDowell, one of Virginia's most insightful political reporters, recalled the phenomenon:

... It was the younger people who had been off in the service and came back with a different view of old Virginia, and they were ready to move it in what they conceived to be forward. They weren't as conservative. They just weren't inclined to be party to something where the word got passed and people got told what to do. There was a sense of independence in those younger men. That generation had been front-line lieutenants, and they were a pretty fiery crowd. There were a whole lot of people who just weren't quite ready to become go-along-in-order-to-get-along Democrats.

I think we get into a lot of trouble the minute we start describing them as "the liberals" or "the conservatives." In terms of the national Democratic party, I think they had some notion that you either ought to belong to a party or not; that you couldn't sit in caucuses in the Congress and go to national conventions and then quietly either sit on your hands or support Strom Thurmond or vote Republican; that there had to be some responsibility in the party. I think in subsequent years we have sort of found that responsibility to the party has fallen apart, but they were standing up for traditional party politics. . . .

The Byrd organization was a rural organization. It was centered in the courthouses and the farmers and the small storekeepers, with a sort of quiet alliance with the Commonwealth Club and the brokers and bankers of Main Street, Richmond. But, fundamentally, it drew its strength and its character out of rural Virginia. These people who began to arise out of the late '40s were urban. They were concerned about public schools. They were well-educated. They weren't rural farmers. They had an intellectual bent. They were concerned about such issues as the poll tax and one-man/one-vote and a lot of things Virginians had risen above for a long time. . . .

There was also a new kind of Republican. I've always figured that was absolutely the same response to the Byrd organization as the . . . so-called "liberal" Democrats. I think they all rose out of the same thing: a recognition that the Byrd organization had been for another time and that Virginia was being held to a lot of old, antiquated, unfair codes of political conduct and power. They didn't think this coziness and benevolent aristocratic rule was the way of a lively state.[57]

---

[57]Charles McDowell, Jr., interview, July 3, 1980.

It was within the dominant Democratic Party that the postwar changes in the Old Dominion first were manifested in intense electoral competition. Harry Byrd's Democratic opponents took great encouragement from President Truman's victory in Virginia in 1948. Looking ahead to the 1949 gubernatorial primary, Colonel Francis Pickens Miller of Fairfax, a leading Byrd organization foe, was confident that the liberals would be able to wrest control of the party from the Byrd men. To Delegate Robert Whitehead of Nelson County, the legislature's foremost critic of the ruling organization, Miller wrote on November 9, 1948, "We are going to take over the leadership of the Party in Virginia with all that implies."[58]

Miller's optimism seemed justified. The organization had hurt itself with its bungled effort to undercut Truman in the state. Many partisan Democrats, especially in two-party competitive southwest Virginia, deeply resented the apparent disloyalty of Senator Byrd and Governor Tuck. And the organization leadership, which had been fatally divided in the 1948 race, appeared headed toward a repetition of the mistake in 1949. Not one, but two, organization stalwarts—State Senator John S. Battle of Charlottesville and Richmond Mayor Horace Edwards—had entered the race for the Democratic nomination for governor. While Battle had received the "nod" from Senator Byrd, Edwards could count on considerable backing from a statewide network of organization friends that he had cultivated during a creditable stint as state Democratic Party chairman. Joining the two Byrd men in the race was the widely travelled and learned Colonel Miller, a former member of the House of Delegates and distinguished veteran of two wars, who promised to be a formidable candidate in his own right. The split in organization ranks opened the way for the liberal Miller to assemble a plurality, and that made his reasonably luminous prospects incalculably brighter.[59]

Miller spoke for a segment of the Democratic Party that had grown rapidly during the war years and those that immediately followed. It included blacks, whose electoral participation climbed markedly in the war's aftermath, and many urban whites who had little enthusiasm for the Byrd organization's tight-fisted stewardship of the state's finances. The wisdom of Senator Byrd's strict pay-as-you-go policy at the state level seemed increasingly dubious to many Virginians who saw pressing needs in public education and other areas go largely unmet while local governments incurred considerable indebtedness endeavoring to provide a minimal level of public services. There were also more union members in Virginia. Though not a large number statewide, significant and growing pockets of support for organized labor did exist, and they were solidly behind Miller. These elements had been brought together before by anti-organization candidates, but they now represented a bigger portion of

---

[58]Henriques, p. 60.

[59]A fourth candidate, Remmie Arnold of Petersburg, was a less significant factor in the contest.

the Virginia electorate, and Colonel Miller gave voice to their concerns in a way that previous candidates had not.

For Miller, the root of the problem in Virginia was the Byrd "machine," and he attacked it with unprecedented ferocity. His was less a campaign to win a term of office than a crusade to cast off the yoke of Byrd organization rule—to "set Virginia free," as he put it.[60] In a typical radio speech, he concluded a sweeping indictment of Byrd, E. R. Combs, and the organization in this way:

> These men are incapable of building a free society because deep in their hearts they do not believe in a free society. They have no real faith in the future of our way of life or of this Republic. They profoundly distrust the judgment of the people. For them the show is over and the curtain is being rung down. They are time-servers—waiting for the sands to run out—half-heartedly fighting a rear guard action for a cause that has lost its meaning. . . . This is why they must go.[61]

The Democratic contenders for governor announced their bids well before the 1948 election, and their contest thus was both unusually hard-fought and long. Miller took his vehement anti-machine message across the state, while Battle, seeking to defuse another anti-organization plaint, stressed his support for significantly increased state funding for education. Edwards, who occupied the middle position in the race philosophically, advocated enactment of a state sales tax to finance increased investment in education, while Battle stressed his opposition to any tax increase.

As if the Byrd organization's problems were not vexing enough already, the Republicans—many of whom usually voted in Democratic primaries for the conservative candidates—were toying with the idea of nominating their own statewide candidates by primary rather than convention in 1949. Such a decision by the GOP almost certainly would aid Miller, since the Republicans could be expected to cast ballots in their own contest on primary election day rather than voting against the liberal Miller in the Democratic race.

The push for the primary as the nominating method came mainly from northern Virginia Republicans and from younger GOP partisans around the state. The Eighth District GOP had nominated its congressional candidate, Tyrell Krum, the previous year by primary, and many attributed his strong showing in the ensuing general election to heightened interest generated by the primary. The state Republican Party leadership understood and respected the thinking of the party's growing youthful contingent. But Ted Dalton, Fred McWane, and Henry Wise feared that the turnout in the GOP primary would be embarrassingly low. For his part, Dalton believed that the Republicans' best strategy would be to schedule a nominating convention after the Democrats' August primary. If the liberal Miller won the Democratic contest, the GOP

---

[60]Miller, pp. 175–178.
[61]Ibid.

could then field its strongest available candidate and have a real prospect of winning the governorship. Other Republicans who were more sympathetic to the Byrd organization, such as Wise, probably harbored no illusions about a GOP win in November but worried that a Republican primary might tip the Democratic contest to Miller.

The delegates to the state Republican convention in Richmond in late April rejected the party leaders' counsel and, by a 376–270 vote, determined that a Republican primary would be held simultaneously with the Democratic one on August 2. In the weeks thereafter, however, hopes for an invigorating GOP primary faded as few Republicans filed as candidates. Walter Johnson, the Northumberland County Commonwealth's attorney, was the sole candidate to seek the nomination for governor. A rather uninspiring race for lieutenant governor developed between Berkeley Williams, a 70-year-old former Richmond postmaster, and E. Thomas McGuire, a College of William and Mary law student. And no Republican showed any interest in taking on incumbent Democrat Lindsay Almond in the election for attorney general. Nevertheless, at the party's central committee meeting in June, the members turned a deaf ear to Ted Dalton's forceful arguments and rejected a proposal to abandon the scheduled primary. With neither of the candidates for lieutenant governor willing to drop out of the race, the Republican primary plans went forward.

Faced with an uncooperative GOP and other adversity, the Byrd organization responded in the last 30 days of the Democratic primary campaign with a demonstration of political prowess that even Miller later described as "brilliant."[62] Throughout the campaign, the Byrd leadership had the benefit of superior financial resources[63] and a talented candidate. Their favorite, John S. Battle, was a thoughtful, dignified, and easy-going man who suffered little in comparison with his two very attractive principal opponents. Late in the campaign, however, another organization asset came pivotally into play: the astute political judgment of Senator Byrd, E. R. Combs, and, especially, Sidney Kellam, the political chieftain of Virginia Beach, who served as Battle's campaign manager. The story of how the organization beat back the frontrunning Miller's potent challenge and made Battle the Democratic nominee for governor in 1949 is among the best illustrations of the savvy political gamesmanship that sustained the Byrd men in power for decades.

The central element of the organization's late-blooming strategy was to portray the reform-minded Miller as a dangerous radical who posed a serious threat to peace and tranquility in the Old Dominion. That was accomplished by tying Miller to "outside labor agitators" who, it was charged, were bent on using him to take over Virginia. In an unusual move three weeks before the

---

[62]Ibid., p. 183.

[63]Battle spent just over $46,000 in the primary race. Miller and Edwards each spent roughly one-third of that amount. Latimer, p. 104.

August primary, Senator Byrd personally took to the hustings in support of Battle and issued the dire warning that a split among conservatives might elect "a CIO-supported candidate."[64] When Miller predictably retorted that the labor issue was a bogus one, the Battle campaign was ready. It had been holding in reserve a copy of a letter from James C. Petrillo, president of the American Federation of Musicians and one of the most unpopular labor leaders in America. In the letter, Petrillo exhorted the union's Virginia members to back "Miller, a liberal and progressive anti-machine candidate."[65] Though the union had only a handful of members in the state, the letter appeared to confirm the takeover charges, and the labor issue became the dominant one as the campaign approached its climax.

Byrd organization leaders then used the growing fear of Miller to squeeze Edwards out of contention and unite the conservative faithful behind Battle. Kellam conceived the slogan, "A vote for Edwards is a vote for Miller," and he effectively executed a strategy designed to portray Edwards as a spoiler who could not win but who might well pull enough votes from Battle to give Miller the win with a plurality of the vote. Roanoke newspaper reporter Buster Carico recalled how it went:

> [T]he cry was, "Horace Edwards is a fine man, but he will keep John Battle from winning. If the good Virginians who are supporting Horace Edwards don't come in and vote for Battle, Miller will win and we'll be run over by niggers and Yankees and union organizers and all them bad things." I can hear it now. And all across the state local people were saying things like, "I love Horace Edwards and this breaks my heart, but Virginia is bigger. We've got to save Virginia."[66]

Positioned between Miller and Battle and initially possessed of a significant bloc of support, Edwards saw the bulk of his backing evaporate as defection after defection from right and left fueled the impression that he could not win. A confidential poll commissioned by Senator Byrd a few weeks before the election projected that Edwards would receive 75,000 votes; if the poll was correct, fully 40 percent of Edwards's support disappeared in the campaign's final weeks.[67]

The organization men also consolidated conservative support behind Battle by turning up the heat on local courthouse officials. Rarely were the subtle pressures that the organization leadership exerted on the loyalists down through the ranks ever disclosed, but the effort to bring Edwards supporters into the Battle camp was intense, and it produced unusually direct confirmation of the long-suspected tactics. In a letter discovered after the primary elec-

---

[62]Latimer, p. 34.
[63]Henriques, pp. 92–93.63
[64]Carico interview.
[65]Henriques, p. 110.

tion, for example, Franklin County Commissioner of Revenue Cam Perdue advised his assistant:

> Mr. Combs, chairman of the Compensation Board, who sets your salary and mine. . ., is very much interested in seeing John S. Battle elected our governor. Since Mr. Combs is a good friend of ours, I think it would be in our interest to get out every vote we can for Mr. Battle.[68]

As the word was passed in increasingly adamant terms, Edwards publicly blasted Combs for turning the Compensation Board into "a political agency, pure and simple."[69] His rather shrill criticism of the respected Byrd lieutenant only served, however, to aid efforts to unite organization followers behind the Battle candidacy.

All of these steps still were not enough to enable the organization to stop Miller. The Byrd men needed help from the Republicans—and they got it. On July 14, 1949, *The Richmond News Leader* printed a statement issued by Henry Wise, the longtime GOP leader, urging Republicans to enter the Democratic primary on August 2 and vote for Battle. It was "the duty of every citizen of this Commonwealth, regardless of party affiliations," Wise said, "to join in this effort to repel this unholy invasion by aliens into our domestic affairs. . . ."[70] Other Republican leaders, including Ted Dalton, criticized Wise's action and urged GOP partisans to participate in their own primary. But Battle labeled Wise's comments "highly patriotic" and made it clear that he welcomed Republican help.[71] Later, Colonel Miller would allege that Wise and Senator Byrd had met secretly to plan Wise's public call for GOP participation in the primary, but the charge was never substantiated and is of doubtful accuracy. Senator Byrd was less than sanguine about providing evidence of organization cooperation with the GOP, and Wise's statement was not certain to increase the number of Republicans voting in the Democratic contest in any event. Indeed, interest in the GOP primary was running so low and opposition to the liberal Miller among Republicans was running so high that a heavy GOP vote for Battle seemed likely even before Wise issued his statement.

Whatever the cause, the magnitude of the Republican "cross-over" on August 2 was striking. Statewide, less than 9,000 voters cast ballots in the GOP primary—fewer than would crowd into the Richmond Coliseum three decades later to nominate the party's Senate candidate by convention.[72] While many

---

[68]Beagle and Osborne, p. 80.

[69]Latimer, p. 34.

[70]Henriques, p. 95.

[71]Ibid., p. 96.

[72]Approximately nine thousand delegates and alternates attended the 1978 Virginia Republican Convention, which nominated Richard D. Obenshain for the United States Senate after six ballots over the course of twelve hours. See Chapter 31. After 1949, Virginia Republicans did not hold another statewide primary for forty years. In 1989, former state Attorney General J. Marshall Coleman defeated former U.S. Senator Paul S. Trible, Jr., and Eighth District Congressman Stanford E. Parris to win the GOP gubernatorial nomination. More than 400,000 Virginians went to the polls to cast ballots in the 1989 contest. See Chapter 35.

Republicans stayed at home on primary day, many others went out to help decide the Democratic contest. In ten of the most Republican counties in the state, 87 percent of those voting cast ballots in the Democratic primary, and Battle won in all ten.[73] Battle received nearly 43 percent of the Democratic primary vote, compared to just over 35 percent for Miller and 15 percent for Edwards.[74] In the view of the vanquished Colonel Miller, the GOP leadership, and most political observers, the Republican vote for Battle easily accounted for his 24,000-vote margin of victory. "Strange as it may seem, the Republican Party in Virginia, though dead on its feet, . . . was the deciding factor in the election of John S. Battle as governor," commented Ted Dalton after the election.

> [Republicans] deserted our own first gubernatorial primary and flocked to the Democratic primary to support Battle. The Byrd organization may deny that it owes its political neck in the state government to the Republicans . . . but the county and precinct workers know otherwise.[75]

The claims of GOP responsibility for Democrat Battle's nomination did little to relieve the acute embarrassment Republicans felt over their own laughable primary. Less than three percent of all primary voters participated in the Republican contest, and in 22 cities and counties across the state the number of Republican voters was less than ten. The party's unopposed candidate for governor, Walter Johnson of Heathsville, averaged less than 100 votes per county and city. Thomas McGuire defeated Berkeley Williams by a 705-vote margin to become the GOP nominee for lieutenant governor.[76] And, adding insult to injury, Democratic Attorney General Lindsay Almond tied for the largest number of write-in votes (seven) in the Republican contest for attorney general and then won the official tie-breaking drawing held by the State Board of Elections, thereby becoming the only Virginian to be nominated by both political parties for the same office in the same election.[77] Though numerous prominent Republicans publicly expressed dismay at the disloyalty of so many active members of the party, a motion calling for the ouster from party committees of all those who had voted in the Democratic primary failed to receive a second at a September 1949 meeting of the GOP state central committee.

With the Democratic primary long tantamount to election in Virginia, the November general elections prior to 1949 typically generated little interest. Few could have been more anti-climatic, however, than the vote held in November 1949. GOP gubernatorial nominee Johnson was extremely conservative even by

---

[73]Henriques, pp. 105–107.

[74]The vote totals were: Battle – 135,436 (42.8%); Miller – 111,697 (35.3%); Edwards – 47,435 (15.0%); Arnold – 22,054 (7.0%). Eisenberg, *Virginia Votes*, p. 180.

[75]*The Washington Post*, September 3, 1950, quoted in Latimer, p. 35.

[76]The vote totals were: McGuire – 4,635 (54.1%); Williams – 3,930 (45.9%). Sabato, *Democratic Party Primary*, p. 66.

[77]Beagle and Osborne, p. 51.

Virginia standards, and his campaign attracted little serious attention from the state's politics-weary voters. The general election tally gave Battle more than 70 percent of the vote, an impressive figure even for a Byrd organization candidate.[78] The GOP effort was a weak one—and unsurprisingly so, since Republicans had helped the Byrd men give the Democratic nomination to one of their most appealing general election candidates in many years.

The events of 1949 mark the year as a critical one in the state's postwar political development. For one thing, it was the year that changing attitudes and demographics in Virginia first manifested themselves in the emergence of a resolute faction within the state Democratic Party determined to bring the conservative state party more into line philosophically with its liberal national counterpart. "Until I met [Francis Pickens Miller in 1949], I was just like most Virginians," commented Henry Howell in 1980.

> I couldn't have cared less. Politics was nothing in Virginia. It was all cut and dried, and the average younger person wasn't invited to take any part and wasn't needed because Harry Byrd, Sr., determined who was going to fill every office. Miller pointed out more graphically [than had others] that our government was a closed society.[79]

Both Howell and Mills Godwin, then a first-term member of the House of Delegates from Nansemond County, played active roles in the 1949 primary campaign. It was a sign of the change to come that neither of these men, who would meet in a titanic gubernatorial struggle in the 1970s,[80] supported the candidate preferred by Senator Byrd in the 1949 contest: Howell backed Miller, while Godwin endorsed party chief Edwards and stood by him throughout the primary contest.

1949 also was the year in which the Byrd organization first joined with like-minded Republicans to put down a perceived liberal Democratic threat. Republicans had voted with Byrd before, but never had their help been indispensable. "Virginia," wrote Colonel Miller in his memoirs, "was being ruled by a coalition of the Byrd party and the Republican party [in 1949]."[81] That year, it was a coalition that helped preserve the Byrd faction's preeminence. In later years, however, as the Byrd organization crumbled and then collapsed under the weight of an expanded electorate and an ever-stronger liberal faction within the state Democratic party, the Virginia Republicans would acquire new strength and then become a strong competitive force in the Commonwealth because of that coalition.

Significantly, 1949 was the last year in which the total vote in the Democratic primary in Virginia exceeded that in the general election. In subsequent

---

[78]The vote totals were: Battle – 184,772 (70.4%); Johnson – 71,991 (27.4%). Eisenberg, *Virginia Votes*, p. 176.

[79]Henry E. Howell, Jr., interview, June 12, 1980.

[80]Godwin defeated Howell in the 1973 gubernatorial election. See Chapter 25.

[81]Miller, p. 188.

years, a smaller and smaller percentage of Virginians took part in the Democratic Party nominating process. As real two-party competition emerged for the first time in the 1950s and then blossomed in the 1960s, Virginia voters began to see the general election as the proper focal point for their electoral participation. To an increasingly moderate-liberal Democratic core constituency was left the party's primaries, a development that eventually facilitated a realignment of Virginia's parties along the lines of their counterparts at the national level.

After the intense political excitement of 1949, the next two years were relatively quiet. Democrats retained their lock on all nine of Virginia's seats in the U.S. House of Representatives in 1950, and in 1951 won their usual lopsided majorities in the State Senate and House of Delegates. The General Assembly that was elected in 1951 contained just four Republicans in the Senate and six in the House.

On the surface, at least, little changed in the Commonwealth. Governor Battle followed through on his campaign pledge to increase state funding for education without raising taxes. The Byrd organization's resolve to maintain Virginia's status as a low-tax state was manifested in the adoption during the 1950 General Assembly session of a measure sponsored by State Senator Harry F. Byrd, Jr., that required an automatic refund to taxpayers of any state budgetary surplus. Demands for state services continued to outpace state spending. Perhaps in response to the strong criticism he received during the 1949 primary campaign, the influential E. R. Combs resigned his post as Compensation Board chairman in 1950, though he retained his other job as clerk of the State Senate. Most Virginians just took a breather from politics during the two years following the bitter 1949 struggle. Few envisioned the storms that would rumble across Virginia's political landscape in the decade ahead.

Chapter 5

Growing Pains:
The Eisenhower Invasion

"We are for General Eisenhower as a man. But if it takes the Republican Party to get him in there—then God bless the Republican Party."[82]

Thomas C. Boushall, 1952

1952 was an unlikely year for a Republican breakthrough in Virginia. Senator Byrd and his Democratic allies seemed to have an unshakable grip on the state's political affairs—they at least enjoyed the support of the Commonwealth's conservative voters—and Colonel Miller and his fellow "national Democrats" appeared to be the only viable political opposition to the Byrd regime. The events of 1949 had provided embarrassing proof of Republican impotence; the GOP dutifully had assisted the Byrd men in putting down a liberal challenge in the Democratic Party and then had marched just as dutifully to a massive defeat in November. As 1952 arrived, most Republicans doubted that their party ever would win a statewide contest in the Old Dominion. Certainly, the year ahead offered little hope. The invincible Senator Byrd would be standing for re-election, as would the state's all-Democratic House of Representatives delegation. That a presidential election loomed ahead lifted some spirits, but the controversial President Truman was stepping aside, and the disappointing 1948 experience suggested that Virginians were unlikely to award their votes to a Republican presidential contender anytime soon.

For a while it seemed that Virginia's Republicans would not have even an internal fight to occupy their energies in 1952. Ohio's conservative United States senator, Robert Taft, had fallen short in his bid for the Republican presidential nomination four years earlier. But, in the wake of Dewey's upset loss to Truman, the popular Taft—nicknamed "Mr. Republican" because of his leadership in the Senate—was favored to win the 1952 nod. In the fall of 1951, he toured the South to test the political waters, and, though he detected considerable bipartisan sentiment for the undeclared candidacy of General Dwight Eisenhower, polls of Republican Party leaders showed Taft to be the heavy favorite for the nomination. That appeared to be the case also in Virginia, where the Ohio Republican enjoyed not only the avid support of

---

[82]Vogt, p. 247.

39

conservative party elders such as Henry Wise and Fred McWane, but the admiration of numerous younger GOP partisans as well.

After his refusal to seek the Presidency in 1948, Eisenhower had been the object of much speculation and pressure concerning the 1952 race. Among his strongest backers nationally was prominent author-editor Dr. Douglas Southall Freeman of Richmond, who privately urged Eisenhower to run and discussed strategies for electing him with another of the general's influential admirers, Senator Byrd. In Virginia, as elsewhere, most of Eisenhower's early support came from outside of the Republican Party. By autumn 1951, Senator Hugh Scott of Pennsylvania had organized local bipartisan Citizens for Eisenhower groups throughout the country, and his efforts were especially successful in the South.

During a swing through Virginia, Scott enlisted the help of Bank of Virginia President Thomas C. Boushall, an influential Democrat and Byrd loyalist, in assembling a state organization to work for the nomination and election of the popular war hero. It did not matter that the revered "Ike" was preparing to mount his bid as the Republican nominee. "We are for General Eisenhower as a man," said Boushall. "But if it takes the Republican Party to get him in there—then God bless the Republican Party."[83] On January 7, 1952, came the long-awaited announcement from Eisenhower that he would accept the nomination if drafted to run by the Republicans. The next day, a group of prominent businessmen and attorneys, most of them conservative Democrats, met at the Hotel John Marshall in Richmond and formed "Virginians for Eisenhower." The unusual contest for the Republican presidential nomination was underway.

Republican Party Treasurer Fred McWane, Taft's chief backer in the Commonwealth, was little concerned as he watched the organizational effort on Eisenhower's behalf. Senator Taft had the support of the GOP regulars, and they—not the Byrd Democrats—would select the convention delegates who would choose the Republican nominee for President. McWane was confident that his Republican colleagues would remain true to their conservative champion and not be swayed by the argument that Eisenhower was more "electable." What he did not appreciate, however, was how much the state GOP had been changing in the years since the war.

During the late winter months and throughout the spring, Virginia Republicans witnessed a hard-fought, often bitter struggle between the Taft and Eisenhower forces. The supporters of Senator Taft had the upper hand among the party regulars and retained it through the state GOP convention, but that did not prevent the Eisenhower enthusiasts from vigorously pressing their case across the state as city and county "mass meetings" were held to select convention delegates. To most observers, the contest pitted the GOP's "new guard"—the younger, more aggressive faction—against the "old guard"

---

[83]Ibid.

that had been controlling the party for years. The party veterans were long-time, loyal supporters of the steadfast Senator Taft. In many cases they were also people who were resigned to the Virginia Republican Party's inability to win elections and who were quite content to have the insular party remain merely an "adjunct of the Byrd organization in time of need"[84] and a funnel for federal patronage. For the new guard, this was the time to build a competitive Republican Party in the state, and the popular Ike was the one who could lay the foundation. Of course, the factional and generational lines did not correspond precisely. Among Senator Taft's most avid fans were a pair of young attorneys who were committed to building a winning GOP—Linwood Holton in Roanoke and J. Calvitt Clarke, Jr., in Richmond.

Since 1948, Republican units across the state had been undergoing something of a changing of the guard. In 1950, for example, Joel Broyhill and Lee Potter made good on their earlier pledge and, with the help of their young business and professional colleagues in the Arlington Optimist Club, succeeded in ousting the aging party leadership and electing Potter as the GOP county chairman. Similar changes occurred in the Shenandoah Valley, where Young Republicans led by Stephen Timberlake of Staunton overcame the "patronage-oriented old timers" in a bruising battle and took control of the Seventh District Republican committee.[85] Perhaps the most bitter contest in 1952 between the old guard and the new was fought in Roanoke, where Holton took on the party elders in a bid for the city GOP chairmanship. Holton emphasized the party's need to field candidates for public office at all levels—especially locally—and he kept his preference for Taft to himself, saying only that he would work actively for the party's presidential nominee no matter who he was. After a protracted struggle, the pro-Eisenhower, new guard forces succeeded in winning the chairmanship for Holton by a narrow margin.

A very different kind of battle was fought between the backers of General Eisenhower and Senator Taft in the Richmond-area Third District. The scene of fractious intraparty strife during the 1940s, the Third District GOP was riddled with personal animosities and factionalism as the 1952 contest began. In contrast to their relatively clear-cut division elsewhere in the state, young activists and older partisans could be found in significant numbers on both sides of the Ike-Taft struggle in the Richmond area. The acrimony was increased several-fold, however, by the influx of Eisenhower's Democratic supporters into the party nominating process. On February 8, 1952, the day of the Richmond City GOP mass meeting, Dr. Freeman used his popular daily radio broadcast to announce that "a very important Eisenhower meeting" would take place that evening. Freeman's ambiguous reference was to the Republican mass meeting, and he urged his listeners to attend "because a good

---

[84]Pearson interview.
[85]See Vogt, p. 225.

many of the Republican leaders in the city favor Mr. Taft, and they might attempt to [pass a motion instructing the elected delegates to vote] for Mr. Taft at the district convention."[86] Freeman's appeal and the efforts of the local Eisenhower clubs bore fruit, as nearly 200 of the general's supporters poured into the John Marshall High School auditorium that evening.

The mass meeting was raucous. With the city Republican chairman, a Taft supporter, wielding the gavel, and state Young Republican Chairman Calvitt Clarke making the motions from the floor, the Taft backers forced through their preferred slate of delegates to the Third District GOP convention. Eisenhower leader Thomas Boushall and his allies vehemently objected to the heavy-handed tactics, and the protests of Eisenhower partisans drowned out much of the proceedings. But the chairman forged ahead, took a series of votes, declared the Taft slate elected, and quickly adjourned the meeting. The incensed Eisenhower backers remained for a rump session and elected a rival slate of delegates and their own set of city GOP officers.

The turbulent meetings and rival slates were the major political news in Richmond and around the state for weeks as the two sides traded charges and counter-charges. The Eisenhower supporters claimed that they were improperly denied an opportunity to speak and vote at the mass meeting, while the Taft partisans insisted that many who had attended the meeting—such as Boushall—were Democrats who had no right to participate. GOP National Committeeman Curtis Dozier, a Taft leader, charged that Dr. Freeman had used his radio broadcast to commit a "fraud" on the Richmond GOP by employing "cautious language and weasel words" to invite Eisenhower supporters to "pack the meeting."[87] *The Richmond News Leader* at first sided editorially with the Eisenhower forces, which it said were victimized by "a ruthless exhibition of parliamentary railroading."[88] The editorial continued:

> If the Republicans of the South had even elementary common sense, they would seize upon the magnificent opportunity that has been handed them to exploit the division within the Democratic party. Theirs is a chance in a lifetime to woo into permanent Republican ranks the many persons who are fed up with the New Deal, the Fair Deal and the Welfare State. But instead of offering these orphan Democrats the welcome mat, the old guard is throwing it in their faces.

The Taft supporters, however, made their case to *News Leader* Editor James J. Kilpatrick, and after a week's reflection he recanted:

> [N]ow that both sides to the dispute have issued full statements it is apparent that the editorial was unfair and the harshest part of our criticism was unwarranted. . . .

---

[86]Ibid., pp. 248–249.

[87]*Richmond Times-Dispatch*, February 14, 1952.

[88]*The Richmond News Leader*, February 12, 1952.

There is a great deal to be said . . . for the side of City Republican Chairman James R. Moore, National Committeeman Curtis Dozier, and so devoted a laborer in the Republican vineyards as J. Calvitt Clarke, Jr., ...

These gentlemen looked over the audience that Friday night and saw an attempted coup in the making; they feared, and with good reason, that an effort would be made by Eisenhower partisans to seize control of the local party machinery. They were about to have their own party taken away from them, and they cannot well be blamed for resisting the move. The pro-Eisenhower faction at the meeting did include a number of Richmonders previously identified with the Republican party, but there is no question that most of those in the Eisenhower group were attending their first Republican meeting, and that their chief interest was not in the Republican party as a continuing political entity, but only in the cause of General Eisenhower.[89]

The Richmond GOP dispute carried over to the Third District convention, where the Eisenhower backers walked out and staged another rump meeting. At the state convention, the matter was resolved temporarily by seating the rival slates and according each of the delegates a half-vote. The issue ultimately was settled at the party's national convention in Chicago, where the pro-Taft Virginia delegates finally were seated. Boushall, who had filed the credentials challenge, chose to remain at home during the national conclave; he bought his first television set with the money he saved by not going to Chicago, and he and his fellow Eisenhower fans watched the proceedings in the comfort of his living room. It was not until well after the national convention that the rival Third District GOP organizations buried the hatchet and joined forces to form a unified campaign committee.

As Eisenhower and Taft followers battled across the state in the early months of 1952, competition for key party leadership posts also developed. In late February, all nine Republican members of the General Assembly joined in a public call for party leadership changes, and they specifically urged the election of State Senator Floyd Landreth of Galax as GOP state chairman and State Senator Ted Dalton of Radford as national committeeman. Though Dalton was unopposed, the chairmanship contest quickly took on overtones of the Taft-Eisenhower struggle. The incumbent, Robert Woods, endorsed Taft and injected himself into the Richmond controversy in support of the pro-Taft delegates, while Landreth, like Dalton, remained publicly uncommitted but was widely suspected of pro-Eisenhower leanings.

At the stormy Republican state convention in Roanoke on May 31, the Taft forces had an apparent majority, but the lengthy and often rancorous session did not go well for them. Nationally, the Taft campaign had suffered setbacks in several primaries, and Eisenhower's growing momentum clearly

[89]*The Richmond News Leader,* February 18, 1952.

was felt at the Virginia Republican gathering. Walter Hoffman, a young Norfolk lawyer and Eisenhower backer, scored a surprise win to become chairman of the convention, and the Taft forces then were able to elect only part of their slate of national convention delegates. In the biggest surprise of the day, Landreth won an upset victory over Woods to become the new state chairman.

As delegates assembled for the Chicago convention in July, the Virginia count stood at nine delegates committed to Taft, four committed to Eisenhower, and ten uncommitted. One of the ten uncommitted delegates who played his cards closest to the vest was Ted Dalton, who wanted the Taft-leaning delegation to elect him national committeeman.[90] That it did, and the very next day Dalton announced his support for Eisenhower. Several other delegates followed Dalton's lead, and Taft on the first ballot received only 14 of the 23 Virginia votes—far from the unanimous support party elders originally had predicted. On the second ballot, when Eisenhower's nomination seemed assured, a voice announced that all 23 Virginia votes were for the general. A scuffle ensued around the Virginia standard, and then another voice was heard correcting the total: there were 19 votes for Eisenhower; four Taft delegates would not switch.

Though Republicans had been voting in Democratic primaries for years, the Taft-Eisenhower battle had prompted the first Democratic foray into the GOP nominating process, and it had been a bruising experience for the participants. The scenario would be repeated again and again in succeeding years as the party grew. Though their GOP had long been little more than a debating society, veteran Republicans guarded their power jealously. If it was not much, it nevertheless was all they had. To charges that they were selfishly and short-sightedly stunting party growth, members of the old guard insisted that they would readily accept genuine converts, but they would not permit Democratic interlopers who were unwilling to pledge fidelity to the GOP to select the party's nominees. It was a reasonable stance in theory, but in practice it would be a major impediment to party growth through realignment. Whether, how, when, and on what terms conservative Virginia Democrats should participate in Republican Party processes would be a matter of great debate in the GOP in the decades that followed.

The process that culminated in the 1952 national convention and the Eisenhower nomination had far-reaching consequences for the Virginia Republican Party. The Eisenhower candidacy and the competition triggered by it had attracted a large number of new people to GOP mass meetings—not just the Democratic interlopers in Richmond, but young professionals, college students, and housewives throughout the state. Much of the local party leader-

---

[90]During this time, and continuing until 1972, the national committeeman and national committeewoman were elected by the state party's delegation to the national convention, rather than by the state convention.

ship had changed hands as the torch was passed—sometimes voluntarily, sometimes not—to a younger group. At the state level, Ted Dalton emerged at the national convention as the preeminent Virginia Republican leader. His statements reflected the determination of the new guard to move forward:

> We want to keep the party alive and fresh and growing. We want it strong, not just for the presidential election, but for local elections as well. We also want to bring harmony to and unify the party, to build good will, and to attract new members. We will seek to bring in independents and former Democrats.[91]

That last sentence probably was the one that stuck in the mind of a teenager from Blacksburg who accompanied Dalton to the Chicago convention. Bringing like-minded Democrats and independents into the GOP made all the sense in the world to young Richard Obenshain.

The long-running, dramatic competition between the venerated "Mr. Republican" and the popular war hero was excitement of the sort that Virginians did not expect from the state's Republicans. It would not be the only exciting and unexpected development in 1952.

---

[91]Vogt, p. 263.

Chapter 6

"Golden Silence" and Presidential Republicanism

"I have found that sometimes silence is golden. . ."[92]

Harry F. Byrd, Sr.

What would Harry Byrd do now? Four years earlier, at his suggestion, Virginia Democrats had endorsed Dwight Eisenhower for President. Now the general was the Republican presidential nominee, and the senator's loyalists had played a part in bringing that about. In fact, Senator Byrd himself privately had given advice to the general's supporters and thereby had aided him in securing the Republican nomination. That had not been an easy thing for Harry Byrd to do; he liked his conservative colleague, Senator Taft, and they were legislative allies. But Eisenhower was a war hero, the kind of popular figure who could capture the imagination of the American people and (most important to Byrd) put an end to two decades of liberalism in the White House. Byrd's personal wishes were clear enough, but what stance would he take publicly? He was, after all, a Democrat—a senior Democrat in the United States Senate and the acknowledged leader of the majority party in Virginia.

While Republicans were choosing between Taft and Eisenhower, Byrd was busy with a battle of his own. The Democratic primary for the U.S. Senate pitted him against Francis Pickens Miller, the formidable 1949 organization foe who now resolved to take his crusade into the heart of the enemy camp. The issues were predictable. Miller blasted away at Byrd's "one-man rule," which he said had resulted in "less freedom of mind in the Commonwealth . . . than any time since 1776."[93] He also questioned Byrd's loyalty to his party, noting that the senator had voted against President Truman more often in 1951 than had "Mr. Republican," Ohio's Senator Taft. "Harry Byrd has sold us down the Ohio River," Miller quipped.[94]

For his part, Byrd was delighted to have Truman as a key issue in the campaign. The senator had become the central figure in the conservative coalition of Southern Democrats and Republicans in the Congress that battled the President, and in 1949, Truman had declared in frustration, "There are too

---

[92]Wilkinson, *Harry Byrd*, p. 85.
[93]Latimer, p. 47.
[94]Ibid.

many Byrds in Congress."[95] Facing fierce opposition from Southern Democrats, Truman decided to forego another re-election bid in 1952, but Byrd continued to hammer away at the evils of "Trumanism." When Miller defended the chief executive in early April with the broad statement, "On every one of the great issues which have confronted him, the President has made the right decision,"[96] Byrd seized upon the statement and sought to make his contest with Miller a referendum on Truman's policies. "I've been asked what kind of Democrat I am," Byrd told one campaign audience. "Well, I still believe in the Democratic platform of 1932—the best platform ever written. I'm a Virginia Democrat, a true Democrat, and if any further definition is needed, I am not a Truman Democrat."[97]

By the time the primary votes were cast on July 15, the contest between Byrd and Miller had become exceptionally shrill and—on Miller's part, at least—quite bitter. Byrd won easily, garnering nearly 63 percent of the vote.[98] Miller's share of the ballots was about what it had been against his multiple opponents in the 1949 race. Though the colonel charged that Republicans in 1952 again invaded the Democratic primary to support his opponent, the situation was very different from what it had been three years earlier. Party Chairman Floyd Landreth publicly had urged members of the GOP to stay out of the Democratic contest, and it is doubtful that Republicans participated in large numbers. It mattered little, however, whether GOP voting was substantial or minimal, because Byrd's margin of victory was so large that no one credibly could claim that Republicans had affected the outcome.

Two days after the primary, Virginia Democrats met in Roanoke for their state convention. They heard former Governor Tuck roundly denounce the Truman administration's policies, and then elected an uncommitted slate of delegates to the Democratic national convention in Chicago. When Senator Byrd, Governor Battle, Tuck, and the Virginia delegation arrived at the convention the following week, they were more concerned about the party's proposed new loyalty oath than about who in the multi-candidate field would emerge with the presidential nomination. In reaction to the desertion of Southern Democrats to "Dixiecrat" Thurmond in 1948, national party leaders were planning to require a pledge of support for the Democratic Party's nominees as a prerequisite to the seating of delegations. That proposal put Eisenhower enthusiasts like Byrd in an untenable position.

The 1952 conclave in Chicago proved to be the last Democratic national convention Harry Byrd ever attended, and it was clear upon his arrival that he was looking for an excuse not to remain for all of that one. Commenting on the

---

[95]Henriques, p. 263.
[96]Ibid., pp. 243–244.
[97]Wilkinson, *Harry Byrd*, p. 88.
[98]The vote totals were: Byrd – 216,438 (62.7%); Miller – 128,869 (37.3%). Eisenberg, *Virginia Votes*, p. 192.

Virginians' unwillingness to sign a loyalty pledge, Senator Byrd declared, "If they want to throw us out, let them. A good many of us would welcome it."[99] As it turned out, the Virginia delegation was seated without taking the oath, but only after Battle took to the podium to offer an eloquent defense of the Virginians' stance. The governor apparently arrived at the rostrum just ahead of a fire-breathing Tuck, who was anxious to lead a Southern exodus from the convention. Reporter James Latimer offered this interpretation of the events:

Neither Byrd nor Tuck would ever admit it, but Virginia newspapermen covering the Virginia delegation believed that Byrd, Tuck and others were trying to get the Virginia delegates rejected or thrown out, so as to put the national party in the position of having kicked out the state party, rather than have Virginia sit through the convention as participants and then put the state party in the position of possibly bolting. It also appeared to the newsmen that Battle knew what Byrd, Tuck and Co. were about, and that Battle, quietly determined, in his gentlemanly way, to avert an open break with the national party, outsmarted the would-be bolters.[100]

With the Virginia Democrats having backed Eisenhower in 1948, Republicans hoped that an open GOP-Byrd organization alliance in support of the general could be arranged in 1952. That hope was dashed, however, by Battle's impressive speech and by the self-serving decision of the Adlai Stevenson camp to back the seating of the Virginia delegation at the national convention. The governor returned to the state triumphantly and, with Senator Robertson, Attorney General Almond, Sidney Kellam, and most of the state's congressmen, proceeded to endorse the Stevenson-Sparkman ticket and to campaign for it.

Virginia Republicans had passed up the opportunity to nominate an opponent for Senator Byrd at their state convention, and the GOP state central committee reaffirmed that decision at a late August meeting in Roanoke. After voting not to field a candidate for Byrd's seat, the committee issued an invitation to Virginia Democrats to join the Eisenhower effort. The GOP resolution recalled "that the Virginia delegates were not welcome at the Democratic National Convention; that they were, in spirit, 'kicked out', but, by the grace of political expediency . . . were suffered to remain in the convention."[101] Though events had precluded Republicans from gaining the help of most of the Democratic leaders in the state, they hoped to pull away enough disenchanted conservatives and Eisenhower admirers to gain a statewide majority for their candidate. As days and then weeks passed with Senator Byrd remaining silent on the race, GOP optimism grew.

The Eisenhower strategy in Virginia was much the same as it was throughout the South. And, for the first time in years, a national Republican campaign

[99]Henriques, p. 286.
[100]Latimer, pp. 50–51.
[101]*Richmond Times-Dispatch*, August 24, 1952.

featured the South prominently in its plans. A confidential memorandum distributed to the Eisenhower campaign's southern operatives provided detailed instructions on how to woo voters who had never been Republican. The remarkable document revealed a well-considered strategy for cracking the solidly Democratic South:

For the South to "bolt" its traditional Democratic voting in 1952 will require a candidate who does not merely campaign under the Republican banner, but AN AMERICAN – worthy of the South's political support.

One must understand and consider carefully the Democratic saga that pervades the Southern mind. Northerners are prone to look askance upon the traditional view that the South still has in its heart the war between the states, and believe that the almost hundred intervening years surely have settled the dust of that conflict. This is especially so as there is practically no living Southerner who could recall, from personal experience, the post-bellum carpet-bagger days, which history teaches did so much to alienate the South from the Republican Party.

True, a great deal of soothing water has passed over the dam that separates the South from the North, but there still remains a hatred and distrust of the Republican Party LABEL when attached to a candidate, particularly in the hearts and minds of those Southerners whose schooling has not been of the advanced type. . . .

Specific suggestions for obtaining Southern support for Eisenhower include:

1. Do not try to sell the Republican Party to Southern voters—sell Eisenhower as the great American he is—whose principles of governing have been accepted by the Republican Party in making him their candidate. . . .

2. Do not try to build a "STATE" Republican Party in the South while seeking to elect Eisenhower. In 1953, with Eisenhower in the White House and hundreds of thousands of Federal jobs available, will be the right time to build a strong Republican Party in the South. . . .

3. Do not harp on that time-worn political tripe that . . . the South needs a two-party system to preserve its freedom in Government. The South has the freest form of Government, for each state within the Democratic Party has not two, but ten and sometimes 20 Party factions to assure uncontrolled free voting at the polls. . . .

4. . . . The South wants a winner as badly as the Republican Party—sell Eisenhower as the one candidate who can win back for the South its pride of being the maker and elector of the President. . .

5. Do not let the negro question enter into the Southern campaign, for there is no negro problem that the South cannot itself take care of. Even if this means alienating some of the negro vote in

populous Northern cities—what of it? The negro vote no longer belongs to the Republican Party as in days of old, for gratitude for freedom from slavery has long been forgotten. In its place, we have 20 years of "handouts" to the negroes by the Democratic Party, which the negro cannot and will not forget at the polls. You cannot teach intelligent voting, except to a small percentage of negroes with higher education. The 136 electoral votes of the South mean more to the Republican Party than the possible loss of a few Northern states, even a big one like Pennsylvania, with its 32 votes. Absolute fairness and opportunity should be accorded the negro, but for the South the question of segregation is holy and must not be disturbed.

6. Look upon the South with reality—recognize that therein lies a people sick of the type of Democratic rule they have had since F.D.R., but still too proud to embrace a Republican Party which would symbolize for them another surrender—another Appomattox. Wean the Southerner TO EISENHOWER, hero of America and the world—give them, in full measure, a hero to worship—they'll love it.

7. Work in harmony with the Dixiecrats—they are anxious to defeat Trumanism. . . .

8. Operate under a "non-Partisan" banner—not a Republican banner—allowing Democrats thereby to work for Eisenhower without sacrificing their Democratic standing in state politics. . . .[102]

The strategy worked well in Virginia. Many of the state's most prominent Democratic civic and business leaders joined "Democrats for Eisenhower" groups, and throughout Virginia the defecting Democrats provided much of the Eisenhower campaign's volunteer manpower and precinct-level organization. The Democrats for Eisenhower were especially effective in the Richmond area, the heart of the state's conservative establishment. There, a group of young lawyers and businessmen who would remain politically influential for years became active in the bipartisan Eisenhower effort. They included FitzGerald Bemiss (later a member of the House of Delegates and State Senate), manufacturer J. Clifford Miller, Jr., and a future United States Supreme Court Justice, Lewis F. Powell, Jr.

On September 26, 1952, Eisenhower ended a 12-day, 12-state whistlestop tour in Virginia. Large crowds lined the train route and heard the war-hero-turned-politician deliver speeches in Roanoke, Lynchburg, Petersburg, and Richmond. At each stop, local Republican and Democrats for Eisenhower leaders participated prominently in the festivities.

---

[102]Copy of memorandum on file at the Republican Party of Virginia Archives (emphasis in original).

The Richmond event was by far the most impressive. More than 30,000 people lined the torchlit motorcade route from the train station to Capitol Square, where another 20,000 jammed in front of the Capitol's south portico to hear the candidate speak. After a rousing introduction by State Senator Ted Dalton, Eisenhower issued a forceful call for an end to Democratic Party domination in the South. But, as he had done at stops earlier in the day, the general lauded Senator Byrd as the true heir to Thomas Jefferson and omitted any reference to GOP congressional candidates. The event was marred only by a mishap that occurred just after the rally ended. As Ike prepared to leave the makeshift platform, the wooden structure collapsed, sending him and several others tumbling to the concrete steps six feet below. Eisenhower climbed up, surprised but unhurt, and issued a smile and wave to the silenced crowd. The event's Republican and Democratic sponsors quibbled among themselves for days over which group was to blame for the accident.

The Eisenhower campaign in Virginia continued to build momentum. The Republican won unprecedented (for a GOP candidate) endorsements from virtually all of the state's major newspapers, and his campaign also took advantage of the new medium of television with an advertising blitz that foreshadowed the expensive media campaigns of the future. The decisive development came in mid-October. Senator Byrd had remained silent for weeks as Virginians speculated about his preference in the presidential race. On October 13, his office in Washington released a statement announcing that the senator would make a radio speech four days later commenting on that subject. By October 17, anticipation about what Virginia's foremost political leader would say had reached a fever pitch. Shortly before the speech, Byrd received a call from Ike. "Don't be too hard on me," the general kidded. "I won't," replied the senator.[103]

The Byrd radio broadcast lasted 30 minutes and was carried statewide on an 11-station network. In the dramatic speech, the senior senator branded "Trumanism" the dominant issue in the presidential race, and he noted that the Democratic nominee, Senator Adlai Stevenson of Illinois, had given no indication that he would depart from Truman's policies. Thus, Senator Byrd concluded, "I will not, and cannot, in good conscience, endorse the national Democratic platform or the Stevenson-Sparkman ticket. Endorsement means to recommend and this I cannot do."[104] The address was to rank among a handful of speeches that changed the course of Virginia politics, and its importance was largely apparent at the time. For thousands of Virginians, the message was clear: it was not only acceptable this time to vote for the Republican nominee; it was the correct thing to do.

---

[103]Alden Hatch, *The Byrds of Virginia* (New York: Holt, Rinehart and Winston, 1969), p. 491.

[104]Wilkinson, *Harry Byrd*, p. 84.

As Republicans, Eisenhower Democrats, and most of the state's newspaper editors applauded Byrd's action, liberal Democrats were outraged. Francis Pickens Miller denounced the senator for "betray[ing] the party" and he later charged that Byrd had made a deal with the GOP to throw the state to Eisenhower in exchange for Republicans' agreement not to oppose him in the Senate race.[105] Governor Battle and Stevenson's other supporters in the Byrd organization had little to say. Battle disagreed politely with the senator's position, but his campaigning on Stevenson's behalf slackened noticeably in the weeks after Byrd's announcement. An elated former Governor Tuck went even farther than Byrd and embraced Ike by name, telling an audience later in October that "the Eisenhower candidacy more nearly conforms to the traditional principles of the Democratic party. . . ."[106]

The result was a historic shift of the Old Dominion into the Republican presidential column on election day. Eisenhower carried the state with more than 56 percent of the vote.[107] Not only did the general improve on the usual GOP totals in rural eastern Virginia, where Byrd's speech was most influential, but he also ran significantly better in the state's urban areas, where the national Democratic Party held decreasing appeal for socially and economically conservative, middle- and upper-income white voters. Eisenhower did not do well among black voters; his open appeal to the Byrd Democrats, coupled with Truman's generally progressive tenure, prompted blacks to move firmly into the Democratic column. The Eisenhower victory cut the new mold into which most subsequent GOP victories in Virginia would fit. To the Republican Party's mountain and valley base, Ike added the support of eastern Byrd conservatives and youthful, right-leaning suburban voters. Seldom in the future would a Republican candidate who failed to capture each of those segments of the Eisenhower coalition win election in the Old Dominion.

On election night, Virginia Republicans celebrated not only their first presidential victory since Herbert Hoover's 1928 win, but also the election of three Virginia GOP congressmen, the party's first in many years.[108] The winners were all members of the Republican youth corps that had become politically active shortly before the 1952 elections: William C. Wampler, 26, in the Ninth District; Richard H. Poff, 29, in the Sixth District; and Joel Broyhill, 33, in the newly created Tenth District. In the Third District, Republican Walter Gambill made a respectable showing in his challenge to moderate

---

[105]Ibid., p. 85; see Miller, pp. 203–204.

[106]Henriques, pp. 312–313.

[108]The vote totals were: Eisenhower (R) – 349,037 (56.3%); Stevenson (D) – 268,677 (43.4%). Eisenberg, *Virginia Votes*, p. 184.

[108]In the twentieth century, Republicans controlled only the Ninth District seat for an extended period of time. Campbell Slemp and then his son, C. Bascom Slemp, represented the southwest Virginia district from 1903 until 1923. From 1923 until 1952, the only Virginia Republicans elected to Congress were two who rode Herbert Hoover's 1928 coattails and served only briefly—Joseph C. Shaffer (Ninth District) and Menalcus Lankford (Second District).

Democratic incumbent J. Vaughan Gary, while most of the other entrenched Democratic congressmen had no GOP opposition. The unopposed Senator Byrd coasted to a massive victory over several splinter party candidates. Republicans also acquiesced in the election of Democratic State Senator A.E.S. Stephens of Smithfield to fill a vacancy caused by the death of Lieutenant Governor L. Preston Collins.

Wampler's win in the Ninth District came over veteran State Senator M. M. Long. His narrow margin of victory—2,300 votes—was the largest of the three successful Republican candidates and, like the others', was attributable to Eisenhower's coattails. Wampler, the state Young Republican chairman in 1950, abandoned a planned legal career and returned to the district to reassemble the precinct organization that nearly elected Republican Eugene Worrell to the seat in 1948. The youthful GOP nominee benefited not only from the surge in Republican activity associated with the Eisenhower candidacy, but also from Democratic division. A Byrd organization loyalist, Long had angered Democratic moderates and liberals with his hard-fought nomination victory over liberal W. Pat Jennings, and many Democrats also resented Senator Byrd's disloyalty to the party's presidential nominee. Dismayed by Byrd's actions, many fiercely partisan Ninth District Democrats apparently threw away their separate Senate race ballots; unfortunately for Long, the House of Representatives contest was on the same ballot.

To the northeast, a law partner of Ted Dalton named Richard Poff clutched to Eisenhower's coattails, and the normally Democratic voters of the Sixth District heeded his call to "send Dick to help Ike" by a margin of 2,000 votes. Though it later came to be viewed as something of a Republican bastion, the Roanoke-centered Sixth District was loyal Byrd country in 1952. Poff's two-decade tenure as the district's congressman would gradually increase pro-Republican sentiment there, but, in 1952, less than 15 percent of the district's voters normally cast Republican ballots, and most of the cities and counties in the district had no local Republican organizations. Poff's upset win was the more impressive because it came over an incumbent Democrat, Representative Clarence G. Burton.

With its rapid wartime and postwar population growth, Virginia became entitled to a tenth seat in the U.S. House of Representatives after the 1950 census. The General Assembly pleased veteran Eighth District Congressman Howard W. Smith by carving the new Tenth District out of the fastest growing and least supportive portion of his district—Arlington County, Fairfax County, Alexandria, and Falls Church. Joel Broyhill and his campaign manager, Lee Potter, had been working on the Republican precinct organization in the area for several years with considerable success. GOP organizing typically was easier there than elsewhere in the Commonwealth because of the influx of Republicans from outside the state and the tendency of many northern Virginia Democrats to align themselves with the more liberal national Democratic Party. While the area had a sizable bloc of Byrd supporters, it was, on the whole, less dominated by the Byrd organization than were localities down-state. In the affluent Fairfax and Arlington suburbs, there was increasing resentment over the tight-fisted organization's refusal to return tax dollars to northern Virginia to pay for desired public services. To the growing Republican base, Broyhill in 1952 was able to add much of the Byrd organization bloc because of a divisive Democratic primary contest won by the more liberal candidate. In a pattern that would be repeated in other congressional districts in the 1960s, Byrd Democrats abandoned their party's liberal nominee after the primary and helped to narrowly elect the conservative GOP contender by a margin of less than 400 votes.

The Republican breakthrough in 1952 in both the presidential and congressional races showed GOP partisans what a little new blood in the party and cooperation with the Byrd Democrats could accomplish. Of course, this was not the first time there had been such cooperation, but it was the first instance in which Republican candidates were the beneficiaries. For party elders Fred McWane and Henry Wise, who long had advocated a coalition with conservative Democrats, the developments of 1952 provided a full measure of vindication. Ironically, however, they and many of their GOP colleagues had viewed Taft, not Eisenhower, as the candidate around whom conservatives in both parties would rally.

Senator Byrd well understood the need for bipartisan cooperation among conservatives. He voiced the concept of coalition himself in a 1951 speech to the Economic Club of Detroit:

> In effect, today, we have three major political parties in this country. We have the Republicans, we have the Constitutional Democrats, and we have the New Dealers and the Fair Dealers. It should be possible to divide the American people into two groups, regardless of party membership; one group comprising those who think in terms of the prime necessity of preserving the basic principles of our constitutional government, and who are willing to make the sacrifices necessary to that end; then in the second group, place those who think in terms of State Socialism and direct personal benefits from the federal government, even at the expense of weakening our system of free democracy.[109]

Those lines were drawn sharply in Congress, where Senator Byrd and other Southern Democrats worked closely with the Republicans. But in Virginia, the case was otherwise. To Byrd, McWane wrote in the fall of 1952 that the "time may conceivably come soon in our State affairs when Virginians of like philosophies should forget party labels and combine under one leadership. . . ."[110]

But McWane knew there was no unanimity on the point among Virginia Republicans. To another correspondent he decried the "politics as usual" approach of the "mountain boys," and added, "We folks who live in Demo-

---

[109]Vogt, p. 178.
[110]Ibid., p. 201.

cratic-controlled sections see many would-be friends who can be wooed by careful handling."[111]

Though he recognized the desirability, and even the inevitability, of Southern realignment, Senator Byrd was not at all enthusiastic about embracing the Republican Party, at least in the Old Dominion. One reason was that he seldom needed to do so. As in the 1949 primary, Republicans rather reliably entered the Democratic contests to help the Byrd organization candidate without demanding or much expecting any favor in return. Also, Byrd wanted to do nothing that would jeopardize his Democratic organization's political dominance at the state and local level. Democratic officials in the courthouses did not mind the senator's legislative cooperation with Republicans, which they deemed understandable given the composition of Congress. But they became exceedingly nervous at any indication of Byrd sympathy for GOP candidates at election time. The local officials' positions hinged on the party loyalty of others, and departures from the party line by the leader of the organization were only likely to encourage more independence down through the ranks. Senator Byrd understood this concern, and he was anxious not to alienate those in his organization who considered themselves "straight-ticket" Democrats. But Byrd also was determined not to stand by idly while, in his view, the country suffered under liberal Democratic rule at the national level.

Senator Byrd's way of accommodating these competing considerations eventually came to be known as "golden silence." For the rest of his life, the senator did not attend another Democratic national convention or support another Democratic presidential nominee. While he did not directly endorse the GOP candidates for President, neither did he leave much doubt about his preference for them. In 1960, when Byrd made reference to his refusal to comment on the presidential race, saying, "I have found that sometimes silence is golden . . . ,"[112] the practice was given its name. Byrd never again went so far as to attack the Democratic nominee and his platform, as he did in 1952, but, then, he never needed to do so. To a Virginia electorate attuned to his cues, the senator's silence spoke with an eloquence that made words unnecessary.

Much of Byrd's resistance to more overt ties with the Republicans was emotional. The Republican Party that he had known since childhood was the party of Reconstruction and black rule in the South and big business in the North. "Good" Virginians simply were not Republicans. J. Harvie Wilkinson III observed that Senator Byrd's "golden silence" stance

> must ultimately be viewed as a product of the peculiar one-party politics of the South. The climate of national and southern politics actually pushed Byrd to the point where silence seemed the only alternative. Critics of this

---

[111]Ibid.

[112]Wilkinson, *Harry Byrd*, p. 85.

policy often made one of two mistakes. Those who denounced Byrd for not joining the Republican Party, "where he really belonged," ignored a century of southern history. Those who saw golden silence as a insidious betrayal of the Democratic party ignored the nature of Harry Byrd.[113]

The nature of Harry Byrd was to put policy and conviction above party. And, though "golden silence" was designed to minimize the adverse impact on the Democratic Party in Virginia, Republicans still benefitted. The most obvious result, of course, was that the state went for Eisenhower in 1952 and for other GOP presidential nominees in succeeding years.[114] In addition, the three successful Republican congressional candidates in 1952 owed their seats to the Eisenhower coattails, and, in Broyhill's case, to even more direct help from Byrd Democrats.

There was, however, a less apparent but nevertheless critical consequence of "golden silence" and the presidential Republicanism it brought to Virginia: voting Republican became increasingly acceptable. Until 1952, many Virginians had gone their whole lives without ever voting for a Republican candidate. Once the barriers of custom and emotion were broken that year, a growing number of Virginians began to give serious consideration to the alternative offered by the GOP at all levels. "[I]t has become quite respectable (in Virginia) to vote Republican," read a 1953 editorial in *The Richmond News Leader*. "[T]hose who went along with GOP candidates last fall have been agreeably surprised to see that lightning did not strike nor were they ostracized socially."[115] The trend would be reinforced every four years when another presidential election came along. With each successive vote for a Republican President, it became easier to vote for GOP candidates in other elections. Senator Byrd was not oblivious to that consequence, but it was a price he was prepared to pay. As former Senator Harry F. Byrd, Jr., later explained, "[E]ach election was judged on its own merits, and despite the fact that it would have an adverse impact on the Democratic Party in the future, Senator Byrd, Sr., concluded to take that position anyway."[116]

To many Republicans in the early '50s, "golden silence" seemed a decidedly mixed blessing. True enough, it enabled Eisenhower to carry Virginia. But Senator Byrd had not switched parties; indeed, he had not even "endorsed" the Republican nominee in 1952. Yet, at the national level the GOP leadership was behaving as if he had fully embraced Republicanism. After they won control of the Senate in 1952, Byrd's Republican colleagues

---

[113]Ibid., p. 86.

[114]The Republican presidential nominee carried Virginia, largely due to Byrd's golden silence, in 1952, 1956 and 1960. In 1964, Byrd again remained silent but the state went into the Democratic column anyway. In 1968, 1972, 1976 and 1980, Virginia returned to the Republican column, with Senator Harry F. Byrd, Jr. either remaining silent or tilting in favor of the GOP nominee. Senator Byrd, Jr., left office in 1983.

[115]*The Richmond News Leader*, June 22, 1953.

[116]Byrd interview.

allowed him to retain the chairmanship of a special committee tasked to recommend ways of reducing nonessential federal expenditures, and President Eisenhower credited Byrd with his Virginia victory. National Republican leaders began to see the Byrd organization—not the state GOP—as the key to winning elections in the Old Dominion, and they went to great pains not to offend the senator. Virginia Republicans soon found that they could count on less than full cooperation from the national party headquarters, particularly when their interests diverged from those of the Byrd organization. Resentment among state Republicans grew, and, in 1953, the state central committee unanimously adopted a resolution criticizing the Eisenhower administration for dispensing patronage in Virginia through Byrd rather than through the GOP leadership.

In the wake of the 1952 elections, there was one new reality in Virginia recognized by virtually everyone: Republican victories on the statewide level could no longer be ruled out. Indeed, the winds of change seemed to some to be blowing briskly in the Republican direction. *The Richmond News Leader* thought it spotted real two-party competition on the Virginia horizon. It proclaimed that "a new political force, made up of thousands of voters who feel no sense of grandfather-worshipping allegiance to the Democratic label, now holds the balance of political power in Virginia."[117] Republicans naturally were exuberant. But, as reporter James Latimer wrote amidst the ballyhoo and predictions of rapid political transformation, this basic problem remained: "How can a Republican Party, which is traditionally conservative, find growing room in Virginia? How can it be more conservative than the Byrd organization?"[118]

The only answer, of course, was a realignment—a move by the Byrd Democrats into the Republican Party. To those who urged him to promote such a restructuring by switching parties, Byrd responded that the suggestion was impractical. Even if he were to switch, Byrd explained, he could not transplant his organization, which included scores of state and local Democratic Party officials, into the state GOP. As *News Leader* Editor James J. Kilpatrick observed in a letter to a Byrd organization friend, there seemed to be no "answer to the dilemma in which conservative Southerners find themselves." He continued:

> It is impossible for many of us to embrace the Republican Party *in the State* for fairly obvious reasons. By and large, the Democrats we have in Congress, in the General Assembly and in State executive offices seem to me immensely superior to any Virginia Republican opposition I have seen on the horizon.

---

[117]Latimer, p. 54.
[118]Ibid.

If you know any rational way out, I'd like to hear it.[119]

No one, of course, had the answer. Essential ingredients for a major political realignment in the Old Dominion—demographic change and electoral reform—were not yet present. And Senator Byrd was not one to sit around pondering such a dilemma while his organization collapsed around him. Statewide elections loomed just ahead in 1953, and it would take considerable skill and effort to counteract the political fallout left from the Republican victories in 1952.

The obvious place for Byrd to start was with the Democrats for Eisenhower. Having observed the energetic activity of that previously apolitical group of prominent young Richmonders during the Eisenhower campaign, Byrd moved to bring them firmly into the organization fold. He invited Lewis Powell, Clifford Miller, and other Eisenhower activists in the Third District to meet with him in Washington, where they discussed ways to place the local Democratic committees in more active and friendly hands. The men returned to Richmond to work on the assignment, and within a year they were in control of the city and district party machinery. Elsewhere, Byrd labored to make certain that his organization men would not deviate from the party line in 1953.

Active support for Republicans in national elections and for Democratic candidates at the state and local level was an awkward and seemingly disloyal tack for the Byrd Democrats to take. But the senior senator had a ready rationalization. He maintained that every state party was autonomous and thus had the right to reject the nominees of the national party. Thus, Virginia Democrats who backed Eisenhower had not been disloyal at all; they simply had been loyal to the state party rather than the national party.[120] To Byrd, states' rights was the essence of constitutionalism, the cause above all causes. Applying that venerable doctrine to political parties was at once consistent with the senator's philosophy and convenient politically.

Virginia's election laws seemed to have been designed peculiarly to conform to the Byrd view of party loyalty. Elections for the state legislature and Virginia's executive offices were held in odd-numbered years. With federal elections held in even-numbered years, any possible coattail effect resulting from a presidential campaign was confined to congressional races. In a year's time, the national issues easily faded from the fore, and Virginia voters participating in elections for state and local offices were little influenced by the political environment beyond the bounds of the Old Dominion. With the state's attorneys general opining from time to time that the Democratic Party loyalty oath did not apply to presidential elections, voters were free to cast Republican ballots in presidential contests and then to participate in Demo-

---

[119]Kilpatrick to James M. Thomson, January 9, 1953, quoted in Vogt, p. 274 (emphasis in original).

[120]Wilkinson, *Harry Byrd*, p. 215.

cratic gubernatorial primaries a year later. The Commonwealth's system of nonpartisan voter registration facilitated the practice. Just as Harry Byrd's organization thrived in Virginia because of institutional devices such as the poll tax, the Compensation Board, circuit judges' appointive powers, and the like, so was it well positioned to withstand presidential Republicanism in the Commonwealth by virtue of the state's unusual election system. It seemed that Senator Byrd had thought of everything.

"Golden silence" was a compromise, to be sure—a halfway approach that allowed Byrd to follow his conscience in national elections while preserving his Democratic organization's control in Virginia. It did not immediately throw open the state's political doors to Republican growth, but it did turn the key. Everybody knew after 1952 that Harry Byrd had voted for a Republican candidate at least once. And, if Harry Byrd had done it, surely the ghost of General Lee did not object.

Chapter 7
The Ted Dalton Phenomenon

"Yes, Virginia, there is a Republican Party. It is still a doubtful quantity in this State; it is still very much the political underdog.... With their platform and plans for an active campaign, the Republican trio may not win. But they may force the Democratic nominees, who in past years have coasted to November victories on the vaguest of vague generalities, into a semblance of debate on major state problems, and thus give the voters a choice."[121]

James Latimer, 1953

Though Senator Harry Byrd went to great lengths in an effort to keep the Republican momentum of 1952 from carrying over into the state elections of 1953, there was something that he had not considered. That was the ability of a man like Ted Dalton to capture the imagination of Virginia voters.

As the Republican nominee for governor in 1953, Dalton was a different sort of Virginia candidate. The 51-year-old Carroll County native had been christened Theodore Roosevelt Dalton, but all who knew him called him "Ted." Possessed of abundant grace and wit, Dalton had a special knack for dealing with people that marked him early for political success. After completing law school at the College of William and Mary in 1924, he began a legal practice in Radford and within a few years was serving as Commonwealth's attorney. In a 1944 special election, he won a seat in the Senate of Virginia representing Radford and the counties of Montgomery, Franklin, and Roanoke—normally a Democratic area. His victory came as a write-in candidate, and his margin was razor-thin. But the relaxed and friendly Dalton won re-election easily in 1947 and 1951, and came to be regarded widely as the GOP's best vote-getter in the state. He was a Republican through and through, as his full name would suggest, but Dalton counted many prominent Democrats among his friends—including Senator Byrd, who occasionally would join him for quail hunting. To reporter Guy Friddell, Byrd once commented that he had never seen anybody like Dalton. During their hunting trips, the senator recalled, Dalton would spot a man working in a field on a far-away hillside and walk all the way over to greet him.[122]

---

[121]*Richmond Times-Dispatch*, June 22, 1953.

[122]Guy Friddell, *What Is It About Virginia?* (Richmond: The Dietz Press, Inc., 1983), p. 75.

"It wasn't an easy choice to jump in and run on the Republican ticket for governor of Virginia in 1953," Dalton recalled years later. "I let it be known that anybody could have the nomination and I'd be glad to withdraw. But they were all urging me, so I got into it."[123] The decision made, Dalton moved quickly to assemble the strongest possible GOP ticket. For lieutenant governor he tapped the Staunton lawyer, businessman, and energetic Republican organizer, Stephen D. Timberlake. And, after a series of telephone calls, he finally persuaded Walter E. Hoffman of Norfolk to join the ticket as the candidate for attorney general. Both runningmates had made bids for congressional seats previously and were regarded as talented campaigners. Interestingly, like Dalton, both had been Eisenhower supporters in the presidential-nomination struggle the year before.

The Republican Party in Virginia had its most attractive ticket in memory—perhaps ever—and across the state it was noticed. "The advantages are all with the Democrats, of course. . .," read a July editorial in the *Richmond Times-Dispatch.*

Yet there is no denying that a fresh political breeze is blowing through the mountains and valleys, the woods and fields of the Old Dominion. It began blowing in 1952, when Virginia not only went for Eisenhower by some 80,000 votes, but three Republican Congressmen out of ten also were elected.

Now the GOP has nominated three absolutely first-rate men . . . from the top rank of Virginia citizenship. In ability, personality and character they can match the three Democrats who are opposing them. . . . It is the civic duty of every adult Virginian to follow this campaign carefully and intelligently. It bids fair to be the most important interparty contest for statewide office held in Virginia during this century.[124]

Predictions of at least a respectable GOP showing were heard throughout the Commonwealth. But the GOP's track record provided little reason to expect that the Republican ticket actually would win. Recalling the "long chronicle of feuds and factions and intraparty squabbles" within the state Republican Party, *The Richmond News Leader* commented, "For 30 years, they have been fighting one another harder than they have fought the Democrats, and the results of this fratricidal warfare have been almost ruinous. . . . The Republicans are 'resurgent,' as the saying goes, but they may yet prove to be largely resurgent against each other."[125]

Indeed, despite Dalton's immense popularity within his party, there was reason to doubt his ability to win full Republican support. Unlike many who were active in the GOP, particularly east of the Blue Ridge Mountains, Dalton was a champion of reform in Virginia. He believed deeply in the need for a

[123]Ted Dalton interview, June 17, 1980.

[124]*Richmond Times-Dispatch*, July 19, 1953.

[125]*The Richmond News Leader*, June 22, 1953.

more forward-looking approach to government in the Old Dominion. From a practical political standpoint, he recognized the futility of attempting to run to the right of the conservative Byrd organization. To be sure, he would not run far to the left of it, either. But thousands of Virginians, he reckoned, shared his conviction that some progress was desperately needed in the state, and he meant to tap that well of public opinion even if it cost him the backing of some Byrd sympathizers in his own party. The central themes of the Dalton campaign were two: to establish a real two-party system in Virginia, and to provide "a progressive, yet sound, government which will be responsive to the needs of the people."[126] It was the latter theme that he pounded home:

I have been in politics long enough to know that we must direct our appeal largely to the young people of Virginia and to the independent and progressive thinking voters for their help in this cause. The courthouse cliques and the old-line politicians will not be moved by our appeals for progress. They will want to retain the poll tax to keep their control; they will never agree for the 18-year-olds, many of whom are sacrificing themselves for our country, to have a voice in selecting the leaders; they will never want to see the schools brought closer to the people, as we contend should be done by having the school board members elected by the people; they will never agree to remove the judges from politics, which we want done; they will not agree to a constitutional convention to revise and modernize our over 50-year-old fundamental law; they will not unite with us in granting the educational and health benefits to the people that the needs require; they will never agree with us in our demand that the best available person should be appointed to serve on the various boards and in the various positions of public service in Virginia; and, in short, they will never agree with us on a progressive, yet sound, program which will be responsive to the needs of the people.[127]

If Dalton's call for progress fell upon receptive ears, the way he expressed it struck a deep emotional chord for many a Virginian. When the gentle and distinguished senator spoke about the state and his hopes for it, he seemed to pour out his whole heart. "He was an extraordinary man," commented reporter Charles McDowell. "Ted Dalton was a man of wit and a magnificent power on the stump. He could make you laugh and then cry about Virginia's failures and problems and the warts on Virginia, and then could speak in the same speech with a pride that made you so proud to be a Virginian you'd want to stand up and wave and shout."[128] He stirred the imagination of his listeners in a way that other state political leaders of the day seldom did. "Man's progress," Dalton liked to say, "is determined by his power to dream and his deter-

---

[126]Text of remarks prepared for publication in "The New Dominion" magazine; copy on file with the author.

[127]Ibid.

[128]McDowell interview.

mination to make those dreams come true."[129] Audience after audience responded to the man and his message.

When they were deliberating over who should carry the Democratic banner, Senator Byrd, former Governor Tuck, and the rest of the organization hierarchy hardly could have anticipated the extent to which Ted Dalton's candidacy would arouse the Virginia citizenry. As it turned out, the Democrat who got the nod was the least well equipped to do battle with the formidable Radford Republican. Fifth District Congressman Thomas B. Stanley was a man of considerable wealth, warmth, and conviction. His credentials were impeccable. He was a highly successful furniture manufacturer and farmer in Henry County; he had served for a number of years as a member of the House of Delegates and for several terms as its Speaker; he had represented the Fifth District in the Congress since 1946; and, perhaps most important, he had been consistently conservative and loyal to the Byrd organization. Few politicians came across better than he in their dealings with people one-on-one. But it was also true that few could turn in a more unexciting, lackluster performance on a campaign platform than Tom Stanley. Despite the length of his political career, Stanley rarely had faced opposition in his previous bids for elective office. Had Senator Byrd known how stark the Dalton-Stanley contrast would prove to be, he might well have backed Attorney General Lindsay Almond, an immensely talented stump orator who was chomping at the bit to run for governor. But Almond had displeased the senator by actively supporting presidential candidates Truman and Stevenson. Besides, Stanley was a fine gentleman who had been waiting patiently for years for his turn. So the nod went to him.

The events of the spring gave hints of the competition that would follow in the fall. Tuck sought Stanley's vacated Fifth District congressional seat in an April special election, and he prevailed by a surprisingly narrow margin over a little-known GOP candidate.[130] In the Democratic gubernatorial primary, Stanley was spared having to face a strong anti-Byrd candidate—Delegate Robert Whitehead had turned aside requests that he run—and the former congressman easily overcame moderate State Senator Charles R. Fenwick of Arlington to gain the nomination.[131] The "almost unbelievably listless"[132] primary campaign was most notable for the absence of substantive issues and the lack of voter interest. *The Richmond News Leader* saw in the "ominous smallness of the [primary] vote" a sign that "a dramatic upset" was possible in

---

[129]Ted Dalton interview.

[130]The vote totals were: Tuck (D) – 16,693 (57.8%); Lorne R. Campbell (R) – 12,182 (42.2%). Latimer, pp. 55–56. Latimer attributed the closeness of the race primarily to dissatisfaction with Tuck's pro-Eisenhower stance among "straight-ticket" Democrats in the western part of the Fifth District.

[131]The vote totals were: Stanley – 150,459 (65.9%); Fenwick – 77,715 (34.1%). Eisenberg, *Virginia Votes*, p. 200.

[132]*Richmond Times-Dispatch*, July 15, 1953.

November, and it called on Stanley "to offer something more than polite evasions and noncommittal 'no comments' to matters of wide state interest" during the general election campaign.[133]

Stanley apparently did not read the editorial, or if he did he was unmoved by it. Like most of the organization leaders, he assumed that victory in November was assured. The Democratic trio, which included incumbents Lieutenant Governor A. E. S. "Gi" Stephens and Attorney General Lindsay Almond, needed only to stress the Byrd organization's tradition of good government and fiscal soundness, it was felt, and Virginians would respond with their usual avalanche of Democratic ballots. Though Almond dissented from that view, contending that Dalton's pronouncements should be answered, the strategy was set. Stanley vacationed in August and then returned to implement the "no comment" game plan with almost religious strictness in the fall. Reporters could pry practically nothing from him but vague generalities; it was nearly impossible to determine where he stood on anything, except that he favored "first, sound business administration, and, second, no increase in taxes."[134]

Meanwhile, Dalton crisscrossed the state stressing his basic themes and advancing a seemingly endless stream of specific proposals. He forcefully urged repeal of the poll tax and reform of the election laws in order to introduce a fuller measure of democracy into the Old Dominion. He called for better public schools, improvements in state hospitals, and the creation of a community college system. Every day, it seemed, there was another new proposal: development of an educational television system; legal limits on campaign spending; a more aggressive state tourism program; a war on tuberculosis; creation of an agricultural commission to study soil, production, and marketing problems; annual General Assembly sessions. Using mostly his own funds, Dalton purchased radio advertising time, and a small amount of television time as well, to get his progressive message across to voters. As the campaign entered its final month, he clearly was gaining on Stanley.

Organization leaders were now duly concerned. In private, Lindsay Almond offered to Senator Byrd the startling prediction that Stanley was headed for defeat.[135] In an effort to salvage the Democrat's sagging campaign, Sidney Kellam of Virginia Beach was brought in as campaign manager, the position he held in Governor John Battle's successful effort four years earlier. Stanley began to remind voters that the Republican Dalton would have a hostile Democratic legislature with which to work if he were elected, and he and his runningmates sought to conjure up images of carpetbaggers and Reconstruction with the charge that the GOP ticket was receiving out-of-state financial support. The usually low-key Stanley even tried to inject some fire

---

[133]*The Richmond News Leader*, July 15, 1953.

[134]Latimer, p. 59.

[135]Beagle and Osborne, p. 83.

into his campaign speeches. But, despite these efforts, organization loyalists at the local level remained unexcited by Stanley and unconvinced that a Republican actually could win. Apathy, as much as Dalton, was about to do in the Byrd organization's candidate.

In the top ranks of the organization there was no little head-scratching and some uncharacteristic hand-wringing as well. It was a source of considerable annoyance to Senator Byrd that James J. Kilpatrick, a stalwart conservative and devotee of the senator's, had thus far declined to give the influential *The Richmond News Leader*'s editorial endorsement to Stanley. When Kilpatrick wrote Byrd in October to give him advance notice of some forthcoming editorial comments critical of Stanley's campaign, the senator fired off a letter suggesting to the young editor that "it might be well to bear in mind that the defeat of the Democratic ticket would destroy that part of the Democratic Party in Virginia that is conservative and turn over the Party to the radicals. . . ."[136] He went on to remind Kilpatrick of the organization's long record of providing sound leadership for the Commonwealth. The response from Kilpatrick must have stunned the patriarch. "Harry," he wrote, "the trouble is that everything is not sweetness and light and sound progressive accomplishment. . . ."[137] He followed with a lengthy recitation of the shortcomings of the state government, department by department. "The sad truth," Kilpatrick concluded, "is that in all too many fields of State government, we have just been coasting—following the lines of least resistance." The newspaperman saved his strongest words, however, for his condemnation of Stanley:

> Tom never indicated the slightest ability to think for himself, to make tough decisions promptly, to speak knowledgeably about the State government. He has shown no imagination, no stature, no drive, nothing to recommend him to the voters. He has been wishy-washy, mealy-mouthed, half-hearted, equivocal; he has stumbled over the slightest expression of opinion. *He is not doing the organization one damn bit of good.*"[138]

If Kilpatrick's judgment seemed harsh, it was one that few around the state would much dispute.

As it turned out, the recriminations were premature. In striking similarity to the developments four years earlier when the organization candidate seemed down for the count in the Democratic primary, a series of events in the closing weeks of the 1953 contest apparently changed the outcome of the election. In mid-October, Sidney Kellam was indicted by a federal grand jury on charges of tax evasion. Kellam maintained his innocence, and, along with Byrd and Stanley, charged that the indictment was the politically motivated work of recently appointed Republican United States Attorney L. Shields Parsons of Norfolk. He nevertheless resigned immediately as campaign manager and was

---

[136]Vogt, pp. 294–295.
[137]Ibid.
[138]Henriques, p. 260 (emphasis in original).

replaced by Fourth District Congressman Watkins M. Abbitt. Though Kellam was acquitted of the charges after the election, the scandal seemed to throw the Stanley campaign off balance. In reality, however, as organization leaders explained later, the episode was just what the Stanley effort needed. Around the state, previously apathetic local Democratic leaders were stunned and moved to action. The Republican threat finally was seen as a real one.

The most critical development in the contest, however, came on October 19 when Ted Dalton delivered a speech in Staunton on the subject of highway construction financing. Throughout the campaign, Stanley had maintained that he was unalterably opposed to a tax increase of any kind, including a gasoline tax hike to fund road construction. Dalton likewise opposed higher taxes, but he believed a tax increase was inevitable unless an alternative source of revenue for needed highway projects could be found. The answer, he concluded, was a $100 million road bond issue, and on a fateful October evening he made his proposal public. The suggestion, recalled colorful reporter Buster Carico, was "dynamite. . . . The whole foundation of the Byrd doctrine was, 'pay as you go' on highway construction. [The Dalton bond proposal] was almost as big an affront as the Pope advocating birth control. . . ."[139] What Dalton had in mind was no radical departure from Byrd orthodoxy. The bonds he proposed would be akin to revenue bonds, with repayment coming from gasoline tax receipts over a ten-year period.[140] But unlike turnpike construction revenue bonds, which were discharged directly with the tolls tendered by turnpike users, the Dalton road bonds necessarily would have been general obligation bonds requiring the state to stand behind them with its full faith and credit. To Harry Byrd, the Radford senator's proposal represented a frontal assault on the citadel of the Commonwealth's fiscal integrity. Dalton had challenged the policy that was the hallmark of Byrd's career and the cornerstone of his organization.

The road financing issue dominated the remainder of the campaign. Senator Byrd, who previously had endorsed Stanley but had little basis on which to criticize Dalton, now took to the stump to denounce the Republican for wanting "to junk the pay-as-you-go plan" and "adopt financing by debts."[141] Other organization leaders joined Byrd on the offensive. Dalton tried gamely to explain the subtleties of his bond proposal, and he charged that the next governor would be forced to raise the gasoline tax if some such solution were not found. But the damage had been done. Byrd now had the issue

---

[139]Carico interview.

[140]Dalton's proposal was akin to the transportation-related "pledge bonds" promoted by Democratic Governors Gerald Baliles and Douglas Wilder more than three decades later. In November 1990, voters overwhelmingly rejected a constitutional amendment that would have authorized the issuance of such bonds by the General Assembly without voter approval. A leading critic of the Baliles-Wilder pledge bond initiative was former Senator Harry F. Byrd, Jr., while State Senator Edwina P. "Eddy" Dalton, Ted Dalton's daughter-in-law, was among its supporters.

[141]Latimer, p. 60.

with which to paint Dalton as a foe of Virginia conservatism, and he was unsparing in his use of it. "It didn't feel good," Dalton later said of his old hunting companion's campaign assault, "but, on the other hand, I understood it. It was his party, and his life's work was in politics. . . ."[142] Ever gracious, an aging Dalton years later could not mask the disappointment—he had given Byrd the sword and Byrd had used it. It had decided the election.

Dalton gave the organization, Senator Byrd would say later, "the closest call we ever had. Until he made that speech he was as good as elected."[141] Dalton agreed. At a GOP central committee meeting after the election, he accepted responsibility for "the great mistake," but told his fellow partisans that he stood by the proposal he made on that "fateful night."[144] "Dalton's way was to take an issue, decide where the right lay, and stand there," wrote columnist Guy Friddell.[145] Warned in advance of the consequences of the speech by his law partner and political ally, Congressman Richard Poff, the Republican standard-bearer nevertheless felt obliged to come forward with his plan. Yet, if he had not underestimated his chances of winning, Dalton might well have postponed or foregone airing the proposal. "Apparently, we all had misjudged what our prospects were for election day at that time," runningmate Walter Hoffman explained. "I am quite confident that had Ted Dalton realized how close it was going to be, he would not have made that speech."[146] It was a costly miscalculation for Dalton and for the Republican Party. Years later, when the Radford Republican encountered Senator Byrd in the corridor of one of the Senate office buildings in Washington, he jovially referred to Byrd as the man who had defeated him. "Oh, no, Ted," Byrd answered, "you beat yourself."[147]

In the wake of the October 19 speech, Dalton's campaign saw crucial financial support dry up, while Stanley's campaign expenditures nearly doubled his foe's. Many conservatives who had been leaning in Dalton's direction, including even some Republicans, began to slip away. Then, on October 21, Colonel Francis Pickens Miller took to the radio airwaves to call on his liberal Democratic followers to vote for the Republican Dalton. The GOP nominee, said Miller, was "a very able and intelligent public servant," and he added that the Dalton platform was "a genuine Democratic document [that reads] like a 1953 version of my 1949 platform."[148] The endorsement undoubtedly sealed liberal support for Dalton, whose stance on the poll tax was particularly appealing to blacks and reform-minded whites. But it provided more

---

[142]Ted Dalton interview.
[143]Friddell, p. 74.
[144]*Roanoke Times*, March 7, 1954.
[145]Friddell, p. 74.
[146]Walter E. Hoffman interview, June 3, 1980.
[147]Friddell, p. 75.
[148]Latimer, p. 61.

ammunition for Senator Byrd, who wondered aloud about the "strange coalition between Mr. Dalton and Mr. Miller," and suggested that Miller's action was motivated by "implacable hatred of me."[149] The 1953 contest, Byrd transparently implied, was merely a replay of the Byrd-Miller battle the year before.

It was a familiar ending to a very unusual campaign. For many Virginians, wrote James Latimer, the contest ultimately seemed to be just "another Byrd vs. anti-Byrd campaign."[150] Stanley received the support of the organization followers and some conservative Republicans. Dalton drew the lion's share of the GOP, black, and liberal vote, and he ran well in the fast-growing suburban areas of the state. Though Dalton's percentage of the vote was the best for a Republican gubernatorial nominee in Virginia in the twentieth century, the breadth of Stanley's winning margin belied the intensity and closeness of the race. Stanley garnered 54.8 percent to Dalton's 44.3 percent in an election that saw voter participation half-again greater than it had been just four years earlier.[151] The comparatively strong showing for Dalton was largely a reflection of his tremendous personal appeal and Stanley's relative weakness as a candidate. Eisenhower's win in 1952 obviously had helped Dalton, but the 1953 elections revealed no Republican trend. Stanley runningmates Stephens and Almond ran well ahead of their ticket leader,[152] and Republican representation in the House of Delegates actually shrank by one, leaving the GOP with just five seats.

Republicans nevertheless were optimistic. Just two years before, they had doubted if two-party competition ever would arrive in the Old Dominion. Since then, they had placed Virginia in the GOP presidential column and had given the Byrd organization a real scare in a governor's race. But the years 1952–1953 were to stand for well over a decade as the high-water mark of Republican renewal, and real two-party politics in Virginia would soon seem as elusive as it had before. Though the undercurrents of growth and change in Virginia continued inexorably if slowly, tangible GOP gains had to await passage of the tragic era Virginians came to know by the phrase, "massive resistance."

Though the GOP's 1952–1953 breakthrough did not trigger a tidal wave of Republican support in Virginia, the developments during that period had exceedingly important implications for the future of the Commonwealth's politics. The Republican Party had received a major transfusion of new blood, and the party's youthful vigor and appeal would have much to do with its eventual emergence as a competitive force. Presidential Republicanism was and

---

[149]9bid.

[150]Ibid.

[151]The vote totals were: Stanley (D) – 226,998 (54.8%); Dalton (R) – 183,328 (44.3%). Eisenberg, *Virginia Votes*, p. 196.

[152]The vote totals in the contest for lieutenant governor were: Stephens (D) – 228,005 (57.7%); Timberlake (R) – 167,336 (42.3%). In the race for attorney general, the totals were: Almond (D) – 235,751 (60.2%); Hoffman (R) – 155,680 (39.8%). Latimer, p. 62.

would remain a fact of life in the politics of the Old Dominion, the first stage in a realignment process that, down the road, would bring Virginia's political parties into line philosophically with their national counterparts. The period also saw the emergence of Ted Dalton as "one of the towering figures" in Virginia politics.[153] Like Eisenhower, Dalton did much to bring respectability to a GOP long regarded as a haven for second-class citizens. An indication of the high esteem in which Dalton was held after the 1953 race was provided in the Senate chamber on the opening day of the 1954 General Assembly session. "[W]hen the tall, silver-haired State Senator from Radford strode into the chamber," reported Guy Friddell, "the entire Senate, most of them Democrats, stood and applauded as Dalton hurried, red-faced, to his seat."[154]

---

[153]Veteran reporter and political columnist Charles McDowell of the *Richmond Times-Dispatch* regarded Dalton as one of three "towering figures" in Virginia politics in the early postwar era. The others were Senator Harry F. Byrd, Sr., and Democratic Delegate Robert Whitehead of Nelson County, the leader of the anti-Byrd faction. McDowell interview.

[154]Friddell, pp. 74–75.

Part Two

Hostage To Massive Resistance
1954 - 1963

Chapter 8

Byrd, *Brown*, and the Politics of Race

"For the past five years, [the organization] had satisfied a
steadily decreasing segment of the Virginia electorate. In the spring
of 1954, however, a new issue appeared on the horizon which was to
retrieve the fortunes of the Byrd organization. The issue was school
desegregation, and under the banner of 'massive resistance' the
Byrd machine quickly refueled its sputtering engines."[1]

J. Harvie Wilkinson III

Having narrowly avoided the calamity of a Republican gubernatorial victory in
1953, Byrd organization stalwarts gathered in Richmond on January 20, 1954,
for what they regarded as the most pleasant of rituals—the inauguration of yet
another stalwart Byrd governor. At this particular gathering, however, a
mixture of relief and unease pervaded the organization's leadership ranks.
With Stanley's victory, the Democratic ruling elders had earned another
four-year political reprieve in the increasingly restive Old Dominion. Yet, the
man who was to be sworn in as governor had stumbled badly during the campaign, and had made it across the finish line only because Senator Byrd carried
him across. He had evinced, at best, a shaky grasp of state issues, and organization leaders understandably were nervous about what the future held for
Virginia under a Stanley administration.

It took almost no time for the new governor to prove that the concerns
were warranted. After stating repeatedly during the campaign that he was
opposed to any tax increase, Governor Stanley was barely into his inaugural
address before he was proposing, to the amazement of nearly all his listeners, a
one-cent increase in the gasoline tax. The reversal seemed to make a prophet
out of Ted Dalton, who had predicted during the campaign that taxes would
have to be raised to finance highway projects. Neither Dalton nor Democratic
legislative leaders imagined, however, that Stanley would renege on his campaign pledge so soon or so dramatically. Many of the legislators themselves
had campaigned in opposition to tax increases. Even so, Stanley's repudiation
of his campaign stance on taxes might not have produced such anger and dismay among his fellow Democrats in the legislature if he had consulted more

---

[1]Wilkinson, *Harry Byrd*, p. 112.

73

than a handful of them in advance. Unlike the remarkably similar but much better-orchestrated turnabout on the same issue by Democratic Governor Gerald L. Baliles three decades later,[2] the Stanley gas tax rise proposal went down to a quick and ignominious defeat.

The new governor also reversed himself on another issue, to the consternation of Democrats in the Ninth District. During the campaign he had promised that he would propose no legislation to toughen the state's Right to Work Law. The subject was a particularly important one in the Fighting Ninth, where Democrats were counting on a large union vote to oust freshman GOP Congressman William Wampler in the fall election. But, midway through the 1954 General Assembly session, Stanley urged the adoption of several bills that would strengthen enforcement of the right-to-work statute, and the legislation was enacted. By this action, Stanley added to his corps of critics most of the Democratic legislators from southwest Virginia.

The Stanley missteps and the resultant appearance of disarray in the high councils of the Byrd organization set the stage for an unusual legislative struggle in the closing hours of the 1954 General Assembly session. The controversy began when it was disclosed that the state's general fund would have a $7 million surplus for the biennium. Under the automatic tax reduction law sponsored by State Senator Harry F. Byrd, Jr., and enacted in 1950, this surplus was to be refunded to taxpayers. But a group of younger members of the House of Delegates, most of them from urban areas, had a different idea. Led by Delegate Armistead Boothe of Alexandria, these "Young Turks" sought to suspend the Byrd tax refund law and amend the budget bill to spend the surplus for improvements at various state educational and mental health institutions.

Proposals to devote additional state funds to such things were not new; virtually every legislative session since the mid-1940s had seen Assembly moderates and liberals challenge the leadership's budget by advocating additional service-oriented state spending, tax hikes, and measures to aid Virginia's debt-ridden local governments. But, until 1954, they never had mustered the votes to get their proposals approved. What was different about the 1954 session was that legislators championing the departure from the Byrd organization party line were not typical organization foes. To be sure, Delegate Robert Whitehead and other vocal organization critics played a prominent role in the 1954 revolt, but they wisely stayed in the background and allowed Boothe and other moderate legislators to take the lead.

Fiscal policy and public services were the issues underlying the Young Turks' initiative, but power was the ultimate objective. The urban legislators

---

[2]Like Stanley, Baliles reneged on his no-tax-hike campaign pledge during his first year in office. However, Baliles did so in 1986 only after a blue-ribbon commission, which he had appointed, recommended higher taxes as a funding source for transportation improvements. See Chapter 36.

knew that if they could muster a majority on the surplus issue, they could force the Byrd organization elders to award them better committee assignments and a greater voice in legislative and political decisions. The Assembly's handful of Republican legislators backed the Democratic upstarts enthusiastically. They were delighted to assist in any effort that could lead to more state spending along the lines advocated by State Senator Dalton in the gubernatorial campaign, particularly when it might have the added benefit of breaking the organization leadership's grip on the legislature. The Young Turks and their allies won a stunning though narrow victory in the House of Delegates, then fell short in the more conservative Senate. It took the deadlocked legislature an extra day following its scheduled adjournment to reach a compromise. The resulting legislation suspended the automatic refund law and appropriated approximately a third of the anticipated surplus.

Though the Young Turk revolt of 1954 was but a single legislative battle without any far-reaching impact on state fiscal policy, it revealed much about the change that was occurring in postwar Virginia. The rapid urbanization trend in the state was having an effect, not only on the demands made upon state government, but on the type of legislators winning elections and the outlook of those who were coming of age politically in the Commonwealth. A progressive coalition consisting of Republicans, Democratic moderates and liberals, and some independent-minded conservatives had come together in the General Assembly, and it had forced concessions. If it could continue to do so, the Byrd organization's principal power base—the state legislature— would be in jeopardy. As the session ended, newspaper editors around the state noted its importance and recognized the choice facing the Byrd organization in its wake. "[T]he old order. . . has changed," wrote the *The Richmond News Leader*, "and the Byrd organization must change with it."[3]

Subsequent General Assembly sessions revealed that the aging Byrd organization leadership was unwilling to yield even slightly to the growing urban appetite for services and the youthful urban legislators' yen for a greater share of influence. Elder Byrd stalwarts, led by House of Delegates Speaker E. Blackburn Moore, responded punitively to the moderates' display of independence by shooting down their bills and by giving them mediocre committee assignments. The harsh treatment helped to drive a wedge that divided the organization and eventually pushed the moderates into a posture of direct opposition to Byrd organization candidates in the 1960s. As Virginius Dabney later explained, "It was a terrible mistake that the Byrd people made by not catering to those fellows and working with them and building the organization around them, because Byrd and his group were all getting old and something had to be done to put new life into the organization. . . ."[4] The error would not be apparent to the Byrd leadership for some time, however, for on May 17,

[3]Latimer, p. 65.
[4]Virginius Dabney interview, June 23, 1980.

1954, the U.S. Supreme Court issued a ruling that completely shifted the focus of political debate in Virginia and throughout the South. The organization would get the "new life" it needed, not by adopting a more liberal approach to state services, but by taking a strident tack on the inflammatory issue of public school desegregation. For the next five years, few other issues would matter much in the Old Dominion.

With Virginia as a party to the lengthy litigation that culminated in the U.S. Supreme Court's landmark rejection of "separate-but-equal" schools in *Brown* v. *Board of Education*, the Commonwealth's Democratic leaders had battled vigorously in court to protect the system of state-enforced segregation. And, as the time neared for the Supreme Court to render its decision, Governor Stanley, Senator Byrd, and the rest of the organization leadership refused to confront the possibility that an adverse ruling might be issued. The Court might mandate further steps to equalize school facilities, they thought, but it would not dare topple the entrenched system of segregation on which the entire social structure of the South was based. When State Senator Ted Dalton and Delegate Armistead Boothe urged during the 1954 session that the governor and legislature begin to study options and possible responses to the impending decision, their suggestions were rejected. The organization steadfastly refused to make preparations, as if ignoring the whole matter could make it go away.

The result was that the Byrd leadership did not speak with one voice when the landmark decision was handed down. In Washington, Senators Byrd and Robertson strongly condemned the ruling as a usurpation of states' rights. The decision was no more popular in Richmond, but it nevertheless brought a temperate response from Governor Stanley:

> I contemplate no precipitate action, but I shall call together as quickly as practicable representatives of both State and local governments to consider the matter and work toward a plan which will be acceptable to our citizens and in keeping with the edict of the Court.
>
> Views of leaders of both races will be invited in the course of these studies. . . .[5]

Attorney General Almond and the state's educational leaders responded in a similarly conciliatory fashion. But, in the weeks after the ruling, other organization figures—especially in racially divided Southside—issued defiant denunciations of the decision, and Stanley was soon backing away from his earlier suggestions of compliance. By late summer, the governor had pledged to "use every legal means at my command to continue segregated schools in Virginia,"[6] and he established a "Commission on Public Education" under the chairmanship of State Senator Garland "Peck" Gray of Waverly to chart a

---

[5]*The Richmond News Leader*, May 18, 1954.

[6]Benjamin Muse, *Virginia's Massive Resistance* (Gloucester, Mass.: Peter Smith, 1969), p. 7.

course of resistance. Despite Stanley's earlier promise that a biracial group would frame the state's response to the Court's mandate, the 32-member "Gray Commission" included no blacks, just two Republicans, and a disproportionately high number of Southside whites.

It took the Gray Commission more than a year to issue its report, and two election days passed in the interim. Congressional elections were held in 1954, and a year later the members of both houses of the state legislature stood for re-election. Neither set of contests, as it turned out, was affected much by the growing desegregation controversy. The Supreme Court had been vague in its initial *Brown* ruling about what steps would be required to dismantle the unlawfully segregated school systems in the South, and various responses were being considered in Virginia and elsewhere. The battle lines were not yet drawn.

Virginia Republicans in 1954 concentrated on preserving the seats they had seized two years earlier with the help of Eisenhower's coattails, while state Democrats targeted the three freshman GOP incumbents. In the Sixth and Tenth Districts, Representatives Richard Poff and Joel Broyhill knew they again would need the support of Byrd Democrats in order to win re-election, but the simultaneous re-election bid of incumbent Democratic Senator Willis Robertson threatened to interfere. If Republicans were to field a candidate against Robertson, Poff and Broyhill would be obliged to support their party's nominee, and the Byrd men backing Robertson undoubtedly would take umbrage. Both congressmen therefore strongly opposed the nomination of a Republican candidate for the Senate, but they found that a Virginia GOP accustomed to waging futile campaigns was reluctant to accede to their wishes. Though it might hamper the re-election bid of his former law partner, Poff, Ted Dalton joined other party leaders in advocating a challenge to Robertson and even took up the search for a suitable candidate. The Radford Republican unsuccessfully entreated Thomas Boushall, the influential Eisenhower Democrat, and several others to enter the race, and he backed off only after it became apparent that no credible contender could be found. Robertson thus went unopposed, and Poff and Broyhill coasted to easy re-election victories.[7]

In the Ninth District, the GOP's other incumbent was not so fortunate. The Byrd men in his district had opposed young W. Pat Jennings of Smyth County fiercely two years earlier and had succeeded in denying him the congressional nomination in the Democratic primary. But, in 1954, Jennings was able to capture the party's nomination, and the Byrd organization fell in line behind him. Though Jennings was too liberal for the tastes of the Byrd men, party loyalty could not be breached in the Fighting Ninth without serious repercussion. Moreover, there was little affection for Congressman Wampler

---

[7]Poff polled 63 percent of the vote against Democrat Ernest Robertson, while in the closely competitive Tenth District, Broyhill garnered 54 percent of the ballots in his contest with Democrat John C. Webb.

among the Byrd followers in southwest Virginia, particularly after he was endorsed for re-election by the United Mine Workers union. The personable young Wampler waged a vigorous campaign, but the combination of high unemployment in the district's coal fields, Senator Byrd's public endorsement of Jennings, and superior Democratic financial resources proved to be too much for the Republican to overcome. Still, he almost certainly would have retained the seat had it not been for the absentee votes received by Jennings. The absentee ballots filed in the contest numbered in the thousands—more than were filed in all of the other Virginia congressional districts combined—and the Jennings margin of victory was just 999 votes. Confident that the election had been stolen, Wampler nevertheless deemed it futile to press his case before the state's Democratic judiciary or in the Democrat-controlled House of Representatives. He determined instead to wait for the next election.

Republican challengers were nominated in other congressional districts, but only in the Richmond area did the GOP candidate make a respectable showing. For the second straight election, Third District Republicans garnered more than 40 percent of the vote for their candidate against incumbent Congressman J. Vaughan Gary. This time it was the energetic young Richmond conservative, J. Calvitt Clarke, Jr., who took on the moderate Democrat, and his strong showing—even without the benefit of presidential coattails—revealed a distinctly conservative and Republican trend in the central-Virginia district. The rapid suburban growth around the capital city was chiefly responsible for the change. That trend would continue, and the Third District eventually would become bedrock conservative territory, delivering huge and often decisive vote totals for successful statewide Republican candidates.

With another round of General Assembly contests just ahead, Ted Dalton and GOP State Chairman Floyd Landreth in April 1955 prevailed upon the party's central committee to hire an executive secretary to spearhead organizational activities for the fall campaigns. The man they had in mind for the job was freshman Delegate H. Clyde Pearson, a 29-year-old Jonesville attorney and—according to Dalton—a real "live wire."[8] Pearson proceeded to criss-cross the state giving speeches, attending party meetings, promoting precinct-level organization, and recruiting candidates. It was a far more active effort than the GOP ever had mounted before, but in the end incumbency still ruled the day. Republicans picked up only one additional seat in the House of Delegates—giving the GOP six of the House's 100 members—and the Republican contingent in the 40-member state Senate remained at three. One bright spot for the GOP, however, was in Roanoke, where another young lawyer named Linwood Holton polled 49 percent of the vote in an unsuccessful bid for a House seat. His stance in favor of gradual compliance with the *Brown* decision had little discernible impact on the race.

---

[8]*Richmond Times-Dispatch*, April 3, 1953.

After a year of deliberation, the Gray Commission finally submitted its report in November 1955. It represented a moderate approach—at least by comparison with what was to follow. Under the "Gray Plan," as the report soon was dubbed, local school divisions were to decide how much integration would occur within their boundaries. The commission recommended that school divisions adopt pupil assignment plans under which students would be directed to attend particular schools on the basis of ostensibly non-racial criteria. There would be token integration, but the Supreme Court's desegregation mandate largely would be circumvented, it was assumed, through inexplicit racially motivated assignments. If the federal courts nevertheless invalidated the local assignments, the Gray Commission had a backstop ready. It recommended that the Commonwealth provide tuition grants for any students who chose to attend segregated private schools rather than racially integrated public ones.

The tuition grant feature of the Gray Plan required amendment of the state constitution in order to modify a provision that barred appropriation of state funds for privately owned institutions. Governor Stanley immediately convened a special session of the General Assembly, and an amendment permitting state support of private schools was approved with little dissent. One of the few to speak out against the measure in the Senate was Ted Dalton. The GOP legislative leader favored the local assignment aspect of the Gray Commission plan, but he worried about the impact of tuition grants on the state's public school system. Moreover, there were ominous signs in some of the public comments of Southside leaders that they opposed even the token integration that could occur under local assignment plans. The tuition grant proposal, Dalton feared, might be the first step toward a stiffer plan of resistance that would lead to an abandonment of public education in order to preserve segregation.

On the floor of the Senate, the Radford Republican sought more than verbal assurances that the commitment to public schools in Virginia would continue. Another provision of the state constitution specifically guaranteed a system of public education in the Commonwealth, and Dalton proposed an amendment to stipulate that nothing in the Gray Plan would diminish or undermine that guarantee. "Unless you insert this provision. . .," contended Dalton, "I have grave doubts that the electorate of Virginia will approve your constitutional amendment."[9] When colleagues responded that his concern about the future of the public schools was unjustified, Dalton replied, "Pray tell me, then, why it would hurt to put in my provision?"[10] His proposal was defeated, and a popular referendum on the constitutional revision was set for January 9, 1956.

---

[9]Buni, pp. 178–179.
[10]Ibid.

The referendum campaign was short but spirited. Dalton worked for rejection of the proposed revision and warned that the tuition grant program would only embark Virginia "on a futile plan that may not stand the test of legality."[11] Joining him in opposition was the articulate senator-elect from Alexandria, Armistead Boothe, whose loosely knit and poorly financed "Society for the Preservation of Public Schools" took the lead in the long-shot campaign to defeat the Gray Plan. Like most of the moderate white political leaders in the state at the time, Dalton and Boothe were avowed segregationists; they publicly criticized the Supreme Court decision that precipitated the controversy and made it clear that they wanted to see as little desegregation occur as possible without jeopardizing the continued operation of the public schools. But most of the other prominent moderates, including University of Virginia President Colgate W. Darden, Jr., supported the referendum proposal, as did liberal Byrd organization foe Robert Whitehead. In their view, the Gray Plan was the most reasonable response that Virginia's conservative leadership was likely to adopt, and they relied on assurances that the local option aspect of the plan would be retained. Local option would permit the school systems in Southside to chart their own course of determined resistance to any integration, while other localities would be free to institute token integration and put the problem quickly behind them.

As the Byrd organization endeavored feverishly to turn out the maximum vote in favor of the referendum proposal, most Virginians came to view the question as one of approval or disapproval of the entire Gray Plan, though only the tuition grant amendment was directly at issue. Governor Stanley embraced all of the Gray Commission's recommendations, but Senator Byrd carefully avoided any endorsement of the local assignment aspect. And, when referendum voters approved the proposal by more than a two-to-one margin, Byrd and other die-hard segregationists immediately hailed it as a mandate in favor of all-out resistance to racially mixed schools. To be sure, that was what the voters of Southside had in mind when they turned out in huge numbers to back the constitutional change. But elsewhere, many voters had cast ballots for a local option feature they thought was implicit in the referendum proposal.

The Gray Commission's middle-of-the-road course was headed for a failure that in retrospect appears inevitable. As one commission member, W. Roy Smith of Petersburg, later explained, the Gray Plan "didn't satisfy the white people in Virginia who said, 'Never!' and it didn't satisfy the black leadership that said, 'Right now!' "[12] As blacks pressed their demands for good-faith compliance with the *Brown* edict, and Southside whites insisted upon unbending resistance to the ruling, the path of moderation became progressively harder to steer. Moderate whites like Dalton attempted to convey a seemingly

---

[11]Ibid., pp. 181–182.
[12]W. Roy Smith interview, July 21, 1980.

contradictory message—that the way to avoid wholesale integration was to permit a token amount of integration to occur. Whatever its merits, that approach sounded far less appealing to most white Virginians than the more simple and direct message of outright defiance coming from Southside and other localities with large black populations. In the racial politics that pervaded Virginia beginning in 1956, there was no middle ground. One was either a segregationist or an integrationist, just as one was either black or white. A willingness to accept even the slightest degree of integration branded one an "integrationist" in the same manner that the slightest black ancestry made one black. Only when Virginians were finally forced to choose between desegregating the public schools and closing them would a politically palatable middle ground reappear.[13]

The stage was set for Virginia's shift away from the Gray Plan to a more hard-line stance by a series of editorials in *The Richmond News Leader.* The newspaper's editor, James J. Kilpatrick, devoted his considerable talents to pillorying the Supreme Court decision, and, in late 1955 and early 1956, he offered a detailed doctrinal justification for refusing to obey the edict. Taking a page from the book of the antebellum champion of Southern states' rights, John C. Calhoun, Kilpatrick argued that Virginia and her Southern sisters had the right to interpose the state's sovereignty so as to nullify the "unconstitutional" ruling by the federal tribunal. The effect of Kilpatrick's extensive writings was to give the advocates of defiance a claim to moral as well as legal high ground. It was much more seemly to take a bold stand on the venerated principle of states' rights than to counsel disobedience to the law of the land for the purpose of perpetuating a system of racial discrimination.

Throughout the South, "nullification" and "interposition" became the watchwords of segregationist resistance. In Washington, Senator Byrd took to the floor of the Senate to praise Kilpatrick and embrace his theory. An orchardist and newspaperman by profession and a champion of state sovereignty by tradition and conviction, Virginia's senior senator knew little of the legal or constitutional niceties that were involved, and he was concerned about them even less. Interposition made good sense, and the *Brown* decision did not, and that was that. It was clear beyond peradventure that all of the opponents of integration had to stand firm and stand together. Coining the phrase that would soon become associated with Virginia's defiant stance, Byrd declared:

> If we can organize the Southern States for massive resistance to this order, I think in time the rest of the country will realize that racial integration is not going to be accepted in the South. . . . In interposition, the South has a perfectly legal means of appeal from the Supreme Court's order.[14]

---

[13]See James Howard Hershman, Jr., *A Rumbling in the Museum: The Opponents of Virginia's Massive Resistance,* Unpublished Dissertation, University of Virginia, 1978, pp. 152–153.

[14]Muse, p. 22.

In Richmond, the Virginia General Assembly adopted an interposition resolution in which it pledged "to take all appropriate measures, legally and constitutionally available to us, to resist this illegal encroachment upon our sovereign powers." A strong popular tide was building behind the resistance movement. Of the 140 members of the General Assembly, only seven voted against the interposition resolution. One Republican, Delegate Vernon S. Shaffer of Shenandoah, was among the opponents, while Ted Dalton and the other GOP lawmakers backed an alternate protest resolution and then abstained on the interposition vote.

Byrd next arranged for a demonstration of Southern solidarity behind his resistance plan. In March 1956, a "Southern Manifesto" bearing the signatures of 101 members of the House and Senate from the South was introduced in both houses of Congress. Given the vocal opposition of State Senator Dalton to the more strident segregationist measures advanced in Richmond, it was noteworthy that both of Virginia's Republican members of the House of Representatives, Joel Broyhill and Richard Poff, were among the Manifesto's signers. Both were quite certain that the vast majority of their constituents, including their many Byrd Democrat backers, favored the declaration and would be unforgiving if their representatives failed to support it.[15] Interestingly, however, Broyhill's Tenth District had been the only congressional district to cast a majority of its votes against the tuition grant proposal in the January 9 referendum.

The contrast between the Dalton and Poff/Broyhill positions reflected the division within the Virginia GOP over the desegregation issue. The party was, in the words of prominent GOP activist Lee Potter, "split right down the middle" on the question.[16] Southwest Virginia and Shenandoah Valley Republicans generally favored gradual compliance with the Supreme Court's mandate. The number of blacks in those areas was small in comparison to other parts of the state, and the Court's decision did not have far-reaching implications there. Typical of the western view was former Congressman William Wampler's. Virginia, he noted, was "about on the bottom rung of the ladder as far as public education was concerned. My feeling was that if we didn't have one good school system, how could we afford to have a dual school system?"[17] To the east, however, most Republicans backed Byrd's hard-line stance. At a February 1956 meeting of the GOP central committee, a proposed endorsement of the General Assembly's interposition resolution appeared headed for passage until party chief Floyd Landreth ruled the motion out of order.

---

[15]Poff's signing of the Southern Manifesto later prevented his nomination to the U.S. Supreme Court by President Nixon. The "Southern seat" on the Court went instead to Richmond lawyer Lewis F. Powell, Jr., in 1972. Poff later was named to the Virginia Supreme Court by Governor Linwood Holton.

[16]I. Lee Potter interview, May 28, 1980.

[17]Wampler interview.

With the re-election campaign of President Eisenhower looming ahead, Virginia Republicans had to walk a tightrope on the desegregation issue. Though Ike had carried Virginia handily four years earlier, the Republican administration was responsible for appointing Chief Justice Earl Warren, author of the detested *Brown* decision. United States Attorney General Herbert Brownell was pressing forward with administration-backed civil rights legislation, and, though the liberal national Democrats also backed the civil rights measures, the Republican President's stance was particularly irritating to Senator Byrd and Congressman Tuck. Their growing hostility to Eisenhower was a worrisome development because Virginia Republicans knew they would need the help of conservative Democrats in order to put the Commonwealth again in the GOP presidential column.

At the party's July state convention in Roanoke, conservative Republicans proposed a resolution that would place the state GOP firmly on the side of states' rights, in favor of the General Assembly's interposition resolution, and in opposition to the administration's civil rights bill. The proposal was derailed in the resolutions committee after moderate attorneys H. Emory Widener of Bristol and Linwood Holton of Roanoke lobbied heavily against it. In its place, the committee approved, and the convention adopted, a far milder and more general statement of support for the principle of states' rights. A few weeks later, Ted Dalton and other Republican moderates found themselves tugging in the opposite direction as they locked horns with proponents of a liberal civil rights plank at the national GOP convention in San Francisco. The liberal plank, they successfully argued, would undermine the party's campaign efforts in the South. Virginia Republicans were trying gamely to straddle the divisive issue. Unwilling to join in the criticism of their party's President or to embrace massive resistance, state GOP leaders nevertheless were determined to keep the state party in the mainstream of pro-segregation opinion in the Commonwealth.

Their efforts, like those of the Democratic moderates, were destined to fail because of the polarizing nature of massive resistance. Though numerous Virginia localities were inclined to choose the path of least resistance and accept token integration, rejection of the Supreme Court's mandate would be ineffective unless there were united and uniform defiance across the state and across the South. Thus the Southside view espoused so bluntly by Congressman William M. Tuck became Byrd organization policy: "If they won't go along with us," Tuck said of certain unnamed Virginia school divisions, "I say make 'em!"[18]

At a secret meeting in Washington on July 2, a group including Byrd, Tuck, Governor Stanley, Congressman Watkins M. Abbitt, and State Senator Garland Gray met to plan how to implement Virginia's massive resistance.[19] In the weeks that followed, a legislative package was drafted, and the governor

---

[18]Muse, p. 22.
[19]Wilkinson, *Harry Byrd*, p. 130.

summoned state lawmakers to Richmond for a special session of the General Assembly. "The Virginia legislature is not generally a body bereft of reason," wrote J. Harvie Wilkinson III, but when the legislators convened on August 27 "extremism was in the air."[20] The gentility and decorum that usually characterized the venerable body were noticeably absent. Inflammatory racial rhetoric abounded. One Byrd lieutenant, State Senator Edward E. Willey of Richmond, later recalled, "We had people whose tongues were wagging faster than their brains were working. That was very prevalent here in those days."[21]

After weeks of controversy and debate, the legislators approved a plan to create a state Pupil Placement Board with authority over school assignments. The legislation provided that if the placement board's segregative decisions were overturned in the federal courts, the governor would order the closing of any schools that were under court order to integrate. Local school divisions that attempted to open schools on an integrated basis—either on their own or under court direction—were to have their state funds cut off completely. Such a school division would then have the choice of operating integrated schools using only local funds (hardly a realistic option) or closing the schools and providing state and local tuition grants for students to attend segregated private schools. The effect was to eliminate even token integration as a viable option for localities under court orders to desegregate. In its determination to preserve states' rights and rigid racial separation, wrote Wilkinson, the Byrd organization had "abandon[ed] the cherished conservative principle that local problems can best be handled by local governments [and had] clamped on every corner of a varied Virginia the racial axioms and attitudes of the Southside and the black belt."[22]

It did so, however, only after a bitter battle. Senators Dalton and Boothe vigorously championed local option at the 1956 special legislative session. Though most of the members of the Gray Commission had abandoned their original position in favor of local pupil assignment plans, two of the commission's members, FitzGerald Bemiss and J. Randolph Tucker, Jr., of Richmond, opposed the package of school closing and fund cutoff laws. As Delegate Bemiss watched the parade of witnesses brought to Richmond by the Byrd leadership to testify in favor of all-out resistance, he grew increasingly disgusted. "These hearings try one's soul!" he wrote to former Governor Colgate Darden in Charlottesville. "Such a dreadful mass of fear, hate, perfidy, ignorance, bigotry—all in the name of 'forefathers,' 'children's children,' 'sacred heritage,' etc., etc."[23] He appealed to Darden, former State Superintendent of Schools Dabney Lancaster, and State Board of Education member Thomas Boushall to come and "save the day" by testifying against the

---

[20]Ibid., p. 131.

[21]Edward E. Willey, Jr., interview, June 6, 1980.

[22]Wilkinson, *Harry Byrd*, p. 133.

[23]Hershman, p. 179.

massive resistance measures. The normally influential men did appear and urged that the local option approach be followed, but the emotional appeals of the resisters drowned them out.

Stanley's massive resistance program passed easily in the House of Delegates. The local option alternative failed in that body by a vote of 59 to 39, with all of the Republicans voting in the minority.[24] In the Senate, however, the vote was much closer. Pitted against local option advocates Boothe and Dalton was the formidable state senator from Nansemond County, Mills E. Godwin, Jr., who served as the floor leader for the massive resistance forces. Godwin had reached the House of Delegates by defeating a veteran Byrd organization legislator in 1947, and he had continued to deviate from the Byrd line by backing Truman in 1948 and Horace Edwards for governor in 1949. But, upon arriving in the Senate in 1952, he had become State Senator Harry F. Byrd, Jr.'s desk mate, and now he was entrusted with the task of steering the organization's most important and controversial piece of legislation through the divided upper house.

Godwin argued that the Stanley program was an essential first step in challenging the validity of the *Brown* decision. At the least, no integration could occur until the legislation was struck down by the courts. Virginians, he exclaimed, "want a basketful of bills, if need be, to preserve segregation."[25] Local option was out of the question. "[I]ntegration, however slight, anywhere in Virginia would be a cancer eating at the very life blood of our public school system," Godwin declared. He then added, "The [Supreme Court] decision is either right or wrong. If we think it is right, we should accept it without circumvention or evasion. If it is wrong, we should not accept it at all."[26] A slim majority agreed, turned aside a local option proposal, and then by a 21–17 vote enacted the entire massive resistance program.

Virginia now had embarked on a course of overt defiance of the nation's highest tribunal, leaving the courts to wrestle with its validity, the state's children to face its consequences, the Byrd organization to ride the political wave it generated, and historians to ponder how and why it happened. The mix of factors and motivations that led Virginia down the path of massive resistance is not easy to sort out—particularly years later, after so much has changed and so many important lessons have been learned. A genuine resentment of steadily increasing federal government power played a part. Racial bigotry, animosity, and fear born of years of rigid societal separation played a part. Political considerations inevitably played a part. The intense pressure from influential Southside Virginia and the pivotal assertion of leadership by the powerful Senator Byrd were obviously key elements. And, against a backdrop of emphatic and often emotional anti-desegregation sentiment among white

---

[24]Wilkinson, p. 132.

[25]*Richmond Times-Dispatch*, September 22, 1956.

[26]Wilkinson, *Harry Byrd*, p. 132.

voters, there was the seemingly irresistible temptation to exploit the potent issue for political advantage.

Throughout the ranks of the massive resisters there were doubts about the constitutionality of the laws passed in that memorable August 1956 session, but there was one overriding goal—delay. Later, after the citadel of resistance came crashing down under the weight of federal and state court pronouncements, the resisters contended that their aim all along had been only to delay the inevitable and to prepare Virginians to accept the change that had to come. They argued that their purpose had been to do all they could legislatively so that the battle would be fought in the courtrooms instead of in the streets. Whether their stand actually served to cushion acceptance or to inflame racial passions was left for historians to debate. For the time being, however, massive resistance gave the Byrd organization a reprieve—both from forced integration of Virginia's schools and from further erosion in the organization's position of political dominance.

Chapter 9

1957: The Massive Resistance Election

"To every question as to what they plan to do when their cut-off-the-funds, close-the-schools program topples in court, [the Democrats] only yell a little louder, 'Little Rock!' "[27]

Ted Dalton, 1957

If it is the duty of the minority party to offer the voters a choice even when the prospects for electoral success are remote, then the gubernatorial campaign of 1957 stands as a lasting testimony to the Ted Dalton-led Republican Party's unfailing devotion to duty. Unlike those in many of the other Southern states, Virginia's politicians generally had not been given to inflammatory, demagogic, emotional appeals regarding race relations before 1957. Only eight years earlier, V. O. Key, Jr., had observed that "politics in Virginia is reserved for those who can qualify as gentlemen. Rabble-rousing and Negro-baiting capacities, which in Georgia or Mississippi would be a great political asset, simply mark a person as not to the manner born."[28] All that changed, however, in 1957—the year in which Harry Byrd's machine "fueled its sputtering engines"[29] on the racial passions and false hopes of Virginia's overwrought white electorate. Ted Dalton was, second only to Virginia's school children, the primary victim of this circumstance.

The stage was set for the 1957 spectacle by the enactment of massive resistance legislation in August 1956. Three months later, Dwight Eisenhower carried Virginia in his successful presidential rematch with Democrat Adlai Stevenson. He did this despite a ringing denunciation of his civil rights policies by his former backer, Senator Harry Byrd, and despite the efforts of a united state Democratic Party leadership, which fell in line behind the Stevenson-Kefauver ticket. Though Byrd again denied the national Democratic ticket his endorsement and kept his "golden silence" on the presidential race, his most conservative lieutenant did not. The irascible Congressman William Tuck reversed his explicit pro-Eisenhower stance of 1952 and warmly embraced the Stevenson candidacy.

---

[27]*The Washington Post*, October 12, 1957.

[28]Key, p. 26.

[29]Wilkinson, *Harry Byrd*, p. 112.

The top Byrd men's racially driven behavior in the presidential contest was enough to raise the ire of some of the organization's backers in the state's business and professional community. In an October letter to the senior senator, Richmond attorney Lewis F. Powell, Jr., sharply criticized those in the Byrd organization who were willing to put "politics above principle" and give "aid and comfort to Stevenson, Kefauver and their allies, Truman, [union chief Walter] Reuther, and the Americans for Democratic Action."[30] Even without the help of the Byrd organization's political leadership, Powell and other veterans of the 1952 Democrats for Eisenhower effort assembled a similar organization and played a similar role in the 1956 campaign. Their well-financed and much-publicized activities were instrumental in stemming the drift of the state's conservative white voters to Democrat Stevenson or to States' Rights Party candidate T. Coleman Andrews. A split within the Byrd organization between its more moderate business and professional adherents and its ardently segregationist, Southside-based political leadership already was apparent, and it became even more pronounced as the desegregation crisis deepened.

The dimensions of Eisenhower's Virginia victory stunned most observers. The Republican incumbent actually improved on his 1952 margin over Stevenson, drubbing the Democrat by more than 120,000 votes. Importantly, however, the Andrews third-party candidacy attracted better than six percent of the ballots cast statewide, and that was enough to keep both major party candidates' vote shares below what they had been in 1952.[31] Predictably, Andrews ran strongest in central Virginia and in the Southside, where the desegregation and civil rights issues loomed largest. But, in a pattern that held true across much of the South, Eisenhower's losses among black-belt whites were more than offset by his sharp gains among black voters. Analyses of selected black precincts in Richmond, for example, revealed that the Republican garnered only 18 percent of the black vote in 1952 but received more than 70 percent four years later.[32] Similar Eisenhower gains were recorded among black voters in Norfolk and Newport News, and apparently were products of the President's pro-civil rights stands and the belligerent posture of the Virginia Democratic Party in the school desegregation controversy. Much more than in 1952, the Eisenhower victory in Virginia in 1956 was assembled in the state's urban areas, where the President received the votes of central-city blacks and moderate-conservative suburban whites.

The black vote for Eisenhower had a very limited spill-over effect on the congressional races. Though the GOP fielded candidates in nine of the ten

---

[30]Vogt, p. 332.

[31]The vote totals were: Eisenhower – 386,459 (55.4%); Stevenson – 267,760 (38.4%); Andrews – 42,964 (6.2%). In 1952, Eisenhower received 56.3 percent of the vote to Stevenson's 43.4 percent. Eisenberg, *Virginia Votes*, p. 208.

[32]Donald S. Strong, *Urban Republicanism in the South* (Birmingham: Birmingham Printing Co., 1960), pp. 9–29.

congressional districts, no seats changed hands. The outcome corresponded closely with the 1954 results: incumbents Poff and Broyhill won re-election comfortably; William Wampler (this time, the challenger) failed narrowly in his Ninth District rematch with Democrat Pat Jennings[33] ; and another GOP challenger made a respectable showing against Third District incumbent J. Vaughan Gary.[34] There was a surprise, however, in the eastern-Virginia First District, where 39-year-old Horace E. "Hunk" Henderson, a former national president of the Junior Chamber of Commerce ("Jaycees"), nearly upset three-term Democratic incumbent Edward J. Robeson, Jr., of Newport News. Henderson was recruited to the GOP in 1953 by Ted Dalton's son, John, who was then a College of William and Mary student. After assembling a strong Republican organization in Williamsburg and winning a place on the city council, Henderson set his sights on a seat in Congress. His energetic, youth-oriented campaign and vigorous attacks on Robeson from the right and left brought him within 1,153 votes of achieving his goal.

Though the 1956 elections brought no Republican gains, the magnitude of Eisenhower's win without the help of the Byrd organization leadership and the surprisingly strong Henderson showing gave GOP partisans considerable encouragement. There were other developments, too, that seemed to warrant optimism. The fruits of several years of active effort to organize Republican women's clubs were apparent at the 1956 GOP state convention, where female delegates comprised more than half of those in attendance. Reflecting the party's growing geographical base, young Lee Potter of Arlington, the tireless Broyhill protege, defeated long-time Republican leader Lester Parsons of Norfolk to capture the party's state chairmanship. The leadership contest was notable for the uncharacteristic absence of rancor and also because it elevated a party-building technician to the top spot and made him the first GOP state chairman ever from populous northern Virginia. There was an atmosphere of good feeling among Republicans, and at some other time that might have been important. But, in 1956, the GOP partisans resembled nothing so much as children frolicking obliviously in the surf as a tidal wave approached.

The dust had barely begun to settle on the presidential and congressional ballot boxes when Attorney General J. Lindsay Almond, Jr., announced on November 17, 1956, that he would seek the Democratic nomination for governor the following year. Though Almond's ambition to be governor was well known, the announcement rather stunned the Byrd organization's high command. The attorney general had not first discussed his plans with Senator Byrd, and, as Almond correctly suspected, the senator preferred others for the state's top job, such as State Senator Garland Gray. For most of the 1950s, Lindsay Almond had led Virginia's legal battle to preserve segregation in the

---

[33]The vote totals were: Jennings (D) – 49,448 (54.1%); Wampler (R) – 41,957 (45.9%). Latimer, p. 85.

[34]Roy E. Cabell, Jr., a Richmond attorney, polled 41 percent of the vote in losing to Gary.

public schools—"one of segregation's ablest legal advocates," *Time* magazine once called him.[35] He came to that role from Congress, where he represented the Sixth District until 1948, when Senator Byrd and Governor Tuck entreated him to fill the unexpired term of deceased Attorney General Harvey B. Apperson. His highly visible role in the desegregation litigation, tireless speechmaking, and fiery oratory won him broad popularity in the state and considerable support in the all-important courthouses. But Almond also had demonstrated a penchant for independent-thinking, and that, in combination with his oratorical flair, made Senator Byrd and his top lieutenants uneasy. They passed him over in 1953 when the nod went to Tom Stanley, and Almond was determined that it would not happen again in 1957.

In the wake of his November announcement, Almond quickly received promises of support from the organization grass-roots. The Byrd leadership remained publicly silent, however, while privately the senator and his men scurried about to determine if Almond could be derailed. Obviously favoring Almond, *The Richmond News Leader* at once warned and taunted the high command: "Before the mystic knights risk civil war in their declining Camelot, they had better be abundantly certain they have a champion more able than he (Almond) to bear their colors in the field."[36] After several weeks, the Byrd leadership concluded that they could not defeat Almond and resolved to embrace him. State Senator Gray announced on December 6 that he would not challenge the attorney general for the gubernatorial nomination, the better to prevent "a division among the proponents of segregated schools."[37] Several days later, Almond received the endorsement of Senator Byrd, who lauded him as "a candidate tried and tested by many years of arduous public service."[38] Byrd made it clear that he wanted a landslide Democratic victory in the general election. The 1957 contest provided an opportunity both to secure a strong public endorsement of the massive resistance policy and to deliver a sharp blow to the resurgent Republicans.

For Virginia's Democratic leadership, then, the 1957 race was to be a "campaign for massive resistance."[39] In some respects, Almond seemed like the natural choice to bear the Byrd standard of defiance. More than any other Virginia leader, he was associated in the public mind with the effort to stave off court-ordered racial integration in the public schools. But Almond was a lawyer, and a good one. The massive resistance legislation enacted in the

---

[35]James W. Ely, Jr., "J. Lindsay Almond, Jr.," in *The Governors of Virginia 1860–1978*, eds. Edward Younger and James Tice Moore (Charlottesville: The University Press of Virginia, 1982), p. 351.

[36]*The Richmond News Leader*, November 27, 1956.

[37]*The Richmond News Leader*, December 6, 1956.

[38]Muse, p. 42.

[39]See James W. Ely, Jr., *The Campaign for Massive Resistance: Virginia's Gubernatorial Election of 1957*, Unpublished Thesis, University of Virginia, 1968.

August 1956 special session was, in his mind, plainly unconstitutional.[40] In fact, he believed this so strongly that he declined to participate in the drafting of the bills and advised Governor Stanley that the program would not stand in the courts. Now, however, the focus had shifted from the legal to the political arena, and the inhibitions of Almond the lawyer gave way to the foot-stomping, podium-pounding fervor of Almond the politician. A firm believer in the rightness of segregation, Almond devoted himself and his superlative stump skills wholeheartedly to the task of securing a vote of confidence in massive resistance—along with his own ascension to Virginia's highest office. Rounding out the Democratic ticket were two others who shared Almond's ambivalence on massive resistance: incumbent Lieutenant Governor A. E. S. "Gi" Stephens and, for attorney general, State Senator Albertis S. Harrison, Jr., of Brunswick County.

Most Republicans had been assuming for some time that Ted Dalton, who mounted such a strong challenge in 1953, would champion their cause again in 1957. But Dalton was by no means anxious to run. The Republicans lacked both money and organization, and the Democrats in Virginia had plenty of both; Almond, the likely Democratic nominee, would be a far more formidable opponent than Tom Stanley had been; and, there was the overriding school controversy, which divided the GOP. A federal judgeship was practically Dalton's for the asking, while the governorship seemed far beyond his reach. On November 11, 1956, in Staunton, the Republican leader stunned a GOP victory dinner audience when he said of the upcoming election for governor, "[I]t is not my turn and my feeling is that someone else should make the race this time."[41] Dalton had planned to make that statement the following day at the state central committee session, but he was moved to do so at the dinner after Congressman Broyhill and others referred to him as the party's gubernatorial candidate. For weeks and then months thereafter, Dalton was besieged by Republican pleas that he consent to run. He remained noncommittal.

The principal reason for his reluctance was the segregation issue. A consistent foe of massive resistance but no advocate of racial integration, the moderate Dalton did not relish carrying the liberal banner against the fiery Almond and the die-hard segregationists who would be manning the fortress of Byrdism in the fall campaign. To Delegate Robert Whitehead he confided fears that he would be branded "a nigger lover by reason of his advocacy of the Pupil Assignment Plan."[42] Indeed, as James Latimer reported, that was precisely what the Democratic leadership had in mind:

[40]Ibid., p. 21.

[41]*Roanoke Times*, December 1, 1956.

[42]James W. Ely, Jr., *The Crisis of Conservative Virginia* (Knoxville: The University of Tennessee Press, 1976), pp. 57–58.

Virtually to a man, high powers among Democrats at the Jefferson-Jackson Day dinner said privately they hoped Republican State Senator Ted Dalton . . . would run again this year. . . . [O]ld pros in the organization are itching to get Dalton into the race. They figure to clobber him so badly as to demolish him and the GOP as a force in state-level politics for years to come. . . . Why were the Democrats so confident? [It] simmered down . . . to one main reason: the issue of racial segregation in the public schools. They aim, quite simply and frankly, to paste the label "integrationist" all over Dalton if he runs—and they're sure they can make it stick through the campaign propaganda battle. . . .[43]

Dalton's reticence was understandable. But his firm conviction that massive resistance was wrong—and his long-held view that the people deserved an opportunity to choose between competing policies espoused by competing political parties—moved him steadily closer to entering the contest.

On June 10, 1957, Dalton declared that he would be a candidate for governor if enough Virginians wanted him to do so, and he invited them to write and let him know their views. To the surprise of almost no one, the Radford Republican announced on July 4 that he reluctantly would mount a campaign in order to, as he put it, "give the people of Virginia an opportunity to save our separate schools."[44] Almond greeted the news matter-of-factly:

He (Dalton) has been running for governor of Virginia for eight years. I am at least glad he has made up his mind, even though he has repeatedly stated that his heart is not in it. My heart and soul are in this fight to defend and preserve Virginia's inherent constitutional rights to govern her own affairs. . . . I am eager to debate this issue with the nominee of the Republican Party.[45]

An ominous indication of what that debate would contain came in Almond's own Fourth of July remarks to an audience in Deltaville, in which he said, "If we believe that the welfare, happiness and interests of both races would be served by intermarriage and production of a hybrid and mongrel race, then our course is the line of least resistance by letting down forever the bars of separation in the schools."[46]

Two days later, delegates to the Republican state convention in Roanoke nominated Dalton by acclamation. Joining him on the ticket were the party's attractive new vote-getter from Williamsburg, Horace Henderson, and an eloquent Republican loyalist from Pearisburg, J. Livingston Dillow. In accepting his party's nomination, Dalton left no doubt that the school issue would be the focus of his campaign. He charged that the state's leaders were "making hostages out of the little school children of Virginia by threatening to close

---

[43]*Richmond Times-Dispatch*, March 29, 1957.
[44]Ely, *Crisis of Conservative Virginia*, p. 57.
[45]Beagle and Osborne, p. 77.
[46]Ibid.

school doors, if necessary, to prevent integration."[47] The inevitable federal court invalidation of massive resistance, he said, would make the school children

the blameless victims of the Democratic leadership's folly.

In this contest the people of Virginia will have the opportunity to decide for themselves whether they favor the cut-off-the-funds program of the Democratic leadership, or whether they favor a locally administered pupil assignment plan. That, in brief, is the school issue.

I charge that the cut-off-the-funds program of the Democratic leadership is taking us down a dead end road that can end only in wholesale integration or the closing of the public free schools of Virginia.

I say to the people of Virginia that there is a way to save our segregated schools. That way is a pupil assignment plan, locally administered. That way was adopted by North Carolina in 1955 and has been tried, tested and approved in the courts. I have twice unsuccessfully co-sponsored such a plan in the General Assembly of Virginia, and from the date of the objectionable Supreme Court decision I have contended that this is our best hope in coping with it.[48]

Dalton went on to praise Congressmen Broyhill and Poff for their stand in favor of states' rights. Then he added, "We not only condemn any and all encroachments to the rights of states, but we also object to the encroachment by the states upon the rights of the localities. . . . The Democratic leadership of Virginia grabbed from the local school boards, whose hearts are dedicated to the cause of education, the right of the localities to say to what schools their children should be assigned."[49] The Tenth Amendment to the United States Constitution, Dalton reminded his listeners, reserved not only to the states, but also to the people in those states, all powers not delegated to the national government.

The lines were drawn clearly. There was to be but one overriding issue in the campaign, and on that issue the two candidates plainly, and often vehemently, differed. Autumn saw one of the most lively and, from virtually all perspectives, one of the most unfortunate gubernatorial contests in the Commonwealth's history. Far from facilitating a rational and sober choice among competing policies by the electorate, the campaign clouded the issues, polarized the citizenry, and left most of Virginia's voters groping about in an orgy of rhetorical excess and near-hysterical public reaction.

From the outset of the campaign, it was apparent that the Republican ticket would face the full fury of the powerful Byrd organization. The able Congressman Watkins M. Abbitt was pressed into service as campaign manager, and Senator Byrd took to the hustings with an intensity not seen

---

[47]Text of speech on file at the Republican Party of Virginia Archives.
[48]Ibid.
[49]Ibid.

since his own bid for the governorship in 1925. Among those joining him on the campaign trail in Almond's behalf were Fifth District Congressman Tuck, Eighth District Congressman Howard Smith, former Governor Battle, and Senator Robertson. The Democratic speakers had many easy targets on which to focus their oratorical blasts: Dalton, the Republican Party, Chief Justice Earl Warren, the U. S. Supreme Court, the state's Republican federal district judges,[50] U. S. Attorney General Herbert Brownell, the Eisenhower civil rights bill, the National Association for the Advancement of Colored People (NAACP), and the perceived horrors of school integration generally. It was not uncommon for all or most of these alleged evils to be lumped together and then roundly excoriated by the Democratic campaigners as if they were part of a single, malevolent conspiracy to bring Virginia's white citizens to their knees.[51]

If, when the campaign began, Dalton had any chance of winning Virginians to his moderate approach of token integration, it melted away in September as events farther south came to dominate the news and then the Virginia political contest. The Dalton campaign already was reeling from the effects of Senate passage of the Eisenhower-backed Civil Rights Act of 1957 in late August when word came that Arkansas Governor Orval Faubus had called out the National Guard to prevent racial integration at Little Rock's Central High School. After several tension-filled weeks, negotiations between Faubus and federal authorities collapsed, and on September 24, President Eisenhower sent troops to Little Rock to compel integration at the school. The reaction in Virginia, as elsewhere in the South, was one of shock and outrage. Civil War and Reconstruction horrors were recalled, and the President was widely condemned. The episode placed Dalton in a difficult situation. He could hardly denounce Eisenhower, a Republican President and a man for whom he had the greatest admiration, but neither could he let the whole matter go by without comment. Virginians were deeply troubled by the dispatching of federal troops to quell a disturbance on Southern soil, and some expression of disapproval by Dalton was essential. After several days of indecision, the Republican nominee sent a telegram to the President requesting the removal of the troops from Little Rock but refraining from criticism of his action in sending them there. "I tell you folks," Dalton declared to one audience, "the Little Rock incident is not a responsibility of mine, and I will not be made a hostage for it nor for the Supreme Court decision nor the civil rights bill."[52]

---

[50]One of the federal judges presiding over local school desegregation cases in Virginia was Dalton's 1953 runningmate, Walter E. Hoffman. Hoffman was appointed to a district judgeship in eastern Virginia in 1954, and he heard the Norfolk school desegregation case in 1956–1958. On February 12, 1957, he held that the state Pupil Placement Act, the first line of defense under the massive resistance program, was unconstitutional. Hershman, pp. 227–231.

[51]See Ely, *Crisis of Conservative Virginia*, pp. 58–59.

[52]*The Richmond News Leader*, October 2, 1957.

Almond, however, wasted no time in capitalizing on the Little Rock situation. A Republican victory in the Commonwealth, he declared, would be regarded "as approval of the invasion . . . of Arkansas" and "an invitation for the creation of many 'Little Rocks' in Virginia."[53] The "sad situation of Little Rock," he solemnly asserted on another occasion, was "a living example" of what would happen in Virginia under Dalton's pupil assignment plan.[54] The Republican countered that it was the Democrats' massive resistance policy that would lead to a Little Rock-style confrontation in Virginia, but he made little headway. The episode in Arkansas fit perfectly with the Democrats' plan to link Dalton to Eisenhower, the Supreme Court, and the NAACP. Even Senator Byrd got into the act, alleging in one speech that Dalton was "working in close cooperation with the national Republican administration, and especially with the political strategist, Attorney General Brownell."[55]

In truth, Dalton did not have close ties to Eisenhower. The President offered no campaign assistance, and he gave only a lukewarm endorsement to the Republican nominee less than a week before the election. That suited Dalton just fine, for Eisenhower's popularity in Virginia had plummeted since the 1956 election due to the civil rights bill, a record peacetime budget, the success of the Soviets' "Sputnik" satellite, and, then, Little Rock. When news of the Eisenhower endorsement reached Dalton, he tactfully expressed his appreciation for the "good wishes" of the President but pointedly noted their differences over the Arkansas matter.[56] Almond campaign chief Watkins Abbitt greeted the endorsement with a smile and a wisecrack. "I hope General Eisenhower does not send his paratroopers to Virginia to carry out his wishes as he did in Little Rock," he quipped.[57]

Dalton found his campaign effort further complicated by the conduct of his aggressive runningmate for lieutenant governor, Horace Henderson. The youthful Henderson was a talented campaigner and electrifying speaker who was unsparing in his verbal assaults on Almond, the Democratic ticket, Senator Byrd, and the Byrd organization. Initially, the Henderson stump performances were beneficial to the GOP ticket. On September 9, for example, the Williamsburg Republican squared off against Democratic Delegate John Warren Cooke before the Mathews County Women's Club. "Today, as never before, the people of Virginia see this powerful machine at its worst," Henderson declared,

> ignoring the people of Virginia, violating the rights of localities and of individuals, and imposing absolute dictatorial power in a state which gave birth to freedom in this great nation. . . . [T]he miserable mess that is our

[53]Ely, *Crisis of Conservative Virginia*, pp. 60–61.

[54]*Richmond Times-Dispatch*, September 25, 1957.

[55]Vogt, p. 351.

[56]Ely, *Crisis of Conservative Virginia*, p. 63.

[57]Ibid., pp. 63–64.

school problem has been made by professional politicians whose main interest is political expediency.

One minute they recognize the law of the land, advocate limited integration, and support the Gray Plan which was approved overwhelmingly by the voters of Virginia. Then the boss speaks, and like a flock of sheep, the machine of Virginia turns completely around—and marches in the opposite direction. And, whoever fails to march immediately with them—is branded an integrationist![58]

After the Little Rock incident, however, Henderson broke with Dalton and publicly defended Eisenhower's actions. Governor Faubus, not the President, was to blame for the confrontation, Henderson declared. "When I said that," he explained later, "well, Dalton and I just parted."[59] Dalton viewed the statements as politically damaging, and he regarded as inexcusable his runningmate's refusal to adopt a position consistent with his own.[60]

Throughout the campaign, Dalton remained on the defensive, pressed to the wall by the charge that he was an advocate—wittingly or unwittingly—of racial integration. Virginia, said Senator Byrd in October, was "the only Southern state wherein the issue has been clearly defined in a state election as between integration and segregation."[61] Congressman Tuck found the choice equally straightforward. "Those favoring mixing of the races will naturally vote for Mr. Dalton. Those favoring separation will vote for Mr. Almond," he said.[62] Almond, who ignited Southside audiences with the promise that he would cut off his right arm before a single black child entered a white school, was given to particularly passionate racial appeals. "[T]he colored vote is going to the Republican Party," he declared, because the Democrats "will not accept amalgamation of races which would lead to mongrelization and hybridization of each race to the destruction of Virginia."[63] Byrd organization supporters around the state followed the candidate's lead. Rather typical was this *Danville Register* editorial:

Let's be honest. Do you know any Virginians for Dalton-Henderson-Dillow who are not members of the N.A.A.C.P.? There may be some. We do not say there are not. We do say, in all sincerity, that we do not know any Danville area voters for D-H-D who are neither Republicans or Negroes.[64]

"It just wasn't a noble period," recalled reporter Charles McDowell.[65]

---

[58]*The Daily Press*, September 10, 1957.

[59]Horace E. Henderson interview, June 12, 1980.

[60]Ted Dalton interview.

[61]*Richmond Times-Dispatch*, October 8, 1957.

[62]Ely, *Campaign for Massive Resistance*, p. 43.

[63]Ibid., pp. 61, 64.

[64]*Danville Register*, October 25, 1957, quoted in Buni, p. 193.

[65]McDowell interview.

Ted Dalton and his supporters continually attempted to ward off the "integrationist" label by pledging support for segregated schools. Party Chairman Lee Potter, who engaged in his own series of heated verbal exchanges with Almond, adamantly insisted that "[o]ur party is for segregation."[66] Dalton declared that massive resistance was a "massive myth leading to a massive retreat and a massive surrender"; it would, he charged, bring "wholesale mixing of races and chaos" to the public schools.[67] With his former law partner, Congressman Poff, doing much of the speechwriting, Dalton late in the campaign accused the Democrats of raising false hopes of a Supreme Court reversal of its desegregation mandate, and he challenged Almond to reveal his "secret plan" for preserving segregation once the federal courts struck down the massive resistance laws. "To every question as to what they plan to do when their cut-off-the-funds, close-the-schools program topples in court," Dalton complained, "[the Democrats] only yell a little louder, 'Little Rock'."[68] The Republican's frequent attempts to inject other issues from his progressive 1953 platform into the campaign were almost completely obscured by the segregation debate.

To the Byrd Democrats, riding the crest of the segregationist wave, it seemed like the good old days had returned. Newspaper endorsements followed one after the other.[69] Campaign contributions poured in at an incredible pace.[70] After the Little Rock episode, recalled Watkins Abbitt, "it was the easiest campaign there's ever been in Virginia to raise money."[71] Support for the Democratic ticket among conservative white Virginians was nearly unanimous. Indeed, it seemed that only some Divine intervention could stem the tide, as the invocation at an Almond rally in Scott County suggested:

> O, Lord, as we thy children are gathered here on this auspicious occasion, we know not how we will vote next Tuesday. But in the absence of any guidance from You to the contrary, we are all going to vote for the straight Democratic ticket. Amen.[72]

To his massive white Democratic support, Almond added the backing of a significant number of conservative Republicans who viewed the contest as a referendum on the massive resistance program. Blacks, whose support was openly solicited by neither candidate, supported Dalton for the same reason that much of white Virginia backed Almond. While the Republican received

---

[66]*Richmond Times-Dispatch*, October 15, 1957.

[67]*The Washington Post*, October 10, 1957.

[68]*The Washington Post*, October 12, 1957.

[69]Dalton was endorsed only by the Norfolk *Virginian-Pilot* and *The Washington Post*. Ely, *Crisis of Conservative Virginia*, p. 63.

[70]Almond's campaign reported spending $78,526, while only $42,801 was spent on the Dalton effort. Latimer, p. 104.

[71]Watkins M. Abbitt interview, June 13, 1980.

[72]Beagle and Osborne, p. 90.

organized labor's endorsement, many rank-and-file workers lined up with Almond because of the school controversy. Liberals and educators supported Dalton, but their numbers were few. In short, the overriding issue in the campaign was school integration, and Almond's was the majority view.

The election brought a record turnout for a non-presidential contest and a huge Democratic victory. All three statewide Democratic candidates were elected. Almond polled 63 percent of the vote in trouncing Dalton, and the Democrat carried every congressional district in the state except the Tenth, which Dalton won narrowly.[73] Despite an unprecedented organizational effort led by GOP chief Potter, the Republicans made no gains in the legislative races. Their number in the House of Delegates remained at six—all from traditional Republican areas in the mountains.

Reviewing the results with reporters, Dalton blamed the Republican losses on the Democrats' emotional appeals. "I couldn't combat the kind of promises Byrd and Almond were making to keep segregated schools, promises that are not realistic," he said.[74] The Democrats, of course, saw in the lopsided results a broad popular mandate to continue the policy of massive resistance. If that conclusion was not completely justified, certainly the majority had expressed in resounding fashion its support for segregated public schools. To be sure, other factors played a part in the outcome. For one thing, it was not a good year for the GOP nationally, and President Eisenhower's popularity was at its lowest point since he entered the White House. The magnitude of the Almond win undoubtedly also was increased dramatically by the riveting events in Arkansas. "Little Rock knocked me down to nothing," Dalton explained. "It wasn't a little rock, it was a big rock."[75] Despite the margin of his defeat, Dalton held to the firm conviction that he had "made a better race . . . in terms of the work done and the results achieved" than he had in the 1953 campaign.[76] He had, he believed, fought a good fight and given the voters a choice.

A year later, Governor Almond wrote to Senator Byrd, "I have tried to avoid running discussions with Dalton, but he was so brazen with some of his statements that I felt I must reply. He has never realized that the votes were counted in the gubernatorial election of 1957. . . ."[77] Still in the State Senate, Dalton accepted the results of the 1957 contest, but he had no intention of acquiescing in a policy that he believed voters had been stampeded into endorsing in that election. He resolved to hold Almond's feet to the fire, and as the NAACP's legal challenges to massive resistance made their way

---

[73]The vote totals were: Almond (D) – 326,921 (63.2%); Dalton (R) – 188,628 (36.4%). Eisenberg, *Virginia Votes*, p. 212.

[74]Ely, *Crisis of Conservative Virginia*, p. 67.

[75]Wilkinson, *Harry Byrd*, p. 138.

[76]Ted Dalton interview.

[77]Wilkinson, *Harry Byrd*, p. 229.

through the federal courts in 1958, things got hotter and hotter for the governor. Senator Byrd and the organization leadership expected Almond to stand firm in his resistance, as he had pledged so forcefully in the campaign. But specific federal court integration orders and school closings were now on the horizon. The bold rhetoric of the fall campaign faded quickly, and difficult choices loomed ahead.

Two years after his second bid for the governorship, Dalton retired from politics to accept a long-expected appointment to the federal bench. Nearly two decades later, he stood on the south portico of the state Capitol—not as governor-elect, but as United States District Judge for the Western District of Virginia—and administered the gubernatorial oath of office to his son, John. It was the closest possible thing to fulfillment of the elder Dalton's ambition. His career had been long and distinguished—a succession of campaigns, checkered by success and failure, full of triumphs and disappointments. Through it all, he seemed to tower above the ordinary and complacent politicians of his day. A person of intellect and conviction, blessed with wit, grace, and courage, Ted Dalton won respect from virtually all quarters of the Commonwealth. He is "one of the ablest political people we have had in Virginia in my lifetime," said former Governor Colgate Darden in 1976. "Ted Dalton has enormous social vision—he's the kind of leader Virginia ought to have...." But, Darden hastened to add, "I never voted for him because he was a Republican."[78] Many other Virginians could have said the same.

"Ted Dalton rode out of the mountains of the west to bring fresh air and a new way to Virginia," recalled columnist Charles McDowell in 1980.

I think the main people who don't appreciate the Ted Dalton tradition are Republicans. What the Republican Party is in Virginia now is some kind of transmutation of the old Byrd Democrats. . . . I should think that modern Republicanism would strike Ted Dalton as a very pale kind of reform. . . .[79]

Perhaps it would, or perhaps the "Mr. Republican" of the 1950s would say that he was merely ahead of his time. Much has changed in Virginia; in many respects, "fresh air and a new way" have come. The "conservatism" of the Old Dominion in the 1970s and 1980s bore a striking resemblance to the "progressivism" championed by Ted Dalton in the 1950s. And therein, perhaps, lies his greatest contribution to the Commonwealth.

---

[78]Conversations with James Latimer, "Living History Makers," WCVE-TV, 1975.
[79]McDowell interview.

Chapter 10

Almond Joyless:
The Collapse and Its Aftermath

"It is not enough for gentlemen to cry unto you and me, 'Don't give up the ship.'. . . If any of them knows the way through the dark maze of judicial aberration and constitutional exploitation, I call upon them to shed the light for which Virginia stands in dire need in this, her dark and agonizing hour. No fair-minded person would be so unreasonable as to seek to hold me responsible for failure to exercise powers which the state is powerless to bestow."[80]

J. Lindsay Almond, Jr.,
January 28, 1959

With Virginia embarked upon a course of massive resistance that invoked memories of and frequent references to the Lost Cause, no one expected Harry Byrd, the leader of twentieth-century Southern defiance, to retire from the field of battle. But that was what he resolved to do, albeit reluctantly, in 1958. On February 12 of that year, Senator Byrd's office in Washington released a statement announcing that he would honor a pledge made privately to Mrs. Byrd in 1952 and retire from the Senate when his term ended in January 1959.

Byrd's announcement was a bombshell. In its wake, organization loyalists hurriedly lined up behind two potential Byrd successors, former governors William Tuck and John Battle. Backing Tuck were the organization's most adamant massive resisters, while Battle enjoyed the support of a majority of Democrats in the House of Delegates and, apparently, Governor Almond. A divisive contest between the two stalwart Byrd men appeared certain until Senator Byrd reconsidered his retirement decision. Shortly after his announcement, the General Assembly adopted a resolution of tribute to the 71-year-old senator, to which it added an amendment offered by State Senator Mills Godwin that earnestly asked Byrd to seek yet another term. The resolution passed unanimously in the House of Delegates and received only one nay vote—Ted Dalton's—in the Senate. To an understanding State Senator Harry F. Byrd, Jr., Dalton explained that he felt it would be inappropriate for him to support such a resolution on the heels of the hard-fought gubernatorial campaign. Concerned about the impending Tuck-Battle schism, and perhaps

---

[80]Beagle and Osborne, p. 117.

by Battle's superior prospects for success, Byrd bowed to the pressure and announced that he would again be a candidate.

Still smarting over its 1957 drubbing and not anxious to sacrifice itself on the altar of another massive resistance referendum, the GOP decided not to nominate an opponent for Senator Byrd in 1958. Given the rancor that normally attended such decisions when the Republicans gathered, there was remarkably little dissent at the state convention in July. The disconsolate partisans could see the handwriting on the wall. There was no money to pay for a campaign. There were no respectable candidates willing to run. Many usually Republican voters were now strongly behind Byrd because of the school issue. And, in the midst of the desegregation controversy, the backlash from a GOP challenge to Byrd might well be enough to knock Poff and Broyhill out of Congress. While the decision was eminently practical, the appearance was one of striking weakness for the state GOP. "All in all," editorialized the *Roanoke World-News*, "it was a rather feeble convention: unwilling and unable to oppose Senator Byrd and shot through the vitals by President Eisenhower's use of troops in Little Rock. The exultation and high hopes which followed 1952 and 1956 now lie in something close to shambles."[81]

Nothing was more demonstrative of the declining competitiveness of the Virginia GOP than the congressional races in 1958. Just two years earlier, the party had sent nine candidates into the field to contest all but one of the state's ten seats in the House of Representatives. But in 1958, Virginia Republicans nominated only three congressional candidates, two of whom were incumbents Poff and Broyhill. With prominent GOP attorneys Glen Williams of Lee County and Livingston Dillow both refusing entreaties to run, Ninth District Republicans failed to nominate a congressional candidate for the first time since the civil war. Across the state, the desegregation issue had Republicans running for cover. "Chairman Potter's 1956 call for a crusade," commented the *Roanoke Times*, "has paled in the hard light of political realism."[82]

November saw the re-election of Broyhill, Poff, and the state's Democratic congressmen, with the exception of the First District's Edward J. Robeson, Jr., who was cast out not by the GOP but by the Byrd organization. Taking their cue from the close Henderson-Robeson fight two years earlier, the Byrd leadership scuttled Robeson and replaced him with Thomas N. Downing, a young Newport News attorney. Joel Broyhill won a fourth term as the Tenth District's congressman by a narrow margin,[83] but the greatest excitement was in the Sixth District, which the new governor, Lindsay Almond, previously had represented in Congress. Almond led Democrats in mounting an all-out assault on incumbent Congressman Richard Poff, but

---

[81]*Roanoke World-News*, July 14, 1958.

[82]*Roanoke Times*, July 10, 1958.

[83]Broyhill won re-election over Democrat Joseph H. Freebill with 53 percent of the ballots and a margin of 4,200 votes.

even with solid Byrd organization backing for his Democratic foe, Poff impressively garnered 57 percent of the vote.[84] The Republican's campaign was ably managed by Roanoke attorney M. Caldwell Butler, whose own interest in a political career was sparked by the hard-fought contest. Senator Byrd, of course, joined the other incumbents in winning re-election, but he was not without opposition. Declaring that "people everywhere, in Virginia as well as in Russia, should have a chance to vote [against] the political machine that has been suppressing them," Dr. Louise Wensel of Augusta County offered herself to the voters as a self-styled "Independent Republican."[85] Roughly one out of every four Virginians who went to the polls voted for her.[86]

Even as Virginia's voters were giving another resounding vote of confidence to the state's conservative Democratic leadership, massive resistance was entering its critical hour. In September 1958, Governor Almond ordered the closing of public schools in Warren County and in the cities of Charlottesville and Norfolk pursuant to the massive resistance statutes. What the Byrd leadership had repeatedly said would not happen was now coming to pass. Federal courts were requiring integration; they were not yielding. And, for the first time, Virginians in large numbers were coming to realize that there was more than rhetoric to massive resistance—that the price of continued segregation actually might be the end of public education in the Commonwealth.

"We face the gravest crisis since the War Between the States," declared Senator Byrd.[87] But the crisis he had in mind was not the closing of Virginia's public schools. It was the inevitable next stage: what Virginia would do when the federal courts declared the school closings—indeed, the whole massive resistance program—to be unconstitutional. To Byrd, continued Southern solidarity in defiance of the federal government, with Virginia gallantly leading the way, was the only acceptable course to follow. He saw the crisis as another act in a drama that most Americans, and most Virginians, thought had closed a century earlier at Appomattox, and he had no intention of letting the curtain fall while he was running the show. But Byrd knew he could not do it alone; he needed Almond to stand firm with him.

In the days and weeks after the September school closings, Byrd, Tuck, House of Delegates Speaker Moore, and others high in the organization ranks pressed Almond to continue the resistance. But the reality of locked school doors and children going untaught wrought a rapid transformation of public opinion during the autumn months, and the moderate political leaders who

---

[84]The vote totals were: Poff (R) – 37,779 (57.0%); Richard F. Pence (D) – 28,530 (43.0%). Latimer, p. 89.

[85]Ely, *Crisis of Conservative Virginia*, p. 18.

[86]The vote totals were: Byrd (D) – 317,221 (69.3%); Wensel (Independent Republican) – 120,224 (26.3%); Clarke Robb (Social Democrat) – 20,154 (4.4%). Eisenberg, *Virginia Votes*, p. 220.

[87]Wilkinson, *Harry Byrd*, p. 141.

had been forced underground during the previous two years emerged to give voice again to the need to preserve public education in the state. To the mounting popular pressure for some sort of tactical retreat was added the behind-the-scenes urgings of some of the most influential business leaders in the state. At a private dinner conference in December 1958, a group of such leaders, including key business and banking figures with longstanding ties to the Byrd organization, met with Almond and Attorney General Harrison to urge an end to the struggle. Even *News Leader* Editor James J. Kilpatrick, the expositor of interposition, now took the position that the resistance laws must be modified "if educational opportunities are to be preserved and social calamity is to be avoided."[88] The state's other major newspapers expressed similar views.

The pressure on the governor from both directions was intense. But probably even more wrenching was the conflict that raged within Lindsay Almond. From the very beginning, he had recognized the unconstitutionality of the massive resistance laws and had doubted that the policy would prevail. Yet, in the 1957 campaign, he had been massive resistance's great champion. He had vowed, in the most adamant of terms, to pay whatever price had to be paid to preserve segregated schools. For more than two years, Almond had been at war with himself over massive resistance. Now events were closing in and he faced a grave choice: to continue the fight, even it if meant defying federal court orders and going to jail on contempt charges, or to sound the call to retreat and to accept the integration that he once vowed would come only with the loss of his own right arm.

On January 19, 1959, came the legal rejection of massive resistance that Governor Almond expected. Both the Virginia Supreme Court of Appeals and a three-judge federal district court ruled, in separate cases, that the anti-desegregation statutes adopted in 1956 were illegal and invalid. When the beleaguered governor went on television two days later to announce his response to the court rulings, his tone was strident and his message was one of continued defiance. An impassioned Almond told Virginians:

> To those in high places or elsewhere who advocate integration for your children and send their own to private or public segregated schools; to those who defend or close their eyes to the livid stench of sadism, sex immorality and juvenile pregnancy infesting the mixed schools of the District of Columbia and elsewhere; to those who would overthrow the customs, morals and traditions of a way of life which has endured in honor and decency for centuries and embrace a new moral code prepared by nine men in Washington whose moral concepts they know nothing about . . . to all of these and their confederates, comrades and allies, let me make it abundantly clear for the record now and hereafter, as governor of this

---

[88]Ibid., p. 143.

state, I will not yield to that which I know to be wrong and will destroy every semblance of education for thousands of the children of Virginia.[89] "I will not yield . . .," the governor had said, and in the legislature the die-hard supporters of resistance were heartened. Until they heard the speech, no one was sure in which direction the governor would lead. Delighted, State Senator Godwin called the executive mansion after the speech to congratulate Almond. He reached Mrs. Almond instead. "Well, just tell him I have always been proud of him, but never more proud than tonight," Godwin told her.[90] There was no speech that Lindsay Almond came to regret more.

Exactly a week later, the governor went before a joint session of the General Assembly and delivered a very different address. Instead of calling for a statewide suspension of public school operations, as many expected, the governor told the legislators that the time for massive resistance was at an end. He called for repeal of the school closing and fund cut-off laws and urged creation of a commission to develop a new legislative package designed to minimize integration in the state's public schools. Tuition grants would continue in revised form, and the compulsory attendance law would be suspended. But federal court orders would be obeyed; there would be no confrontation, no forcible closure of the schools by the National Guard, no "futile" penal sentence for the governor. All had been done that was reasonable to do, a calm and steady Almond explained, and it was time to move on. In the Senate, a coalition consisting of Republicans, anti-organization liberals, former Young Turks, and a handful of Byrd organization adherents joined together to sustain the Almond position and reject a move to continue the resistance measures. The vote was 22 to 17. Several weeks later, the Senate adopted a local option proposal advanced by the governor's commission. Again the resisters were overcome, but by only a 20–19 vote. By that time, integration had already begun, under court order and without incident, in several Virginia localities.

The governor's abrupt reversal left many of the massive resisters bitter. Years later, Mills Godwin offered the opinion that Almond's action was "both right and wrong." He explained:

From a legal standpoint, time had run out. The change was going to have to be done, but the way he went about it was completely wrong. . . . Here he was leading the troops, and when we got there he went the other way. It was like going up to the mountaintop with him leading the parade and just before he got there, he turned around and came down. The rest of us were standing up there.[91]

Almond candidly conceded several years later that his fiery television speech of January 21 had been a mistake. "I don't know why I made that damn

---
[89]Beagle and Osborne, p. 113.

[90]Ibid., p. 114.

[91]Mills E. Godwin, Jr., interview, September 9, 1979, September 18, 1984, and May 8, 1990.

speech," he said in 1964. "I saw the whole thing crumbling. I was tired and distraught. I agonized and gave vent to my feelings, which never should have been done."[92] Even without that speech, however, Almond's failure to fight to the last would have earned him the unbending enmity of Senator Byrd. "If Lindsay had gone to jail, he would have had more power than I have," the senator later opined.[93] But it was not Almond's popularity that concerned the organization leader. The governor had reneged on his promises, defied Byrd's leadership, and let down the state. It was something the senator and the organization high command would never forgive.

Many others, of course, viewed Almond's abandonment of massive resistance as a courageous, if tardy, act of leadership. For Ted Dalton, it contained a measure of vindication. Before the episode reached its climax, the Republican leader made the point directly. "Through this crisis," Dalton said in December 1958, "Virginia's Republicans have faced the facts. We told the truth when it hurt, but in the long run the people will remember we stood for right at all times regardless of the political cost." He added that it was "a tragic fact that the Democratic politicians have always known privately that the state could not defy the United States government. But to gain political ends, they raised false hopes by promising to keep the schools open and entirely segregated. . . ."[94] Whether Dalton's token integration approach would have achieved his stated aim of preserving segregation will never be known because it was never tried. Nor can it be said with complete assurance that Virginia's adjustment to the imperative of school desegregation would have been eased by adoption of the policy advocated by the Republican leader. But the correctness of one of Dalton's assertion was beyond dispute: massive resistance raised false hopes of a Supreme Court reversal, and the Byrd Democrats derived immense political gain from those hopes. It was not Dalton's style, however, to rub salt in the wounds of a person who had been through an ordeal like Almond's. When the governor sought support from Republican lawmakers in repealing the massive resistance program, they gave him their votes and refrained from gloating, at least publicly.

The political consequences of massive resistance were far-reaching. Republicans bore the brunt of the political impact during the controversy. A Virginia GOP that a few years earlier seemed poised to capitalize on presidential Republicanism and waning support for the Byrd organization had, by 1959, been sapped of its strength and vitality. Its most attractive and capable candidate had been tarnished in the bitter massive resistance campaign of 1957. And, with the GOP placed in the "liberal" camp by virtue of the Dalton and Eisenhower positions on the over-arching issue of school desegregation, there was little to cause conservative Virginians to gravitate toward the Republican

---

[92]Wilkinson, *Harry Byrd*, pp. 146–147.

[93]Beagle and Osborne, p. 120.

[94]*Richmond Times-Dispatch*, December 14, 1958.

Party. The modest trend toward realignment had been interrupted, and the result was a Virginia GOP that exited the 1950s in a state of disarray. In the 1959 General Assembly elections, Republican strength dipped to its lowest level in many years—just two senators and four delegates.

For the Democratic Party, the long-term consequences of massive resistance were more significant. The state's political preoccupation with the desegregation controversy had halted temporarily the Byrd organization's decline and the growth of the Democratic Party's moderate-to-liberal faction. Yet, the massive resistance era ended much as it had begun. The legislative majority assembled by Governor Almond to repeal massive resistance in 1959 was remarkably similar to the moderate coalition put together by the Young Turks in their 1954 revolt against Byrd organization fiscal policy. The demise of massive resistance emboldened some organization foes, and it made new foes out of some moderates who deviated from the Byrd line and were subsequently disciplined for it by the organization leadership. The demise also forced the conservative Byrd organization leadership to confront the new political realities of a changing Virginia.

One of those realities, the extent of which was revealed by the 1960 census, undoubtedly was a source of acute dismay for Virginia's political patriarch. Upon completing his term as governor in 1930, Harry Byrd had declared that Virginia's "rural population has been the bulwark of the State in the past, and agriculture should be advanced in every practical and reasonable way."[95] But, by 1960, Virginia was more urban than rural and more industrial than agricultural. Though the school desegregation controversy had masked its political effects, a major demographic transformation had been steadily eroding the organization's base.

The 1960 census revealed that the rapid urban growth of the 1940s had continued through the 1950s. Virginia's population climbed nearly 20 percent between 1950 and 1960, a rate of growth comparable to that of the previous decade. Even more important, however, was the pattern. The state's rural areas averaged only two-percent growth during the '50s, and many rural counties—particularly in Southside Virginia—experienced sharp drops in population. The moderate-sized cities and smaller metropolitan areas of the state recorded an average population increase of 13 percent. But in Virginia's five largest metropolitan areas, the average rate of growth between 1950 and 1960 approached 40 percent—nearly twice the statewide rate of increase.

Northern Virginia again experienced the biggest population jump by far, but there were also large gains in the Richmond area and the Tidewater cities. Virginia's growth was centered in the urban corridor that stretched from the suburbs of Washington, D.C., down to Richmond and over to Norfolk and Virginia Beach. From 1940 to 1960, the growth in this curving tail of the northeastern megalopolis far outpaced population increases in the rest of the state,

---

[95]Wilkinson, *Harry Byrd*, p. 157.

and the trend would continue through the next two decades. By 1960, a majority of the state's people (55 percent) already resided in urban areas, and before the '60s closed, 63 percent of Virginians would be urban dwellers.[96]

The steady stream of Virginians and non-Virginians into the state's urban areas reflected the changing nature of the Commonwealth's economy. By 1960, fewer than one out of ten citizens in the state were employed in agriculture. Nearly twice that number worked for the federal government. Manufacturing industries were the single largest employer and accounted for 20 percent of the state's labor force. Virginia, like the other Southern states, was benefiting from corporate decisions to decentralize and move production and warehousing facilities nearer to eastern markets. Labor-intensive industries from the North and Midwest also were also attracted by the comparatively cheap labor in the South, where unions were weak and agricultural mechanization left many people in search of work. The industrial development in Virginia was geographically broad-based and varied. New manufacturing plants sprang up all around the state, and the development in the Shenandoah Valley and the Roanoke area even outpaced that in the traditional manufacturing centers of eastern Virginia. The types of products manufactured were diverse as well. The three largest categories—textiles, chemicals, and food products—accounted for only 37 percent of the total manufacturing work force.[97]

With urbanization, industrialization, and economic prosperity inevitably came political change in the Old Dominion. The ruling Byrd organization drew its strength from, and geared its policies toward, rural Virginia. The people who accompanied new industry—business executives, plant managers, and factory workers—came with varied backgrounds and political inclinations. Some were moderate or liberal Democrats; others were moderate or conservative Republicans—but few had much in common with the rural, conservative Byrd Democrats. That also was true of the young whites who flocked from Virginia's rural areas to the burgeoning suburbs, and of the rural blacks who migrated to the central cities. Though the middle-class suburbanites tended to be conservative in their outlook, and central-city blacks typically were liberal, both quickly became unsatisfied with the low level of public services provided by the state's conservative leadership. With urbanization came a host of urban wants and needs—better schools, better streets, a better system of public transportation, and so forth. Organization leaders seemed unwilling to help local governments cope with the steadily rising demands made upon them.

By 1960, the situation facing Virginia's urban localities was acute. The state government had carefully safeguarded its own fiscal integrity;

---

[96]See William J. Serow and Charles O. Meiburg, "The Average Virginian As Seen by the Census," *University of Virginia News Letter* (Charlottesville: Institute of Government, University of Virginia), February 15, 1973.

[97]See Wilkinson, *Harry Byrd*, pp. 161–163.

"pay-as-you-go" had kept Virginia out of debt. But the state's unwillingness to tax, borrow, or spend sufficiently to relieve urban pressures had left local governments in dire financial straits. Gross county debt in Virginia had soared from just over $20 million in 1947 to more than $165 million in 1956. The largest expense was for new school construction, and the fast-growing urban localities bore the heaviest burden. Of the $165 million in county debt, 62 percent was owed by the six largest urban counties (Arlington, Fairfax, Henrico, Norfolk, Princess Anne, and Chesterfield). The Young Turk revolt at the General Assembly in 1954 had been a reflection of the growing urban frustration over low levels of state spending, and, as the '60s began, the localities' plight was even worse. A growing bloc of moderate, urban legislators was ready to force action in order to provide some relief.

The 1960 General Assembly session saw a continuation of the sharp division that had emerged with the demise of massive resistance a year earlier. Much as they had done in the wake of the Young Turk revolt, the senior Byrd organization leaders in the Assembly—chief among them House Speaker Moore—dealt harshly with junior legislators who deviated from the hard-line Byrd stance on massive resistance. A number of younger, moderate-conservative legislators from urban areas had sided with Governor Almond in pulling back from the precipice in 1959. Normally supportive of the organization, these lawmakers now found themselves on the outside looking in. Though urban moderates were growing in numbers in the legislature, the Byrd leadership seemingly had no interest in reaching an accommodation with them. In a 1980 interview, one member of the moderate bloc, former State Senator FitzGerald Bemiss of Richmond, recalled the situation:

[T]he Byrd organization, despite the fact that they had a very tight grip until about that point, had its foundations coming loose. And the threat [in the General Assembly] was not so much the Republican Party, because the numbers didn't change there. The threat was urbanization and, therefore, liberals.

I remember a funny instance. When I came over to the Senate, I was, in effect, punished or disciplined for my bad behavior in the House in opposing massive resistance, and so I got lousy committee assignments and I had lots of trouble getting anything done. One time I said to [State Senator Garland "Peck"] Gray, "Peck, you really ought to be nicer to me than you are because you don't really have the choice between me and somebody better. You have a choice between me and somebody worse." He laughed and said, "You know, Gerry, I simply can't imagine that. I'll have to take my chances."

This is a relevant story, because I was succeeded [in the Senate by J. Sargeant] Reynolds. Now, however you judge Sarge, Sarge was bound to be "worse" from Peck Gray's point of view than Bemiss, because he was a notch to the left. It just didn't do any good for Peck to polish me off. He wasn't going to get some nice, affable country boy in my place, you see, because of the urban setting.[99]

Determined to reinstate discipline in organization ranks and to put the maverick Governor Almond in his place, the conservative General Assembly leadership mounted a full-scale assault on the governor's budgetary proposals in the 1960 session. State Senator Harry F. Byrd, Jr., took the lead in opposing the three percent sales tax sought by Almond. A frequent proposal of Democratic moderates and liberals in the '40s and '50s, the sales tax was embraced by Governor Almond as a means of financing additional state programs. But the combination of entrenched conservative opposition to new taxes and antipathy toward Almond in the Byrd ranks doomed the measure, and it died in committee. Most of Almond's budget, however, survived the assault by the Moore-Byrd-Godwin-Gray faction. In the Senate, Democrats split, 19–19, and the votes of Republicans James C. Turk and Floyd Landreth provided the margin of victory for the governor's recommended expenditures for education and other state services.

Virginia Republicans watched these developments anxiously. Even though their party had not been faring well lately, things had not been going smoothly for the Byrd organization, either. First, there was the ignominious end of massive resistance. Then, the factional lines within the Democratic Party seemed to harden in the 1960 General Assembly session. Governor Almond emerged as the leader of a moderate group that was contending for power with the aging Byrd high command. The situation seemed ripe for Republican exploitation, but the debilitated Virginia GOP had a long way to go before it would be back in a position to capitalize on the Democratic division.

Republican State Chairman Lee Potter saw in the end of massive resistance and the onset of another presidential election campaign an opportunity at last to achieve some of his ambitious organizational goals for the party. The Virginia GOP was united behind Vice President Richard Nixon's bid for the Presidency, and Potter used the presidential campaign to recruit new party workers. To foster participation by Democrats and independents in the Republican effort, he formed ostensibly nonpartisan "Nixon for President" clubs as adjuncts to local GOP committees. A key Southern strategist for the Republican National Committee, Potter executed a game plan across the region that closely resembled the 1952 Southern campaign for Eisenhower. As in the two Eisenhower efforts, Democratic business and professional leaders in Virginia rallied behind the GOP presidential nominee.

Virginia Republicans also took a page from their 1952 playbook in deciding to forego a challenge to incumbent Senator A. Willis Robertson in 1960.

---

[99]FitzGerald Bemiss interview, June 25, 1980. After Reynolds ran successfully for lieutenant governor in 1969, the Senate seat formerly occupied by Bemiss was held for 16 years by L. Douglas Wilder, a black attorney who was considered the most liberal member of the State Senate during much of his tenure there. Wilder moved on to the lieutenant governorship in 1986, and to the governorship in 1990.

Potter, like most of his GOP colleagues at the national level, held both of Virginia's conservative United States senators in high regard. And, with confidant Joel Broyhill, the party chief labored to derail potential challenges to the 73-year-old junior senator. As always, the decision to concede a major office to the Democrats was a controversial one in the GOP, but the interests of the Republican presidential ticket and the state's two congressional incumbents combined with the absence of a viable Senate contender to seal the decision. Delegates to the 1960 state Republican convention re-elected Potter as state chairman and overwhelmingly approved a committee report recommending that no one receive the GOP nomination for Senate.

At the Republican national convention in Chicago, the Virginia delegates bristled at a pro-civil rights platform plank agreed upon by Vice President Nixon and his erstwhile foe, liberal New York Governor Nelson Rockefeller. After a half-decade of electoral setbacks attributable to civil rights issues, Virginia Republicans were anxious to secure the adoption of a middle-of-the-road provision that would be politically palatable in the South. Republican National Committeewoman Hazel Barger of Roanoke, a Southern leader on the convention's platform committee, had worked diligently toward that end, only to see the effort collapse as part of a Nixon- Rockefeller reconciliation. Though the delegation's vice chairman, Linwood Holton, applauded the strong civil rights plank and even urged that Rockefeller be nominated for Vice President, few of the Virginians agreed with him. The liberal plank brought a strong denunciation from Sixth District Congressman Richard Poff, and, for a while, Virginia joined other Southern delegations in threatening to withdraw support from Nixon and give it instead to the conservative Arizonan, Senator Barry Goldwater. Only a private delegation meeting with Nixon and a unity appeal by Goldwater forestalled the move.

The general election contest in 1960 pitted Nixon and his runningmate, Ambassador Henry Cabot Lodge, against Democratic Senators John F. Kennedy of Massachusetts and Lyndon B. Johnson of Texas. Over the objections of Governor Almond, who had grown fond of Kennedy when they served together in Congress in the late '40s, the Virginia delegation to the Democratic national convention was formally instructed by the state convention to support Johnson for the presidential nomination. The Virginia delegates came away from the national Democratic convention less disenchanted, on the whole, than in previous years. While Kennedy had defeated Johnson, the Texas senator had been placed on the ticket as a gesture to the South, and the Virginia Democrats felt they had an inside track to the Kennedy campaign in the person of William C. Battle, son of the former Virginia governor and a close Kennedy friend.[99] Battle was chosen to head the Kennedy-Johnson campaign in Virginia, and his quiet, effective efforts on Kennedy's behalf did

---

[99]Battle met Kennedy when they served together in the Pacific during the Second World War. When the boat under Kennedy's command, PT 109, was rammed and sunk by a Japanese destroyer, a boat under Battle's command rescued Kennedy and part of his crew.

much to quell dissent within the state's Democratic Party. Working closely with him were State Senator Thomas H. Blanton of Bowling Green, the Democratic state chairman, and Governor Almond, who stumped energetically for his party's ticket not only in Virginia but throughout the South.

Almond shifted his campaigning into high gear immediately after the GOP ticket was nominated. He chided the Virginia delegates returning from the national Republican convention for "embracing Mr. Nixon's ultra-liberal civil rights program," and he roundly denounced the "Nixon-Rockefeller liberal philosophy" embodied in the party platform.[100] GOP State Senator James C. Turk of Radford, a member of the Dalton law firm there, responded to the governor's attack by pointing to the Democrats' national platform, which he said was "markedly more socialistic than any . . . ever submitted to the American people."[101] Almond's support for the liberal Kennedy platform should not surprise Virginians, Turk added derisively, "inasmuch as no platform has ever worried him. Soon after his election as governor he repudiated the platform (massive resistance) on which he had been elected. . . ."[102] Then, trying out a theme Republicans would use in the fall campaign in an effort to exploit Democratic division, Turk asked, "Could it be that the answer to the recent activity of the governor in support of Kennedy and his platform is that he is seeking to take away from U.S. Senator Harry Byrd control of the Democratic Party in Virginia?" The gloves had come off well before the traditional Labor Day start of the fall campaign.

In the wake of the national conventions, the big question concerned whom Senator Byrd and his conservative Democratic followers would support. There was considerable talk in Virginia and throughout the South about a possible conservative third-party ticket composed of Byrd and Senator Goldwater. But the Republicans moved swiftly to nix that idea. On August 30, Goldwater flew to the Old Dominion to kick off the Nixon-Lodge campaign in the state with a series of well-attended, enthusiastic GOP rallies in Charlottesville, Norfolk, and Richmond. While ruling out a third-party bid with Byrd, Goldwater lavished praise on the senior senator. At each stop, he reminded his audience about Byrd's recent criticism of the Democratic platform. "I don't know how a man could be more explicit," opined the Arizonan. "I believe if I were a Virginia Democrat, I'd catch on in a hurry."[103]

A good many apparently did. At his annual picnic in Berryville, Byrd made it clear that he would not embrace his party's national platform or ticket. Coining the phrase that became the label for his policy of non-support of Democratic presidential nominees, the senator said:

---

[100]*Roanoke Times*, July 31, 1960.

[101]*Roanoke Times*, August 1, 1960.

[102]Ibid.

[103]*Roanoke World-News*, August 31, 1960.

When I want to speak out, I do, and when I don't, I don't. I have found that sometimes silence is golden. . . .

These parties come and go. Some are conservative, some are radical, but the Constitution remains, and the oath I have taken (to support and defend the Constitution) is my platform.[104]

To thousands of conservative Virginians, Senator Byrd's "golden silence" signalled support for the GOP nominee. While William Battle made significant strides in pulling together anti-organization and pro-organization Democratic officials under the Kennedy standard, he was much less successful in his efforts to mobilize the state's business and financial community for the Democratic ticket. Late in the campaign, overt race-baiting returned to Virginia when House Speaker E. Blackburn Moore wrote to Battle seeking assurances that the Democratic nominee would not appoint a black federal judge in Virginia if elected President. Though the tactic alienated some blacks who otherwise might have backed Nixon, the public release of the letter by Moore, one of Senator Byrd's closest confidants, was widely seen as a further cue that the senator strongly preferred the Republican candidate. Fears of a Democratic assault on the state's Right to Work Law, appointment of black federal judges, and Kennedy's Catholicism sent many conservative white Virginians reaching for the Republican lever on election day.

That Virginia was a key battleground in the presidential election was apparent from the vigorous efforts of both sides and from the visits to the Commonwealth by Nixon, Kennedy, and Johnson. Predictions of a close race were borne out by the returns on November 8.[105] Nixon's 52 percent of the Virginia vote was enough to prove that the preceding Eisenhower victories had not been solely a reflection of the heroic general's personal popularity, but the result represented a victory for the Nixon Democrats and "golden silence" more than for the Republicans. It was apparent that conservative Democrats once again had delivered the state over to presidential Republicanism, and few saw in the returns any sign of a Virginia GOP resurgence. Though Congressmen Poff and Broyhill won re-election, Republicans fielded only four other candidates and mounted no serious challenges to any of the state's eight incumbent Democratic congressmen. Predictably, Senator Robertson rolled up more than 80 percent of the vote against two splinter-party challengers.[106] All in all, it was another weak showing for state Republicans, and Kennedy's narrow nationwide win made the situation even gloomier for the minority party.

---

[104]Friddell, p. 76.

[105]The vote totals were: Nixon (R) – 404,521 (52.4%); Kennedy (D) – 362,327 (47.0%). Eisenberg, *Virginia Votes*, p. 224.

[106]The vote totals were: Robertson (D) – 506,169 (81.3%); Stuart D. Baker (Independent) – 88,718 (14.2%); Clarke Robb (Social Democrat) – 26,783 (4.3%). Eisenberg, *Virginia Votes*, p. 228.

As thoughts turned to another impending gubernatorial election, the long shadow of massive resistance continued to cast a pall over hopes for a Republican resurgence. Once loosed on the Virginia electorate in 1957, overtly racial politics seemed to become a permanent fixture of campaign discourse and a perpetual bar to Republican acceptance and success at the state levels. Though the racial ploy by House Speaker Moore apparently aided Nixon in 1960, Virginia Republicans knew that racial polarization would be used by the Byrd men to forestall any significant GOP gains at the state and local level. Unless the Byrd-Almond schism provided an unexpected opening, it would be some time before Republican prospects again seemed as bright as they had during the heady days of 1952 and 1953.

Chapter 11
Governor Harrison and the "Happy Bridge"

"The Harrison years were a very happy bridge between two eras in Virginia's political history."[107]

Carter O. Lowance

Virginians needed a respite after the bitter political clashes of the late 1950s, and the administration of Governor Albertis S. Harrison, Jr., occasioned one. An island of tranquility in a sea of political upheaval, the Harrison years provided what Carter Lowance, a trusted adviser to a succession of Virginia governors, termed "a very happy bridge between two eras in Virginia's political history."[108] The Byrd organization remained in control—its "Indian summer," according to J. Harvie Wilkinson III[109]—but the growing strength of Republicans and left-leaning Democrats made it clear that the venerable machine's days were numbered.

Shortly after the 1960 presidential election, Lieutenant Governor A. E. S. "Gi" Stephens of Smithfield announced that he would be a candidate for governor in 1961. For years a staunch Byrd man, Stephens had served more than two terms as lieutenant governor and, like other ambitious organization followers before him, had grown impatient waiting for Senator Byrd's nod of approval for a bid for governor. His relations with several key Byrd insiders, including Congressman Tuck and House Speaker Moore, had been strained for years, and worsened considerably when Stephens supported Almond's shift away from massive resistance in 1959. With his early announcement, the lieutenant governor obviously hoped to duplicate Almond's 1957 feat and lock up the nomination before other potential candidates could get their efforts underway. But Stephens had neither the popularity nor the bevy of political IOUs that had enabled Almond to preempt the field four years earlier, and in the weeks after his announcement it was apparent that the Stephens candidacy was not generating much enthusiasm inside or outside the Byrd organization.

Within the Byrd ranks, there was support for possible gubernatorial bids by State Senators Harry F. Byrd, Jr., and Mills E. Godwin, Jr., and Attorney

---

[107]Carter O. Lowance interview, June 11, 1980.
[108]Ibid.
[109]Wilkinson, *Harry Byrd*, p. 240.

General Harrison. The die-hard segregationists generally preferred Byrd or Godwin to Harrison because the attorney general, too, had supported Governor Almond's abandonment of massive resistance. After listening to the urgings of his colleagues, State Senator Byrd met privately with his father to discuss a possible run for governor. The elder senator reportedly responded that it would be inappropriate for two members of the same family to simultaneously hold high statewide office, and he offered to resign his U.S. Senate seat if Byrd, Jr., wished to seek the governorship. The younger Byrd was unwilling to ask his father to do such a thing and decided to forego the opportunity.[110]

With an apparent recognition of the need for a period of calm and reconciliation after the tumultuous massive resistance years, Senator Byrd, Sr., then lent his support to Albertis Harrison. Gentlemanly, distinguished, attractive, and articulate, Harrison seemed to be right for the times. His legislative career and his middle course on massive resistance while attorney general gave him an appeal that reached across the Democratic Party's factional divide. On the Byrd organization ticket with him, however, were two state senators regarded as stalwart members of the organization's most conservative faction: Godwin and Robert Y. Button of Culpeper.

The sudden death of Delegate Robert Whitehead in 1960 deprived anti-organization Democrats of the talented leader that most assumed would be their gubernatorial candidate in 1961. The Byrd foes thus had little choice but to embrace the Stephens candidacy, and, in March 1961, State Senator Armistead Boothe of Alexandria, the former "Young Turk" and massive resistance foe, agreed to run for lieutenant governor on a ticket headed by Stephens. T. Munford Boyd, a University of Virginia law professor, joined the pair as the candidate for attorney general. The lines were drawn for a typical pro-Byrd versus anti-Byrd Democratic primary campaign. Stephens adopted the usual anti-organization themes—broader participation in government, poll tax repeal, more state services—while Harrison coupled the normal organization rhetoric of frugality and honesty with a progressive-sounding emphasis on industrial development.

While the Democrats vied for support in the winter and spring of 1961, the search was on for a Republican standard-bearer. The situation at first was somewhat reminiscent of the days before the Second World War when the Virginia GOP offered up only token candidates for statewide office. In those days there rarely was any competition for the party's nomination, though occasionally there was something resembling competition as prominent Republicans sought to foist on each other the unwanted responsibility of carrying the party's banner in the fall campaigns. It was an indication of how devastating the racial politics of the massive resistance period had been for the Virginia GOP that the party's most prominent figures could not be coaxed into running

---

[110]Hatch, p. 516.

for governor in 1961. Republicans pressed State Senator Turk, party vice chairman Linwood Holton, and others to make the race, but they would have none of it.

Holton did, however, accede to GOP Chairman Lee Potter's request that he head a search committee charged with finding a willing and able candidate to lead the Republican ticket. After canvassing the potential candidates, Holton and Potter agreed that Horace Henderson, the party's 1957 nominee for lieutenant governor, was the strongest candidate available. After the unsuccessful 1957 campaign, Henderson had accepted a post in the U.S. State Department and had moved to McLean. He was reluctant to switch gears and undertake a long-shot gubernatorial bid, but, ambitious, Henderson found it impossible to reject the persistent and persuasive appeals from Holton and Potter. He agreed to run, and virtually everyone who attended the 1961 state GOP convention came with the expectation that Henderson would receive the party's gubernatorial nomination.

At the July convention, however, Henderson suffered a shocking upset at the hands of former Delegate H. Clyde Pearson of Lee County. Pearson, the man Ted Dalton had recruited to be the GOP's executive director in 1955, toppled Henderson by adding unexpected backing in northern Virginia to his western Virginia base. Henderson seemed to be the victim of his own and the party leadership's over-confidence. He also suffered from criticism of his performance during the 1957 campaign; many Republicans in the western part of the state shared young John Dalton's view that Henderson had undermined Ted Dalton in 1957 by making stridently anti-segregation statements that conflicted with the ticket leader's more measured and guarded pronouncements. The state's Young Republican federation, which John Dalton chaired in 1959–1960, was especially vocal in its opposition to Henderson during the convention weekend.

The sudden and decisive movement to Pearson did not occur until the day of the balloting, and his unanticipated win threw the convention into pandemonium. The delegates still faced the task of nominating candidates for lieutenant governor and attorney general, but no one was sure how to proceed. Pearson had come to the convention with no expectation of winning, and he had given little or no consideration to whom should be on the ticket with him. Infuriated by the turn of events and confronted with a convention that was behaving like an unguided missile, party chairman Lee Potter quickly concluded that the sooner the whole thing was over the better it would be. He arranged for a motion for adjournment to be made; it carried amid the confusion, and the convention ended without any candidates having been nominated for the second and third spots on the ticket.

The quick adjournment had the effect of tossing the decision about the Pearson runningmates into the lap of the party's central committee. It was not altogether an unpremeditated move, for a number of GOP leaders believed that it would be wise to await the outcome of the Democratic primary contests before selecting the Republican candidates for lieutenant governor and attorney general. Harrison appeared certain to be the Democratic gubernatorial nominee, but the Godwin-Boothe and Button-Boyd races were regarded as too close to call. If the anti-organization candidates won either or both of those contests, the GOP would have a good chance of picking up organization support in the fall campaign. Under those circumstances, such viable Republican candidates as State Senator Turk or party treasurer John Dalton might be persuaded to join the Pearson ticket. The difficulty was one of timing, however. The Democratic primary was set for July 11 and that date also was the deadline for party nominations. If the GOP wanted to complete its slate, the state central committee would have to act before midnight on that date. Thus, the Republican committee session was set for nine o'clock on the evening of July 11.

The Democratic competition had been at center-stage for months, but it commanded surprisingly little interest on the part of the Virginia electorate as primary day approached. Harrison generated considerable enthusiasm for his candidacy, and he held an apparently insurmountable lead over Stephens in the campaign's closing days. Given his record as a Byrd organization adherent for much of his career, Stephens's anti-organization rhetoric never rang quite true. The contest for lieutenant governor, however, provided a clear choice between a hard-line conservative and an urban moderate. Both were men of stature and substance, and each had his own committed corps of supporters. Both also waged vigorous campaigns—Boothe assailed Godwin's prominent role in massive resistance and his tight-fisted approach to fiscal matters, while Godwin charged that Boothe opposed Virginia's Right to Work Law and had been "the great apostle of integration."[111]

When the primary votes were tallied, Godwin had defeated Boothe, but his 54 percent of the vote was far below the typical share for Byrd candidates in previous elections. Harrison polled nearly 57 percent of the vote in winning the gubernatorial contest, while Button received approximately 52 percent against Boyd and a little-known third candidate.[112] The significance of the outcome lay not so much in the fact that the Byrd men had won yet again, but in the closeness of the contests. A moderating trend within the state Democratic Party was in evidence, and Godwin would not fail to notice it.

The Byrd organization victories were, of course, bad news for the members of the Republican central committee who had assembled in Richmond on

---

[111]James L. Bugg, Jr., "Mills Edwin Godwin, Jr.," in *The Governors of Virginia 1860–1978*, eds. Edward Younger and James Tice Moore (Charlottesville: The University Press of Virginia, 1982), p. 375.

[112]The vote totals in the election for governor were: Harrison – 199,519 (56.7%); Stephens – 152,639 (43.3%). The vote totals in the election for lieutenant governor were: Godwin – 187,660 (54.4%); Boothe – 157,176 (45.6%). The vote totals in the election for attorney general were: Button – 178,134 (51.9%); Boyd – 150,755 (43.9%); Eugene C. Adkins – 14,236 (4.1%). Latimer, p. 100.

primary election night to choose runningmates for Clyde Pearson. Disappointment with the Democratic primary results, frustration over the refusal of the party's younger leaders to join the ticket, and dissatisfaction with the party leadership for permitting the awkward situation to develop in the first place combined to make the committee session rancorous. Members traded criticisms and wrangled over their limited array of options until the midnight deadline for nominations arrived. When it was pointed out that midnight was still an hour away according to eastern standard time, the members tussled for an additional hour before throwing in the towel. Several days later, Pearson held a press conference to announce two independent candidacies that would round out a *de facto* GOP ticket. The party's national committeewoman, Mrs. Hazel Barger of Roanoke, entered the race for lieutenant governor, and the 30-year-old Commonwealth's attorney of Russell County, Leon Owens, became a candidate for attorney general. The GOP central committee reconvened soon thereafter and endorsed the pair.

Despite its inauspicious beginning, the Republican ticket had a youthful look that reflected the important role that younger partisans now were playing in the GOP. The presence of Mrs. Barger on the ticket similarly evidenced the considerable influence of women in the party. Both were characteristic of a new Republican Party in Virginia. But in most other respects, the 1961 GOP ticket—comprised wholly of southwest Virginians—resembled the token Republican candidacies of earlier years. The 36-year-old Pearson traveled around the state making speeches while a pair of campaign staff workers pounded out press releases in the dusty attic of the Roanoke GOP headquarters. They worked tirelessly, but with a total budget of $15,000 and only a handful of campaign personnel, the Pearson campaign looked more like a bid for a seat in the state legislature than a serious try for statewide office.

The Republican nevertheless went on the offensive, and he was able to gain considerable press attention. He blasted Godwin for championing massive resistance, and challenged Harrison to defend or renounce the school-closing policy. Republican lawmakers, Pearson reminded voters, had supplied "the margin by which disaster was avoided" when massive resistance reached its critical hour.[113] Pearson also predicted a Harrison tax hike, blamed the Byrd organization for state government waste and autocratic rule, and linked the state Democratic ticket with the "big-spending" national Democrats and President Kennedy, whom Harrison backed in 1960. The Republican nominee sought to cast himself in the Ted Dalton mold; the GOP was held out as the forward-looking, reform-minded alternative to the stagnation that had attended the Byrd organization reign.

Harrison's response to Pearson was straightforward—he simply ignored him. As he had done in the primary campaign, the Democratic nominee stressed the organization's record of sound, honest, and fiscally responsible

---

[113]*Roanoke World-News*, July 13, 1961.

government as well as the need for measures to spur industrial development in the state. As for massive resistance, both Harrison and Godwin espoused the view that the policy had bought time for Virginia to adjust to the inevitable desegregation of its public schools and that, because of the policy, Virginia's adjustment had been free of violence. As the nominee of a largely united Democratic Party, Harrison hardly needed to answer Pearson's attacks. There was no overriding issue in 1961 to shake up the normal alignments, and a youthful GOP upstart was bidding for the reins of state government against one of the most attractive, accomplished, and respected of the venerable organization's cadre of public servants. Pearson could expect a fair number of anti-Byrd protest votes from liberal Democrats, but not enough to make him a real contender in November.

The result was a resounding mandate for Albertis Harrison on election day and a humiliating setback for Virginia Republicans. Harrison's nearly 64 percent of the vote resembled the massive, old-style Byrd organization victories that were common in the years before the Second World War, and runningmates Godwin and Button also won easily.[114] Republican legislative candidates won in only five House of Delegates districts. The poor GOP showing triggered an avalanche of recriminations, with some alleging that party leaders had not backed Pearson fully after his upset nomination victory while others countered that, had Henderson been nominated, he would have fared markedly better. It was all quite unpleasant, so no one was surprised a few months later when party chief Potter announced that he was resigning his post in order to devote more time to his Southern party-building efforts for the Republican National Committee. To fill the chairmanship vacancy, Potter recommended—and a nearly unanimous state central committee in April 1962 elected—the man who had been denied the gubernatorial nomination, Horace Henderson.

Given the magnitude of the GOP defeat in 1961, there was little reason to look for a Republican renewal in Virginia anytime soon. But the congressional elections of 1962 and the legislative races the following year presented new opportunities for two-party competition, and the Virginia GOP's youthful corps of enthusiastic partisans was undaunted. In large measure it was the political quietude achieved during the Harrison tenure and the preeminence of major national issues that served to enliven Republicans and revive their sagging hopes.

---

[114]The vote totals in the election for governor were: Harrison (D) – 251,861 (63.8%); Pearson (R) – 142,567 (36.1%). Eisenberg, *Virginia Votes*, p. 232. The vote totals in the election for lieutenant governor were: Godwin (D) 251,223 (65.7%); Barger (R) – 131,437 (34.3%). The vote totals in the election for attorney general were: Button (D) – 247,931 (65.3%); Owens (R) – 131,774 (34.7%). *Votes Cast for Governor, Lieutenant Governor and Attorney General, General Election, November 7, 1961* (Division of Purchase and Printing, Commonwealth of Virginia, 1962).

A party leadership battle in the northern-Virginia Tenth District in June 1962 attested to the GOP's vitality, though the partisans there had their guns aimed at one another rather than at the dominant Democrats. At issue was the vacant chairmanship of the Tenth District GOP. The Republican organization in northern Virginia had been expanding steadily since the election of Joel Broyhill to Congress in 1952. The area's sustained, rapid population growth attracted more Republicans each year, and Broyhill's hard-fought re-election campaigns every two years provided a strong impetus for ongoing GOP organizational efforts. By the 1960s, the Tenth District bore little political resemblance to Virginia's other nine congressional districts. It was two-party competitive, tended to follow national political trends, and had partisan alignments more akin to the rest of the nation than to the South. Broyhill continued to cater to his substantial Byrd Democratic following, though he was becoming increasingly dependent for re-election upon the district's Republican-leaning federal government workers and his own precinct organization, which was far stronger than GOP organizations elsewhere in the state. As the number of Tenth District Republicans increased, competition for party leadership posts and factional strife grew, too. A sizable element within the party deemed Congressman Broyhill to be too conservative, too solicitous of the Byrd Democrats, and insufficiently aggressive in pushing Republicans for local offices. In 1962, Broyhill's personal choice for chairman of the Tenth District GOP, Arlington party chief Robert J. "Jack" Corber, was opposed by Glenn A. Burklund, a freshman member of the House of Delegates.

On June 5, Fairfax County Republicans gathered in the Falls Church High School auditorium for what was to be one of the most colorful GOP meetings in the party's history. At issue was which candidate for district chairman—Corber or Burklund—would receive the county's 62 votes at the Republican district convention. The county GOP chairman was allied with the Burklund (anti-Broyhill) faction, and, as a fierce thunderstorm raged outside, he gaveled the meeting to order. Seconds later, a 20-foot piece of metal pipe came crashing down from the ceiling onto the stage, gaining the immediate attention of everyone in the boisterous, packed auditorium, including the county chairman, whose life had been spared by inches. Things went downhill from there.

It quickly became apparent that the Corber forces had a clear majority. On a series of voice votes, however, the county chairman ruled in favor of the Burklund position, flagrantly misinterpreting the will of the majority. After the third such vote, cheers, jeers, and boos drowned out the proceedings completely. A large group of fist-shaking, umbrella-waving Corber supporters angrily surged toward the front of the auditorium; one Corber zealot seized the microphone briefly before a melee on stage knocked out the sound system; lightning flashed; thunder boomed; the astounded members of a jazz band on hand for the event fled for their lives; and then, as if on cue, electrical power was lost, and the hall went dark. Within moments, the howl of police sirens could be heard over the din. A small army of uniformed officers arrived, restored order, and, when the lights came back on, even counted the ballots. The Corber forces prevailed, and Corber went on to become Tenth District chairman at the district convention. Two years later he became the GOP state chairman.

On hand for the wild evening in Fairfax, party chief Henderson must have wondered whether a growing state GOP was such a good idea after all. But he enjoyed grass-roots organizing and rhetorical jousting with the Democrats, and the party chairmanship provided almost unlimited opportunities for both. Henderson stumped across Virginia with evangelistic fervor proclaiming the GOP as the party of the future. While he advocated electoral reforms and progressive policies at the state level, Henderson was most vocal in assailing President Kennedy and the liberal policies of the national Democrats. He predicted (almost prophetically) that when Senator Byrd, Sr., passed from the scene and legal challenges to the poll tax and other electoral restrictions succeeded, the state Democratic Party would move to the left and conservatives would be forced to realign themselves with the GOP. Henderson's "party of the future" theme seemed all the more appropriate in light of the surge in Young Republican membership that paralleled his tenure as state chairman.

A major reason for the Young Republicans' sharp membership gains was the leadership of Richard D. Obenshain, a Richmond lawyer who presided over the statewide GOP youth federation from 1961 until 1964. Like Henderson, Obenshain was a traveler, and he crisscrossed the Commonwealth "spreading the gospel," as he put it,[115] with an intensity that even the state party chairman could not match. The "gospel" that Obenshain took to Young Republican club meetings and other party gatherings was chiefly philosophical, but he also advocated a strategy for Republican growth. A native of southwest Virginia, Obenshain's roots were in the traditional, progressive Republicanism of the mountain region. But, while at New York University, he had encountered a law professor, Sylvester Petro, whose conservatism significantly influenced his thinking. Young Obenshain became a conservative true-believer, compelled to political activism by an abiding belief that government expansion posed a mortal threat to individual liberty, the health of the nation's economy, and the fabric of American society. He never lost the progressive social outlook, particularly on racial matters, that were products of his western upbringing, but it was Obenshain's conservative creed that pervaded his thoughts, motivated his actions, and comprised his message. The intensity of his conviction and his ability to articulate it marked him as unique even as his active role in the Republican Party was just beginning.

If conservatism was the ultimate objective, party realignment was the means to achieve it. As he traveled around the state promoting Young Republican growth, Obenshain coupled his stirring conservative rhetoric with a call

---

[115]Mrs. Richard D. Obenshain interview, June 30, 1980, and July 18, 1982.

to like-minded Virginians to gather under the Republican banner. The key to the party's future, he contended, was in attracting conservative Democrats (and young conservatives without party affiliation) to the GOP. In a March 1963 letter to the editor of *The Richmond News Leader*, Obenshain wrote:

The proper question for young Virginians is, simply, "How can the victory of conservative principles be assured?" The only realistic answer is for American conservatives to unite in the Republican party, the only national party which can be returned to the basic tenets of constitutional government and individual freedom. . . . Only if we Southerners will unite with conservative Republicans across this nation . . . can we attain the nationwide strength essential for political victory.

The News Leader recently suggested that this union of Southern conservatives might be prevented because we Republicans would be unwilling to surrender positions of party leadership to "apostate Democrats." Such a reluctance would have been true even in the recent past, but the leadership of the Republican party in the South is passing to the younger men, most of them motivated by an intense concern for the ultimate conservative victory. Instead of rebuffing Democrats, we have consistently welcomed all new Republicans—if anything, we accord higher honor to those who have the courage to break with the Democratic label and thus lead the transformation to a Republican South.[116]

Obenshain devoted himself single-mindedly to promoting that transformation, and his efforts bore fruit a decade later.

With Obenshain's vigorous organizational efforts, it was apparent in the early '60s that the state GOP's new breed included many strongly conservative young activists, in addition to the youthful moderates and progressives like Linwood Holton and Clyde Pearson who had been streaming into the party since the days of the Eisenhower and Dalton campaigns. The young conservatives were strongest in the Richmond area and in northern Virginia; the progressives were more numerous in Tidewater and western Virginia. But throughout the state, a new generation of Republicans, their ranks greatly swelled with Democratic converts, was coming of age. Though the differing perspectives of these young activists would produce significant factional divisions within the GOP in the '70s, those lines were not apparent in the early '60s.

Advocates of a conservative/Republican realignment in Virginia found considerable cause for optimism in the outcome of the 1962 congressional elections. The GOP nominated four challengers as well as incumbents Poff and Broyhill, and the Republican candidates received an impressive 49.5 percent of the total vote in the six contested congressional races. Significantly, the two challengers who came closest to winning—Third District nominee Lewis H. Williams and Seventh District candidate J. Kenneth Robinson—ran

---

[116]*The Richmond News Leader*, March 10, 1963.

as unabashed conservatives. They made the liberal policies of the increasingly unpopular Kennedy administration the focus of their campaigns, and they sought to position themselves firmly to the right of their Democratic foes. Williams, a 35-year-old Richmond obstetrician,[117] failed to unseat incumbent Representative J. Vaughan Gary by only 343 votes out of more than 58,000 votes cast, while orchardist Robinson of Frederick County came within 598 votes of overcoming Byrd Democrat John O. Marsh, Jr., in their battle for the seat of retiring Congressman Burr Harrison. Both men would go on to play key roles in the state GOP successes of the next decade—Robinson, as a member of the State Senate and then Congress; Williams, as a party leader and Obenshain confidant.

The strong GOP showing in the congressional races encouraged Republicans and stunned Democrats. Much of it was attributable to displeasure with Kennedy, a widespread feeling that led to Republican gains throughout the South in 1962. But there were clearly other forces at work, and reporter Buster Carico identified two of them in his election *post mortem*:

1. Young people have taken over the Republican Party and have built up organizations that are willing to check registration books for names of new voters, ring doorbells, stamp envelopes, and work at the polls, while the Democratic organization that was once young and vigorous, too, is showing its age.

2. Some Democrats privately blame Senator Byrd for what is happening. They claim if he had gone ahead and supported the Democratic candidates for President in 1952, 1956 and 1960, Democrats might not be so inclined to vote for Republicans for Congress now.[118]

Assessing their near-misses, Williams and Robinson stressed grass-roots organization and conservative philosophy as the keys to success for the state GOP. Both expressed the hope that the national Republican Party in 1964 would heed the Southern message and nominate a resolute conservative, like Arizona Senator Barry Goldwater, rather than a Rockefeller-type liberal for President.

Before the resumption of presidential politicking, however, Virginians faced elections for both houses of the General Assembly in the fall of 1963. The GOP badly needed to make gains; its contingent of five delegates and two state senators in 1962 constituted less General Assembly representation than the party had a decade earlier. Party chief Henderson tapped Kenneth Robinson to chair a candidate-recruitment committee, and the two men convened a group of 75 prominent state Republicans in Lynchburg in January 1963 for a series of campaign seminars and a strategy session concerning the upcom-

---

[117]Williams was active in the Virginia GOP from the 1960s to the 1980s, but he gained the most notoriety in 1991, when he acknowledged having hired a private investigator to probe allegations of drug-related and sexual misconduct by Charles S. Robb during Robb's tenure as governor from 1982 to 1986. See Chapter 36.

[118]*Roanoke Times*, November 7, 1962.

ing legislative races. A few months later, Robinson reported to the state central committee on the progress of his recruitment efforts, and he made a pitch for help in enlisting viable GOP candidates. "[The Republican Party] must become a party that is active at all levels of government," Robinson declared. Only then, he added, would the GOP become more than the "Byrd bucket brigade" with its only job being "to put out the brush fires that erupt occasionally in the Democratic organization."[119]

In the fall, the Virginia Republicans sent 14 Senate and 35 House of Delegates candidates into the field. The GOP contenders generally positioned themselves near the political center, running to the left of the Byrd organization on state issues and to the right of the national Democrats. The results were impressive. Total Republican strength in the legislature was doubled; seven new members were added, for a total of 11 in the House and three in the Senate. The Virginia GOP, declared chairman Henderson, now was making "consistent progress toward a two-party state."[120] Outwardly unconcerned, Governor Harrison rejected suggestions that Republican gains in Virginia presaged a state GOP win in the ensuing presidential contest. But, with the youthful President Kennedy expected to be in the picture in 1964 and the aging Senator Byrd, whose term was to expire that year, expected to be out, GOP prospects seemed bright. Neither expectation would prove correct.

The Republican advances of 1962 and 1963 gave only a slight hint of the political transformation to come. The Harrison tenure brought no major reforms in Virginia, and, on the surface at least, little changed. The state continued to rank at or near the bottom of the national listing in terms of the individual tax burden and per capita expenditures on most categories of public services. There was little momentum for reform in the General Assembly and little legislative controversy of any kind. Governor Harrison directed his energies toward attracting new industry to the Commonwealth, and in that he achieved considerable success. But perhaps his most important contribution was his role in restoring order, moderation, and reasoned public discourse to Virginia's political life in the wake of the massive resistance period. Politics in the Commonwealth during his tenure reflected his easy-going personality and dignified, deliberate style.

The seeds of the change that soon would blossom in the state nevertheless were present during the early 1960s. Population growth and economic development were proceeding apace, and Virginia's suburbs were rapidly expanding. The urban corridor was well on its way to becoming the politically dominant area of the state by virtue of its soaring numbers. The civil rights movement, which would transform American politics, was building momentum throughout the South. Virginians watched with the rest of the nation as the boycotts, demonstrations, and violent clashes in Alabama and

[119]*Roanoke Times*, April 28, 1963.
[120]*Richmond Times-Dispatch*, November 6, 1963.

Mississippi brought the issue to the political fore. The Old Dominion was spared the ugly scenes of physical conflict and confrontation, but Virginia blacks were by no means sitting out the struggle. While there were some sit-ins and demonstrations in the Southside, the more important civil rights developments in the Commonwealth occurred in the courtrooms. There, the targets included the hated poll tax and legislative malapportionment, and Republicans joined blacks in seeking to overturn the Byrd organization's electoral restrictions.

In Washington, Senator Byrd was at the peak of his power in the United States Senate; he was the acknowledged leader of a congressional conservative coalition that was endeavoring resolutely to thwart the initiatives of the liberal young chief executive in the White House. The senator, however, already had announced his retirement once—before he was persuaded to reconsider in 1958—and most assumed that he would step aside when his term expired in 1964. There was a sense among political observers in Virginia that his imminent departure would open the floodgates of change in the Old Dominion.

By 1963, the pressures for reform and progress at the state level had been mounting for some time, and the rigid fiscal codes that were the hallmark of Harry Byrd's Virginia appeared to remain intact less because of their perceived merit than because of the power and esteem enjoyed by the organization chieftain. In a February 1963 article in the *University of Virginia News Letter*, former Governor Colgate W. Darden, Jr., single-handedly breathed new life into the long dormant debate over the wisdom of the state's "pay-as-you-go" policy. Darden used the article, entitled "Virginia's Indirect Debt,"[121] to challenge state and local capital project funding methods that were being used in lieu of general obligation bond financing. That so well-respected a Byrd man would speak the unspeakable was a sign of the change to come. Another Byrd tenet—opposition to a state sales tax—was giving way even before the Harrison tenure came to an end. In his final budget message, the outgoing governor proposed enactment of the tax, and his successor proceeded to steer it through the General Assembly.

The Harrison years were calm, but it was a false calm. Just below the surface, swirling currents were working a transformation the extent of which few could foresee at the time. In a short while, forces of change would converge to sweep away the old order and usher in a period of stormy uncertainty. Virginia, in 1963, was poised for a dramatic political realignment. It would take more than a decade, however, for anything resembling a stable new order to emerge from the chaos.

---

[121]Colgate W. Darden, Jr., "Virginia's Indirect Debt," *University of Virginia News Letter* (Charlottesville: Institute of Government, University of Virginia), February 15, 1963.

Part Three

A New Democratic Coalition Emerges
1964 - 1967

Chapter 12
Suddenly, An Expanded Electorate

"Every close urban-rural conflict which in the past has resulted in a rural victory will now be an urban victory. I do think the urban strength reflected in the reapportionment plans could bring us almost into the 20th century."[1]

M. Caldwell Butler, 1964

Virginia's rapid population growth, concentrated in the urban corridor that stretched from northern Virginia south to the Richmond area and then east to Hampton Roads, created a host of new public needs and new political issues with which Virginia's aging Byrd organization leadership seemed unwilling and even unable to cope. The influx of new voters from other states gave Virginia a more cosmopolitan electorate, and with the broader perspective came increased expectations of government responsiveness. Far from endeavoring to curb the growth, Governor Albertis Harrison and Lieutenant Governor Mills Godwin worked actively to promote Virginia's industrial development. The shift from an agricultural to a manufacturing-oriented economy did not comport with Senator Byrd's vision of an agrarian Virginia, but the trend was viewed positively by the Commonwealth's business and professional community. If the state's pro-business policies seemed fully consistent with its longstanding conservative proclivities, those policies nevertheless contained the seeds of the Byrd organization's destruction. A machine centered in rural courthouses and dependent upon a restricted, almost homogenous electorate was ill-equipped to absorb the twin shocks of urbanization and industrialization.

In its intolerant treatment of the "Young Turks" and the moderates who refused to toe the line on massive resistance, the Byrd organization leadership had shown itself loathe to adapt to the new political conditions brought about by the rapid postwar urban growth and industrial development. Rather than cultivate the support of the growing number of youthful lawmakers from urban areas, the senior Byrd men had rebuffed them. Of course, the organization's ability to resist change in such a stubborn manner was derived directly from the immense political strength it drew from the emotional desegregation

---

[1]Wilkinson, *Harry Byrd*, p. 249.

controversy. Once that polarizing dispute subsided, the ruling Democratic elders no longer had the luxury of turning a deaf ear to the increased demand for public services that was the inevitable by-product of the significant demographic and economic changes occurring in the state. As would soon become clear, even so devoutly conservative an organization man as Mills Godwin could, when confronted with the choice of adapting or perishing, see his way clear to adapt.

There was, however, no way for the Byrd organization to adapt to the rapid expansion of the Virginia electorate that occurred as a result of major legal reforms in the mid-1960s. The dominant Democratic Party power structure was dependent upon the disfranchisement of large numbers of blacks and, to a lesser extent, white Republicans and Democratic liberals, who did not share Byrd's conservative tenets. When the legal impediments to political participation were eliminated, the influx of new black voters and liberals into the Democratic Party dislodged the Byrd Democrats from their position of dominance within that party and left them without a political vehicle. As the Virginia Democrats began to move to the left, many right-leaning Virginians began to move away from the Democratic Party.

Though the more egregious of the discriminatory registration and election practices had ended in Virginia by the '60s, the poll tax remained. It was the cornerstone of the Democratic organization's electoral restriction structure, and few failed to recognize its pivotal importance in assuring continuation of Byrd hegemony. The organization had fended off several assaults on the poll tax by blacks and Republicans since the Second World War, but it was apparent by 1963 that the levy's days were numbered. Congress had passed and submitted to the states for ratification a constitutional amendment that would bar poll taxes in federal elections, and with most states—even in the South—having already abolished the tax, ratification was a virtual certainty. In November 1963, Governor Harrison acted to avert the impending calamity for the organization. He convened a special session of the General Assembly, and secured passage of a new statute requiring would-be voters to file a certificate of residence six months before the election if they did not pay the poll tax.

On the verge of relief from the long-detested poll tax (though only in federal elections), Republicans were incensed by this new attempt by the Byrd organization to preserve its sympathetic, restricted electorate. Anticipating the enactment of the residency-certification requirement, the GOP central committee asked J. Livingston Dillow of Pearisburg, the party's 1957 nominee for attorney general, to assemble a legal team to challenge the law. The Republicans previously had focused their efforts against the poll tax in the political and legislative arenas. But the new sentiment of the partisans was voiced by former state GOP chief I. R. Dovel, who declared, "It's time we quit letting the anti-organization Democrats and the NAACP fight our legal battles against the Byrd machine."[2] A lawsuit was filed on behalf of party Chairman Horace Henderson and Roanoke County Young Republican Lars Forssenius as plaintiffs, and Dillow's litigation team included such Republican legal luminaries as future federal judges James Turk, Emory Widener, and Walter Hoffman, and future GOP candidates Linwood Holton, John Dalton, and Richard Obenshain. On May 29, 1964, a three-judge panel ruled unanimously that the residency certification law violated the United States Constitution and could not be implemented.

The 24th Amendment to the Constitution had been ratified on January 23, 1964. By the fall registration deadline, removal of the poll tax had brought 224,305 new potential voters onto the federal election rolls. The turnout in the 1964 presidential election in Virginia exceeded a million voters for the first time, and the total constituted an increase of 35 percent over the level of voter participation in the 1960 Kennedy-Nixon contest. The impact of poll tax abolition was greatest in the black community. More than 125,000 Virginia blacks were estimated to have gone to the polls on election day in 1964, and the largest increases in turnout occurred in the rural Southside counties with large black populations. Many of the blacks casting ballots were first-time voters; new black voter registration in Virginia in 1964 was estimated at 55,000.[3]

The increased registration and voting by blacks were due in large measure to the efforts of black voter groups, which moved to capitalize on poll tax repeal by undertaking vigorous registration drives and organizational activities. The migration of rural blacks to the cities, a trend which had been underway since the Second World War, produced urban concentrations of black citizens who could be organized easily for political participation. The Crusade for Voters, a Richmond-based black political action group formed during the massive resistance controversy, was instrumental in registering and organizing blacks in the capital city. By the late '60s, the number of registered Richmond blacks had reached 30,000—compared with just 4,000 in 1956—and the Crusade for Voters had become a potent statewide organization. Passage of the federal Voting Rights Act in 1965 and federal court invalidation of the poll tax in state and local elections in 1966 opened the door to further gains in black participation. Before the end of the decade, the number of blacks registered to vote in Virginia had risen from approximately 100,000 to more than 250,000.[4]

With the changes of the mid-'60s, the Byrd organization's carefully constructed electorate rapidly came unglued. Not only the abolition of the poll tax and other electoral restrictions, but also the continued fast pace of population growth in the state, drastically altered the Old Dominion's political landscape. Blacks were not the only ones registering and voting in greater numbers; Virginians of all colors, regions, and political persuasions were doing

---

[2]*Roanoke Times*, September 28, 1963.
[3]See Wilkinson, *Harry Byrd*, pp. 258–261.
[4]See Buni, pp. 221–223.

so. By 1969, the gubernatorial election turnout would be 350 percent higher than it had been only two decades earlier. A small, relatively homogenous electorate was converted into an unmanageably large and cosmopolitan one. Republicans were cheered because they saw in these changes an essential ingredient for GOP growth in Virginia: the emergence of an increasingly liberal constituency exerting pressure on state Democrats to adopt a more liberal stance on major issues.

The same reasoning underlaid, at least in part, the Republicans' enthusiasm for population-based reapportionment. The Byrd Democrats who controlled the Virginia General Assembly did not want to transfer legislative seats to the state's fast-growing urban areas. Besides jeopardizing various venerable incumbents, such a transfer inevitably would bring more recalcitrant urban moderates and liberals into the legislature's upper and lower houses. It also would pave the way for the election of more Republicans, since GOP candidates who tended to draw much of their strength from the suburbs also would be able to capitalize on the nomination of left-of-center Democrats in urban settings. Despite the political objections of the organization men, the landmark decision of the U.S. Supreme Court in *Reynolds* v. *Sims*[5] in June 1964 left them with no choice but to apportion the legislature strictly on the basis of population. The effects of the decision, moreover, would be lasting, since the constitutional "one person-one vote" rule necessitated decennial districting revisions that promised to translate future urban growth into additional legislative seats for the heavily populated localities. As much as the partisan ramifications, the implications of the new rule for public policy buoyed House of Delegates Republican leader M. Caldwell Butler of Roanoke. "Every close urban-rural conflict which in the past has resulted in a rural victory will now be an urban victory," he predicted. "I do think the urban strength reflected in the reapportionment plans could bring us almost into the 20th century."[6]

The rules by which the political game was played in Virginia thus were being revised extensively at mid-decade—not by Virginians, but by federal courts and through federal enactments. As the presidential election year of 1964 opened, both political parties were struggling to keep abreast of the rapidly changing political situation. Their focus was on two incumbents—Lyndon Johnson, who recently had assumed the Presidency after the assassination of President Kennedy in Dallas, and Senator Byrd, who, it seemed, had been around forever. For all the change that abounded, the issues seemed remarkably familiar: Republicans debated what to do about Byrd—whether or not to contest his re-election—while Virginia Democrats wrestled with whether to endorse another liberal Democratic presidential nominee. Neither party ultimately followed the usual course.

---

[5]377 U.S. 533 (1964).
[6]Wilkinson, *Harry Byrd*, p. 249.

Chapter 13

Identity Crisis:
The Goldwater GOP Battles Byrd

"Can you imagine Patrick Henry at St. John's Church saying, 'I
know not what course others may take, but, as for me, silence is
golden. . .'?"[7]

Lewis H. Williams, June 28, 1964

The 1964 presidential contest found Virginia Republicans uncharacteristically
united. Senator Barry Goldwater of Arizona enjoyed enthusiastic support
from the party's more conservative element, and a majority of the GOP
moderates also fell in line behind his candidacy. The breadth of the Arizonan's
support in Virginia was partly the result of the comparative liberalism of his
principal opponents for the nomination, Governor Nelson Rockefeller of New
York and Governor William W. Scranton of Pennsylvania. In addition, most
Republican moderates who might have preferred one of Goldwater's opponents recognized the futility of challenging the highly organized Goldwater
campaign in Virginia. Goldwater backers were passionately committed to their
candidate, and moderates like Linwood Holton, who hoped to carry the party's
standard in the future, recognized the wisdom of not incurring the conservatives' wrath.

Interestingly, two Virginia Republicans who dared to absent themselves
from the Goldwater consensus had been competitors for the GOP gubernatorial nomination three years earlier—Clyde Pearson and party Chairman
Horace Henderson. Pearson accepted the assignment as Rockefeller's
Southern coordinator, while Henderson stayed publicly neutral and
attempted to deliver an uncommitted Virginia delegation to the national
convention in San Francisco. Henderson had made an undisclosed decision
not to seek re-election to the chairmanship when his term came to an end in
June 1964, and, during the preceding winter, he approached Walter Gambill of
Richmond, leader of the Goldwater forces in the state, with a proposal:
Henderson would step aside as party chief and would back Gambill for the
chairmanship in return for Gambill's cooperation in sending an uncommitted
delegation to San Francisco. The irascible Richmonder would have nothing to
do with the proffered deal and proceeded to rally Goldwater partisans on the

---

[7]*Richmond Times-Dispatch*, June 28, 1964.

central committee to strip Henderson of his power over convention committee appointments. Though the Goldwater forces controlled the June convention as expected, Gambill paid a price for his firmness. Tenth District GOP chief Jack Corber of Arlington garnered the support of western moderates and won an upset victory over Gambill to become the party's new chairman.

Among the most vocal Goldwater supporters during the spring competition were Richard Obenshain and the state's Young Republicans. The Young Republican federation gave the Arizona senator an early endorsement, and state "YR" chairman Obenshain was rewarded for his efforts by selection as a delegate to the national convention. Two student activists who were to become GOP rivals in the '70s lined up on different sides of the 1964 nomination contest. J. Marshall Coleman, student body president at the University of Virginia and a former chairman of the Young Republican club there, served as chairman of Young Southerners for Rockefeller, while Wyatt B. Durrette, Jr., who was pursuing a graduate degree in political science at Johns Hopkins University, served as executive director of Youth for Goldwater in Maryland. Durrette went on to become the principal spokesman for Goldwater in that heavily Democratic state during the fall campaign.

The sparring over the presidential nomination was, however, but a sidelight to the real controversy that gripped the Virginia GOP in the spring and summer of 1964. It had become increasingly apparent as 1964 approached that Senator Byrd would not retire after his term expired. Many had come to suspect that the senator was preparing to run one more time, after which he would resign and leave the choice of an interim successor to Governor Harrison. Republicans differed strongly over what the party should do in the event the aging senator did stand again for re-election. Not since 1946 had the GOP nominated an opponent for Byrd. Yet, in some ways, 1964 presented a new situation.

The opponents of nomination and their arguments were familiar enough. The leader was Congressman Joel Broyhill, whose alliances with Byrd Democrats in Congress and in the Tenth District were legendary. Broyhill reminded Republicans that Byrd had helped push Virginia into the GOP presidential column in 1952, 1956, and 1960, and he argued that Republican opposition to the senator might well prompt a strong straight-ticket campaign by Democrats that could cost Goldwater the state and jeopardize the incumbent GOP congressmen. Futile candidacies against popular conservative Democrats would not strengthen the Virginia GOP, Broyhill maintained. To the contrary, such challenges only would strain relations with like-minded Byrd men, impede realignment, and make the Republican Party in the state appear much weaker than it actually was. The Tenth District congressman found the most support for his position in Richard Poff's Sixth District and in the Southside, where many GOP leaders had close ties to the Byrd organization at the local level.

The advocates of nominating a Republican candidate for Byrd's Senate seat sounded the familiar themes about the virtues of two-party competition and the responsibility of a political party to offer voters a choice. If Byrd wanted to join the GOP, that would be fine, they said, but in the absence of such a move he had to have Republican opposition. Party chief Henderson was perhaps the most outspoken of this view's exponents, but many mountain-valley Republicans and GOP moderates from around the state voiced agreement. Interestingly, the party's younger element—both moderates and conservatives—also favored the nomination of an opponent for Byrd. The same state Young Republican convention that re-elected Richard Obenshain as federation chairman in 1963 called for the nomination of a GOP Senate candidate in 1964 "regardless of the identity of the Democratic nominee."[8] The young partisans, Broyhill recalled later,

wanted to beat their breasts a little bit. They thought the Republican Party was growing a little faster than it was actually growing and felt that it would grow faster by [challenging Byrd]. That was the Goldwater year and the conservatives were licking their chops a little more than normal.[9]

One of the young conservatives who favored a challenge to Byrd was Emporia attorney D. Dortch Warriner. An Obenshain associate, Warriner was eager to demonstrate to traditional Republicans around the state that the GOP conservatives in eastern Virginia and the Southside were not more committed to Byrd than to the Republican Party. But "real Republicans" like Warriner were the exception rather than the rule in Southside Virginia. Most in the Southside GOP were simply "safe Republicans"—people who supported Republican candidates for national office, received patronage, and were careful not to do anything (or to let the GOP do anything) that would be harmful to the Byrd organization at the state or local levels. The pro-Byrd feeling among these Southside Republicans was notorious within the party, so few were surprised when local GOP leaders blasted party chief Henderson for declaring the party's intention to oppose Byrd in the fall Senate race.

Henderson had a plan, however, for dealing with his Southside critics. "The Fourth District was the bedrock of the 'Republocrats'—the Byrd Democrats who were occupying all of the Republican committees," the party chief later recalled.

I cleaned out all of Southside Virginia. At the state central committee meeting [on January 25, 1964], I got them to unsuspectingly approve a resolution that if there was any city or county [Republican committee] that did not hold a legally authorized mass meeting, then the state chairman could declare the party offices vacant and call a mass meeting. They approved it unanimously. They didn't know what I was up to. Then, the

[8] *Richmond Times-Dispatch*, February 23, 1963.
[9] Joel T. Broyhill interview, April 11, 1984.

minute the mass meetings occurred and there hadn't been any in all of Southside Virginia, I vacated every one of [the local party offices].[10] Henderson, in effect, fired 17 of the 19 GOP unit chairmen in the Fourth District. He also declared the district chairmanship vacant, thereby ousting Harry H. Vaughan of Hopewell, who had held the position for 26 years.

On April 3, 1964, the GOP state central committee met at the Hotel Petersburg to decide whether Henderson's action would stand. The specific issue was whether the chairman had the authority to take the steps he had taken, but the focus of much of the debate was on the proper role for the GOP in Southside Virginia. Henderson maintained that Republicans were obliged to nominate willing candidates who stepped forward to run for local offices. But Vaughan reminded the committee that much of the Byrd organization's leadership hailed from his part of the state. "We have the entire Democratic Party to buck," he complained to a chorus of boos. "Our vote in presidential years is built up by Democrats and we're not about to stab the boys at the court-house in the back."[11] At the close of the stormy six-hour session, the central committee voted by a narrow margin to sustain Henderson's action. "[T]his is a great positive step for the Republican Party in Virginia," the chairman declared after the vote.

It demonstrates we mean business in filling our responsibility as a vigorous opposition party in the state. The last sanctuary of the Democratic organi-zation is now challenged. . . . Even more important is the fact that one-tenth of the people in Virginia will now begin to have the benefits of a choice of candidates which is an essential right in a democracy.[12]

Though Henderson later reappointed many of the ousted officials to their former positions on the condition that proper mass meetings would be held, the episode gave impetus to the involvement of a new, younger group of Southside Republicans. "[The] mass firing," recalled Warriner, "opened up the Fourth District for the Republican Party on an organizational level."[13] It also added to the growing momentum behind the move to nominate an oppo-nent for Senator Byrd.

The state GOP convention on June 13 was the scene of a lengthy and bitter parliamentary struggle over the Senate nomination. The majority's sentiment was reflected in the keynote address by J. Kenneth Robinson, who called upon Republicans to fight for their "political independence" in Virginia. "We can never achieve this independent status . . . ," Robinson declared, "so long as we grovel every four years to seek the sanction and support of the one-faction, one-party organization that currently controls our state polit-

---

[10]Henderson interview.

[11]*The Virginian-Pilot*, April 4, 1964.

[12]Ibid.

[13]Interview with D. Dortch Warriner conducted by Deborah L. Wood on behalf of the Republican Party of Virginia.

ically."[14] But it was late in the day when the convention finally turned to the issue of the Senate nomination; many exhausted delegates already had left the hall, and many others soon departed as Congressman Broyhill and his conservative northern Virginia lieutenants delayed the proceedings with a series of motions and quorum calls. Though convention chairman James Turk eventually succeeded in getting the balloting underway, the votes were split among several candidates and none garnered a majority. After hours of parliamentary maneuvering, the convention adjourned just before 11 p.m. without nominating a Senate contender.

The Broyhill, pro-Byrd forces had won an apparent victory, but the situation soon changed dramatically. Newly elected party chairman Corber interpreted the will of the convention to be in favor of a Senate nomination, so he promptly declared his intention to find a candidate who would be acceptable to the central committee. His stance shocked most Republicans, chief among them Joel Broyhill, because Corber had been a close ally of the Tenth District congressman, had served as his campaign manager, and generally owed his rapid rise through GOP ranks to Broyhill's support. Corber knew that Broyhill believed the nomination of a Republican foe for Byrd might place his Tenth District seat in jeopardy, but the chairman shared the conviction of other Republicans that the party had a duty to oppose the Democratic senator. Shortly after the convention, Corber urged the party's two strong 1962 congressional candidates, J. Kenneth Robinson and Lewis H. Williams, to consider running against Byrd. Neither would agree to do so.

When the central committee met on June 27 to choose a nominee, 30 votes split evenly between Lynchburg attorney Frank L. McCann, a 37-year-old conservative, and 68-year-old moderate Richard A. May of Gloucester, while a 24-vote bloc signalled their opposition to the nomination of a candidate by abstaining. The rhetorical highlight of the meeting came when Dr. Lewis Williams placed McCann's name in nomination. Responding to the claim that the GOP owed its successes in presidential elections to Senator Byrd, Williams criticized the "fallacy" of "golden silence." "Can you imagine," he asked the committee members, "Patrick Henry at St. John's Church saying, 'I know not what course others may take, but, as for me, silence is golden. . .'?"[15]

Though a number of the young conservatives preferred having no candidate to fielding the elderly and moderate May, McCann felt otherwise. At Linwood Holton's urging, the Lynchburg attorney ensured the nomination of a candidate by withdrawing after the first ballot and throwing his support to May. May garnered a majority two ballots later, with the Broyhill allies arguing unsuccessfully that a two-thirds vote was necessary to nominate. In the wake of the four-hour battle, Broyhill evoked a storm of controversy and a torrent of

---

[14]*Richmond Times-Dispatch*, June 14, 1964.

[15]*Richmond Times-Dispatch*, June 28, 1964.

condemnation from fellow partisans by questioning the validity of May's nomination and even threatening legal action. Within a few weeks, however, May and Corber were able to cool tempers, and the entire GOP leadership, including Broyhill, endorsed the Republican candidate for the Senate seat that Harry Byrd had owned for 32 years.

One final item of internal business awaited Republicans before the onset of the fall campaign. After a late-blooming, unsuccessful bid in 1960 to become the Republican national committeeman from Virginia, John Dalton had decided to go all-out for the position in 1964. It was the same post that his father, Ted, had won a dozen years earlier. The younger Dalton had political ambitions of his own, yet the path to elective office was virtually closed to him. After he finished law school and joined his father's firm in 1957, one of his law partners, Richard Poff, was his congressman. First his father, then another law partner, James Turk, represented him in the State Senate. And his next-door neighbor, Mrs. Charlotte "Pinky" Giesen, held the House of Delegates district in which the Daltons voted. Obliged to await his turn, John Dalton channeled his political energy into Republican Party activities, serving as state Young Republican chairman, state party treasurer, and legal counsel. When he decided to challenge incumbent National Committeeman Niles Straughan in 1964, Dalton did not know that another Republican heavyweight, former state party chairman I. Lee Potter, also was interested in the post. At the national convention in San Francisco, the Virginia delegation voted by secret ballot, and the delegation's 30 votes were split evenly between Dalton and Potter. After several ballots, Richard May secretly switched, and Potter was elected by a 16–14 vote. It was Dalton's last bid for a party office and the last contest of any kind that he would lose. The next year, he won election to the House of Delegates and began his steady climb to the governorship.

Delegates to the San Francisco convention returned to Virginia full of energy and enthusiasm, not yet aware that "extremism in the defense of liberty"[16] made better statesmanship than politics. The Virginia GOP had united behind the conservative favorite in the presidential race, but it simultaneously had broken with recent tradition and nominated a moderate Senate candidate to oppose Virginia's conservative patriarch. The actions seemed contradictory, and they were; they reflected a lack of strategic consensus within the growing party. Virginia Republicans differed over whether the best way to build the party was by attracting Byrd Democrats and assembling a conservative coalition primarily around national issues, or by attracting more moderate and liberal voters and assembling a progressive coalition chiefly around state issues. The former approach probably was the majority view in the state GOP in 1964. But, even among those who favored the realignment

---

[16]In accepting the presidential nomination, Goldwater proclaimed, "Extremism in the defense of liberty is no vice, and . . . moderation in the pursuit of justice is no virtue." See Barry M. Goldwater, *Goldwater* (New York: Doubleday, 1988), p. 186.

strategy, there was disagreement. Would Republicans have greater success attracting Byrd Democrats by using a carrot or a stick? In 1964, they opted to use both—offering Goldwater to conservative Democrats as a carrot, and demonstrating their willingness to use a stick by mounting opposition to Byrd. These issues would continue to divide a Virginia GOP in search of both identity and mission.

Chapter 14
Aboard The Lady Bird Special

"Let's be Democrats from the courthouse to the White House."[17]

W. Pat Jennings, 1964

While Republicans were unexpectedly opposing Senator Byrd in 1964, members of the state's majority party were acting conspicuously unlike good Virginia Democrats, too. Twelve years of "golden silence" had not sat well with many Democrats, and not only the moderate and liberal straight-ticket faithful were displeased. Many Democratic conservatives also had begun to worry about the growing competitiveness of Republicans at the state and local levels, a development they attributed in large part to Byrd's tacit support of GOP presidential nominees every four years. As the state Democratic convention neared, there was considerable sentiment for an endorsement of Lyndon Johnson's candidacy for re-election and uncertainty about Senator Byrd's view on the matter.

There was some reason to believe that Johnson might be acceptable to Byrd. After all, the President was a Southerner, and Virginia Democrats had supported him for the presidential nomination in 1960. But Johnson, while vice president, had taken increasingly liberal stands on civil rights issues, and after Kennedy's death in 1963 he pressed for passage of the Civil Rights Act of 1964. Byrd was unalterably opposed to the Texan by the summer of 1964. When, on the eve of the Virginia Democratic convention, the senator learned that Governor Harrison planned to offer a mild resolution endorsing Johnson's candidacy, he was enraged. If such a resolution were presented to the convention, Byrd declared, he would take to the floor to oppose it. The adamant senator had his way. Harrison reversed his stance and secured from the resolutions committee a statement that merely acknowledged Johnson's likely nomination and called upon him to support "Jeffersonian principles" in his campaign.

Harrison and Byrd organization leaders could not control the convention, however. As soon as the governor read the noncommittal resolutions committee statement, the pro-Johnson delegates erupted in opposition. A

---

[7]Wilkinson, *Harry Byrd*, p. 253.

141

substitute resolution endorsing the President's re-election bid was offered from the floor, and a furious demonstration and debate ensued. In the sweltering July heat of the Richmond Mosque, delegates heard Ninth District Congressman W. Pat Jennings implore them to "be Democrats from the court-house to the White House."[18] They did not hear from the esteemed leader of the courthouse Democrats, Senator Byrd, because he remained in seclusion down the street at the Hotel John Marshall. Without him, the loyalty tide could not be stemmed. In an unprecedented rejection of Byrd organization leadership, the delegates voted, 633.5 to 596.5, to place the state party on record in favor of Johnson's re-election. The action represented a significant step toward a closer alignment of the state Democratic Party with its national counterpart.

The fall campaign saw Virginia's Democratic leadership nearly as divided on the presidential race as the convention had been. Senator Byrd maintained a steely silence on the race; he thought about politics little after the death of his beloved wife, Sittie, in late August. Reporters and political observers looked in vain for a clue as to whether his silence this time was as laden with pro-Republican meaning as it had been in prior years. Signals from the organization leadership were conflicting. Congressman Tuck, State Senator Byrd, Jr., State Senator Garland Gray, and House Speaker Blackburn Moore all mimicked the senior senator's silence. A group of 17 conservative state legislators, including Delegates W. Roy Smith of Petersburg and D. French Slaughter, Jr., of Culpeper, announced that they could not support President Johnson and stopped just short of endorsing Senator Goldwater. Other Democratic lawmakers, however, heeded the pro-Johnson urgings of stalwart Byrd lieutenant Sidney Kellam of Virginia Beach, who served as Virginia campaign manager for the Johnson-Humphrey ticket. Many state Democrats simply kept their heads down and avoided the fight.

The most notable and controversial development of the presidential campaign in Virginia came when the nation's First Lady, Mrs. Johnson, whist-lestopped across the state in early October aboard the Lady Bird Special. Among her guests on the train were two women destined to become Virginia first ladies—Katherine Godwin and the future Lynda Johnson Robb—but it was the presence of Lieutenant Governor Mills Godwin and, briefly, Governor Albertis Harrison, that created the stir. Godwin had warm words for the President and First Lady at a send-off ceremony in Alexandria, then rode on the train later as it journeyed through Southside Virginia. Harrison boarded the Lady Bird Special in Richmond, where he made a pro-Johnson speech that was widely regarded as more effusive than required for politeness. Neither man discussed the train ride with Senator Byrd, before or after.

For Godwin, who was planning a bid for governor in 1965, visible support for the national Democratic ticket had obvious political significance. For three

---

[18]Ibid.

years as lieutenant governor, he had travelled throughout the state, and he had his finger on the pulse of the party. The Democratic Party in Virginia was moving toward the center, pressures for more progressive policies were mounting, and patience with the part-time party loyalty of some of the Byrd leaders was wearing thin. Climbing aboard the Lady Bird Special was a calculated political risk that Godwin elected to take partly because of his own political self-interest and partly because he viewed Goldwater as a bit too far to the right. "It wasn't the easiest thing I ever did," said Godwin of the decision.[19] But it proved to be a smart political move for him, and gave a big boost to the Johnson campaign in the state.

A variety of alignments occurred in the presidential and senatorial contests. Republican loyalists backed Goldwater for President and May for senator. Conservative Republicans and many organization Democrats lined up behind Goldwater and Byrd. Straight-ticket Democrats supported Johnson and Byrd. And, some anti-organization Democrats and Republican-leaning moderates went with Johnson and May. Both national tickets sought to tie themselves to the popular Senator Byrd; one bumper sticker read "Barry and Harry," while another urged "Vote for Johnson-Byrd November Third."[20] In the inverted political world of the Old Dominion, ticket-splitting was approaching an art form.

Despite the confusion, one thing about Virginia was clear to Goldwater's strategists: it would be impossible to carry the state without the help of conservative Democrats. So, when Senator Byrd advised the Goldwater camp that a visit to the state by the presidential candidate would be awkward and unwise in light of the contested Senate race, the Arizonan heeded the advice. Instead, South Carolina Senator J. Strom Thurmond, a new convert to Republicanism, was pressed into service. In Southside Virginia, Richard T. Short of Virginia Beach had been laboring for the Goldwater-Byrd "ticket," but the energetic young Byrd lieutenant found many Southside conservatives confused by the pro-Johnson stance of the region's two statewide leaders, Harrison and Godwin. Thurmond's Democratic background and record of opposition to civil rights measures made him the ideal Goldwater surrogate for the region, so Short hastily arranged for the South Carolinian to make an extensive tour across Virginia's southern counties.

As Thurmond stumped in Southside, the emphasis was on conservatism, not Republicanism. The Fourth District had never supported a GOP presidential nominee—it was the only Virginia district that did not do so at least once in 1928, 1952, 1956, or 1960—and the Republican label was a heavy burden for any candidate there to bear. Recognizing this, the Thurmond planners went to extraordinary lengths to downplay party affiliation. When the senator came to Emporia, for example, local GOP chairman Dortch Warriner was informed

---

[19]Godwin interview.
[20]See Wilkinson, *Harry Byrd*, p. 256.

that he could not introduce Thurmond and would not even be allowed to sit on the platform while the senator spoke. In order to meet the Thurmond staff's demand that the senator be introduced by the local "Virginians for Goldwater-Byrd" chairman, Warriner had to designate someone to assume that role for a 24-hour period. The indignity to Republicans was great, but the tour strongly aided the Goldwater effort in the region.

The racial issue was a potent one in the Southside, where surging black voter registration and civil rights pressures stoked white fears of social upheaval and a political takeover. While Goldwater's record was not one of racial intolerance, his opposition to the Civil Rights Act of 1964 helped his backers in appealing for the support of Southside whites. Elsewhere in Virginia, however, racial politics did not play so well, and other issues dominated. Goldwater's sharp tone, his image as a warmonger, and fears that he would cut back or even abolish Social Security benefits, all cost him Republican-leaning moderate and conservative votes. As was the case nationwide, Goldwater's fiery conservatism (rather than Johnson's liberalism) became the preeminent issue in the campaign. Reflecting on his defeat years later, a more mellow if still cantankerous Goldwater noted, "The whole campaign was run on fear of me. In fact, if I hadn't known Goldwater, I'd have voted against the s.o.b. myself."[21] A record number of Virginians turned out on election day, the majority of them determined to do exactly that.

Virginia returned to the Democratic presidential column on November 3, 1964, for the first time since 1948. Political observers, who had been expecting a very close race, were surprised by the size of Johnson's victory in the state. The incumbent's ticket polled 53.5 percent of the popular vote and amassed a winning margin of more than 75,000 votes.[22] The Virginia totals paled in comparison to Johnson's record-breaking 61.3 percent of the popular vote nationally, but it was nevertheless a solid win for the party-first Virginia Democrats.

Johnson's victory came primarily in urban areas; by the mid-'60s, it had become almost axiomatic that the candidate who prevailed in urban Virginia—particularly the urban corridor from northern Virginia through Richmond and down to the Tidewater cities—won election. Johnson ran well ahead of the normal Democratic presidential vote in the suburbs of Washington, D.C., and in Hampton Roads. The conservative suburban counties of Henrico and Chesterfield provided their predictably hefty GOP majorities, but Goldwater's Third District margin was diminished by a large Democratic vote in Richmond and was insufficient to offset his urban losses elsewhere in the Commonwealth.

---

[21]*Richmond Times-Dispatch*, May 13, 1984.

[22]The vote totals were: Johnson (D) – 558,038 (53.5%); Goldwater (R) – 481,334 (46.2%). Eisenberg, *Virginia Votes*, p. 240.

Both parties experienced significant defections from their usual bases of support. In the traditional Republican strongholds of the Valley, Goldwater ran well behind the Nixon and Eisenhower totals. On average, the GOP vote share in the area was off more than 13 percent from the 1960 showing. In Harrisonburg, for example, Goldwater received slightly more than 50 percent of the vote, compared to 72 percent for Nixon in 1960; in Waynesboro, where Nixon had polled nearly 70 percent of the vote, Goldwater received only 47 percent. The Republican totals fell short of the usual mark in southwest Virginia as well. The normally closely divided Ninth District turned in a Johnson winning margin in excess of 16,000 votes.[23]

The Democrats needed those inroads in traditionally Republican areas to offset their losses in the once-reliable Southside. Goldwater carried 16 counties and five cities in that region, some by margins in excess of 60 percent, while the Democrats staved off the GOP challenge in ten counties and four cities. The GOP ticket's unprecedented dominance in the Byrd organization heartland was significant. At first glance, it appeared to be little more than an aberration owing to the predominance of racial concerns in Southside. Virginia reflected a Southern phenomenon in that respect. Goldwater had broken the longstanding Democratic grip on several states of the Deep South—South Carolina, Georgia, Alabama, Louisiana, and Mississippi—but had failed to carry the border states which had backed Republican presidential nominees in previous elections. Similarly, in Virginia, Goldwater picked up new support in the black belt counties—the part of the state most like the Deep South—but forfeited mountain-valley and suburban GOP votes. The long-range significance of Goldwater's feat in Southside, however, lay in its opening of the door to Republican acceptability in the region. Racial preoccupations would fade, but if Virginia was to undergo a political realignment, the bedrock conservative Southside would have to overcome its hostility toward Republicanism. It began to do so with the Goldwater candidacy.

Another development with momentous implications for the future of Virginia politics was the magnitude and homogeneity of the black vote in the 1964 presidential election. The removal of the poll tax and the intense political organization drives in the black community accounted for most of the increase in the number of blacks who went to the polls. But the impact of the black vote in the 1964 contest was a function of the blacks' bloc-voting behavior as well as their numbers. Spurred by President Johnson's support of civil rights and anti-poverty legislation, the presence of civil rights leader Hubert Humphrey on the Democratic ticket, and fear of Goldwater, blacks went to the polls and voted with a degree of unanimity virtually unparalleled in the Commonwealth's political history.[24] Predominantly black precincts registered incredibly lopsided totals on election day. One Richmond precinct voted 2,138-to-14

---

[23]See Ralph Eisenberg, "The 1964 Presidential Election in Virginia: A Political Omen?" *University of Virginia News Letter* (Charlottesville: Institute of Government, University of Virginia), April 15, 1965.

[24]See Buni, pp. 219–220.

for Johnson; Newport News' Jefferson Park precinct gave Johnson 1,325 votes and Goldwater none. Most precincts delivered well over 90 percent of the vote to the Democratic ticket. The votes of blacks were essential for Johnson's urban corridor advantage, and they easily exceeded the President's statewide margin of victory.

The presidential contest also revealed the emergence of a new winning coalition within the state Democratic Party. In contrast to the Byrd organization victories in previous statewide elections, the Johnson triumph did not depend on huge majorities in rural Virginia. Rather, the main components of the Democratic presidential win were a greatly swollen black vote (particularly in the urban areas), the support of organized labor, and the ballots of anti-organization liberals, restive moderates, and a fair number of conservative Byrd Democrats. It was a coalition that spanned the political spectrum. To some, the outcome seemed to be mostly the product of the masterful political hand of Sidney Kellam, Johnson's campaign chief in Virginia, and the surprising efforts of Harrison and Godwin. Like all elections, the 1964 contest was decided by the convergence of a set of unique events, personalities, and circumstances, but subsequent events would confirm that the result was no fluke. The diverse and fragile Democratic coalition first assembled in 1964 would last for several years and then collapse. In the 1970s, faction-ridden state Democrats would boost realignment and help usher in a period of Republican dominance by embracing the most liberal nostrums of the national Democratic Party. But, in the 1980s, Lyndon Johnson's centrist son-in-law, Charles S. Robb, would assemble a winning coalition quite similar that constructed in 1964 and thereby restore the Democratic Party to a position of preeminence in Virginia politics.

In the congressional elections of 1964, there were few surprises. The decision in the Senate race, of course, was a foregone conclusion. The 77-year-old Byrd and his 68-year-old challenger barely crossed swords during the campaign. Byrd did not need to campaign, and with all the other political news to cover, the press gave little attention to the GOP's Richard May. A lifelong Republican, May had grown up in Massachusetts and moved to Virginia after serving on General Douglas MacArthur's staff during the Second World War. He had been an executive with General Motors, and he turned to politics after his retirement in the small Tidewater town of Saluda. His defeat by Byrd was decisive enough to quell even the most passionate of political ambitions, and it brought May's late-blooming political career to an abrupt end. Byrd rolled up 64 percent of the vote to the Republican's 19 percent, with the remainder distributed among several independent candidates.[25] May's bid did not prove threatening enough to the Byrd men to cause the backlash some Republicans had feared in the House of Representatives races. Split-ticket voting was suffi-

---

[25]The vote totals were: Byrd – 592,260 (63.8%); May – 176,624 (19.0%). Eisenberg, *Virginia Votes*, p. 244.

ciently widespread to keep GOP Congressmen Poff and Broyhill in office even as Goldwater and May were going down to decisive defeats. Democratic congressional incumbents were also successful except in the Third District, where Representative J. Vaughan Gary retired following his razor-thin 1962 win over the GOP's Lewis Williams. Gary's departure opened the door for the expected candidacy of Democrat David E. Satterfield, III, son of the popular Byrd Democrat who had represented the district in Congress prior to Gary. The Republicans tapped young Richard D. Obenshain, who reluctantly decided to make the race on the eve of the nominating convention. The increasingly large suburban vote in the district gave Republicans reason to believe they could capture the seat, but the campaign was complicated by the presence of a formidable third candidate, liberal State Senator Edward E. Haddock of Richmond. With Haddock campaigning as a pro-Johnson "Independent Democrat" and receiving the support of the local black political organization, Obenshain could not hope to garner the anti-Byrd protest vote from blacks that had swollen Republican Williams's total two years earlier.

Obenshain's strategy was to make the race principally a contest between himself and the liberal Haddock. He embraced the Goldwater candidacy and platform, chided Satterfield for his noncommittal stance on the presidential race, and sought to tie his Democratic foe to the national Democrats. Voting for Satterfield, Obenshain warned, would split the conservative bloc and risk the election of a liberal. The contest occasioned frenzied organizational activity on all sides, and was heated by a series of confrontational joint appearances between the candidates. Despite Obenshain's efforts to link Satterfield with Johnson and the national Democrats, the conservative Democratic establishment in the Third District stood by their party's congressional nominee, and the result was a fairly even three-way split in the electorate.

If Satterfield had some uncomfortable party associations at the national level, Obenshain had problems of his own closer to home. Goldwater's decision not to come to Virginia deprived Obenshain of a powerful endorsement. And, in bidding for conservative Democratic votes, the Republican was hardly aided by the presence of a runningmate who was opposing Senator Byrd. May understandably wanted to stump in the vote-laden suburban areas of the Third District and did so frequently, but Obenshain always managed to have a scheduling conflict or other excuse for not appearing with him. Finally, Obenshain's fierce party loyalty and the increasing awkwardness of the refusals led him to reject the advice of his associates and agree to join May for a campaign event shortly before the election. Obenshain's close friend and adviser, Lewis Williams, thought the better of it, however, and he purposely misinformed both campaigns of the time at which the rally was to begin. When the congressional nominee arrived, the Senate candidate already had come and gone. "Peculiar, isn't it?" Obenshain asked when he learned of May's earlier departure. Williams did not disagree—and never explained.[26]

---

[26]Lewis H. Williams interview, June 4, 1980, and August 30, 1984.

Obenshain's first run for public office in 1964, like the others that followed, yielded significant returns for the GOP in terms of the organizational advances it occasioned and the commitment and enthusiasm it generated among Republican activists. But, also like the other Obenshain bids to follow, it did not yield success for the candidate. The Republican trailed Satterfield by only 654 votes, with Haddock a few thousand votes behind.[27] It was a heartbreaking defeat for Obenshain and a disappointment for the GOP, which increasingly was looking to the Richmond suburbs as a critical part of its base. The installation of a Byrd Democrat who reflected the Third District majority's conservative views would postpone for well over a decade the GOP's capture of the seat.

In the wake of Johnson's landslide victory, Virginia Republicans differed over the reasons for their defeat. Conservative partisans insisted that the outcome was a reaction to the traumatic Kennedy assassination and not a rejection of conservative policies. But moderate Republicans blamed Goldwater's fiery brand of conservatism and his seemingly racist stances. Just four years earlier, the progressive Nixon posture on civil rights had been blamed for the GOP's defeat. If the Republican Party "had quit trying to appease these minority groups," Congressman Broyhill had declared in 1961, "we would have a Republican in the White House today."[28] But the tack suggested by Broyhill apparently had led to electoral disaster in 1964, and moderates now had the initiative in the Virginia GOP.

With their sights fixed on the coming gubernatorial election against the former massive resister Godwin, Republicans made a much-publicized move in May 1965 to regain some of the party's lost ground among black voters. With the GOP central committee's support, party chief Corber appointed Clarence Townes, Jr., a black insurance executive from Richmond, as special assistant to the chairman. It was a notable development—the first appointment of a black to a position of statewide prominence by either party in modern times.[29] But the gesture had little impact in the Goldwater campaign's aftermath. Large numbers of blacks were beginning to acquire and exercise voting rights, and it was quickly apparent that they meant to reward their Democratic civil rights sponsors with virtually unswerving party loyalty. After his ride on the Lady Bird Special, even ex-massive resister Godwin suddenly seemed irresistible to black Democrats.

---

[27]The vote totals were: Satterfield (D) – 43,880 (34.7%); Obenshain (R) – 43,226 (34.2%); Haddock (Independent Democrat) – 39,223 (31.0%). Buni, pp. 226–227.

[28]*Richmond Times-Dispatch*, July 8, 1961.

[29]Buni, p. 171.

Chapter 15

The Godwin Revolution

"[The people of Virginia] are expectant. They have given their
assent in many places to the tapping of whatever new sources of
revenue are needed. . . .
"We make a mistake, as their leaders, if we get too far ahead of
our people. But we make a greater mistake if we fall behind them.
"I have made a compact with myself that my own errors will be
in the former category."[30]

Mills E. Godwin, Jr.
Inaugural Address, 1966

"[A] little rebellion, now and then," wrote Thomas Jefferson to James
Madison in 1787, "is a good thing, and as necessary in the political world as
storms in the physical." Judging from the dramatic change that his administration
brought to the once-staid Old Dominion, it may be assumed that
Governor Mills Godwin placed considerable stock in his predecessor's words.
But a comparison to the *recipient* of Jefferson's missive may be more appropriate,
because as Godwin debarked the Lady Bird Special in 1964, he seemed to
have undergone a transformation on the subject of federal-state relations as
profound as Madison's journey from *The Federalist* to the *Virginia Resolutions*.
The former champion of defiant resistance to federal desegregation orders
had, by 1964, become a cheerleader for the most aggressive wielder of federal
power since Roosevelt, and his own administration as Virginia's governor
would bring unprecedented activism as well. Godwin could certainly agree
with Jefferson's assertion that an occasional rebellion was healthy. But the
sage of Chuckatuck no doubt would have elaborated that the desirability in
every instance hinged upon the revolt's being led—or at least managed—by
the right people.

Godwin was certain that he was the right person to lead the revolution
that was coming to Virginia in the mid-1960s. The resilient Democrat had
gained favor with the Byrd high command and statewide prominence through
his pivotal work on behalf of the massive resistance program, and this had catapulted him to the second spot on the Democratic ticket in 1961. Many,

---

[30]*Selected Speeches of The Honorable Mills E. Godwin, Jr., Governor of Virginia, 1966–1970*,
p. 4.

however, attributed the difficulty of Godwin's primary victory that year to his reputation as a segregationist and his strict adherence to Byrd fiscal codes. Godwin sensed the changing mood of his party and his state. In 1964, his endorsement of Johnson won him applause from moderate and liberal Democrats and was a key factor in the formation of the expansive coalition that enabled the incumbent President to carry Virginia. As 1965 approached, Godwin made it clear that he would pursue more progressive policies as governor than had his predecessors. The result was broad support for his candidacy within the Democratic Party—so broad, in fact, that neither he nor his runningmates, State Senator Fred G. Pollard of Richmond and incumbent Attorney General Robert Y. Button, had any opposition in the primary elections.

In his fascinating account of the 1965 gubernatorial election, J. Harvie Wilkinson III examined Godwin's career to that point and concluded that he was "a master practitioner of the political art."[31] Writing after Godwin's second term as Virginia's governor—he held office again, as a Republican, from 1974 to 1978—Guy Friddell called him "a man for all seasons."[32] Like a long distance runner in hilly country who must peer ahead and change course periodically in order to stay on ridges and avoid valleys, Godwin had an uncanny knack for discerning political trends and adjusting to them. It was a skill that served him well in a postwar political environment in which change often seemed the only constant in Virginia. Even in 1965, well before Virginia's political upheaval reached its climax and the extent of Godwin's versatility became apparent, many could see that he was a consummate politician.

Though some observers commented pejoratively on Godwin's agility, most recognized that his political realism and capacity for compromise complemented his guiding beliefs and principles. He seemed to have a natural instinct for leadership, and he resolved to lead in the direction that he regarded as best for the state. Effective governance and effective politics, he knew, went hand in hand; neither was possible without the other. And so Godwin looked, more meticulously and more successfully than most, for ways to advance both himself and his principles.

Godwin seldom approached the fine line between astute political leadership and self-interested opportunism because his stands ultimately were rooted in conviction. Though critics would charge that expediency drove his evolution from "massive resister" to "education governor," the inconsistency was more apparent than real. The political benefit of each stance in its time was undeniable, but so was Godwin's sincerity. He had opposed public school integration primarily because he, like most Southside whites, had been convinced that it would upset the delicate relationship between the races and trigger a prolonged period of social strife. Though the rigid racial code of his region and insensitivity to black aspirations had prompted that stance,

---

[31]Wilkinson, *Harry Byrd*, p. 263. For a description of the 1965 campaign, see pp. 263–284.
[32]Bugg, p. 391.

Godwin's position also reflected a genuine, if misplaced, concern about the impact of desegregation on the state's public education system. In the mid-1960s, when he moderated his image and became a leading proponent of educational advances and other improved public services, Godwin was responding to a political climate favorable to progressive measures he believed were needed. "[T]he people of Virginia were in the mood for a move forward," he later recalled in a conversation with James Latimer, "and I had a program to challenge them."[33] If his progressive impulses seemed too long restrained, it was because, for Mills Godwin, politics was the art of the possible.

To Republican conservatives who were more interested in converting than in defeating Byrd Democrats, Godwin's embrace of his party's liberal national ticket in 1964 had been at once infuriating and encouraging. Though Godwin had helped deny the GOP Virginia's electoral votes, his stance had given the Republicans an issue with which to encourage conservative defections from the state Democratic ticket in 1965. At a November 1964 meeting of the GOP central committee, partisans applauded when Richard Obenshain referred to Godwin's support for Lyndon Johnson and declared that Virginia should no longer be governed by "turncoats like Albertis Harrison and Mills Godwin."[34] Republicans, he continued, should nominate a solidly conservative ticket in 1965 so that right-thinking Virginians could "reap retribution of the people who betrayed us [in the presidential election]."[35] At about the same time, Lewis Williams touched off a whirlwind of controversy with the then-radical suggestion that Republicans seek the conversion of a prominent conservative Democrat to run as the party's candidate for governor. The GOP conservatives also repeatedly urged Congressman Broyhill to enter the race.

In the aftermath of Goldwater's defeat, however, conservative influence within the GOP was at a low ebb. The Republican Party in Virginia remained in large measure a party of progressivism at the state level. For many traditional Republicans, high-sounding conservative rhetoric about individual freedom and limited, constitutional government did not send hearts pounding or competitive juices flowing nearly as quickly as did blistering attacks on the Byrd "machine," its electoral restrictions, and its stingy fiscal policies. Suburbanites, who often took sharply conservative positions on national issues, tended to favor a progressive approach at the state and local levels. The GOP's growing suburban base included many who shared the traditional Republicans' belief that the Byrd organization's mode of operation and policies were better suited to days past. They were ready to support a Republican for governor who championed change.

---

[33]Conversations with James Latimer, "Living History Makers, Part III: Harrison, Godwin and the 1960s," WCVE-TV, 1982.

[34]*The Richmond News Leader*, November 23, 1964.

[35]*Richmond Times-Dispatch*, November 22, 1964.

Linwood Holton fit the bill. The party's western region vice chairman was an attractive candidate and an effective campaigner—a veteran of two strong bids for the House of Delegates from Roanoke in the 1950s. The 39-year-old Holton was a native of Big Stone Gap in far southwest Virginia; he had served in the Navy and attended Washington and Lee University and Harvard Law School before settling into a legal practice in Roanoke. He also had long been active in GOP affairs and was well known to Republicans around the state. Virtually all understood him to be a mountain-valley Republican in the progressive Ted Dalton tradition, a moderate on racial issues, and a passionate believer in two-party politics. Most also sensed his ambition, so few were surprised when he stepped forward to seek the party's nomination for governor. Holton did so with an awareness of Godwin's advantages and the bleak prospects for a Republican victory, but he hoped that a foundation could be laid for a successful bid for governor in the future. The nomination was his without opposition.

The Holton ticket was geographically and philosophically balanced. Northern Virginia, the locus of much of the new suburban Republican strength in the state, was represented by 35-year-old McLean businessman Vincent F. Callahan, Jr., the nominee for lieutenant governor. Callahan had run unsuccessfully for the House of Delegates in 1963 and was a veteran Tenth District activist. D. Dortch Warriner, 36, of Emporia, who enjoyed the support of the party's conservative wing, joined the ticket as the candidate for attorney general. Warriner had declared his candidacy primarily to draw attention to the party-building efforts of the Republicans in Southside Virginia, and he was somewhat surprised when no other GOP candidate stepped forward to seek the post. Just eight years earlier, he had emerged from law school and had rejected the counsel of friends who predicted his legal practice would suffer if he openly avowed his Republican sympathies. Now Warriner was his party's nominee for election as the Commonwealth's chief legal officer.

The Virginia GOP was united and, for the first time, ready to wage a serious statewide campaign on behalf of its candidates. The strong Ted Dalton bids in 1953 and 1957 had been individual performances in which the party had played a minimal role. By 1965, however, the state GOP apparatus had something to offer Holton and his youthful runningmates. In addition to the use of its headquarters and full-time executive secretary, the party organized a series of seminars for Republican workers that served to bolster the ticket's precinct-level campaign. The GOP's organizational wizard, National Committeeman Lee Potter, agreed to serve as campaign manager for the Holton ticket, thus guaranteeing ample campaign assistance from the Republican National Committee. With these assets, Holton laid out a strategy for defeating Godwin. He figured to gain blacks' support by reminding them of Godwin's role in massive resistance and to attract conservative backing because of his opponent's efforts on behalf of Johnson in the recent presidential race.

The time was right, however, for Mills Godwin. His shift to the political center enabled him to reassemble the broad coalition that had formed behind President Johnson's candidacy. Blacks, labor leaders, veteran Byrd organization foes, and stalwart organization adherents all climbed aboard the Godwin bandwagon. It was a phenomenon that left Republicans scratching their heads. How could a candidate previously identified with his party's most conservative faction garner support spanning the political spectrum? Holton publicly marveled at the "incredible logic under which [Godwin] was able . . . to send Armistead Boothe to Arlington to proclaim him a liberal in the finest tradition of the Great Society while he was also able . . . to send Bill Tuck to Danville to attest he was a true conservative in the tradition of Harry Byrd."[36] Though GOP leaders derided Godwin's as a "chameleon candidacy,"[37] the charges fell on deaf ears.

Most striking was the former massive resister's support among blacks. Holton had solid credentials as a social progressive and supporter of civil rights, and he actively and openly appealed for black support by pillorying the Byrd organization's voting restrictions and support for segregation. Such direct appeals for black support would have been seized upon by Democrats to rally white voters in earlier elections, but observers expected 100,000 blacks to vote in 1965, so Godwin joined Holton in wooing black political leaders. The Democratic lieutenant governor dismissed talk of massive resistance as outdated and contended that the policy had "bought valuable time during which people were able to adjust to conditions that were inevitably to come."[38] He then moved on to surer footing, emphasizing his leadership role in the successful Johnson re-election campaign and advocating increased education expenditures and other improvements. Both candidates proposed progressive measures, but the Democrat had the edge in seeking support from blacks because he appeared the likely winner. Blacks were not confident of Godwin's sincerity, but, as Dr. William Thornton of the Crusade for Voters put it, they supported him hoping "that he would realize we'd helped him to win and therefore would do something for us."[39] Moreover, the centrist Godwin candidacy afforded an opportunity for blacks to demonstrate the wisdom of the Democrats' progressive strategy and the continuing viability of the new Democratic coalition assembled in 1964—a coalition in which black voters were an indispensable element.

---

[36]Jack R. Hunter, *Linwood Holton's Long Quest for the Governorship of Virginia and its Impact on the Growth of the Republican Party*, Unpublished Thesis, University of Richmond, 1972, p. 32.

[37]*The Richmond News Leader*, May 14, 1965.

[38]Jack Bass and Walter DeVries, *The Transformation of Southern Politics* (New York: Basic Books, Inc., 1976), p. 350.

[39]Neal R. Peirce, *The Border South States* (New York: W.W. Norton and Company, 1975), p. 58.

The thinking of Virginia's labor leaders was much the same. They believed that the state GOP was headed toward alignment with the "regressive policies" of the national Republican Party, while Virginia Democrats were moving in a more moderate direction. "[A]n atmosphere is developing in the Democratic Party nationally and in Virginia," opined AFL-CIO Vice President Julian Carper, "where management, labor, and government can work more closely together."[40] Long the politically impotent whipping boy of the Byrd Democrats, organized labor sensed an opportunity to back a winner and gain some much-needed credibility in the state. Godwin was an exceedingly unlikely vehicle for labor. In responding to the AFL-CIO's endorsement of his opponent during the 1961 primary campaign, Godwin had rued the arrival of any new day in the Commonwealth "molded and fashioned by the labor union bosses of Virginia or by any who do their bidding."[41] But, four years later, Godwin was bidding for votes and labor was bidding for influence in a drastically altered political environment, so pragmatism ruled the day. For the first time in many years, organized labor backed the Byrd organization candidate.

Notwithstanding his liberal support, Godwin held most of the Byrd organization as well. Many in the courthouses had little enthusiasm for the candidate's new moderate image, but they recalled his yeoman service during the school desegregation controversy and they were willing to give him considerable leeway in adjusting to the shifting political winds. Most who doubted Godwin's conservative convictions had been sobered by the breadth of his support within the party, and they had pledged their support well before the onset of the general election campaign. For a great many organization sympathizers in the business community, Godwin's readiness to lead Virginia forward and to improve her standing among the states in various categories of governmental services was a welcome development. The Commonwealth's attractiveness to new business and industry depended, to a large extent, on such services, and increased state expenditures for education, roads, mental hospitals, and the like could be counted upon to return healthy dividends. In September, a group of 14 "eminent Virginians"—prominent Byrd supporters who had played important roles in "Democrats for Eisenhower" in 1952 and 1956—announced their support for Godwin. Most of these key business leaders would never back another Democrat for governor.

Godwin pledged increased teacher salaries, capital outlays for institutions of higher education, industrial development measures, improvements in mental hospitals, steps to combat pollution in the state's growing urban areas, and other initiatives. In so doing, he mimicked the progressive GOP platforms of the preceding two decades. But it was the Republicans who, in 1965, were perceived as running the "me too" campaign. Holton advocated many of the same programs, and his slogan—"Make Virginia First Again"—touched the

---

[40]Hunter, p. 31.
[41]Wilkinson, *Harry Byrd*, p. 267.

correct chord, but many Virginians simply believed that Godwin was better situated to produce the desired results. He had government experience, his party controlled the General Assembly, and, as a confirmed Byrd man, he was in a position to lead the state away from some of the no-longer-cherished tenets of Byrdism. What were "dangerous" and "irresponsible" fiscal policies when promoted by Republicans or Democratic liberals suddenly became "sound" and "prudent" steps forward when advanced by the stalwart Godwin. Long an advocate of a vigorous two-party system in Virginia, *The Richmond News Leader* editorially captured the prevailing sentiment when it commented, "The time for a change . . . is not yet."[42]

The *News Leader* was counseling delay in changing parties, but a substantial group of ardent conservatives opposed the dramatic policy shifts that were being urged by both major-party candidates. In July, a number of Byrd Democrats in Southside Virginia formed the "Conservative Party" and nominated a ticket headed by Chesapeake Assistant School Superintendent William J. Story, Jr. The Conservatives wanted to retain "pay-as-you-go" financing, eliminate federal intrusion into public education and state affairs generally, and, most important, "investigate and expose subversive influences."[43] A member of the right-wing John Birch Society, Story warned that both political parties were leading the state "down the road to socialistic, Communistic, Marxist control."[44] Principally, however, the formation of the group was a reaction to Godwin and his embrace of President Johnson, whose civil rights policies were anathema to Southside conservatives. "The Virginia Conservative Party was a direct outgrowth of [the Lady Bird Special]," recalled Richard Short, the group's finance chairman. "If that train had never come through Virginia with Godwin aboard in 1964, I don't believe there ever would have been a Virginia Conservative Party."[45]

Story's candidacy turned Southside Virginia, the one-time bastion of Byrd organization strength, into a political battleground. The backlash there from Godwin's role in the 1964 presidential campaign was much sharper than he had expected. "Despite the fact that I had gone the extra mile in supporting certain (massive resistance) legislation that they had proposed to the General Assembly, they didn't ever forgive me for riding on that train," Godwin later remarked.[46] To cut his losses, Godwin relied upon campaign assistance from Southside Congressmen Watkins Abbitt and William Tuck. In late October, Abbitt joined the Democratic nominee for a rally in Buckingham County. A vote for Story "would be utterly futile," the congressman declared, "even though many of us agree with what has been said by the Conservative candi-

---

[42]*The Richmond New Leader*, October 30, 1965.

[43]Wilkinson, *Harry Byrd*, p. 271.

[44]Ibid.

[45]Richard T. Short interview, June 10, 1980, and August 26, 1988.

[46]Latimer, "Living History Makers, Part III."

date."[47] Abbitt went on to remind the audience of Godwin's role as the leader of the massive resistance forces in the State Senate. "[W]e are not going to forget those hectic days," he added.

While Godwin strove to counter the Conservatives in Southside, he was careful not to offend other even more important elements of his coalition, especially in more populous regions. Once politically dominant, the rural Virginia black belt had been politically expendable in 1964, and it would be so again in 1965 if Godwin's strategy proved successful. The Democrat thus stressed the progressiveness of his platform and derided Story as one who "wants to turn the clock back" and "sees a Communist behind every tree."[48] Story proved to be a useful foil for the centrist-sounding Godwin throughout much of Virginia, while Godwin relied on his own Southside roots and conservative past to generate the vote he needed from that region.

Complementing Godwin's other advantages in the race against Holton was a substantial edge in contributions. The Democrat spent more than $215,000, while Holton's campaign invested less than $80,000.[49] By Virginia standards, it was an extremely expensive race. The incumbent governor had spent less than $30,000 during the 1961 general election campaign, and the seven-fold increase in just four years was a reflection not only of rapidly escalating campaign costs but of the seriousness with which Democrats viewed Holton's challenge. Most of the increased expenditures went for the relatively new innovation of media advertising—television, radio, newspaper, and billboard advertisements. Financial constraints, however, forced Holton to rely more on publicity generated through personal interviews, press releases, and public events. He benefited significantly from appearances on his behalf by former President Eisenhower, former Vice President Nixon, and House of Representatives Minority Leader Gerald Ford. Godwin, by contrast, made sure he was nowhere near when Vice President Hubert Humphrey came to Virginia Beach in autumn to address a Municipal League convention.

The result was a sizeable Democratic victory on election day. But, even with his spectral coalition, Godwin became the first Virginia chief executive in the twentieth century to fail to amass a majority of the vote in winning election. Godwin received 47.9 percent of the vote to Holton's 37.7 percent and Story's 13.4 percent.[50] The Democratic victory again demonstrated the critical importance of the urban corridor. Godwin carried most of the cities and counties in the corridor, thanks to a hefty majority of the black vote—estimated at

---

[47]Buni, pp. 239–240.

[48]Wilkinson, *Harry Byrd*, p. 273.

[49]Ibid.

[50]The vote totals were: Godwin (D) – 269,526 (47.9%); Holton (R) – 212,207 (37.7%); Story (Conservative) – 75,307 (13.4%); George L. Rockwell (American Nazi Party) – 5,730 (1.0%). Eisenberg, *Virginia Votes*, p. 248.

75 percent—and a respectable showing in the suburbs.[51] The Conservative inroads into the usual Byrd organization vote in the Southside exceeded pre-election forecasts, however, and were responsible for holding Godwin to a mere plurality statewide. Story carried 11 counties, including vote-rich Chesterfield, and won absolute majorities in three of them. In other counties south of the James River he prevented Godwin from receiving the support normally accorded Byrd organization standard-bearers.

For Republicans, the returns were a source of some encouragement. Holton's showing was the best by a GOP candidate for governor since Ted Dalton's 1953 bid; moreover, unlike Dalton, Holton had not been the beneficiary of a liberal anti-Byrd protest vote. The 1965 GOP total thus appeared to reflect an enlarging Republican base in the state, an interpretation reinforced by the similar shares of the vote received by Holton's two runningmates.[52] Traditionally Republican areas in the mountains and in the Shenandoah Valley, which had balked at Goldwater's candidacy in 1964, were put firmly back in the GOP column by Holton. In addition, the Republican nominee demonstrated strength in the suburbs. He carried northern Virginia's Tenth District and Henrico County in the Third District, and he outpolled Godwin by 10,000 votes in the state's five largest suburban counties. But the traditional GOP strongholds and the suburbs were just two of the three segments of the electorate that Holton and his strategists had targeted. He hoped to get at least half of the black vote—Republican Clyde Pearson had received an estimated 70 percent of blacks' ballots four years earlier[53]—and his inability to do so cost him the election.

Despite passage of the Voting Rights Act and continued voter registration drives by blacks, the turnout among blacks was lower in 1965 than in 1964. When voters went to the polls on election day in 1965, the judicial invalidation of the state poll tax was still several months away. Despite a significant rise in population throughout the state, fewer than 563,000 total votes were cast in the 1965 governor's race—roughly half the 1964 total and only nine percent above the previous high for a state election set in 1957. Still, Godwin's 75-percent share of the black vote—estimated conservatively at 60,000—was enough to provide his margin of victory. Though the governor-elect seemed reluctant to admit it in the election's wake, support from blacks had been a decisive factor in his success. Moreover, the influence of blacks in future state-

---

[51]Ralph Eisenberg, "Gubernatorial Politics in Virginia: The Experience of 1965," *University of Virginia News Letter* (Charlottesville: Institute of Government, University of Virginia), March 15, 1969.

[52]The vote totals in the election for lieutenant governor were: Pollard (D) – 272,425 (50%); Callahan (R) – 202,053 (37%); Reid T. Putney (Conservative) – 69,941 (13%). The vote totals in the election for attorney general were: Button (D) – 274,445 (51%); Warriner (R) – 184,899 (34%); John W. Carter (Conservative) – 80,542 (15%). *Votes Cast for Governor, Lieutenant Governor and Attorney General, General Election, November 2, 1965* (Division of Purchase and Printing, Commonwealth of Virginia, 1966).

[53]Vogt, p. 368.

wide contests promised to increase dramatically following abolition of the poll tax applicable to state elections.

That the Democratic ticket had won yet another gubernatorial election was far from remarkable, but the composition of the 1965 victory, like the Johnson win in 1964, gave pause to even the most inveterate political observers. The ballots barely had been tabulated before doubts were being expressed about the durability of the fragile new Democratic coalition. The magnitude of the political task facing the new governor was noted by James J. Kilpatrick, editor of *The Richmond News Leader*:

> Were ever such bedfellows united in one boarding house? Here were Byrd Democrats, anti-Byrd Democrats, Goldwater Republicans, Negroes, whites, pro-labor and anti-labor, somehow tented together in an uneasy coalition based upon respect for Senator Byrd, Democratic habit, pure pragmatism, respect for Mr. Godwin, and a good deal of what's-in-it-for-me. Mr. Godwin's fearfully difficult and delicate task, as governor, will be to keep this political structure from becoming altogether unglued.[54]

The 1966 congressional elections would present the first test for the Godwin coalition in the electoral arena. But, with a dynamic new chief executive in the Capitol, public attention first was riveted on the General Assembly, where the governor's bold campaign rhetoric would either be translated into landmark legislation or be consigned to the junk heap.

Those who knew Godwin well had no doubt that he would follow through on his campaign pledges. Few, however, could have anticipated the sweeping nature of the initiatives the erstwhile die-hard conservative would propose. "Spending money for the demonstrated needs of the state doesn't mean you are less conservative," Godwin explained in a 1969 interview. "The change is a natural evolution of the times, . . . the result of industrialization and intellectual concern for public education. We're convinced a majority of Virginians want responsive conservatism."[55] To many, it seemed that Godwin had come to that view rather late. Popular support for educational advances and improvements in other public institutions had surged as the state's population and economy expanded rapidly in the postwar period, but Godwin and his Byrd organization allies had remained unresponsive for nearly two decades. By 1966, however, the popular mood was apparent. "A moderation set in," Godwin recalled. "[T]he people were ahead of the politicians, I found out in 1964 and 1965."[56] He resolved never to let that happen to him again, and he said so in his inaugural address:

---

[54]See Wilkinson, *Harry Byrd*, p. 283.

[55]George M. Kelley, "The Changing Style of Virginia Politics", *University of Virginia News Letter* (Charlottesville: Institute of Government, University of Virginia), February 15, 1969.

[56]Ibid.

[The people of Virginia] are expectant. They have given their assent in many places to the tapping of whatever new resources are necessary. They are able and they are willing to channel greater private means toward greater public service.

We make a mistake, as their leaders, if we get too far ahead of our people. But we make a greater mistake if we fall behind them.

I have made a compact with myself that my own errors will be in the former category.[57]

Godwin's inaugural message made clear his intention to "move Virginia forward everywhere." Schools, colleges, roads, hospitals, parks, and prisons—all would receive major improvement during his tenure. "If there is a watchword for our time," the governor declared, "it is to move, to strike out boldly, to reach for the heights." Education, however, was unmistakably his principal concern:

If there is a universal enemy, if there is a main root to the excesses and to the inertia which get in our way, if there is a handmaiden to poverty and failure, it is ignorance. Let us marshall our resources against it.[58]

The first step in the marshalling of resources for education and other improvements was adoption of a sales tax, and Godwin skillfully maneuvered the tax legislation through the 1966 General Assembly session. Doing so represented a dramatic about-face; just six years earlier, Godwin had joined State Senator Harry F. Byrd, Jr., and other Byrd organization stalwarts in defeating Governor Lindsay Almond's sales tax proposal. But times had changed; legislative reapportionment in 1966 had brought more urban legislators to the General Assembly, and escalating demands for public services could no longer go unanswered.[59] The sales tax revenues and surplus from the previous biennium enabled Virginia's government to take new action on a number of fronts. In education, as in other areas, the reform-minded Godwin seemed determined during his own tenure to make up for decades of governmental neglect. Funding for public education for 1966–1968 was increased 37.5 percent over the preceding biennium. Appropriations for highways, ports, corrections, public safety, welfare, conservation, and state parks all rose substantially during Godwin's term. In those four years alone, the state budget climbed nearly 42 percent. But Godwin also promoted industrial development and modernization of transportation facilities in the hope that the Commonwealth's economic expansion would help fund the new initiatives.

Before Godwin's administration ended, the most fundamental of the Byrd fiscal maxims was cast aside in the push for progress. The "pay-as-you-go" policy was synonymous with Harry Byrd. He abhorred debt and

---

[57]Selected Speeches of The Honorable Mills E. Godwin, Jr., Governor of Virginia, 1966–1970, p. 4.

[58]Ibid., pp. 2–4.

[59]For a detailed discussion of the momentous 1966 General Assembly session and enactment of the state sales tax, see Wilkinson, Harry Byrd, pp. 285–304.

devoted most of his political career to combatting it. But Byrd died in 1966, and a good many Virginians seemed to feel that the limitations on debt financing, like the senator himself, belonged to a bygone era. Mills Godwin was one citizen who held that view. In 1968, he won legislative and then popular approval of $80 million in capital fund bond issues for education and mental health programs. The following year he endorsed the recommendation of a constitutional revision commission that the Commonwealth's debt policy be liberalized and that constitutional borrowing limitations be eased. It was a "most traumatic experience" for Godwin, as he later explained:

> Of course, I had been very much part of the Byrd organization, and I still considered myself part of its leadership. I knew Senator Byrd during his career had opposed that type of (borrowing) program. It was not an easy thing to do—to support it as vigorously as I did, to see it successfully concluded—but I thought it was the right thing to do.[60]

Republican legislators, many of them from the moderate GOP strongholds of western Virginia, applauded Godwin's progressive initiatives. House GOP Leader M. Caldwell Butler and freshman Delegate John Dalton energetically supported the sales tax proposal in the 1966 General Assembly session and worked with the new governor to secure its passage. The GOP had for years been advocating progressive policies at the state level, and finally it appeared that its call was being answered. Though their party was not yet benefitting from the changed political environment, Republican leaders—including their 1965 standard-bearer—believed they deserved a significant share of credit for the progress that was being achieved under Godwin. Butler made that point in a summary of the 1966 legislative session published in the *University of Virginia News Letter*:

> [In 1965], for the first time in recent history, the Democratic candidates for Governor and the General Assembly of Virginia were forced by a vigorous, articulate, and responsible Republican campaign and outstanding Republican candidates at all levels to get out and campaign among the people . . . .
>
> The sudden and dramatic changes came about because the people let it be known in the campaign and election of 1965 that they expected them. The two-party system came of age in Virginia with the 1966 General Assembly.
>
> Republicans take pride in comparing accomplishments of this General Assembly with the platform adopted at their convention of May 1965. . . . [T]he change was the result at least in part of an emerging two-party system and the efforts of the Republican Party.[61]

---

[60]Latimer, "Living History Makers, Part III."

[61]M. Caldwell Butler, "A Republican Looks at the 1966 Virginia General Assembly, *University of Virginia News Letter* (Charlottesville: Institute of Government, University of Virginia), August 15, 1966.

If a two-party system had arrived in Virginia, the Byrd organization leadership in the General Assembly seemed unaware of it. House Speaker Blackburn Moore continued to deny seats on any of the body's active committees to Republican legislators, a policy that rendered the GOP members largely ineffective in influencing legislation. Republicans denounced the practice as undemocratic, and divided responsibility for auditing the major committees. "We would attend the committee meetings until they went into executive session and kicked us out," recalled Delegate A. R. "Pete" Giesen of Augusta County, "and then we'd go to the press and scream and holler about being ejected. . . . "[62] Journalists who themselves had been ousted by the Democratic bosses often reported the GOP complaints. "Republicans had not [complained publicly] in the past because they thought it called attention to the fact that they were not effective legislators," Giesen explained. "We felt that the system was so bad that the public would react to it, [and] they did."[63]

Republicans added two members (one in each house) in the 1965 legislative elections, for a total of 12 in the House of Delegates and four in the Senate. Delegate John Dalton was tapped to head the GOP legislative campaign in 1967, and the vigorous effort waged that year yielded two new seats in each house. With these improving numbers gradually came an added measure of respectability and influence for Republican legislators. Their proposals began to receive serious consideration rather than peremptory rejection. Still, GOP legislators in the lower house were not awarded meaningful committee assignments until 1968, when John Warren Cooke of Mathews succeeded Moore as Speaker. The Virginia legislature had been a bastion of Byrdism for 40 years, and the aging organization loyalists who dominated leadership posts would have to pass from the scene before Republicans in the General Assembly could achieve anything approaching full participation in the legislative process.

Though Republican legislators conscientiously supported most of Godwin's program and gladly joined him in ushering in an era of progressivism, they and their fellow partisans stood on the sidelines and watched gleefully as the disparate elements of the governor's diverse political coalition came, inevitably, into conflict. Godwin's failure to hold together that coalition, which in 1964 interrupted a string of GOP presidential victories in the state, and which in 1965 swept him into the Executive Mansion, was in some ways as striking as the governor's legislative successes. The 1966 elections would spell the end of the Byrd era in Virginia politics, and the 1969 gubernatorial contest would set the stage for a Republican renaissance in the Old Dominion.

---

[62]Arthur R. Giesen interview, June 19, 1980.
[63]Ibid.

Chapter 16
1966: End of an Era

"The Byrd tradition continues in at least the expectation of high standards of fiscal and ethical integrity among officeholders. But as a cohesive, dominant, controlling force in the political life of Virginia, the Byrd machine is dead. . . ."[64]

Jack Bass and Walter DeVries

It is difficult to mark precisely the demise of the Byrd organization. Overseen by a single, acknowledged leader in Harry Byrd, Sr., the organization was a political power structure anchored in the courthouses of rural Virginia, dependent upon a restricted electorate, largely unconcerned with and unaffected by modern campaign techniques, and philosophically committed to "pay-as-you-go" financing even at the expense of necessary public services. By the late 1960s, not one of those characteristics applied to the Democratic Party in Virginia, nor would any of them apply to either state party thereafter. Many conservative traditions continued; a distinctive philosophical conservatism—though tempered by long-restrained progressive impulses—remained a salient feature of the state's political life; and many of Senator Byrd's prominent supporters went on to play pivotal roles in Virginia's continuing political development. But the Byrd organization itself expired sometime in the mid-'60s.

Scholars and political professionals of the era would debate whether the Byrd organization could have withstood the shocks of change in the '60s by embracing younger, urban lawmakers, and by moderating its policies to meet the demands of an increasingly urban and industrial society. But the debate was largely beside the point. The organization's aging leaders, chief among them the senator himself, were neither so discerning nor so willing to adjust to the winds of political change in the Old Dominion as was Mills Godwin. And, as the 1966 congressional elections approached, the old guard bosses found themselves pitted against the resurgent moderate and liberal elements of the state Democratic Party. J. Harvie Wilkinson III explained:

The senator held around him a corporal's guard of lifelong conservatives who still played prominent roles in the commonwealth's politics.

---

[64]Bass and DeVries, p. 340.

Senator Robertson, Congressmen Abbitt, Tuck, and Smith, state legislators Gray, Moore, and Byrd, Jr., formed the hard-core element of the old Byrd organization which clung to the orthodoxies of Byrd conservatism in spite of change. This element had systematically alienated certain social, economic, and political forces throughout Virginia. The Tuck labor wars, the massive resistance program, the Young Turk struggle, and fiscal deprivations under pay-as-you-go had turned labor, Negroes, and many young and urban Virginians against the machine. These forces, when first alienated, were somewhat anemic, but by 1966 they had become dragon slayers. . . .[65]

As long as the organization leadership acquiesced in the election of liberals like Johnson or moderates like Godwin, cooperation with the party's centrist and left-leaning elements was possible. But, for a variety of reasons, common ground proved unattainable in 1966. With their ranks swollen by demographic changes and the removal of electoral restrictions, the anti-Byrd forces in the Democratic Party were ready to assert themselves. They would do so with telling effectiveness.

The 1966 campaign opened, in effect, just after election day in 1965 when Senator Harry F. Byrd, Sr., announced his retirement. Tired, plagued by arthritis, and robbed of his zest for life by the death of his wife the previous year, Byrd could go on no longer. His resignation on November 11 received nationwide attention, and he was lavishly praised from both sides of the aisle. Many Americans knew little about what Harry Byrd's organization had meant to Virginia; its record of integrity, stability, low taxation, and low levels of public services was largely unknown beyond the Commonwealth. But many Americans knew about Harry Byrd, and to them he was Virginia. He was the symbol of states' rights, of opposition to big government and deficit spending at the federal level, and of defiant Southern resistance to school desegregation and civil rights. The recurring congressional battle of the postwar years had been between the Democratic liberals and the conservative coalition of Republicans and Southern Democrats. Byrd was the latter's foremost leader, and so his retirement portended the end of an era not only in the Old Dominion, but nationally.

Virginia would not long be without a Byrd in the United States Senate, however. The choice of an interim successor fell, apparently by design, to lame-duck Governor Harrison, who had neither a diverse coalition to satisfy nor a legislative agenda that could be disrupted by a controversial appointment. To virtually no one's surprise, Harrison chose State Senator Harry F. Byrd, Jr. The appointment, however, was not universally applauded. To many, the junior Byrd was every bit as conservative as his father. He had battled the Young Turks in 1954, was a leading massive resister in 1956–58, and torpedoed the Almond sales tax in 1960. He had given no sign of enthusiasm for the

[65]Wilkinson, *Harry Byrd*, p. 305.

progressive Godwin platform of 1965. With the senior senator finally out of the way, the last thing moderate and liberal Democrats wanted was to install a younger Byrd as a fixture in the Senate. Moreover, the appointment had dynastic overtones that rubbed many Virginians the wrong way. "These are the times for political giants, not the shadows of once great men," exclaimed GOP Chairman Jack Corber.[66] Senator Byrd, Jr., thus faced a tough test in 1966—he would have to convince wary voters to award him the four years remaining of his father's term.

Also in 1966, the term of Virginia's junior U.S. senator, A. Willis Robertson, was due to expire. A devout conservative but never a member of the Byrd organization inner circle, Robertson had worked in the shadow of Harry Byrd for more than two decades. Now, at age 79, the still-robust senator at last had the opportunity to assume center-stage. Party leaders, however, had grave doubts about the viability of a Robertson re-election bid. The senator's age and the stern conservatism of a Byrd-Robertson ticket would make it exceedingly difficult to assemble anything resembling the broad Godwin coalition in either the Democratic primary or the general election. Meeting at the Waldorf-Astoria in New York City following a Chamber of Commerce meeting, Virginia's Democratic leaders—including Harrison, Godwin, Byrd, Jr., and Kellam—discussed possible replacements for Robertson. A favorite scenario had First District Congressman Thomas Downing, a 48-year-old urban moderate with organization ties, making the race. But Robertson was determined to run for re-election, and Downing decided not to challenge him. What may have been the only opportunity to keep the expansive new Democratic coalition intact for at least another year thus went by the board.

Pitted against the two stalwart conservatives were a pair of former Young Turks. Armistead Boothe of Alexandria and State Senator William B. Spong, Jr., of Portsmouth opposed Byrd and Robertson, respectively, and, though all four ran separate campaigns, the two contests quickly took on the cast of a traditional organization versus anti-organization struggle. The Byrd-Boothe contest received the most attention and focused on a variety of issues—fiscal policies, school desegregation, and labor relations—that for years had divided Byrd organization loyalists and foes. The game and nimble Boothe exploited concerns that his opponent was running on his father's coattails rather than his own merit, while the affable "Little Harry" generally ignored Boothe's salvos and stressed the virtues of his and the organization's conservative record.

By contrast, the race between Spong and Robertson centered on issues of age and experience more than philosophy. The incumbent's slogan proclaimed "Robertson – Gets Results," and the elderly senator seldom passed up a chance to remind voters of his seniority and his influence as chairman of the Senate Banking and Currency Committee. The 45-year-old Spong responded with a thinly veiled exploitation of the age issue, portraying himself as a "Man

---

[66]Ibid., p. 308.

of Today" whose youthful energy and moderate outlook were needed in changing times. Though the Spong-Robertson contest inevitably divided largely along pro- and anti-organization lines, Spong had the advantage of not having been an especially vocal critic of the Byrd regime. And, though Robertson enjoyed broad support among the state's conservative voters, he had no great reservoir of loyalty among Byrd lieutenants in the courthouses. The confident Robertson made a serious miscalculation early in the primary campaign when he rejected suggestions that he and Byrd run as a ticket with a joint campaign organization. As the primary voting neared, many local Democratic leaders gave Byrd's campaign their principal attention and devoted little energy to Robertson's bid.

When the votes were counted on July 12, the once indomitable Byrd organization was shaken to its very foundations. Harry Byrd, Jr., survived, but Boothe led in the returns for most of election night, and the weary senator did not join his supporters to claim victory until just before midnight, when the tally showed him leading by about 8,000 votes. The other Senate race was even closer, and Spong eventually was declared the victor by a margin of 611 votes out of more than 433,000 cast.[67] The voting patterns in the two races were nearly identical. Spong and Boothe both carried the urban corridor by running up hefty margins in northern Virginia and Hampton Roads. The two moderates also ran well ahead of their opponents in southwest Virginia. The Byrd-Robertson strength was in the rural areas across the state—Southside, Tidewater, and central Virginia—as well as the Shenandoah Valley and the Richmond suburbs.

The contests were so close and the voting patterns were so similar that any of several marginal issues may have accounted for the edge given Byrd and Spong. Byrd's name, Robertson's age, over-confidence in the Robertson camp, Spong's ability to avoid the anti-organization label while amassing moderate and liberal support—all were factors that might account for Byrd's doing slightly better than Robertson and Spong's garnering a few more votes than his *de facto* runningmate Boothe. Also significant may have been the manner in which the primary campaign ended. On July 8, four days before the vote, Byrd, Jr., canceled his campaigning in order to be at his father's bedside; the victim of a brain tumor, the elder Byrd lay unconscious and near death at his Berryville home. The other candidates ceased their politicking as well, bringing the hard-fought campaign to an abrupt close.

The two Senate primaries had given voters choices similar to those they had frequently faced for four decades: strong Byrd organization conservatives versus more moderate Democratic challengers. But unlike previous contests, the primary races in 1966 were close, and a veteran conservative senator was ousted. The explanation lay chiefly in the vastly changed Democratic primary

---

[67]The vote totals were: Byrd – 221,221 (50.9%); Boothe – 212,996 (49.1%); and Spong – 216,885 (50.1%); Robertson – 216,274 (49.9%). Eisenberg, *Virginia Votes*, pp. 260, 264.

electorate. With the poll tax gone, voter participation had increased dramatically. Turnout in the 1966 primaries eclipsed the previous record—433,000 in the 1961 Democratic primary—by more than 80,000 votes. Urbanization and industrialization had brought many new Democratic voters into Virginia and had moderated the views of many others. These blocs joined newly enfranchised blacks and a growing labor constituency in rejecting the hard-line conservatism of the Byrd organization.

By 1966, too, Republicans—who for years had entered Democratic primaries to help defeat anti-organization liberals—were pursuing an independent course. Two-party competition was an impending reality, and the GOP had no interest in invading the Democratic primary to stem the majority party's leftward drift. That drift could only enhance the prospects for Republican victories in ensuing elections. Also, it was apparent that an increasing number of Virginians who had voted for Republican presidential candidates now were beginning to take a serious look at GOP candidates at the state level. The prospect of a meaningful choice in general elections diminished the importance of the Democratic primaries, and local conservative Democratic leaders found it increasingly difficult to find individuals who were willing give their time and energy to assist Byrd-type conservatives in primary campaigns. The advantage in the primary contests thus was ceded to the more moderate and liberal elements of the Democratic Party, a phenomenon that enabled Republicans to reap the harvest of disaffected conservatives in November. It was a nascent trend in 1966, but insightful observers of both parties could see what was beginning to happen.

Ironically, the Byrd organization could have withstood the assault and re-nominated both Byrd and Robertson in 1966 if not for the defection of Southside conservatives. Angered by the Harrison-Godwin support of Johnson in 1964 and Godwin's heresies in 1965 and early 1966, some leaders of the Conservative Party resolved to signal again their displeasure by fielding candidates for the Senate. By what logic Byrd and Robertson were too "liberal" for these Conservatives remains a mystery. Nomination of the two conservative incumbents would have demonstrated the infeasibility of assembling Democratic tickets with centrist appeal akin to Godwin's, but, rather than enhancing conservative control of the Democratic Party, the Southside hard-liners dealt their soul mates a fatal blow. While many of the 75,000 Virginians who had voted for William Story in 1965 voted for Robertson on July 12, 1966, many more than the 612 needed to re-elect the senator heeded their leaders' call to boycott the Democratic primary.

Robertson's defeat was a shock, but nothing stunned the Byrd organization like the defeat of Eighth District Congressman Howard W. Smith. The venerable Judge Smith, powerful chairman of the Rules Committee in the House of Representatives, had been the senior Senator Byrd's counterpart as chieftain of the conservative coalition in the lower house. A veteran of 18 terms in Congress, the 83-year-old Smith was toppled in the primary by a little-known liberal member of the House of Delegates from Fredericksburg, George C. Rawlings, Jr. Rawlings waged an aggressive and hard-hitting campaign that emphasized the incumbent's age and conservatism, and he managed a slim, 645-vote victory largely because the previous year's reapportionment had placed a sizable portion of moderate, suburban Fairfax County in Smith's district.[68] The result was but another indication that federal courts and the new "one-person, one-vote" rule were changing the nature of politics in Virginia and the entire country.

As voters turned their sights to the general election of 1966, it was apparent that the Byrd organization had suffered a crushing blow. In less than a year, its three most senior leaders had departed, taking with them nearly a century of congressional seniority. Still, the primary results were a mixed bag. If Spong's victory showed that the center-left elements of the 1965 Godwin coalition could go it alone and succeed, Byrd's win demonstrated the continuing appeal of the Byrd name and Virginia's abiding conservatism, particularly on national issues. Through no one's design, the two Democrats who emerged from their party's nomination battles represented an appealing duo with something to offer the divergent elements of the Johnson and Godwin coalitions. GOP partisans rapidly were learning that the long-awaited demise of the Byrd organization would not automatically lead to Republican electoral success in the Old Dominion.

The choice of GOP nominees for the two Senate seats was complicated by the timing of the Democratic primary, which again fell on the last legally permissible date for party nominations. That meant that Republicans would meet in convention to choose their candidates before the identities of their Democratic foes were known. GOP conservatives wanted Joel Broyhill to enter the contest if Boothe or Spong were nominated, and they considered fielding a stalking horse who would step aside and permit Broyhill to become the candidate if either primary turned out as hoped. But Broyhill and Linwood Holton, also widely rumored to be a possible candidate, disavowed interest, so the GOP delegates proceeded to nominate two little-known contenders. Mayor James P. Ould, Jr., of Lynchburg opted to seek the Robertson seat, and party chief Corber persuaded Lawrence M. Traylor of Heathsville, a former Eighth District congressional candidate, to accept the GOP nod for Byrd's seat. Though tempted to do so, Republicans declined to change nominees after they saw the weaker-than-expected showings of the Byrd organization candidates in the Democratic contests.

The Democrats went on to comfortable, if not lopsided, victories in November. The Republican team campaigned vigorously, using the unpopular Johnson administration as their principal target, and they got valuable late campaign help when former Vice President Nixon stumped in the state. But

---

[68]The vote totals were: Rawlings – 27,115 (50.6%); Smith – 26,470 (49.4%). Wilkinson, *Harry Byrd*, pp. 314, 332–333.

the GOP found its task complicated by Ould's attempt to run to the right of Spong while Traylor positioned himself to Byrd's left. Local Democratic organizations backed both of their candidates, and Spong and Byrd proved to be a formidable combination. Spong pulled Byrd along somewhat in the urban areas, while Byrd helped his more liberal runningmate in the organization's rural strongholds.

Though both Democrats won in the urban corridor, Spong won there, as he did statewide, by a larger margin. He carried the corridor with 63 percent of the vote and received nearly 59 percent of the statewide tally, while Byrd polled slightly more than 53 percent in the urban corridor and won a similar share of the statewide vote.[69] The patterns of support for the two Democrats were quite different statewide, but the most striking difference was in their respective showings among black voters. Spong garnered 96 percent of the vote in selected black precincts analyzed by the University of Virginia's Ralph Eisenberg, while Byrd polled only less than 14 percent in those same precincts.[70] Traylor's stronger performance than his more attractive Lynchburg runningmate thus appeared to be largely the result of an anti-Byrd protest vote by blacks. If the GOP had pitted Ould or some other more prominent Republican against Byrd, it might well have seized the new senator's seat.

The 1966 elections were not without their bright spots for Virginia Republicans. In the Ninth District, former Congressman William C. Wampler overcame his old nemesis, incumbent W. Pat Jennings, in a race dominated by Wampler's attacks on the Johnson administration's increasingly unpopular Vietnam and Great Society policies.[71] And, in northern Virginia, conservative Fairfax Republican William L. Scott easily captured the Eighth District seat by harvesting the votes of thousands of Byrd Democrats who were furious over Judge Smith's ouster by the liberal Rawlings in the Democratic primary.[72] The Wampler and Scott victories doubled GOP membership in the state's House of Representatives delegation and helped Republicans poll an impressive 56 percent of the total vote in the six contested congressional races. The Fifth District results also were a source of encouragement to the GOP. In garnering nearly 44 percent of the vote in his race against veteran incumbent Congressman William Tuck, Republican Robert L. Gilliam raised GOP hopes of

---

[69]The vote totals were: Spong (D) – 429,855 (58.6%); Ould (R) – 245,681 (33.5%); F. Lee Hawthorne (Conservative) – 58,251 (7.9%). Eisenberg, *Virginia Votes*, p. 252. In the other race, the vote totals were: Byrd (D) – 389,028 (53.3%); Traylor (R) – 272,804 (37.4%); John W. Carter (Conservative) – 57,692 (7.9%). Ibid., p. 256.

[70]Ralph Eisenberg, "1966 Politics in Virginia: The Elections for U.S. Senators," *University of Virginia News Letter* (Charlottesville: Institute of Government, University of Virginia), May 15, 1967.

[71]The vote totals were: Wampler (R) – 49,413 (53.7%); Jennings (D) – 42,571 (46.3%). Ralph Eisenberg, "1966 Politics in Virginia: The Elections for U.S. House of Representatives," *University of Virginia News Letter* (Charlottesville: Institute of Government, University of Virginia), June 15, 1967.

[72]The vote totals were: Scott (R) – 50,782 (57.2%); Rawlings (D) – 37,939 (42.8%). Ibid.

eventually capturing the once solidly Democratic district situated in the western portion of Southside and in the foothills of the Blue Ridge.

The 1966 elections produced a host of contradictory results: a moderate Democrat toppled a veteran conservative senator, while a conservative senatorial incumbent overcame an attractive moderate Democratic challenger; Republicans remained uncompetitive in the Senate races, while in the House contests there was a renewal of the pattern—inaugurated by Broyhill in 1952—of Republicans capitalizing on Democratic primary divisions and liberal victories to win in November. Despite these contradictions, several new political realities were apparent from the 1966 results. Spong's victory in the general election, like Godwin's the previous year, demonstrated that a centrist Democrat who could minimize defections from his right and left flanks could win easily in Virginia. Byrd's narrower advantage in the November contest against a less-than-formidable GOP opponent revealed the vulnerability of any conservative Democratic candidate who was unable to retain the support of his party's liberal wing. And Rawlings's landslide loss to Republican Scott provided convincing evidence of the inviability of a liberal candidacy unacceptable to Democratic conservatives. The seemingly simple prescription for state Democrats was to nominate moderate candidates who could unite the party from left to right. Whenever they failed to do so, Republicans would have a chance to win.

On the way to a philosophical realignment of Virginia's political parties with their national counterparts, the state's Democrats had hit upon a new formula for electoral success. It represented an astute and nimble adjustment to changing political terrain, and it was charted principally by the visionary Governor Godwin. But it would not last long. Elements of the coalition were too divergent; the combination of factors that produced it were too fleeting; the range of common acceptability to the left and right wings of the party was too narrow; and the nominating process was too uncontrollable for viable centrist candidacies to emerge with any consistency. With the traditional and emotional attachment of conservatives to the Democratic Party breaking down, and with moderates and liberals assuming more and more influence in Democratic primaries, the conservative element of the Godwin coalition was destined to slip away. At the other end of the spectrum were strong personalities and committed liberal activists who had no intention of stopping halfway in their effort to remake the Virginia Democratic Party in the image of its leftward-lurching national counterpart.

Though the future was uncertain, it was clear in 1966 that the Byrd organization was a creature of the past. The patriarch passed away on October 20, 1966, and, though he left an heir, the junior Byrd had no interest in assuming leadership of the organization. The organization had been his father's creation; its members had owed their personal loyalty to him. They would support Byrd, Jr., because he shared their philosophy and views, but there was no guarantee that the new senator could command the same degree of authority over party matters as had his father. Moreover, Byrd, Jr., did not want the responsibility. He had worked closely with his father on organization business over the years and had no desire to continue. Years later, the younger Byrd recalled his thinking:

I had seen the headaches and the heartaches and the vast problems and difficulties associated . . . with being the political leader. . . . I saw first-hand that for years [Senator Byrd, Sr.] tried to get out from under that role. He wanted to devote more time to the Senate and less time to the so-called political organization. He was never able to get out from under it, so he finally toward the end just sort of threw up his hands and said, "Okay, I'll just continue on."

I felt that I didn't want to get in that same fix. And I'd either have to get out of it in the beginning or I probably would never get out of it until I got defeated or they threw me out. So I concluded that I just did not want to assume that role. . . .[73]

The senior senator's personal leadership—his meetings, his correspondence, his extensive local visits and contacts with courthouse officials—had been the glue that held his political organization together. Without him, the organization would not long last. But even if Harry Byrd, Jr., had been willing and able to assume the mantle, the organization's time had past. The electoral restrictions that had ensured one-faction, one-party rule in Virginia since 1902 were gone. The state's electorate was not only greatly expanded; it was heterogeneous. Blacks were voting. Republicans were voting. Urban and suburban dwellers now comprised an electoral majority. Virginia's legislature had been reapportioned to reflect a more accurate image of the state's changing face. Massive resistance and the pervasive politics of race, like the state's tight-fisted fiscal policies, were now things of the past. Virginia was plunging headlong into the future, leaving the battered remnants of the once-invincible machine in the dust.

If the full extent of the benefit state Republicans would derive from all this was not immediately apparent, it was nevertheless tremendous. The end of the poll tax and discriminatory registration practices had added thousands of new GOP voters to the rolls. Industrialization had brought in many thousands more. "Golden silence" and presidential Republicanism had converted others, while the rapid growth of suburban Virginia had sharply increased the GOP's base. The once-moribund party now had a realistic mission—to bring full two-party competition to Virginia and to translate Republican principles into governmental policies. Successes in congressional races complemented presidential victories, and the prospects for a GOP breakthrough at the state level had been enhanced considerably. A party with a purpose, Republicans now had a youthful appeal that promised improving GOP fortunes in the future. In addition, thousands of conservatives maintained an unnatural,

---

[73]Byrd interview.

uneasy, and ultimately unsustainable alignment with the Democratic Party. Breeding enough Republican voters to take control of Virginia's government would take years, but the GOP could do a lot in a short time with converts.

Virginia in the late '60s was poised to enter a new era of two-party competition. A candidate's victory in the Democratic primary would not again be "tantamount to election" in the Old Dominion.[74] Indeed, the primary, which for years had stymied Republican growth, would prove to be the Democrats' Achilles' heel. Discord and disunity in Democratic ranks would, in a short time, quicken the pace of Virginia's political realignment. A stable new order was still several years away, but a series of Republican firsts was right around the corner.

---

[74]For an insightful analysis of the demise of the Democratic primary in Virginia, see Sabato, *Democratic Party Primary*, pp. 72–98.

Part Four

Triumph and Turmoil: The Holton GOP

1968 - 1971

Chapter 17
Prologue: Republican Resolve, Democratic Division

"We offer a party united behind a united ticket, a party fighting for Virginia rather than with itself."[1]

Linwood Holton, 1969

Linwood Holton had long wanted to be governor of Virginia and to be the first Republican to accomplish that feat in modern times. Shortly after arriving in Roanoke in 1949 to start his legal career, he had reinvigorated the Republican Party organization there. Twice—in 1955 and 1957—he had waged energetic but unsuccessful bids for a seat in the House of Delegates, and for some time he had played a prominent role in statewide Republican affairs. His spirited bid for the governorship in 1965 thrust him to the forefront of state politics. He and his party seemed inexperienced then in the ways of government, and Mills Godwin's left-to-right Democratic coalition left them little room to maneuver. Yet, Holton's showing had been respectable, and he approached the 1969 gubernatorial election with enhanced stature. Few Republican activists or political observers entertained serious doubt about his intentions. Holton was running—and running hard.

Big Stone Gap is a long way from Richmond. The mountains and coalfields of far southwest Virginia—the land of Linwood Holton's youth—are closer to eight other state capitals than to Virginia's. But distance is but one facet of the remoteness. A world away from tradition-bound Tidewater, the rugged Southwest tends to instill individualism in those who struggle and strive there. Personal achievement and fortitude in the face of adversity, more than blood line or social rank, determine one's standing in the eyes of his fellows. Sensing the differences, and frequently magnifying them, the mountain folk have long cast a wary eye to the east. To many westerners in the late 1960s, the preoccupation with racial issues and governmental frugality among politicians east of the Blue Ridge seemed to guarantee perpetual unresponsiveness to the pressing needs of the western region—jobs, roads, and schools.

Holton's personality reflected his mountain roots, and so did his political philosophy. Despite his broader perspective, an ingrained suspicion of the motives of the eastern Virginia gentry remained very much a part of his

---

[1]Copy of Holton campaign brochure on file at the Republican Party of Virginia Archives.

outlook. To him, the Byrd organization was less the conservator of Virginia virtues than an instrument of reactionary control wielded by the lowland aristocracy. Its stinginess he resented. Its racial intolerance he abhorred. Its techniques for self-perpetuation he had spent a career combatting. Though he regarded his own philosophy as conservative, the political convictions he shared with the Byrd Democrats easily were overshadowed by the deep-seated differences. Holton's heart was with the crusading progressivism personified by Ted Dalton, and to him two-party competition meant, first and foremost, the presence of a viable alternative to Byrd-style conservatism. He thus had little enthusiasm for the party-building strategy championed by conservative Republicans in eastern Virginia who were anxious to attract Byrd Democrats to the GOP. Holton partially doubted, and partially feared, that such a strategy would succeed.

Much of the Virginia Republican Party shared Holton's centrist priorities. GOP moderates were prevalent west of the Blue Ridge, in the cluster of cities around Hampton Roads, and in portions of suburban northern Virginia. But the '60s had seen the growth of a more conservative strain of Republicanism in many areas of Virginia. The Broyhill enthusiasts in northern Virginia and the younger GOP partisans in the Third District and Southside were its core. The emphasis of these party members was on national issues—the vast increase in domestic social spending under the Kennedy and Johnson administrations, the extending arm of federal government regulation into areas previously reserved to the states, and the worldwide fight against communism. Such concerns, they believed, overshadowed differences with the Byrd organization.

Though it was not widely recognized at the time, the premises of Republican progressivism in Virginia were becoming increasingly unsound as the '60s drew to a close.The more objectionable aspects of the Byrd organization were fading into the past: massive resistance was far behind; the last electoral restrictions recently had been removed; and levels of public services at the state level were being increased dramatically by the Godwin administration. A leftward-edging state Democratic Party was becoming increasingly attractive to liberals and increasingly uncomfortable for conservatives. Nationally, the philosophical divergence between the parties was widening as sharp differences emerged on a wide array of economic, social, and foreign policy issues. Opportunities for a conservative realignment beneficial to Virginia's Republicans were beginning to emerge in the Commonwealth.

None of this mattered much to Holton. The differing philosophical and strategic views within the ranks of his party were matters he was confident he could handle. If GOP conservatives were not wildly enthusiastic about his candidacy, neither did they pose much of a threat to his nomination. Except for Congressman Broyhill, who evinced no interest in running, there was no other Virginia Republican with name recognition or demonstrated campaigning ability to match Holton's. Moreover, Holton's popularity within the party was broad. The sandy-haired, square-jawed mountaineer was an attractive candidate, and his easy-going stump style made him an unusually effective campaigner. Republicans liked him—and they wanted a winner. They sensed that Holton had a chance.

The Roanoke GOP leader figured to benefit significantly from the 1968 presidential election. After former Vice President Richard Nixon campaigned for him during the 1965 governor's race, the two men had stayed in fairly close contact. A friendship developed, and when Nixon started laying the groundwork for his 1968 run for the Presidency, he called on Holton. The Virginian played prominent regional roles in the Nixon nomination and general election campaigns, and his high profile helped to create the widespread impression that he was a Nixon intimate. The association not only enhanced Holton's standing with much of the Virginia electorate; it also helped to solidify his support among GOP conservatives.

While Holton carried out his high-level assignment for the Nixon campaign, the task of coordinating Nixon's Virginia effort was performed by Emporia attorney Dortch Warriner and Alexandria Councilman Harry S. Fleming. Though Nixon's nomination in 1968 was far from certain in the early stages of the presidential jockeying, the middle-of-the-road frontrunner picked up impressive early support from both Virginia GOP moderates and conservatives against his two left-of-center competitors for the nomination—Michigan Governor George Romney and New York Governor Nelson Rockefeller. A late-blooming bid by California Governor Ronald Reagan had little impact on the Virginia delegates, who backed Nixon overwhelmingly at the party's Miami Beach convention.

Though the Nixon umbrella united the Virginia GOP in 1968, a split between the party's emerging moderate and conservative factions developed over the state chairmanship. The decision of party chief Jack Corber to forego seeking re-election at the June 1968 state convention set the stage for a hard-fought contest between Fairfax County GOP Chairman Samuel Carpenter and Richmond Republican Henry Sutliff, Jr., a wealthy tobacco product manufacturer and veteran member of the party's central committee. The race found the Nixon campaign's Virginia captains on opposing sides: Holton led GOP moderates toward the northern Virginian's camp, while Warriner joined party conservatives in central Virginia and the Southside in backing Sutliff. The Holton-backed candidate emerged the winner at the state convention with approximately 58 percent of the delegate votes, and several weeks later party moderates also installed a Holton protege, Cynthia Newman, as national committeewoman. Rounding out the GOP leadership trio was Arlingtonian Lee Potter, who won another term as the party's national committeeman. The leadership contests reflected both the dominance of the Holton-led moderate wing of the party and the geographical shift in the party's base. For the first time, all three top party positions were held by Republicans from northern Virginia.

State Democrats, meanwhile, were locked in a leadership struggle of their own that was a harbinger of bitter battles to come. Virginia Democratic Chairman Watkins Abbitt, the Fourth District congressman, narrowly won re-election over liberal Joseph Fitzpatrick of Norfolk at the party's state convention, and moderate State Senator William B. Hopkins of Roanoke prevailed in the contest to succeed retiring National Committeeman Sidney Kellam. The gathering revealed the rapidly escalating hostility between the Democratic Party's conservative, moderate, and liberal factions. Many of the liberal delegates actually jeered Governor Godwin as he addressed the state convention, and Godwin later would cite the conclave as a watershed event. It was then that many Democratic conservatives first came to recognize the inevitability of liberal domination of their traditionally conservative state party.

During the fall campaign, Godwin confined his political efforts to speeches in support of the bond issue referendum for mental health and education. The governor's lack of effort on behalf of the national Democratic ticket of Senators Hubert Humphrey and Edmund Muskie was in marked contrast to his controversial advocacy of the Johnson-Humphrey slate aboard the Lady Bird Special only four years earlier. Other Byrd Democrats resumed their quadrennial activity on behalf of the national GOP ticket, but with state Republican regulars this time assuming the more prominent leadership roles.

The challenge for the Nixon backers was to make certain that the candidacy of Alabama Governor George C. Wallace, nominee of the fledgling "American Independent Party," did not split Virginia's conservative vote and give the state's electoral votes to Humphrey. Wallace's candidacy, like Strom Thurmond's third-party bid two decades earlier, reflected the South's discontent with the liberal social agenda of the national Democratic Party as well as its lingering wariness of the Republican label. In 1948, Harry Truman had won a surprise victory in Virginia over the opposition of Senator Harry Byrd, Sr., precisely because of such a division in conservative Democratic ranks. Fearing a replay of the 1948 fiasco, the conservative *Richmond News Leader* warned editorially that a vote for Wallace would aid the liberal Humphrey. The same message was delivered by the mostly Democratic "Virginians for Nixon" and their chairman, Richmond financier Lawrence Lewis, Jr. In the end, conservative defections to Wallace were minimized, and his racial and anti-establishment appeals actually may have pulled more normally Democratic blue-collar votes from Humphrey than conservative votes from Nixon.

Richard Nixon's plurality win in Virginia restored presidential Republicanism to the Old Dominion. Nixon and his runningmate, Maryland Governor Spiro T. Agnew, polled 43.4 percent of the statewide vote to the Humphrey-Muskie ticket's 32.5 percent.[2] The Wallace vote was 23.6 percent of the statewide total—a record showing for a third-party presidential candidacy in

---

[2]The vote totals were: Nixon (R) – 590,319 (43.4%); Humphrey (D) – 442,387 (32.5%); Wallace (American Independent) – 321,833 (23.6%). Eisenberg, *Virginia Votes*, p. 268.

Virginia, but the Alabamian's smallest share of the vote in any Southern state. In Virginia, as throughout the South, the pre-Goldwater GOP presidential voting pattern was re-established. The Republican ticket carried the border states but lost the black belt to Wallace. In the Commonwealth, the GOP team ran well in traditional Republican areas and in the suburbs, but was bested by the Alabama governor in most of Southside.

More good news for state Republicans came in the 1968 congressional election returns. For the second time in as many years, GOP candidates for the House of Representatives collectively received a larger share of the vote in the major-party contested races than did their Democratic opponents.[3] In addition to returning the four Republican incumbents, the GOP elected G. William Whitehurst, an Old Dominion University history professor and dean of students, to the Second District seat vacated by retiring Democratic incumbent Porter Hardy, Jr. An influx of suburban dwellers during the '60s had made the Hampton Roads district progressively more receptive to GOP candidates, but Whitehurst also owed his win to his high name recognition and to Democratic division. Though a political novice, the personable Whitehurst was well known in the Hampton Roads area because of his daily commentary on a local television evening news broadcast. His opponent, liberal Democrat Frederick T. "Bingo" Stant, Jr., survived a bitter primary battle only to suffer widespread moderate and conservative Democratic defections to Whitehurst in the general election.[4]

The 1968 elections awarded the Virginia GOP half of the state's 10-member House of Representatives delegation for the first time in more than a century and returned the White House to Republican control. The developments greatly encouraged most Virginia Republicans, but none more than Linwood Holton. Aided by lessons learned in his previous statewide race, he proceeded to plan his 1969 campaign with great care and thoroughness. Rather than confirm his intentions publicly, however, Holton injected some useful suspense into the campaign preliminaries by fostering speculation that he might forego a second gubernatorial bid and accept a federal judicial appointment. It was a page out of Ted Dalton's strategy book, and it worked well. A "draft-Holton" effort took shape, and an added measure of excitement surrounded the state convention as Republicans assembled in Roanoke in late February.

The GOP nominating conclave was held earlier than usual in order to give the party's ticket additional time to campaign and added visibility during the anticipated multi-candidate competition for the Democratic gubernatorial nomination. Holton's campaign team placed considerable importance on the

---

[3]In the seven contests featuring both Democratic and Republican candidates, the GOP polled 49.7 percent of the vote to the Democrats' 47.4 percent. Larry J. Sabato, *Virginia Votes 1969-1974* (Charlottesville: Institute of Government, University of Virginia, 1976), p. 27.

[4]The vote totals were: Whitehurst (R) – 51,188 (54%); Stant (D) – 43,224 (46%). *The Virginian-Pilot*, November 6, 1968.

convention because a successful event would project a confident and competent party image and give the ticket important early momentum. By previous state GOP standards, the 1969 convention was large. The Hotel Roanoke ballroom was overflowing, and the delegates were effervescent with enthusiasm. A television crew hired by the campaign's new media consultant, the Robert Goodman Agency of Baltimore, moved through the crowd capturing the excitement for a series of fall campaign commercials. The hottest commodity in the Republican Party nationally, California Governor Ronald Reagan, was on hand, and he brought the GOP faithful repeatedly to their feet with a rousing keynote address. After the convention's work was done, exuberant Republicans cheered their beaming nominee while he held in his arms his youngest son, Dwight, whose namesake—Dwight D. Eisenhower— had given the Virginia GOP a rebirth nearly two decades earlier.

Holton knew that he needed a united Republican Party in order to win the governorship. Virginia Republicans had a well-deserved reputation for fighting among themselves, and there was no lack of friction in the party in 1969. Holton's task was to keep the disagreement safely below the surface and out of public view through November. The nature of the division within the GOP was illuminated by veteran reporter Charles McDowell in a magazine article:

> Joel T. Broyhill of Arlington, the crafty panjandrum of Virginia Republicans in Congress, is not particularly fond of Linwood Holton, and vice versa. Broyhill considers Holton an opportunist, a Rockefeller-type Republican who worked his way into the Nixon camp to enhance his gubernatorial ambitions. One gets the clear impression that the conservative Broyhill regards himself as the logical leader of Virginia Republicans.
>
> [Holton] believes the future of the state party is tied to the national party, and that he falls into the moderate range of the Republican spectrum with President Nixon. His identification with Nixon, for better or worse, is the heart of his campaign strategy in Virginia.
>
> . . . The Broyhill version of the future of Republicanism in Virginia is as the conservative successor to the Byrd machine, with which he has cooperated quietly in the tenth district for years. He dreams, sometimes aloud, of converting Senator Harry F. Byrd, Jr., to Republicanism and joining with him as the head of a Broyhill-Byrd alliance that would keep Virginia in conservative hands for decades.
>
> Pending that unlikely marvel, the Broyhill types can be expected to help Holton this year as long as he sticks to the Nixon-identification strategy.[5]

The need to retain the support of Broyhill and the party's more conservative faction was very much on Holton's mind as he set about recruiting his run-

---

[5]Charles McDowell, "Notes from the Mountains and Valleys on the Resurrection of the Grand Old Party and the Ambitions of Linwood Holton," *The Washingtonian*, September 1969, p. 44.

ningmates before the state convention. State Senator J. Kenneth Robinson, a conservative with support in all segments of the party, was the clear favorite for the nomination for lieutenant governor. In fact, many conservatives quietly urged Robinson to challenge Holton for the top spot on the ticket. But an illness in the Frederick County legislator's family prevented him from joining the ticket in either capacity. Holton urged several other GOP office-holders to join the ticket before State Senator H. Dunlop "Buz" Dawbarn of Waynesboro finally agreed to become the candidate for lieutenant governor. The affable Dawbarn recently had gained his Senate seat by scoring an upset victory over veteran Democratic lawmaker George Cochran of Staunton, and he had won the respect of his legislative colleagues in Richmond. Though he had little interest in being lieutenant governor, Dawbarn acceded to Holton's urgings only after becoming convinced that his presence on the ticket would enhance GOP prospects for victory in the governor's race.

In order to cement party unity, Holton still needed a prominent conservative on his ticket. His first choice was Richmond lawyer Richard D. Obenshain. A central figure in the party's growing conservative camp, Obenshain had proved his campaigning skill in his strong congressional bid in 1964. After traveling widely and speaking at GOP gatherings of all sorts for eight years, he was well known and well liked throughout much of the party. His presence on the ticket would be especially helpful to Holton in the increasingly Republican and conservative Richmond area.

There was, however, a catch. Obenshain doubted that the moderate Holton could win in the conservative Old Dominion, and he was reluctant to join a ticket that he feared had little prospect of success. Signing onto the Holton ticket would force Obenshain to abandon his legal practice—he was a member of the Richmond law firm of McGuire, Woods & Battle, as was Democratic gubernatorial contender William C. Battle—and that would leave him and his family in a precarious financial position. Through Weldon Tuck of Halifax, an Obenshain protege and Fifth District GOP leader, Holton conveyed assurances that a job in state government or the Nixon administration would be available to Obenshain if he were unsuccessful in his bid for attorney general. With those assurances, and with strong encouragement from political allies who felt the GOP ticket needed a resolutely conservative voice, Obenshain tilted toward making the race. On the eve of the convention, he finally resolved to run—but not just to help Holton. Obenshain was in it to win.

Holton had thus succeeded in accomplishing the first objective of his campaign. He had united the party and assembled a balanced and attractive ticket. In their literature, Holton, Dawbarn, and Obenshain were dubbed "The Victory Team," a label that previously would have earned Virginia Republicans only laughter and derision. A Holton quotation printed in a campaign pamphlet reflected the emphasis on party harmony: "We offer a party united behind a united ticket, a party fighting for Virginia rather than with itself."[6] The GOP solidarity was in marked contrast to the bitter struggle being waged for the Democratic gubernatorial nomination. Though Holton and the Republicans had positioned themselves well, events unfolding in the Democratic contest would prove decisive in the fall.

The 1969 Democratic primary campaign showed how quickly conditions can change for a political party. Just four years earlier, Mills Godwin had brought together the divergent forces within the Democratic Party for an impressive victory. Optimistic partisans then felt that the dynamic Godwin had ushered in an era of good feeling among Democrats that would enable them to withstand the shocks of political change in the Old Dominion. But the discord of 1966 had presaged the dissolution of the broad Democratic coalition, and by 1969, neither Godwin nor any other Democratic leader could keep it from crumbling. Three formidable Democratic candidates—one representing each of the party's three major factions—stepped forward to seek the gubernatorial nomination.

The choice of conservatives was Lieutenant Governor Fred G. Pollard, a skilled legislative leader who was as knowledgeable about state government as anyone, with the possible exception of Governor Godwin and his venerable aide, Carter Lowance. Though there was little question about Pollard's qualifications, the former Richmond legislator was not an effective stump speaker or a warm one-on-one campaigner. In days past, he might have been regarded as a Democratic moderate—he had opposed massive resistance and sided occasionally with the advocates of increased state spending—but, in 1969, he was perceived as being the farthest to the right in the Democratic field. Some organization strategists, including the governor, seriously doubted Pollard's ability to win in such circumstances.

Pollard's main problem was William C. "Bill" Battle. A son of the Byrd organization governor of the '50s, Battle was a leading Democratic moderate in the '60s. His friendship with President Kennedy, which stemmed from their wartime service in the Pacific, had been highly publicized during the Kennedy administration. Battle had led John F. Kennedy's Virginia campaign in 1960 and then had managed William Spong's successful effort to topple incumbent U.S. Senator Willis Robertson in 1966. Though his only governmental experience was as ambassador to Australia during the Kennedy administration, Battle was determined to run for governor in 1969. The nature of Godwin's victory in 1965 and Spong's win a year later convinced Battle, Spong, and other Democratic moderates that the party needed a candidate of their ilk in order to retain the governorship. Battle's campaign slogan, "Not Left or Right—Forward!" reflected his strategy. He would steer the middle course, stress the need for new leadership, and avoid controversial specifics.

---

[6]Copy on file at the Republican Party of Virginia Archives.

State Senator Henry E. Howell, Jr., of Norfolk was the energetic leader of Democratic liberals in Virginia. He had cut his political teeth in the 1949 campaign of Byrd organization foe Francis Pickens Miller, whose vision of dramatic change in the state had been frustrated by Battle's father. In 1969, Howell was the self-proclaimed leader of a "people's campaign" against "the establishment." Elect him, his slogan declared, and he would "Keep the Big Boys Honest." After a series of successful challenges to state-regulated utility and insurance rates, and a legal victory over the Godwin administration in a suit over the state's use of federal education funds, Howell could lay claim to being Virginia's foremost consumer activist and populist crusader. His favorite campaign targets were the Godwin administration's sales tax on food and nonprescription drugs and the rates charged by VEPCO, the electric power utility. Blacks liked Howell's earlier stand against massive resistance, and organized labor appreciated his unabashed embrace of public sector collective bargaining and opposition to the state's Right to Work Law. The rhetorically gifted and flamboyant Howell could excite liberals like no other, and he came to personify their cause.

Governor Godwin was adamantly opposed to Howell. The two differed diametrically in almost every respect—background, philosophy, style, and temperament—and the governor was determined that Howell would not be his successor. It was obvious to Godwin that the presence of both Battle and Pollard in the race played into Howell's hands, and both he and Senator Harry F. Byrd, Jr., endeavored feverishly for months to arrange some sort of accommodation between the moderate and conservative camps. Byrd sought unsuccessfully to persuade esteemed former Governor Albertis Harrison to run for another term.[7] Trial balloons also were floated for possible compromise bids by T. Marshall Hahn, president of Virginia Polytechnic Institute, and First District Congressman Thomas Downing, but neither got far off the ground. The effort to avert a moderate-versus-conservative split was plagued—and ultimately doomed to failure—by the intransigence of Battle and his supporters. Though Pollard expressed a willingness to step aside if Battle would do likewise, Godwin found the former ambassador and his chief backer, Senator Spong, unwilling even to discuss such a move. Battle and his associates were convinced, with considerable justification, that he had the edge and would win the primary.

With the collapse of efforts to avoid the fight, Godwin assumed a position of neutrality in the primary campaign. It was well known that he did not favor Howell, but he remained silent as to his preference between Pollard and Battle. That silence proved detrimental to Pollard, who, as Godwin's lieutenant governor, generally was expected to receive his support. Pollard's presence on the 1965 ticket had aided Godwin's bid for support from blacks in Richmond, and many in the Pollard camp were shocked that Godwin would

---

[7]*The Virginian-Pilot and The Ledger-Star*, January 10, 1988.

overlook that debt in 1969. The governor, however, insisted later that he "did everything I could for Fred short of endorsing him publicly," and that he refrained from an outright endorsement out of concern about Howell.[8] Doubting Pollard's prospects in the primary even with his open support, Godwin worried that his intervention on the lieutenant governor's behalf would only pull more votes from Battle to the advantage of the Norfolk liberal. Moreover, if none of the three candidates received a majority of the vote in the primary, Godwin wanted to be in a position to campaign in support of Battle over Howell in the run-off contest. He believed he would be less persuasive in that eventual effort if he were to oppose Battle in the initial race.

Godwin's expectation of a Battle-Howell run-off was confirmed when the results came in on July 15. Battle polled a 39-percent plurality, but Howell was close behind with 38 percent.[9] Pollard's distant third-place showing—he garnered a little better than 23 percent of the vote—was surprising, but it was Howell's strength that most stunned political activists and observers. The liberal's populist, anti-establishment themes brought him support from an unusual coalition of blacks, blue-collar workers, and farmers. Most impressive was his showing in the urban corridor, where he polled more than 44 percent of the vote. Unlike in the 1968 presidential election, when the suburbs cast the larger share (58 percent) of the metropolitan area vote, central-city ballots comprised more than 54 percent of the metropolitan area vote in the July 1969 primary. Howell's strong performance in the urban corridor thus resulted from a disproportionately high turnout in the cities.[10]

The vote pattern on July 15, 1969, revealed much about what was happening to Virginia Democratic primaries generally. Central-city blacks and low-income whites were participating in growing numbers, while more conservative voters in the suburbs were sitting out the primary contests. The suburban voters increasingly were focusing their attention on the general election. Republican nominee Holton and GOP State Chairman Carpenter encouraged that trend by urging voters to "save their votes" for November and "let the Democrats settle their own family affairs" in the primary.[11] As a result, the turnout in both the July primary and the August run-off were considerably below expectations. Despite population increases, registration drives, and poll tax repeal, total participation in the July primary was 30,000 votes less than the turnout in the 1966 Spong-Robertson race. Even the more exciting August run-off exceeded the 1966 total by only several hundred votes.

---

[8]Godwin interview.

[9]The vote totals were: Battle – 158,956 (38.9%); Howell – 154,617 (37.8%); Pollard – 95,057 (23.3%). Sabato, *Virginia Votes 1969-1974*, p. 125.

[10]Ralph Eisenberg, "1969 Politics in Virginia: The Democratic Party Primary," *University of Virginia News Letter* (Charlottesville: Institute of Government, University of Virginia), February 15, 1970.

[11]*The Richmond News Leader*, July 20, 1969.

If there were lingering doubts about the demise of the Byrd organization, the July 1969 Democratic primary removed them. The organization had fielded the only ticket in the primary races—Pollard was joined by Delegate W. Carrington Thompson of Pittsylvania County as the candidate for lieutenant governor and by Fairfax County Delegate Guy O. Farley, Jr., as the contender for attorney general. None of the Byrd candidates fared well. Youthful, moderate-liberal State Senator J. Sargeant "Sarge" Reynolds of Richmond polled nearly 64 percent of the vote to defeat Thompson,[12] while moderate Andrew P. Miller, an Abingdon attorney and son of the 1949 gubernatorial candidate, led Farley in the race for attorney general. Miller polled 41 percent of the July 15 vote, Farley garnered 35 percent, and two other candidates divided the remainder.[13] That sent Farley into a run-off with Miller and made the Fairfax delegate the only candidate on the Byrd organization ticket who even remained in the chase after the primary.

The Battle-Howell competition in the run-off was hard-fought and bitter, and much of the strong feeling was triggered by Governor Godwin's involvement. After the primary, the governor shifted swiftly from his neutral posture to one of strong and active support of the moderate Battle. Godwin's energetic campaigning and frequent attacks stirred Howell's ire; the uniting of the moderate and conservative wings, declared the Norfolk senator, could mean only one thing: "the Big Boys have made their deal."[14] Howell and his supporters were particularly incensed by Godwin's emphatic refusal to promise support for Howell if he were to prevail in the run-off.

With the bulk of the Pollard support expected to come his way, Battle was confident of victory in the run-off. Though most of those who had voted for Pollard in July did vote against Howell in August, a sizable bloc of Pollard supporters who were angry at Battle for undercutting their candidate apparently sat out the run-off contest. "The feeling," explained Pollard manager and legislative veteran W. Roy Smith, "was that Battle was the one who had messed up and, because of his own political ambition, had defeated a good man."[15] Battle won the run-off, but by the surprisingly narrow margin of 52 percent to 48 percent.[16] Howell again demonstrated his ability to energize a large urban liberal constituency. He polled an impressive 54 percent of the urban corridor vote—59 percent in the central cities—but was overcome by large Battle margins in the Southwest and in most of rural Virginia. In northern Virginia, Battle picked up crucial additional conservative votes and

---

[12]The vote totals were: Reynolds – 242,085 (63.9%); Thompson – 89,765 (23.7%). Sabato, *Virginia Votes 1969-1974*, p. 129.

[13]The vote totals were: Miller – 151,991 (41.2%); Farley – 129,241 (35.0%); Bernard Levin – 47,003 (12.7%); C. F. Hicks – 41,084 (11.1%). Ibid., p. 133.

[14]*The Richmond News Leader*, July 18, 1969.

[15]Smith interview.

[16]The vote totals were: Battle – 226,108 (52.1%); Howell – 207,505 (47.9%). Sabato, *Virginia Votes 1969-1974*, p. 137.

was able to carry areas that had provided Howell with pluralities in the July primary.[17]

Battle had emerged the winner, but only after a prolonged and exhausting fight that seriously depleted the financial resources of his campaign and his party. Joining him and Sargeant Reynolds on the Democratic ticket was Andrew Miller, who attracted the support of moderates and liberals and coasted to an easy win in his run-off duel with Guy Farley.[18] The Democrats had nominated a middle-of-the-road ticket, but at a considerable cost. Not only had their campaign coffers been depleted, but the party was sharply divided and the prolonged and shrill Democratic infighting had taxed public patience. The Republicans were campaigning hard and proclaiming the virtues of a two-party system to an increasingly receptive electorate. Linwood Holton was poised to reap the harvest of disaffection sown by the Democrats.

---

[17]Eisenberg, "The Democratic Party Primary," *University of Virginia News Letter*, February 15, 1970.

[18]The vote totals were: Miller – 257,622 (63.2%); Farley – 150,140 (36.8%). Sabato, *Virginia Votes 1969–1974*, p. 141.

Chapter 18
"It's Time for a Change"

> "A decade of political irony reached its peak in 1969. The Republican governor-elect was given his margin of victory by one or both of two dissident groups of former Democrats. A group from the conservative right was motivated by hopes of [promoting] a realignment of parties along conservative versus liberal lines. A group from the liberal left . . . turned to the GOP gubernatorial candidate in hopes of stomping out the last trace of the Byrd organization. . . ."[19]
>
> James Latimer, 1969

In the gubernatorial contest four years earlier, Linwood Holton had positioned himself to the left of Mills Godwin. Like previous Republican candidates for governor, he had presented himself in 1965 as a progressive alternative to the Byrd organization candidate. But Godwin had moved to the center and had been able simultaneously to capture the conservative vote and to deny Holton the anti-Byrd protest vote that Democratic liberals usually gave Republican contenders.

In 1969, the tables had turned. Battle, like Godwin before him, was attempting to occupy the middle ground, but it was Holton who was poised to draw votes from both left and right. The Republican this time positioned himself to the right of his Democratic opponent and appealed successfully for backing from disenchanted conservatives. At the same time, the divisive Democratic primary struggle enabled the moderate Holton to reach out to resentful liberals. His campaign theme—"It's Time for a Change"—appealed to both groups of dissidents and struck the right chord for a populace eager to turn away from one-party rule. As the beneficiary of Democratic defections from both ends of the political spectrum, Holton was able to assemble a coalition comprised of elements just as divergent—and ultimately as incompatible—as those put together by Godwin in 1965.

The differences between Battle and Holton on issues affecting state government were not notable, and neither candidate seemed particularly

---

[19]James Latimer, "The Coming Decade: A Political Sphinx," *Richmond Times-Dispatch*, December 21, 1969, reprinted in Weldon Cooper and Thomas R. Morris, *Virginia Government and Politics: Readings and Comments* (Charlottesville: The University Press of Virginia, 1976), p. 115.

eager to accentuate the points of disagreement that did exist. Battle seemingly believed that, with the primary contest decided, Virginians would dutifully proceed to elect him because he was a Democrat. Holton sought to focus attention on national issues and thereby to create the perception that he, not Battle, was the candidate who embodied the convictions of conservative Virginians of both parties. Battle's well-known ties to the Kennedy administration made him especially susceptible to the charge that he was a liberal national Democrat at heart, while Holton could exploit his own affiliation with President Nixon. A steady stream of national GOP luminaries, including the President, Vice President Agnew, and Governor Reagan, appeared in Virginia on Holton's behalf and reinforced the Republican nominee's conservative image. Holton also was helped in the conservative Third District by Obenshain's presence on his ticket and by the emphatic and unprecedented (for a Republican) editorial support he received from *The Richmond News Leader*.[20]

The conservative thrust of Holton's campaign and Battle's Kennedy connections made it easy for disenchanted Democratic supporters of Lieutenant Governor Fred Pollard to back Holton. Many Byrd organization loyalists resented not only Battle's defeat of the capable and conservative Pollard, but also his leadership role in the 1966 Spong victory over conservative stalwart Willis Robertson. While the Pollard supporters had gotten behind Battle to defeat Howell in the run-off, they now felt little obligation to support him over Holton in the general election. The November voting gave them an opportunity to settle a score. A notable example was the influential Delegate Roy Smith, who took no public position on the fall contest but "told everybody that asked [him] that [he] was voting for Holton."[21] Many other prominent Democratic conservatives simply sat out the race.

A number of influential Byrd Democrats went significantly farther, however. On October 1, a group of 166 conservative businessmen, attorneys, and financial leaders, most of them from the Richmond area, endorsed Holton and the Republican ticket. For them, preservation of the already-crumbling local political structure paled in importance compared to the pressing national issues that seemed to divide the two candidates and, increasingly, their respective parties. Describing themselves as "former Eisenhower and Nixon supporters who have been statewide and local Democrats," the members of the group adopted the label "New Republicans" and declared their intention "to work within the Republican Party in Virginia to elect Mr. Holton and his runningmates."[22] Led by Lawrence Lewis, Jr., of Richmond, the group seemed to

---

[20]The *News Leader* endorsement of Holton and his runningmates was its first endorsement of a GOP gubernatorial ticket. The *Richmond Times-Dispatch* and most of the other major newspapers in the state backed Battle.

[21]Smith interview.

[22]Hunter, p. 103.

embrace the Republican Party without reservation or condition. The symbolic value of their endorsement was significant, but their principal contribution to Holton was financial. Just prior to their announcement, the Holton campaign had been strapped financially, and the candidate had ordered staff cutbacks in order to avoid indebtedness. The infusion of new funds enabled the GOP campaign to press forward at full steam in the contest's crucial final month.

The financial backing of Lewis and the New Republicans, in combination with funds raised mostly from out-of-state sources by J. D. Stetson Coleman, a wealthy Republican financier from The Plains in Fauquier County, enabled Holton to outspend his Democratic opponent in the fall campaign.[23] It was the first time that a GOP candidate for governor had done so. Looking back on his winning campaign during a 1980 interview, Holton described the New Republicans as "a very, very necessary part of the coalition" that elected him in 1969. "That conservative support," said Holton, "was extremely important from a money standpoint because . . . that's the only group that puts up any real money for political races in Virginia."[24] Some traditional Republicans bristled at the idea of a GOP campaign being funded by Byrd Democrats, but the benefit to Holton was undeniable. Moderate Roanoke Republican Caldwell Butler, Holton's law partner, labeled the New Republicans "opportunists," but quickly added, "Obviously, Linwood needed them."[25]

Old foes do not easily become allies, and many moderate Republicans such as Holton had spent years combatting the Byrd organization. But, unhappy Byrd Democrats were now turning to the conservative-sounding Holton, and political expediency dictated that GOP moderates swallow hard. The pill had been made considerably less bitter by the recent changes in the Democratic Party. "The more progressive Godwin administration," explained GOP Delegate A. R. "Pete" Giesen of Augusta County, "made it more acceptable for those people to come into the Republican Party and easier for us to accept them. [Godwin] paved the way to a degree for Lin Holton's election."[26] Though many of the issues that had divided the GOP and Democratic conservatives in previous years were declining in relevance, the scars of old battles remained. The 1969 contest was the first state election to occasion a major step toward a philosophical realignment of the political parties in Virginia, but many moderate Republicans and Byrd Democrats would find the going far from easy in succeeding elections as they headed haltingly toward the altar.

With the Democratic Party moving perceptively leftward during much of the '60s, the long-discussed realignment of the Virginia parties along the con-

---

[23]Holton reported expenditures of approximately $387,000, while Battle and his running-mates collectively spent only $321,000. Battle, however, spent another $425,000 in his pursuit of the Democratic nomination. Cooper and Morris, p. 103.

[24]Holton interview.

[25]Hunter, p. 69.

[26]Giesen interview.

servative-Republican/liberal-Democrat lines of their national counterparts had seemed increasingly likely. The defection of Democratic conservatives to the Republican Holton in 1969, while an historic first, was therefore not an altogether surprising development. What shocked observers was the fact that Democratic liberals bolted to the GOP candidate at the same time.

The bruising primary and run-off competition left many Howell supporters embittered—not only at the Democratic nominee, but also at Governor Godwin. As Battle later recalled, Godwin "came out [during the run-off campaign] and made a lot of speeches, but rather than being positive for me, he was anti-Howell. He just hated Howell so badly that when he got on the stump what came out was castigation of Howell."[27] It was not a bad theme, Battle added, "but it didn't help when I then had to run against Holton." The volatile Howell would do nothing to assuage the resentment among his partisans, and even seemed to inflame it. While conceding that he was obliged to back the party's nominee, Howell said publicly that his supporters were "free spirits" who would do as they pleased in the fall.[28] He subsequently defended that much-publicized statement as an attempt to make clear that his backers were a diverse lot whose support would have to be solicited by Battle based on policy positions rather than merely an appeal to party loyalty. But, however intended, the statement appeared to be an invitation to the Howell constituency to back Holton.

If Howell was decidedly unhelpful in healing the Democratic rift, Battle and Godwin also made little effort to reach out to Howell and party liberals. Any possibility of a rapprochement disappeared in October when Godwin and Democratic Chairman Watkins Abbitt blocked the seating of Howell at the head table during a party unity dinner and even declined to recognize him when the dignitaries were introduced. The snub was the final blow for many of Howell's supporters. They already felt little obligation to back the party's nominee, since Godwin himself had indicated during the run-off that he would not support Howell even if the liberal were to win the nomination. Now the message from Godwin and Battle was that there was no room in the Democratic Party for Howell and his followers. If that was the way Godwin and his allies felt, the Howell backers reasoned, the party leaders could try to elect a Democrat as governor without the liberals' help. Responding to pleas that he act to halt defections by his supporters, Howell insisted that Democratic moderates must first "sit down and talk with me about the kind of Democratic Party we should have."[29] Quietly, he coached emissaries from the Holton camp on how to obtain his backers' support.

For many of Howell's supporters—blacks, organized labor, and liberals—Battle's candidacy offered little hope for change. The Democratic

27William C. Battle interview, November 4, 1988.
28Bass and DeVries, p. 353.
29Hunter, p. 71.

nominee seemed to be firmly under the thumb of Godwin and Abbitt, whom they regarded as unreconstructed Byrd men. Rather than helping to perpetuate conservative control of the Democratic Party, the Howell Democrats decided to seize the opportunity to "nail the coffin shut" on the Byrd organization once and for all by defeating Battle.[30] Though the frustrated Democratic nominee reminded disaffected liberals that he had parted ways with the Byrd organization many years earlier and bore no responsibility for its misdeeds, Battle's protests fell largely on deaf ears.

The Virginia AFL-CIO, which had backed Godwin over Holton in 1965, resisted pro-Battle pressure from national union leaders and Massachusetts Senator Edward Kennedy, and instead endorsed Holton. "Our reply was simply this: 'We've been waiting a lifetime to kill the Byrd machine and this is our chance and we're going to do it,'" said state AFL-CIO chief Julian Carper.[31] Organized labor's long-range strategy was apparent from Carper's statement: "The best way to make sure that the Byrd machine is eliminated completely is to elect a Republican. [That would force] a restructuring of the state Democratic Party" in the image of the national party and pave the way for election of a liberal Democrat in 1973.[32] While there was little enthusiasm in the ranks of organized labor for Holton, and actually some dissension over abandonment of the Democratic ticket, most union members apparently shared Carper's view and backed the Republican nominee.

Prominent black leaders did likewise. In 1965, they had taken a chance by supporting Godwin, and they had found his gubernatorial tenure profoundly disappointing. Dr. William Thornton of Richmond, who played a decisive role in the 1965 endorsement of Godwin by the Crusade for Voters, said he "kicked [himself] for it for four years."[33] "Godwin had promised that he would do a number of things . . .," Thornton recalled in a 1980 interview.

He told us that he had changed—that we could see the difference after he was elected. And we supported him. After he was elected we went down to him with a menu of things that we thought he should do . . . . We presented to him in writing the things we'd like to see done. He said he'd get back to us. . . . He hasn't gotten back to us yet.[34]

Particularly upsetting to blacks was Godwin's refusal to back Oliver Hill, a prominent black civil rights attorney, for a Richmond judgeship following Hill's endorsement by several black bar groups. Having once supported a moderate-sounding Byrd Democrat with unsatisfactory results, black leaders were disinclined to try it again with Battle in 1969.

30Ralph Eisenberg, "The Emergence of Two-Party Politics," in *The Changing Politics of the South*, ed. William C. Havard (Baton Rouge: Louisiana State University Press, 1972), p. 79.

31Peirce, p. 63.

32Hunter, p. 65.

33Peirce, p. 63.

34William S. Thornton interview, June 3, 1980.

By contrast, Linwood Holton's candidacy held some appeal for the black political leadership. Convinced that his failure to get a larger share of the black vote had kept him from pulling off an upset victory in 1965, Holton had since devoted considerable time and effort to cultivating ties in the black community. By 1969, black leaders not only believed that Holton could win; they also trusted him to follow through on his pledges if he succeeded. Appealing to disgruntled Byrd Democrats while vying for black support was not easy for Holton, but the political breezes were just right for him to walk the tightrope successfully. Had blacks not been preoccupied with the perceived sins of the Byrd machine in 1969, they might have been less tolerant of Holton's embrace of Nixon and his jabs at Battle for his national Democratic connections. But Holton was savvy enough to stress his audience's foremost concern when he appeared before black groups. "Mr. Battle will be obligated," Holton told one gathering of blacks, "to those who put in the governor before him, and the governor before him, all the way back to 1925."[35] Declaring that "a vote for Battle would be a vote for the Byrd machine," the Crusade for Voters endorsed Holton in late September.[36]

Though all three members of the Republican ticket benefited considerably from the conservative Democratic defections, support for Holton from the liberal wing of the Democratic Party did not extend to his GOP running-mates. The AFL-CIO, the Crusade for Voters, and other Howell supporters backed Sargeant Reynolds and Andrew Miller, whose nominations had been accompanied by far less rancor than had Battle's. Most of the GOP's resources went into the Holton effort, leaving Dawbarn and Obenshain without the funds for radio and television advertising necessary to increase their name recognition and to garner support from a narrower moderate-conservative coalition. In late September, however, Obenshain received significant financial help from J. D. Stetson Coleman, Lawrence Lewis, and others, and this enabled his campaign to conduct a separate media advertising effort in the contest's closing weeks.

The toughest assignment in the fall campaign appeared to be Dawbarn's, for he faced the youthful and charismatic "Sarge" Reynolds in the race for lieutenant governor. The GOP state senator from Waynesboro was not overly concerned, however, because he never seriously entertained hopes of winning. Dawbarn worked hard on behalf of Holton, and his easy-going style and refreshing candor won him many admirers. Indicative of his approach was this encounter with a reporter, which Dawbarn recalled years later:

> A week or two before the election someone asked me how the campaign was going. And I said that I thought Holton would get elected unless he goofed in the last few days and that I thought Obenshain was gaining rapidly on Andy Miller but I didn't know whether there were

[35]*Richmond Times-Dispatch*, November 1, 1969.
[36]Hunter, p. 64.

enough days left for him to catch him. Then someone said, "Well, how are you and Sarge going to make out?" And I said, "He's going to clobber me." And they said, "Do you mean you want to make that statement?" And I said, "Well, do you want me to lie to you?" And they said, "Well, you're not supposed to say that." And I said, "You shouldn't have asked me the question then . . . ."[37]

Dawbarn's candid assessment proved to be on target. Linwood Holton garnered 52.5 percent of the vote on November 4, 1969, and became the first Republican in a century to capture the Virginia governorship.[38] Though unsuccessful in his bid for attorney general, Obenshain polled more than 400,000 votes—next to Holton's, the highest vote total that had been amassed by a GOP candidate for statewide office in Virginia.[39] With approximately 50,000 votes separating the candidates, the Obenshain-Miller contest was the closest of the three races. Reynolds, as expected, easily out-distanced Dawbarn in the race for lieutenant governor, though the Waynesboro Republican received more than 40 percent of the vote.[40] Ticket-splitting, which previously had been common in Virginia only in presidential election years, was widespread in 1969; more than a third of the state's localities gave majorities to statewide candidates of different parties on November 4.[41] And, Republicans made large gains in the legislative races. They added ten new delegates to bring GOP strength in the House of Delegates to 24 members, and they also won a special election to add a seventh Republican senator.

The turnout in the 1969 general election exceeded 915,000 voters and dwarfed previous vote totals in non-presidential elections. The number voting in the governor's race was nearly 63 percent higher than in the 1965 general election, and was more than twice the turnout in the August 1969 primary run-off. Repeal of the poll tax in state elections and rapid population growth both contributed to the vast increase. The locus of most of the new voter participation and two-party competition was the state's urban corridor, which, when combined with the vote in the only two metropolitan areas outside of the corridor, provided nearly 60 percent of the votes cast in each of the three state-

---

[37]H. Dunlop Dawbarn interview, June 21, 1980.

[38]The vote totals in the race for governor were: Holton (R) – 480,869 (52.5%); Battle (D) – 415,695 (45.4%); Beverly B. McDowell (Conservative) – 10,596 (1.2%); William A. Pennington (American Independent) – 7,382 (0.8%); George R. Walker (Independent) – 1,182 (0.1%). Sabato, *Virginia Votes 1969-1974*, pp. 142–145.

[39]The vote totals in the race for attorney general were: Miller (D) – 455,264 (52.1%); Obenshain (R) – 402,382 (46.1%); Flavius B. Walker, Jr. (Conservative) – 9,725 (1.8%). Ibid., pp. 150–153.

[40]The vote totals in the race for lieutenant governor were: Reynolds (D) – 472,853 (54.0%); Dawbarn (R) – 371,246 (42.4%); Samuel J. Breeding, Jr. (American Independent) – 16,839 (1.9%); Louis A. Brooks, Jr. (Conservative) – 10,557 (1.7%). Ibid., pp. 146–149.

[41]Ibid., p. 13.

wide races. All three winners—Holton, Reynolds, and Miller—polled majorities in the urban corridor and ran better there than in the state as a whole.[42]

The GOP ticket exhibited markedly increased strength beyond the traditionally Republican areas of western Virginia. The trio demonstrated the party's growing suburban appeal and its ability to attract conservative voters previously aligned with the Byrd-dominated state Democratic Party. All three Republicans won majorities of the state's suburban vote and carried massive Fairfax County in northern Virginia and the two large suburban counties adjacent to Richmond. The GOP team also improved significantly on previous Republican performances in Southside. All this was evidence that the Democratic shift to the left was prompting changes in voting behavior in state contests similar to what had been happening in presidential elections since the 1950s. Republican voting was now becoming respectable at all levels. An expanded GOP base was evident in 1969, and the potential for further gains through realignment was apparent.

In the wake of the 1969 election, analysts quibbled over whether defections by conservative or liberal Democrats were responsible for the election of Virginia's first GOP governor in the twentieth century. Much of the discussion missed the crucial point—that support from both ends of the Democratic spectrum had been essential to Holton's win. The support of the Democratic conservatives enabled Holton and his runningmates each to poll more than 40 percent of the vote—something GOP statewide candidates rarely had done in the past. It was the additional vote that Holton received from various elements of the Howell constituency that made the difference between victory for him and defeat for his two runningmates.

Even with the backing of key black leaders and organizations, Holton was unable to garner a majority of the votes cast by blacks in the race for governor. Still, the estimated 37 percent of black support received by Holton represented a significant incursion into the usual Democratic base in the state's cities. Holton polled majorities of the vote in normally Democratic Alexandria, Hampton, Newport News, Richmond, Roanoke, and Virginia Beach, and he held Battle to slim margins in other urban areas. The Republican even garnered a 51-percent majority of the central-city vote statewide. By contrast, Dawbarn and Obenshain received five and seven percent of the black vote, respectively, and their opponents rolled up majorities approaching 60 percent in the central cities.[43]

Holton also ran well among the segment of the Howell constituency that had supported the Independent presidential candidacy of George Wallace in 1968. Howell, the populist, had demonstrated an appeal beyond the usual liberal Democratic circles in the 1969 primary contests. His anti-establishment

---

[42]Ralph Eisenberg, "1969 Politics in Virginia: The General Election," *University of Virginia News Letter* (Charlottesville: Institute of Government, University of Virginia), May 15, 1970.

[43]Sabato, *Virginia Votes 1969–1974*, p. 18.

"people's campaign" tapped the same reservoir of resentment towards big business, big government, and big institutions in general that had been the source of much of Wallace's support in 1968. Many of the Wallace-Howell voters were urban residents with blue-collar occupations and below-average incomes, and they apparently backed Holton in the general election largely because of their disenchantment with Howell's defeat in the primary. Interestingly, while urban Wallace voters were helping Holton carry the central cities, rural Wallace backers also supported the Republican. Particularly in Southside, many conservatives who had supported Wallace in 1968 and Fred Pollard in the July 1969 primary turned to Holton in the fall.

When the dust settled after the lengthy and tumultuous series of campaigns for the Virginia governorship in 1969, a debate began that would occupy Republicans during much of Holton's tenure as governor: Was Holton's victory the product of masterful coalition-building by the candidate, or was it just that Holton was in the right place at the right time? And, more to the point, could the Holton coalition be duplicated by subsequent GOP candidates?

Writing shortly after the election, James Latimer commented that a "decade of political irony reached its peak in 1969."[44] He offered this succinct explanation:

The Republican governor-elect was given his margin of victory by one or both of two dissident groups of former Democrats. A group from the conservative right was motivated by hopes of transplanting remnants of the old Byrd organization into the Republican party, to promote a realignment of parties along conservative versus liberal lines. A group from the liberal left, including Negro and labor organizations, turned to the GOP gubernatorial candidate in hopes of stomping out the last trace of the Byrd organization as the first step in rebuilding the Democratic party to elect a liberal governor in 1973.[45]

"We almost didn't have to go out to seek support," recalled J. Harvie Wilkinson III, a speech writer for Holton.[46] "People were just sore. They kept coming to Linwood Holton—loads of disenchanted voters on both ends of the spectrum—and Linwood Holton reaped the harvest." "It was," Wilkinson added, "a very hard year for Holton to lose."

It was not necessary to diminish Holton's contribution to his own victory in order to make the case that his was a coalition of the moment—the product of events and circumstances little foreseen and virtually impossible to duplicate. Holton was, of course, vitally important, if not essential, to the GOP victory in 1969. A less attractive candidate, a less capable campaigner, a leader less able to unite the state Republican Party, a nominee without simultaneous personal

[44]*Richmond Times-Dispatch*, December 21, 1969, quoted in Cooper and Morris, p. 115.
[45]Ibid.
[46]*Richmond Times-Dispatch*, December 5, 1982.

ties to the conservative Republican leadership in Washington and the liberal black leadership in Virginia—in short, a GOP candidate with any of those shortcomings—might well have been unsuccessful in 1969. But the relevant inquiry for Virginia Republicans looking to future elections was whether the conditions that made Holton "electable" in 1969 could and would repeat themselves.

Those conditions, if not unique, certainly were unusual enough to cast serious doubt on the feasibility of re-creating a coalition like Holton's on a consistent basis. Only rarely, one could safely predict, would circumstances permit such diverse and normally incompatible elements as the New Republicans and the Crusade for Voters to join in the pursuit of a common short-term goal while seeking to advance wholly incongruous long-term ends.[47] Even amid all of the GOP exuberance in the election's wake, thoughtful Republicans recognized that it was unlikely that political conditions in the Old Dominion would continue to afford their party the best of both worlds. In the future, the Virginia GOP would have to choose. It could continue to seek support from a coalition of moderate mountain-valley Republicans, blacks, organized labor, and liberals, or it could seek to grow by appealing chiefly to conservatives who were disenchanted with the Democrats' lurch to the left. With a historic realignment transforming politics not only in Virginia but throughout the South, the former course would set the GOP against the tide; the latter would permit it to ride the wave.

That was not, however, how Linwood Holton saw things. He would have the Republican Party cling tenaciously to the strategy that elected him in 1969 until the reins of party leadership were seized from him midway through his tenure as governor. Holton's attitude may well have stemmed from the fact that the alternative party-building strategy—joining forces with the Byrd Democrats—was one that was emotionally and philosophically untenable for him regardless of its merit pragmatically. Or, perhaps, as veteran reporter Charles McDowell suggested, Holton seriously envisioned an all-inclusive GOP that would span the philosophical spectrum in the Old Dominion. "I think Linwood Holton might well argue," ventured McDowell in 1980,

that the Democratic Party was so far to the right, so closed, so confused, that he had a chance to proclaim a party that really swept across this whole scope—that it was a coalition that he put together and thought you might conceivably keep together. That was unrealistic of him, I suspect. But if you had a view of the Democratic Party as old, withered, in-grown and not reaching out to anybody, Holton's notion that you could sweep nearly everybody into the Republican Party was a very bold and dramatic notion. I

<hr>

[47]See Louis M. Seagull, *Southern Republicanism* (Cambridge, Mass.: Schenkman Publishing Co., Inc., 1975), p. 135.

guess he misfigured it, but I don't think that in his mind [his coalition in 1969] was a fluke.[48]

Whatever may have been Holton's vision for the future of the Virginia GOP, it is clear that his election gave great impetus to realignment of the political parties in the state. There was, of course, more than a little irony in that. Having spent a career fighting the Byrd organization, Holton now found himself swept into office at least in part by the votes and campaign contributions of a group bent on transplanting Byrd conservatism to the Virginia GOP. There was irony in it, too, for blacks, organized labor, and liberals, who had hoped to smash the Byrd organization by backing Holton. Soon, it would become apparent that they had only dented the machine and may even have contributed to its partial survival as part of the GOP-led conservative coalition that would emerge in the '70s. By pulling the rug from under the moderate Battle in 1969, Democratic liberals put their party on a course that, in a few years, would take it far to the left of the Virginia electorate and thereby open the way for a decade of conservative Republican successes.

There was a measure of irony in the election outcome for Governor Godwin as well. After four years of fast-paced progress greeted with apparent enthusiasm by most Virginians, a strong sentiment for further change had manifested itself in the first Democratic gubernatorial defeat in a century. Godwin watched his former GOP foe assemble a broad coalition not dissimilar from the one Godwin himself had put together to defeat Holton in 1965. The governor backed the losing Battle ticket in 1969, but he understood as well as anyone the implications of the election returns. To a close political friend he confided, "We had some defections from the right. . . but if the control of our party ever gets into the hands of the real liberal element, we will see tremendously large defectors—perhaps even including me."[49]

Most of the *post mortem* assessments overlooked one of the crucial factors in Holton's victory. When, for example, Governor Godwin met with reporters to canvass the reasons for his party's defeat in the gubernatorial race, he cited the divisive Democratic primary, Democratic defections to Holton from the left and the right, Nixon's active support of the Republican nominee, and Holton's "It's Time for a Change" campaign theme.[50] What Godwin ignored—and what Virginia Democrats would continue for years to ignore—was the new campaign technology used by Republicans.

Television and radio advertising, professional campaign consultants, extensive air travel, polling, and public relations personnel had been standard features of political campaigns in other states for several years, but 1969 saw that new campaign technology come to Virginia for the first time. No longer could "passing the word" around the courthouses be counted upon to produce

[48]McDowell interview.

[49]Bugg, p. 383.

[50]Hunter, p. 58.

winning campaigns in the Old Dominion. The Holton campaign's successful fundraising efforts enabled it to make extensive use of television and radio messages produced by the Baltimore-based Goodman Agency, a leading national media consulting firm. The Holton effort included other innovations, such as a helicopter tour of major media markets, extensive use of advance men, and a press relations/policy development/speech-writing operation led by Staige Blackford, a former political reporter for the Norfolk-based *Virginian-Pilot*, and J. Harvie Wilkinson III. The candidates themselves travelled more widely and campaigned more intensely than had previous statewide candidates of either party, and even their wives took to the stump. National Committeewoman Cynthia Newman coordinated a joint tour by the three spouses that gained widespread favorable publicity.

In August 1969, the Holton team imported a professional campaign manager from Texas who recently had steered John Tower through a successful U.S. Senate election. Already in place when the new manager arrived, however, was a well-organized campaign structure erected by Holton aide John Ritchie of Charlottesville and Tenth District GOP Chairman William Stanhagen. Using the Tower campaign manual and an organization plan honed in Congressman Joel Broyhill's biennial re-election battles, Holton campaign officials had plotted a sophisticated statewide effort involving an intensive voter registration drive, precinct-level organization, precinct targeting, and a get-out-the-vote operation. Manuals were prepared; seminars were conducted; and hundreds of volunteers recruited from across the state were equipped, for the first time, with the tools for waging a technically proficient campaign.

Another innovation by the Holton campaign—and one with significant consequences for the GOP's future—was its organizational drive on the state's college campuses. The effort was directed by William Royall, a Young Republican and Tazewell County native who had cut his political teeth in William Wampler's 1966 campaign for Congress. Schooled in campus organizational techniques by veteran conservative activist Morton C. Blackwell of Arlington, Royall knew how to identify Republican-leaning students and turn them out to vote in campus mock elections. His efforts resulted in highly publicized Holton victories in 20 of the 22 contests held at state colleges and universities during the fall campaign. News of the mock election victories in the campaign's closing weeks helped to demonstrate to skeptical voters that a GOP candidate for governor could win in Virginia. Moreover, Republican leaders discovered a reservoir of youthful enthusiasm and volunteer manpower on the campuses that the party would continue to tap in subsequent campaigns.

Another key factor in the 1969 election became more apparent after the decennial census was completed. The 1970 census revealed that Virginia's postwar industrialization and urbanization trends had continued apace during the preceding decade. The state's population grew 17.6 percent between 1960 and 1970, and much of the increase resulted from migration. The growth was centered in the state's urban areas, and, especially in the suburbs. By 1970, nearly 60 percent of the Commonwealth's population was located in its six Standard Metropolitan Statistical Areas. The northern Virginia suburbs were spreading southward and westward to encompass a second tier of Piedmont counties; suburban Virginia Beach was growing rapidly; the counties surrounding Roanoke and Richmond were experiencing large population increases; and most other urban corridor localities also were growing steadily. Of the 15 fastest-growing localities during the '60s, all were either suburban counties or newer cities that served in effect as suburbs of older cities.[51]

The political trend in the vote-rich suburbs was distinctly conservative and increasingly Republican. Virginia's economic expansion had hiked the median family income in the state by nearly 40 percent (after inflation) between 1960 and 1970, and the percentage of male Virginians engaged in white-collar jobs climbed from approximately 33 percent to 50 percent during that decade.[52] The suburbs were the locus of much of the new affluence in the Commonwealth. The younger, mostly white, middle-class, business and professional persons who typically resided in suburban areas tended to have a moderate-to-conservative political outlook. In northern Virginia, where expansion of the federal government accounted for much of the population increase, the presence of the Pentagon and other defense-related facilities on the Virginia side of the Potomac attracted residents who tended to be more conservative than those in neighboring Maryland, where many residents worked for federal agencies administering social programs. Richmond's suburbs were comprised of a high percentage of native Virginians, and drew much of their sharply conservative character from the presence of a large portion of the state's business and financial leadership and from the consistently conservative editorial views of the Richmond newspapers.

It was clear by 1969 that the Virginia Republican Party owed its modern resurgence largely to the establishment of a suburban base. Roanoke's suburbs had been the first to assume a Republican cast, followed by northern Virginia in the '50s. By the mid-1960s, the counties of Henrico and Chesterfield adjacent to Richmond evidenced growing Republican sympathies. Many suburban voters had been drawn to the GOP in earlier years by its more progressive stance on education and other public services of importance to urban residents. As state services were expanded and became less of an issue in the '60s, suburban voters' conservative proclivities on national economic and foreign policy issues continued to push them toward the Republican camp. The

---

[51]See William J. Serow, "Population Change in Virginia, 1960–1970," *University of Virginia News Letter* (Charlottesville: Institute of Government, University of Virginia), May 15, 1971.

[52]William J. Serow and Charles O. Meiburg, "The Average Virginian as Seen by the Census", *University of Virginia News Letter* (Charlottesville: Institute of Government, University of Virginia), February 15, 1973.

support of suburbanites had been the key to the successful GOP presidential campaigns in the Old Dominion since 1952, and it provided the foundation for Linwood Holton's historic victory in 1969. Future Republican candidates in Virginia would have to win in the suburbs or they would not win at all.

Chapter 19

Linwood Holton and the Burden of Being Governor First

"[T]he great Holton contributions were symbolic and intangible: a new air of openness in state government, two-party democracy in action, and, above all, racial understanding through personal tolerance and goodwill."[53]

J. Harvie Wilkinson III

The inauguration of the man who ended a century of Democratic rule in the Old Dominion was a joyous occasion for Virginia Republicans. For those who had labored a lifetime in pursuit of respectability as much as power, the sight of Linwood Holton raising his hand to take the oath of office was a source of spine-tingling pride. Veteran Republican workers and youthful enthusiasts joined in celebration of a triumph not of philosophy or personality, but of party.

The changing of the guard brought "no thunderbolt, no deluge, no cataclysm of any kind," wrote Charles McDowell of the *Times-Dispatch*.[54] There was, however, an unmistakably fresh breeze blowing through Capitol Square, and all were alert to see what further changes might come with the next gust. Holton viewed the success of his administration as the central factor in determining the fortunes of his party for the foreseeable future. Unless he governed well, the first Republican governor in a century might well be the last for years to come. The Roanoke Republican brought to the office no detailed legislative agenda, no bold vision of sweeping reform. But, aided by his own casual style, good humor, and fresh perspective, he meant to open up Virginia's government—to give it a new and friendly face. After the progressive Godwin tenure, Holton's aim was not so much to change the direction of the ship of state as to enlarge its crew—to include Virginians of all ranks, races, and regions in state government at all levels. To some, the objective might have seemed a modest one, but to Holton, who often appeared more apologetic than proud of Virginia's past, it would be a contribution of historic

---

[53]J. Harvie Wilkinson III, "Linwood Holton," in *The Governors of Virginia 1860–1978*, eds. Edward Younger and James Tice Moore (Charlottesville: The University Press of Virginia, 1982), p. 407.

[54]Ibid., p. 397.

dimension. Success, however, required an administration that was not only open but effective. And, to be effective meant getting along with the Democrats who dominated the legislature.

Governor Holton did not know personally most of the members of the General Assembly. Having never served in the legislature or in state government, he lacked the personal relationships with key legislative leaders upon which his predecessors had been able to draw. Holton recognized the problem, and devoted considerable time and energy to cultivating close ties with the Assembly leadership. He liked Lieutenant Governor Reynolds, the presiding officer in the Senate, and worked well with him. He also developed a good working relationship with House of Delegates Speaker John Warren Cooke and House Appropriations Committee Chairman W. Roy Smith. Cooperation with and from the influential Smith was vital if the governor was to gain support for any of his legislative initiatives. Delegate M. Caldwell Butler, Holton's former law partner and a member of the Appropriations Committee, played a key role in facilitating that cooperation and in serving as a bridge between the governor's office and the legislature during the first half of Holton's term.

With a Republican governor on the third floor of the Capitol, the GOP legislators on the second floor saw their role change drastically. No longer were they the vocal minority slinging arrows at Democratic legislation that was certain to pass; suddenly they were the conciliatory minority sponsoring and championing legislation backed by the governor, much of it winning approval by the Democratic majority. By 1970, Republicans were afforded at least modest representation on all major House and Senate committees and had become active participants in the legislative process. Relations between the governor and the legislative leadership, and between lawmakers of both parties, were so good that Senate Minority Leader James Turk of Radford praised the less-partisan air at the State Capitol in a published commentary on the 1970 legislative session.[55]

Two of the principal reasons for Holton's success in creating an atmosphere of amiable nonpartisanship were his modest legislative agenda and his selective approach to exercising leadership on matters before the General Assembly. In many if not most of the legislative struggles during his governorship, Holton was little more than an observer. The strategy paid off, however, in that the governor won support for a number of proposals he regarded as important. At his urging, for example, legislators approved state expenditures for local sewage treatment plants, community mental health centers, port development at Hampton Roads, and special assistance to the state's poorer public school districts. The pattern of tax increases inaugurated by Governor

---

[55]See James C. Turk, "A Republican Looks at the 1970 Virginia General Assembly," *University of Virginia News Letter* (Charlottesville: Institute of Government, University of Virginia), August 15, 1970.

Holton's predecessor was continued by the Republican chief executive. Though lawmakers rejected his proposal for a higher levy on cigarettes, they approved increased taxes on alcoholic beverages, gasoline, and corporate and personal incomes. The governor achieved mixed results in his environmental initiatives. His administration secured funding for sewage treatment and imposed stringent new restrictions on private pollution of public waterways, but Holton's wetlands protection and strip-mining proposals fared poorly. Perhaps Holton's most significant legislative achievement was enactment—by razor-thin margins in both houses of the Assembly—of a measure to reorganize state agencies and establish the governor's Cabinet.[56]

At the top of the Holton agenda, however, was the fostering of better race relations in Virginia. That objective was the new governor's central theme as he delivered his inaugural address. "Here in Virginia," he declared, "we must see that no citizen of the Commonwealth is excluded from full participation in both the blessings and responsibilities of our society because of his race. Let our goal in Virginia be an aristocracy of ability regardless of race, color, or creed."[57] Just as Governor Godwin before him had seemed determined in a single gubernatorial term to remedy years of Byrd organization neglect of public education and other services, Holton was committed to turning the page on Virginia's race-preoccupied past. His goal was to make the Commonwealth "a model in race relations," and he moved to do so by bringing black citizens into state government. During his tenure, the number of blacks employed in state government rose 25 percent, and several blacks were appointed to high-level positions in the administration.

Somewhat ironically, to this racially progressive Virginia governor fell the difficult task of coping with the explosive school-busing controversy. The school desegregation issue had faded into the background during much of the '60s, but in the early '70s it was brought quickly back to the fore in Virginia by federal court orders mandating student reassignment and transportation to eliminate numerical racial imbalances in several city school systems. The court orders aroused deep parental concern and stirred racial passions anew. Nowhere was the reaction from whites more bitter than in the Richmond area, where it was feared that court-ordered desegregation would mean long bus trips between the predominantly black City of Richmond and the mostly white surrounding suburbs.

The controversy presented a personal dilemma and a serious political problem for the governor. He was opposed to busing. Even before many of the deleterious effects of the practice—the resultant "white flight" and urban resegregation—were widely appreciated, Holton regarded the busing of

---

[56]See Wilkinson, "Linwood Holton," pp. 398–399, 403–406. Critical support for Holton's cabinet proposal came from key Democrats at opposite ends of the political spectrum. Delegate Roy Smith patroned the legislation in the House, while State Senator (and future Governor) Douglas Wilder's vote provided the winning margin in the upper chamber.

[57]Ibid., p. 397.

students in order to achieve racially balanced schools as wrongheaded. But the dispute could not be divorced from its historical context. Much of the vocal opposition to busing was motivated, in Holton's view, by the same racial bigotry that for years had pervaded Virginia society and politics. He had no desire to jump on that bandwagon by excoriating federal authorities and stirring racial antagonisms in the manner of several of his predecessors. He thus refrained from public criticism of the federal courts and resisted pressures to have the state intervene in local desegregation litigation.

To an enraged and even frenzied white citizenry, Holton's inaction was infuriating. They expected the governor to take the lead, but instead he remained inside the comfortable confines of the Capitol, strangely silent, as the furor grew. On the opening day of classes in the fall of 1970, however, Holton acted. His was an act of leadership, to be sure, but it was not what the busing foes had in mind. In a gesture of compliance with federal authority, the governor escorted his 13-year-old daughter, Tayloe, to the mostly black Richmond high school to which she had been assigned under the court's busing plan. This profoundly symbolic event received nationwide attention and was widely hailed as a signal that Virginia finally and firmly had turned away from massive resistance.

Given the emotionalism of the moment, it is not surprising that Holton's dramatic gesture drew widely divergent reviews. Many within Virginia and without lauded it as a courageous act of statesmanship—"the most significant happening in the Commonwealth in my lifetime," former Governor Colgate Darden called it.[58] But conservatives were shocked and even disgusted. To them, it seemed that Governor Holton had enthusiastically embraced the busing policy and was receiving national accolades for doing so. "I think the conservative people . . . would have had me get up on top of the Capitol every day and scream at Washington," Holton recalled later, "but the way I saw my job was to keep the schools open and to keep the people as calm as possible in handling what really was a crisis . . . ."[59] That Holton did, but at considerable political cost.

Never a favorite of conservatives anyway, Holton was generally regarded after the busing controversy as something of a liberal. Those with whom he worked in the General Assembly viewed his handling of fiscal matters and his gubernatorial tenure generally as responsible, moderate, and often conservative. But the familiar maxim about perception being more important than reality in matters political applied with particular force to Holton. His seeming sympathy for court-ordered busing reinforced lingering doubts among conservatives about other aspects of his political outlook, and, as a consequence, his support among Democratic, independent, and Republican conservatives, especially in eastern and central Virginia, plummeted.

---

[58]Bass and DeVries, p. 359.
[59]Linwood Holton interview, May 28, 1980, and April 19, 1990.

For his part, Holton never sought to downplay his differences with some conservatives on racial matters:

I think that it is incumbent on this democracy to integrate itself to the extent that black citizens be given an opportunity to use their full talents. I've never advocated government subsidy of them and I don't even advocate busing. I do advocate opportunities for them to compete with everybody else and to have no disadvantage because of the color of their skin in that competition . . . .

. . . The distortion of the meaning of the word "conservative"—to take it and construe it as an instrument of white supremacy—I resent terribly because "conservative" doesn't mean that and yet it has been used that way.[60]

Some conservatives, of course, did not share Holton's progressive attitude on race relations. Other conservatives abhorred racial prejudice but were simply unwilling to assign civil rights the preoccupying importance that often seemed to characterize Holton's approach to racial matters. Thus, in ways subtle as well as direct, the busing controversy early in Holton's term drove a wedge between him and much of conservative Virginia.

As had been the case with his immediate predecessor, Holton's largely successful tenure as the Commonwealth's chief executive was not accompanied by comparable successes as party leader. Excessive expectations on the part of the GOP rank-and-file, inattention to party matters by the governor, strategic miscalculations, electoral reverses, and real and perceived philosophical differences combined to make Virginia's first Republican governor unpopular among many activists in his own party. Though Holton's election represented a historic breakthrough for the state Republican Party and sent the hopes of GOP partisans soaring, it did not take long for the glow to begin to fade.

Shortly after his election, Holton moved to place the state GOP apparatus in more effective hands. He shunted aside recently installed state party chief Samuel Carpenter, whose performance had satisfied few Republican leaders, and replaced him with hard-working and organizationally skilled Seventh District Chairman Warren French of Edinburg. He also gained the support of the GOP central committee for the hiring of a full-time, salaried executive director in the person of Republican activist Edd Shull of Roanoke. But, despite the personnel changes, emphasis on grass-roots organization, and ambitious plans for the 1970 congressional campaigns, it was soon apparent that all was not well in Linwood Holton's Republican Party.

No Republican in Virginia in 1970 had experienced a GOP gubernatorial administration, so many partisans assumed that the presence of a Republican in the Executive Mansion would open the door to all manner of power, patronage, and perquisite. Those anticipating an abundance of political spoils

---

[60]Ibid.

heard sobering words from the governor-elect at a morning gathering of enthusiastic partisans before the inaugural ceremony. Holton began with the familiar salutation, "My fellow Republicans," then, after a pause, went on to explain that he would not again use that phrase because, as governor of all Virginians, he would belong to no party.[61] Their leader's words no doubt sounded curious to some and ominous to others. He had provided a glimpse of the rather peculiar attitude toward party affairs that would characterize his governorship.

Holton, the veteran party activist, proved disinterested in using his office to reward party workers or to strengthen the GOP. Foremost in his mind was working harmoniously and effectively with the Democrat-dominated General Assembly and state bureaucracy, and that aim seemed to preclude virtually any display of partisanship. Such things as political speeches, appearances at Republican events, social occasions for GOP stalwarts at the mansion, and other gestures of goodwill and appreciation toward the party were given a low priority and frequently were neglected. As the months went by, Republicans began to grumble that the governor was ignoring them. Holton had time, it seemed, to hobnob with the wealthy and powerful, but was always too busy to spend time with the people who had helped him achieve his lofty position. An increasing number complained that Holton had forgotten his roots.

The focus of much of the GOP discontent was the governor's appointments to state agencies, boards, and commissions. Holton made much of his opening of state government to minorities, women, and persons from regions of the state—the Southwest and northern Virginia—previously neglected. But he placed too little emphasis, in the view of many GOP partisans, on appointing Republicans. To them, it often seemed that the governor felt more indebted for his election to black Democrats than to members of his own party. Also vexing was the fact that several key posts in the administration went to non-Virginians. The resentment was particularly strong in Holton's native southwest Virginia, where party passions ran deep and expectations of patronage ran high. The more the governor and his aides talked about the importance of having a successful first Republican administration and the need to appoint only well-qualified individuals to state posts, the more the GOP faithful took offense. The inference was that qualified Republicans were not available, and party activists thought they knew otherwise. Moreover, Holton had been elected governor without previous governmental experience, and his insistence upon exceptional qualifications for his appointees thus had a rather hollow ring.

Though the governor, with the assistance of Secretary of the Commonwealth Cynthia Newman, did succeed in placing a large number of Republicans in governmental positions, the expectations of party workers

---

[61]Warriner interview.

were not met. Perhaps they were simply too great. Holton aide John Ritchie recalled:

> When Holton was elected governor, he was the first Republican governor in the lifetime of any active Republican. And [his election] conjured up appetites that were not unlike those of the Gauls when they were sacking a Roman city. The dreams of the political rewards far exceeded the reality of what could be accomplished. It was a party that had been out of power for almost a century, and when they got back in, they just had visions of rewards that far exceeded anything that could be accomplished.[62]

"But, in all candor," added Ritchie, "it would have been possible to be more partisan than the Holton administration was."[63] The failure to be so would contribute mightily to Holton's impending political difficulties.

One appointment not made by the governor was to have an especially profound impact on the course of Republican Party affairs. Having reluctantly taken on the race for attorney general in 1969 after receiving assurances of post-election job opportunities, Richard Obenshain fully expected to assume an important role in the Holton administration. Indeed, as Obenshain's friend, Dortch Warriner, recalled in 1984, Holton's guarantees to Obenshain had been "three-deep and ironclad."[64] After the election, however, discussions between Obenshain and Holton dragged on for weeks and then months, with Obenshain receiving no firm offer of a position he regarded as acceptable. One post of particular interest to Obenshain, that of Commissioner of Motor Vehicles, was vetoed by the governor, who was intent upon hiring an expert in the field from another state. Other possible assignments were floated for Obenshain's consideration by Holton aides, but offers of employment were not forthcoming. The governor eventually expressed a willingness to appoint the Richmond conservative to the Alcoholic Beverage Control Board or to promote him for appointment to the federal bench, but Obenshain was committed to pursuing a political career and knew that neither post would advance his goal. Finally, after months of frustration, uncertainty, and financial insecurity, Obenshain concluded that Holton had no intention of awarding him a significant post in his administration and began a new law practice.

His mistreatment by Holton was a source of deep resentment for Obenshain, but Obenshain's friends and supporters reacted to the episode with an intensity that had more far-reaching political ramifications. Never great admirers of Holton, the conservative GOP activists who looked to Obenshain for leadership had already been somewhat displeased with the way the gubernatorial candidate had monopolized the Republican ticket's resources in 1969. Their mild displeasure turned to bitter hostility, however, as it became clear that the governor was not going to reward Obenshain for

---

[62]John Ritchie interview, June 30, 1980.
[63]Ibid.
[64]Warriner interview.

joining the ticket. The fact that the appointment matter went unresolved for months while their anguished friend waited without a source of income only served to heighten the animosity. It was a fateful misstep by Holton—one that contributed significantly to his growing corps of dedicated and determined foes within the GOP. It also had the effect of leaving Obenshain outside of the Holton administration, where he would be free to criticize the political misadventures that were to come in rapid succession during the first years of Holton's tenure.

Despite his difficulties with GOP regulars and some conservatives, Linwood Holton would leave office as a successful governor by almost any measure. Upon his successor's inauguration in January 1974, public opinion polls put Holton's popularity at nearly 80 percent, and even his harshest critics acknowledged that he had governed well. One of those frequent critics, *Richmond News Leader* Editor Ross Mackenzie, cited Holton's notable achievements in race relations: "Linwood Holton has helped to create a suitable climate in which every Virginian can advance on the basis of ability alone. For a mere four years, that is achievement enough for anyone."[65] It was the broad approval of his service as governor that made Holton's drastically diminished political standing all the more curious. A leading figure nationally following his 1969 election, Holton saw his political career end, for all intents and purposes, even before he left the governorship. As Virginia's first Republican governor, he put governing first and—ironically, for an inveterate champion of "two-party government"—ignored the imperative of party leadership. His one-time campaign aide, J. Harvie Wilkinson III, rendered this verdict:

Holton, while governor, inhabited the dream world where good government automatically makes good politics, and where lofty policy decisions somehow become detached from the need to remember first names, placate precinct chairmen, send letters of congratulations or condolence, or, if the governor cannot personally do those things, have lieutenants around who will. Yet in Holton the ideal and the practical never quite conjoined. The lesson of Linwood Holton is that it may never be enough simply to govern well.[66]

For Republicans, Holton's failure to reconcile the ideal with the practical in 1970 and 1971 would spell electoral disaster.

---

[65]*The Richmond News Leader*, January 10, 1974.
[66]Wilkinson, "Linwood Holton," p. 407.

Chapter 20
1970: Opportunity Lost

"I've seen speculation in the papers that you'll go home having done nothing. Frankly, I can't believe it. We're the biggest, strongest and the best party in Virginia . . . . Doing nothing would be like having the biggest, shiniest, newest fire engine and not taking it to the fire."[67]

Governor Linwood Holton
Virginia Republican Convention, 1970

Still basking in the glow of their historic victory in the 1969 governor's race, members of the GOP's state central committee assembled in Richmond early in 1970 and heard the University of Virginia's foremost political analyst, Ralph Eisenberg, offer a promising assessment of the party's condition. The Virginia Republican Party, he reported, was "at the apex of its success in this century," and the 1969 election had "firmly established two-party competition in the state."[68] With another round of congressional elections slated for the fall, the prospect of continued division in Democratic Party ranks fueled the Republicans' optimism. Harry F. Byrd, Jr., only narrowly had won his party's nomination for the United States Senate in 1966, and already Fredericksburg liberal George C. Rawlings, Jr., a former member of the House of Delegates, was gearing up to challenge Byrd's re-nomination in the July 1970 Democratic primary.

It was not long, however, before political developments refuted Eisenberg's confident prediction of normal two-party competition in Virginia. On March 17, 1970, Senator Byrd stunned Virginians with the announcement that he would depart the party of his fathers and seek re-election to the Senate as an Independent. The ostensible reason for his action was his party's new loyalty oath, which would require him to pledge in advance his support for the Democratic slate of electors, and thus the Democratic nominee for President, in the 1972 election. Byrd regarded the loyalty oath as intolerable, but his decision to bypass the Democratic primary also was based on a keen appraisal of the Virginia political landscape. It was clear that many conservative and middle-of-the-road voters no longer were inclined to participate in Demo-

---

[67]Wilkinson, "Linwood Holton," p. 399.
[68]Text of remarks on file at the Republican Party of Virginia Archives.

cratic Party balloting, and the resultant moderate-liberal domination of the party process placed Byrd's re-nomination in doubt. Even if he were to win the primary, his liberal Democratic foes probably would back the Republican candidate in the November general election. By running as an Independent, Senator Byrd could avoid those perils and seek the support of conservative Virginians of all political persuasions.

For conservative Republicans, young and old, who had been dreaming of a Byrd-GOP alliance in Virginia, Senator Byrd's announcement was taken as a signal that he was at last ready to lead the large corps of disenchanted Democratic conservatives into the Republican camp. All that remained, they assumed, was for the GOP to make the appropriate entreaties to Byrd, and he would make the switch. Public invitations to join the Republican Party and seek re-election as its nominee were issued to Senator Byrd by President Nixon and Governor Holton, and many of Byrd's Democratic friends and Republican allies urged him to accept. To their considerable surprise and chagrin, however, the senator refused. He would neither become a Republican nor pledge to vote with the Republicans in organizing the Senate. The noncommittal Byrd would say only that he would "welcome a Republican endorsement."[69]

GOP leaders then split over whether to endorse Byrd's Independent candidacy for re-election or to nominate a Republican to run against him. Governor Holton assumed a leadership role in the effort to put forward a GOP contender for the seat, and a decade later he offered this explanation:

This had been my life—to build a two-party system in Virginia. And one year after we'd first elected a statewide candidate was not the time to throw up our hands and concede the election to an Independent.

If Byrd had wanted to run as a Republican and thereby play within the two-party system, I wouldn't have been exuberant about the idea because we just have two different kinds of thinking. I like Harry Byrd personally, but his thinking and my thinking are different, particularly on this race issue. So it wouldn't have been any great cause for celebration for Byrd to become a Republican, but if he had come over and agreed to run as a Republican, the party clearly would've nominated him and I would've supported him. But the third-party idea simply breaks up the two-party system, and I would not support him [as an Independent]. And I insisted that the party not fall for that . . . .[70]

---

[69]Wilkinson, "Linwood Holton," p. 399.

[70]Holton interview conducted by Ms. Wood for the Republican Party of Virginia. In a separate interview with the author, Holton elaborated on his differences with Byrd and Byrd's ally, Mills Godwin, on the subject of race relations:
I never thought you could build a party on the right wing. Segregation inevitably would be a part of it, and I could not support that. . . . This was right on the heels of massive resistance, and that is what [Byrd and Godwin] stood for. I felt that they would be bad influences on the Republican Party, and that if the Byrd-Godwin group controlled the Republican Party, it would have to be phased out just like the Byrd organization.

Holton's view was generally supported in the traditionally Republican mountain-valley region of western Virginia. Despite their shared convictions with Senator Byrd on matters such as fiscal policy and national defense, many party regulars in the west had long regarded the Byrd organization as their principal political opposition. It would have been difficult enough for them to accept Senator Byrd if he had come to the GOP as a willing suitor, but they, like Governor Holton, could never justify giving Byrd their support without his first publicly embracing the party. Among those who came to the support of Holton on the Byrd question were party chief Warren French and a number of GOP legislators from the western part of the state who had worked closely with the governor during the 1970 General Assembly session. State Senators H. D. "Buz" Dawbarn and James Turk, Delegates Caldwell Butler and John Dalton, and other Holton allies from western Virginia were dubbed the "mountain and valley boys," and they provided crucial backing for the governor's stance.

On the opposite side of the issue was Tenth District Congressman Joel Broyhill, a longtime Byrd ally on Capitol Hill and a veteran of earlier GOP battles over whether to challenge Senator Byrd, Sr. Broyhill and other eastern Virginia conservatives hoped that the party would endorse Byrd or at least refrain from nominating a candidate so that Republicans would be free to vote for the senator in the November election. Two prominent GOP lawmakers—conservative Delegates George Mason Green of Arlington and Benjamin F. Woodbridge of Fredericksburg—took the lead in mobilizing grass-roots Republican support for Byrd, and Lawrence Lewis and his group of New Republicans also played an active role in the pro-Byrd effort. The increasingly influential Richard Obenshain opposed the nomination of a Byrd foe, but he remained publicly neutral on the issue after agreeing to chair the state GOP convention at which the matter would be decided.

Those favoring nomination of a Republican candidate for the Senate were thought to have the early advantage, but their arguments were premised on the availability of a credible GOP contender. Soon after Byrd's announcement, Governor Holton tried and failed to persuade freshman Congressman G. William Whitehurst of Norfolk to enter the race, and two other potential candidates—northern Virginia Delegates Vincent F. Callahan, Jr., and Stanford E. Parris—also decided against running. In need of a stalking horse or two to keep the contest alive while he searched for a viable statewide contender, Holton encouraged 36-year-old Delegate Ray L. Garland of Roanoke and Kenneth M. Haggerty, a member of the Arlington County Board of Supervisors, to become candidates. Though, as Holton intended, both men succeeded in garnering commitments of support from their respective regions, neither was a political heavyweight with a serious prospect of statewide success. As the weeks rolled by without a prominent Republican stepping forward to assume the challenge, some of the mountain and valley boys, including Delegate John Dalton, began to question the wisdom of fielding a candidate. As the convention approached, the Byrd backers abandoned hope of winning a GOP endorsement of the incumbent, but the prospects for averting the nomination of a Byrd foe seemed good.

The absence of a prominent and credible GOP candidate did not deter Governor Holton. He was committed as a matter of principle to mounting Republican opposition to Byrd, and he insisted that his wavering supporters stand with him. The governor knew how to touch the chord of party pride that makes refraining from nominating a candidate the most difficult of tasks for a political convention. In a memorable and probably decisive banquet speech the night before the convention session, Holton urged delegates to send a GOP candidate into the field:

> I've seen speculation in the papers that you'll go home having done nothing. Frankly, I can't believe it. We're the biggest, strongest, and the best party in Virginia. . . . I can't believe we'll do nothing. Doing nothing would be like having the biggest, shiniest, newest fire engine and not taking it to the fire.[71]

Ray Garland, the eventual beneficiary of Holton's persuasive appeal, did not hear the governor's "fire engine" speech. He was busy preparing for a television appearance on a local Richmond station following the late news. Early the next morning, however, he called Holton at the Executive Mansion. Confident that the stage had been set for the nomination of a candidate, Garland reiterated his willingness to step aside in favor of a better-known candidate, such as Dawbarn, Turk, or Butler. Holton advised that the others remained unwilling to run, and he counseled Garland to forge ahead.

Several hours to the north, a Republican of some prominence was awaiting word from Richmond on the convention outcome. President Nixon had often discussed with his savvy Southern strategist, South Carolinian Harry Dent, his hopes for bringing about a massive political restructuring in the South, and the chief executive regarded Virginia's Senator Byrd as the key to it. The Old Dominion had been the leader of the Confederacy, and for a half-century Harry F. Byrd, Sr., had been the central figure in a United States Senate dominated by Southern Democrats. As a congressman, then as Vice President, Nixon had observed and come to admire the elder Byrd. "The Byrd name was synonymous with good government and conservatism," recalled Harry Dent in 1988, "and Nixon felt that if a man of Byrd's stature came over [to the GOP] other Democratic leaders throughout the South would follow."[72] That it was the junior Senator Byrd whose political affiliation was at issue mattered little. With Byrd would come the Byrd organization, Nixon and Dent believed, "and all of a sudden the state would be turned right-side-up

---

[71]Wilkinson, "Linwood Holton," p. 399.
[72]Harry S. Dent interview, October 26, 1988.

politically."[73] The shock waves from such a shift would be felt throughout the South.

The President and his political aide did not stand by wishfully on the sidelines. It was an early request from the President that prompted Holton's initial invitation to Byrd to join the GOP. Byrd declined, and a Republican endorsement of his candidacy then seemed unlikely. But, as the convention approached, Nixon met secretly with Byrd at the White House to explore the prospects for the senator's caucusing with the Republicans in the next Congress if the Virginia GOP were to refrain from opposing his re-election. Would Byrd take that critical step by 1972, if not before, the President asked. Byrd's response was oblique and ostensibly noncommittal, but Nixon and Dent construed the cues as an affirmative response.

Some of Byrd's supporters—including his friend and confidant, former Governor Godwin—were not enthusiastic about the prospect of a Byrd affiliation with the GOP: their Democratic colleagues in the courthouses would find it hard to accept. But Byrd, like his father before him, had worked closely with the Republicans in Congress, and he felt at home with them philosophically. He knew that the long-term interests of conservatism in the Commonwealth—indeed, in the South and the nation—would be advanced significantly by his joining the GOP. Virginia Republicans could pave the way for Byrd to take that step by embracing his Independent candidacy for re-election, but the senator could not and would not publicly elicit such an embrace.

The problem for Byrd was one of appearances. To offer to run as a Republican, or to appeal for GOP support by declaring how he would align himself on the forthcoming votes to reorganize the Senate, would cast the proud senator in the role of enlistee when what he needed was a draft. "I had made a commitment to the Virginia people on March 17th that I was going to run as an Independent," Byrd recalled later, "and I didn't feel very comfortable on some subsequent date . . . in effect reversing my position."[74] Moreover, Holton and some of his allies had made no secret of their lack of affection for the senator even as they issued the obligatory invitations to him to join the GOP, and Byrd was hardly interested in crashing their party. Finally, there was Byrd's consideration of the feelings of loyal Byrd men throughout Virginia. It would be difficult enough to justify his acceptance of a GOP draft to many of the courthouse Democrats, but Byrd would never be able to explain his going hat-in-hand over to the Republican side. Byrd had met the Republicans halfway—he had taken the bold step of leaving the Democratic Party—and it was up to them to come the rest of the distance.

Into the breach stepped President Nixon and master-strategist Dent. They would not permit Republican pride or Linwood Holton to stand in the way of the historic opportunity they saw to spur a Southern realignment—one

---

[73]Ibid.
[74]Byrd interview.

they felt could be consummated in a transforming presidential election two years hence when Nixon would be standing for re-election. After their meeting with Senator Byrd indicated that the popular Virginian could be moved to join the GOP, the President summoned Governor Holton to the White House for a conference. Nixon, recalled Dent, left no doubt about the importance he attached to opening the door for Byrd to align himself with the Republicans:

The President showed Holton what we were seeking to do and why, and the importance of it. He made it clear that he wanted it done. I don't remember the exact words Holton used, but I know we (Nixon and Dent) left the meeting convinced that Holton was going to cooperate. This was all he had to do—cooperate and not be an obstructionist.[75]

Convinced that Holton would take the steps necessary to preclude nomination of a Republican opponent for Byrd, Dent conveyed the good news to the Virginia senator and, with Nixon, took no further action.

The state GOP convention followed a few weeks later. Dent arrived in Richmond and was "shocked and amazed" by news of Holton's "fire engine" speech and his efforts to promote the nomination of a foe for Byrd.[76] In the convention hall, Byrd banners and posters were in abundance, but a strong tide was running in favor of nominating a Byrd opponent. As Congressman Broyhill dutifully appealed for support for a motion calling for no nomination, he was greeted with a wave of boos and jeers from the emotionally charged delegates. It was an unpleasant and unfamiliar experience for the veteran congressman and GOP leader. He had come to Richmond hoping and expecting that Senator Byrd would make a statement or positive gesture toward the GOP that would make a tacit Byrd endorsement palatable to the delegates. But no such gesture had been forthcoming, and Broyhill found himself forced to stand essentially unarmed before the Republican mob. When the speeches were over, delegates rejected the "no-nomination" motion by a vote of 634.8 to 419.2, and then proceeded to give the party's nod to Garland over Haggerty.

Garland's nomination was a major triumph for Governor Holton, whose leadership had been decisive in thwarting the pro-Byrd effort. By so doing, Holton believed that he had kept the state GOP in a posture in which it could continue to appeal to the more progressive elements of the coalition that had elected him governor in 1969. Though Garland was not well known around the state, Holton knew him to be knowledgeable and articulate, and he was confident that the two-term Roanoke legislator would make a respectable showing. That Garland defeat Byrd in November was not crucial—it was enough that the state Republican Party had discharged its obligation to give voters a choice. Win, lose, or draw, the GOP would have fulfilled its responsibility as part of the emerging two-party system in Virginia.

---

[75]Dent interview.
[76]Ibid.

Many conservative Republicans and Byrd Democrats—including the New Republicans who had brought crucial financial and organizational support to Holton's campaign only a few months earlier—disagreed with the governor's reasoning. In their view, running the little-known Garland against the popular Byrd was the height of folly. Worse, it risked the election of a liberal Democrat by siphoning off moderate and conservative GOP votes from Byrd. More fundamentally, Republican opposition to the man whose name was synonymous with traditional Virginia conservatism revealed a philosophical unsoundness on the part of the governor and his allies that distressed devout conservatives. Already somewhat suspicious of the new chief executive, many of them henceforth would regard Holton with contempt.

What was most unsettling to conservatives was the opportunity it appeared to squander. *The Richmond News Leader* expressed that view shortly after the convention in an editorial entitled, "They Blew It". The Republicans, it stated,

> could have joined hands with the conservatives and formed a practically unbeatable coalition in Virginia politics. But their pride was too much for them. They refused to keep their appointment with the conservatives at the altar. And thereby they invited their own ignominious defeat.[77]

The *News Leader* was quick to point out, however, that Governor Holton and the Republicans were not solely responsible for the abortive union. Senator Byrd, whom the Republicans had courted for months, was by no means left waiting at the altar.

Indeed, Byrd's unwillingness to provide meaningful public encouragement to his GOP suitors had effectively doomed efforts to prevent the nomination of a Republican candidate. Broyhill could not answer critics who charged that he had no assurances, public or private, that Byrd would cooperate with the GOP if endorsed or unopposed by the Republicans. When Broyhill publicly opined during the convention that Byrd would vote with the Republicans to organize the Senate when Congress reconvened, Byrd felt obliged to set the record straight in a telegram that—while thanking Broyhill for his efforts at the convention—made it clear that the senator had made no commitment of any sort. "Had [Byrd] been a little more helpful in his public pronouncements," Broyhill flatly declared later, "we would have endorsed him at that convention, Mr. Holton's approach to the contrary notwithstanding."[78]

Byrd's apparent unwillingness to blaze a trail for others by going all the way into the Republican camp not only disappointed conservative Republicans; it left many restless Byrd Democrats frustrated as well. "You can't build

---

[77]*The Richmond News Leader*, June 29, 1970.
[78]Broyhill interview.

a damn thing as an Independent," observed former Democratic State Senator FitzGerald Bemiss of Richmond. "You're just in limbo and it doesn't do anybody any good at all."[79] Especially among conservative business leaders around the state, there was a widespread feeling that the Republican Party offered the best vehicle for the long-term advancement of their views. Byrd's seeming failure to recognize and encourage recognition of that new reality was a puzzle to them.

Nowhere, however, was the displeasure over the events at the GOP convention more keen than in the Nixon White House, and the anger there was directed entirely at the recalcitrant Governor Holton. Less than a year earlier, candidate Holton had stumped across Virginia invoking the President's name and attesting to the closeness of their relationship. Following a series of forays into the state by prominent national Republicans, President Nixon himself had made a much-publicized pitch for Holton at a Roanoke rally late in the 1969 campaign. Immediately after the election, Holton had been invited to the White House where he received the President's personal congratulations. But, when it came time to aid, or at least acquiesce in, Nixon's realignment strategy, Holton had played the obstructionist. What infuriated the President was his belief that Holton had misled him. "We thought we had Lin set," recalled Harry Dent. "When he was in there with the President he didn't do all this kicking and bucking and jumping, but then he went back down to Richmond and pulled those shenanigans."[80] Holton flatly denied any deceit:

> I never gave them any indication that I would accept an endorsement of Byrd as an Independent or would support the party's refraining from nominating a candidate to oppose him. I am confident that every indication I gave them was that Byrd would have to run for re-election as a Republican or he would face a three-way race.[81]

Later, when Holton could have used a friend in the White House to help fend off a challenge by conservatives to his leadership of the state GOP, Nixon no doubt remembered the 1970 episode. "You just don't do that to a President," said Dent, still marveling two decades later at Holton's maneuver.[82]

While the Holton-led GOP was nominating Garland, Democrats were throwing their support behind flamboyant Fredericksburg liberal George Rawlings, the giant-killer who had unseated veteran Eighth District Congressman Howard Smith in 1966. Rawlings was backed for the Democratic Senate nomination by State Senator Henry Howell, and narrowly bested Fairfax Delegate Clive L. DuVal II and a third candidate in the mid-July primary elec-

---

[79]Bemiss interview.
[80]Dent interview.
[81]Holton interview.
[82]Ibid.

tion.[83] The primary was most noteworthy for its low level of voter participation. Less than 130,000 Virginians cast ballots in the contest (just 29 percent of the number that voted in the 1969 primary), reflecting both the increasing popular focus on general elections and the party's loss of Democratic conservatives to the Independent Byrd.

The attitudes of Republicans about their Senate nominee ranged from wildly enthusiastic to downright distraught. Though a significant segment of the party's rank-and-file preferred Byrd over Garland, virtually all of the GOP leadership in the state backed the party's nominee. The campaign was co-chaired by State Senator James Turk and Delegate Vincent Callahan. In northern Virginia, a joyless Congressman Broyhill lent both his personal support and his Tenth District Republican organization to the Garland effort. Most other conservative Republican leaders, including Richard Obenshain, gave at least nominal support to Garland, and the nominee received enthusiastic GOP backing in the mountain and valley areas. A "Republicans for Byrd" organization formed largely by the Byrd campaign and the New Republicans failed to attract many prominent GOP leaders after the state convention, though it did achieve some success in creating the appearance of Republican disunity.

The two most important Republican leaders, however, were unwilling or unable to provide Garland with the help he needed. Making no secret of his displeasure with the Virginia Republicans' opposition to Byrd, President Nixon favored Byrd with a pair of high-profile meetings—one at the White House and another at a lavish California banquet in honor of the Apollo 11 astronauts—and he pointedly refused to endorse Garland's candidacy. Perhaps even more damaging to the Republican nominee was the unwillingness of the President and Republican National Committee operatives to allow funds from national GOP sources to flow to Garland's campaign. With the conservative Virginia business and financial establishment not backing him, Garland could not hope to finance a serious statewide campaign without out-of-state Republican support. The predicament was a familiar one to older Republicans: Byrd, like his father, was receiving help from Republicans at the national level without giving anything in return to the Virginia GOP.

Governor Holton was willing but largely unable to assist Garland because of the school busing controversy, which became the dominant political issue in much of the state in the summer of 1970. Holton's highly publicized gesture of acceptance of the federal busing edict for Richmond came only weeks after the state GOP convention, and from then on the Republican governor and his hand-picked Senate candidate were inextricably linked in the public mind to

---

[83]The vote totals in the primary were: Rawlings – 58,874 (45.7%); DuVal – 58,174 (45.1%); Milton Colvin – 11,911 (9.2%). Sabato, *Virginia Votes 1969–1974*, p. 157. Though DuVal was legally entitled to a run-off because Rawlings's plurality margin was less than one percent of the total primary vote, he waived his right and endorsed Rawlings.

the unpopular racial mixing policy. Garland tried in vain to cut his losses in the Third District's normally Republican suburbs by voicing his opposition to busing, but his comments had little effect other than to hamper his efforts to garner black support. In the end, Governor Holton's personal popularity among blacks proved non-transferable to Garland. Democrat George Rawlings already had cultivated strong support in the black community, where his liberal views were favored and his 1966 ouster of conservative stalwart Howard Smith was still appreciated.

Holton and Garland had hoped to isolate Rawlings on the extreme left and to make the contest a two-man fight between the conservative Independent and the moderate Republican. But it was soon apparent that they had overestimated the size of the Republican base vote in the state, underestimated Rawlings's support among moderate and liberal state Democrats, and grossly undervalued Senator Byrd's personal appeal among conservative voters of both parties. Garland spoke frequently during the campaign about the dangers of "extremism from the right and left,"[84] but many Republicans obviously perceived the far greater threat to be from the left. Much of Garland's GOP support disappeared late in the campaign as fears mounted that he would split the conservative vote with Byrd and elect Rawlings by a plurality. "We must not risk the election of an irresponsible, far-out ultra-liberal," Byrd warned in a highly effective election-eve statement. "The only way such a person can be elected in Virginia is by the Republican candidate pulling votes from me."[85]

On election day, Virginians went to the polls in record numbers and vindicated the senator's daring strategy. Just seven months earlier, *Time* magazine had reflected the consensus among pundits when it reported, "Young Harry is out of step [with Virginia . . . . His] chances are poor, and Byrd may well finish third in a three-way race."[86] But when the votes were tallied, Byrd had scored a stunning victory. He received 54 percent of the statewide vote, won handsome majorities in both the suburbs and the central cities, and carried all but 11 counties and three cities.[87] Rawlings finished second with 31 percent of the ballots, and Garland—in the worst GOP showing in a major statewide election since the inception of the Byrd organization—garnered a dismal 15 percent of the vote. Rawlings's second-place finish was secured with the support of more than 90 percent of black voters, but he failed to duplicate the performance of his populist friend and ally, Henry Howell, among low-income whites who had preferred Independent George Wallace in the 1968 presidential election.

---

[84]*Richmond Times-Dispatch*, August 20, 1970.

[85]*The Richmond News Leader*, November 2, 1970.

[86]*Time*, March 30, 1970.

[87]The vote totals were: Byrd (I) – 506,633 (53.5%); Rawlings (D) – 295,057 (31.2%); Garland (R) – 145,031 (15.3%). Sabato, *Virginia Votes 1969–1974*, pp. 159–161.

University of Virginia political analyst Larry Sabato found that Senator Byrd garnered more than 60 percent of the vote in sample Wallace precincts.[88]

There was, however, some much-needed good news for the GOP in the House of Representatives election returns. All five Republican incumbents were re-elected by sizable margins, and a sixth, State Senator J. Kenneth Robinson of Frederick County, scored an easy victory in the race to succeed retiring Seventh District Democrat John O. Marsh, Jr. Robinson had lost to Marsh in 1962 by less than 600 votes, but he rolled up almost 62 percent of the vote in the 1970 contest against little-known Democrat Murat Williams. His election gave the GOP its first majority of the state's House of Representatives delegation in modern times.

Republican congressional candidates in 1970, as in the two preceding campaigns, received more votes in the contested races than did their Democratic opponents.[89] Incumbents everywhere coasted to re-election, and the four conservative Democratic incumbents posted especially large victories. In the Third District, conservative incumbent David Satterfield rolled up 76 percent of the vote in turning back a spirited challenge by Holton protege J. Harvie Wilkinson III. The 25-year-old Wilkinson, then a University of Virginia law student, was something of a celebrity because of his recently published book about Harry Byrd, Sr., and his organization,[90] but his youth and inexperience were easy targets for the popular Satterfield. The incumbent's massive margin was, however, chiefly a product of the Republican candidate's unhelpful links to Holton and Garland at the height of the busing furor. GOP challengers also were trounced by incumbents Watkins M. Abbitt and W. C. "Dan" Daniel in the Southside Fourth and Fifth Districts, respectively, and no Republican opposed First District incumbent Thomas N. Downing. Until the conservative incumbents were to step aside voluntarily, there would be no GOP victories in the four congressional districts still held by Democrats.

Almost unnoticed amidst all the attention given the Byrd landslide and the Republican congressional gains was the passage of Virginia's revised constitution in a popular referendum. The constitutional changes had been fashioned during the Godwin administration, and their approval by the electorate in the fall of 1970 was little more than a formality. Still, it represented a historic landmark. Virginia officially turned away from "pay-as-you-go" financing, and the last vestiges of the electoral restrictions adopted in 1902 were eliminated. Thus, two central tenets of the old Byrd organization were abandoned, without fanfare or a fight, even as the heir to the Byrd legacy was

---

[88]Ibid., pp. 28–32.

[89]GOP candidates received a 49.7-percent plurality of the vote in the party-contested races, while the Democratic contenders managed a 51.4-percent majority of the total congressional election vote. Sabato, *Virginia Votes 1969–1974*, p. 27.

[90]Wilkinson's *Harry Byrd and the Changing Face of Virginia Politics, 1945–1966* was published in 1968.

scoring yet another impressive victory for the conservative cause. As had been the case since mid-century, Virginia politics remained a peculiar blend of constancy and change.

Chapter 21
The Reynolds Tragedy

"Virginia has lost more than she presently realizes. . . .
[J. Sargeant Reynolds] held out hope for people who had not yet
begun to participate in the affairs of the state, and he served as a
unifying element for young and old, black and white, rich and
poor."[91]

State Senator L. Douglas Wilder, 1970

Though analysts make much of political trends and tides, the course of history
is often transformed in incomprehensible ways by a sudden and unexpected
event. Twice during the 1970s, tragedy was to befall youthful political stars in
Virginia at the very moment when their aspirations seemed certain to be
crowned with success. In 1978, Republicans lost their party leader, Richard
Obenshain, in an airplane crash as he campaigned for the United States
Senate. But in 1971, it was Democratic Lieutenant Governor J. Sargeant
Reynolds—the man almost universally regarded as destined to win election as
governor two years later—who died tragically, the victim of an inoperable
brain tumor. Only 34, Reynolds seemed to have it all—intellect, charisma,
youthful energy, good looks, wealth, and broad political support. As he moved
swiftly up the ladder from delegate to state senator to lieutenant governor, his
gifts were apparent. His death on June 13 deeply saddened Virginians, who
had shared the young lieutenant governor's ordeal as he struggled coura-
geously with his illness for months.[92]

The loss of Reynolds, "the only foreseeable catalyst for the state's
strife-torn Democratic Party,"[93] altered the course of Virginia politics in ways
that will long be a subject of speculation. Its immediate effects were to necessitate a special election for lieutenant governor in November 1971 and to
breathe new life into the gubernatorial ambitions of State Senator Henry
Howell. The death of the attractive and reassuring Reynolds, and the resultant
ascension of the liberal and polarizing Howell, was to have a profound impact

---

[91]Donald P. Baker, *Wilder: Hold Fast to Dreams* (Cabin John, Maryland: Seven Locks Press,
1989), p. 78. Following Reynolds's election as lieutenant governor in 1969, Wilder had won a
special election to succeed him as one of Richmond's two representatives in the State Senate.

[92]See Cooper and Morris, p. 83; Wilkinson, "Linwood Holton," pp. 401–402.

[93]Peirce, p. 61.

on the state's partisan realignment and the emergence of two-party competition. Virginia Democrats were about to enter the political wilderness, where they would wander for a decade.

Reynolds's death in June meant that the special election campaign to choose his successor would be a short one. Governor Holton wasted little time in indicating his desire to see George P. Shafran, a freshman member of the House of Delegates from Arlington, become the GOP nominee for the post. Though Delegate John N. Dalton of Radford had more experience, a better-known political name, and a serious interest in running, Shafran's assets included a northern Virginia base, a reputation as a highly successful real estate executive, and considerable personal wealth. In his first two legislative sessions, Shafran had proven to be a quick study and an effective ally in promoting Holton's legislative agenda. Holton saw advantages to having a fresh face in the field for the fall; the northern Virginia legislator might be able to bridge the growing divide between the "mountain and valley boys" and the conservatives to the east; and, most important, he could fund his own campaign. With the governor's wishes clear, Dalton agreed to head Shafran's campaign, and it briefly appeared that Holton's early signal might produce an uncontested nomination.

Holton was wrong, as he later would acknowledge, on almost every count. Richard Obenshain and many who a year earlier had fought the nomination of a Republican foe for Senator Harry Byrd, Jr., rallied quickly behind another Arlingtonian, Delegate George Mason Green, Jr. Green, like Obenshain, was a conservative true-believer, a former chairman of the state's Young Republican federation, and an advocate of building the GOP by recruiting disaffected Democratic conservatives. Though a number of conservative Republicans urged Obenshain to enter the race himself, he chose instead to serve as chairman of the campaign of his friend and ally, Green. His leadership role on Green's behalf represented Obenshain's first public split with Governor Holton, and it signalled more than just a challenge over the nomination for lieutenant governor. Green, declared Obenshain, was a man of strong principle who would appeal to the large bloc of non-aligned Virginia voters who backed Byrd in the preceding election—"the people," Obenshain noted, "who have left the Democratic Party because of its steady progress toward radicalism and are now waiting in political limbo."[94] Attracting those conservative Democrats to the GOP—in spite of Holton, if necessary—was Obenshain's foremost goal.

With Obenshain leading the effort, the Green candidacy occasioned the formation of a statewide network of GOP conservatives who were determined to give the party a new, conservative image. They met regularly to plan strategy and coordinate activities during the Green campaign, and the next year they would mount a direct assault on Holton's control of the party machinery. But at the 1971 GOP convention, Holton demonstrated that he was still in charge.

---

[94]Text of Obenshain statement on file at the Republican Party of Virginia Archives.

Shafran emerged the narrow victor, his success assured through heavy lobbying by the governor and his lieutenants. But the tactics employed by the chief executive, including the thinly veiled threat that he might not provide fundraising help if the nominee were not to his liking, generated bitterness that deepened the party's factional rift.[95]

The GOP battle behind, Holton and his hand-picked nominee figured to prevail in the fall against a divided Democratic Party. Another three-way race loomed, with State Senator Henry Howell, the liberal Democratic leader, now vying as an Independent, and Delegate George J. Kostel, a moderate from Clifton Forge, carrying the Democratic standard. Howell opted for an independent bid after the Democratic central committee voted to choose its nominee by convention rather than primary for the first time in 25 years. Though the bruising 1969 primary battles and the low turnout in the 1970 senatorial primary were reasons enough to abandon the traditional Democratic nominating method, Howell correctly construed his party's decision as an effort to derail his candidacy. An unannounced but unabashed candidate for governor in 1973, Howell saw the lieutenant governorship as an opportunity to gain statewide credibility and legitimacy in preparation for his run for the top spot. As an Independent, he would accomplish an end-run around the conservatives and moderates who still dominated Democratic Party councils, and appeal to Virginia's increasingly independent-minded electorate as a free agent.

While Howell's exit was a source of relief for many Democratic leaders, most were sobered by the realization that the flamboyant populist would be a formidable contender in the fall. Efforts to unite the party behind veteran State Senator Edward L. Breeden of Norfolk, who had no aspirations for the governorship, met with initial success. But Democratic moderates and liberals caucused and pronounced Breeden and Hampton State Senator Hunter B. Andrews, another potential candidate, unacceptable. The contest then splintered, as four delegates (D. French Slaughter, Jr., of Culpeper, George N. McMath of Accomac, Carrington Williams of Fairfax, and Kostel) and one state senator (Robert C. Fitzgerald of Fairfax) announced their candidacies for the nomination. Kostel, 43, who was favored by many moderate supporters of the late Sargeant Reynolds, entered the race only eight days before the August convention and portrayed himself as the "unity" candidate. He prevailed over the more liberal Delegate Williams on the fourth ballot, when backers of McMath, Slaughter, and Fitzgerald switched to him as a compromise choice.[96]

With moderate candidates having emerged the victors over conservative challengers in both major parties, the stage was set for liberal Henry Howell's first—and only—statewide victory. He polled 40 percent of the vote, defeating

---

[95]Edd Shull interview, May 27, 1980.

[96]Sabato, *Virginia Votes 1969–1974*, pp. 39–42. Fitzgerald, who had the support of Governor Godwin, finished a distant third. The bulk of his supporters switched to Kostel after the third ballot.

Kostel by nearly 30,000 ballots and Shafran by more than 150,000. Kostel, with 37 percent of the tally, made a strong second-place finish, while Shafran captured the remaining 23 percent.[97] The GOP nominee carried only 12 counties and two cities (mostly in traditional Republican strongholds), and he received a plurality in just one congressional district—the northern Virginia Tenth. In the Third District, where Republicans had been gaining steadily and Holton had won every precinct in 1969, Shafran failed to carry even one precinct.

The GOP campaign suffered from myriad maladies—among them poor organization, an inexperienced candidate, internal division, a shortage of funds, and perhaps most significant, the lack of a coherent message. Though Shafran had sponsored anti-busing legislation in the General Assembly, the perception of him as "Holton's candidate" frustrated attempts to use the busing controversy to rally conservatives to his side. Kostel emphasized his own opposition to busing, and, with very visible support from former Governor Mills Godwin and Senator Harry Byrd, Jr., the Democratic nominee seemed the more credible conservative. Kostel hammered home the message that he was the only viable alternative to Howell, and, though Shafran's tally dwindled as a result, the Republican still garnered enough anti-Howell votes at Kostel's expense to allow the Independent to win the election.

"I wished many times that I had just stayed out of that damned thing," Holton later said of the contest for the GOP nomination for lieutenant governor in 1971. "I encouraged my supporters to support George Shafran, and they did. And without that he never would have been nominated . . . . But, boy, I made a big mistake in gauging his capabilities as a candidate."[98] From Holton's perspective, Shafran almost single-handedly had turned opportunity into disaster. "He (Shafran) couldn't remember from today until tomorrow what he ought to do or what position he ought to take . . .," recalled Holton. "His performance . . . (was) absurd."[99] For his part, Shafran did not dispute complaints that he performed as a political novice; his lack of campaign experience, he correctly noted, was known to all at the time he was nominated. But Shafran also cited the inactivity of GOP conservatives and "the label of Linwood Holton" as reasons for his poor showing. "I always considered myself a conservative," explained Shafran, "but I was labeled a Holton moderate against my wishes, and I could never get out of it."[100]

Shafran's defeat triggered an avalanche of criticism directed at Governor Holton. The conservative *Richmond News Leader*, which endorsed Holton in 1969, was merciless in its denunciation:

---

[97]The vote totals were: Howell (I) – 362,371 (40.0%); Kostel (D) – 334,580 (36.9%); Shafran (R) – 209,861 (23.1%). Ibid., p. 44.

[98]Holton interview.

[99]Ibid.

[100]George P. Shafran interview, May 27, 1980.

The steepness and swiftness of the Republican nose dive cannot be overstated. Here you have an organization purporting to be one of Virginia's two major political parties, and the best that it can average in two consecutive Statewide elections is a measly 19.5 percent of the vote. . . . If he were to run for office today, it is doubtful that Mr. Holton could be elected State dogcatcher.

The conservatives of this State elected Mr. Holton, and since his ascendancy to the Mansion he has thrown them nary the smallest chicken bone. Indeed, he has done practically everything he could do to disdain them and defeat their candidates. He has forced them away from the Republican party—the party in which conservatives properly belong. And in the process the Republican party has become a sick joke. . . . Mr. Holton really has done a job on the Republican.party.[101]

Not even Holton's usual GOP allies could resist complaint. "I had been led to believe by pre-convention super salesmanship that the Shafran Campaign would be thoroughly professional and well-organized," wrote Sixth District GOP Chairman William B. Poff to State Chairman Warren French, "but after the campaign [started,] I began hearing stories about an amateur organization and a lamentable lack of finances."[102] Organizationally, financially, strategically, and emotionally, the Virginia GOP was flat on its back. Nearly everyone blamed Linwood Holton.

"[R]etrospect gives you a whole lot better view than looking ahead," remarked former Governor Holton ruefully in 1984 as he prefaced his admission of error in promoting Shafran as the party's candidate.[103] But a retrospective view exonerates Holton from responsibility for the fact, if not the magnitude, of his party's 1971 defeat. With two credible moderate-conservative candidates in the race, a victory for the liberal Howell was virtually assured from the beginning, regardless of whom the major parties nominated. Indeed, the choice of Republican conservatives, Mason Green, later concluded that he, too, likely would have lost if nominated.[104] Only the absence of a GOP nominee could have thwarted Howell's bid, and no one in the Republican camp was seriously recommending that in 1971. The hapless Shafran was the next best thing, however. By sending him into the fray at Holton's behest, the Republicans did a minimum of damage to Kostel's cause and probably maximized the chances of denying Howell the lieutenant governorship. Understandably, no one was advancing that argument in Holton's defense.

By expending most of his remaining political capital to dictate the GOP nominee for lieutenant governor in 1971, Governor Holton did his conservative Republican foes a colossal favor. He took an impossible situation—a

[101]*The Richmond News Leader*, November 4, 1971.
[102]Letter on file at the Republican Party of Virginia Archives.
[103]Holton interview.
[104]George Mason Green, Jr., interview, May 28, 1980.

three-way race involving Henry Howell—and made it appear to be another major setback for his centrist approach to Republican party-building. In the process, he solidified the impression that he was unalterably hostile to GOP conservatives' appeal for support from disaffected Byrd Democrats, engendered new bitterness in conservative ranks through his forceful tactics, and prompted his critics to coalesce into a well-organized and highly motivated opposition. The historical and geographical divisions in the Virginia GOP had taken on a more philosophical cast during Holton's stewardship, and the "mountain and valley boys" who loyally followed the governor's lead now found themselves isolated from the determined conservatives in northern Virginia, the Richmond area, and the Southside. After the 1971 repeat of the 1970 debacle, even Holton's admirers in traditionally Republican areas were reluctantly conceding that the GOP needed a new approach.

While Republicans and Democrats alike were thrashing about in disarray in the aftermath of the 1971 contest, Lieutenant Governor-elect Henry Howell was confidently eyeing a second bid for the governorship in 1973. Taking a cue from Senator Byrd, he had extricated himself from the faction-ridden Democratic Party and appealed to a Virginia electorate that was finding party affiliations increasingly confusing and almost meaningless. By the early 1970s, many Virginia voters had been alternating between support for Republican and Democratic nominees with regularity, and a 1971 poll revealed that less than 60 percent of Virginians identified with either major political party.[105] With both parties uncertain of their direction and divided from within, Howell would have a good chance of repeating his plurality victory two years later. As lieutenant governor, he would acquire enhanced stature and would have an opportunity to cultivate a less strident image than that which had catapulted him to prominence in the '60s.

Interestingly, Howell shared more than partisan independence with Senator Byrd. Though the Norfolk Democrat's liberal, pro-black, and pro-labor views were anathema to Byrd and other conservative Democrats, many Byrd supporters showed up in the Howell column in the 1971 election. In his analysis of the special election returns, University of Virginia political scientist Larry Sabato found that Howell in 1971 improved upon his performance in rural Virginia relative to his 1969 Democratic primary showing, and much of the improvement was among voters who preferred George Wallace for President in 1968 and Harry Byrd for the Senate in 1970. Sabato's analysis in 1971 revealed that Howell polled better than 57 percent of the vote in selected precincts carried by Wallace.[106] With his opposition to the sales tax on food and nonprescription drugs and his emphasis of consumer issues, Howell's populist appeal transcended the usual political alignments. Many voters who found big government menacing and backed conservatives like Byrd

---

[105]Peirce, p. 64.
[106]Sabato, *Virginia Votes 1969–1974*, pp. 49, 56.

responded favorably to Howell's rhetorical assaults on big business. The Norfolk Democrat cast himself as a champion of the powerless. And, without racial tensions or national issues to polarize the electorate, many blue-collar whites were receptive to Howell's appeal along economic class lines.

The addition of a bloc of normally conservative white voters to Howell's constituency of blacks, labor, and national Democrats made the populist liberal an unusually formidable figure in Virginia politics. And, in 1971, it seemed that the rest of political Virginia was playing into Howell's hands. On the Democratic side, the defeat of moderate William Battle in 1969 and the unexpected death of Lieutenant Governor Reynolds in 1971 left a leadership vacuum that guaranteed continued infighting. On the Republican side, the moderate chief executive was busy dealing with a growing conservative clamor in his own party. While both parties in the state searched for philosophical definition, the Commonwealth's preeminent political leader, Senator Harry Byrd, Jr., had made the Independent label palatable, even appealing, just in time for Howell to borrow it. To many moderate and conservative Virginians, the prospect of a Howell administration was unthinkable. But, unless the political landscape in the Old Dominion changed quickly and drastically, Henry Howell could be the next governor.

The years 1968–1971 were the Virginia Republican Party's bittersweet Holton years. Presidential Republicanism returned in 1968 with Nixon's win in the state, and the GOP's long postwar march toward respectability and competitiveness culminated in Holton's impressive gubernatorial victory in 1969. But the new Republican governor had badly misjudged the political breezes that were blowing across the Commonwealth. Though his campaign and his administration trumpeted change, Holton seemed unalterably wedded to the Republican politics of the past. His vision of the GOP as a progressive alternative to Byrd-style conservatism ignored the reality of post-Byrd Virginia: liberal pressures were buffeting the state Democratic Party, and Virginians in growing numbers were searching for a viable vehicle for the advancement of their largely conservative views. Holton prevented the GOP from capitalizing on that opportunity, and humiliating Republican defeats in 1970 and 1971 were the results. Two years after the 1969 GOP breakthrough, most Republicans believed that it was—to borrow the governor's winning slogan—time for a change.

Virginia in 1971 was poised for a major political realignment. During the Holton years, the Commonwealth had "wander[ed] between two worlds, one dying, the other powerless to be born."[107] In Virginia, as in much of the South, the period of conservative Democratic hegemony had passed, but a stable new political system had not yet emerged. The consecutive independent candidacies by the conservative Byrd and the liberal Howell were indicative of a

---

[107]Peirce, p. 68. The description was borrowed from the nineteenth-century English poet and literary critic, Matthew Arnold.

political system in transition, as were the ideological cleavages within the Virginia parties. By 1971, forces were mobilizing to bring both state parties into philosophical congruence with their national counterparts, and those forces soon would assert themselves with sudden and surprising effectiveness. For Democratic and Republican conservatives, the resuscitated gubernatorial ambitions of Henry Howell would supply a powerful impetus and a heightened sense of urgency to the process of realignment.

Part Five

Obenshain, Godwin, and the Rapid Realignment

1972 - 1975

Chapter 22
The Realignment That Might Have Been

"There were two main impediments to Nixon's Southern [realignment] strategy—Watergate and a fellow named Linwood Holton."[1]

Harry S. Dent, Special Counsel to President Richard Nixon

If ever there was a man with a mission, he was Richard Dudley Obenshain. A native of southwest Virginia, Obenshain was a Republican by inheritance. But the fire that burned inside him—the passion that stirred him to action and guided his uncommon and unrelenting efforts—was philosophical more than partisan. Through him and his leadership, Republicans and conservative Democrats would find common ground and join forces to dominate Virginia politics during the 1970s.

The well-read Obenshain was a student of philosophy, theology, economics, and history, and for him the sole object of political endeavor could be summarized in a word, *Freedom*. In a brief essay so titled he made his purpose plain: "The most important goal in my life is to have some significant impact in preserving and expanding the realm of personal freedom in the life of this country."[2] The philosophy of freedom, he explained, was a "radical and dynamic idea to turn loose creative capacities." Personal liberty and moral rectitude, the ethic of individual initiative, free markets, limited constitutional government, states' rights, the principle of equality under law, the international struggle for democratic principles and capitalism—all flowed from the same powerful idea. For Obenshain, the American experiment in freedom was real; a dangerous twentieth-century trend toward "socialism and state-directed activity" had placed it in jeopardy; and Virginians had a unique responsibility to come to its defense.[3]

The impassioned conservative had a gift for conveying his convictions. Obenshain was friendly, good-humored, youthful in spirit, a bit shy. He often found small talk uncomfortable and tedious. But on the subjects he cared about he could inspire. "When Dick spoke you got the feeling that this was not

---

[1]Dent interview.
[2]*Richmond Times-Dispatch*, December 26, 1976.
[3]Ibid.

just some abstract philosophical debate, liberals versus conservatives," recalled Edward S. DeBolt, a political consultant who worked with him on several campaigns. "He was convinced that this was a titanic struggle, good against evil, and we had to start fighting now before it was too late."[4] To Lawrence Lewis, the influential leader of the New Republicans, Obenshain exhibited a missionary's zeal. "He spoke my language as a conservative," said Lewis. "He had charisma, conviction—real fire in his soul about what he was doing. . . . And he could get that across to people."[5]

Obenshain the philosopher and orator had another attribute that would prove crucial to the Virginia GOP in the 1970s: He was an insightful political strategist. Before most Republicans and Byrd Democrats began to think about it seriously, he discerned the potential for a new majority coalition in Virginia. The keys to advancing his conservative principles and revitalizing the state Republican Party, Obenshain knew, were one and the same: a realignment of the political parties. He had been busy spreading that message since he led the state Young Republicans in the early '60s. "The proper question for young Virginians," he had written in March 1963,

is simply, "How best can the victory of conservative principles be assured?" The only realistic answer is for American conservatives to unite in the Republican party, the only national party which can be returned to the basic tenets of constitutional government and individual freedom. . . .[6]

Democratic conservatives would be welcomed warmly into the GOP, Obenshain predicted: "[I]f anything, we [Republicans] accord higher honor to those who have the courage to break with the Democratic label and thus lead the transformation to a Republic South."[7]

Nearly a decade later, significant numbers of Virginia Democrats finally were beginning to leave the house of their fathers. But, to Obenshain's immense chagrin, the Holton GOP had rolled up the welcome map. A historic opportunity to promote conservative solidarity and Republican growth was being missed. Determined to help forge a new conservative purpose and image for the GOP, Obenshain initially planned to seek the seat of incumbent Senator William B. Spong, Jr., in 1972, but associates persuaded him to run for the party chairmanship instead. It was a decision with far-reaching ramifications. Within little more than a year's time, Obenshain and his conservative allies had wrested control of the GOP from the sitting Republican governor, thrown open the party's doors to disaffected Byrd Democrats, elected the state's first Republican U. S. senator in this century, seized seven of the state's ten seats in the House of Representatives, and persuaded former Governor Mills Godwin to switch parties and oppose Henry Howell for the governorship

---

[4]*The Washington Times*, August 2, 1983.
[5]Lawrence Lewis, Jr., interview, November 2, 1988.
[6]*The Richmond News Leader*, March 10, 1963.
[7]Ibid.

in 1973 as a Republican. Obenshain was not alone responsible for any of those achievements, but plainly he was indispensable in each of them.

The years 1972 and 1973 proved to be pivotal ones in the emergence of the Republican Party as a consistently competitive force in Virginia politics. Dramatic changes in both political parties during that time began to surmount partisan affiliations based on tradition and disposition, and the resultant realignment yielded immense benefits to the Virginia GOP. The presidential candidacy of the ultra-liberal George McGovern in 1972, the success of liberal activists in winning control of the state Democratic Party machinery that year, and the polarizing gubernatorial bid by Henry Howell the next year combined to trigger a mass exodus of Democratic conservatives from their traditional party home. The Obenshain-led Republican Party invited them in, and many came. With the help of factional division in the Democratic camp, the GOP scored a surprising victory over incumbent Senator Spong in 1972. And the following year, Mills Godwin, the durable Byrd Democrat, and John Dalton, the energetic mountain-valley Republican, ran successfully as the GOP team for the two top state posts. A dominant new force in Virginia politics—a Republican/Byrd Democrat coalition—emerged.

The GOP gains were huge, and they came in rapid succession. But, ultimately, the Republican progress of 1972 and 1973 has to be evaluated, not in terms of what was, but in comparison to what might have been. As the decade wore on, realignment in Virginia would mean a new receptiveness on the part of the Commonwealth's traditionally Democratic electorate to Republican candidates for statewide office. It would mean Republican identification with many of the state's venerated conservative symbols. And it would mean a gradual rise in the percentage of Virginia voters who considered themselves Republicans. But, with the notable exception of Mills Godwin and a handful of others, realignment would not mean a transfer of partisan allegiance by state and local Democratic officeholders. The failure to win significant converts in the courthouses and in the General Assembly would have profound long-term implications for the state GOP.

When they tried to recruit Senator Harry F. Byrd, Jr., in 1970, President Nixon, Congressman Broyhill, and other conservative Republicans had high hopes that a Byrd alignment with the GOP would trigger a massive switch-over to the Republican Party by prominent Democratic conservatives at the state and local levels. But that was not to be. Rather, there would emerge during the 1970s an amorphous body of conservative former Democratic officeholders, business leaders, and Byrd organization loyalists who would come to be known, appropriately enough, as the "Coalition." They would straddle the parties, giving valuable support to conservative Republican candidates during the '70s, but reserving—and ultimately exercising—the right to return to the Democratic fold if and when that party nominated candidates to their liking.

Though the emergence of the Coalition and the remarkable string of Virginia Republican successes in the '70s was not duplicated in other Southern states, the Virginia experience nevertheless fit the basic pattern of Southern realignment. As Professors Earl and Merle Black noted in their seminal 1987 study of Southern politics,[8] there has been a region-wide trend toward greater identification with the Republican Party—from 76 percent Democratic and 10 percent Republican in 1952, to 40 percent Democratic and 25 percent Republican in 1984. While this transfer of loyalties has been significant, it is noteworthy that more conservative Southern Democrats have moved to an independent position than actually have adopted the Republican label. The second largest bloc—35 percent of all Southern voters—described themselves as independent in 1984, compared to just 14 percent who identified with neither party in 1952. The pattern of rather rapid Democratic dealignment followed by a more gradual realignment of conservative voters with the Republican Party has been experienced in every Southern state, including the Old Dominion. The observations of the Professors Black regarding Southern politics in the mid-1980s were applicable to Virginia beginning in the 1970s:

There is no majority party in the modern South. . . . Outcomes of most statewide elections now hinge upon whether Democratic or Republican candidates can attract sufficient numbers of independents to form winning coalitions. . . . [GOP candidates] have learned to compete (and sometimes win) by assembling coalitions of Republicans, independents, and disaffected Democrats.

. . . The old Democratic majority has collapsed, but it has yet to be replaced by a Republican party that has attracted a new majority or even a new plurality of the electorate. . . . As of the mid-1980s, the southern party system remains fundamentally dealigned, though the process of partisan realignment is moving forward.[9]

Could the more swift and sweeping realignment contemplated by President Nixon for Virginia and the rest of the South in the early '70s have come to pass? The answer is, quite possibly. The realignment of the Southern parties—the trend toward philosophical alignment with their national counterparts—was a current that ran through American politics from the New Deal of Franklin Roosevelt to the conservative administration of Ronald Reagan. But the South was poised uniquely for dramatic change in the early '70s. The presidential campaigns of General Eisenhower, and, in the Deep South the conservative crusade of Barry Goldwater, had given realignment a major boost by rehabilitating Republicanism in the eyes of many Southern voters. Lyndon Johnson's Great Society and the civil rights and antiwar movements of the late '60s supplied another powerful push by discrediting the national Democrats in the eyes of those same Southern voters. The stage thus

---

[8]Earl Black and Merle Black, *Politics and Society in the South* (Cambridge, Mass.: Harvard University Press, 1987).
[9]Ibid., pp. 233–237.

was set for Nixon—who appealed primarily to the South's patriotism and anti-communism—to transform Southern politics. What went wrong? "There were two main impediments to Nixon's Southern [realignment] strategy," answered Nixon aide Harry Dent in 1988, "—Watergate and a fellow named Linwood Holton."[10] Watergate's devastating impact on Republican fortunes regionally and nationally is well known, but Nixon's 1970 "Byrd strategy" and Holton's role in derailing it have not been previously disclosed. The failure of the Holton-led Virginia Republicans to cooperate with Nixon's plan for a gradual Byrd move into the GOP denied the President the breakthrough he thought would precipitate a cascade of Southern Democratic switch-overs in connection with the 1972 presidential election. After that election, the unfolding Watergate scandal neutralized Nixon, the most potent agent for political change in the South, and tarnished the Republican label in the process.

It is impossible, of course, to assess reliably the impact that a Byrd switch would have had throughout the South in the early '70s. But the Southern strategists in the Nixon White House were not alone in sensing a historic opportunity. South Carolina Senator Strom Thurmond, who switched to the GOP in 1964, encouraged White House efforts to recruit his Virginia colleague and advised the junior Byrd to make the move. "If Byrd had switched, with the good reputation the name 'Byrd' had and deserved," Thurmond commented,

it would have had a tremendous impact [in the South]. Robert E. Lee was always so popular, and he was from Virginia. The people of the South have always looked to Virginia for leadership to a great extent. And if Virginia had [gone Republican] that would have helped [realignment] a great deal.[11]

That view was echoed by Senator Byrd, Jr.'s close friend and Senate ally, North Carolina's Jesse Helms. A switch by the prominent Virginian, Helms noted, would have had significant political repercussions throughout the region at a critical time.[12] It would have given other Southern Democrats in the Congress "the courage to [switch parties]," explained former Senator Carl Curtis of Nebraska, "[and] it would have also put the fear into them" by making it harder for them to justify their continuing Democratic affiliation to conservative constituents.[13] With Watergate, however, the chance for a rapid transfer of partisan loyalties in the South quickly disappeared.

Whatever may have been the effect of the 1970 Byrd misfire and the Watergate scandal in the other Southern states, the GOP opportunities forfeited in Virginia were tremendous. Watergate came at a most inauspicious time. During 1972, conservative businessman and Byrd confidant Richard

---

[10]Dent interview.

[11]J. Strom Thurmond interview, January 31, 1989.

[12]Jesse Helms interview, January 31, 1989.

[13]Carl Curtis interview, February 10, 1989.

Short of Virginia Beach worked assiduously with White House aide Dent to pave the way for prominent Virginia Democrats to back Nixon's re-election bid and move into the GOP. Conservative business leaders from Virginia were invited to the White House for a series of meetings in early 1972. In July, Mills Godwin, Richard Obenshain, and two dozen state legislators—all conservative Democrats—met with the President in the Oval Office to discuss Virginia's political future. Before the series of most damaging Watergate revelations began to filter out, hopes were high for a move into the GOP by several of the state's conservative Democratic congressmen and enough Democratic state legislators to shift control of at least one house of the General Assembly.

The guest roster for the private White House huddle read like a "Who's Who" of conservative Virginia Democrats. Among those in attendance were a number of prominent Democratic lawmakers who would go on to play major roles in Virginia politics in the '70s and '80s, some as Republican converts and others as Democratic loyalists. In addition to Godwin, who switched to the GOP in 1973, the group included Delegate D. French Slaughter, Jr. (later a Republican congressman from the Seventh District), State Senator Herbert H. Bateman (later a GOP congressman from the First District), Delegate George N. McMath (later chairman of the state Republican Party), J. Smith Ferebee (later finance chairman of the Virginia GOP), and former Seventh District Congressman John O. Marsh, Jr. (later Counsellor to President Ford and Secretary of the Army under President Reagan). Among those who met with Nixon but thereafter remained in the Democratic camp were Delegates Edward E. Lane (Democratic nominee for attorney general in 1977) and Richard M. Bagley (Secretary of Economic Development during the administration of Governor Gerald L. Baliles and briefly a candidate for governor in 1985), and State Senate kingpins Edward E. Willey of Richmond, William F. Parkerson of Henrico, and Frederick T. Gray of Chesterfield.[14] A central figure in the White House meeting was Delegate W. Roy Smith, then-chairman of the powerful House of Delegates Appropriations Committee, and later a leader in the gubernatorial campaigns of Republican Governors Godwin (1973) and Dalton (1977), Democratic Governor Robb (1981), and unsuccessful GOP gubernatorial candidates Wyatt B. Durrette, Jr. (1985) and J. Marshall Coleman (1989). Though most of the Democrats were actively considering an eventual party switch when they came to the Nixon meeting, the Watergate disclosures shortly thereafter caused all but a few to abandon the notion. As a Republican candidate for governor a year later, Mills Godwin received the overwhelming support of Byrd Democrats, but only a few

---

[14]Also present for the White House meeting were State Senators Paul W. Manns and Leslie D. Campbell, Jr.; former State Senator FitzGerald Bemiss; Delegates Walther B. Fidler, William M. Dudley, Calvin W. Fowler, Robert B. Ball, Sr., Lacey E. Putney, B. R. Middleton, Russell M. Carneal, and Charles W. Gunn, Jr.; former Delegates R. Maclin Smith and Thomas R. Glass; J.D. Stetson Coleman, James F. Olmsted, Richard T. Short, and Harry Dent.

Democratic officeholders followed his lead and adopted the increasingly unappealing Republican label.

While Watergate caused many leading Virginia Democrats to reassess their willingness to move toward formal alignment with the GOP—and thereby deprived state Republicans of much of the benefit they otherwise would have realized from the conversion of Godwin—the failure to recruit Byrd in 1970 also looms larger in retrospect because of the scandal. Had Senator Byrd joined the GOP before the 1972 election, as President Nixon envisioned, many other conservative Democrats in the state—including prominent Byrd allies in the General Assembly—likely would have entered the party then, too. Once in, they doubtless would have remained to weather the Watergate storm rather than seeking cover in partisan neutrality. And, instead of a loose coalition between Republicans and Byrd Democrats during the 1970s, there may well have been a fusion.

Capturing Senator Byrd for the GOP remained a preoccupying goal for Obenshain and Republican conservatives throughout the '70s as they sought to solidify the new relationship between the GOP and remnants of the Byrd organization. Though a subject of continual speculation, the Byrd switch never came. And 1970 may well have represented the only realistic opportunity for an overt Byrd-GOP alliance.

In the wake of the 1970 election, Senate Democrats welcomed Byrd back to their fold, essentially ignoring his independent status in the campaign and permitting him to keep his valuable seats on the Finance and Armed Services committees. Spurned by the Republican leadership in Virginia and embraced by his Democratic colleagues in Washington, Byrd had little incentive and even less justification to side with the Republican minority on the key votes to organize the Senate. In a memorandum to President Nixon in December 1970 in preparation for an upcoming Nixon-Byrd meeting, Harry Dent astutely anticipated the long-term implications of the senator's impending action: "If Senator Byrd does not move now, he may continue to enjoy his independent status and continue as a nominal Democrat for seniority and committee assignment purposes. Thus, we may never get him across the line."[15] Despite Nixon's protest to Byrd that caucusing with the Democrats "would undo all the good that has been done by [Byrd's] breaking the ice as an Independent on the way to becoming a Republican before 1972," the Virginia senator was unmoved.[16]

Byrd soon found his neutral perch quite comfortable, as Dent had predicted. Veteran political commentator Charles McDowell of the *Richmond*

---

[15]Memorandum, Harry Dent to President Nixon, December 10, 1970; copy on file with author.

[16]Memorandum, Harry Dent to President Nixon, December 11, 1970; copy on file with the author.

Times-Dispatch, speaking in 1980, described the considerable advantages afforded by the senator's independent status:

> The fact is, our most secure politician is Harry Byrd, Jr., and one of the reasons he is secure is that he is disentangled from the political parties. . . . He is the genius of our age because he learned, ahead of most Americans, that the two political parties are sinking—that they are less and less effective and have less and less power. And he got disentangled fast.
>
> Now [Senator Byrd] has the best of all worlds. He sits in the Democratic caucus, gets good committee assignments from the Democrats, supports the Democrats on organizational issues, and then votes with the Republicans. He doesn't ever have to run in primaries or take sides in factional fights. He just runs in one nice general election as the Byrd candidate. And it's beautiful, . . . it's brilliant. [He] must indeed sit at home and laugh!
>
> I have covered the "Will Harry Byrd turn Republican?" story since I was a very small boy. He's never turned. And I fully expect to pass on to one of my children the responsibility to cover that story. Why in the world would [Byrd join the Republican Party]? There would seem to be no reason at all.[17]

There was, of course, one potential reason: a Byrd switch would provide a powerful impetus for realignment in the Old Dominion. And the senator very much wanted to see Virginia's transition to conservative Republican leadership take place. As early as November 1970, he shared with Dent his hope that Mills Godwin would switch parties because—as Dent relayed it to Nixon— "this would put Virginia in the GOP column for the next decade or more."[18] But Godwin, unlike many of the senator's other trusted advisors, was unenthusiastic about a switch by either Byrd or himself, especially while Linwood Holton was governor. Though Nixon, at Byrd's instigation, met with Godwin in late November 1970, the former governor considered suggestions of a switch at best premature.[19]

Later, when Obenshain became the Republican state chairman and Godwin entered the GOP, Harry Byrd, Jr., already had settled into his unique role as the Senate's Independent Byrd Democrat. He would not turn his back on those Democratic Senate colleagues who had indulged his part-time party loyalty and saved a place for him in their caucus. Moreover, as Byrd watched the '70s progress, Virginia Republicans were winning elections, and realignment seemed to be proceeding just fine without an overt move by him. As for the long term, well, the future looked bright there, too. The dynamic and prin-

---

[17]McDowell interview.

[18]Memorandum, Harry Dent to President Nixon, November 27, 1970; copy on file with the author.

[19]Godwin interview; Memorandum, Harry Dent to President Nixon, December 10, 1970; copy on file with the author.

cipled Richard Obenshain had many good years ahead of him, and he would be the one to carry the conservative banner for a new generation of Virginians. Or so it seemed.

Harry Byrd's independent status and Watergate profoundly affected the course of realignment and the development of Republicanism in Virginia. The popular senator's refusal to formally align himself with the GOP not only deprived the Republican Party of a strong stimulus for Democratic conversions; it had the opposite effect in that it showed many disenchanted Democratic conservatives at a critical time the existence of an alternative to the two parties. Unlike Lawrence Lewis and his New Republicans, who in 1969 declared their intention actually to enter the GOP, most disenchanted Democratic conservatives after 1970 followed Byrd's lead and remained unaffiliated. Watergate soon thereafter seemed to confirm the wisdom of disentanglement. The ensuing emergence of the loose-knit "Coalition" consisting of non-aligned Byrd organization alumni and admirers was not a natural or inevitable development, but the product of a political environment in which independence from the parties was deemed a virtue—by the state's independent senior senator and by the large bloc of Virginia voters who supported him and his father before him. "I vote for the man" became the familiar refrain of the 1970s, and it evidenced almost a disdain for traditional notions of party loyalty. While the weakening condition of political parties was a national trend and partisan dealignment was rampant across the South, plainly nowhere in America were party ties less meaningful than in Virginia.

The realignment trend continued in the Old Dominion, as throughout the South, because demographic trends and the wide philosophical divergence of the national parties guaranteed at least a gradual transition. Beginning in 1972, cooperation between Virginia's Republicans and Byrd Democrats yielded the GOP an impressive string of statewide electoral successes that lasted through the decade. But conservative Virginia's enthusiasm for partisan independence hampered the consolidation of Republican gains in the '70s, fostered GOP factionalism, and paved the way for a strong Democratic resurgence in Virginia in the '80s.

Chapter 23
1972: Obenshain Takes Charge

"[With] the McGovern crowd in control, only the hard-core liberals still feel at home in the Democratic Party.... What we must do is use these next six months to dramatically increase the strength of the Republican Party in Virginia."[20]

Richard D. Obenshain, April 1972

Though retrospect yields tantalizing clues about achievements that might have been, most Virginia Republicans in late 1971 could not have dreamed of the successes the GOP actually would experience during the dizzying next two years. Another presidential election promised another Republican win, but the real prizes were up for grabs in the state contests, and those did not look promising at all. Incumbent Senator William Spong seemed a shoo-in to win a second six-year term, and, though there were persistent rumors that former Governor Godwin might come storming back in 1973 to "save the state" from a Henry Howell governorship, there was little expectation that he would switch parties. After the paltry GOP showings in the 1970 and 1971 statewide contests, the Virginia Republican Party seemed to have precious little to offer.

The situation looked bleak but not desperate to Richard Obenshain. His longstanding personal ambition was to preach the virtues of conservatism from the floor of the United States Senate, and he had long focused on the seat held by Senator Spong. From the beginning of Spong's congressional tenure in 1967, the middle-of-the-road Democrat had been a favorite target of Obenshain's biting rhetoric at Republican meetings around the state. Though Obenshain was unsuccessful in his 1969 bid for attorney general, his strong showing and Holton's breakthrough that year heightened the Richmonder's senatorial ambitions. The GOP setbacks in 1970 and 1971 sapped much of the up-and-coming party's momentum, and Obenshain knew a race against Spong in 1972 would be an uphill battle even with the aid of President Nixon's coattails. But if the Virginia GOP was to become the rallying point for conservatives of both parties, someone had to raise the flag. And none of the state's conservative Republican congressmen—with the exception of the rather

---

[20]*The Richmond News Leader*, April 28, 1972.

obscure William Scott of the Eighth District—had expressed an interest in opposing the seemingly formidable Spong.

Obenshain was thus tilting toward a Senate candidacy in December 1971 when northern Virginia GOP activists Hugh Mulligan and Kenneth Klinge approached him at the party's annual candidate appreciation dinner in Richmond and asked him to join a few of their mutual friends after dinner for an impromptu caucus. Obenshain thought the purpose of the huddle was to begin laying plans for a Senate campaign, but the group had something else in mind. With George Mason Green and several other veterans of the 1971 Green campaign, Klinge and Mulligan had conceived a bold idea: seizing the reigns of the state GOP. "We decided that the only way to stop what was happening was to get control of the mechanism—the party—and the only way to do that was Dick Obenshain," Klinge recalled. "Dick was articulate enough to make it happen."[21] The group's suggestion that he forego the Senate race and run instead for GOP state chairman stunned and initially disappointed Obenshain. But, as those present elaborated the reasons—the need to give the party a leader other than Holton, to articulate the virtues of realignment, and to recruit Godwin—Obenshain began to ponder the possibilities. When the participants adjourned, however, few were optimistic he would concur.

Obenshain immediately canvassed his other close associates and found them largely in agreement. Among those strongly urging him to take on the chairmanship challenge was Dortch Warriner, the Fourth District GOP chief and one of Obenshain's closest friends. "I told him I thought it would give us a chance in eastern Virginia to develop a party—that without it we would be an insular party in the mountains and valleys with an enclave in northern Virginia, and that would be all," Warriner remembered a decade later. "[I said] that if he were chairman we would become a statewide party, and then he could run for the Senate and hope to win."[22] Obenshain was persuaded, and in January 1972, a group of approximately 50 Republicans from around the state—nearly all of them long-time Obenshain admirers and losing combatants in the 1970 and 1971 GOP convention battles—assembled in Richmond to begin the planning.

Thus was born the "Obenshain group" or "conservative caucus"—the corps of key GOP activists that would make nearly all of the major decisions for the state Republican Party for the remainder of the decade. Among the dozen or so leaders were some who would play increasingly important roles in party affairs, including Warriner, Klinge, Judy Peachee of Chesterfield, William Stanhagen of Arlington, Hugh Mulligan of Alexandria, Donald W. Huffman of Roanoke, John E. Alderson, Jr., of Troutville, and William H. Hurd of Charlottesville. The group's January 1972 meeting was held at the Virginia Inn north of Richmond, and the participants reassembled there

---

[21]J. Kenneth Klinge interview, May 27, 1980, and August 30, 1984.
[22]Warriner interview.

frequently during and after the chairmanship campaign. The hotel, owned by conservative businessman J. Smith Ferebee, also played host to Godwin, Byrd, and other conservative Democrats and independents as they caucused in 1972 and 1973 concerning their own political plans. Perched atop a hill overlooking the northern approach to Richmond on Interstate 95, the Virginia Inn seemed a fitting place for conservatives of both parties to plot their defense of Virginia values against the advancing armies of liberalism and change.

The existence, membership, and meetings of the Obenshain group remained largely unknown except to the participants, but the challenge to Holton's leadership of the Republican Party was not long a secret. In late February, Obenshain announced his candidacy for the chairmanship, and before that, Dortch Warriner and Fifth District Republican Chairman Weldon Tuck visited the governor at the Executive Mansion to apprise him of Obenshain's plans. "We told him that Dick was going to win," recalled Warriner,

> and that he was going to win either over the governor's opposition or with his graceful acquiescence. We thought it would be much better for the party if he had the governor's graceful acquiescence—that the mountain and valley boys would be more reconciled to it and the governor himself would be sending the signal that everybody, from the Holton wing all the way through, was going to welcome the New Republicans into the party.
>
> He asked us [what our vote count was], and we told him. And he told us he thought we were wrong and that he was going to be able to control the convention. And he wished us well, and we wished him well.[23]

Spurred by Holton's challenge, the insurgents went to work recruiting new activists and endeavoring to persuade party veterans that the GOP needed new direction from the top. Their efforts met with quick success for a variety of reasons.

A principal factor was Obenshain himself. With his family roots in southwest Virginia and his adulthood home in Richmond, his personal ties bridged the GOP's factional divide. And, for more than a decade, he had been crisscrossing the Commonwealth promoting the Republican Party, conservative doctrine, and his realignment strategy. As state Young Republican chairman in the early '60s, a congressional candidate in 1964, and the GOP's nominee for attorney general in 1969, Obenshain had gotten to know Republicans in every part of Virginia. He was the loyal soldier, always stumping for this Republican candidate or that one, attending local party meetings, providing uncompensated counsel when the party or its local committees got into legal scrapes, speaking at banquets, energizing the faithful at rallies—and in the process earning political IOUs, memorizing names, and making friends. While not every Republican shared his philosophical fervor or enjoyed his sometimes strident rhetoric, virtually all recognized his talents and appreciated his

---

[23]Ibid.

dedication. "You can always count on Dick," they often would say, and almost everyone seemed to like him.

It is doubtful, however, that the fondness for Obenshain would have translated into enough support to overcome incumbent party chief Warren French if not for the successive electoral debacles suffered by the GOP while following Governor Holton's lead during the preceding two years. Obenshain's realignment strategy offered hope for improvement, and that appealed even to traditional Republicans who were wary of what an influx of Byrd Democrats might do to their party. Moreover, the specter of a Henry Howell governorship greatly strengthened the case for some sort of cooperation with Democratic conservatives. Obenshain's vision of bringing like-minded Virginians of both parties together set some Republican hearts pounding faster than others, but to most in the GOP that approach seemed superior to any alternatives then being suggested. For moderate Delegate Vincent Callahan, who lined up Republican legislators for Obenshain and later gave the Richmonder's nominating speech at the state convention, the overriding concern was putting the GOP back in a position to win.[24]

What made many mountain-valley Republicans nervous about all the realignment talk, however, was the seeming emphasis on philosophy over party. The mission of a political party in a two-party system, the western partisans argued, is to run candidates so that voters are given a choice. If the Republican Party were to defer to independents like Harry Byrd—or, as some suspected, Mills Godwin—simply because they were conservative, the party's purpose would effectively disappear and the two-party system would crumble. Unlike Holton, many traditional Republicans in western Virginia had no visceral negative feeling toward Senator Byrd and his Democratic allies, and they saw the wisdom of combining forces. But, as Warren French explained, the issue was on what terms the alliance would be formed:

> I am one who is willing to welcome Democrats into the party if they want to be Republicans. But I am not willing to turn the party over to them just for their votes. That's just my philosophy: I believe in running candidates against all Democrats. If they're going to be Democrats, then we have a responsibility to oppose them. I believe in a two-party government more than I believe in a conservative or liberal philosophy.[25]

The Obenshain-French contest in 1972 was not a liberal-versus-conservative battle, emphasized Republican Delegate Pete Giesen of Augusta County, who backed French. "It was a difference . . . as to the way the party ought to function."[26]

For many Republicans—and to many outside observers—the chairmanship contest seemed to have less to do with Obenshain, French, and their

---

[24]Vincent F. Callahan, Jr., interview, May 29, 1980.
[25]Warren French interview, June 18, 1980.
[26]Giesen interview.

respective approaches to party-building than with the controversial Governor Holton. The chief executive's problems went beyond the Garland and Shafran defeats. In eastern Virginia, conservatives of both parties were seething over his failure to lead the fight against court-mandated busing to achieve school desegregation. In western Virginia, Holton's natural political base, Republican activists were still smarting over his lack of partisanship as governor and, particularly, his failure to appoint large numbers of Republicans to state government posts. French, the governor's loyal supporter, knew his bid for re-election was in trouble from the very beginning.[27] Though the incumbent chairman was viewed almost uniformly by GOP leaders as a conservative-thinking, hard-working, and capable party captain, his sponsor in the governor's mansion had aroused a corps of critics who were determined to send him a message.

This was especially true of Obenshain's inner circle. Like their leader, Obenshain's close associates were concerned chiefly with making the GOP a safe and inviting haven for the Byrd conservatives—especially Godwin—who were increasingly uncomfortable and unwanted in the Democratic Party. But there was no concealing these partisans' ill will toward the governor. Some felt that Holton should have shared more campaign funds with Obenshain when the two ran together on the GOP ticket in 1969. All believed that Holton had effectively reneged on assurances to Obenshain concerning a post-election job in his administration. They had found it especially galling in 1970 to watch their friend twist in the wind for months while waiting for Holton to offer him an acceptable position. The governor's forceful put-down of the Green candidacy in 1971, and his unconcealed disdain for the Obenshain backers and their party-building notions, only reinforced the antagonism. If, as Obenshain liked to say, "an army moves on its stomach . . . [but] a political party is moved by emotions,"[28] Holton had supplied ample impetus for those moving against him.

When Republicans assembled in Roanoke in June 1972 for their state convention, Obenshain claimed the chairmanship by a lopsided, 769–288 vote. His conservative followers re-elected incumbent National Committeewoman Cynthia Newman, but rejected another Holton-backed candidate for the national committeeman post in favor of William Stanhagen, the Tenth District GOP chairman. The inevitability of the Obenshain triumph had been apparent as the delegates assembled in Roanoke, and conventioneers thus witnessed few fireworks. The will of the party was plain, and a gracious Warren French joined a conciliatory Obenshain in promoting harmony. The unity theme also was emphasized by the defeated Governor Holton, who told delegates before the vote, "You do what you want to about the party leadership. Whatever you do, when we come out of this convention, I'm going to be with

[27]French interview.
[28]See *The Richmond News Leader*, June 5, 1972.

you."[29] The governor later was elected chairman of the Virginia delegation to the GOP national convention in Miami.

The change in Republican leadership brought predictable expressions of jubilation from the conservative quarter. "This is a great day for Virginia's conservative majority," exulted *The Richmond News Leader*, "and we have Dick Obenshain to thank for it."[30] But Obenshain sought to play down talk of a conservative takeover of the party and instead insisted that the GOP merely had signalled its desire to welcome disenchanted Democrats into its ranks. He had especially reassuring words for party moderates who feared the new chairman might back an independent gubernatorial bid by Mills Godwin in 1973. Referring to Republican Congressmen J. Kenneth Robinson and G. William Whitehurst as potential gubernatorial contenders, Obenshain told reporters in late June that the GOP would have a nominee of its own for governor the next year. And, yes, he confirmed, some Republican overtures were being made to former Governor Godwin.

"When they left the [state GOP] convention, there were a lot of people who felt the whole thing was going to be a Byrd Republican Party, that there would be a bunch of conservative Democrats in charge and the Republican Party as it had been known for years had gone down the tubes," recalled Alan T. Rains, Jr., the GOP executive director appointed by French. "But, to Dick's credit, in a very short time after he was chairman it became apparent that he was really building the party and working very hard to bring various factions in. And it worked."[31] Obenshain retained Rains as the party's executive director, and the two took to the road in July to meet with local Republican committees. Obenshain delivered the inspirational message, and Rains briefed party workers on the mechanics of the GOP's new voter-registration drive.

While Republicans were installing new party leadership, decisive changes also were occurring in the Democratic Party hierarchy. Aided by national party rules that mandated greater participation by minorities and women, supporters of the presidential candidacy of Senator George McGovern of South Dakota marched through local party meetings and easily controlled the state Democratic convention. They denied the party's most recent governor, Mills Godwin, a delegate seat at the state convention and replaced moderate and conservative party officials with veteran liberal activists. Joseph T. Fitzpatrick of Norfolk assumed the party chairmanship, and two other allies of Lieutenant Governor Henry Howell—George Rawlings and Ruth Harvey Charity—were elected to seats on the Democratic National Committee. Not surprisingly, the dramatic convention triggered divergent reactions from interested partisans. "The takeover of the Democratic Party by the forces supporting Senator McGovern's candidacy had a devastating effect upon what

---

[29]*The Richmond News Leader*, June 3, 1972.
[30]*The Richmond News Leader*, June 5, 1972.
[31]Alan T. Rains, Jr., interview, July 3, 1980.

was left of the moderate forces in the Democratic Party," recalled Senator Spong many years later. "[T]he mechanisms employed were far more severe than anything previously complained of about the Byrd organization."[32] A great many loyal Democrats were alienated from the party by the developments at the 1972 state convention, recalled Andrew Miller.

You had many people in leadership positions in the party in previous years—and I am not talking about people who were obviously [Byrd] organization types; I am talking about people who were involved in Bill Battle's campaign, Sarge Reynolds's campaign, my campaign in 1969—who were just tossed out of any party position they might have held. It was done in such a way that you had literally thousands of Virginians saying, as a consequence of what occurred at the Roanoke convention in 1972, that [they] might never be involved in the Democratic Party again. And they haven't been, by and large.[33]

From Henry Howell's perspective, however, the convention brought changes that were long overdue. It was a great victory, he crowed, for the Democrats "who believed in life after birth and did not like this decadent Democratic Party [in Virginia] that really had a Republican philosophy."[34]

The two Roanoke conventions in the summer of 1972 represented an important milestone in Virginia's realignment. For the first time, the philosophical orientation of the political parties in the state more or less mirrored the national parties. And new GOP Chairman Obenshain saw in the dramatic changes a unique opportunity to move beyond presidential Republicanism. Since 1952, when Senator Byrd, Sr., publicly repudiated his party's national ticket and Eisenhower carried the state, many conservative Democrats had worked actively for Republican presidential candidates. But in the past they always had scurried back into the Democratic camp for the ensuing state and local contests. Though some had backed Holton for governor in 1969, most had returned to the Democratic fold to support George Kostel's bid for lieutenant governor in 1971. In an April 1972 speech, Obenshain spoke of breaking that cycle:

[W]ith George Rawlings and the McGovern crowd in control, only the hard-core liberals still feel at home in the Democratic Party. . . .What we must do is use these next six months to dramatically increase the strength of the Republican Party in Virginia. . . . For 20 years Virginians have been voting for Republican Presidents and Republican congressmen, only to drop back into the Democratic Party for four more years. It is time for all of us who believe in limited, economical government to unite within the Republican Party. If we stay divided—some of us as full-time Repub-

---

[32]William B. Spong, Jr., interview (written responses), September 23, 1985.
[33]Andrew P. Miller interview, July 24, 1980.
[34]Howell interview.

licans and some of us as presidential Republicans—then the Howells and Rawlings will continue to dominate the politics of Virginia.[35]

The import of Obenshain's words probably was little noticed or appreciated. As usually occurred in Virginia, even amidst the presidential campaign most thoughts were focused on the gubernatorial contest that would come the following year. But when Obenshain spoke of "us[ing] these next six months," he meant it. Before the governor's race there would be a Senate election, and Obenshain believed the political climate was right to elect a Republican United States senator from Virginia. He and William Scott may have been the only two people in the Commonwealth who held that view.

Obenshain and Scott did not know each other well, and they had first talked about the Senate race in 1971 at a time when Obenshain was still thinking about making a run himself and Scott already was a committed candidate. Scott made it clear that he had no intention of changing his plans, and Obenshain's decision to vie for the party chairmanship headed off a clash between them for the nomination. Scott did not have the option of seeking re-election to his Eighth District seat in the House of Representatives because Democrat-sponsored redistricting legislation the previous year had placed his residence in the Tenth District of incumbent Congressman Joel Broyhill. Many Republicans and Byrd conservatives (including Senator Byrd himself) urged Broyhill to take on Spong, but the congressman declined to risk his considerable seniority in the lower house on a long-shot bid for the Senate. Democratic Delegate D. French Slaughter, Jr., of Culpeper also turned aside suggestions that he switch parties and take on the uphill fight. Only the idiosyncratic Scott seemed interested in the nomination, and that merely reinforced the view of most that Spong was unbeatable.

Shortly after the state GOP convention, Obenshain summoned a handful of his closest associates to his Richmond home to plot strategy. Several months earlier they had stunned Obenshain with the suggestion that he run for party chairman, and now it was his turn to surprise. "We are going to elect Bill Scott to the Senate," he declared to colleagues Warriner, Klinge, and Stanhagen, who responded with jocular derision. To their queries about how he proposed to accomplish such a feat, Obenshain replied that they would need to take charge of the Scott campaign committee so that they could run a state-of-the-art campaign free from Scott's managerial whim. To questions about financing the campaign, Obenshain responded that retired industrialist J. D. Stetson Coleman of Fauquier County, a prominent fundraiser in national Republican circles, was chomping at the bit to raise money in an effort to oust Spong and capture the seat for the Republicans. But would Scott, a two-term congressman with a persona that many found less than compelling, be taken seriously by voters? Obenshain did not have a persuasive answer for that question, but he insisted that it was well worth the effort because a victory or

---

[35]*The Richmond News Leader*, April 28, 1972.

even a strong showing in the Senate race would be extremely helpful in convincing Mills Godwin to run as a Republican for governor in 1973.

The next five months proved to be the most frustrating and difficult of Obenshain's political career. He proceeded to implement the plan he had described to his colleagues: a Scott-for-Senate Committee was formed with Obenshain in command; Obenshain's conservative organization was mobilized in Scott's behalf; and efforts began to enlist the wealthy Coleman's financial help. But Obenshain soon found Scott argumentative, uncooperative, and virtually intractable on almost every point of campaign policy and strategy. "Dick resigned every weekend" over one dispute or another with Scott, recalled his widow, Helen.[36] The biggest battles were over campaign funding.

Raising money for Scott proved difficult. Obenshain contacted Lawrence Lewis, Smith Ferebee, and other pillars of the conservative financial establishment in Richmond on behalf of Scott and argued forcefully that Spong was too liberal, that Scott could beat him, and that a GOP win would dramatically advance realignment. Governor Holton assisted the effort by conveying to Ferebee in not-so-subtle terms that any chance of GOP backing for a Godwin gubernatorial bid the next year would hinge on financial support for Scott from the former governor's conservative Democratic friends. Lewis thereafter invited dozens of prominent Virginia conservatives to meet Scott at his Charles City County farm. But Scott "left most everybody cold," according to Lewis,[37] and much of the conservative community, including the influential Richmond newspapers, declined to embrace his long-shot candidacy. With the election barely six weeks away, Scott's campaign coffers were almost empty.

The financial problems did not deter Obenshain. As he, conservative cohort Hugh Mulligan, and a handful of other senior GOP advisers read the campaign's latest poll, Scott's deficit appeared daunting indeed. But they noticed something even more important: Spong, the well-known incumbent, was favored by less than 50 percent of the voters sampled.[38] A well-crafted media blitz portraying Scott as a viable conservative alternative could send the dissatisfied undecided voters scurrying to the GOP candidate. The data and plan were presented to Stetson Coleman, who responded by advancing $200,000 to a newly formed "Virginians for Scott" committee for the purpose of purchasing the needed television advertising time. With such a large "loan" coming from a single supporter, Obenshain anticipated that Coleman's investment would produce some adverse public reaction. But he did not expect the adamant opposition that came from, of all people, the candidate. Scott interpreted Coleman's loan offer as an attempt to purchase influence, and he would hear none of it. A flabbergasted Obenshain quickly assembled a meeting with Scott, key campaign advisers, and associates of Coleman. Heated

---

[36]Mrs. Richard D. Obenshain interview.

[37]Lewis interview.

[38]Hugh Mulligan interview, January 10, 1990.

words were exchanged, and the candidate gave his assent to the financial assistance only after he was assured that Coleman would not call on Scott, or even set foot in his senatorial office, if he were elected. Only that was sufficient to convince the irascible congressman that Coleman's only ulterior motives were the ouster of Spong and the recruitment of Godwin for the 1973 race.[39]

Coleman's late loan enabled Scott to saturate the airwaves with a simple message—that Scott was conservative and Spong was not. Previous television advertising by the Scott campaign had introduced the little-known congressman as an experienced lawmaker, a conservative, an adamant foe of busing, and an ardent Nixon supporter. But the October messages assailed Spong's alleged liberalism, his voting record in the Senate, and his party ties to McGovern. While ads linking Scott to Nixon and Spong to McGovern ran statewide, other attacks on the incumbent were targeted regionally. For example, Spong was hammered in the Southwest and in Southside Virginia for his support of gun control measures, in Richmond for his position on voting rights legislation and his failure to oppose mandatory busing forcefully, and in the Hampton Roads area for his lack of support for defense spending and the Vietnam War effort. The messages were simple and hard-hitting, and there were a lot of them. "Bill Spong did not realize he was in a fight until it was too late," recalled his close friend and 1966 campaign manager, William C. Battle.[40] Scott's media blitz took Spong by surprise, and the attacks came too late for response. Spong's own advertising had been less issue-oriented and specific, and it failed to insulate the senator from Scott's October onslaught. As Old Dominion University political scientist David Hager noted after the election, "[T]he arcane, courtly, Byrd-controlled politics of Virginia [had been transformed into a] media-dominated pattern," and Scott's campaign was on the cutting edge.[41]

In the view of most observers, however, the outcome of the contest was not solely or even principally a product of Scott's media campaign. University of Virginia professor Ralph Eisenberg called the late media blitz "frosting on the cake",[42] and analysts agreed that the Scott ads merely had reinforced other major factors in the election. Chief among those was the presidential contest. Though Nixon did not make a campaign visit to Virginia—he declined to campaign against any Senate incumbents—Scott clung to the President's coattails from start to finish. His campaign materials told Virginians that they had a "rare opportunity to cast two votes for President Nixon"—one in the presidential column and one for Scott in the Senate race. As point man for Scott, Obenshain repeatedly linked the moderate Spong to his party's liberal presidential nominee.

---

[39]Ibid.; Short interview.
[40]Battle interview.
[41]*Richmond Times-Dispatch*, September 16, 1973.
[42]*Richmond Times-Dispatch*, November 19, 1972.

Spong made the worst of the situation. Rather than simply acknowledging nominal support for McGovern as the nominee of his party, the incumbent Democrat repeatedly declined to answer reporters' questions about his position on the presidential race. "Bill seemed to be having a hard time making up his mind if, when, and how he was going to handle that," remembered Battle, ". . . and it cost him."[43] The senator seemed at best ambivalent on the issue and, at worst, supportive of McGovern but unwilling to admit it. The latter interpretation, which Republicans encouraged, gained credence late in the campaign when Spong answered the persistent queries of a liberal-sounding Ferrum College student by commenting privately that he planned to vote for McGovern. The student proved to be no campus radical, but a Republican activist and editor of the college newspaper, and the Spong remark received wide dissemination in the final days of the campaign. Obenshain later pointed to Spong's Ferrum remark as the "catalyst" for Scott's late surge.[44]

Scott, meanwhile, benefited from a parade of visiting conservative and Republican national leaders. His biggest boost came on the eve of the election when Vice President Spiro Agnew, on his second campaign swing through Virginia, keynoted a large and enthusiastic campaign rally for the Senate candidate in the Richmond Coliseum. As Scott's momentum became apparent during the campaign's closing weeks, Spong suffered significant defections from the conservative ranks of his party. Many Byrd Democrats recalled unfavorably the incumbent's defeat of Willis Robertson six years earlier, and when they sensed midway through the campaign that Spong could be toppled by the more conservative Scott, they were anxious to help. In the Fifth District, a key battleground, Scott benefitted from kind public words by Democratic Congressman W. C. "Dan" Daniel and an outright endorsement days before the election by former Governor William Tuck. Former Congressman Howard Smith, whom Scott had succeeded in the Eighth District, also endorsed the GOP nominee.

Spong's dilemma was obvious—in 1972, he had even less middle ground to stand on than there had been for fellow-moderate Battle in 1969. Many of Spong's centrist Democratic supporters had been dislodged from their party posts and dispirited by the actions of the heavy-handed McGovern forces during the spring. Most Democratic conservatives were lukewarm if not hostile in their attitudes toward him, and the liberals controlling the Democratic Party machinery were only slightly more enthusiastic about him than were the conservatives. "The nominating convention left me pretty much alone and on my own in the re-election campaign," Spong recalled in 1985.[45] He added that the Scott endorsements by prominent Democratic conserva-

---

[43]Battle interview.
[44]*Richmond Times-Dispatch*, November 19, 1972.
[45]Spong interview.

tives late in the campaign were especially unhelpful. "I did not solicit such support, and perhaps I should have," Spong commented,

[but] any public embracing of many such figures would have brought cries of dissatisfaction from the supporters of Henry Howell, who was then the most active and vigorous politician in Virginia. On the other hand, any public embracing of Howell would, in many instances, have deprived me of the support of my closest friends and associates.[46]

In a polarizing political period in Virginia, the intellectual and deliberate Spong was caught in the middle.

Aided by Nixon's election-day romp in the state, which netted the incumbent President nearly a million votes,[47] Scott upset Spong by a hefty 75,000-vote margin. In becoming the first Republican senator from Virginia since 1889, Scott carried 79 of 95 counties, 20 of 39 cities, and seven of ten congressional districts (Spong won only in the Second, Fourth, and Tenth Districts). The Republican nominee polled 51.5 percent of the statewide vote to Spong's 46.1 percent. The remaining 2.4 percent went to former GOP state chairman Horace Henderson, who, dismayed by the increasingly conservative direction of the state Republican Party, waged a largely symbolic campaign as an Independent.[48]

Reviewing the results of the Senate contest, political analyst Larry Sabato cited four principal factors in Spong's defeat at the hands of the underdog Scott: (1) the Nixon coattails and the takeover of the state Democratic Party by the liberal McGovern forces; (2) the view of many wealthy and influential conservative Democrats that a win by Scott would help convince Mills Godwin to run for governor in 1973; (3) the financial support provided to Scott by Stetson Coleman[49] and the media blitz it funded; and (4) the overconfidence and disorganization in the Spong camp.[50] Sabato's assessment reflected the thinking of most observers, and the participants disagreed only as to emphasis. Spong stressed the impact of Scott's media blitz: "The message of the media was that I was too liberal for Virginia, and a majority of those voting accepted that."[51] Scott cited the candidates' differences on key issues, downplayed the impact of the Coleman loan and media blitz, and added, "[Obenshain] was given substantial credit—and justly so—for my winning."[52]

---

[46]Ibid.

[47]The vote totals were: Nixon (R) – 988,493 (67.8%); McGovern (D) – 438,887 (30.1%); Louis Fisher (Socialist Labor) – 9,918 (0.7%); John G. Schmitz (American Independent) – 19,721 (1.4%). Sabato, *Virginia Votes 1969–1974*, p. 60.

[48]The vote totals were: Scott (R) – 718,337 (51.5%); Spong (D) – 643,963 (46.1%); Henderson (Independent) – 33,913 (2.4%). Sabato, *Virginia Votes 1969–1974*, pp. 59–61.

[49]Scott outspent Spong in the campaign, $619,908 to $380,921, and the aggregate loans and contributions provided by Coleman more than accounted for the Scott advantage.

[50]Sabato, *Virginia Votes 1969–1974*, pp. 59–60.

[51]Spong interview.

[52]William L. Scott interview, May 28, 1980.

Nixon's landslide victory in Virginia, as elsewhere in the nation, brought together Goldwater's 1964 constituency and the suburban and traditional Republican support assembled in previous elections by Nixon and Eisenhower. In Virginia, the President's campaign was structured so as to give representation to each of the major elements of the winning Republican coalition—GOP conservatives, Republican moderates, and Byrd Democrats—through a managerial triumvirate comprised of Dortch Warriner, Cynthia Newman, and former Democratic State Senator FitzGerald Bemiss. Under this trio's direction, parallel Republican and "Virginians for Nixon" organizations were established in localities throughout the state. The "Virginians" nomenclature—which would be used in GOP campaigns throughout the '70s and into the '80s—allowed Democrats, former Democrats, and independents to participate without making any assertion, express or implied, of affiliation with the Republican Party. In his first active role on behalf of a GOP nominee, former Governor Mills Godwin served as the Virginians for Nixon chairman. And Delegate George McMath, who publicly announced early in the year that he was leaving the Democratic Party, was the group's organization director. With McMath recruiting Byrd Democrats, and Obenshain protege Judy Peachee organizing Republican regulars, local Nixon campaign co-chairmen (consisting of one Republican and one "Virginian") were appointed throughout the state. It was a successful exercise in coalition-building and an approach that maximized active participation in Nixon's re-election bid.

The President's strategy of courting conservative Democrats paid handsome dividends. His 1972 campaign achieved the first Republican presidential sweep of the South, and his margins in many Southern states, including Virginia, rivaled those of Franklin Roosevelt, the last Democrat to carry the region solidly. In the Old Dominion, the Republican President accomplished the unprecedented feat of carrying every city and all but one county. Only tiny and heavily black Charles City County backed the Democrat.

In addition to propelling Scott to a surprisingly easy win over Spong, Nixon's coattails extended to GOP candidates for the House of Representatives and General Assembly. Already in possession of a majority of the state's congressional seats, the principal task for Republicans was to weather reapportionment and retain their hard-won gains. In the re-configured Eighth District vacated by William Scott, Delegate Stanford E. Parris polled 44 percent of the vote to win a hard-fought, three-way battle.[53] In another three-candidate contest, Roanoke Delegate M. Caldwell Butler garnered 55 percent of the ballots to capture the seat of Republican Richard H. Poff, who had resigned to accept appointment by Governor Holton to the Virginia

---

[53]Parris defeated Democratic Commonwealth's Attorney Robert F. Horan, Jr., of Fairfax County and Independent William R. Durland, a liberal who had the support of State Senator Henry Howell.

Supreme Court. GOP congressional incumbents William Whitehurst, Kenneth Robinson, William Wampler, and Joel Broyhill posted easy wins over their Democratic challengers, and Republican candidates ran unopposed in two state legislative districts that had been vacated by GOP incumbents. The two new lawmakers, State Senator John N. Dalton of Radford and Delegate J. Marshall Coleman of Staunton, were destined to hold their legislative posts for only a short time before moving up the political ladder.

Republicans gave conservative Democratic Congressmen Thomas Downing, David Satterfield, and Dan Daniel little trouble, but they seized the opportunity presented by the retirement of Fourth District incumbent Watkins M. Abbitt of Appomattox. There, the GOP claimed a seventh congressional seat with the surprising victory of Republican Robert W. Daniel, Jr., over a splintered field that included a Democrat and three Independents. The district had become distinctly more urban and Democratic as a result of redistricting, but the conservative Daniel rode the Nixon wave and carried 13 of 17 localities. He polled an impressive 47 percent of the vote, and even managed a plurality win in normally Democratic Portsmouth, Senator Spong's hometown. With Daniel's victory and wins by the six other successful GOP contenders, Republicans amassed 54 percent of the cumulative major-party vote in the contested congressional races.[54]

"The Year of the Republican", as the University of Virginia's Larry Sabato dubbed it,[55] drew to a close with GOP spirits soaring. More than 700 activists attended a state party "Victory Dinner" in Richmond, where they celebrated the congressional gains and Nixon landslide and also paid tribute to former party chief Warren French. Since the decisive June convention, Obenshain's stewardship of the party had reassured wary Holton Republicans, and the GOP electoral gains had exceeded even the conservatives' expectations. Meeting in December 1972, the party's central committee overwhelmingly adopted a resolution endorsing the realignment strategy and inviting conservative Democrats and independents to join the GOP. As the unified Republicans looked to the momentous gubernatorial election looming ahead, they had confidence that their party finally had become competitive at the state level. The two major Republican leaders could claim a share of credit for the accomplishment—Holton, for helping to legitimize a Republican vote through his 1969 victory, and Obenshain, for demonstrating through Scott's win the viability of the conservative coalition approach.

[54]Sabato, *Virginia Votes 1969–1974*, pp. 76–79.
[55]Ibid. p. 59.

Chapter 24

Mills Godwin, Reluctant Republican

"As one of you . . ."

Mills E. Godwin, Jr.
Virginia Republican Convention,
June 9, 1973.

Mills Godwin never wanted to become a Republican. Discussion of a second bid for the governorship by the popular former chief executive began shortly after Henry Howell was elected to succeed the late Lieutenant Governor Sargeant Reynolds in 1971. The topic occupied more than 200 leading business, civic, and governmental figures of both parties who gathered at Richmond's venerable Commonwealth Club in January 1972 to honor several retiring state legislators and hear speeches by Godwin and Senator Byrd. "There are many who probably would say that because of his great record, his future is past," said a smiling Byrd in presenting Godwin to the group, "but from talking here tonight, many of you seem to think his future is in the future."[56] A prolonged standing ovation ensued, and Godwin's subsequent remarks seemed to signal his plans: "The transcendent need, as I see it, in Virginia now is a consolidation of our thoughtful citizens into a solid front of political strength to confront anyone who would use our electorate for their own selfish purposes or political gain."[57] For the assembled bipartisan conservative leadership of the Commonwealth, the gentlemanly jargon did not obscure the message. They had to work together and spare no effort to stop Henry Howell, and Godwin seemed ready to lead the way.

The assignment was not one the 57-year-old former governor coveted. His first term had been marked by unparalleled achievement and marred by profound grief over the accidental death of the Godwins' only child, Becky. He could not hope to repeat the level of achievement, and neither he nor his devoted wife Katherine wanted to relive the painful memories that awaited them in the Executive Mansion. But Henry Howell seemed to embody the antithesis of everything in which Godwin believed, and the former governor

---

[56]*Washington Star*, January 11, 1972.
[57]Ibid.

worried that both the state's conservative traditions and its measured progressive strides of recent years would be jeopardized by Howell's election:

> I was interested in seeing [a continuation of the] momentum that had been generated during my first term as governor and carried forward to a large degree during Holton's term. . . . I felt that the election of Howell would have brought a dramatic change to Virginia's political thinking, [and] that he would have been a disruptive influence as governor and would have retarded the momentum and the growth that Virginia was enjoying.[58]

With pledges of campaign money from conservative business and political leaders who insisted that only he could stop Howell—and with the reluctant support of the former First Lady—Godwin resolved during 1972 to enter the race. He wanted to run as an Independent.

The reasons for Godwin's preference for an independent bid were both emotional and practical. He had been a Democratic officeholder for more than two decades; during that time, his party had bestowed upon him many honors, including the highest, the governorship. Aside from his own mixed feelings about severing that tie, the inevitable appearance of ingratitude was a nagging source of concern. By running as an Independent like Byrd, Godwin merely would be absenting himself from the Democratic Party; if he joined the GOP, he would be repudiating it. Worse, he would be under pressure as a Republican to support all of the nominees of his new party, including those who ran against his Democratic allies. Godwin had many friends in the Democratic courthouses and state legislature who would not accept any proffered justification for such a supreme act of disloyalty as affiliation with the rival Republicans. And he valued those friendships.

On the practical side, the former governor understood that he had to walk a tightrope in order to win the election. It would have been difficult enough to bring long-time Republican and Democratic antagonists together for concerted action against a conventional liberal foe, but Henry Howell posed special problems. Howell's populist appeal cut across the usual philosophical lines; he had garnered backing in previous races not only from blacks, labor, and liberals, but also from a significant number of Wallace and Byrd voters. Godwin could hope to amass a majority only by retaining as much of his old moderate and conservative Democratic support as possible while adding to it the traditional and suburban Republican base. He was uneasy about the prospects for getting die-hard Republicans to support an old nemesis, and he knew that moving all the way into the GOP camp would alienate many of his past supporters in the Democratic Party. The best resolution of those competing considerations, it seemed to Godwin, was for him to run as an Independent and for Republicans to forego fielding a candidate.

---

[58]Godwin interview.

There was only one problem with that approach: nobody in a position of leadership in the Virginia Republican Party—not Richard Obenshain, not Dortch Warriner, and certainly not Linwood Holton—was willing to go before the GOP convention in 1973 and ask its delegates to do what Godwin wanted. When Obenshain and his conservative Republican allies huddled at the Virginia Inn late in the summer of 1972 to discuss Godwin and the upcoming gubernatorial race, Warriner forcefully asserted that the former governor should seek the GOP nomination and run "as a Republican" or the party should offer another candidate. The issue of whether the Republican Party was going to nominate candidates had been settled at the 1970 convention, Warriner declared, and that battle should not be fought again. Some of the assembled, including Obenshain, bristled at the idea of giving the proud Godwin any sort of ultimatum, and the new party chairman argued for a more flexible approach. But all agreed that a formal Godwin affiliation with the GOP was essential in order for the arrangement to succeed.

A few weeks later, Obenshain and Warriner went to see the former governor at Cedar Point, Godwin's home on the James River in Nansemond County, now Suffolk. Obenshain, who would lead numerous GOP delegations to Cedar Point and engage in a series of lengthy one-on-one discussions with Godwin during the next nine months, joined Warriner in emphasizing the importance of a Republican bid by the former governor. Godwin was "cordial but condescending," Warriner later recalled, and he lectured the two Republican leaders on the need for them to be less preoccupied with building the Republican Party and more interested in what was best for Virginia. An agitated Warriner retorted that "Virginia was going to be here long after the likes of Dortch Warriner and Mills Godwin were dead and gone, . . . that the welfare of Virginia depended upon a strong Republican Party, and that we were thinking of Virginia when we were thinking of building the party."[59] The irascible Emporia attorney thereafter decided to leave the delicate direct negotiations with Godwin to the more deferential and diplomatic Obenshain.

Though Warriner was a Southside conservative, his reaction to Godwin's reluctance to embrace the GOP mirrored that of many partisans in traditionally Republican areas. "It seemed to me that he was putting us down," Warriner explained, "and I had worked too dad-blamed hard for something that I was proud of to have this man put it down." [60] Having endured social slights and all manner of indignity over the years for his partisan affiliation, Warriner was in no mood to accept Godwin on Godwin's terms. "He wanted our endorsement but he didn't want to call himself a Republican," Warriner added. "It was as though we were good enough for him to go to bed with but not good enough to marry."[61] That Godwin adopt the Republican label became an

---

[59]Warriner interview.
[60]Ibid.
[61]Ibid.

intense matter of principle as well as pride for Warriner, and, as the discussions went forward between the former governor and Obenshain, Warriner took it upon himself to represent the feelings of the many Republicans who, he was certain, felt the way he did.

During the fall and into the winter of 1972, Obenshain organized a series of expeditions to Cedar Point, all designed to persuade Godwin to become the Republican candidate for governor. The visitors included various GOP activists and legislators, conservative business leaders, and even some prominent General Assembly Democrats. They delivered two principal messages. Republicans sought to convince the former governor that he would be embraced fully and supported actively by local party workers if he joined the GOP, while Democrats and independents favoring the conversion sought to reassure Godwin that a GOP affiliation would not cause any erosion of his support among their colleagues. In his separate visits and communications with Godwin, Obenshain stressed the former governor's ability to advance realignment, the difficulty of rallying Republicans without his wholehearted embrace of the GOP, and the importance of the Republican precinct organization to the campaign against Howell.

The long-running discussions between the party chairman and the former governor resulted in the development of a relationship of mutual confidence and admiration between them, and Godwin later reported that Obenshain's influence had been decisive in his eventual decision to run as a Republican in 1973. It was a most unlikely scenario: a twice-defeated highland Republican, the aristocratic Godwin's junior by more than 20 years, advising one of the most popular and successful of Virginia's Democratic governors that he now had to switch parties in order to win election to that office again. As fall turned to winter and the relationship deepened, Obenshain became convinced that Godwin was moving toward an eventual affiliation with the GOP. But the terms of the arrangement remained unsettled.

Throughout this period, Godwin also was counseled to run as a Republican by his close associate, Senator Harry F. Byrd, Jr., and by his key fundraisers in the conservative business community, J. Smith Ferebee. Ferebee was summoned to Cedar Point in mid-1972, and he recommended unreservedly that the former governor go all the way into the Republican camp. Lawrence Lewis, Jr., Thomas C. Boushall, James C. Wheat, Jr., Richard Short, John T. "Til" Hazel, and other Godwin supporters in the Virginia business establishment echoed that view. Their advice was prompted initially by fear that a refusal by the former governor to enter the GOP would produce a three-way race that would guarantee Howell's election. As that prospect diminished, there remained the problem of garnering active and enthusiastic Republican support for Godwin's bid. The agitation by GOP conservatives like Warriner for a wholesale Godwin switch bolstered Obenshain's argument that the former governor could not count on vigorous support from either of the Republican factions unless he came all the way over. Godwin's key financial supporters

never doubted that they could raise the money he would need, recalled Ferebee, "but we felt he also had to have the Republican organization [and the traditional GOP base in southwest Virginia] behind him. . . . [We had] to be
united, and you couldn't get united with the Republicans if you didn't embrace
them."[62]

With the arrival of the gubernatorial election year, interest in Godwin's
plans mounted. Entreaties to the former governor to run as a Republican
came from a variety of quarters. GOP legislative leaders held a press conference to publicly urge him to become the party's nominee, and Congressman
Stanford Parris announced formation of a "Committee to Nominate Mills
Godwin as a Republican" which a large number of northern Virginia Republicans joined. The party's other potential candidates for governor—most
notably Congressmen Joel Broyhill, Kenneth Robinson, and William
Whitehurst—declined suggestions that they run and expressed support for a
Republican bid by Godwin. State Senator John Dalton, who earlier had
written to Godwin expressing the "hope that you would consent to letting the
Republican Convention nominate you,"[63] visited the former governor in
February 1973 and expressed a desire to run on the GOP ticket with him. Ironically, while the conservative Warriner was taking a hard line on Godwin's
embrace of Republicanism, "mountain and valley boy" Dalton was assuring
the former governor that he would back him whether he ran as an Independent or as a Republican.[64]

The General Assembly's adjournment in late February signalled the
opening of a new political season in the Commonwealth, and Godwin shortly
thereafter issued a public statement confirming that he would again seek the
governorship. Though Godwin made no reference to party affiliation,
Obenshain, Ferebee, and others felt that great strides had been made in
persuading the former governor to come into the Republican camp, and a
further statement by Godwin regarding his partisan intentions was set for early
March. Godwin planned to limit his subsequent comments to a declaration of
his willingness to accept a Republican endorsement or nomination if it were
offered to him. But that did not satisfy Dortch Warriner, who feared that
Godwin would accept the GOP's support and then remain independent.
Obenshain deemed his friend's concern unjustified, but he recognized that
many Republicans would share Warriner's antagonism toward Godwin if the
former governor persisted in eschewing the Republican label.

For months, Obenshain had been the key negotiator, shuttling back and
forth between Richmond and Cedar Point, sharing the party's perspective with
Godwin, and arguing Godwin's position to Warriner and their GOP

---

[62]J. Smith Ferebee interview, June 4, 1980, and August 30, 1984.

[63]Letter, Dalton to Godwin, dated December 1, 1972; copy on file at the Republican Party
of Virginia Archives.

[64]John N. Dalton interview, July 1, 1980, and September 10, 1984.

colleagues. He later likened his experience to that of a ping pong ball, with Godwin and Warriner furiously wielding the paddles. But time now had run out. Godwin's clarification of his party status was nearing; the former governor's intention regarding the GOP remained purposely ambiguous, and an angry Warriner resolved to draw the line. Godwin either would use the words, "I will run as a Republican," at his press conference on March 4, the Emporia Republican declared, or Warriner immediately would announce his own candidacy for the GOP nomination. The one thing everybody seemed to understand was that a three-way race would spell disaster, and if a threat by Warriner was needed to make that scenario a plausible one, the Emporia warrior would readily oblige. One could debate the wisdom of the GOP's nomination of Ray Garland in 1970, but at least the act clearly had shown that state Republicans were capable of sending futile candidates into the field as a matter of principle. That fact, plus Warriner's renowned volatility, made his threat one that could not be taken lightly.

On the eve of Godwin's announcement, Obenshain left for Atlanta to fulfill professional obligations. Though the fruits of his labors remained uncertain, the party chairman told associates he had done all that he could do. That evening, Warriner called Governor Holton and urged him to convey to Godwin the message that the GOP would oppose him unless he announced that he was "running as a Republican." Holton demurred; Godwin never listened to him, Holton protested, and the governor had no desire to initiate a political discussion with his disagreeable predecessor. But Holton did call Smith Ferebee to pass along Warriner's threat, and Ferebee contacted Godwin to reiterate the necessity of his fully embracing the GOP and the infeasibility of any arrangement other than a wholesale party switch. "Godwin is not a guy you can *force* to do anything," Ferebee explained later, "but he is a very practical guy. If he believes you and what you say makes sense, then he has to make the choice of whether he is going to go ahead and do it, or not be elected."[65]

The players in the drama, *sans* Obenshain, converged the next day on Richmond's Hotel John Marshall, where Godwin was to make his announcement. Warriner was there to listen and, if necessary, to carry out his threat by telling the assembled press corps that he, too, would be a candidate. He immediately encountered Ferebee in the lobby and inquired about Godwin's plans. Ferebee disclaimed knowledge but returned a short time later with a copy of the former governor's prepared remarks in his hand and a forced smile on his face. "I think you are going to like it," he said with feigned enthusiasm, and then handed Warriner the text.[66] The pertinent passage read:

> I think the vehicle to achieve the goal of an uninterrupted good
> government in Virginia is something that, to me, is far more important

---

[65]Ferebee interview.
[66]Ferebee, Warriner interviews.

than either or both of our political parties . . . . I believe today that the Republican Party in Virginia supports that goal, and I welcome their support, and I will accept their nomination or endorsement if tendered to me at their Convention next June.[67]

"That's not it, Smith, and you know it," said Warriner. "You tell him (Godwin) that's not it."[68]

As luck would have it, a seething Warriner and a worried Ferebee found themselves a short time later standing side-by-side in the rear of the hotel meeting room as Godwin made his remarks. In his distinctive rolling cadence, the former governor delivered the words just as Warriner had read them: ". . . I believe today that the Republican Party in Virginia supports that goal, and I welcome their support, and I will accept their nomination or endorsement if tendered to me at their Convention next June. . ." Then, pausing, his eyes fixed on Ferebee and Warriner, Governor Godwin strayed from his prepared text and uttered, ever so haltingly, the magic words: ". . . and, of course, having accepted that nomination, if it is forthcoming, I intend to run as a Republican in the campaign next fall for governor."[69] Ferebee and Warriner embraced and began to dance around until the curious gaze of reporters prompted them to compose themselves. "It was," said Ferebee, "the happiest day in politics I ever had."[70] Warriner, who narrowly had escaped an unwanted campaign for governor, agreed.[71]

The months of often agonizing interplay between Godwin, Obenshain, Warriner, and their various associates had been worth the effort. Personal relationships had been strained more than once, and on numerous occasions the whole enterprise teetered near collapse. Obenshain's determination to forge an agreement, and his patience with the exceedingly strong-willed players on both sides, were the keys to the success of the negotiations, but Ferebee and Warriner also proved indispensable in sealing the deal. Assurances of support from moderate and conservative Republicans, the business community, and senior Democrats in the General Assembly helped convince the former governor that he could safely make the switch. Ultimately, the advice of Godwin's longtime confidant, Carter Lowance, and the former governor's confidence in the political judgment of Obenshain guided his decision.[72]

If uttering the words Warriner had demanded wrought a transformation in Godwin, it was not immediately apparent. The former governor continued to tell reporters thereafter that he "[did] not consider [himself] to be a Repub-

---

[67]Copy of statement on file with the author.

[68]Warriner, Ferebee interviews.

[69]Transcript of remarks on file with the author.

[70]Ferebee interview.

[71]Warriner interview.

[72]Godwin interview.

lican at this time," that such a self-description would depend upon the action of the upcoming Republican state convention, and that he would accept, but was not seeking, the GOP nomination for governor.[73] Godwin had reconciled himself to making the switch, but he was determined to do so in a manner that would not unnecessarily alienate his Democratic sympathizers. "It would have been nothing short of foolish, in my judgment," he insisted later, "to have embraced Republicanism up and down the line and thereby caused a disaster among some of my good Democratic friends who stayed with me in the election."[74] Godwin's uneasiness about Republican affiliation did not go unnoticed in GOP ranks, however, and matters worsened when the presumptive nominee told a reporter in April that he might have to reassess his plans if the unfolding Watergate scandal continued to deepen. As the June GOP convention neared, Obenshain labored to guard against insurgencies and prevent Republican resentment toward the former Democratic governor from breaking out into open view.

When the party faithful gathered in Richmond, the mood was somber. "The delegates understand and accept, in their heads, the political strategy involved in recruiting Godwin into their party at the very top of it," wrote columnist Charles McDowell. "They seem to believe in the concept of a conservative coalition and realignment of the parties in Virginia. But there is no mistaking that nominating an old Democratic foe is still a joyless business for most of these Republicans."[75] Godwin, who shared the mixed emotions, hardly reassured the wary Republicans by referring to them repeatedly as "you people," and to himself as "your nominee," in his appearances at district caucuses at the convention. Many of the delegates made their feelings known by donning buttons on the convention floor bearing the words, "I'm proud to be a 'you people'."[76] But when it came time to cast their ballots, the assembled Republicans made Mills Godwin their nominee by a vote of 1253 to 208.

For many of the GOP partisans from western Virginia, the only thing that made the events in Richmond that weekend palatable was the candidacy of John Dalton for lieutenant governor. The son of Virginia's "Mr. Republican" of the 1950s, "Johnny" Dalton had been a loyal mountain and valley boy and had developed a significant GOP following in his own right. Though he had supported Governor Holton on party matters through 1971, the Radford legislator had taken no position on the Obenshain-French chairmanship battle in 1972, and he saw opportunities for himself as well as his party in the realignment strategy being pursued under Obenshain's leadership. Dalton correctly believed that his presence on the Godwin ticket would enthuse traditional

---

[73]Transcript of press conference on file with author.
[74]Godwin interview.
[75]*Richmond Times-Dispatch*, June 10, 1973.
[76]Ibid.

Republicans in the Valley of Virginia and the Southwest, and it was a belief that Godwin, Obenshain, and many of their associates shared.

Some GOP conservatives, especially in northern Virginia, disagreed. They worried that the moderate Dalton was too closely aligned with Holton and would turn the party away from its new conservative stance at the first opportunity. Stetson Coleman, George Mason Green, and other Obenshain allies urged the party chairman to seek the second spot on the ticket himself, and Obenshain, though strongly disinclined, was weighing their request when Dalton announced his candidacy. Dalton's move preempted Obenshain—their families were long-time friends and a contest between the sons was unthinkable—and the episode produced an unspoken breach between the two Republican leaders that never would close completely. Dalton's announcement brought a private reproof and then a public excoriation from Coleman, but Obenshain moved to quash resentment toward Dalton by quickly disclaiming interest in the race. After a brief, abortive "draft Obenshain" drive, Mason Green, Dortch Warriner, and other GOP conservatives parted ways on the lieutenant governor nomination. Green and his northern Virginia allies threw their support to conservative Arlington Delegate Herbert Morgan, while Warriner, Lewis Williams, and other Obenshain associates to the south supported Dalton. Warriner placed the Radford state senator's name in nomination at the state convention, and Dalton easily gained the nomination over Morgan and youthful State Senator A. Joe Canada, Jr., of Virginia Beach.

The unenviable task of opposing popular incumbent Attorney General Andrew Miller fell to conservative State Senator M. Patton Echols, Jr., of Arlington, who assumed the third spot on the GOP ticket. During the spring, Obenshain had led a small delegation that visited conservative Democratic legislator D. French Slaughter, Jr., of Culpeper and urged him to run for attorney general as a Republican. Slaughter declined, opining that "one convert on your ticket is probably enough,"[77] and efforts to round out the ticket thereafter subsided. At the convention, there was considerable feeling among the Republican leadership that the wisest course would be to field no foe for the formidable Miller, since a GOP ticket effort might drive Miller's moderate Democratic supporters into the Howell camp. But few seriously thought the assembled delegates would permit that. "You can't really do what the insiders know is smart politics [at a convention]," noted Echols. "You get a convention hall full of people . . . and they're all shouting and screaming and thinking they can eat tigers for breakfast, [and they are] going to nominate somebody."[78] Recognizing that, party leaders reluctantly turned to Echols, who easily defeated Eighth District GOP Chairman Gant Redmon and joined the ticket.

---

[77]Klinge interview.

[78]M. Patton Echols interview, May 30, 1980.

Mills Godwin made his first appearance at a Virginia Republican convention on June 9—as the party's nominee for governor. The historic moment did not disappoint. Before mounting the stage, the former governor showed Dortch Warriner the opening line of his remarks and suggested that an ovation following the salutation would help convey the enthusiastic acceptance of the former Democrat by the GOP partisans. Warriner, delighted by what he read, concurred instantly and spread the word to the others on the platform. Following an introduction by Congressman Parris, the former Democratic chief executive strode to the podium and uttered words the party faithful desperately wanted to hear. "As one of you . . .," he began, and with that all on stage leapt to their feet and the delegates answered with a thunderous and prolonged ovation. The moment was just what Godwin had planned: an unmistakable signal that he had accepted the Republicans and, through their boisterous response, an affirmation of their acceptance of him. After more than a few moments, the convention hall returned to order, and Godwin formally accepted the party's nod. He issued a summons to Virginians to join an effort that transcended party allegiances and then, his arms raised with his Republican runningmates, basked in the delegates' adoration.

Chapter 25
Armageddon, Virginia-Style

"Buckle up your armor and join a people's crusade.... We must restore power to the people of Virginia!"[79]

Lieutenant Governor Henry E. Howell, Jr., April 1973

On the morning after the 1973 Republican state convention, the *Richmond Times-Dispatch* hailed the marriage of Godwin and the GOP and proclaimed the dawn of a "new era" in Virginia politics. "Now that Godwin, Virginia's most recent Democratic governor, has made the change," read the newspaper's editorial, "the GOP can expect many more former Democrats to knock at its doors. The result should be a potent political organization dedicated to responsibly progressive government."[80] But before the potent new organization could take the reins and guide Virginia along its traditional path, it had to overcome the formidable and very untraditional Henry Howell.

For much of the period since the Second World War, the theme of Virginia politics had been the disintegration—at first, gradual, and by the late 1960s, total—of the stable and staid political order known as the Byrd organization. By 1973, the Republican Party had replaced the old organization as the vehicle of conservatism in Virginia, and many of the inveterate Byrdites had climbed aboard or were running alongside. But the issue in the 1973 election was much more fundamental than vehicles or labels. The populist-liberal Lieutenant Governor Howell was prepared to mount a direct assault on the conservative precepts and monied interests that long had dominated Virginia politics. This contest—"Armageddon," it aptly was named[81]—was to be a battle for Virginia's political soul.

With the leadership changes of 1972, forces loyal to Howell had taken control of the Democratic Party. But Howell decided for his 1973 gubernatorial bid to retain his Independent status, the better to avoid the

---

[79]Larry J. Sabato, *Aftermath of "Armageddon": An Analysis of the 1973 Gubernatorial Election* (Charlottesville: Institute of Government, University of Virginia, 1975), p. x.

[80]*Richmond Times-Dispatch*, June 10, 1973.

[81]The label was first applied by Charles McDowell. See Charles McDowell, Jr., "When the Experts are Undecided," *Richmond Times-Dispatch*, October 28, 1973, quoted in Sabato, *Aftermath of "Armageddon,"* p. 1.

"McGovernite" epithet that had proved so damaging the previous year. Though both candidates for governor had been Democrats for most of their lives, the long-dominant Virginia party for the first time had no nominee. Howell was the Democrats' *de facto* candidate by virtue of his support among the party's liberal constituency groups, and his supporters arranged for the Democratic state central committee to adopt a resolution "commending" his candidacy. The actual Democratic ticket consisted of two moderates—State Senator J. Harry Michael of Charlottesville for lieutenant governor and incumbent Attorney General Andrew P. Miller, who sought re-election.

The gubernatorial candidates' rhetoric left little doubt about their divergent political perspectives. Though Howell sought to temper somewhat the strident language that had characterized his 1969 bid and also to take advantage of his enhanced stature as lieutenant governor, he did not depart from his anti-establishment, populist themes. "Buckle up your armor and join a people's crusade . . .," he beckoned in April. "We must restore power to the people of Virginia!"[82] Howell relished verbal blasts at the "king makers," who, he charged, had anointed Godwin and were attempting to govern "the affairs of Virginia [from] behind the closed doors of the Commonwealth Club."[83] The lieutenant governor's populist platform centered on opposition to the sales tax on food and nonprescription drugs, which had been enacted during Godwin's first term as governor, and objections to rates charged by the state's electrical and telephone utilities. Like Senator Hubert Humphrey, who Howell admired and supported, the lieutenant governor was a happy warrior whose often electrifying personality on the campaign trail energized his supporters.

Godwin responded to Howell's affronts to the business community and the affluent with apocalyptic warnings of radical change. "Unless we all face up to what is at stake . . .," he declared in late May, "we must be prepared for drastic change in the kind of responsible, stable government to which we have become accustomed."[84] An unapologetic spokesman for the "establishment," Godwin was serious, even austere, on the stump. His dark business suits seemed to match the clouds his dour speeches discerned on Virginia's horizon. Despite his progressive record as a Democratic governor, Godwin was cast in 1973 in the untenable political role of naysayer. That he needed to sound the alarm in order to defeat Howell was plain, but the difficulty Godwin faced was in defining just what about Henry Howell was so alarming. With the effervescent Howell campaigning for "the people," and with Godwin seeming to carry water for powerful business interests, the GOP watched its candidate's early lead in the polls transformed into a deficit by Labor Day.

---

[82]Sabato, *Aftermath of "Armageddon,"* p. x.

[83]*The Richmond News Leader*, May 31, 1973.

[84]Sabato, *Aftermath of "Armageddon,"* p. x.

As the general election campaign began in earnest, many Virginians came to view the contest as little more than a grudge match between the state's two political titans. There was more than a little reality behind that perception. The two men had been at cross-purposes, and often bitterly so, throughout their careers. Howell had begun his involvement in politics as a soldier in Francis Pickens Miller's 1949 anti-Byrd crusade, while Godwin had been a Byrd organization leader since the '50s. During the first Godwin administration, Howell had sued the governor successfully over the state's use of federal education funds. The two candidates had clashed in 1969 over the Democratic gubernatorial nomination, and Godwin had been instrumental in defeating Howell in the primary run-off. Following Battle's loss that November, they had traded charges of culpability for the outcome. Then, in 1972, the former governor had been denied a seat at the state Democratic convention when liberal forces allied with Howell took control. The personal hostility between the two candidates was apparent to all in 1973, and the resultant departure from Virginia's traditionally genteel political competition seemed to repel many voters.

The motivational problems were most acute, however, among the Republicans. In his post-election comments on the race, GOP chief Obenshain explained that the Nixon administration's deepening Watergate scandal had sapped much of the usual Republican enthusiasm. "The campaign in some ways was almost like walking through a mine field because every two or three weeks another explosion at the national level would take place," he said.[85] In the summer there was the disheartening spectacle of the Senate hearings into the Watergate break-in and related issues, during which the existence of the secret Oval Office tape recordings was first disclosed. As Senate investigators and the special prosecutor thereafter attempted to obtain the tapes, the Nixon White House stonewalled. In the campaign's closing weeks, the country was rocked by the resignation of Vice President Agnew because of tax evasion charges, followed by Nixon's firing of Watergate Special Prosecutor Archibald Cox in the "Saturday Night Massacre." It was a traumatic time for Americans generally, and it was especially distracting and demoralizing for Republican activists.

The Watergate developments served to worsen the already widespread lethargy in Virginia GOP ranks. Mixed feelings about the nomination of the former Democrat Godwin did not disappear overnight for many old-line Republicans. While the Democrat-turned-Republican enjoyed the unanimous bipartisan support of the state's congressional delegation, the backing of incumbent Governor Holton and a large majority of state legislators, editorial support from every major state newspaper, and the active campaign efforts of the state Republican Party leadership, the grass-roots GOP workers whose efforts would be needed to turn out the Godwin vote were slow to stir. Noting

---

[85]*The Virginian-Pilot*, February 10, 1974.

the malaise in Republican ranks, columnist Charles McDowell predicted in early September that Godwin would be seen more in the company of running-mate John Dalton. "It's Dalton's coattails that are beginning to look crucial, to hear some of the Republicans tell it," he wrote.[86]

Godwin's campaign organization was a major part of the problem. Carter O. Lowance, a remarkable man who had served ably at the right hand of a succession of Virginia Democratic governors, chaired the effort and staffed the campaign with veteran Byrd organization operatives. As chairman of Democrats for Godwin, former Congressman Watkins Abbitt of the Southside was given a central role. But the courthouse-based, "pass-the-word" style of campaigning that had served the Byrd organization well for decades had become hopelessly outdated by 1973. The electorate had expanded tremendously; many new people had come to the state; the urban corridor now held the key to elections; and, targeted voter identification and turnout operations had displaced the "pass-the-word" technique. As the "token Republican" in the Godwin campaign organization, Judy Peachee found herself constantly calling Obenshain for help. "Dick and I would go in and sit down with Carter [Lowance], and Dick would pound on the desk about how they had to run as a Republican and [they could not do that] by letting Watt Abbitt run everything," Peachee recalled.[87]

The Godwin campaign's problems were not limited to the Republican front. Despite the magnitude of the Howell threat in the eyes of political insiders, much of the conservative business community initially failed to take the race seriously. Godwin's support seemed so broad, and the GOP-Byrd Democrat alliance so formidable, that few gave the liberal Howell much of a chance. The over-confidence proved highly damaging to the Godwin campaign's fundraising program, and that in turn constricted its organizational efforts and media advertising. The Republican nominee also had problems retaining his conservative Democratic base. Partisan Democrats, especially in southwest Virginia, could not brook his party switch. In the Southside, where Godwin had been viewed with a measure of suspicion since his 1964 embrace of the Johnson-Humphrey ticket and his progressive program as governor, Howell's populist appeals seemed to be making substantial inroads among low-income white voters who previously had backed Wallace and Byrd.

The situation thus looked as bleak for Godwin in September 1973 as it had for John S. Battle at a comparable stage in the tumultuous 1949 Democratic primary fight, when the conservative establishment in Virginia had last faced a resolutely liberal foe. Then, a flurry of late campaign issues and the combined energies of the Byrd organization and the state GOP had shifted the campaign momentum dramatically in the contest's closing weeks and produced a conser-

---

[86]*Richmond Times-Dispatch*, September 13, 1973.

[87]Judy F. Peachee interview, September 14, 1979, August 30, 1984, and September 20, 1984.

vative victory. Much had changed in Virginia since 1949, but the galvanizing issues in the fall of 1973—labor, race, and fiscal policy—were familiar. Instead of Sidney Kellam as master strategist, Godwin had Richard Obenshain. And the outcome was remarkably similar.

The dramatic turnaround in 1973 began in late September with Howell's disclosure of a campaign poll that showed the lieutenant governor leading his Republican foe by more than nine percentage points. Howell thought that release of the encouraging data would contribute to his campaign's growing momentum. It had the opposite effect, however, in that it immediately jolted Democratic conservatives, Republican regulars, and the business community from their complacency. Dollars flowed into the Godwin campaign's coffers, precinct organizational activity picked up, and the Republican National Committee dispatched a team of veteran politicos to join a campaign salvage operation spearheaded by Obenshain.

For months, Howell had been on the offensive, and now it was the GOP's turn to seize the initiative. Obenshain launched a two-pronged attack, moving decisively on both the organizational and public relations fronts. Kenneth Klinge, who recently had been installed as the party's executive director, masterminded the organizational efforts with assistance from the Republican National Committee. He assembled a field staff of experienced campaign operatives, established seven regional telephone banks, hired callers to canvass voters in targeted pro-Republican precincts, and saw to it that more than 250,000 calls were made to identify favorable voters. Campaign literature was mailed to the undecided respondents, and more than 100,000 voters who indicated support for Godwin were called again in the 48-hour period preceding the close of the polls on November 6. The expansive program was made possible through the innovations of the State Board of Elections under the chairmanship of Holton-appointee Joan S. Mahan; lists of registered voters had been computerized for the first time and made available to the public in 1972.

Telephone banks had been used in previous Republican and Democratic campaigns, but the sophisticated GOP program established by Klinge—with its use of computerized lists of voters, precinct targeting, paid callers, and direct mail—dwarfed earlier efforts. It yielded a Republican technological advantage that would persist and expand throughout the '70s, and its pivotal importance in the 1973 race was reflected in a post-election analysis by the GOP. The party's internal report concluded:

By September, 1973, it was apparent that the normal campaign efforts to identify and get out the vote were not being mounted. The reasons for the unusual apathy and lack of precinct activity will be left to historians. Watergate was unquestionably a factor; so, too, in certain areas was the novel coalition that resulted in the Republican ticket .... [The program undertaken by the state Republican Party] was designed to use a comprehensive telephone blitz in our known favorable urban precincts to mobilize the maximum urban turnout for the Republican ticket. . . .

[W]e believe . . . the key to victory was the drive *to increase the turnout in our favorable precincts.*[88]

The success of the telephone canvassing program was apparent in the election returns from the targeted areas, and Obenshain and Klinge were lauded for the achievement in the election's wake. "That phone bank more than anything else gave birth to the legend of Dick Obenshain as the consummate party mechanic," observed Edward S. DeBolt, who served as a Godwin campaign consultant.[89]

Obenshain was most active, however, on the public relations front. He established a surrogate program and, with Congressman J. Kenneth Robinson and several prominent Democratic state senators, took to the stump on Godwin's behalf. During the campaign's final weeks, Obenshain relentlessly assailed Howell for a variety of political sins, including his ties to organized labor, opposition to the state's Right to Work Law, embrace of McGovern's candidacy in 1972, support for gun control measures, and seemingly sympathetic statements concerning court-ordered busing. Along with the party chairman's verbal blasts, the GOP blanketed the state with inflammatory anti-Howell campaign literature focusing on those issues. The target of the attacks later pointed to Obenshain's efforts in explaining the election outcome. Citing the Republican chairman's "instinct for the jugular," Howell commented that "Obenshain turned defeat into victory by his last-minute attacks on me in 1973."[90]

The lieutenant governor later conceded, however, that his own campaign missteps had sealed his fate. The sales tax on food had been his most potent political issue, but a Howell initiative announced in mid-October allowed Godwin and the Republicans to turn the tables. To replace the revenue that would be lost through repeal of the unpopular tax on food sales, Howell proposed a hike in the tax on alcoholic beverages, a new levy on bank and corporate stock dividends, an increase in the corporate income tax, and a ceiling on state spending. It was "as simple as ABC," the lieutenant governor said, referring to his plan to target alcohol, banks, and corporations with new levies. But Godwin and W. Roy Smith, chairman of the House of Delegates Appropriations Committee, immediately denounced the Howell "ABC" plan as irresponsible and unworkable. Godwin warned that its enactment would "stymie the growth of the state," and at Republican headquarters fliers assail-

---

[88]Copy of memorandum on file at the Republican Party of Virginia Archives (emphasis in original).

[89]*The Washington Times,* August 2, 1983.

[90]John Stanley Virkler, *Richard Obenshain: Architect of the Republican Triumph in Virginia,* Unpublished Thesis, Auburn University, 1987, p. 72.

ing the proposal as a "tax on jobs" were prepared and distributed almost over-night.[91]

The Godwin campaign surged in the closing days of the climactic contest. Howell's ammunition seemed to have been spent by early October, and so was the lion's share of the Independent's campaign money. An early Howell lead in fundraising quickly was erased, and Godwin was able to outspend his opponent heavily on television and radio advertising in the campaign's critical final weeks.[92] While Obenshain, attorney general candidate Echols, a host of surrogates, and a bevy of television, radio, and newspaper ads bashed Howell down the stretch, Godwin emphasized his own accomplishments and his positive prescription for Virginia's future. Organized and highly visible support from college students gave the former governor a more forward-looking image, and his handlers managed to persuade Godwin to exchange his dark suits and ominous exhortations for more colorful attire and upbeat rhetoric. With his own uncommon campaigning skills, the former governor proved highly effective on the stump during the stage of the contest when it mattered most.

"By the end," commented Obenshain after the election, "our strongest weapon was the difference between Henry Howell during the campaign and Henry Howell during his previous political career."[93] The Independent presented himself to the voters as a populist and sought to downplay the litmus-test issues that had earned him the fervent support of blacks, organized labor, and Democratic liberals. His efforts to move to the middle met with initial success, but by October the GOP campaign was dramatically calling attention to issues that long had motivated Virginia's largely conservative electorate. Howell's attempts to dodge those criticisms were branded flip-flops by the Godwin camp, and for Virginia voters familiar with Howell from his several recent campaigns, the GOP's charge of inconsistency had the ring of truth to it.

Not surprisingly, Howell viewed the GOP's negative blitz differently. It injected phony issues into the campaign, he argued, and he saw the "scare tactics" in historical perspective:

> The organization always turns up the burner when you get close to November, just like when [Ted] Dalton was almost beating [Thomas] Stanley [in 1953]. . . .
> They wait and turn on the busing situation towards the end. They take the gun issue and they begin to move it in October during hunting season.

---

[91]Sabato, *Aftermath of "Armageddon,"* p. 20.

[92]Godwin outspent Howell, $1,093,866 to $987,316. More than 40 percent of the total spent by both candidates was used for television, radio and other advertising, and in that category of expenditure Godwin's campaign exceeded Howell's by more than $164,000. See Sabato, *Aftermath of "Armageddon,"* pp. 84–85; Melville Carico, "'73 Campaign Floated on a Sea of Cash," *Roanoke Times*, February 10, 1974, reprinted in Cooper and Morris, pp. 145–149.

[93]*The Virginian-Pilot*, February 10, 1974.

And that's when they get out all the ghosts and start scaring people—direct mail, television spots, [popular Washington Redskins football star] Sonny Jurgensen on the radio in northern Virginia saying, "One of the candidates wants to send my son to school in the District of Columbia. . . ."

That's their tradition. They like to be the gentle plantation owners as long as they can, but when it gets close they get mean. They are going to slug; they are going to kick; they are going to do anything to win the fight.[94]

Howell's complaints about the GOP-Byrd organization fusillade in the closing weeks of the 1973 campaign may have had at least some merit. But, in reality, the coalition arrayed against him included not only conservatives of both parties, but leading Republican and Democratic moderates as well. GOP Governor Linwood Holton warmly embraced Godwin in the campaign's final days as "the man I want to succeed me,"[95] and the man Holton defeated in 1969 with Howell's help, Democrat William C. Battle, also endorsed the Republican nominee. "The fact of the matter is that in order to win a statewide campaign in Virginia, you have to appeal to significant segments of the Virginia community," commented Andrew Miller, who avoided the Godwin-Howell choice by declaring his intention to cast a write-in vote for House of Delegates Speaker John Warren Cooke. "If you decide, as Howell did very early in his career, that you are going to run against substantial segments of the community and create a confrontation with them, you're not going to be elected."[96]

Howell almost defied Miller's axiom. Opposed by nearly every major political figure in the state, all of the major newspapers, and the vast resources of the Virginia business community, he came within 15,000 votes of defeating a popular former governor with ties to both parties.[97] Voter turnout exceeded more than one million for the first time in a Virginia gubernatorial election, and nearly every statistical comparison reflected the closeness of the contest. Godwin received 50.7 percent of the total tally to Howell's 49.3 percent. The Republican carried 49 cities, and Howell won in 46. Twenty cities gave majorities to Godwin, while Howell received the most votes in 19. Godwin carried six congressional districts (though both northern Virginia districts turned in razor-thin Godwin majorities), while Howell polled majorities in the three southeastern Virginia congressional districts and in the southwestern "Fighting Ninth." In the critical urban corridor, the candidates divided the vote almost evenly—Godwin's 55-percent suburban advantage approximately

---

[94]Howell interview.

[95]*Richmond Times-Dispatch*, October 24, 1973.

[96]Andrew Miller interview.

[97]The vote totals were: Godwin (R) – 525,075 (50.7%); Howell (I) – 510,103 (49.3%). Sabato, *Virginia Votes 1969–1974*, p. 83.

offset Howell's 57 percent of the central-city vote—while Godwin managed a slim, 51-percent majority in rural areas.[98]

Though voting tendencies in Virginia had been in transition for several years, the 1973 results reflected a wholesale departure from the usual patterns. Godwin's party switch, Howell's populist appeal, and reaction to Watergate were contributing factors. Clearly, however, it was Howell's ability to divide the electorate largely along economic lines that created the most upheaval and contributed most directly to his strong showing. "His populist approach . . . had the effect of blurring the traditional distinctions between conservative and liberal," Obenshain noted in the election's aftermath.[99] Howell used the 1968 presidential election results to make a similar point: "I have always said the Humphrey and Wallace precincts were joined together, and that's why I came so close."[100] Precinct-by-precinct analysis in the election's wake confirmed those assessments. According to Professor Larry Sabato, the populist Independent in 1973 polled well over 90 percent of the black vote while also improving upon his previous showings in precincts that Wallace had carried. Howell's tally even exceeded Harry Byrd's 1970 share of the Wallace vote in some places—an impressive feat given the Godwin campaign's emphasis of the racially charged busing issue. Howell's vote in some urban Wallace precincts exceeded 60 percent, while in rural precincts that Wallace had carried, Godwin outpolled Howell only narrowly.[101]

The unusual nature of the 1973 voting was apparent also in the other two statewide races. Ticket-splitting was rampant, and, though Virginians narrowly rejected Howell's bold assault on Byrd organization orthodoxy, they gave large majorities to the sons of the two most formidable organization challengers of the previous generation—Ted Dalton and Francis Pickens Miller. Neither John Dalton nor Andrew Miller exhibited the crusading spirit that had been trademarks of their fathers, and it could be argued on behalf of each that a crusade no longer was warranted. The moderate and measured approach of both men in 1973 seemed to reflect Virginia's gradual transition from the staunch conservatism of their fathers' day to a more progressive or pragmatic period.

Dalton polled 54 percent of the vote and carried every congressional district on his way to becoming Virginia's first Republican lieutenant governor.[102] He rolled up his biggest margins in the traditionally Republican areas of the Sixth, Seventh, and Ninth Districts, and clearly helped running-

---

[98]Ibid., pp. 82–91.

[99]*The Virginian-Pilot*, February 10, 1974.

[100]Howell interview.

[101]Sabato, *Virginia Votes 1969–1974*, pp. 88–95.

[102]The vote totals were: Dalton (R) – 505,729 (54.0%); Michael (D) – 332,990 (35.5%); Flora Crater (Independent; endorsed by the Virginia Women's Political Caucus) – 98,508 (10.5%). Sabato, *Virginia Votes 1969–1974*, p. 83.

mate Godwin in those regions, while he was the beneficiary of the former governor's coattails in the conservative and largely Democratic Southside. The Godwin-Dalton duo proved to be a potent combination. Courthouse Democrats rewarded Dalton's assistance to Godwin on the Republican ticket by including the GOP nominee for lieutenant governor on the informal but highly influential "Southside ticket."[103]

Attorney General Miller's re-election victory was the most impressive.[104] The Democrat carried every city and county in the state—a feat not accomplished even by President Nixon in his landslide victory the preceding year—and in most localities the Miller margins were huge. Miller's GOP opponent, former State Senator M. Patton "Pat" Echols, Jr., of Arlington, entertained little or no hope of winning from the beginning, but his 29-percent showing was worse than it could have been. Concerned that association with Echols might hurt them among Miller partisans, Godwin and Dalton excluded their runningmate from most campaign appearances other than those in northern Virginia and in some partisan Republican strongholds. Echols's totals presumably were depressed further as a result of his prominent participation in the anti-Howell assault in the campaign's closing weeks. Echols, the dedicated partisan, had done his duty, but in the process the incumbent Democratic attorney general was awarded a landslide victory that made him appear the giant on the state political scene.

The Godwin-Dalton victory made 1973 another Republican year, but the returns in the fall did not fulfill the rosy predictions of the spring. Godwin's difficult and narrow win prompted more sighs of relief than shouts of joy in the GOP camp, and the legislative elections brought real disappointment. Earlier in the year, there had been confident talk of impending party switches by a number of prominent Democratic state legislators. A Republican or joint GOP-Independent majority in the House of Delegates even appeared within reach. But most of Godwin's legislative supporters either sought re-election as Independents or retained nominal Democratic status, and the fall elections resulted in a net loss of five GOP legislative seats. Voters installed 65 Democrats, 20 Republicans, and 15 Independents in the House of Delegates. Only one incumbent, Delegate George N. McMath of Onley, switched to the Republican side and was re-elected. A principal reason for the disappointing 1973 results was the Watergate scandal. And it would get much worse.

---

[103] John Dalton interview.

[104] The vote totals were: Miller (D) – 662,568 (70.6%); Echols (R) – 276,383 (29.4%). Sabato, *Virginia Votes 1969–1974*, p. 83.

Chapter 26

Watergate: Realignment Reassessed

"I had great difficulty forgiving [President Nixon] for [Watergate]. He was taking himself out, but it would have been so much better had he not taken a bunch of guys like me out with him. If he had just been honest with me, maybe I would not have lost."[105]

Rep. Stanford E. Parris,
on the 1974 congressional elections

When Mills Godwin and two dozen Democratic state legislators met with President Nixon at the White House in 1972, no one was certain how many of the assembled would one day become Republican. But there seemed a real possibility that the whole group eventually would move *en masse* into the GOP. With Godwin apparently preparing to make the switch, Delegate George McMath counted at least 48 members of the lower house who either already were Republicans or actively were considering a switch to the GOP.[106] Rumors abounded that as many as 12 Democratic conservatives in the Senate—nicknamed the "Dirty Dozen"—also were toying with a transfer of allegiances.[107] The lingering issues were how, when, and whether enough members could be enlisted to shift partisan control in one or both houses. A Republican majority would mean that senior lawmakers who switched could retain their influential committee chairmanships.

While McMath hosted a series of meetings during which the conservative House Democrats weighed their options, several Senate Democrats approached Richmond Senator Edward E. Willey, the powerful president pro tempore and Finance Committee chairman, about jointly moving into the GOP. Willey had attended the White House conference, but he had no intention of switching parties. Years later, a feisty and cantankerous Willey recalled the episode:

They asked me about it, and I said, "Y'all are crazy. In the first place, you were elected as Democrats. Now if you want to be Republicans, you resign from the Senate and run as Republicans. You can't go out here now and

---

[105]Stanford E. Parris interview, September 26, 1984.

[106]George N. McMath interview, August 19, 1980.

[107]Peachee interview.

change parties in the middle of the stream." I said, "Don't come around here asking me to change from a Democrat to a Republican because I'm not going to do it." I would have had them all kicked out of office [if they had switched].[108]

Willey's opposition impeded the effort, but a large number of switches still seemed inevitable until the Watergate scandal unfolded in late 1972 and throughout 1973.

The 1972 gathering of Virginia Democratic lawmakers in the Nixon White House proved to be "the high water mark for the realignment effort in Virginia," in the retrospective assessment of Mills Godwin.

If we could have gotten that group to switch, it would have brought a lot of other people over quickly. But then Watergate intervened. I had many people tell me that the stigma from Watergate was the reason they did not want to take on the Republican label.[109]

By the time Godwin formally joined the GOP in June 1973, most of his friends on the Democratic side of the aisle already were seeking re-election as Independents or Democrats.

The scandal's impact became even more apparent after the fall elections. Fifteen Independents won House of Delegates races in 1973, including a number of senior lawmakers who had chaired committees as Democrats during the previous legislative session. But when the General Assembly reconvened in January 1974, several of the legislators successfully sought readmission to the Democratic caucus.[110] The new governor—hardly a stickler for party labels in the best of times—recognized that Watergate was making Republican affiliation a serious political liability, and he did not encourage his Democratic friends in the General Assembly to switch parties. To the contrary, Godwin urged them to stay where they were, lest their forfeiture of key committee chairmanships impede passage of his legislative initiatives. With no realistic prospect of achieving GOP legislative majorities in the foreseeable future, party switches by Godwin's powerful Democratic friends would only serve to diminish their influence and hasten the elevation of more junior—and liberal—Democratic legislators.

As Nixon's Watergate problems worsened in the months leading up to his resignation in August 1974, public sentiment toward the Republican Party turned sour nationally. The 1972 break-in at the headquarters of the Democratic National Committee by operatives linked to Nixon's re-election committee—the Democratic offices were in the Watergate office complex in Washington, thus supplying the scandal's name—was only a small part of the

---

[108]Willey interview.

[109]Godwin interview.

[110]One delegate who ran as an Independent in 1973 and thereafter retained that status was Eva Scott of Amelia. In 1979, Delegate Scott affiliated with the Republican Party and successfully sought a seat in the Virginia Senate—the first woman to serve in that body.

myriad disclosures and charges that streamed out in late 1973 and the first half of 1974. New allegations of partisan "dirty tricks," campaign finance abuses, misuse of public office, and obstruction of justice at the highest levels of the Nixon administration were daily fare for months. The damage to Republican officeholders and to the GOP was compounded many times over by the vigorous, long-running partisan defense of the President. With the revelations of presidential culpability in the summer of 1974, many of Richard Nixon's staunch Republican defenders were perceived by voters as gullible or even corrupt.

The 1974 congressional elections brought sharp Democratic gains nation-wide. The cumulative effects of high inflation, severe recession, and high-level corruption—all attributed to Republican malfeasance in Washington—ensured a strong anti-GOP tide. And, voter hostility toward Republicans was exacerbated significantly by the decision of the new President, Gerald R. Ford, to grant his disgraced predecessor a full pardon. The demoralization within GOP ranks was as damaging to Republican candidates as was the negative feeling directed toward the party from outside. In district after district and state after state, dazed and dispirited Republican activists and voters simply sat out the 1974 congressional contests, while Democratic candidates reaped the harvest of voters bent on expressing their displeasure with the GOP.[111]

The nationwide Republican debacle extended to Virginia and breathed new life into a state Democratic Party that had been gasping for five years. In northern Virginia, where the *The Washington Post*'s daily Watergate disclo-sures had an especially significant impact, Democratic challengers toppled congressional veteran Joel T. Broyhill and freshman member Stanford E. "Stan" Parris. Broyhill had planned to retire from Congress in 1974, but he recognized that it would be difficult for Republicans to retain his Tenth District seat in the adverse political climate, so he acceded to entreaties by then-Vice President Ford and others that he seek one more term. Despite his long service, however, the dean of the Southern Republicans in the House of Representatives suffered an upset loss to Democrat Joseph L. Fisher, a liberal economist and member of the Arlington County Board of Supervisors. Fisher polled nearly 54 percent of the vote, and rolled up his biggest margin in suburban and normally Republican Fairfax County.

In the neighboring Eighth District, Stan Parris was buried by liberal Democrat Herbert E. Harris. Parris had won the seat in 1972 with a slim plurality, but Harris amassed a 58-percent majority against the incumbent in 1974. Unlike Broyhill, Parris had recognized that his seat was in serious jeopardy as the Watergate scandal deepened, and he had become increasingly critical of President Nixon in his private conversations with fellow Virginia congressmen. To Representative William Whitehurst, Parris complained of receiving large amounts of anti-Nixon mail and of the political damage

---

[111]Congressional Democrats picked up 47 seats in the House of Representatives.

inflicted by the *Post*'s Watergate coverage.[112] Despite the avalanche of bad publicity, however, Parris stood behind the embattled President publicly until the final disclosures that brought Nixon down. A week before Nixon's resignation, Parris received the President's personal assurance that he was not involved in the Watergate cover-up. "I had great difficulty forgiving him for that," the congressman commented in 1984. "He was taking himself out, but it would have been so much better had he not taken a bunch of guys like me out with him. If he had just been honest with me, maybe I would not have lost."[113]

The Virginian most directly involved in the Nixon controversy survived his re-election campaign. Freshman Congressman M. Caldwell Butler of the Sixth District had received a rather unprestigious assignment to the House Judiciary Committee upon his arrival in Washington in early 1973, but by mid-1974 he was at center-stage nationally as the committee weighed the evidence proffered in support of several articles of impeachment directed at Nixon. As late as several weeks before Nixon's resignation on August 9, Butler had assured his Virginia colleagues that press accounts exaggerated the case against the President, but additional disclosures prompted him to express publicly on July 25 his view that Nixon should be impeached. The statement triggered an immediate backlash against Butler among Sixth District Republicans; fellow GOP Congressman William Wampler, back home the next morning in his neighboring Ninth District, found that most GOP constituents thought it was Butler who should be impeached.[114] But the Sixth District incumbent picked up some Democratic votes because of his action, and he managed to poll a 45-percent plurality to overcome two opponents.[115]

Democrats almost defeated two other Republican incumbents. Congressman J. Kenneth Robinson, widely regarded as entrenched in the largely conservative and Republican Seventh District, won with only 53 percent of the vote against an energetic and affable Democrat, George H. Gilliam of Charlottesville. Robinson's share of the vote was nearly 14 percent less than his 1972 showing, and the drop was attributable primarily to a lack of participation by Republicans. In the partisan Ninth District, Wampler polled 51 percent of the vote to survive narrowly a bitterly contested race against Democratic liberal Charles J. Horne.

The bright spot for the GOP was in the Fourth District, where freshman GOP Congressman Robert W. Daniel retained his seat because of another split in Democratic ranks. A multi-candidate race had produced a Daniel

---

[112]See G. William Whitehurst, *Diary of a Congressman* (Norfolk: The Donning Company, 1983), p. 105.

[113]Parris interview. Parris returned to Congress in 1981 after a successful rematch with Herbert Harris, and served there until he was defeated in 1990.

[114]Whitehurst, pp. 112–113.

[115]Butler's two challengers, Democrat Paul Puckett and American Independent Party candidate Warren D. Saunders, divided the remaining votes almost evenly. Sabato, *Virginia Votes 1969–1974*, pp. 103–104.

victory in the largely Democratic district in 1972, and two liberal Democratic rivals—white Delegate Lester E. Schlitz of Portsmouth and black minister Curtis Harris of Hopewell—enabled the Republican incumbent to post a 47-percent plurality win in 1974. With Daniel's success, and with easy wins by the other incumbent congressmen, the Virginia GOP managed to hold on to half of the state's ten seats in the House of Representatives.

Fallout from Watergate and the national economic recession contributed to Democratic victories in several special state legislative elections in 1974, and also to further General Assembly gains by the majority party in 1975. Republican representation after the 1975 elections dipped to 17 in the House of Delegates and five in the Senate, while ten Independent seats reverted to Democratic hands. By mid-decade, it was clear that the Virginia General Assembly would be resistant to the realignment pressures that had been evident in the recent state and national contests. The fortification of that Democratic bastion, coupled with the Democratic congressional advances in 1974, forestalled the party's further decline and signalled the return of stability to the Virginia political scene.

As political analyst Larry Sabato noted in his summary of 1974 electoral developments, "[t]he specter of Watergate overshadowed all other issues . . . and permitted the state Democratic party to shed the millstone of McGovernism."[116] Nearly a decade of preoccupation with the leftward drift of the national Democrats and the ascendancy of avowed liberals within the state Democratic Party had provided a powerful impetus for realignment, and Virginia Republicans had moved decisively to capitalize on the opportunity in 1972 and 1973. But the pressures for philosophical realignment and the resultant downward spiral of Democratic fortunes in Virginia were arrested by two new preoccupations in 1974 and 1975—scandal and recession. Those developments intervened in time to prevent an influential body of Democratic conservatives, including many elected officials and prominent business leaders, from formally aligning with the GOP. For the next ten years, the balance of political power in Virginia would be held by independents whose moderate-conservative views would ensure measured progress and preclude drastic change in the Old Dominion.

As realignment took an intermission at mid-decade, the cast of characters on the Virginia political stage underwent some changes. In September 1974, newly inaugurated President Ford tapped Virginia GOP Chairman Richard Obenshain to become co-chairman of the Republican National Committee. The appointment was suggested by former Seventh District Congressman John O. Marsh, Jr., Ford's counsellor and a close friend from their days together in Congress. In addition to Obenshain's proven record as a party leader, the conservative Virginian could be counted upon to shore up the President's right flank, which had sagged upon his selection of liberal former

---

[116]Sabato, *Virginia Votes 1969–1974*, p. 118.

Governor Nelson A. Rockefeller of New York to be Vice President. To replace the departing Obenshain as party chairman, the conservative activists controlling the Virginia GOP installed a recent convert to Republicanism, Delegate George McMath. McMath's candidacy for the party post averted a factional showdown between Holton protege William Poff of Roanoke and Arlington conservative Hugh Mulligan, and it sent another strong signal of GOP enthusiasm for realignment.

1974 also saw the departure from the political scene—albeit temporary—of Governor Linwood Holton. Though his gubernatorial tenure had been marked by political setbacks and a loss of influence over his own party, Holton left office with widespread popular approval and a solid record of achievement. For his party, the mountain-valley Republican leader had accomplished several things. He had proven that it could win a state election, and that a Republican could govern the Commonwealth successfully. Both had been subjects of widespread doubt only a few years before. And even Holton's failures as party leader while governor may have yielded significant benefit to the GOP. "My judgment is that if we had let Senator Byrd run as an Independent [in 1970] without any opposition," Holton asserted in 1987,

> then Mills Godwin would have run to succeed me as an Independent, . . . and we would not have built the Republican Party. As it was, they saw that we were going to insist on running candidates from that day forward. And, when Mills Godwin decided to run again for governor in 1973, after much pulling and tugging from both Dortch Warriner and Dick Obenshain, . . . I think that is what made him run as a Republican. Had we not done it that way, we would have had a scattering of the parties and I am not sure when we would ever have gotten to the two-party democracy that had been my life's work.[117]

While it can be argued persuasively, if only speculatively, that Holton's actions in 1970 actually impeded development of a strong two-party system by preventing movement into the GOP by Senator Byrd and many of his independent followers, it is beyond dispute that the first Republican governor was guided throughout by his longstanding commitment to the ideal of "two-party democracy."

Several others who affected the course of Virginia's realignment also exited in 1974–1975. Henry Howell, whose liberal threat had caused conservatives to coalesce, found himself out of office for the first time in a decade, though he would not stray far from the political action. Two Republican conservatives who had been among the most instrumental recruiters of former Democrats stepped aside as well. Veteran party leader Joel Broyhill, whose Byrd/Republican coalition in northern Virginia had preceded the budding conservative coalition downstate by nearly two decades, retired from politics

---

[117]Conversations with James Latimer, "A Different Dominion: The Republican Renaissance," WCVE-TV, 1986.

following his defeat in the 1974 congressional contest. And Dortch Warriner, a key figure in the GOP since the early '60s, realized his longstanding ambition to be a federal judge.

The most prominent Virginia Republican leaders at mid-decade, of course, were Governor Godwin and Lieutenant Governor Dalton. There was little doubt that the experienced and versatile new governor would administer the state's affairs with skill and effectiveness. But few Republicans expected from ex-Democrat Godwin—who had to be coaxed, cajoled, and coerced into the GOP—a notably partisan tenure as governor. Even in his acceptance speech at the state Republican convention, the former governor had made it clear that he would not work for the defeat of longtime Democratic allies who shared his conservative convictions. His approach to realignment as a Republican governor would be similar. He would appoint ample numbers of Republicans to posts in his administration, but GOP complaints would not deter him from giving key positions to conservative Democrats as well. He would participate in partisan political activities only when they did not represent an affront to his Democratic friends. And, he would work with Obenshain and Dalton to keep the GOP in harmony with the state's independent and conservative-minded business community. Where party affiliation was concerned, Godwin was not out remake Virginia.

John Dalton, on the other hand, was a lifelong Republican who identified the party's fortunes with his own. He shared Richard Obenshain's enthusiasm for building the GOP, and, by 1973, he also shared the party chairman's belief that realignment was the way to do it. As the natural successor to Holton's mantle as leader of the mountain-valley Republicans, the new lieutenant governor was able to persuade most remaining doubters and dissenters that the party's conservative message and its efforts to recruit disenchanted Democrats were prudent and politic. Dalton, in fact, went out of his way to refute the party-building stratagem of Governor Holton:

> [Republicans] might occasionally get some support from the left. But when you can get it, it's because of whom the Democrats happen to have nominated. And you can't build the party on that. You can build the party . . . by putting together the people who used to be conservative Democrats and the people who were old-line Republicans. . . . [T]he mountain and valley Republicans, the old traditional Republicans who have been Republicans all their lives, have got to realize that we can't win with just straight-line Republicans. Once you move out of the I-81 corridor, you have got to have some people who used to be Democrats.[118]

Dalton worked hard to promote the realignment strategy; he knew that his own hoped-for elevation to the governorship in the next election would depend upon his ability to reassemble the conservative coalition that had

---

[118] John Dalton interview.

propelled him, Senator Scott, and Governor Godwin to their recent statewide victories.

Like Godwin and Dalton, many moderate and conservative Virginia Democrats and Virginia Republicans emerged from the transition period of the early '70s more convinced of both the feasibility and the desirability of cooperation and coalition than they had entered it. To a large extent, the liberal leadership of the state Democratic Party had helped the GOP surmount the emotional and historical impediments to realignment—a development to which Godwin alluded in his address at the 1973 GOP convention. "The sharp reversal in philosophy and leadership of [the Virginia Democratic Party]," he noted, "has made it impossible for me, as well as many others, to continue under its banner. It has brought into focus the great potential good for Virginia that can come through a regrouping of voters with similar convictions."[119] But the question looming at mid-decade was how the new conservative coalition would fare when it faced a moderate, mainstream Democrat, such as popular Attorney General Andrew Miller. The issue lurking behind that question was whether state Republicans in the 1970s were building a durable party organization or merely assembling transitory coalitions.

---

[119]Text of speech on file at the Republican Party of Virginia Archives.

Part Six

Conservative Coalition, Republican Renaissance 1976 - 1980

Chapter 27

The Enigmatic "Coalition"

"The same conservative values and traditions which guided a
limited electorate under machine control also cue a greatly
expanded electorate under no one's control. The new surge of
Republicanism and the decline of Democratic fortunes in Virginia
represent no sharp break with the past. Old ties still bind, but those
ties are cultural, social and philosophical conservatism, rather than
party labels."[1]

Larry J. Sabato, 1979

As the United States at mid-decade prepared to celebrate the completion of
two centuries of independence gained through the oratory of Henry, the pen
of Jefferson, the sword of Washington, and the vision of Madison and Mason,
Virginia no longer was counted in the national vanguard. Indeed, the Old
Dominion in 1976 even seemed to be out of step politically with the rest of the
South. While the nation's and the South's voters were turning back to the
Democratic Party for leadership in the second half of the 1970s, Virginians
were embracing Republicanism with both arms. The Virginia GOP would
leave the decade as the strongest and most successful state party in the
country, Republican or Democratic. And the Commonwealth, which had been
a uniquely one-party, one-faction state as recently as the 1960s, would experience a full flowering of two-party competition as the 1970s unfolded.

Indeed, Republicans proved so successful in the '70s that many observers
were moved to question whether Virginia had been rapidly transformed from a
one-party Democratic to a one-party Republican state. Some found in the
GOP winning streak evidence that the Byrd organization had withered and
died only to be reincarnated as the new, conservative Virginia Republican
Party. Such characterizations were not wholly groundless, but neither did they
rest on a solid analytical foundation. They tended to misrepresent both the
nature and the extent of the newly acquired GOP strength in the Commonwealth. While real two-party competition had indeed arrived in Virginia, the
apparent Republican "dominance" of state politics was illusory. The Virginia

---

[1]Larry J. Sabato, *Virginia Votes 1975–1978* (Charlottesville: Institute of Government, University of Virginia, 1979), p. 4.

GOP had hit upon a winning formula under the conditions then prevailing, but there was no guarantee that the chemistry always would be right.

While there were many factors, four elements were central to the success of statewide Republican campaigns in the 1970s: conservatism, coalition, suburbanization, and organization. The Commonwealth's cultural, social, and political traditions are distinctly, even uniquely, conservative. And from 1972–1973 through the end of the decade, the Virginia GOP had sole custody of the important "symbols of conservatism"[2]—familiar conservative themes and leaders—to which a majority of the state electorate regularly would respond. That the GOP should have such a monopoly was a reflection both of the Republicans' unity of purpose and of the Democratic Party's inability to muzzle or modulate the resolutely liberal voices within its ranks.

Because neither major party since the mid-'60s has commanded the allegiance of a majority (or even a clear plurality) of the Commonwealth's voters, the name of the game in Virginia politics has been coalition. Following the collapse of the Byrd organization, Democrats forged a winning coalition by combining liberals, blacks, the weak organized labor elements in the state, white Democratic moderates, and a significant number of conservatives who were willing to embrace left-of-center Democratic candidates out of long-standing party loyalty and the hope that the party eventually would move back toward the center.

Beginning in 1972–1973, with the installation of Richard Obenshain as GOP chairman, the conversion of Mills Godwin to Republicanism, and the election of the Godwin-Dalton ticket, the GOP was able to assemble a philosophically oriented coalition of conservative and conservative-leaning Virginians of both parties. Conservative Republican partisans, mountain-valley GOP moderates, and former Byrd Democrats practiced successful coalition politics by achieving unity despite their diversity, primarily through the like-minded leadership of Obenshain, Dalton, and Godwin. Republican coalition-building efforts during the '70s also were facilitated by factional infighting among the divergent elements of the state Democratic Party.

Demographic changes in Virginia worked to enhance the GOP's advantage. The state's population increased more than ten percent in the '70s, and most of that increase was in the suburbs. The once-rural Old Dominion had experienced rapid suburban growth for several decades, and the conservative proclivities of suburban voters combined with their burgeoning numbers to significantly expand the Republican base. While GOP candidates found the prosperous suburbs squarely in their corner during most of the '70s—mostly because of the primacy of economic and national security issues—the largest suburban bloc consisted of independent-minded voters for whom social issues such as education, public safety, race relations, and personal privacy also could weigh heavily in voting. Depending upon the circumstances, the issues, and

---

[2]Ibid., p. 1.

the candidates, these suburban swing voters could side with either party. Their strong support for a series of GOP contenders was a key element in the string of Republican victories in the 1970s.

GOP wins during the decade also were a product of superior political organization. The Republican Party and the successive GOP campaigns cultivated an effective precinct-level organization and complemented it through the development and use of modern technology for raising campaign funds, targeting precincts, identifying favorable voters, communicating with the undecided, and getting to the polls those willing to cast Republican ballots. The Republican Party's financial, technological, and organizational edge was only a temporary one, but the GOP used its window of opportunity to full advantage before Democrats were able to close the gap in the early '80s.

Even with these various advantages, Republican victories did not come easily in the second half of the '70s. All of the contests either began or ended as close ones. And, as developments in the early '80s later confirmed, even at the height of its winning streak the GOP was only a misstep or two away from defeat. Virginia's political environment was a truly competitive one, and, though voting tendencies were becoming significantly more Republican, the balance of political power remained in the hands of a large bloc of non-aligned voters, many of whom had considered themselves Democrats at some point in their lives. If there remained after Watergate a chance for a more complete and permanent realignment of Virginia's conservative majority with the GOP, it vanished with developments in the late '70s—most notably the sudden arrival of Charles Robb on the state political scene in 1977 and the tragic departure of Richard Obenshain in 1978.

Virginia politics in the late '70s was, as ever, an odd mixture of change and continuity, and one's ability to decipher the developments depended upon an understanding of the Byrd-era legacy. During the half-century reign of Senator Harry F. Byrd, Sr., as the Commonwealth's political chieftain, Virginia was solidly Democratic like her Southern sisters. But the Old Dominion's dominant Democrats never succumbed to the allure of populism, nor was there the multi-factionalism that typified Democratic politics elsewhere in the South. Unsympathetic observers commonly described Virginia politics by reference to the Byrd "machine," but, as the followers of the senior senator were always at pains to point out, Virginia's Democratic organization bore little resemblance in manner or method to the big-city political machines of the day. Conservative orthodoxy and rural traditions were the glue that bonded the Byrd men.

The self-effacing descriptions used by Senator Byrd and others when discussing the organization gave it an aura of mystery and an appearance of informality. Though everyone seemed to accept that something called the "Byrd organization" existed, there rarely was tangible proof. Only infrequently was it possible to distinguish developments that occurred through design and direction from those that emerged naturally from the broad-based conservative consensus among the state's voters and elected officials. Byrd organization Governor John S. Battle offered the most often-recited disclaimer during his 1949 campaign, when he said:

As for this so-called iniquitous machine, it is nothing more nor less than a loosely knit group of Virginians who usually think alike, who are interested in the welfare of the Commonwealth, who are supremely interested in giving Virginia good government and good public servants, and [who] usually act together.[3]

Virginia's political structure was an enigma, and that was the case even before realignment came along to complicate the situation.

Beginning in 1952, with Senator Byrd, Sr.'s repudiation of the national Democratic ticket, and continuing during the ensuing years of his "golden silence," a considerable segment of the Byrd organization turned its attention and energy quadrennially to aiding the election of Republican candidates for President. This crack in Democratic Party loyalty became a chasm in 1969 and the 1970s, as Byrd conservatives also actively supported GOP candidates for office at the state level. But the bonds of philosophy, friendship, social and economic status, Democratic heritage, and common political enterprise that had linked the Byrd organization leaders and lieutenants to one another withstood the shocks of political change. As Virginia emerged from the chaotic, transforming period of the late '60s and early '70s, the remnants of the Byrd organization coalesced to exert influence and confound observers anew through an even more enigmatic and nebulous non-entity known as the "Coalition."[4]

The genesis of the "Coalition" nomenclature is not known, and the label's tendency to confuse may explain the perpetrator's preference for anonymity. As journalists and political analysts struggled after 1973 to convey the intricacies of Virginia politics to the unschooled, they faced the linguistic hurdle of distinguishing the majority coalitions assembled by candidates in successive elections from the particular group of Byrd conservatives commonly referred to as the "Coalition." The confusion was exacerbated by the fact that the latter was but an element, albeit a key one, of the former. Thus, a person could refer to the success of the conservative coalition in the '70s and mean the ability of GOP candidates to mobilize a coalition consisting of traditional Republican moderates in the western region, GOP conservatives in suburban central and northern Virginia, and the remnants of the Byrd Democratic organization throughout the state. Or, by referring to the conservative coalition, one could intend an allusion solely to the former Byrd Democrats who now referred to themselves as the "Coalition." For the veteran Byrd strategists who for years

---

[3] *Richmond Times-Dispatch*, May 24, 1949, quoted in Henriques, p. 82.

[4] The convention of using a capital "C" when referring to the loosely organized group of former Byrd Democrats known as the "Coalition" has been employed in this book as a convenient way of distinguishing that specific use of the term from the broader, generic uses of the word "coalition."

had fostered the organization's outward ambiguity and had amused themselves and perplexed others by communication through obtuse signals, the "Coalition" nomenclature opened new horizons of obfuscatory mischief.

Governor Battle's benign characterization of the Byrd organization as a "loosely knit group of Virginians who usually think alike . . . [and] usually act together" applied equally well to the Coalition. Three decades later, Mills Godwin needed to alter Battle's formulation little in describing the Coalition; it was, he told a reporter, merely a "loosely knit group of like-minded people who want to see responsible people elevated to public office."[5] But the Coalition was far from monolithic. It included an odd mixture of young and old businessmen and professionals, rural and urban notables, and current and former Democratic elected officials. Because of the varying individual responses to the changes in Virginia's political parties, Coalition adherents ran the gamut from virtual Republicans (such as Governor Godwin, Smith Ferebee, Lawrence Lewis, and the 1969 New Republicans), to avowed Independents (such as Senator Byrd, former Delegate D. French Slaughter, Jr., of Culpeper, and former Delegate W. Roy Smith of Petersburg), to lingering Democrats (such as Sidney Kellam of Virginia Beach and former Congressman Watkins Abbitt). There was no fixed membership roll for the Coalition—just a network of personal relationships and a shared political philosophy. Especially at the Democrat-leaning end of the spectrum, the ability to mobilize Coalition support for GOP candidates would depend from election to election on the degree of the major party contenders' divergence on philosophy and policy.

Along with the litmus-test issues around which conservative Virginians regularly rallied, the influential "symbols of conservatism" that fueled GOP victories during the '70s were the recognized leaders of the Coalition: Godwin, Byrd, Smith, Slaughter, and—whenever Henry Howell was running—Abbitt and Kellam. To Virginia's many conservative independent voters, particularly in rural Virginia and the Richmond area, the nod from such respected former Byrd organization figures gave Republican candidates enhanced credibility and unassailable conservative credentials. The Coalition leaders raised the "Virginians for _____ " banner and organized prominent independent and Democratic business and community leaders around the Commonwealth to back statewide GOP candidates. Lists of the supporters' names were circulated via mail and newspaper advertisements as testimony to the breadth of conservative establishment support for the Republican contenders.

In addition to influencing non-aligned conservative voters, the Coalition wielded decisive fundraising power. To Republican candidates in the '70s, the financial support extended by the state's business and financial establishment—much of which was headquartered along Richmond's Main Street—was a political lifeline. Without it, GOP candidates could not have financed their campaigns and the Republican Party could not have funded the

---

[5]*The Washington Post*, November 14, 1980.

technological innovations that significantly advantaged its nominees. In a 1980 interview, veteran political observer Charles McDowell noted the extent of the business leaders' influence:

Neither party in Virginia has the vitality of Main Street, Richmond when they're fired up on a political issue. They go out and meet at [former State Senator FitzGerald] Bemiss's house, and 40 people with power and brains suddenly can be more important than either party. They were more important than either party when they decided to ditch massive resistance out at that house. And they were more important than either party when they decided to go with Godwin [for governor in 1973] in a switch of parties . . . .

From their point of view, they have been very wise to swing from one party to the other, and to assert their influence for a Democrat at one time and for a Republican in another race. They've tried to get the best conservatives they can find, and they haven't let this transition freeze their thinking into, "Which are we—Republicans or Democrats?"

. . . I think we are talking about a group of people who have come upon the secret which gets rediscovered every few years around America that relatively few dedicated people who will really work at it can have an awesome impact on politics. In this case, you have the representatives of some of the largest business interests in the state who therefore have influence that produces contributions and support.[6]

The foremost leader of the Coalition unquestionably was Governor Godwin. Unlike Senator Byrd, who spent most of his time in the nation's capital, Godwin had been the political leader in Richmond and had worked closely and regularly with the state's business leaders and the conservative Democrats and independents in the courthouses. In his first term, Godwin reflected many of the progressive impulses of the business establishment, which long had been more supportive of investment in schools, roads, and other public services than had the political leadership of the Byrd organization. Though recession, budget shortfalls, a severe energy shortage, and other crises occupied Godwin's attention and necessitated retrenchment during his second term, the governor retained the complete confidence and enthusiastic support of the business community. At the same time, Godwin's conservative social outlook and his refusal to adopt a particularly partisan brand of Republicanism preserved for him the respect, affection, and support of many of the Byrd men in the courthouses.

Though Governor Godwin was not an aggressive party leader following his switch to the GOP in 1973, he worked actively with Richard Obenshain and Lieutenant Governor John Dalton to solidify the coalition that had carried him to an unprecedented second gubernatorial election victory. It was a coalition assembled around conservative precepts, with the Republican Party as its

---

[6]McDowell interview.

vehicle. Importantly, the mainstream conservatism of Virginia in the '70s was markedly more progressive—"responsive" was the word Godwin often used—than in the days of the Byrd organization. Virginia's government, like the state's urban and suburban localities, had experienced rapid growth. State expenditures for education and other services had risen sharply. Avenues for political participation had been extended to the once-disfranchised, introducing more diverse viewpoints into the state's governmental processes. And, with those changes, the divide between the mountain-valley GOP moderates and the pro-Byrd conservatives to the east narrowed. Some saw in the coalition strategy and the conservative political rhetoric of Godwin and Dalton in the 1970s evidence of a calculated departure from the more centrist and pragmatic views each had previously espoused. But such appraisals overlooked the changes that had taken place in Virginia and Virginia's government. The conservative coalition that elected Republicans in the '70s was the reflection of a broad moderate-conservative consensus in the Commonwealth in favor of sustained economic progress and opposed to drastic social change.

While the conservative coalition strategy brought the Virginia GOP remarkable success in the '70s, there was inherent in the concept of coalition an acknowledgement that a complete realignment of conservatives with the Republican Party had not been, and perhaps could not be, achieved. Had realignment been consummated, the former Democrats who comprised the Coalition would have been assimilated into the GOP, its adherents would have come to regard themselves as Republicans, and the state's conservative voting majority would have come to identify more strongly with the Republican Party. None of those things happened, though Republicans made limited progress on each of those fronts between 1972 and 1980. With the Democratic resurgence in the '80s, it would become painfully apparent to Virginia Republicans that they had failed to institutionalize much of their advance during the '70s.

Reflecting on the course of realignment at the close of the decade, former Governor Godwin offered this description of the developments in the 1970s:

The prospects [for realignment of Virginia's conservative majority with the GOP] were extremely good a few years ago. The first obstacle that arose to a more substantial alignment than has taken place was, of course, the Watergate affair. This was occurring when I was running for governor in 1973 and climaxed in 1974 with Nixon's resignation. This almost closed the door as far as a cross-over of Independent conservatives and Democratic conservatives to the Republican Party. Had it not been for Watergate and matters associated with it, such as Agnew['s resignation], I think there would have been a greater movement over to the Republican Party at that time.

Since then, I think there has been an understanding by conservatives that they would support those candidates for statewide and national office who were convincing as to their conservative or moderate-conservative labels, regardless of party. And, therefore, we have seen . . . a willingness on the part of people who thought alike to act in concert, and it has been to the benefit of the Republican Party where it has occurred because it has enabled their candidates to win. They have been nominating responsible, reasonably conservative people, and this has appealed to the majority of the Virginia electorate more than the kind of candidates the Democrats have offered.

There has been some continuing movement over to the Republican Party, but it has slowed. And, depending on who is nominated in the next few years, we will see how much that has progressed. I have a feeling that about 25 percent of the people who vote in Virginia are basically Republican; about 35 percent of them are Democrats; and those percentages are going to vote for their respective nominees almost without exception, whether they are liberal, moderate, or conservative. But [the voters that comprise] this other 40 percent are going to vote for the candidate they perceive to be the most moderate or conservative in their political thinking.[7]

The reasons for the unwillingness of some former Democrats to embrace the GOP formally were varied. There were the historical and sentimental attachments and, for some, the lingering hope that the conservative Virginia Democratic Party of old one day would return. "There has always been this crowd—[House of Delegates Speaker] A. L. Philpott is one; [former House Speaker] John Warren Cooke is another—who have this notion that the Democratic Party is a very valuable thing and can be brought back into a more sensible political alignment," commented former Democrat FitzGerald Bemiss in 1980.

[They think] they are doing a very valuable thing by hanging in there with the Democratic Party rather than turning it over to the George Rawlings and the Henry Howells. I don't think that makes any sense, but it has been a considerable deterrent [to Republican Party growth].[8]

For other conservatives, observation and experience had taught that both parties were philosophically transient and therefore unreliable. Independent status provided the flexibility to cope with shifting partisan currents while holding to one's conservative moorings.

Moreover, with numerous conservatives still serving in constitutional and legislative offices at least nominally as Democrats, many conservative Democrats and independents who regularly supported Republicans for state and federal offices resisted formal alignment with the GOP, lest such affiliation unduly complicate matters at the local level. The presence of conservative Democratic Congressmen David Satterfield in the Third District and Dan Daniel in the Fifth provided additional reasons for their backers to straddle the partisan fence. And the state's conservative business leaders—who

---

[7]Godwin interview.
[8]Bemiss interview.

generally were more inclined toward overt Republican activity than were the former Democratic officeholders in the Coalition—ultimately preferred an independent posture because of the advantages it yielded in lobbying for pro-business legislation from the Democrat-controlled General Assembly and Congress.

It could be debated which was the cause and which was the effect, but the reality was that, like the Coalition, much of the state's conservative electorate regarded itself as independent. As long as there was an independent conservative constituency, there would remain a strong incentive for Senator Harry Byrd, Jr., and the business and political leaders in the Coalition to maintain that status as well. From that position, they could evaluate both parties' candidates and, by their endorsements and contributions, exert a powerful influence over the large bloc of independent voters and thus over election outcomes. "All through my time watching Virginia politics, the conservatives have managed to control most things," commented Charles McDowell in 1980:

> Maybe that's because they didn't resist the rise of Republicanism, but they didn't all run over and take a pin and say, "I'm a Republican", either. They kept their options. They stayed in the middle and floated and laid in their power where it was needed at a given time. [It was] a very slick transition from their point of view.[9]

What did indeed seem to be a "slick" response to the changing political conditions of the '70s nevertheless had detrimental long-term consequences for the realignment process. As long as respected conservatives were seen holding office variously as Republicans, Democrats, and Independents, the state's largely conservative electorate would continue to perceive party labels as unreliable guides and would deem voting "for the man rather than the party" to be the responsible course. Thus, the independent-minded Coalition became an inertial more than a realigning force in Virginia politics. "There has been a very definite realignment," commented Senator Harry F. Byrd, Jr., in 1980. "On the other hand, I think in Virginia—and maybe I had something to do with this—the people as a whole are more independent of parties than in most other states."[10] Largely because of the Coalitionists' insistence upon independence, realignment in Virginia would stall as soon as the leftward-leaning state Democratic Party ventured back toward the political center.

To the GOP's Obenshain, the goal always had been a durable conservative Republican majority in Virginia, and the coalition among conservatives was but a necessary means to that end. He very much wanted the former Democrats to affiliate formally with the GOP, not only to advance realignment, but so they could help ensure the nomination of reliably conservative Republican

---

[9]McDowell interview.
[10]Byrd interview.

candidates through their active participation in party processes. Obenshain recognized that so long as Coalition leaders like Godwin, Smith, Slaughter, and (occasionally) Byrd were lending support to GOP candidates, the immediate object of electing Republicans could be achieved. In such circumstances, there was merit in the Coalitionists' contention that it really did not matter what they called themselves. But it was vitally important, in Obenshain's view, that Virginia move beyond the transitional phase so that the Republican Party permanently would become *the* political party for conservative Virginians. Achievement of that objective was impeded by the shortsighted persistence of Harry Byrd and most of the Coalition in avoiding the Republican label. "Dick's message all along," recalled Judy Peachee, "was that unless the conservatives stay together under one banner and work together, ultimately we will splinter [and that will] give the moderate-liberal element the upper hand."[11]

The independence of the Coalition also guaranteed further division within the GOP over how much, if any, influence those non-Republicans should exert in GOP affairs. The former Democrats' financial support and their conservative seal-of-approval were essential for Republican victories in the '70s. But, since 1952 when realignment began apace, the question of whether and how Byrd Democrats should participate in the GOP had been a subject of controversy. In 1952, Byrd organization Democrats supporting Dwight Eisenhower had turned out *en masse* for Republican mass meetings and had triggered a tidal wave of resentment and opposition. Two decades later, little had changed. Though Virginia Republicans were anxious to have the Byrd support for their candidate in the fall, they nevertheless guarded their party prerogatives and processes jealously. Suggestions from the Coalitionists about who should be awarded GOP nominations rarely were well received by Republican regulars.

During the 1970s, however, the leadership of Dalton and Obenshain prevented the latent grass-roots Republican resentment toward the influential Coalition independents and Main Street fundraisers from becoming a major obstacle to formation of winning coalition campaigns. Both party leaders emphasized the importance of cooperation with the former Democrats as the way to build the GOP. "Obenshain tried to take a role and dominate the party rather than letting it go to Mills Godwin and other [conservative former Democrats]," observed Charles McDowell.

> However closely allied they were supposed to be, I think that Mills Godwin represented who Obenshain in the long haul thought should be replaced and that real Republicans ought to run the Republican Party. I think it was very smart of him to identify quickly with the New Republicans and the business interests and assert himself as a Republican. That's what

---

[11]Peachee interview.

John Dalton has done, certainly, and that is what some of the Republican congressmen have done.[12]

So long as the Virginia GOP had leaders like Dalton and Obenshain, who simultaneously enjoyed the confidence of Republican regulars and of the Byrd Democrats and business leaders who comprised the Coalition, conservative solidarity and Republican victories would be attainable. Without their unifying leadership, factionalism and partisan infighting would make effective coalition-building and even GOP solidarity impossible.

---

[12]McDowell interview.

Chapter 28

The State-of-the-Art GOP

"[Some suggested that] we were adopting a Republican creed because the Jaycees had a creed. We were talking about some organizational techniques [on another occasion and] they said "it sounds like the Jaycees again." Well, maybe so, maybe not. The Jaycees have been pretty successful, and if you involve people and win elections, I guess that's the name of the game."[13]

Former GOP Chairman George N. McMath, 1980

At a Republican leadership conference at Staunton in June 1974, GOP Chairman Richard Obenshain sounded an optimistic note even at the height of the Watergate furor. Mills Godwin's conversion and victory had given the realignment strategy an important boost, he reported, and the Republican Party had a "fantastic opportunity to establish itself as the dominant force in Virginia for decades to come."[14] Yet, Obenshain knew that campaign technology and organization had been indispensable components of the GOP's winning efforts in 1969, 1972, and 1973, and he emphasized them as he addressed the assembled party leaders. "[O]ur ability to realize the [party's new] promise," the party chairman stressed, "is going to depend on whether we develop and continue to practice the capacity for hard, precinct-level, local political activity that is going to be the price of future victories."[15]

Both realignment and party organization were thus on the minds of the GOP's conservative leadership caucus a few months later when they turned to Delegate George McMath to succeed Obenshain as party chief. When Vice Chairman Hugh Mulligan of Arlington called McMath in September 1974 with the news that the party's conservative leaders wanted McMath to be the new state chairman, it came as a bolt out of the blue. McMath had been a Republican for little more than a year, and he had never even set foot in the party's headquarters in Richmond. But, with Obenshain's sudden elevation to the national Republican co-chairmanship, the conservatives wanted a chairman who would reinforce the party's new ties to the Byrd Democrats and

---

[13]McMath interview.
[14]Virkler, p. 82.
[15]Ibid.

297

also bring a strong managerial hand to the party helm. McMath fit the description perfectly. The personable Eastern Shore legislator had built a successful newspaper business, been a prominent and effective leader of the state's Junior Chamber of Commerce (the "Jaycees"), managed Senator Byrd's 1970 re-election campaign, and organized the strong "Virginians for Nixon" effort in 1972. As one of very few conservative Democratic officeholders who actually had joined the GOP, he would be acceptable to Republican regulars. With support from Governor Godwin, Lieutenant Governor Dalton, Senator Scott, outgoing chairman Obenshain, and the party's leadership structure, McMath was—scarcely a week after Mulligan first called him to broach the idea—the consensus choice for state chairman.

McMath assumed his post under the most difficult of circumstances. Bedeviled by Watergate, a sagging economy, and a strong Democratic campaign effort, the GOP was deep in debt and also confronted with a severe deficit of energy and enthusiasm. By 1976, however, McMath had the Republican organization back on its feet and stronger than ever. Shortly after arriving on the scene in 1974, he loaned the party $20,000 in personal funds to pay off current bills and meet the payroll. Within a year and a half, he had reorganized the staff structure, hired a full-time finance director, communications chief, and field staff, moved GOP headquarters to a more suitable office suite on Richmond's Main Street, and quadrupled the party's annual operating budget to more than a half-million dollars.

The party chairman found his new position to be a full-time job, and he later decided to forego re-election to the House of Delegates in order devote more time to party-building activities. He traveled throughout the state exhorting the GOP faithful to "Think Big!"—a large wooden pachyderm bearing those words helped him make the point—and he instituted numerous other innovations designed to enhance the party's self-image and *esprit d'corps*. The GOP's annual dinner in 1975 was dubbed the "Commonwealth Dinner" (in earlier times it had borne the name of President Lincoln), and those present at the well-attended April gathering heard remarks by President Gerald Ford. McMath also succeeded in spurring the central committee to formally adopt a Virginia Republican Creed that espoused fidelity to conservative principles. "I was accused on one occasion of being too Jaycee-like," recalled the chairman after his tenure,

> [Some suggested that] we were adopting a Republican creed because the Jaycees had a creed. We were talking about some organizational techniques [on another occasion and] they said "it sounds like the Jaycees again." Well, maybe so, maybe not. The Jaycees have been pretty successful, and if you involve people and win elections, I guess that's the name of the game.[16]

---

[16]McMath interview.

It was a game McMath played with exceptional energy, determination, and skill.

McMath's tenure saw an increase in the size and level of activity of local Republican committees, and the party's auxiliaries also experienced sharp membership gains. The growth of the College Republican Federation of Virginia and the Virginia Federation of Republican Women was especially significant. As in the early '60s, the influx of young activists and female volunteers gave the party new vigor and enthusiasm. The College Republican organization, led in 1976 by University of Richmond student David Robertson, would grow rapidly throughout the '70s and yield a well-trained corps of GOP operatives for future campaigns. The effects of the campus organizational efforts were felt during McMath's tenure through well-publicized mock election victories, large numbers of student absentee ballots, and precinct-level volunteer manpower. Under the leadership of veteran GOP organizer Virginia "Ginny" Lampe of Arlington, the women's federation also expanded sharply in size and assumed an increasingly prominent and active role in state and local Republican campaigns.

McMath was able to attract an energetic, youthful corps of trained operatives to staff the state Republican headquarters. In late 1975, he tapped William Royall, 29, a veteran of several GOP campaigns and of the Republican National Committee's communications department, to serve as the party's new executive director. A few months later, 25-year-old Karl Rove of Alexandria, then chairman of the College Republican National Committee and a former aide to national GOP Chairman George Bush and Co-Chairman Obenshain, joined the staff as finance director. For Royall, Rove, and the other members of the McMath team, the priorities were development of the party's direct mail fundraising program and refinement of its computerized registered voter lists. More effective regular communication with local GOP units through a newsletter and other devices also received emphasis. When he was not shepherding the party's ambitious direct-mail and telephone-bank fund solicitation effort, Rove was busy assembling precinct-organization and campaign manuals for distribution to Republican troops in the field.

Virginia Republicans of necessity looked to former Byrd Democrats and the independent conservative business establishment to finance party operations and Republican campaigns, but the GOP was prepared to supply its own indispensable ingredient of the winning formula—organization. The conservative former Democrats and Republican regulars manning the precinct brigades would be backed during the second half of the '70s by a technically proficient, state-of-the-art GOP operation unmatched by anything remotely comparable on the Democratic side. Well-financed, well-organized, sure in its strategy, and intent upon harmony, the Virginia GOP was a model for state party organizations throughout the country.

It would take all of the Virginia Republican Party's considerable assets to mount a winning campaign in 1976. In the aftermath of Watergate and his pardon of Richard Nixon, President Gerald Ford was waging an uphill battle to retain the White House, while in Virginia and the rest of the South the presence of former Georgia Governor Jimmy Carter at the top of the Democratic ticket made Republican victories unlikely. The difficult situation was complicated by the presidential candidacy of former California Governor Ronald Reagan, champion of the Republican right, which occasioned the renewal of the GOP's moderate and conservative factional divisions across the country.

The Ford-Reagan struggle sharply divided Virginia Republicans. Most of the Obenshain-led conservative faction lined up behind the Californian, while Ford's support came primarily from the party's moderate wing. Spearheading the Reagan campaign were three Republican legislators—State Senator A. Joe Canada, Jr., of Virginia Beach, Delegate Wyatt B. Durrette, Jr., of Fairfax, and Delegate Raymond R. Robrecht of Salem. McMath and Senator William Scott also lent Reagan their support. Richard Obenshain, who resigned from his national party post in mid-February ostensibly to spend more time with his family, privately preferred Reagan but remained publicly uncommitted during most of the nomination campaign. The Ford forces in the state were led by former Eighth District Congressman Stanford E. Parris, who had served with the President in Congress. Ford also received important early endorsements from Governor Mills Godwin and Congressmen J. Kenneth Robinson and G. William Whitehurst.

The view of Parris, Godwin, and Lieutenant Governor John Dalton—who announced his own support for Ford shortly before the national convention—was that the President, by virtue of his office, record, and mainstream views, had a better chance of winning the general election than did the more philosophically oriented Reagan. Though the articulate former California governor inspired conservative true-believers, Republican moderates and many of the state's independent business leaders feared a repeat of the 1964 Goldwater debacle if Reagan were to become the nominee. The support Ford received from the business segment of the Coalition was "pragmatic," explained FitzGerald Bemiss.

> These [business] people are not all that hard right wing. . . . [They] are more moderate than they look sometimes, and they are looking to see which of the guys is going to win since there is not much real philosophical difference there. In 1976, [they] just felt that Ford was more likely to win than Reagan.[17]

In most of the Southern states, the support of GOP moderates and pragmatic conservatives was sufficient to give Ford a majority of the national convention delegates, though in several states the competition was fierce. In Virginia, however, Reagan's candidacy was backed solidly by the conservative forces that had delivered the party chairmanship to Obenshain in 1972 and had dominated state GOP councils since. As his underdog candidacy began to gain

---

[17]Bemiss interview.

momentum nationally, Reagan stumped in the state and attended the party's annual Commonwealth Dinner in late March, and thereafter his Virginia loyalists dominated the delegate selection process. With the exception of Godwin and Dalton, who were included for reasons of protocol, most of the Virginia delegates to the national convention were thought to be supporting Reagan. Shortly before the convention, however, a handful of delegates who earlier had expressed a preference for the Californian announced that they instead would vote for Ford. The contest for the presidential nomination was exceedingly close, and the potentially significant switches infuriated Virginia Reagan organizers.

The national convention in Kansas City thus proved to be an especially acrimonious affair for the Virginians in attendance. Tempers flared when Governor Godwin, who had been awarded the delegation chairmanship over Senator Scott, gave a seconding speech for Ford. And, when the roll was called, Herbert Morgan of Arlington—with the assent of Obenshain and the other Reagan backers—wrested the microphone from Godwin and demanded that the Virginia delegates be polled individually. The delegation cast 35 votes for Reagan and 16 for Ford, and the polling of the group on national television guaranteed that each of the delegates would be held accountable to the folks back home. It was, as former GOP executive director Kenneth Klinge recalled in 1983, "a very bitter convention. There are still people who are not speaking to each other as a result of those floor fights."[18]

Gerald Ford and Senator Robert Dole, his sharp-tongued runningmate from Kansas, began the general election campaign with a large deficit in the polls. Jimmy Carter's strong regional appeal undercut the Republican Southern strategy inaugurated by Richard Nixon, and the GOP ticket's disadvantage in the South was exacerbated by the inactivity of many Reagan partisans who sat on their hands after the bruising nomination fight. But in that respect, too, Virginia was different.

Shortly after the acrimonious convention, a leadership team was assembled for the Ford campaign in Virginia, and the essential elements of another winning conservative coalition were represented. Lieutenant Governor Dalton, former party chief Obenshain, and Coalition leader W. Roy Smith were named co-chairmen of the statewide effort; GOP Executive Director William Royall became the campaign manager; and Judy Peachee, the newly elected Republican national committeewoman from Virginia, took a leave of absence from Governor Godwin's staff to serve as organization director. Virginia was one of only two states in which the national leadership of the Ford campaign entrusted administration of the campaign effort to the state GOP organization. "Our strategy," recalled Royall,

> was for them (the national Ford campaign) just to leave us alone. We knew the coalition that was necessary to put the campaign together; we had just

---

[18]*The Washington Times*, August 2, 1983.

done it [in the 1973 Godwin campaign]. We had a good group of people all pulling together. And Obenshain, Dalton and Roy Smith—as well as [FitzGerald] Bemiss, who was close to [Ford campaign manager James] Baker—said, "Look, just give us our budget; give us a little bit of money, and let us do it, and we'll win."[19]

With the Virginia GOP already recognized as one of the premier Republican organizations in the country, the unusual request was granted.

The keys to the success of the Virginia GOP's effort for Ford were conservative solidarity and Republican unity. In much of the South, conservative Democrats who had abandoned Hubert Humphrey in 1968 and George McGovern in 1972 rallied around native son Carter in 1976. But in Virginia, which gave birth to Southern presidential Republicanism during the Eisenhower campaigns, the Byrd Democrats stayed with Ford. With Governor Godwin as the titular head of the state GOP, Roy Smith as Ford's state co-chairman, and former Democratic Congressman John O. Marsh, Jr., as a senior official in the Ford White House,[20] there was no lack of confirmation that the incumbent was the favorite of Virginia's conservative Democratic establishment. In late October, the President came to Richmond following a televised debate with former Governor Carter in Williamsburg, and he was joined at an enthusiastic Capitol Square rally by two other conservative icons—Independent Senator Harry Byrd, Jr., and former Democratic Governor William Tuck. Carter's Southern and agrarian appeal was strong in many conservative rural areas of the state, and the impressive display of Coalition support for Ford helped to hold down the Democrat's totals in the Southside and other Byrd strongholds.

After the divisive nomination fight, Republican unity was far from inevitable. But, as William Royall emphasized later, there was a concerted effort by Reagan's Virginia leadership to put the spring battles behind and meet the Carter challenge:

The greatest thing was that the party came together after the convention. From Jerry Ford's acceptance speech on, you had all of these died-in-the-wool Reagan people who stood up and said, "We're going to go back home and work like hell for Jerry Ford." And they did. No one worked harder than Dick Obenshain and Judy Peachee, and people like that had really wanted Reagan to be the nominee. I think that was the single greatest factor [in Ford's win in Virginia].

That didn't happen in Mississippi. It didn't happen in Texas. If all of the Reagan-dominated party organizations in the Southern states had supported Ford as hard as Virginia did, Ford would have been President. But they didn't.

---

[19]William A. Royall interview, June 5, 1980.

[20]Marsh, who as Seventh District congressman served with Ford in the House of Representatives from 1962 until 1970, joined the White House staff in 1974 as Counsellor to the President with Cabinet rank.

... Dick Obenshain was just a classic example of someone who led the conservative wing of the party in his state and yet was a Republican first and foremost.... God bless him, he really worked. He spoke; he held news conferences; he did everything we asked him to do.[21]

Recognizing that it was a key battleground state, the Carter campaign mounted a strong effort in Virginia as well. While Ford was appealing for conservative support in Capitol Square, the Democratic nominee was addressing an even larger crowd in Alexandria. His presence in northern Virginia was noteworthy. Like the populist appeal of his friend and supporter Henry Howell, Carter's non-ideological message cut across the ordinary philosophical lines in the independent-minded Commonwealth. But his better-than-usual support (for a Democrat) in much of Virginia was not matched by strength in the vote-rich northern Virginia suburbs. There, Carter's anti-Washington, anti-bureaucracy rhetoric did not sit well with the thousands of federal workers for whom the presidential choice had potentially far-reaching personal consequences.

While Ford had to come from far behind nationally, the race was close in Virginia from Labor Day forward. A Ford campaign poll in September gave the President a two-percent lead in the state. And, though Obenshain, Dalton, and College Republican Chairman David Robertson held a news conference in late October to trumpet Ford's 62 percent of the statewide vote in campus mock elections—Obenshain called it a "weathervane of the general election"[22]—both sides knew the race was a dead heat and could go either way. The numbers on election night matched the expectations. The intense race to the finish line ended with Carter winning narrowly nationally and losing in Virginia by the closest presidential vote in the state in nearly a century.

Jimmy Carter delivered the White House back into Democratic hands with the help of a nearly solid South. Virginia, the erstwhile leader of the Confederacy, was the lone exception. "When faced with the choice of supporting a southern Democratic moderate or a non-southern Republican conservative," wrote the University of Virginia's Larry Sabato, "the right-leaning Commonwealth, unlike her neighbors, went with her head and not her heart."[23] Ford's Virginia margin—23,000 votes—was less than 1.5 percent of the nearly 1.7 million ballots cast in the state.[24] The suburban vote again was key, and Ford polled nearly 54 percent of it; his success in the two congressional districts in northern Virginia and in the conservative Richmond suburbs provided his winning margin. Carter made the race close by dupli-

[21]Royall interview.

[22]*Richmond Times-Dispatch*, October 30, 1976.

[23]Sabato, *Virginia Votes 1975-1978*, p. 9.

[24]The vote totals were: Ford (R) – 836,554 (49.3%); Carter (D) – 813,896 (48.0%); Peter Camejo (Socialist Workers) – 17,802 (1.0%); Thomas J. Anderson (American) – 16,686 (1.0%); Lyndon H. LaRouche (U. S. Labor) – 7,508 (0.4%); Roger L. MacBride (Libertarian) – 4,648 (0.3%). Ibid., p. 10.

cating Howell's coalition of blacks, blue-collar urban whites, and low-income rural voters. The geographic distribution of the vote in the state closely resembled the 1973 Godwin-Howell pattern. The Democrat received a majority of the vote in Wallace precincts,[25] and he held Ford well below the usual GOP presidential vote totals in the Southside and the Roanoke Valley.

While the Virginia outcome was different, the distinctive Southern voting patterns in the presidential contest were nonetheless evident in the Old Dominion. Carter's inroads in the conservative, normally Republican-voting rural areas of Virginia reflected a regional phenomenon. The greatest shift into the Democratic column from the 1972 contest was among low-income Southern whites. As Republican analyst Kevin Phillips noted, "The real key [to Carter's victory] lay in the working-class and lower-middle-class constituencies— perhaps 15 percent of the national electorate—routinely ignored by Gerald Ford-type Establishment Republicanism."[26] Carter's strength among Southern blacks also was apparent in Virginia—he received better than 91 percent of the black vote in the Commonwealth.[27] Black voter turnout rose sharply in the South in 1976, and there were increases in Virginia as well. But Carter, like other Democratic candidates in the state during the 1970s, suffered from the tendency of Virginia's black voters to go to the polls less often, on average, than whites. Without this differential, the Democratic ticket would have carried Virginia and made a clean sweep of the South.

The largest Virginia vote-getter in 1976, however, was not President Gerald Ford but Independent Senator Harry F. Byrd, Jr., who won his most lopsided re-election victory ever. Though there were 140,000 fewer ballots cast in the Senate contest, 50,000 more Virginians voted for Byrd than for Ford. Against retired Admiral Elmo R. "Bud" Zumwalt, a former chief of naval operations, and Martin H. Perper, a GOP fundraiser from McLean, Byrd carried eight of ten congressional districts and rolled up a hefty 57-percent majority.[28] To the extent it attracted any interest, the contest was chiefly between Byrd and Democrat Zumwalt; Perper, who described himself as an "Independent Republican," ran a shoe-string campaign after he was denied the GOP nomination at the party's June convention.

With GOP leaders Obenshain and Dalton opposed to the nomination of a Senate candidate and with no credible Republican contender available, there was never any chance of a repeat of the 1970 controversy, when the party's moderate and conservative wings squared off over whether to nominate a

---

[25]Sabato's study concluded that Carter received 53.5 percent of the vote in selected precincts carried by American Independent Party candidate George Wallace in 1968. Ibid., pp. 15, 19.

[26]Kevin Phillips, *The American Political Report*, February 4, 1977, quoted in Harry S. Dent, *The Prodigal South Returns to Power* (New York: John Wiley & Sons, 1978), pp. 16–18.

[27]Sabato, *Virginia Votes 1975–1978*, p. 15.

[28]The vote totals were: Byrd (I) – 890,778 (57.2%); Zumwalt (D) – 596,009 (38.3%); Perper (I) – 70,559 (4.5%). Ibid., p. 10.

candidate against the independent Byrd. Perper's bid at the 1976 convention garnered only token support from a smattering of Republican regulars in the far western region of the state. But GOP Chairman McMath, who had managed Byrd's 1970 bid, was hopeful for many months that the senator would become the Republican nominee in 1976. Early in the year, he and former chairman Obenshain jointly wrote to Byrd and made the case for a switch to the GOP. "The point we tried to make," recalled McMath, "was the contribution he could make to future generations by helping to build a strong Republican Party."[29] The Republican leaders' letter followed a December 1975 central committee resolution that, for the first time, formally invited the senator to join the GOP.

To McMath's considerable disappointment and mild embarrassment, the senator announced on May 18 that he would seek re-election as an Independent. Committee assignments, senatorial seniority, and the political advantages of independence again were the principal factors. Though McMath branded the GOP convention's decision not to oppose Byrd a "tacit endorsement" of his candidacy,[30] the independent senator also could count on significant help from the Democratic side. Like the Republicans, Virginia Democrats extended an early invitation to Byrd to join their ranks, and in the fall the Democratic National Committee contributed equal amounts ($5,000 each) to the Byrd and Zumwalt campaigns. More important, there was a substantial overlap in the Byrd and Carter constituencies. The two jointly carried 49 counties and 19 cities, garnered much of the same support in the Southside, and suffered similar fallout in suburban northern Virginia from their anti-government stances.[31] Though Byrd did appear with Ford at the Capitol Square rally in late October as the presidential race tightened nationally, he maintained characteristic "golden silence" on the contest from start to finish and thereby minimized any backlash in the Carter camp. Rather than seize the opportunity to advance Republicanism in Virginia, Byrd chose the independent path that would assure him a comfortable re-election victory.

The contests for the state's House of Representatives seats provided yet another indication that Virginia was out of step with regional and national trends. Despite a bruising primary fight against two liberal opponents, moderate Democrat Robert E. Quinn of Hampton was favored to win the First District seat being vacated by his retiring friend and supporter, Representative Thomas N. Downing. The conventional wisdom was that Quinn's prospects were improved significantly by the GOP's nomination of Essex County Commonwealth's Attorney Paul S. Trible, Jr. The 29-year-old Trible surprised observers in the spring by overcoming Democrat-turned-Republican Herbert H. Bateman of Newport News and another opponent in a spirited convention

---

[29]McMath interview.
[30]*Richmond Times-Dispatch*, July 18, 1976.
[31]See Sabato, *Virginia Votes 1975–1978*, p. 21.

battle. Bateman, a respected moderate-conservative state senator, had switched parties and sought the GOP nomination at McMath's urging, but he was defeated when Republican regulars unexpectedly united behind Trible.

In the fall, the youthful GOP nominee confounded the experts again by narrowly defeating Quinn even as Democrat Carter was edging Ford in the district.[32] With help from disaffected supporters of black Newport News Councilwoman Jessie Rattley, who had lost to Quinn in the Democratic primary, Trible was able to garner a surprising 30 percent of the district's black vote. Noting the unusual nature of his achievement—it resembled Holton's in 1969—the young congressman-elect declared after the voting that the "black people of Virginia never again will be neglected by the Republican Party and never again [will be] taken for granted by the Democratic Party."[33] In addition to his inroads into the Democratic base, Trible's victory was attributable to his aggressive and energetic campaigning, which was in stark contrast to the performance of his overconfident Democratic opponent. The GOP nominee also received valuable campaign help from the state Republican headquarters.

In becoming the First District's first GOP congressman since Reconstruction, Trible also became the only Republican to wrest a Southern congressional seat from the Democrats in 1976. His win continued a pattern of GOP congressional victories following divisive Democratic primaries in Virginia, and it gave Republicans another majority of the state's House of Representatives delegation. Incumbents coasted in the other nine congressional districts. In northern Virginia, Democratic liberals Herbert Harris and Joseph Fisher, who had toppled GOP incumbents in 1974 at the height of Watergate, each consolidated his position by soundly defeating a Republican foe.[34] Conversely, two Virginia GOP congressmen who only narrowly had survived the 1974 Watergate debacle—Robert Daniel and William Wampler—overcame Democratic challengers by solid margins.[35] For the sixth consecutive time, the GOP won a majority of the major-party congressional vote statewide, but it passed a milestone by also winning its first plurality of the total congressional vote in the state.[36]

---

[32]The vote totals were: Trible (R) – 71,789 (48.6%); Quinn (D) – 70,159 (47.4%); Mary B. McClaine (I) – 5,887 (4.0%). Sabato, *Virginia Votes 1975–1978*, p. 24.

[33]*The Richmond News Leader*, November 3, 1976.

[34]In the Tenth District, Fisher polled nearly 55 percent of the vote to defeat Republican Vincent F. Callahan, Jr., while Harris topped the GOP's James R. Tate in the Eighth District with nearly 52 percent of the ballots. Sabato, *Virginia Votes 1975–1978*, p. 24.

[35]Daniel garnered his first absolute majority in a congressional bid by polling 53 percent of the ballots in his Fourth District race with Democrat J. W. "Billy" O'Brien. In the Ninth District, Wampler received more than 57 percent of the vote in his rematch with Democrat Charles J. Horne. Ibid.

[36]See generally Alexander J. Walker, "The Virginia Congressional Delegation Since 1965," *University of Virginia News Letter* (Charlottesville: Institute of Government, University of Virginia), October 1978.

The 1976 elections contributed to the growing acclaim enjoyed by the Virginia GOP in national Republican circles. As the only Southern state to give its electoral votes to Gerald Ford and the only one to capture a formerly Democratic congressional seat, the Old Dominion stood apart. Its Republicans had achieved unity of purpose when other GOP organizations were divided from within. The Virginia Republican Party was proficient technologically, organizationally, and financially while GOP organizations elsewhere remained in the throes of post-Watergate retrenchment and malaise. Virginia was quickly coming to be viewed as one of the most Republican states in the country. In much the same way that moderate Democrats across the country would look to the winning formula of Chuck Robb and Douglas Wilder a decade later as the blueprint for a party resurgence, conservative Republicans throughout the nation were beginning to focus on Virginia and GOP leaders Obenshain, Godwin, and Dalton as possessors of the secret for success. In conservative Virginia, the "Reagan Revolution" had arrived a few years early.

Chapter 29

Henry Howell Strikes Again

"So far, the leaders of the bipartisan conservative establishment
that has dominated Virginia elections for almost a century have
been unable to solve the latest problem in state political
triangulation: whether Republican Dalton or moderate Democrat
Miller would be the best bet to stop the liberal Howell."[37]

James Latimer, November 1976

John Dalton grew up with politics; he learned from a master; and he practiced the art well. Ted Dalton, Virginia's original "Mr. Republican," never became governor himself, though he came the closest of any modern GOP contender before Holton. But in 1977, the elder Dalton's aspirations rode the shoulders of his adopted son, John. They were steady shoulders indeed.

The younger Dalton's gifts did not match his father's, but he made up for the deficit with determination, methodical planning, boundless energy, and relentless effort. His sixth sense for politics impressed all who knew him. He could reel off the vote counts and percentages from the most obscure of past contests; he could recite the factors affecting the outcomes of literally hundreds of political races; he had a facility for remembering names and faces, and, in case he should ever forget, he kept a voluminous card file of political contributors, supporters, and acquaintances. To say that John Dalton was driven by a desire to become governor would perhaps leave the wrong impression. But he clearly had his sights fixed on that goal from a very early age. He would spare no effort to succeed, and he meant to leave nothing to chance.

Of course, chance has its way of altering the political landscape so as to frustrate even the most meticulous of planners. In Dalton's case, he freely acknowledged later that unexpected events had placed him on the brink of achieving his goal in 1977. He would not have run for lieutenant governor in 1973 unless Mills Godwin had been at the top of the ticket, and Mills Godwin would not have been at the top of the ticket if the bright career of moderate J. Sargeant Reynolds had not been extinguished prematurely by an inoperative brain tumor. Lieutenant Governor Reynolds's death and Henry Howell's election to fill that vacancy had hastened the Virginia electorate's partisan realign-

---

[37]*Richmond Times-Dispatch*, November 7, 1976.

309

ment. The Republican Party's successes in 1976 had signalled the end of the reverses caused by Watergate. And now Dalton, as Mills Godwin's logical successor, was in a position to assemble a coalition of Republicans and former Democrats that could elect him governor.

As the son of a prominent Byrd organization foe, Dalton at first blush seemed an unlikely candidate for the conservative Coalitionists to pin their hopes on in 1977. Early on, in fact, there was some casting about by the Byrd men for one of their own to make the race. State Senator Elmon Gray of Waverly, a Democrat and son of organization stalwart Garland "Peck" Gray, was the subject of frequent discussion at the Commonwealth Club and in the corner offices on Richmond's Main Street during 1976. But the presence of Dalton as the heir-apparent on the Republican side precluded a repeat of Godwin's switch-and-run routine. And the Democratic field already was crowded. The two Democratic titans, former Lieutenant Governor Howell and Attorney General Andrew Miller, were gearing up for a primary campaign that promised to be a battle royale.

The unease about a Dalton bid among certain Coalition leaders reflected little displeasure with the man. A few conservatives worried that Dalton's mountain-valley roots eventually might resurface and alter the GOP's rightward direction. But, as lieutenant governor, Dalton had worked well with Godwin during the latter's second term as governor, and he now was wholly committed to the conservative coalition strategy advocated by Godwin and party strategist Richard Obenshain. As he paid his visits to the business leaders on Main Street during 1976 and early 1977, Dalton found them receptive and even somewhat supportive. But the question on all of their minds was, "Could he win?" For most of the conservative Virginia establishment in 1977, stopping Henry Howell again was the top priority. But, unlike in the showdown with Howell four years earlier, there was uncertainty and division in conservative ranks over who could best get the job done. "So far," wrote veteran reporter James Latimer in late 1976,

> the leaders of the bipartisan conservative establishment that has dominated Virginia elections for almost a century have been unable to solve the latest problem in state political triangulation: whether Republican Dalton or moderate Democrat Miller would be the best bet to stop the liberal Howell.[38]

For Dalton, the establishment's preoccupation with the Howell threat initially posed a serious problem. "The business community was just determined to beat Henry Howell," Dalton later recalled,

> and my problem early on in that campaign was the fact that Andrew Miller was perceived as the strongest person to keep Virginia from going to Henry Howell. Along in the '76 and early '77 period, Miller had worked the business community. He had been to see many of the people on Main

---

[38]Ibid.

Street that finance conservative-type campaigns and was getting commitments from a lot of those people on the basis that he was the savior to keep Henry Howell from being governor. And his track record looked good. He carried every city and county in [his race for attorney general] in 1973, and I don't recall anybody doing that even in Harry Byrd's heyday.[39]

Dalton and his strategists were deeply concerned that, once on board with Miller in the primary, many moderate and conservative business leaders were likely to stick with the Democrat in the fall contest. Miller was not only successful; he was capable, intelligent, and eminently reasonable. Plainly, he would be the toughest of the Democrats for Dalton to overcome in November.

While some of the Coalitionists had doubts about Dalton's ability to win, others had more fundamental suspicions of Miller. The moderate attorney general was, after all, the son of one of the Byrd organization's most vehement critics, Colonel Francis Pickens Miller. Unlike Ted Dalton and Harry Byrd, Sr., who always had remained quite cordial despite their political differences, the fights between Byrd and Miller were marked by vitriolic exchanges and undisguised mutual contempt. Andrew Miller had adopted a less strident approach than his liberal father's and had aligned himself with the moderate Spong-Battle wing of the Democratic Party. But concern about Miller's "tendency to the left," as elderly banker Thomas C. Boushall put it, was enough to keep many business leaders from siding with him though they thought Miller had the best chance of beating the far more liberal Howell.[40]

Dalton announced his candidacy on March 7, 1977, in a radio address that promised a "progressive and prosperous Virginia" and invoked the names of Holton, Godwin, and his father, Ted. Throughout the spring, Governor Godwin, GOP chief George McMath, and Coalition leaders Roy Smith, Smith Ferebee, Lawrence Lewis, and Bruce Gottwald labored, with considerable success, to mobilize independent conservative support behind Dalton. The candidate himself spent the bulk of his time courting business leaders and wooing potential contributors away from Miller or off of the fence. As the party's June convention approached, Dalton was preoccupied not only with fundraising, but with the selection of his runningmates as well. His attention also turned frequently to the Democratic contest where, to Dalton's chagrin, polls showed that Henry Howell was far behind Andrew Miller.

As the consensus nominee of a Republican Party that he had spent a lifetime serving and building, Lieutenant Governor John Dalton might have been expected to wield substantial influence in the selection of his runningmates. He certainly tried to do so. With Godwin and Obenshain, Dalton recognized the need to reach out to the Byrd Democrats, who would be the swing bloc in the probable race against Miller in the fall. But neither Fairfax Delegate Wyatt B. Durrette, Jr., nor State Senator J. Marshall Coleman of Staunton, the two

---

[39]John Dalton interview.
[40]Thomas C. Boushall interview, June 6, 1980.

lifelong Republicans vying for the GOP nomination for attorney general, would fill that role. And State Senator A. Joe Canada, Jr., of Virginia Beach, the lone declared candidate for the second spot on the ticket, was unacceptable to several key Coalition leaders—primarily because of his past bouts with the conservative Democratic faction in Virginia Beach led by Byrd loyalist Sidney Kellam.

Efforts to give the Coalition representation on the Republican ticket focused early on the spot sought by Canada, but GOP and Coalition leaders were unable to settle upon a candidate. Canada had announced his candidacy for lieutenant governor in early January 1977, and the field had been cleared for him when former Congressman Stanford Parris of Fairfax withdrew from consideration after publicly flirting with a bid for more than a year. As the spring months rolled by, Canada remained formally unopposed while Dalton, Godwin, Obenshain, and their Coalition allies searched in vain for an alternative. There was talk of persuading State Senator Elmon Gray of Waverly or State Senator Frederick Gray of Chesterfield to switch parties and make the race. Thomas T. Byrd, the youthful son of Senator Harry F. Byrd, Jr., and manager of the family's newspaper business, also was mentioned. And many Richmond business leaders favored a bid by former State Senator FitzGerald Bemiss. Two prominent recent converts to Republicanism, party chief McMath and State Senator Herbert Bateman of Newport News, also were frequent subjects of discussion. But, ultimately, none was willing to make the venture.

For John Dalton, the situation was disconcerting and grew more frustrating with each passing day. "The Coalition people indicated to me that they wanted someone besides Joe Canada [for lieutenant governor], and I told Joe that," Dalton later recalled.

> There was not anything personal against Joe. I like Joe. But everybody told me that Joe could not finance a campaign. . . . The general consensus was that Joe would probably lose to Chuck Robb, [who was then vying for the Democratic nomination for lieutenant governor,] and if Robb wasn't the nominee, it would probably be [Richard S. "Major" Reynolds, III]. So you had to have somebody who could match the Johnson or Reynolds money or at least have some access to big money. . . . I told Joe that I was concerned about his ability to raise the money that had to be put up, from what the Main Street people were telling me. I laid it right out for him. But he felt like he wanted to run anyway.[41]

Indeed, Canada felt that his time had arrived. First elected to the State Senate in 1971 from mostly Democratic Virginia Beach, the youthful and energetic Republican had gained notoriety within the GOP during his good-natured bid for the nomination for lieutenant governor in 1973. After aligning himself with Obenshain's conservative faction, Canada had been

---

[41]John Dalton interview.

rewarded with co-chairmanship of Ronald Reagan's Virginia campaign in 1976. Except for a misstep on the Equal Rights Amendment—he initially favored it and then abruptly switched his stance during the 1976 General Assembly session, prompting charges of political expediency—the Virginia Beach senator had played his cards well. The suggestion that he step aside when there was no opposition candidate in the field seemed preposterous to him and his key supporters.

Enter Walter W. Craigie, Jr. A Richmond investment banker and former state treasurer and secretary of finance under Governor Holton, Craigie was well known in the business and financial circles of the capital. As finance chairman of the Dalton for Governor campaign, he had been at the center of efforts by Dalton and Obenshain to recruit a candidate for lieutenant governor who would appeal to the wealthy Main Street contributors and conservative independents around the state. After weeks of hand-wringing over the unavailability of a suitable contender, Craigie stepped forward with a solution—himself. Accounts differ as to where the suggestion for a Craigie candidacy originated, but Obenshain and Dalton were quickly, albeit somewhat reluctantly, on board. What followed was an episode that almost dethroned Obenshain as *de facto* party leader and led to an embarrassing repudiation of Dalton by Republicans on the very day he became their nominee for governor.

Craigie resigned his post as Dalton finance chairman and announced his candidacy for lieutenant governor on April 15, scarcely six weeks before the nominating convention. His bid was supported by an unusual group of past antagonists. With the exception of Senator William Scott, who backed Canada, Craigie's supporters included virtually the entire top echelon of the state GOP. Governor Godwin and former Governor Holton publicly endorsed Craigie. Lieutenant Governor Dalton told reporters that he planned to vote for the Richmonder at the convention. And former party chiefs Richard Obenshain and Warren French jointly signed a letter recommending Craigie's candidacy to the GOP delegates. Even with his late entry into the race, Craigie had such strong support from leaders in both party factions that his nomination seemed likely.

"Had I known there was going to be a candidate fielded by Lieutenant Governor Dalton," recalled Canada, "I would have never gotten into it. But when I was told what was happening, I said, 'Well, you're probably going to win, but you're going to know you're in a race.'"[42] The Virginia Beach Republican had but one strategy available to him, and it packed an emotional punch that reflected his own pique. He would incite and exploit grass-roots GOP resentment toward the party's ruling elders, and especially toward the pseudo-Republicans on Main Street, the "fat cats" who, he charged, were outsiders trying to run roughshod over the hard-working Republican activists who had labored long in the party vineyards.

---

[42]A. Joe Canada, Jr., interview, June 12, 1980.

Canada's anger at the party leaders' efforts to derail him was shared by many Republicans around the state, especially among the conservative allies of Obenshain, and especially in northern Virginia. The choice of Craigie was particularly annoying. Craigie had been aligned with the Holton camp in the early '70s, and, in 1976, he had backed the moderate Ford. How Obenshain could turn his back on Canada, a Reagan supporter and conservative loyalist, was a mystery to many of the former party chief's allies. Had Obenshain and the conservative Republicans in Richmond "sold out" to the Main Street financiers who supported GOP nominees only when it suited them? It was a question that some previous Obenshain allies were reluctantly asking.[43]

In the Third District, Obenshain's associates stood by him and backed Craigie, who also had the advantage of being the hometown candidate. But, as the convention neared, Obenshain had difficulty in other parts of the state pulling his troops behind the investment banker. "What happened was, Dick [Obenshain] and Judy Peachee went with Craigie, and they did it without consulting the conservative troops in the field. And a lot of those troops left them for Canada," recalled George Mason Green.[44] Others backed Craigie only with great reluctance. "The thinking on the part of many around Dick," noted Kenneth Klinge, "was that he (Obenshain) had made a mistake by supporting Craigie. But they felt Dick's prestige was on the line and so they had to support him."[45] Acknowledging years later the political fallout to Obenshain from his bid, Craigie commented, "Dick really put the party before himself personally. Here was a clear example, I think, of where he made a tough decision with respect to me because he thought it was in the best interest of the party. . . . He never once asked me for a commitment in return as to the future plans that he had."[46]

Except for its role in the fragmentation of Obenshain's conservative faction, the late-blooming contest for lieutenant governor might not have been so consequential for the GOP had it not been for its impact on the Durrette-Coleman battle for the attorney general nomination. As the year opened, the contest between the Fairfax delegate and the Staunton senator looked like just another duel between the party's dominant conservative wing and its declining moderate faction. Durrette, also a state co-chairman for Reagan in 1976, had the blessing of Obenshain, whom he had backed for party chairman in 1972. Coleman, who hailed from the Shenandoah Valley and had allied himself with the GOP partisans from that area, had backed French in 1972 and Ford in 1976, and was supported by Linwood Holton. Since Durrette's faction controlled the GOP in 1977, he began the race with a clear edge.

---

[43]John E. Alderson, Jr., interview, September 24, 1984.
[44]Green interview.
[45]Klinge interview.
[46]Walter W. Craigie, Jr., interview, September 19, 1984.

Their contrasting factional orientations notwithstanding, Coleman and Durrette actually were remarkably similar candidates—perhaps too similar to become anything other than rivals. The two men were gifted with keen intellects, were roughly the same age (mid-30s), had been in the General Assembly for approximately the same length of time (five or six years), and had similar voting records in the legislature (moderately conservative). While Coleman had been aggressively partisan at the Capitol, Durrette had adopted a less confrontational approach. Durrette viewed government through a more abstract, philosophical lens, while Coleman had almost a scientific fascination with governmental processes and the development of practical solutions. Had circumstances been different, Durrette the philosopher and Coleman the technician might have made powerful allies. But both men were ambitious, articulate, hard-charging politicians, and they were on a collision course.

The favorite in the race received an early campaign boost in February when Ronald Reagan brought his famed three-by-five cards and his crowd-pleasing rhetoric to Richmond for a Durrette fundraising reception. Then, throughout the spring, Coleman and Durrette dueled in a lengthy series of joint appearances before local Republican committees and gatherings. The main issues in the race were standard fare for a GOP nomination contest; the crucial concerns were which of the two men was most likely to win in the fall, and which was the more conservative. On the former issue—the term "electability" was commonly used to describe the elusive attribute—Durrette trumpeted his vote-rich northern Virginia base, while Coleman emphasized his electoral track record, which included his upset victory over an incumbent Democratic state senator in 1975. Coleman sought to blur the party's factional lines by calling attention to less-than-conservative aspects of Durrette's legislative record, while the Fairfax frontrunner generally refrained from attacking Coleman in order to minimize the residue of rancor that would remain in the fall.

The 3,000 GOP delegates assembled in the Roanoke Civic Center for the party's state convention on June 4. For months it had seemed that the Coleman-Durrette clash would supply the only excitement at the convention, but the late-blooming Craigie-Canada confrontation suddenly assumed preoccupying importance for many of Obenshain's lieutenants who were backing Durrette. With the assumption that Durrette was comfortably ahead, they turned their attention to the contest for the second spot on the ticket. The Craigie candidacy and the split among conservatives that it caused were just the help Coleman needed.

Anticipating the fireworks to come in the contested races, convention planners made John Dalton's coronation as the party's gubernatorial nominee the first order of business. Governor Godwin had the first word, proclaiming 1977 a "time of opportunity" for Republicans and declaring, "Those Virginians not attached to any party hold the key and the answer to who will be Virginia's next governor. Let's go home and get them. . . . I pledge to you my best efforts in that regard."[47] Godwin placed Dalton's name in nomination, and a unanimous convention vote followed. The gubernatorial nominee deferred his appearance and acceptance speech until after the selection of his running-mates, and so the delegates quickly turned to the weekend's two principal tasks.

First up was Richard Obenshain. Observing with notable understatement that it might be better for him personally to "stay out of this hot battle," the former party chairman proceeded to nominate Walter Craigie for lieutenant governor. "Nothing is more important than to elect John Dalton governor of Virginia this year," Obenshain declared, before insisting that Craigie's nomination would give the GOP "the best, the strongest ticket."[48] Obenshain was followed a few minutes later by Delegate George W. Jones of Chesterfield, who delivered a blistering attack on Craigie in the course of placing Canada's name in nomination. Jones struck the sharp-edged theme of the weekend for the Canada forces when he lauded the Virginia Beach senator as "a self-made man, . . . [one] not born with a silver spoon in his mouth."[49]

As Delegate Raymond R. "Andy" Guest, Jr., of Warren County took to the platform to second Canada's nomination, all seemed to be going more or less as expected. But then something both unexpected and unprecedented happened. Guest spoke only briefly and then yielded the remainder of his time to Canada's most effective advocate—Canada himself. Visibly angered but clearly in control, the candidate challenged the party leadership directly, blasting its attempt to force on the party faithful candidates "anointed in smoke-filled rooms," and at one point advising the delegates, "Don't let them shove you around. Shove back!"[50] It was a defiant appeal to the GOP regulars' spirit of independence and their sympathy for the underdog, divisive in a sense but highly effective. It was prompted, Canada said later, by the last-minute appearance of Craigie campaign literature featuring endorsements by party elders and by John Dalton's active arm-twisting on Craigie's behalf at the convention. Canada explained:

> We thought long and hard about making that speech. But when I discovered that people were being pulled off the floor and leaned on in the strongest terms [by Dalton], plus some of the [Craigie] newsletters that went out, I felt it was just time to tell the truth. And that's what my speech was about—that the party is not run by just one person or by a handful of people, but by all the people at the convention center. The tactics [the leadership] used backfired on them completely.[51]

[47]*Richmond Times-Dispatch*, June 5, 1977.
[48]Ibid.
[49]*Roanoke Times & World-News*, June 5, 1977.
[50]Ibid.
[51]Canada interview.

Canada's dramatic speech not only appealed to emotions but showed the extemporaneous state senator at his oratorical best—clearly superior in that regard to Craigie, who had little stump-speaking experience. Its impact was palpable and almost certainly decisive in the contest. "You could feel the tide turn [as Canada spoke]," Craigie recalled.[52] The balloting immediately thereafter produced a result that stunned observers. Canada carried the First, Second, Fourth, Eighth, and Tenth District delegations and bested the leadership's choice by a reasonably comfortable 100-vote margin out of approximately 1,800 delegate votes.

As the delegates turned to the Coleman-Durrette contest, the tide now was running strongly against the Richmond-based GOP leadership and independent business community. Though Dalton had remained neutral in the contest for the attorney general nomination, many of those in the forefront of the Craigie venture also were leaders of Durrette's campaign, and the Fairfax Republican felt the backlash. Coleman benefited not only from the conservative faction's split over the Craigie-Canada choice, but also from the realization by moderate mountain-valley Republicans that this volatile convention presented an opportunity to break the conservatives' five-year-old grip on the GOP and to repudiate Obenshain's leadership.

Following Canada's lead, both Durrette and Coleman seconded their own nominations. Both made articulate appeals to the party faithful, and both then proceeded to poll approximately the same number of delegate votes. It was high drama. The roll was called by congressional district, with local county and city delegations first polling themselves and then reporting the results to their respective GOP district chairmen, who in turn tallied the votes and reported them to the chair. As the remarkable closeness of the contest became increasingly apparent, confusion mounted. Some districts reported when the roll was called, but others passed. A number of local units requested the opportunity to caucus anew to check the accuracy of their tallies and to open the way for some more arm-twisting. Soon districts that had reported their votes were asking the chair for the opportunity to revise their tallies. The roll was called, and called again, and again. "The race was so close . . . that it was a fraction of a vote difference," recalled the youthful convention chairman, State Senator Nathan Miller of Bridgewater, "and the difficulty as chairman, when you have 3,000 delegates out there, is to maintain some degree of decorum and order when the intensity is so great that people just get very, very emotional."[53] Indeed, as the balloting went on for more than an hour, the situation approached pandemonium.

In what GOP Chairman McMath later lauded as "a masterful job,"[54] Miller continued the roll call until, for one fleeting moment, all ten GOP

---

[52]Craigie interview.

[53]Nathan Miller interview, June 19, 1980, and September 20, 1984.

[54]McMath interview.

district chairmen had reported their district's totals and none was in the process of re-caucusing. Though even then several district chairmen were seeking permission to re-caucus, Miller worried that such maneuvers would continue interminably and would undermine the integrity of the entire process, leaving the nomination subject to challenge by whomever was not declared the winner. He thus slammed the door shut on the balloting, and, after determining the results of the tally, promptly announced that Marshall Coleman had been elected the nominee for attorney general. Coleman had 905.46 votes to Durrette's 896.71, with 7.83 abstentions. The Staunton senator led his opponent by less than nine votes, but, even more significant, he had gained an actual majority and averted a second ballot by less than a single vote. A stunned and disappointed Durrette dismissed aides' plaints that the roll call had been handled improperly and could be challenged, and instead took to the podium to move that Coleman's nomination be made unanimous.

The fireworks suddenly concluded, John Dalton and his two surprise runningmates made their way quickly to the platform to bask in the conventioneers' applause and to strike the traditional pose with raised, clasped hands. Most eyes were on the victors, Canada and Coleman, until the gubernatorial nominee began his acceptance speech by directing the delegates' attention to a smiling federal judge seated in the visitors' section. Ted Dalton rose and waved as the delegates gave him a prolonged ovation in what was a nostalgic, emotional moment for many of the assembled. His son then proceeded to warmly welcome his runningmates onto the ticket and to profess indifference concerning the outcome of the Democratic primary campaign scheduled to end ten days later. "We are going to beat either the big spender (Miller) or Howling Henry (Howell) because I don't think the people of Virginia will believe that either of them represents the philosophy of the vast majority of the people," Dalton declared.[55]

The lieutenant governor spent most of his first day as the GOP nominee for governor fending off reporters' queries about why the delegates had repudiated his choice for the second spot on his ticket. On his return from Canada's headquarters where he had gone to extend congratulations after the balloting, Dalton insisted to reporters that Canada was "an excellent candidate" who would win in November. His "stirring speech," Dalton opined with feigned nonchalance, had carried the day.[56] Publicly unfazed, Dalton privately viewed the convention developments as an unmitigated disaster. Democrats would gloat that the GOP gubernatorial nominee lacked sufficient clout in his own party to name his runningmates. Canada seemed to bring nothing to the ticket and had little chance of winning. The effort to derail the Virginia Beach senator had divided the party and provided a public forum for Republican regulars to denounce the Main Street crowd and Byrd Democrats for trying to

[55]*Richmond Times-Dispatch*, June 5, 1977.
[56]Ibid.

tell the GOP what to do. And Coleman's success had compounded the damage since, of the two candidates for the attorney general nomination, Durrette enjoyed the greater support among the Coalition leaders allied with the party's conservative wing. Plainly, it was an inauspicious beginning for what promised to be a very difficult campaign.

Republican insiders understood, however, that the biggest loser at the Roanoke convention was Richard Obenshain, who had staked his considerable prestige on two ultimately unsuccessful candidates. The conservative group that had carried him to the party chairmanship in 1972 and dominated GOP affairs since then had splintered, with many of his past supporters angrily rejecting Obenshain's leadership. "We were split all over the map," recalled William Stanhagen. "The 1977 convention was the first instance of the 1972 conservative caucus not hanging together."[57] The disarray came at a critical time for Obenshain, who was then contemplating a bid for the seat of retiring Senator William Scott the next year. "I have just seen my political life pass before my eyes," a dejected Obenshain told ally John Alderson as the Roanoke convention neared its close.[58] To confidant Lewis Williams, he was even more emphatic. "This convention has made the decision for me," Obenshain said, "There isn't any way I am going to run for the Senate."[59] With the conservatives divided and many of them furious at him, the Richmonder doubted that he could gain the party's Senate nomination the following year. And the nomination probably would be worth little anyway, since Andrew Miller was likely to be governor and some Miller-style moderate likely would be tapped as the Democratic nominee for the U.S. Senate.

The 1977 GOP state convention was the first of three consecutive quadrennial conclaves from which Virginia Republicans would depart angry and divided. The bitter infighting and factionalism that would characterize the 1981 and 1985 GOP nominating contests would debilitate the party and set the stage for back-to-back Democratic statewide sweeps. Fortunately for John Dalton and Marshall Coleman, developments in the Democratic primary would spare the GOP a similar fate in 1977. After several years of successful coalition-building, Republican regulars had rejected the sound strategy of their leadership and had invited electoral disaster. In November 1977, they would win again in spite of themselves, but in a few years the seeds of discord would blossom into disarray and defeat.

There was little reason to expect Henry Howell to overcome Andrew Miller in the Democratic gubernatorial primary on June 14, 1977. Published polls had been giving the popular two-term attorney general a sizeable advantage since December 1975, when the race began. Except for a brief truce during the Carter presidential campaign in the fall of 1976, the two Democrats

---

[57]William Stanhagen interview, September 27, 1984.

[58]Alderson interview.

[59]Williams interview.

had subjected their party and fellow citizens to a highly public and divisive feud. Republicans hoped for a harvest of disaffection regardless of who prevailed in the primary, but they knew that a win by the liberal underdog Howell would aid Dalton most.

During much of the spring, Howell's campaign appeared outwardly to be on the verge of collapse, primarily because of a large Miller advantage in reported fundraising. The two men engaged in a lengthy series of debates and joint appearances that primarily served to convey to the public the visceral nature of their mutual dislike. Howell made campaign finances and alleged "dirty tricks" by the Miller camp a principal issue,[60] and he also attacked Miller's record of high spending as attorney general.[61] Miller countered with volleys aimed at Howell's past disloyalty to the Democratic Party and also at his liberal legislative record, including his support for collective bargaining for public employees. The labor-related attacks may well have backfired on Miller, because it was the strong and active backing of the state AFL-CIO and the Virginia Education Association that enabled Howell to offset much of Miller's financial advantage. With organized labor and the Crusade for Voters, the preeminent black political organization in the state, handling the get-out-the-vote effort for his campaign, Howell could count on a strong liberal turnout on primary day.

Poll data compiled for the Dalton campaign in February 1977 confirmed Miller's lead in the Democratic contest, but it also indicated the moderate Democrat's vulnerability. Howell actually had a five-percent advantage among those voters who felt most strongly about voting in the primary. The former lieutenant governor's liberal following constituted the core constituency of the Democratic Party—the Democrats who would turn out to vote in the primary regardless of the circumstances. On the other hand, the poll showed Miller's supporters to be far less dedicated. The Miller Democrats tended to have highly favorable opinions of Republican Governor Godwin and Independent Senator Byrd, and a plurality had voted for Gerald Ford over Jimmy Carter in the presidential contest a few months earlier. In fact, among 1976 Ford voters, Miller was running neck-and-neck with Dalton in the early sampling. In short, the moderate Miller was held in high esteem among the expansive middle of the Virginia electorate. That guaranteed him a big lead in the polls and a victory in the Democratic primary if a reasonably large number of voters came out to cast ballots. But if the turnout were small, Howell would have a real chance for an upset.

The Dalton pollsters also provided this sobering information to the Republican candidate and his strategists. Anti-Howell feeling among conser-

---

[60]*Richmond Times-Dispatch*, May 21, 1977.

[61]The extensive changes in the organization of the Office of the Attorney General during Andrew Miller's tenure are described in Thomas R. Morris, "The Office of Attorney General in Virginia," *University of Virginia Newsletter* (Charlottesville: Institute of Government, University of Virginia), April 1980.

vative voters was running so strong that they might enter the Democratic primary in large numbers "upon the theory that they may be putting Henry Howell away for the last time."[62] The pollsters added that "Dalton will find it very difficult to keep Republican support from crossing over and voting for Miller in June." Adding to the risk was the fact that Dalton's image with voters remained vague, and his views were largely undelineated. Without a strong Dalton base outside traditional Republican circles, the danger was that moderate and conservative voters would see the Miller-Howell race as their principal opportunity to express a choice for governor. The Dalton campaign recognized early that voter attention had to be directed to the contest that awaited in the fall.

The possibility of Republican "cross-over" voting in the Democrats' open primary was a much-discussed topic throughout the primary campaign. Speculation focused not only on how many would cross over, but also on how they would vote. Despite data suggesting a greater likelihood of anti-Howell voting by Republican-leaning Virginians, the widespread belief that Howell would be a weaker foe for Dalton led to much talk about possible GOP voting to boost the liberal's candidacy. Six weeks before the primary election, Miller publicly charged that an "unholy alliance" had been formed between the Dalton and Howell camps to that end.[63] The accusation was reminiscent of those leveled by Miller's father during his 1949 and 1952 campaigns, and it brought a sharp response from Dalton. Miller's remarks, said the Republican, were "those of a desperate man whose attempts to be all things to all people have cost him the support of committed conservatives."[64] A few days later, Dalton leveled a charge of his own; he told reporters that Miller was "scared to death" and "wants Republicans and conservatives to go into that primary and bail him out."[65] For the record, Dalton reiterated his request that his supporters stay away from the polls on July 14.

Behind the scenes, there was some pro-Howell activity by Republicans, but it was neither on a large scale nor particularly orchestrated. J. Smith Ferebee, the conservative fundraiser and Godwin intimate, was so doubtful of Dalton's ability to rally conservatives against Miller in the fall that he secretly raised funds for the financially ailing Howell campaign. "In my own mind, it was easier to fight a known hazard, recognized by everybody—[Howell]—than it was to convince people that Miller was not the conservative guy he was pretending to be," Ferebee later explained.[66] But Ferebee found other major

---

[62]The poll and accompanying analysis by Decision Making Information (DMI) are on file at the Republican Party of Virginia Archives.

[63]*The Richmond News Leader*, May 5, 1977.

[64]Ibid.

[65]*Richmond-Times Dispatch*, May 8, 1977.

[66]Ferebee interview.

Republican benefactors, such as Lawrence Lewis, unwilling to risk the possibility that Howell might win in November if they helped him succeed in June.

The Howell camp also received ad hoc assistance from individuals on the Dalton campaign staff, mostly in the form of technical advice and voter lists.[67] Dalton campaign chief William Royall and Howell manager Paul Goldman had a number of conversations prior to the primary voting, but suggestions from Miller that there was high-level collusion were baseless, according to Royall. The Republican operative said that an active conspiracy was unnecessary because the two camps independently had obtained reliable polling data which showed that the moderate Miller could be squeezed from the left by Howell and from the right by Dalton.[68] What Howell needed was for Dalton to rally conservatives, and that is exactly what the Republican did during the ten days between the GOP convention and the Democratic primary.

The "Ten Days in June" campaign was an idea conceived by Dalton organization director Judy Peachee as a means of decreasing primary turnout by focusing the attention of conservative voters onto Dalton and the November election rather than the imminent primary. Immediately after the convention, the GOP ticket went on the road for a high-profile, ten-day campaign tour of the state. Accompanying the much-ballyhooed jaunt by the newly nominated trio was a $30,000 radio ad campaign that featured Mills Godwin, a popular figure among Miller supporters, urging voters to "save" their votes until November when John Dalton would be on the ballot. The widespread airing of Godwin's praise for his lieutenant governor sent a clear message to the Coalition and the broader conservative community throughout the state: November would be soon enough to save Virginia from Henry Howell.

The turnout on election day confirmed the worst fears of the Miller camp. Moderate and conservative voters stayed away from the polls in droves, leaving the Democratic Party business to the liberal "Howell people," who handed their hero a dramatic upset victory.[69] Statewide, slightly less than 25 percent of all registered voters (less than 14 percent of the voting age population) came to the polls. The urban corridor, which Howell carried with a 55-percent majority, accounted for nearly two-thirds of the total vote. Rural areas, where Miller prevailed by a similar margin, turned in less than a third of the statewide ballots. Turnout was lowest in the suburbs, and Howell had a slim advantage there. The strong vote for Howell in the cities, especially in his native Tidewater, was the result of his lopsided victory among black voters—he polled better than 85 percent of the vote in selected black precincts—as well as his lingering support among blue-collar whites.[70] Only in the rural areas did

---

[67]William Bayliss interview, June 20, 1980.

[68]Royall interview.

[69]The vote totals were: Howell – 253,373 (51.4%); Miller – 239,735 (48.6%). Sabato, *Virginia Votes 1975–1978*, p. 129.

[70]Ibid., p. 39.

Howell's populist appeal among low-income whites show signs of wearing thin.

The impact of Republican voting in the primary was difficult to measure. Though Miller found in the results "significant signs that there was an organized effort among the Republicans" for Howell,[71] a study by several College of William and Mary political scientists concluded that a majority of the GOP interlopers had cast ballots for the more conservative Miller.[72] Moreover, the turnout was so low as to preclude the existence of extensive Republican "cross-over" voting. The impact of GOP efforts, if any, was reflected in the widespread abstinence of would-be conservative voters on primary day. The Dalton handlers had succeeded in giving their candidate a high profile at a critical time, and that reinforced the tendency of all but the most active Democratic partisans to forego participation in nominating contests. As Dalton had urged, Virginia's vast moderate-conservative majority left the June 14 primary to "the liberal-thinking people of the state who consider themselves Democrats."[73]

In his post-election analysis of the Miller-Howell contest, Professor Larry Sabato of the University of Virginia put the primary turnout and outcome in historical perspective:

While many factors contributed to [Howell's upset win], the underlying structural reason is clearly the unique nature of the primary electorate. With the growth of the Republican party and the development of a mass electorate in Virginia, the Democratic party primary has ceased to be tantamount to election. The average voter, less party oriented and more independent in political outlook than ever before, has begun to look upon the primary as a preliminary procedure, reserved for party activists; he prefers to delay his electoral participation until the November general election, when the "real" decision is made. Thus, the Democratic party primary in Virginia has become much like primaries in other two-party competitive states around the country.

This change in voter attitude toward the primary has had a significant effect on turnout. A low participation rate in the primary has allowed the Democratic party activists (liberals, organized labor, blacks and urban voters) to dominate the party nominating process to a degree far surpassing their strength in the electorate as a whole. These activist groups are the most important components of the Howell coalition, a fact that makes Howell's 1977 triumph less surprising.[74]

---

[71] Andrew Miller interview.

[72] Alan Abramowitz, John McGlennon, and Ronald Rapoport, "Voting in the Democratic Primary: The 1977 Virginia Gubernatorial Race," in *Party Politics in the South*, eds. Robert Steed, Laurence W. Moreland, and Tod Baker (New York: Praeger, 1981), pp. 89–91.

[73] *Richmond Times-Dispatch*, June 3, 1977.

[74] Sabato, *Virginia Votes, 1975–1978*, pp. 32, 36.

Indeed, an awareness of the growing liberal domination of Democratic Party nominating processes had been the chief reason for Senator Harry F. Byrd, Jr.'s decision to run for re-election as an Independent in 1970. By failing to heed that lesson and, in their over-confidence, also failing to mount a massive get-out-the-vote drive, Miller and his strategists had squandered the candidate's immense popularity and irreparably damaged his once-promising political career.

In stark contrast to the outcome in the gubernatorial contest, a pair of attractive right-of-center candidates won contested races to join Howell on the Democratic ticket. Charles S. "Chuck" Robb, the moderate-conservative son-in-law of former President Lyndon Johnson, had aligned himself informally with Miller during the primary campaign, but he benefited from the presence of two liberal opponents in the race for lieutenant governor. Richard S. "Major" Reynolds III, brother of the late Lieutenant Governor J. Sargeant Reynolds, and Arlington Delegate Ira M. Lechner divided the liberal vote and allowed the millionaire political novice Robb to win with a 39-percent plurality of the ballots.[75] The repeal in 1971 of the state law imposing a majority-vote requirement had obviated the need for a run-off primary, and Robb was among the first beneficiaries of the change.

Rounding out the ticket was a conservative legislative veteran, Delegate Edward E. Lane of Richmond, chairman of the powerful House of Delegates Appropriations Committee and a one-time Byrd organization lieutenant. Lane became the nominee for attorney general with only 35 percent of the primary vote, but he far out-distanced his three Democratic opponents.[76] As the most conservative Democratic nominee for statewide office since Attorney General Robert Y. Button ran for re-election on Mills Godwin's 1965 ticket, Lane was something of a political anomaly in the Virginia of the 1970s. At the opposite end of the political spectrum from Howell, Lane's presence on the Democratic ticket made the team a philosophical rainbow, and almost immediately the trio was dubbed the "Rainbow Ticket."

Republicans gathered in Richmond's Hotel John Marshall on the evening of June 14 ostensibly to welcome the Dalton-Canada-Coleman team back from their "Ten Days in June" tour, but most in attendance simply referred to the gathering as the GOP "victory party." That indeed was the atmosphere as the several hundred jubilant Republican activists in attendance cheered every news report showing Howell leading during the evening. When a buoyant Richard Obenshain arrived midway through the party, the grinning party

---

[75]The vote totals were: Robb – 184,887 (39%); Reynolds – 156,151 (33%); Lechner – 132,520 (28%). Ibid., p. 133.

[76]Lane's opponents were moderate Delegate Erwin S. "Shad" Solomon of Bath County, liberal Arlington Delegate John L. Melnick, and consumer advocate John Schell of Fairfax County. The vote totals were: Lane – 152,215 (35%); Solomon – 99,841 (23%); Melnick – 92,319 (22%); Schell – 85,990 (20%). *Official Election Results 1977* (State Board of Elections, Commonwealth of Virginia), p. 47.

leader approached a group of friends and asked in a whisper, "So, did you all do it?" There were sheepish nods all around; these devout Republicans had been Howell supporters for a day.

Both the smallness of the turnout and the composition of the Democratic ticket pleased the Republicans. But, in the primary's aftermath, there were some sobering realities to digest. The Democrats' "Rainbow Ticket" was undeniably an odd combination, but the party emerged from the intense competition at least outwardly unified behind its team, on which all party factions were represented. The Democratic trio would be aided by the efforts of a reasonably popular leader in the White House. And television advertising during the Democratic primary campaign had boosted the name recognition, and hence the standing, of all three successful Democratic contenders. The first poll numbers following the primary were anything but encouraging to Dalton, as he recalled years later:

> Our poll in February showed that [Howell] was 15 points ahead of me. And when we did a poll in June after the Democratic primary, that one showed that he had jumped up to 21 points ahead of me. And I was devastated. I could not believe what I was hearing, because here was the man that I thought I wanted to run against, and we had gotten him, [yet] he had increased his margin by six points.[77]

The initial post-primary polling, however, reflected little more than Howell's greater familiarity among state voters after an unprecedented six statewide campaigns in eight years. But Howell was in the lead, and to many observers it looked as though his third bid for governor just might be the charmed one.

Howell's primary victory and his large lead in the polls guaranteed a full and early mobilization of the conservative political establishment behind the GOP's Dalton. In July, the now-familiar umbrella organization for conservative independents and Democrats was organized again under the banner, "Virginians for Dalton." Influential Coalition leader Roy Smith of Petersburg became the "Virginians" chairman, Lawrence Lewis, Jr., signed on as the Dalton campaign's new finance chief, and contributions began flowing in. "All I had to do was make the call," Lewis recalled, "and they asked how much he (Dalton) needed."[78] As the campaign unfolded, other prominent Byrd men, including former Governor William Tuck and Compensation Board Chairman Fred Pollard, climbed aboard the Dalton bandwagon. Though Senator Harry F. Byrd, Jr., made no public endorsement, he sent ample signals to indicate his preference. And Governor Godwin became increasingly active during the fall. By late September, Godwin had released an impressive list of 49 present and former members of the General Assembly—all Democrats—who had agreed

---

[77]Conversations with James Latimer, "A Different Dominion: The Republican Renaissance," WCVE-TV, 1986.

[78]Lewis interview.

to back Dalton, and the popular governor took to the hustings furiously on behalf of his former runningmate.

The year had begun with Dalton, Obenshain, and their GOP allies struggling to rally independent-minded conservatives behind a third consecutive Republican candidate for governor. Their dubious prospects for success had dimmed further at the GOP state convention when efforts to assemble a ticket to the Coalitionists' liking were unceremoniously rebuffed by the Republican faithful. But suddenly by mid-summer solidifying the influential Virginia conservative establishment behind the Dalton candidacy no longer was a concern. Only Henry Howell could have produced such a remarkable rallying of the conservative guard around the erstwhile mountain and valley boy.

Chapter 30
1977: The Dalton Dream Fulfilled

"I do solemnly swear that I will support the Constitution of the United States, and the Constitution of the Commonwealth of Virginia, and that I will faithfully and impartially discharge all the duties incumbent upon me as Governor, according to the best of my ability, so help me God."[79]

Judge Ted Dalton, January 14, 1978
Administering the oath of office to
Govenor-Elect John N. Dalton

It all had fallen into place for John Dalton. With his eyes firmly fixed on the goal of the governorship, he had moved swiftly through the ranks to the forefront of his party. In 1973, he had teamed up with the popular ex-Democrat, Mills Godwin, and had made his own important contribution to the formation of a strong conservative coalition in the state. Democratic moderate Andrew Miller threatened to rehabilitate the traditional party for Virginia conservatives in 1977, but Henry Howell's come-from-behind win in the Democratic primary guaranteed conservative solidarity behind the GOP nominee. The Radford Republican was riding the crest of a wave, but it was not in John Dalton's personality to be over-confident. He had seen the close call that Henry Howell gave the popular Godwin in 1973, and he knew the populist crusader was not to be underestimated. He also had experienced the highs and lows of Ted Dalton's gubernatorial bids, when late developments like the highway bond proposal in 1953 and the dispatch of federal troops to Little Rock in 1957 had snatched defeat from the jaws of victory. A tough-as-nails politician who had seen it all, John Dalton was not about to let up for an instant.

Neither, of course, was Henry Howell. Counted out by many political participants and observers only a few months earlier, he had brought down the seemingly invincible Miller, and now he had "Johnny-boy," as he derisively called Dalton, squarely in his sights. Indeed, his Rainbow Ticket's chances of a sweep of the statewide offices seemed not at all remote during the summer months. Howell had tossed or tempered the more liberal items on his policy agenda, and pre-Labor Day polling data revealed that the Democrat was perceived as nearer to the moderate middle of the Virginia electorate than was

---

[79]*Richmond Times-Dispatch*, January 15, 1978.

327

the conservative Dalton. As the two candidates sparred in a series of July and August joint appearances before various civic and business groups, the nimble and flamboyant Democrat invariably seemed to come away the winner. In attacks reminiscent of the Byrd organization's assault on Francis Pickens Miller and other liberal challengers, the GOP candidate humorlessly hammered Howell for his organized-labor backing and his past statements supporting public-sector collective bargaining and repeal of the state's Right to Work Law. But the Democrat brushed Dalton's criticisms aside with a deft mixture of wit and sarcasm, and, with the help of coin toss wins that almost always allowed him to speak last, he managed to fire off closing volleys at Dalton that generally found their target.

Somewhat surprisingly, Howell chose the state AFL-CIO convention in late August as the forum for his sharpest attack on Dalton, and the speech would prove to be his undoing. Ignited by the cheers of the exuberant supporters who filled the Roanoke convention hall, the effervescent Democrat alternately accused and taunted his rival. The thrust of the Howell speech was a new charge—that Dalton had violated conflict-of-interest proscriptions as a state legislator and "[had used] public office for private gain." Referring to "rumors" from unidentified sources, Howell charged:

> There are those who say he (Dalton) attempted to feather his nest by the bills he put in and the bills he tried to get passed. Now, if you were attempting to use public office to feather your nest, Johnny, you'd better get out of the race. . . . Shades of Watergate we want nothing of in Virginia.[80]

Howell provided no specifics to support his charge, but instead gave Dalton four days to make a complete personal financial disclosure and to answer questions about his conduct as a state legislator.

The Dalton camp rejected the vague Howell allegation and invoked a statement by Andrew Miller during the preceding spring that "attacks on the motives and integrity of others for reasons of political expediency have been the foundation of Mr. Howell's career."[81] The Republican ignored Howell's deadline, and as days passed the Democrat declined to produce evidence to support his charge other than general statements that Dalton had introduced banking legislation as a member of the General Assembly at a time when he had a financial interest in banks. Five days after Howell's AFL-CIO speech, veteran *Richmond Times-Dispatch* reporter Shelley Rolfe published details of the Dalton legislative record that largely refuted Howell's conflict-of-interest charge. Dalton, who had a financial interest only in two federally chartered banks, had patroned legislation in 1972 to permit state-chartered banks to increase fees for processing certain loans.[82] In response to the report, Howell

[80]*The Washington Post*, August 30, 1977.

[81]*Richmond Times-Dispatch*, August 21, 1977.

[82]*Richmond Times-Dispatch*, August 25, 1977.

campaign manager William Rosendahl acknowledged the absence of impropriety by Dalton, and he sought to defend his candidate's AFL-CIO speech on the ground that "Howell was merely trying to 'tease' Dalton into revealing his financial wealth."[83]

Editorial reaction to the unsupported Howell allegations was sharply critical of the Democrat, and the Dalton camp moved quickly to capitalize on the opportunity. Declaring "trust" to be the most important issue in the campaign, Dalton charged Howell with deliberately misleading Virginians by leveling the false charge. He demanded that his foe back up the allegation or apologize, and he challenged Howell to meet him at the State Capitol a few days later to settle the matter. On the appointed day, Dalton appeared at the Capitol to denounce Howell as untruthful and to declare that his foe's lack of trustworthiness henceforth would be "the focal point of the campaign," while in a hotel across town Howell met with reporters, cited other allegedly improper Dalton bills, and steadfastly refused to acknowledge error.[84]

The episode reinforced the most negative aspects of the rabble-rousing image that Howell had been struggling to tone down since his purposely shrill 1969 gubernatorial bid, and it also aided the Dalton campaign's pre-determined strategy of portraying Howell as a liberal who was attempting to deceive voters about his real views in order to win election. To most observers, including strategists in both camps, the late August misstep by the excitable Howell appeared in retrospect as the turning point in a campaign that until then had been going his way. But Howell remained loathe to admit his mistake, as reflected in this exchange during a 1980 interview with the author:

Q: That speech before the AFL-CIO that caused such a stir—what motivated you to do that, [and] did it hurt your campaign?

A: Surprisingly enough, it did. We were kicking off the campaign for the general election, and Dalton had been anti-consumer, and we had done ... preliminary research on some of his votes. And I told [a staff person] to check his votes on banks and so forth. [We found] this bill that Dalton was patron of which changed the interest that could be charged by a state bank, and he was on the board of a bank and owned significant stock ...

Q: It turned out to be a national bank, didn't it, that would not have been affected by the bill?

A: That was never decided. I can't forget that. I went up to the Federal Reserve, and none of them knew. But the newspapers—Shelley Rolfe wrote a story that was erroneous; I can't go over all the details. But at the time my staff man didn't know all of the intricacies of federal and state banks. And when we looked into it, ... you know, I didn't know it, and I just wanted to get this group of working people. So, as a reason I

---

[83]*The Ledger-Star*, August 25, 1977.
[84]*Richmond Times-Dispatch*, August 29–30, 1977.

said, 'Now, a banker shouldn't put in a banking bill. I say to you that he's been feathering his nest,' and so forth.

So [the press] went to work on it. And I think for a banker to put in a banking bill is a conflict of interest, whether he's putting it in for a national bank or a state bank. If you own dominant stock and you're on the board of directors of a bank and you're a legislator, you should let other people further the banking interests. But nobody thought that. They were just trying to find a way to stab me for picking on the banks. Power of the press—they never look for anything. But let me make one little mistake on something, and you would have thought I crucified Jesus, that I was Judas who betrayed him . . .[85]

Virginia's rough-and-tumble politicking often belies the state's genteel image and the rules of gentlemanly conduct that govern other pursuits in the Old Dominion. But the 1977 gubernatorial campaign had become unusually acrimonious and personal, and Labor Day had not even arrived. Referring to Dalton's allegations of organized labor's control over Howell and to Howell's conflict-of-interest charges against Dalton, reporter James Latimer asked, "Haven't the major party candidates for governor . . . both begun to inject a bit of demagoguery into the 1977 campaign? And if they keep it up, what will they be saying about each other by election day?"[86] The criticism from Latimer and other reporters little influenced the candidates and their handlers, however, and their heated joint appearances continued for several more weeks.

What was to be the last of nine personal encounters between the gubernatorial candidates came on September 14, when they appeared jointly at a forum sponsored by the Richmond Jaycees. Howell used his closing remarks—he won the coin toss again—to attack Dalton bitterly, at one point accusing him of "running the most deceitful and deceptive campaign in the history of Virginia."[87] Howell's complaint was with Dalton's assertions that the Democrat had backed gun control measures, tax increases, collective bargaining rights for government employees, and abolition of the state's Right to Work Law during his political career. Three days later, the Democrat called a news conference to blast the Dalton campaign's mailings to registered voters; he compared the GOP missives to Nazi propaganda and charged the Republican with waging the "most poisonous, divisive hate campaign" in the Commonwealth's history.[88] Dalton had had enough, and on September 19, the lieutenant governor convened a news conference to announce that he no longer would share a platform with his foe. Howell's "headline-seeking, issue-ducking, character assassination brand of politics" made further debates pointless, Dalton said, and he charged his rival with making "personal,

---

[85]Howell interview.

[86]*Richmond Times-Dispatch*, August 28, 1977.

[87]*The Richmond News Leader*, September 14, 1977.

[88]*Richmond Times-Dispatch*, September 21, 1977.

unfounded attacks on me and my family."[89] To reporters' queries, Dalton responded indignantly, "I don't have to sit there with him and have him stick his finger in my eye and listen to him say these things."

The debate cancellation was a bold stroke, though few of the nervous Republican activists who called the Dalton headquarters to complain saw it that way. Among the members of Dalton's large campaign steering committee, only former Governor Holton and a handful of others applauded the move. But there were seven additional meetings, including a televised encounter, scheduled for the final six weeks of the campaign, and Dalton had not been faring well in those that already had been held. Howell seemingly had supplied a credible excuse to terminate the exchanges, and the GOP camp was astute enough to seize upon it. The idea was Dalton's, and it was embraced immediately by his campaign manager. In part the decision was a product of John Dalton's very real outrage over Howell's attacks, recalled Republican campaign chief William Royall, and in part it was guided by tactical considerations.[90] The action had the effect of extricating Dalton from the counter-productive appearances and, in the process, made the GOP candidate appear decisive while highlighting Howell's shrillness.

The public reaction to the debate cancellation decision divided, predictably, along party lines. Privately reticent, Republicans were strongly supportive of Dalton's action in their public comments, while Democrats charged that the Republican was hiding behind a pretext. Howell seemed somewhat taken aback by Dalton's announcement, and he responded with uncharacteristic blandness, observing only that Virginians "don't like quitters."[91] The Democrat and his aides knew that the GOP camp wanted to revive his "Howling Henry" image, and they quickly took steps to modify Howell's demeanor and to temper both his flamboyance and stridency. In the ensuing weeks, the Democratic nominee generally emphasized conservative themes such as fiscal restraint and donned dark, pin-striped suits on the campaign trail.

Several weeks after Dalton broke off the joint appearances and made "trust" his principal campaign issue, there was another major development in the race, and this one put the Republican camp on the defensive. A group of northern Virginia conservatives, ostensibly acting independently of the Dalton campaign, announced that it would seek to raise nearly $100,000 to fund hard-hitting anti-Howell television advertisements. The "Independent Virginians for Responsible Government" (IVRG), as they identified themselves, felt that the Dalton campaign had been ineffective in making Howell and his record the issue in the gubernatorial contest. In much the same way that Richard Obenshain and operatives from the Republican National

[89]*Richmond Times-Dispatch*, September 20, 1977.

[90]Royall interview.

[91]*The Richmond News Leader*, September 20, 1977.

Committee had intervened to save the Godwin campaign four years earlier, the IVRG protagonists meant to boost what they saw as a sagging Dalton effort. To raise the needed funds, the group recruited Seventh District Congressman J. Kenneth Robinson as signer of a provocative letter to 15,000 conservative contributors around the state.

Unfortunately for Dalton, the IVRG letter included several inflammatory and inaccurate statements concerning Howell's record and policy positions, and the adverse publicity that attended release of the text of the letter gave new credence to Howell's repeated charges that the Dalton campaign was distorting his stands and exploiting groundless fears in its mailings. Most objectionable was the letter's false assertion that Howell once had urged the busing of Virginia school children into Washington, D.C. Attacks on Howell's alleged pro-busing stance had been a controversial mainstay of the Godwin campaign's fusillade four years earlier, but the issue had not previously been injected into the 1977 discussion. Sensing the opening, Howell blasted the "hate letter" as a "fear and smear tactic" and charged that the busing references were a blatant attempt "to evoke emotions and set blacks against whites and undo everything we've achieved in Virginia."[92] IVRG chairman John T. "Terry" Dolan of the National Conservative Political Action Committee (NCPAC) was forced to acknowledge that the letter contained several significant inaccuracies.

Dalton and his campaign had declared trustworthiness the touchstone in choosing a governor, and now they were being charged with telling untruths about Howell. The GOP nominee responded to the furor by denying that he or his staff had any foreknowledge of the IVRG letter, a claim that raised further doubts about the Republican's credibility. Dalton personally had been in the dark about the letter and believed the same was true of his staff, but manager William Royall in fact did have considerable advance knowledge concerning the independent group's plans.[93] Howell continued to hammer away on the issue for two weeks and succeeded in keeping his GOP foe on the ropes. In addition to demanding repudiation of the independent group by Dalton, Howell charged that former party chief Obenshain and current chairman McMath had formed a "right-wing partnership" with the IVRG to repeat the successful "fear campaign" waged by Republicans in 1973. He challenged GOP moderates—"Holton Republicans," he termed them—to repudiate the tactic.[94] Only in mid-October, after Dalton finally issued a public request that the independent group not air their controversial television ads, did the issue fade away.

---

[92]*Richmond Times-Dispatch*, October 2, 1977; *The Washington Post*, October 1, 1977.

[93]John Dalton, Royall interviews.

[94]*Richmond Times-Dispatch*, October 10, 1977. Obenshain and McMath steadfastly denied any involvement with the IVRG.

Such sparring dominated the Dalton-Howell campaign, and it left little time for serious discussion of the programs and policies favored by the two candidates. Personality—especially Howell's—loomed larger than issues throughout the race, and, to the extent that issues were presented, the Dalton campaign generally succeeded in making Howell's previous liberal stands the focus. The problem for the populist Democrat was that his image was too well defined in most voters' minds. That had some beneficial aspects, of course, but on balance it was a major liability. A lifetime of often provocative statements could be used against Howell, while Dalton's uncontroversial record gave Democratic strategists little ammunition. The Dalton handlers were free to mold the image of their lesser-known candidate as they wished, and they made him a portrait of enlightened conservatism.

"Virginia's Next Great Governor" and "New Energy for Virginia" were the two Dalton campaign slogans. The former linked Dalton to the immensely popular outgoing governor, Mills Godwin, and to Virginia's conservative tradition, while the latter emphasized the youthful vigor and forward-looking approach of the Dalton ticket. While wrapping the Radford Republican in the Godwin-Byrd mantle, GOP strategists were careful not to submerge the strain of progressivism that also was Dalton's heritage. The candidate was pictured often with young people and benefited from a very successful GOP campaign on college campuses around the state. An active Republican effort also was mounted in the black community, and the emphasis there was on Dalton's moderate outlook on race relations and his partisan affiliation with former Governor Linwood Holton, who retained a reservoir of goodwill among numerous prominent black political leaders. Though Dalton made few numerically significant inroads against Howell among blacks, the balanced profile helped the GOP candidate counter the appeal of Howell's progressive populism among suburban white voters.

If it had not been for a major surge in Dalton's support in the northern reaches of the state late in the campaign, the 1977 gubernatorial election might have been reasonably close. But the Dalton campaign's polling data one month before election day showed that fully 50 percent of all undecided voters in the state were northern Virginia residents, and that information prompted Dalton's handlers to redirect campaign resources, including the candidate's time and television advertising purchases, to that theater. The GOP's crucial northern Virginia offensive came at a time when the Howell campaign was financially incapable of responding.

The effects of the costly Democratic primary battle were apparent in the fall, as Howell found his base of financial support stretched thin. Even with the help of a September fundraising visit by President Jimmy Carter, the Democrat was able to raise less than a million dollars for the general election contest. In contrast, the Dalton campaign could tap the well-heeled and fully mobilized conservative business community, and it also broadened its contributor base substantially by mounting an unprecedented direct-mail fundraising program. By election day, Dalton's campaign spending approached two million dollars. The GOP fundraising effort dwarfed previous records and yielded the party an expanded financial base for subsequent campaigns.[95]

In addition to the GOP's significant financial advantage, the Dalton campaign made superior use of available campaign technology. Technical and organizational proficiency had been a hallmark of John Dalton's previous campaigns, and his gubernatorial bid was no exception. The extensive use of broad-based appeals for money and support through the mails was a first in Virginia, and it was accompanied by a large and sophisticated telephone program to contact voters, persuade the undecided, and make certain that the supportive went to the polls on election day. Though Dalton invariably would ask Republican audiences to volunteer time at the local GOP telephone bank—he liked to recall for listeners his own volunteer phoning during the Eisenhower presidential campaigns—his campaign made extensive use of paid telephone callers to identify favorable voters in the most heavily populated Republican-leaning areas of the state. After observing organized labor's success at getting Howell's supporters to the polls during the primary contest, the GOP would spare no effort to turn out Dalton voters.

Dalton's financial, technical, and organizational advantages were supplemented by the efforts of his seemingly tireless sponsor, Governor Godwin, who took to the stump in October with a frequency and intensity that left no doubt about his interest in the outcome. Godwin had one more chance to "save Virginia" from Henry Howell, and the chief executive clearly meant to make the most of it. No candidate could ask for a more talented advocate than Godwin, and the easy-going Dalton had the luxury of staying largely positive and statesmanlike in his stump speeches while Godwin barnstormed the state pummeling Howell. For the GOP faithful who regularly criticized the former Democrat for not being "partisan enough" after his conversion to Republicanism, Godwin's rolling blasts at Howell had a musical quality.

Election day produced a stunning Dalton win. Unhampered by the adverse conditions that nearly had stymied Godwin four years earlier (Watergate revelations and resentments over the nominee's party-switching, chief among them), Dalton assembled a broad moderate-conservative majority. GOP traditionalists in the western part of the state backed him as one of their own; conservative Democrats and independents backed him because he was not Henry Howell; and moderate suburban voters backed him because he

---

[95]Howell reported expenditures of approximately $778,000 in the general election contest and $567,000 in the primary. Dalton's expenditures—$1,864,000 plus another $90,000 that his campaign contributed to his runningmates—easily exceeded Howell's combined primary and general election totals. Richard W. Hall-Sizemore, "Money in Politics: Financing the 1977 Statewide Elections in Virginia," *University of Virginia News Letter* (Charlottesville: Institute of Government, University of Virginia), August 1980.

The previous record for gubernatorial campaign spending was set by Mills Godwin's 1973 campaign, which reported expenditures of approximately $1.1 million. See Sabato, *Virginia Votes 1975-1978*, p. 71.

seemed more reasonable, more predictable, and more gubernatorial than his rival. With turnout up sharply from the 1973 gubernatorial contest, Dalton polled nearly 56 percent of the statewide vote and buried Howell by an unprecedented 158,000-vote margin.[96] The Republican carried every congressional district except Tidewater's Second and Fourth, and won in 63 of 95 counties and 29 of 41 cities.

The pattern of the vote reflected the GOP's superior organizational efforts. Dalton collected approximately 60 percent of the suburban ballots, and the suburbs accounted for nearly 40 percent of the total statewide vote.[97] He also polled large majorities in the rural Fifth District, a conservative stronghold, and in the Sixth and Seventh Districts, the traditional Republican base. As compared with his 1973 performance, Howell lost the most ground in the state's rural areas—an indication that his once-appealing populist pose had evolved into a more conventional liberal posture. Howell retained his strong support among black voters—by some accounts, he did better among blacks against Dalton than he did four years earlier against Godwin[98]—but black voters were not successfully mobilized. According to a survey by *The Washington Post*, blacks supplied less than ten percent of the ballots cast in the 1977 election though they constituted roughly 19 percent of the state's population.[99]

In addition to giving Dalton a landslide win, voters set the stage for a gubernatorial showdown four years later by electing two attractive and ambitious young men—a Democrat and a Republican—to the other two statewide posts. Charles S. "Chuck" Robb and Marshall Coleman won election to the offices of lieutenant governor and attorney general, respectively, by comfortable margins. Democrat Robb had been heavily favored to dispatch of the GOP's under-funded Joe Canada, and his 54-percent share of the vote actually was somewhat smaller than expected.[100] Republican Coleman had begun as the underdog in his race against legislative veteran Edward Lane, and his nearly 54 percent of the ballots cast for attorney general surprised and impressed most observers.[101] The election of the two skillful politicians with

[96]The vote totals were: Dalton (R) – 699,302 (55.9%); Howell (D) – 541,319 (43.3%); Alan R. Ogden (U.S. Labor) – 10,101 (0.8%). Sabato, *Virginia Votes 1975–1978*, p. 48.

[97]Ibid., p. 65.

[98]An analysis of selected black precincts by Professor Larry Sabato of the University of Virginia indicated that Dalton polled only 5.0 percent of the black vote in 1977, compared to an estimated 5.7 percent for Godwin in 1973. Ibid., p. 66.

[99]*The Washington Post*, November 10, 1977. The lower turnout rate for blacks reflected a decade-long trend, which hampered Democratic candidates throughout the 1970s. A reversal of that trend would prove to be an important element in the Democratic resurgence during the 1980s.

[100]The vote totals were: Robb (D) – 652,084 (54.2%); Canada (R) – 550,116 (45.8%). Sabato, *Virginia Votes 1975–1978*, p. 145.

[101]The vote totals were: Coleman (R) – 617,628 (53.6%); Lane (D) – 535,338 (46.4%). Ibid., p. 149.

similar outlooks but divergent backgrounds guaranteed a contest in 1981 that largely would determine the state's political direction for the next decade.

Though by a smaller margin than some had forecast, Robb's win nevertheless was impressive. Not only did he buck the strong Republican tide that swamped his runningmates, but he did so on his maiden political voyage. That Robb was a political novice was not difficult to glean. On the stump he looked the candidate's part, and he moved easily among crowds of well-wishers and the curious, but his rambling and disjointed speaking style frequently left audiences with the impression that either he was confused, or they were, or both. A steady, likeable man, Robb was no crusader—he and runningmate Howell were opposites in that regard, as well as most others. His partisan affiliation had more to do with matrimony than philosophy, and, as a celebrity and heir to Lyndon Johnson's considerable political connections and wealth, Robb could get by without a clear sense of his own policy goals. As a Democrat in a conservative state, Robb could even turn that apparent shortcoming to advantage.

The pattern of Robb's victory over Canada showed state Democrats how one of their own could win in post-realignment Virginia. He held enough conservative Democrats in line to carry the rural areas by a respectable margin, swept the heavily Democratic central cities with more than 60 percent of the vote—almost ten percentage points better than Howell's showing in those areas—and also eked out a narrow victory in the suburbs despite the GOP gubernatorial nominee's massive victory there. If Robb could deprive his Republican opponent of a suburban victory in an adverse year like 1977, and also could retain the Democrats' liberal urban base, he was certain to be a formidable contender in any future contest. Of course, a major reason for Robb's success in 1977 was his hefty financial advantage over Canada. Not counting the Democrat's extensive primary campaign expenditures, Robb's $447,000 in fall spending easily eclipsed Canada's $289,000, and nearly half of the Democratic expenditures were funded by Robb's personal loans.[102]

Canada emerged from his unsuccessful campaign with a $110,000 debt, for which he largely blamed runningmate Dalton. Pursuant to an arrangement agreed upon shortly after the GOP convention in June, Canada and Coleman were each to receive 12.5 percent of all funds raised by the Dalton campaign. But nearly $2 million was raised for the Dalton effort, and his runningmates each received only $45,000 of that. To Canada, this was a breach of faith, and it was especially galling because the shortage of funds kept his campaign message off of the airwaves in late October, when polls showed him swiftly making up ground against Robb. To Dalton, however, Canada's plight was of his own making; the Virginia Beach senator had sealed his fate by ignoring Dalton's warnings and insisting upon a place on the GOP ticket without any prospect of sufficient financial backing. A large portion of the funds contributed to the Dalton campaign came from the Coalition—from the "Main Street

---

[102]Hall-Sizemore, "Money in Politics."

fat cats" that Canada had derided at the June convention—and the money came with specific instructions that it be used by Dalton and not his running-mates. The agreed-upon formula for dividing resources among the ticket did not include such earmarked funds, according to Dalton and his campaign manager.

Marshall Coleman did not let the lack of financial assistance from Dalton get in his way. The Staunton senator knew that he would have to win the contest for attorney general largely on his own. His opponent was a veteran legislator, a respected conservative and Coalition insider, a close friend of Mills Godwin and Roy Smith, and a popular politician in the heavily Republican Third District. Indeed, Delegate Edward Lane seemed like a perfect runningmate for Dalton—except that he was a Democrat and, in 1977, on Henry Howell's ticket. To win, Coleman knew that he would need to assemble a coalition at variance with Dalton's. Without any hope of garnering support against Lane from prominent Byrd Democrats, Coleman aimed to hold the Republican and Republican-leaning voters and to chip away at Lane's left flank.

Coleman's campaign had a conservative thrust—he wanted to cut the size of the attorney general's staff by ten percent, to restrict parole and make criminal sentencing more uniform, and to vigorously defend the Commonwealth's interests in court against what he portrayed as unwarranted federal intrusion. He promised to be an active, aggressive attorney general—to be "the people's lawyer"—but the intended contrast was more one of style than of substance. Indeed, Lane himself spent much of the fall campaign pledging action on consumer issues and sounding a distinctly populist tone. When it came to outflanking Lane on the left, however, Coleman reached for an outdated but still inflammatory issue—massive resistance. Lane had come to the General Assembly in 1954 and had supported the Byrd organization line on most issues, including its staunch opposition to public school desegregation. Coleman, on the other hand, had backed several civil rights measures during his much shorter legislative career, and he contrasted his progressive record on racial issues with Lane's support for massive resistance. That issue, along with Coleman's personal wooing, won him endorsements from the influential black Virginia Crusade for Voters and from the liberal Virginia Education Association. The tactic succeeded in making significant inroads into Lane's support among black Democrats and liberals, and it also made Lane's conservative friends furious at Coleman.

In the end, Lane was out-flanked on both sides by Coleman. The GOP candidate polled an estimated 33 percent of the black vote[103]—the best showing for any Republican since Holton garnered more than a third of the black vote in the peculiar circumstances of 1969. Coleman also cashed in on the heavy Republican turnout for Dalton and the increasing popular identification

---

[103]Sabato, *Virginia Votes 1975-1978*, pp. 66-67.

of the GOP as the more conservative political party in the state. Lane had been expected to do very well in the Richmond-area Third District and the Southside Fifth, where the Coalition's influence was greatest. Former Byrd organization loyalists Fred Pollard and Watkins Abbitt organized and publicized a "Virginians for Dalton-Robb-Lane Committee"; GOP Governor Godwin publicly endorsed the Democrat; and Harry Byrd's *Winchester Star* gave Lane its editorial nod. But, despite the best efforts of the Coalition's senior leadership, it was Coleman who harvested a majority of rural and suburban conservative votes on election day. He almost bested Lane in the Democrat's home district and carried the Fifth District—formerly a Byrd stronghold—by a comfortable margin.

Most impressive, however, was Coleman's win in northern Virginia. His share of the vote exceeded 60 percent in the Eighth and the Tenth Districts, a showing that easily surpassed Dalton's and Robb's. In both style and substance, Coleman appealed to the suburban voters of the region, while Lane generated little enthusiasm there in the primary contest and seemed to fade further in the fall. Key campaign strategy decisions aided Coleman as well. His campaign manager, Anson Franklin, was a youthful but experienced GOP operative, and he recognized early that television advertising would be the most critical use for the campaign's limited resources. The Coleman effort thus economized by foregoing the usual field organization, and fully half of the husbanded advertising dollars were directed to vote-rich northern Virginia. Though television advertising was far more expensive there than elsewhere in the state, it was in the state's cosmopolitan northern suburbs that Lane's advantages as the establishment candidate were least palpable. The Coleman campaign's 21-day television blitz came at the very end of the contest when many northern Virginians were just turning their sights to the state races; it portrayed Coleman as a talented, energetic, young activist, and it was very effective.

A fundraising gap also partly explained the outcome of the contest for attorney general. Lane raised more money than Coleman, but the Democrat was forced to spend much of it in winning his party's nomination, and the GOP candidate actually managed to raise and spend more than Lane during the fall campaign. Though the Democrat received financial help from conservative leaders Byrd and Godwin, Coalition fundraisers were occupied with helping Dalton overcome the Howell threat, and Lane suffered from over-confidence among his conservative backers. He was handicapped also by his forced association with runningmate Howell, which dampened enthusiasm for his candidacy in the business community. The lack of funds for campaign advertising in turn made it difficult for Lane to project a positive image in areas where he was not well known, especially northern Virginia.

With his upset win in the contest for attorney general, Coleman joined Robb as his party's heir apparent, an almost-certain nominee for governor in 1981. But, while Robb's victory had left him with few political scars, Coleman was badly bruised. To become the first GOP attorney general in Virginia history, the mountain-valley Republican had twice overcome the choice of the conservative establishment—first Durrette in the GOP nomination contest, and then Lane in the general election. In both instances, he had achieved his goal through a combination of glib speeches, tireless personal campaigning, and strong attacks on his foes' records. While many conservative Durrette partisans harbored lingering resentment over Coleman's shots at a fellow Republican, it was the reaction of Godwin and the Coalitionists to the campaign against Lane that was most damaging. "The factor that was most important in generating ill will toward Marshall," recalled Roy Smith,

> was his bringing into the campaign Ed Lane's voting in the 1956, 1957 and 1958 sessions of the General Assembly—the massive resistance days. Those of us who were there and knew Ed Lane's activities at the time knew full well that Marshall has been able to greatly over-emphasize and exaggerate Ed's part in that whole era. [Lane] came to the General Assembly in 1954 . . ., and he was in no sense among the top leadership [of the legislature during massive resistance]. . . . [Coleman's] campaign, both in his attacks on Ed Lane and in the groups to which he addressed his appeal, cast some doubts about his general political philosophy.[104]

"I was not happy with having the opponent I had [in the 1977 general election]," answered Coleman.

> I didn't pick him. He was not the kind of standard target that Republicans have had success going against. . . It gave me a very difficult hand to play.
>
> Obviously, I wanted to appeal to the Republican Party and to like-minded people around the state, which we were able to do. I also felt that it would be an advantage for me whenever I could to reach across and seek votes from any group that would be a part of a natural Democratic constituency. . . . I tried to show the black community that a Republican candidate for statewide office was acceptable—accessible and open to their points of view. I never was required to submit to demands or to say or do anything for that group different from what I said or did for any other group. . . .
>
> I took an approach in seeking the Crusade [for Voters endorsement] very much like I did in Roanoke in getting the [GOP] nomination. I got a list of members and called and made personal visits to the leadership. And I was able to have an impact. I got some good, strong support there [even though Richmond Mayor] Henry Marsh made a blistering attack on me at the [endorsement] meeting and accused me of being a right-wing Republican. . . . But I still had my own supporters, and I largely played on the [massive resistance] theme. I said, "Let's look at the record. Here's a man (Lane) who says that he wants your support and your vote, but where was he when you needed him?"[105]

---

[104]Smith interview.

[105]J. Marshall Coleman interview, June 4, 1980, and September 17, 1984.

Coleman had played the hand he was dealt in 1977. He had played it boldly, played it to win, and played it well. Like Mills Godwin in 1965 and Linwood Holton in 1969, he had reached across the philosophical divide and had captured a significant share of the liberal Democratic vote. But winning against the odds had its price, and both Durrette and Lane had friends who would be lying in wait for the new attorney general the next time around.

With Dalton's landslide and Coleman's surprising victory, Virginia Republicans celebrated another hugely successful campaign on election night, 1977. A multi-purpose bond issue backed by Godwin and Dalton passed easily, and the Republican contingent in the House of Delegates increased by four members (to 21). Though all three statewide Republican candidates emerged with campaign debts and the Virginia GOP also went into the red, the party was in excellent health. A new Republican governor, this one more partisan than the last, soon would take office. And the GOP technological advantage had been increased dramatically with the acquisition of additional computer capability, major programming refinements, and significant data expansion.

John Dalton was sworn in as the Commonwealth's 63rd governor on January 14, 1978, the constitutional oath administered by his father, Judge Ted Dalton, as his hand rested on a Bible held by his wife, Eddy. It was the pinnacle for the First Family of Virginia Republicanism—the fulfillment of the dreams of father and son—and the younger Dalton used the moment to sound the progressive, business-like themes that would characterize his administration. The just-concluded election represented a verdict in favor "of moderation, of prudence, of reliance on time-tested principle," he declared. And he concluded by summoning a vision of a "new dominion of freedom, justice, progress and opportunity for all."[106] Even before the inaugural address was given, Dalton had reached across the color line that had long divided Virginians and had been much in evidence in the 1977 gubernatorial election. Dr. Jean Harris, Dalton's designate as secretary of human resources, would be the first black and the first woman to serve in a Virginia governor's cabinet. Racial moderation, taut fiscal conservatism, strongly pro-business policies, and active partisanship were the common expectations for the Dalton administration.

With the successor of his choosing affirmed by the voters, Mills Godwin retired a second time to Cedar Point and the role of elder statesman. His second term had been marked, not by great advances as in his first, but by a succession of externally generated crises that had required a different sort of leadership. Inflation, recession, an oil embargo, discharges of deadly kepone pollution into the James River, and a series of natural disasters had necessitated a steady gubernatorial hand more than vision, and Mills Godwin had responded. He left office with a reservoir of popular affection and goodwill greater even than that which remained at the end of his extraordinarily

---

[106]Text of remarks on file with the author.

progressive first term. In his final address to the General Assembly as governor on January 11, 1978, he compared his two terms as the Commonwealth's chief executive:

From the vantage point of my final message eight years ago, we could look back on an incoming wave of public affluence and public expectations that carried us to new heights: major new accommodations at our state-supported colleges and universities; a new community college system; the first general obligation bond issues in this century for higher education and for mental health; a revision of our state constitution and other advances long delayed.

Now, as we look back, we find that wave has receded, leaving behind during these last four years a real threat of deficits in our budgets; the first threat of cold homes and stalled automobiles; the first major contamination of Virginia's waters; the first restrictions on the use of drinking water in many, many years; and a succession of ten major floods and seven minor ones.

I leave to history and to your judgment and that of the people of Virginia, the quality of our response.

But in making that judgment, I would suggest that the real test of statesmanship is not how far we can ride an incoming tide, but how well we can keep the ship of state from running aground when that tide goes out.[107]

As a satisfied and relieved Godwin prepared to leave public life, there was a broad consensus in the Commonwealth that he had been one of a handful of truly great Virginia governors. Even so, few understood the full extent or nature of the impact that this confident, often controversial, and occasionally contradictory "man for all seasons"[108] had on the Old Dominion's politics during his three remarkable decades of public service.

The contest that elected the third consecutive Republican governor in Virginia also rang down the curtain on the colorful political career of Henry Howell. Described by one of his past supporters as "a flamboyant, testy, mercurial populist, a political gadfly of non-Bourbon origins and demeanor, anything but bland, and quintessentially un-Virginian,"[109] the Norfolk Democrat had left unmistakable footprints in the political fields he trod during three decades of engagement. He left some constructive contributions in his path. But his three consecutive bids for governor had paralleled the Virginia Republican Party's string of gubernatorial victories, and few construed that as coinci-

---

[107]*Leadership in Crisis: Selected Statements and Speech Excerpts of The Honorable Mills E. Godwin, Jr., Governor of Virginia, 1974–1978*, p. iii.

[108]See Bugg, p. 370.

[109]The description was supplied by Larry Sabato, who, before embarking on a fruitful career as a scholar and political analyst, worked as statewide youth coordinator in Henry Howell's 1971 campaign for lieutenant governor and again in his 1973 gubernatorial campaign. See Sabato, *Virginia Votes 1975–1978*, p. 82.

dence. Each time that the irrepressible liberal had tried to reach his goal his attempt had been beaten back by a coalition of Republicans and ex-Democrats, conservatives and moderates, who, if denied him as a cause to rally against, might have headed off in their own separate directions.

Though few had neutral feelings about the happy warrior from Norfolk, he seemed best able to stir the ire of the moderates in his own party. As they viewed it, Howell had thrown the 1969 election to the Republicans after he failed to have his way in the primary and run-off. Then in 1973, and again in 1977, he had blocked Andrew Miller's path to the governorship. By 1977, the Miller-Howell feud went far beyond personal animosity and amounted to an enduring and debilitating factional breach among state Democrats, with liberals following Howell and moderates coalescing around Miller. With Dalton's election by a wide margin in 1977, the Miller Democrats could plausibly claim that their party had suffered another avoidable setback because of the insatiable ambitions of Howell. Miller himself suggested half-jokingly in 1980 that Republicans should place a plaque honoring Howell on the front of their new party headquarters.[110]

"That's horsefeathers!" replied Howell,

I haven't elected [three consecutive GOP governors]. The very Democrats [who are blaming me] elected them. Plus, the Republicans got a lot of money together, and Obenshain put together an excellent political organization. I haven't elected [Republican governors]. I got a half million votes—more votes than a Democrat ever got before. The only trouble was that Godwin got 14,000 more and Dalton got a hundred and some thousand more. And I didn't get any support from [the other Democratic faction] after I won the Democratic nomination. I didn't get a mailing list; they did not raise five dollars for me. . . .

[There is] nothing wrong with Andy Miller—I supported him [in 1969 and 1973]. If he had just had sense enough to support me in 1973 instead of recommending a write-in vote for [House of Delegates Speaker] John Warren Cooke, I would have been governor, and I would have been through. And he could have carried on in the United States Senate or what-have-you . . .[111]

Henry Howell's exit in 1977 was the first step in ending a Democratic rift that had been a bonanza for the Virginia GOP throughout the '70s. Andrew Miller, however, had one more run left.

---

[110]Andrew Miller interview.
[111]Howell interview.

Chapter 31
The "Great Indoor Primary" of 1978

"The greatness of this party, the reason we've been stacked here to the rafters with this enthusiasm, is because of our commitment to the great, historic, fundamental principles of Virginia. Thousands of Virginians are here today because of that commitment of our party. And thousands and thousands more are waiting around the state . . ."[112]

Richard D. Obenshain
Virginia Republican Convention, 1978

The Republican Party of Virginia would never be the same after 1978. Only a few decades earlier the fledgling GOP had held its conclaves in small banquet rooms, and in many areas of the state the proverbial meeting in a telephone booth would have been possible. But, in 1978, Virginia's ascendant Republicans would host the largest political convention in terms of delegates assembled that had ever been convened in the free world. Not only the numbers participating (nearly 9,000 delegates and alternates), but the intensity of the competition and the unity in its wake, would attest that the party had come of age. But barely two months after the tumultuous and exhilarating convention, the party would know supreme tragedy. And, three months after that, it would overcome adversity to win another important statewide victory. The events of 1978 would supply unmistakable proof that two-party competition had flowered fully in the Commonwealth and that Virginia's moderate- conservative majority, at least for the time-being, preferred Republican leadership. But, most of all, 1978 would forever change the Virginia GOP because of what was lost when a small airplane crashed in Chesterfield County late on August 2.

The stage had been set for the dramatic 1978 developments two years earlier by the Commonwealth's junior senator. Virginians who wanted solidly conservative representation in Washington had no reason for complaint with William Scott, but the senator's penchant for generating "bad press" had severely eroded his standing among the majority of voters. Copy-hungry members of the news media delighted in the conservative lawmaker's verbal

---

[112]Transcript of speech on file with the author.

gaffes, and as they began to watch him more closely following his arrival in the Senate in 1973, he seemed to oblige them regularly. By 1976, Scott and his wife, Inez, had resolved to withdraw from the field of battle. His announcement that he would retire at the end of his term was greeted in GOP circles with widespread applause and near-universal relief. Scott had won an important victory for the party in 1972, but polls indicated that a re-election bid by the freshman senator in 1978 would have presented Virginia Republicans with a herculean task.

Jockeying for the GOP nomination to succeed Scott began immediately in the wake of his 1976 retirement announcement, and, by November 1977, four candidates were prepared to enter the fray. Richard Obenshain, Linwood Holton, former Navy Secretary John Warner, and State Senator Nathan Miller all wanted the seat, and their competition for the nomination in 1978 would occasion one of the most exciting and colorful battles in the Commonwealth's rich history of political warfare.

From the outset, Obenshain was regarded as the frontrunner. After the GOP central committee voted in March 1977 to choose the party's senatorial nominee in 1978 by convention, the conservative leader's control over the party machinery made him the clear favorite. Privately, however, Obenshain was uncertain. He frequently alternated between moods of ambition and introversion, and, though the Senate long had been his foremost goal, a part of him resisted mightily. To Obenshain's personal ambivalence was added the fallout from the 1977 convention fights in which Walter Craigie and Wyatt Durrette, both candidates he actively backed, were defeated. His conservative group split over the contests, and many of his usual GOP allies were upset with him. Moreover, the hard-working Richmond lawyer worried about the financial strain on his young family of back-to-back nomination and general election campaigns. Thus, while most Republicans assumed that Obenshain would seek and win the GOP Senate nomination, Obenshain himself during much of 1977 hovered close to a decision not to make the race.

Obenshain eventually came to terms with his doubts and committed himself wholeheartedly to the political enterprise that would be his last. With the assistance of George Mason Green and other conservative hard-liners, he labored methodically to repair the strained relationships among his followers while, in Richmond, Judy Peachee hastily drafted a Senate campaign plan. On November 12, the conservative leader was ready, and, surrounded by cheering young partisans from campuses around the state, dozens of Richmond-area friends and professional colleagues, prominent conservative GOP activists from throughout Virginia, and the pillars of the conservative business community centered in the Third District, Obenshain formally launched his drive for the nomination. His brief speech stressed the principles and themes that had been his focus through two decades of political life—individual freedom, limited government, and free enterprise. Obenshain's strategy for becoming his party's Senate nominee was simple. He would rally conservative Republican regulars by articulating his ideas; he would point to his role as the architect of the GOP's recent victories and emphasize his own ability to reassemble that winning coalition; and he would call on the many Republican friends whom he had met and helped during his long labors in the party vineyards.

Linwood Holton also was an ambivalent candidate. After leaving the governorship in January 1974, he had gone to Washington to serve as Secretary of State Henry Kissinger's assistant secretary for congressional relations. The job was unsatisfying, and Holton had left it a year later to join the Washington, D.C., law firm of Hogan and Hartson. Friends and family members observed his restlessness, and urged him to re-enter the political arena. The former governor had higher name recognition among Virginia voters than other potential GOP candidates for the Senate and could cite favorable poll numbers to convince Republicans that he was the most "electable" candidate they could nominate. But the easy-going Holton never had a burning desire to be in the United States Senate, and a race for the nomination against the likes of Obenshain and Warner was not something to be undertaken casually. Moreover, Holton worried that his own entry into the race might merely divide the party's more moderate faction to Warner's detriment and Obenshain's advantage.

Holton, however, had known John Warner since their college days at Washington and Lee University—he was a law student there while Warner was a freshman—and nothing about Warner then or thereafter particularly impressed him. Though he viewed the political novice as less doctrinaire, and therefore less objectionable, than Obenshain, Holton simply did not expect the Warner candidacy to take hold. Nor did Holton at that point have any inkling that Warner could and would invest a half-million dollars of personal funds in his campaign.[113] The former governor thus resolved his own doubts in favor of a bid and kicked off his campaign on December 19. If brevity had been the object, the entire Holton announcement speech easily could have been reduced to three words—"I can win." Heartened by the 1977 Republican state convention, which had demonstrated that it was possible to blur the factional lines that guaranteed the Obenshain forces party hegemony after 1972, Holton downplayed his moderate, mountain-valley roots and played up his "electability." With Andrew Miller as the likely Democratic foe in the fall, Holton argued that only his own positive statewide image and proven vote-getting ability would be a match for the formidable former attorney general. That the twice-defeated Obenshain already had lost one election to Democrat Miller—the 1969 contest for attorney general— strengthened Holton's case immeasurably.

As Republican activists and political observers turned their attention from the 1977 contests to the impending Senate battle, most expected Holton and Obenshain to be the principal combatants. They could be forgiven for under-

---

[113]Holton interview.

estimating John Warner. A University of Virginia School of Law graduate, Navy and Marine Corps veteran, former assistant federal prosecutor, and Washington lawyer, Warner had little political experience. He had worked with the 1960 Nixon presidential campaign as an advance man, and then had headed the arm of Nixon's 1968 campaign that organized "citizen groups"—doctors, lawyer, real estate brokers, and the like—to support the GOP presidential nominee. After participating in Holton's gubernatorial campaign, he had become under-secretary of the Navy in 1969, and then was secretary of the Navy from 1972 until 1974, when President Nixon tapped him to head the American Revolution Bicentennial Administration. In addition to his Washington experience, two marriages had left Warner with political assets that markedly enhanced his electoral prospects. His marriage to Catherine Mellon, daughter of billionaire industrialist Paul Mellon, had ended in 1973 with an amicable divorce, but Warner emerged from it a millionaire with a Middleburg country estate and a home in the exclusive Georgetown section of Washington, D.C. Though reporters typically portrayed Warner's wealth as a product of the divorce, some of it actually was acquired during the course of the marriage through Warner's own legal practice and successful business ventures.[114] In 1976, he married Elizabeth Taylor, and the two quickly became Virginia's foremost celebrity couple. With his high-profile leadership of the Bicentennial completed, Warner and Taylor took to the Virginia hustings in 1977 to attract crowds and raise money for John Dalton and his ticket. It was a highly successful effort—one that drew many star-struck, celebrity-seeking Virginians to political activity for the first time—and there was little doubt that Warner was laying the groundwork for a Senate bid the following year.

Warner entered the race formally on January 5, 1978. In touting his own candidacy, he stressed his Washington experience and his ability to win the general election contest. Though the latter claim never had been tested in a political race, Warner, like Holton, could cite polls that suggested he would fare better in the fall than Obenshain. As with Holton's strong showing in opinion surveys, the poll numbers cited by Warner generally reflected his higher name recognition among voters—a product chiefly of his much-publicized marriage to Elizabeth Taylor. Nevertheless, Warner looked the part of a senator, and he was burdened neither by Obenshain's poor electoral track record nor the conservative leader's image as a rigid right-winger. He thus was an appealing alternative for some Republicans who doubted Obenshain's

---

[114]Warner revealed in 1990 that the divorce settlement effectively made him custodian of the real estate assets for the benefit of the couple's children, and he received substantial disposable funds only during the ten-year period prior to the youngest child's reaching adulthood. Though Warner and his former wife shared custody, the children lived with Warner in their Georgetown home. Out of a desire to protect the children, Warner chose for many years to forego correcting the frequent news media characterizations that overstated the value and overlooked the conditional nature of the interests he acquired pursuant to the divorce agreement. John W. Warner interview, June 27, 1980, and May 17, 1990.

ability to win but were not ready to give the Senate nomination to the moderate Holton.

In truth, however, Warner began the race without a significant base of support within the GOP. Obenshain and Holton each had sizeable followings among the activists who normally decided Republican nominations, but Warner did not. To be competitive, the newcomer had to bring new people—first-time activists—into the process. That was no easy task; there had been no large-scale invasion of the Virginia GOP by outsiders since 1952, when hero-worshipping Eisenhower partisans overcame the Republican "old guard" and Senator Robert Taft in a titanic presidential nomination struggle. But, as the 1978 contest proceeded, the celebrity appeal of Warner's wife and the candidate's generous financial support of his own campaign enabled the outsider to identify and mobilize supporters to a far greater degree than anyone, including Obenshain and Holton, had anticipated.

The reaction of Virginians to Elizabeth Taylor Warner, and vice versa, intrigued political and non-political observers alike. Second District Congressman G. William Whitehurst watched Republicans' response to her at a Dalton campaign luncheon in March 1977 and made this entry in his diary:

> Neither John Dalton nor Mills Godwin caused the rubbernecking in that ballroom that Liz Taylor did. . . . Those faithful who had plunked down $25 apiece for gravy-laden hamburger were obviously determined to get more for their money than indigestion and an earful of conservative rhetoric. They did. There is an awful lot of Liz Taylor. A beauty in her youth, she has suffered from the propensity of many women in their forties. In a word: she is fat. Nevertheless, if she has not shed any pounds, neither has she lost her magnetism. Throughout the speech-making, the audience stared alternately at her and at the speakers.[115]

The famed actress's draw extended well beyond Republican circles, and it was that broader appeal that proved critical to Warner's success. The curious came to investigate at political gatherings where the Warners were scheduled to appear, and for many the exciting first encounter with a glamorous stage and screen star was also their first encounter with the drama and excitement of politics. It was an electrifying mixture that brought a large number of them back again and again.

The actress found the role of a real-life political wife to be her most challenging; she commented afterwards that politics "[made] acting look like a kindergarten exercise."[116] But she played the part with warmth and sincerity, and the Virginians she met on the campaign trail usually responded in kind. "The campaign was harder than anything I'd done in my own career," Taylor wrote several years later,

---

[115]Whitehurst, p. 235.

[116]Elizabeth Taylor, *Elizabeth Takes Off* (New York: The Berkley Publishing Group, 1987), p. 37.

but I must admit there was something exhilarating about the experience. I could be spontaneous in public because I was working for someone other than myself, and the people of Virginia were just wonderful. They welcomed me, made me feel at home, and supported me generously. I still get a warm feeling from them.[117]

"Virginia is a sophisticated state, and [Virginians] are not people who get unduly excited about celebrities," observed John Warner. "Virginians sort of took her in stride, with a measure of doubt, and just wanted to watch her and see what she did. Undoubtedly, she contributed to larger crowds [than I otherwise would have had]."[118]

The field for the Senate race was completed by Nathan Miller, the 33-year-old state senator from Bridgewater in the Valley of Virginia. The boyish-looking lawyer had won election to the House of Delegates for the first time in 1971, and, in 1975, he had upset veteran Democratic incumbent George S. Aldhizer, II, to gain a seat in the Virginia Senate. When Miller declared his candidacy for the U.S. Senate nomination shortly after the November 1977 election, most Republicans construed the youthful lawmaker's bid as an effort to lay a foundation for some subsequent campaign for statewide office. Miller, however, was in the race to win. With three major candidates in the contest, he felt that a deadlocked convention was a realistic possibility. By seeking to be every delegate's second choice, he could position himself as a viable compromise candidate for the Senate nomination while also cultivating support for possible future bids for statewide office.

Throughout the winter and spring months of 1978, the four candidates displayed their wares almost every evening at a series of joint appearances before GOP unit and district committees, Republican women's clubs, and campus and Young Republican groups. The occasions were uniformly polite and upbeat, with the candidates in turn stressing their positive points and consistently refraining from leveling criticism at one another. As the Republican "road show" proceeded, it soon became apparent that the two GOP veterans, Obenshain and Holton, had developed a genuine camaraderie despite their past rivalry, while the newcomer Warner seemed the odd-man-out. Holton and Warner were the most obviously antagonistic, primarily because each resented the other's presence in the race, but both Holton and Obenshain became miffed over Warner's showmanship, frequent exaggerations, and misleading rhetoric. "All of us were kind of laughing at John because he was such a clown [during the joint appearances]," recalled Holton,

He had obviously taken some lessons on how to campaign [and] Dick and I would just giggle at him. It got him awfully mad, but it was a friendly race. Dick and I had been competing a long time on these things, and we were

---

[117]Ibid., p. 41.
[118]Warner interview.

just determined that when the nomination went to somebody it would be worth having. We were not going to have an intra-party fight on an individual, personal basis . . ., though John tempted us with that clowning and putting out stuff that just wasn't so.[119]

"There was some friction between us on one or two occasions," Warner acknowledged; "It was unfortunate, but it never persisted."[120] "We came out of it without any real problems," agreed Holton.

I talked with him pretty plainly [after the nomination contest] to say, "John, this is straight business. You don't go around trying to fool people, and there's no point in doing any acting. You're a good guy—just be yourself." I was trying to help him, and I think it did help him.[121]

Indeed, as the least-experienced candidate in the field, Warner's campaigning skills clearly were improved the most by the grueling nomination contest.

In a multi-candidate race in which no contender is able to assemble a first-ballot majority, the delegates' second choice becomes a critical factor. In that situation, the relationships between and among the various camps and candidates take on immense importance. Such was the case in 1978 as the Republican contenders dueled, first in joint appearances, and then at city and county mass meetings where the convention delegates were to be chosen. The personal friction between Holton and Warner carried over to their respective partisans and promised to be a factor at the convention. Also significant, however, was the collaboration of the Holton and Warner campaigns in an effort to prevent Obenshain's supporters in some areas from formally binding whole delegations to vote for the conservative party leader. The tactic of binding delegations through "instruction" resolutions[122] occasioned a number of bitter battles, particularly in the vote-rich Third District; one notable result was increased cooperation between the Holton and Warner camps and shared resentment toward Obenshain and his lieutenants.

The competition at local mass meetings was fierce not only in the Richmond area but throughout the state. Warner's campaign was well-funded and well-organized, and his reliance on out-of-state professionals to guide him through the byzantine Virginia GOP nominating process proved no disadvantage whatsoever. At meeting after meeting, dozens and dozens of new

---

[119]Holton interview.

[120]Warner interview.

[121]Holton interview.

[122]Though a frequent source of controversy and rancor in the GOP, the practice of "instruction" was sanctioned by party rules which allowed a majority at a local mass meeting or convention to adopt a resolution binding all of the unit's delegates to an ensuing convention. Alternatively, the party's rules permitted a local majority to elect a slate of delegates favoring a particular candidate. Either action could have the effect of making local mass meetings winner-take-all affairs. Because the practices were discretionary and the rules were not widely understood by many participants, use of the "instruction" and "slating" devices tended to produce emotional charges of unfairness, acrimonious debate, and widespread grass-roots dissension.

faces—the "Warner people"—showed up to get a glimpse of the celebrity couple and to secure delegate slots for the big event scheduled for Richmond in June: the party's state convention. Obenshain's operatives countered the Warner influx, not only by turning out the conservative GOP faithful, but also by tapping their own source of new activists: the conservative businessmen and Byrd Democrats with whom Obenshain had established close ties during a decade of coalition building. In Obenshain's behalf, many prominent Coalitionists and conservative followers of Mills Godwin and Harry Byrd were willing to compromise their independence and formally participate in GOP party processes for the first time.

The vigorous competition thus had the very beneficial consequence of rapidly swelling the ranks of active Republican partisans, and attendance estimates for the June convention soared as the event neared.[123] Party Chairman George McMath eyed the unfolding developments with nervous excitement. In hopes of increasing convention participation, he had gained approval by the GOP central committee for an increase to 3,081 in the number of delegate votes. And, with the party rules permitting each of those delegate votes to be divided among as many as five persons, there was little practical limitation on the number of individuals who could participate as convention delegates. As the mass meetings were held over a four-month period from February to May, the cumulative convention attendance estimates reported by the local GOP committees soon reached well into the thousands. With GOP Executive Director Jeff Gregson, McMath searched in vain around the country for guidance concerning how to organize such a mammoth conclave. "We knew there would be no in-between there. It was either going to be an efficient operation or absolute chaos," McMath recalled.[124] The situation was unprecedented, and, as the candidates hurried toward the convention finish line, the sponsors raced to avert disaster.

In competitive politics everybody loves a winner, and so it was not surprising that the two words spoken most often in late spring as Republicans prepared for their tumultuous state convention were "electability" and "momentum." The former concerned which of the four contestants most likely would win in November if nominated, and the latter concerned which was poised to win in June. For frontrunner Obenshain, the case for electability rested on his superior ability to reassemble a winning coalition of GOP conservatives, mountain-valley Republican moderates, and former Byrd Democrats. Obenshain's backers argued that his two earlier electoral defeats, both by narrow margins, were party-building exercises that had paid handsome divi-

---

[123]For an in-depth examination of the background, philosophy, and other characteristics of the delegates at the 1978 Republican state convention, see Alan Abramowitz, John McGlennon, and Ronald Rapoport, *Party Activists in Virginia: A Study of Delegates to the 1978 Senatorial Nominating Conventions* (Charlottesville: Institute of Government, University of Virginia, 1981).

[124]McMath interview.

dends for the GOP in the '70s, and they dismissed as defeatist the familiar plaints that the former party chairman was, like Goldwater and Reagan, simply "too conservative" to be elected. Warner's promise of November victory rested on his celebrity appeal, wealth, glamor, senatorial good looks, and the fact that, unlike Obenshain, he neither had lost an election nor been stereotyped by the news media as an arch-conservative. To suggestions from the opposing camps that the staid Virginia electorate would dismiss their man as an unaccomplished, star-chasing dilettante, Warner's promoters scoffed. The Holton campaign, which presented the only candidate who actually had prevailed in a previous statewide race, entreated delegates to "Win With Lin Again!" and sought to rebut arguments that Holton's 1969 election merely had been a fluke produced by an unusually divisive three-way Democratic nomination battle. As for the dark-horse candidate, Nathan Miller, well, if he miraculously won at the convention, anything was possible in November.

If the elusive quality known as electability took on talismanic importance for the delegates eyeing November, momentum was the mystical force that impelled those caught up in the contest at hand. In physics, momentum is the product of an object's mass and linear velocity, but in politics, the phenomenon does not lend itself to such precise definition. It may be described as the added impetus that a candidate gets from the growing expectation that he will win—that is, a self-fulfilling prophesy. Or, it may be said that momentum supplies in politics what adrenalin and desire together supply in human physical endeavor. However defined, momentum in the realm of politics is an abstract and elusive concept, but for the thousands who convened in the Richmond Coliseum on June 3, it would become a palpable, almost irresistible force. Every candidate and campaign operative competing at the 1978 Republican state convention knew that, there and then, momentum would be everything.

Predictions and expectations were exceedingly important. On the eve of the convention, the Obenshain camp predicted that their candidate would lead on the first ballot with 1,200 votes and would exceed the 1,541-total needed to win on the third ballot. Both Holton and Warner acknowledged that Obenshain was the leader in the race, but each claimed to be in second place. The Holton backers predicted a victory for their man on the second ballot, while the Warner campaign, whose vote projections seemed the more realistic, predicted that the former Navy secretary would get the votes he needed on the third ballot. Nathan Miller, staking his hopes on a three-way deadlock, talked of a sixth ballot victory; he was not particular, though, insisting only that he would be in "first place on the last ballot."[125] The most striking prediction of all came from GOP Chairman McMath: nearly 10,000 people were expected to attend the convention, and it would be the "largest political convention in terms of delegates assembled ever held in the United States."[126]

[125]*Richmond Times-Dispatch*, June 3, 1978.
[126]Ibid.

The thousands converged on Richmond throughout the day on Friday, June 2. After a brief, largely ceremonial convention session that afternoon, the candidates and their families, campaign operatives, party officials, delegates and alternates, news reporters, concessioners and hotel workers began the long night that was to precede the very long day. The candidates hustled from place to place pressing the flesh, giving news interviews, addressing delegates in congressional district caucuses, making the obligatory appearances at various functions, and, finally, hosting their own "hospitality" parties. Delegates were wined, dined, coaxed, cajoled, persuaded, dissuaded, and persuaded again. Behind the scenes, veritable armies of volunteers and paid operatives worked feverishly to gather intelligence, update vote counts, choreograph candidate movements, bolster the confidence of supporters, sway the undecided, "spin" the press corps, and supply the most impressive entertainment for the delegates. Though few of the convention participants were genuinely undecided about their first choice, every delegate was a potential vote on the second and subsequent ballots. So, telephone lines buzzed, walkie-talkies crackled, anxious partisans pounded urgently on elevator buttons, and smoke-filled hotel rooms overflowed into smoke-filled hallways as every one of nearly 9,000 delegates and alternates became either a prize to be won or a foe to be shunned.

With the last revelers carrying on obliviously, campaign operatives worked through the wee hours of Saturday morning making final preparations. Just before dawn, a corps of Obenshain volunteers fanned out to every hotel and motel in the Richmond area and slipped the latest issue of the campaign's convention newsletter under each guest's door. Many Republicans were puzzled by what they read the next morning. Instead of confident boasts of impending victory, the Obenshain newsletter contained predictions of an extremely long and very difficult battle, with victory coming only after many ballots. The tone of the missive surprised Holton and Warner strategists—one Warner tactician told reporters that it was a "stupid" move—but it became clear much later in the day that the Obenshain strategy of reduced expectations had been a wise one.[127]

By 10 a.m. Saturday, all of the excitement, energy, and emotion that had been dispersed throughout the capital the preceding evening was packed into the constricting confines of the Richmond Coliseum. The usually cavernous arena was—as Obenshain would observe triumphantly some 14 hours later—literally "stacked to the rafters" with delegates, alternates, and hundreds of guests. To the left of the stage was erected a battery of television cameras like nothing ever seen before in Virginia politics. National and even international television network crews were on hand to capture the drama of the world's largest political convention with a cast that included the renowned Elizabeth Taylor in her most unlikely role. The coliseum was a mass of humanity, ban-

[127]*Richmond Times-Dispatch*, June 4, 1978.

ners, signs, and color from floor to ceiling. And there was noise—more noise than one can imagine.

Governor John Dalton, who had remained scrupulously neutral throughout the hard-fought nomination battle, made the first speech—a carefully worded appeal for party unity amid the most intense competition the surging GOP had ever witnessed. The lanky young attorney general, Marshall Coleman, appeared briefly to thank delegates for their support during the previous fall's campaign: "When I was hungry, you fed me. When I was lost, you found me. . . . And each night I slept in a Republican house, in a Republican bed . . ."[128]

And then the really important speeches began: Congressmen William Whitehurst and Caldwell Butler nominating and seconding, respectively, the Holton candidacy; former Congressman Joel Broyhill rising to place Warner's name in nomination and Warner himself rising to second that motion; former Governor Mills Godwin presenting Obenshain as the architect of Virginia's "great coalition"; and then Nathan Miller. After each candidate's name was placed in nomination, his supporters quickly spilled into the narrow aisles, each group attempting to outdo the other's demonstration as if decibels rather than votes would decide the contest. While the Obenshain show had a cast of thousands, the Warner march was the most exciting because it featured the candidate himself, a rousing rendition of "Anchor's Away," Elizabeth Taylor in a sailor's cap, and the day's worst crush of bones and television cameras. The prize for creativity, however, went to Miller, who, with no armies for a floor demonstration, came up with a better idea. After Delegate Bonnie Paul of Harrisonburg placed his name in nomination, the hall suddenly went dark and a mammoth movie screen dropped from the ceiling behind the podium. In moments, the hushed masses were watching a lively slide presentation with spine-tingling music and myriad scenes of the youthful Senator Miller in action. At its conclusion, a spotlight replaced the images on the huge screen and then descended to find standing at the podium in the flesh, the only illuminated object in the arena, Nathan Miller—media candidate and star of the future. What he said didn't matter; every delegate would remember the glitter.

And then it was time for business. Thousands upon thousands of delegates, apportioned among ten congressional districts, divided into more than a hundred local units, most casting fractionalized votes, many unrested and otherwise impaired after a raucous evening, dazed by passionate appeals by their peers, and anxious to the breaking point, were about to distribute their votes among four candidates. The ballots then would be tallied in the delegations, reported, tallied again, and announced by the convention chairman, after which the entire process would be repeated again and again until someone, someday mustered a fraction more than half of the total delegate

---

[128]Ibid.

votes. At that point, the air would rush out of the balloon, the survivors would rush out of the coliseum, and it all would be a memory. Could it be done? "I never thought it could be pulled off," recalled Roanoke newspaper reporter Buster Carico, who had watched the Republican Party grow from a tiny western enclave.[129] "At the largest political convention in the history of the world, the Great Indoor Primary, it has been a long day—about a month and a half in the real world . . .," began newspaper columnist Charles McDowell many hours later, forced by deadlines to file his report even while the outcome remained in doubt.[130]

As the balloting got underway, it quickly was apparent that George McMath, Jeff Gregson, and the Virginia GOP's supporting cast had met the organizational challenge. The party chairman's decision to ban beer sales at the coliseum and his systematic ballot-counting procedures proved crucial in facilitating an orderly process. But his most insightful action was to place the convention gavel in the hands of Herbert Bateman. The state senator from Newport News knew parliamentary procedure forwards and backwards, but, even more important, he knew how to wield the gavel in a manner at once decisive yet scrupulously fair. His knack for presiding had been honed over the years as chairman and general counsel for the Jaycees, which held large and often intensely competitive national conventions. Early in the spring, when McMath first named him, some in the Warner and Holton camps expressed concern that Bateman was an Obenshain partisan. But the senator reassured each of the campaign managers personally, and by June he enjoyed the full confidence of all of the contending camps. As a result, the historic Richmond gathering occasioned less parliamentary maneuvering and procedural controversy than almost any other contested GOP convention, before or since. "I was extremely proud of the way the convention operated [because] I know how very fraught with danger it was," Bateman recalled years later.[131] The convention chairman's performance won near-universal praise from those who witnessed it, hour after wearying hour.

The first ballot began a little after noon, and it was completed in two and a half hours. Obenshain received just eight votes less than the 1,200 he had predicted. The all-important second-place position went to Warner, who garnered 853 votes; Holton, with 780, was not far behind; and Miller polled 252. Though he had been edged only narrowly by Warner, Holton's third-place showing dealt his candidacy a damaging blow. As the next ballot began, the former governor hustled over to the Ninth District section of the convention hall to appeal for support from his native southwest Virginia. But it was too late. With second-place honors in the first round went the right to challenge Obenshain for the prize, and the former governor watched his total slip

[129]Carico interview.

[130]*Richmond Times-Dispatch*, June 4, 1978.

[131]Herbert H. Bateman interview, June 11, 1980, and September 18, 1984.

slightly on the second ballot. Nathan Miller's share declined even more precipitously as Warner and Obenshain strategists recalled votes that had been "deposited" in Miller's column on the first ballot in order to create the appearance of momentum when retrieved on the second.

It was after 5:00 p.m. when the second ballot was concluded, and Obenshain and Warner indeed had the momentum. Their partisans poured out on the convention floor to shout, wave signs, and demonstrate their conviction that victory would soon be theirs. From one portal, a waving Dick and Helen Obenshain strode out to greet the applauding delegates as if for the first time that day. The appearance of the candidate fired the Obenshain demonstrators anew, inspiring loud chants of "We want Dick" and "Ohhhh-ben-shain" as red signs sporting large white "O"s covered the convention floor. Moments later, the Warners made their own entrance to a rousing "Warner Will Win" refrain; red-white-and-blue posters bearing the candidate's rustic profile were hoisted once again; and sailor's hats filled the aisles. The battle was joined.

After a time, State Senator Bateman gaveled the convention to order, the demonstrators retired to their various delegations, and the third ballot began. To serve as a command post, each campaign had been assigned a wooden perch constructed in a corner overlooking the convention floor. Each was equipped with telephones, walkie-talkies, adding machines, and a lot of very tense people who were in constant communication with their respective tacticians and number-crunchers located in separate rooms in the bowels of the coliseum. The Warner and Obenshain platforms were now the scene of frenzied activity; the third ballot was expected to produce significant movement by the delegates. And when the roll was called, the numbers confirmed that the Holton cause was lost. Obenshain's total stood at 1,338, Warner's at 996, Holton's at 620, and Miller's at 122. Within minutes, the former governor took to the stage, accompanied by his wife and four children, to bow out gracefully. "Fellow Republicans: Jinx, Tayloe, Anne, Woody and Dwight are very happy to join you in welcoming me to the role of elder statesman," Holton declared. Saying that he was "inspired and thrilled" by the support he had received in his Senate campaign, Virginia's first GOP governor in the twentieth century concluded, "We now abide by your will, and withdraw from the race."[132]

The prolonged applause for Holton gradually faded into a resumption of the competing Obenshain and Warner partisan refrains, as sign-waving, foot-stomping delegates again poured onto the convention floor. There were now hundreds of delegate votes up for grabs, and strategists for both Obenshain and Holton expected the former governor's exit to put the frontrunner over the top. "After Linwood dropped out, I voted for Obenshain because I felt that we owed it to him," recalled Holton protégé Caldwell

---

[132]*Richmond Times-Dispatch*, June 4, 1978.

Butler.[133] The common background of party service and the evident rapport that had recently developed between the two GOP veterans led many of the Holton partisans to switch to Obenshain. But, when the fourth-ballot votes were counted, the movement to the frontrunner fell short of expectations. Perhaps the remnants of the past Holton-Obenshain factional clashes and the underlying ideological differences were less easily surmounted than some had believed. But the more plausible explanation was that, for most of the delegates, electability was the overriding concern. Recalled long-time Holton ally Cynthia Newman:

> A lot of people I know began looking for a winner, and I think they just thought John Warner had a better chance of winning than Dick Obenshain did. Looking back on it, I am not sure they were correct. But I really think it was a practical move on their part. I voted for John Warner and I liked Dick Obenshain better. But, there again, I thought he had a better chance of winning.[134]

As anxious partisans on all sides held their breath, the fourth ballot totals rolled in. When all of the delegations had reported, Obenshain remained a hair short of his goal. With 1,541 votes needed to win, he had 1,521. John Warner had picked up a majority of the Holton votes and now was at 1,338. Nathan Miller also had gained significantly, increasing his total from 122 votes on the third ballot to 201 on the fourth. It was now that Miller became the decisive player. Since he first entered the Senate race, it had been well known that Miller mostly drew votes that otherwise would have been Obenshain's, especially in the conservative Seventh District. Without Miller in the contest, Obenshain certainly would have won the nomination on the fourth ballot. But Miller had stayed through the fourth ballot, and he now resolved to stay for the fifth as well. As the balloting resumed at approximately 8:30 p.m., the discerning in the Richmond Coliseum knew that Obenshain's campaign was beginning to stall. The momentum—that all-important force—was no longer with him.

The young Senator Miller was in a quandary. Holton's withdrawal had not been part of the expected scenario; Miller had counted on a three-way deadlock to deliver him a compromise nomination. But, with Holton's withdrawal, the Bridgewater senator had picked up votes. No one withdraws when they are picking up votes. But, then again, what realistically were the chances of a deadlock now? Obenshain had not gone over; he was probably dead in the water. But what about Warner? Warner was moving up fast. What if Miller, by staying in the race, succeeded only in holding Obenshain back and allowing Warner to win? That result would be contrary to the wishes of a majority of Miller's own supporters. The Obenshain people—from the candidate on down—were furious at him already, and a private visit from Governor Godwin at the begin-

---

[133]M. Caldwell Butler interview, April 5, 1984.
[134]Cynthia Newman interview, July 2, 1980.

ning of the fifth ballot made it clear that Miller would be held accountable if Obenshain were to lose. The ambitious state senator could kiss the conservative vote goodbye in any future race if that happened. Of course, Warner would be none too pleased with him if he pulled out now, either. What to do? . . .

"It was a fairly incredible scenario . . .," wrote Charles McDowell,

[A]t 8:30 an excited, weary, hungry, dry convention was voting for the fifth time. A rereading of Obenshain's morning [newsletter] at this point indicated he believed all along he had to win it on the fifth or never. . . . Obenshain needed about 20. Warner needed about 103. And there was Nathan Miller, the boyish bachelor from the Shenandoah, the audio-visual politician, the hope for the future, sitting on 201 and a fraction.[135]

Suddenly, Miller's good-natured, innovative, long-shot Senate bid ran the very real risk of damaging his political future, perhaps fatally.

When the fifth ballot results were in, a wave of momentum for Warner swept through the convention hall. The movement had been slight, but for the first time Obenshain's total actually decreased—by five votes—as a handful of his exhausted elderly supporters left for home. Though the crack in the frontrunner's previously rock-solid support had a major psychological impact, more significant numerically was the fifth-ballot decline in Miller's total and the resultant increase in Warner's. Obenshain now had 1,516 votes, Warner had 1,393, and Miller had 166. The deafening Warner demonstration that followed was spurred in large measure by the antics of the candidate himself. In a surge of emotion, the charging Warner leaped atop the wooden platform that was his campaign's command post and exhorted the delegates by waving his suit coat and then a campaign placard high over his head to the roaring approval of his partisans. It was a moment that was emblazoned in the memory of every person in the arena—the dashing candidate in multi-colored suspenders, caught up in the excitement, jumping up and down, leading the cheer. It was not typical for traditional Virginia, but, then, neither was his candidacy, his famous wife, nor this convention.

"There is strong speculation that I would have won on the sixth ballot," commented Warner in an interview years later:

That's because people watching a convention like that were seeing the top guy slip back and the other guy coming forward with the momentum. And I got up and did that famous speech on the table-top, which some people have described as absolutely ridiculous and others as the most heroic thing they have ever seen in politics. The criticism and the accolades go the full spectrum. But, anyway, that got that audience up on their feet unlike they had been in hours. The Obenshain people, I believe to this day, felt they were going to lose on the sixth ballot . . .[136]

---

[135]*Richmond Times-Dispatch*, June 4, 1978.
[136]Warner interview.

Seated across the coliseum watching the surging Warner were an exhausted and nearly dispirited Richard Obenshain and his wife. The fear and fatigue were almost overwhelming, recalled Helen Obenshain, until the couple looked up to see a smiling supporter, former Democratic Delegate Guy O. Farley, Jr., of Fairfax, who assured them in a whisper that "God is on your side."[137] It was at that nadir that something unexpected and wonderful happened for the Obenshain forces, . . . at that zenith that horror filled Warner and his corps of masterful tacticians. There, in the distance, preparing to mount the platform at the front of the convention hall, was Nathan Miller.

"I stayed in there until the fifth ballot when I started losing ground," recounted Miller. "And after that I realized that I could not gain anymore, and there was no reason to be a spoiler, so I withdrew."[138] It was widely suspected then, and later confirmed privately by his closest associates, that Miller preferred Obenshain for the nomination and withdrew so that the stumbling frontrunner could win.[139] Though his withdrawal came too late to spare him the ire of many Obenshain partisans, the state senator's move had the predict- able effect. As Miller announced his withdrawal with the declaration, "It's time for this convention to work its will,"[140] Obenshain, Warner, and their top lieutenants rushed to the area where the Seventh District delegates, and the bulk of the now-freed Miller backers, were located. The hunt for the last crucial votes was on.

It was after 10 p.m., and Warner's weary pros huddled to discuss the tactic of interposing parliamentary objections in order to delay the proceedings past midnight. It was thought that some of the Obenshain partisans from the Shenandoah Valley might decline for reasons of religious conviction to remain in the arena once the Sabbath arrived, and that could tip the balance in the close contest. Warner recalls a "feverish conference in the bowels of that coli- seum" on the subject—one that he terminated. "I made the decision right there and then that it would be wrong," he said later. "We had conducted that campaign ethically, fairly, honestly every step of the way, and I would not at that late hour reverse the policy that I had in effect since the first day. So we . . . let the sixth ballot go forward."[141]

In a flash, the almost unbelievably long and dramatic battle was done. Warner fared well among the Miller partisans, but not well enough. The final tally, shortly before midnight, made Obenshain the party's Senate nominee with 1,579 votes—just 38 more than the number needed to win. Even before the votes all were tabulated, Warner strode briskly to the rostrum to laud Holton as the party's elder statesman, acknowledge Miller as a promising

---

[137]Mrs. Richard D. Obenshain interview.

[138]Nathan Miller interview.

[139]Bayliss interview.

[140]*Richmond Times-Dispatch*, June 4, 1978.

[141]Warner interview.

candidate for the future, and move that Obenshain's nomination be made unanimous. The motion passed as a satisfied State Senator Bateman quickly banged the chairman's gavel. Moments later, the Obenshains mounted the stage. Praising his opponents and pledging his best efforts to unite the GOP after this "longest, most exciting, most tenacious competition we've ever had in this Virginia party," the triumphant nominee declared:

> The greatness of this party, the reason we've been stacked here to the rafters with this enthusiasm, is because of our commitment to the great, historic, fundamental principles of Virginia. Thousands of Virginians are here today because of that commitment of our party. And thousands and thousands more are waiting around the state of Virginia for this campaign to take to them the message of the principles and the strengths that the Republican Party of Virginia offers to this state, and also offers for constructive leadership to the United States of America.[142]

Obenshain had prevailed over formidable foes in a convention unprecedented in its size, its length, and the intensity of its competition. His victory was the more impressive because of Warner's tangible advantages—massive free media attention and campaign money coffers nearly three times the size of Obenshain's.[143] The experience was especially satisfying for the veteran party leader because his "troops"—the conservative party regulars—had stayed with him until the end, their intense devotion never really having been in doubt. "We had waited eight or ten years to elect our man to office," recalled Judy Peachee. "There was no way we were going home. And when it was over we were riding on a high. . . . [T]here was no stopping us now."[144] Obenshain carried the hopes of many, but his hard-fought nomination victory lifted from his shoulders a heavy personal burden; after the tumultuous 1978 convention, he could no longer be branded a "loser," the label that had haunted him since his unsuccessful bids for public office in the '60s.

For Warner, the long-shot newcomer who had come from nowhere to the brink of a tumultuous convention victory in a span of less than a year, there was satisfaction, too, though even greater disappointment. Warner and his crafty, well-organized campaign had been underestimated at every turn, but as ballot followed ballot on the decisive day, nearly everything fell into place as they had planned. Warner had taken on two of the most accomplished Virginia GOP leaders; he had attracted literally thousands of people to Republican Party activity for the first time; he had turned out his supporters for the state convention in record numbers; he had converted backers of Linwood Holton

---

[142]Text of remarks on file with the author.

[143]Warner spent more than $590,000 on his campaign for the party nomination, most of it coming from his personal funds. Obenshain's campaign reported expenditures of approximately $212,000, and Holton's listed spending of approximately $114,000. Nathan Miller spent just over $50,000. Sabato, *Virginia Votes 1975-1978*, p. 91.

[144]*The Washington Times*, August 2, 1983.

and Nathan Miller as his campaign steadily gained credibility and momentum; he had come close—ever so close—to capturing the prize. To his credit and eventual reward, John Warner kept his disappointment in check. From his convention speech seeking acclamation for Obenshain to his appearance with the nominee the next morning, at which he pledged his support and presented the candidate with a $500 campaign contribution, the defeated Warner rang the bell for party unity.

"The happiest part of the convention," Obenshain wrote to a correspondent several weeks later, "was the amazingly united and friendly spirit which emerged. Lin Holton, John Warner and Nathan Miller have all expressed, in the strongest terms, their willingness and intent to help in any possible way."[145] Somewhat surprisingly, the actual GOP harmony in the convention's wake was as genuine as the contenders and party officials claimed. State Democrats had hoped to capitalize on residual bitterness in the losing camps following the intense Republican nomination battle; Andrew Miller, the frontrunner for the Democratic Senate nomination, branded Obenshain an "extremist" after the GOP conclave and called on Holton Republicans to join him (Miller) "in the mainstream."[146] But, instead of engendering strife, the competition for the GOP nomination seemed to have strengthened bonds among the Republicans. The losing candidates deserved much credit for the harmony, but so did Obenshain, who always had been among the first to put intra-party squabbles behind once the issues had been settled.

One week after the Republicans chose Obenshain, Democrats convened in Williamsburg to give Andrew Miller their party's nod. Only twice previously—in 1946 and 1971—had Virginia Democrats nominated statewide candidates by convention, and in both instances the departure from the traditional primary election method had been occasioned by an unexpected vacancy.[147] But after their 1969 and 1977 primary debacles, Democrats concluded that the Republicans' successful track record using the convention method might not be purely coincidental. The Democratic delegate selection process differed from the GOP's in several significant respects, however. The Democratic delegates were selected in mass meetings held on the same day at the same hour (noon on Saturday, April 15); they were divided proportionally among the candidates in relation to the number of supporters that assembled for each candidate at each mass meeting; they were bound to support their

---

[145]Letter to the author dated June 16, 1978; copy on file with the author. Holton and Warner, with former Governor Godwin and former Delegate W. Roy Smith, became the honorary co-chairmen of the Obenshain campaign. Miller was appointed chairman of the Obenshain Advocates Committee.

[146]*Richmond Times-Dispatch*, June 11, 1978.

[147]Democrats held conventions to nominate candidates to fill the vacancies caused by the deaths of U.S. Senator Carter Glass in 1946 and Lieutenant Governor J. Sargeant Reynolds in 1971. See Sabato, *Democratic Party Primary*, pp. 54–60, 83–84.

chosen candidate on the first ballot at the state convention; and, each delegate had one full vote at the convention.[148]

The differing rules guaranteed that the Democratic gathering would feature fewer delegates and less fireworks. Miller was the heavy favorite, though the presence of numerous other candidates in the race prevented him from securing the necessary majority of delegate votes until after the third ballot. The former attorney general's chief opponent was liberal State Senator Clive L. DuVal II of Arlington, and the next largest first-ballot vote-getter was G. Conoly Phillips, a Norfolk councilman and automobile dealer who brought hundreds of fellow "born-again" Christians into the party nominating process for the first time.[149] Except for Miller's gradual gains, there was little movement by the delegates from ballot to ballot. And, with Miller just a few votes shy of the 1,397-vote majority needed to win the nomination on the third ballot, all seven other Democratic candidates acknowledged the inevitable and jointly withdrew from the race with the request that the frontrunner be nominated unanimously.

A short time later, Andrew Miller appeared before the unified and enthusiastic convention to accept his party's nomination. He paused only to praise his Democratic rivals and to acknowledge the presence in the gallery of his father and mother, Colonel and Mrs. Francis Pickens Miller, before sounding the battle cry for a strong and strident campaign. He blasted GOP candidate Obenshain as "an extremist . . . [and] an ideologue of the radical right" and urged "homeless Holton Republicans" to join his campaign.[150] Before the determined Miller was an assemblage of Virginia Democrats with views ranging from very conservative to very liberal, a fact confirmed by three College of William and Mary political scientists who surveyed the partisans.[151] But, despite their varying outlooks, virtually all could agree that Miller, the only living Democrat elected statewide between 1966 and 1977, represented the party's best chance to break its long losing streak in major state contests.

Among the most noteworthy developments at the Democrats' Williamsburg conclave was the presence of hundreds of conservative-thinking political novices, mostly from Tidewater, who attended to support Conoly

---

[148]Under the Democratic rules, any candidate who produced more than twenty percent of the attendees at a mass meeting received committed (for the first ballot) delegates in proportion to their strength at the meeting. Those attendees whose candidate did not receive twenty percent of the vote at the mass meeting were permitted to join uncommitted caucuses or to join with the supporters of other candidates. Votes were not fractionalized. See Abramowitz, McGlennon and Rapoport, *Party Activists in Virginia*, p. 21.

[149]The first ballot totals were: Miller – 1,222; DuVal – 587; Conoly Phillips – 412; former Fairfax County Supervisor Rufus Phillips – 240; former Fairfax Delegate Carrington Williams – 150; Hampton State Senator Hunter Andrews – 139; Frederick Babson of Virginia Beach – 11; women's rights activist Flora Crater – 10. Abramowitz, McGlennon, and Rapoport, *Party Activists in Virginia*, p. 104.

[150]*Richmond Times-Dispatch*, December 31, 1978.

[151]See Abramowitz, McGlennon and Rapoport, *Party Activists in Virginia*, p. 33.

Phillips because of their shared religious perspective. Reverend M. G. "Pat" Robertson, son of the late U.S. Senator A. Willis Robertson and head of the Virginia Beach-based Christian Broadcasting Network (CBN), placed Phillips' name in nomination at the convention. In so doing, he foreshadowed the increase in political activism of fundamentalist and evangelical Christians that would occur in the '80s. The evangelical Christians, Robertson declared to the quizzical Democratic regulars, were a "great sleeping giant coming into the political process."[152] Though their first foray was into the Democratic Party's nominating process—a predictable development in light of President Carter's widely publicized "born-again" faith—these conservative Christians and others like them soon would have a major impact on the internal dynamics of the state GOP.

Miller's nomination set the stage for a rematch of the 1969 contest for attorney general in which the Democrat had prevailed. Both contestants were fierce party loyalists who had spent their entire adult careers in partisan political endeavor. Miller had gotten his start as state president of the Young Democrats, and Obenshain had begun as leader of the state's Young Republicans. The former Democratic attorney general's moderate approach represented his party's best hope for the future, and Miller seemingly had walked a primrose path in politics until his 1977 defeat at the hands of Howell. Obenshain, in contrast, had endured early setbacks to see his dream of realignment and conservative coalition realized in the '70s. The Miller-Obenshain confrontation resembled an encounter on adjacent escalators: Obenshain's was on the way up; Miller's, on the way down. But, with Republicans apparently having placed philosophy ahead of electability through the selection of their most conservative candidate, most observers gave the centrist Democrat a slight edge.

---

[152]*Richmond Times-Dispatch*, December 31, 1978.

Chapter 32

The Obenshain Tragedy

"Richard Dudley Obenshain was 42 and on his way to the heights—very likely to the United States Senate, and possibly beyond. . . . Far less than most, he deserved a hurried death. For here was a man whose every considerable achievement was the result of fierce adherence to principle.[153]

Ross Mackenzie
The Richmond News Leader, August 4, 1978

"If every day could be like this, there'd be no stopping us!" Obenshain declared to his driver and confidant, 23-year-old Bradley B. Cavedo, as the pair approached Winchester for the candidate's appearance on August 2. The day that would be Richard Obenshain's last had been marked by enthusiastic crowds and some of the upbeat nominee's most passionate and inspiring speeches. Asked by a member of one audience whether he thought one person could make a difference in Washington, Obenshain had given his inner reasons for running for the Senate as Cavedo had never heard him previously. "We have to let the nation hear the voice of Virginia, the voice of freedom, just as the nation heard it 200 years ago!" he had exclaimed. And then he added, to the puzzlement and consternation of his buoyant aide, "And even if we don't succeed we must go down fighting."[154] Obenshain's appearance in Winchester brought "one of the most moving speeches I've ever heard," recalled liberal Democratic Delegate Lewis P. Fickett, Jr., of Fredericksburg, his party's congressional candidate in the Seventh District. "The essence of the speech was the necessity of individual freedom and the vitality of private initiative, which are the cornerstones of American democracy."[155] That was the essence of Richard Obenshain.

The candidate's excitement on August 2 was justified. In the 60 days since his tumultuous convention victory, Obenshain had pulled together a winning campaign organization, and had positioned himself to achieve the electoral victory that previously had eluded him. Against Miller, the formidable

---

[153]*The Richmond News Leader*, August 4, 1978.
[154]*The Virginian-Pilot and The Ledger-Star*, August 5, 1978.
[155]*The Richmond News Leader*, August 3, 1978.

moderate, two-term attorney general, the conservative GOP leader had begun the race perceived as the underdog. But Obenshain was a master at exploiting Democratic weaknesses, and by early August it was clear that he had found Miller's.

The Democrat was vulnerable on several counts. First, there was the national setting. Virginians had long evinced distinctly conservative attitudes on national issues such as foreign policy and economics, and, though Miller's party was in power in Washington, both President Carter and Congress were out of favor in Virginia. Defense spending cuts, inflationary tax hikes, budget deficits, the treaty ceding the Panama Canal back to the tiny isthmus nation—all were easy targets for Obenshain and burdens for Miller to bear. Miller's general image as a moderate would be of little aid when he was called upon by Republicans to account for the actions of the liberal Democratic majority in Congress that he hoped to join.

Second, there was Miller's recent track record. The loss to Howell in 1977 tarnished the former attorney general's image of invincibility and seemed to diminish his confidence as well. Observers found Miller a less affable and appealing candidate in 1978 than he had been a year earlier. "He was a more embittered candidate after that [1977 loss to Howell]," recalled Chuck Robb. "I never saw the old flair that Andy had earlier."[156] In addition, some financial supporters who had seen their investment in Miller go for naught the previous year were reluctant to invest heavily in him in 1978.

Finally, there was the public perception of Miller. As the incumbent in 1973, Miller had carried every Virginia city and county in the race for attorney general, a fact that attested to his broad popularity among voters. An Obenshain campaign poll in spring 1978 found that, of the nearly two-thirds of Virginians who said they had an opinion of Miller, more than 50 percent had a favorable attitude while only 15 percent viewed him unfavorably. Yet, in response to the question, "What do you like best about Andrew Miller?" more than two-thirds said they did not know. And nearly half of those polled could not classify the Democrat as liberal, moderate, or conservative. Miller's high, positive name recognition insulated him from early negative attacks by Obenshain—that was the good news. But the candidate was not perceived as standing for anything; Virginians did not associate him with any particular idea, policy, or characteristic that they cared strongly about. And that fact meant that he could be defeated by someone perceived as standing for something voters wanted.

Miller's strategy was simple enough; he meant to seize the center and portray Obenshain as a right-wing extremist. That the former attorney general would run an aggressive campaign designed to do just that was apparent from his pointed public pronouncements which began immediately upon Obenshain's convention victory. For Obenshain and his consultants, however,

---

[156]Charles S. Robb interview, October 5, 1984.

the strategic calculus was more complicated. They had to make up a deficit in name recognition, mobilize the conservative financial establishment to fund the GOP campaign, and simultaneously moderate the Republican's image in order to capture enough middle-of-the-road voters to assemble a statewide majority.

The first two Obenshain objectives were addressed in early July in a campaign strategy memorandum that began with this four-point premise: (1) that Obenshain had a severe name recognition deficit; (2) that Miller was a "non-polarizing candidate" (that is, he was neither hated nor feared); (3) that there was little "Republican money" in Virginia, but there was a conservative financial establishment that gave to Republicans "only if either the Democratic candidate is hated or feared, or if the Republican candidate looks like a winner"; and (4) that "Obenshain probably cannot win without the support of this establishment and therefore he must soon begin to look like a winner."[157] To achieve the latter goal and thereby "win the active involvement and support of the conservative financial community establishment before they drift to Miller,"[158] the Obenshain handlers launched a late July radio advertising campaign featuring regionally targeted endorsements by Dalton, Godwin, Warner, Holton, and other popular Republicans. The radio advertisements followed closely on the heels of a widely publicized Richmond dinner for conservative business leaders that Coalition kingpin Roy Smith hosted in honor of Obenshain, Dalton, and Godwin. The Obenshain moves produced the desired results, and it was apparent as July drew to a close that the influential remnants of the Byrd organization and the powerful Main Street financiers were falling in line solidly behind the GOP nominee.

The financial support from the conservative business community would fund the campaign, but the GOP camp knew that Obenshain could not win with conservative support alone. Miller was no Henry Howell; his moderate platform would enable him to cut sharply into the GOP's suburban and rural voting blocs. The Obenshain planners thus plotted to move their man toward the political center while also targeting elements of the Democratic base constituency to which the Republican candidate might direct an appeal. Part of the positioning was stylistic—Obenshain abandoned his heavy black horn-rimmed eye-glasses for a more contemporary-looking metallic pair; his wardrobe was updated; and he dropped the philosophy-laden verbal blasts at his opponent in favor of a greater emphasis on bread-and-butter concerns. Perhaps most important, Obenshain scheduled several well-publicized speeches before audiences that were improbable for a conservative Republican, and he spelled out several policy positions that also were unconventional. The objective was to make the Richmond lawyer seem open-minded,

---

[157]Copy of memorandum on file at the Republican Party of Virginia Archives.
[158]Ibid.

accessible, reasonable, and innovative—exactly the antithesis of the doctrinaire Obenshain image that Miller was working to create.

With polling data confirming that a majority of Virginians saw economic issues as the most important facing the country, Obenshain made his support for the Kemp-Roth tax cut legislation[159]—a proposed 33-percent reduction in individual income tax rates over three years—a central plank in his platform. In that respect, the Virginian's campaign resembled the Reagan presidential campaign that would follow two years later—though, in 1978, the proposal for a one-third tax cut was a novel, almost radical, idea. For Obenshain, the tax relief initiative was a concrete manifestation of his strong *laissez faire* philosophy, and was also tailor-made to appeal to blue-collar workers who seldom backed Republicans.

In late July, Obenshain and his handlers resolved to defy the conventional wisdom and take the Republican's message of tax relief, reduced inflation, and economic opportunity to the AFL-CIO, first at a meeting of the organization's political arm (the Committee on Political Education, or "COPE") and then—scheduled for late August—at the state AFL-CIO convention. "Jimmy the Greek at Las Vegas would have laid odds that I would not have shown up here," Obenshain said as he began his remarks at the COPE meeting, relieving the tension.[160] Acknowledging candidly the major policy differences between them, Obenshain nevertheless stressed his "mutual commitment with labor to assure greater economic growth despite disagreement on specific issues." His presence, humor, and candor were appreciated by the assembled labor leaders, according to state AFL-CIO President Julian Carper, who later lauded the Republican as "a man of high principles [and] a courteous gentleman of exceptional ability."[161]

Obenshain's strategists also targeted the education establishment as a source of usually Democratic votes that could be weaned away from Miller. The Democrat had angered the leaders of the Virginia Education Association (VEA) during his 1977 primary campaign, when he had blasted it and Howell for together seeking collective bargaining rights for public school teachers. That history provided an opening for the GOP, and though Obenshain was fiercely opposed to public-sector bargaining rights, he had no problem embracing creation of a federal Department of Education—a Carter administration initiative strongly supported by teacher unions. Obenshain also actively courted the individual members of the VEA's political action committee board. The goal was merely to prompt a non-endorsement by the usually

---

[159]The legislation was proposed in the House of Representatives by New York Congressman Jack Kemp and in the Senate by Delaware's William V. Roth, a former Virginia resident and state chairman of Virginia's Young Republican federation in 1952. A modified version of the Kemp-Roth proposal was enacted in 1981 as the cornerstone of the Reagan administration's growth-oriented economic program and thereby gained the nickname, "Reaganomics."

[160]*Richmond Times-Dispatch*, August 22, 1978.

[161]Ibid.

Democratic group and in the process to convince political observers that the GOP candidate was not the ideologue that Miller and some members of the news media were suggesting. For the most part, Obenshain promised the educators only straight talk and an open door; it was enough to remind them of Miller's waffling on key VEA issues and his recent attacks on the organization for supporting Henry Howell.

Speeches before black political organizations also were scheduled by the Obenshain camp in an effort to broaden the candidate's appeal. And, by the end of July, when Obenshain met with the GOP's executive committee to present a campaign progress report, the candidate was ebullient. The Republicans' early objectives had been substantially achieved. The party was unified, and GOP local committees were hard at work. The business community was virtually locked in, and that meant that the Obenshain effort would have the funds it needed to wage another technologically and organizationally proficient campaign. News media references to Obenshain as an "arch-" or "ultra-conservative" had given way to descriptions of his unusual, candid, and even courageous appeals to traditionally Democratic groups. Obenshain's easy-going personality and good humor had seemed to disarm a previously hostile press corps, producing a rapport that further bolstered the candidate's confidence and performance. On the key topics of tax relief and economic growth, Miller had placed himself squarely against the Kemp-Roth proposal, thereby creating a major pocketbook issue that Obenshain and his aggressive press operation already were hammering home and planned to exploit throughout the fall. The Democratic nominee and his campaign seemed to be doing little, and almost nothing right. By late July, the GOP campaign's polling was showing a sharp upward trend for Obenshain. Everything was going well.

And then suddenly it was over. On the return home from Frederick County at the end of that heady and hectic August 2, Obenshain's airplane crashed in the trees a fraction of a mile short of the Chesterfield County airport. The 42-year-old candidate and two others were killed, the fiery wreckage strewn about the woods.[162] Virginians awakened to the tragic news on Thursday, August 3, and mourned the loss of a man whom most were just beginning to know. The human dimensions of the tragedy sank in quickly. Obenshain had left a widow, Helen, and three young children—Mark, 16, Anne Scott, 12, and Kate, 9. The tremendous political implications of the loss became evident more gradually.

"Your Daddy died pursuing a dream. He tried to do what he thought was right. You can hold your heads high when you remember that," the Reverend

---

[162]Killed with Obenshain when the twin-engine Piper PA34 aircraft crashed were pilot Richard Neel, 42, of Alexandria and flight instructor Ronald A. Edden, 28, of Camp Springs, Maryland. Following its inquiry, the National Transportation Safety Board attributed the accident to pilot error. The Board found that the pilot had attempted a visual landing in bad weather and cited his unfamiliarity with the aircraft. Virkler, p. 133.

Albert Curry Winn gently told the Obenshain children as a tearful throng at Richmond's Second Presbyterian Church listened on Saturday, August 5.[163] Mr. Winn's simple eulogy seemed to console many whose grief was magnified by a sense of the tremendous potential that had been lost, of the dream that would go unfulfilled. "Life is measured more truly by the depths of our involvements than the lengths of our years," he said, adding, "Dick Obenshain lived more fully in 42 years than other people do in 82."[164]

The funeral service was over a half-hour after it began. Obenshain's flag-draped coffin was borne by Governor John Dalton, Judge Dortch Warriner, Dr. Lewis Williams, and other close friends. Behind it followed a composed Helen Obenshain, who paused occasionally to give a tearful friend a reassuring whisper or touch, and the three children, their hands clasping them firmly to one another. And then the honorary pall-bearers—Linwood Holton with his wife, Jinx, Nathan Miller, and John and Elizabeth Warner—followed by hundreds of mourners, including Senators Byrd and Scott and Democratic Senate candidate Miller. From Richmond, Obenshain's body was taken to Botetourt County and laid to rest next to his forebears.

The calamity brought predictable expressions of tribute and sympathy from all quarters. Obenshain was hailed in death, as in life, as the architect of the modern Virginia Republican Party and its winning conservative coalition, and as a singularly articulate and devoted apostle of conservative tenets. "Richard Dudley Obenshain was 42 and on his way to the heights—very likely to the United States Senate, and possibly beyond . . .," editorialized *The Richmond News Leader*. "Far less than most, he deserved a hurried death. For here was a man whose every considerable achievement was the result of fierce adherence to principle. . ."[165]

That Obenshain was on the brink of achieving his lifelong goal of a seat in the United States Senate is a point on which, in hindsight, there is broad, bipartisan agreement. "Dick would have been elected to the Senate. We had just gotten a poll back [and] Andy Miller was dead in the water. . . . We had everything going for us," said campaign manager Judy Peachee.[166] "He without a doubt would have won. He would have defeated Miller hands down," agreed former Governor Godwin.[167] "At our convention," state Democratic Chairman Joseph T. Fitzpatrick recalled,

> many of the delegates were jubilant [about Obenshain's nomination]. They said, 'It's Johnson-versus-Goldwater again.' I told them not to be so

---

[163]*The Washington Post*, August 6, 1978.

[164]Ibid.

[165]*The Richmond News Leader*, August 4, 1978.

[166]B. Scott Tilley, *Richard Obenshain: Visionary and Engineer of the Rise of the Republican Party in Virginia*, Unpublished Paper, University of Virginia, 1988, p. 18; copy on file with the author.

[167]Ibid.

cocky. . . . I told them that Obenshain was smart and tough, and that he was the strongest possible candidate that the Republicans could have nominated. I felt Obenshain would have defeated Andrew Miller . . ."[168] "Those who were watching the campaign closely knew that everything was falling in place for Dick, and barring the unforeseen he was going to win by a decisive margin," recalled veteran GOP activist William Hurd, Obenshain's press secretary.[169] "Dick was going to win; he would have clobbered Andy Miller, absolutely decimated him," agreed William Royall, then a top aide to Governor Dalton.[170] Observers as diverse as veteran political reporters Shelley Rolfe and Buster Carico, former Democratic Lieutenant Governor Henry Howell, former Congressmen Joel Broyhill and Caldwell Butler, conservative financier Lawrence Lewis, Jr., gubernatorial advisor Carter Lowance, and former Governor Linwood Holton offered similar assessments.[171] Andrew Miller, unsurprisingly, disagreed; he ventured that Obenshain would have lost in November if tragedy had not intervened.[172] "Before the nomination he had been portrayed often as highly vulnerable in being 'too far to the right,'" wrote Guy Friddell. "But a deepening trend to conservatism in the electorate and Obenshain's steady march to victory now made him appear to have been the ideal candidate all along."[173]

The Senate campaign stood in abeyance while Obenshain was interred and the GOP gathered itself to select a new nominee to carry the party's standard. Upon learning of Obenshain's death, Andrew Miller suspended his own campaign efforts indefinitely. A day later, his own family was bereaved as his father, Colonel Miller, the passionate and intellectual Byrd organization foe, passed away at age 83.

The task of choosing the party's new Senate nominee fell, under state law, to the GOP central committee, which was dominated by conservative partisans who had been loyal to Obenshain. On Friday, August 4, less than 48 hours after Obenshain's death, campaign manager Judy Peachee and two close associates of Mills Godwin—Roy Smith and Smith Ferebee—traveled to Suffolk to ask the former governor to pick up the fallen candidate's mantle. Godwin gave the trio a polite hearing, but by the end of the conversation the visitors were pessimistic about the prospects for an affirmative response. The former governor was departing later that day for a long-planned business trip to Austria, and he promised to give them his answer shortly. But, with his trusted

---

[168]Virkler, p. 132.

[169]William H. Hurd interview, May 4, 1989.

[170]Royall interview.

[171]Shelley Rolfe interview, June 5, 1980; Carico, Howell, Broyhill, Butler, Lewis, Lowance, and Holton interviews. Holton initially thought Obenshain could not win but revised his opinion after seeing the lackluster general election campaign waged by Andrew Miller.

[172]Andrew Miller interview.

[173]Friddell, p. 105.

advisor Carter Lowance and the former First Lady opposing further political ventures out of concern for Godwin's health, there was little chance that he would accede to the request.

Speculation in the aftermath of the airplane crash centered on the convention runner-up, John Warner, but the Obenshain loyalists who would determine the new nominee were in no mood to surrender to the Middleburg politician the prize they had captured over his opposition just 60 days earlier. To them, Warner was untested; he had not labored in the party vineyards; he seemed more the celebrity socialite than the Virginia statesman; and, he appeared to possess precious little of the philosophical commitment that they had so admired in Obenshain. The idea of Warner as keeper of the flame was not only unappealing to many grief-stricken Obenshain partisans; it was downright offensive. Most of them were determined to find someone else—preferably Godwin, but if not him, someone other than Warner. Even Obenshain's long-time GOP foe, Linwood Holton, was preferable to Warner in the view of some of Obenshain's followers.

The Warners had been in New Hampshire for an appearance arranged by the Republican National Committee when news of Obenshain's death flashed across the television screen early in the morning. After completing a scheduled speech they returned to Middleburg and went into seclusion, emerging only to attend the Obenshain funeral services. That Warner was a likely replacement for the deceased nominee was much discussed in the news media, but the prospective candidate maintained his silence and made no telephone calls to promote his expected candidacy. The vacancy would be filled by the conservative-dominated Republican central committee on which Warner had little clout, and he concluded that his best course was to maintain a respectful silence while the situation sorted itself out.

Shortly after Obenshain was buried in Botetourt County on Saturday, August 5, the conservative leader's top lieutenants met at the nearby home of Roanoke attorney Donald W. Huffman to review their options and decide on a course of action. They agreed that Godwin was their first choice and that Seventh District Congressman J. Kenneth Robinson was the next-best option. All present recall the Godwin-Robinson consensus, but recollections vary about what was to be done if both of them declined. There was ample sentiment voiced that other options should be explored before turning to Warner, and there was considerable discussion about tapping party chief George McMath as the third alternative. Others argued, however, that Warner was the only logical choice under the circumstances, and that an effort should be made to establish a satisfactory working relationship with him. Some left the Huffman home convinced that there was a consensus in favor of Godwin, Robinson, and McMath, in that order,[174] while others felt that there was

---

[174]Alderson interview.

agreement only on the first two.[175] The conflicting interpretations and expectations that stemmed from the meeting were to be the genesis of a large misunderstanding—one that would quickly blossom into major division within the ranks of Obenshain's leaderless followers.

The next day, Linwood Holton called party chief McMath to inform him that he would not be a candidate for the Senate nomination. Holton wanted to remove his name from consideration quickly in order to avoid further press speculation. "I never really had that much interest in the Senate job as such, and when I made that [convention] speech about being the elder statesman, that was it in my mind," explained Holton. "I was ready to let the younger people do the running and be glad to help, counsel and advise. . . . My wife, particularly, felt that we really had made our contribution to Virginia politics as far as being a candidate was concerned."[176] Holton probably did not realize that he was preferable to Warner in the eyes of many Obenshain backers on the central committee, and a conversation with Governor Dalton had left him with a clear sense that Warner probably would be the nominee unless Godwin acceded to the draft. The easy course for the former governor was simply to stand aside, and that he did.

On Sunday, August 6, Judy Peachee and Robert Russell of Chesterfield County, a long-time Obenshain ally and the finance chairman of his campaign, went to Washington, D.C., to discuss a possible Senate bid with Congressman Robinson. They explained that Governor Godwin already had been approached and appeared certain to decline. They then told the congressman that the conservative Virginia GOP leadership was unanimous in its desire that Robinson assume the nomination, and that the votes necessary to accomplish that at the forthcoming central committee meeting already were in line. The Seventh District congressman had long been a favorite of Republican conservatives, including Obenshain, and, though Robinson rarely had involved himself in the party's internal processes, he seemed the most willing and able to carry forward the party's philosophically based mission. Though impressed by the conservatives' confidence and earnest appeal, Robinson was uninterested in a Senate bid. He could do more good for Virginia and the nation, he explained, as a senior minority member of the Defense Subcommittee of the House Appropriations Committee than as a freshman senator. Having devoted his considerable energy and ability in Congress to the cause of rebuilding America's defenses and intelligence-gathering capability, Robinson concluded that the midpoint of the seemingly disastrous Carter administration was no time to risk his seniority and House seat on an uphill campaign for the Senate. He promised his visitors a firm answer within 24 hours but gave them no encouragement.

---

[175]Peachee interview.
[176]Holton interview.

The disappointed pair left their meeting with Robinson and traveled across the Potomac to confer with another Obenshain intimate, former GOP executive director Kenneth Klinge. Klinge noted the widespread rumors that Warner was about to declare his candidacy and advised Peachee to meet with Warner in an effort to delay his announcement. If the man from Middleburg entered the race, any chance of delivering an uncontested nomination to someone else would evaporate. And, if Warner was to be the eventual nominee, that ought to be accomplished in a better way—by consensus among the Obenshain followers rather than through a preemptive move by Warner. Moreover, Warner had a right to be apprised of what the Obenshain aides were doing; they were, after all, attempting to decide his future. Peachee called Wyatt Durrette, the Obenshain associate on the best terms with Warner, and within minutes a meeting was arranged. That evening, Peachee, Durrette, and Russell drove out to Atoka, Warner's Middleburg estate, for what was to be a three-hour discussion with the prospective candidate and his wife, Elizabeth.

Meanwhile, in Richmond, Governor Dalton was speaking by telephone with former Governor Godwin, who was still in Austria. Dalton told his predecessor that the nomination would be his if he were willing to accept it, but Godwin responded that he would not. The two men then discussed John Warner, and they found themselves in agreement. "[Warner] got the next highest number of votes at the convention. He was the choice of almost half of the delegates. And I felt that [nominating him] was about the only thing the party could do," recalled Godwin.[177] Dalton elaborated:

> It appeared to me that Warner had two big things going for him that would dictate that he would be the candidate after Obenshain was killed. The first thing was that he had come in second at the convention, and if Mills Godwin was not going to run, Warner certainly ought to have the first call on it because the delegates had just assembled from throughout the state and he had gotten more votes than either Holton or Miller.
>
> Second, I thought we had to have someone who could put the money up himself. It's one thing to start in late May or June running for the U.S. Senate and get a financial organization together to raise your money. And it's something entirely different to start one in September. . . . In a federal election you can't contribute but a thousand dollars before the convention and a thousand dollars after the convention, and you cannot sign a note for somebody. So the only person who could sign a note was the candidate himself. John Warner was a man of substantial means who could go to the bank and arrange the financing that had to be arranged immediately.[178]

---

[177]Godwin interview.
[178]John Dalton interview.

Unlike Dalton, Godwin was prepared to back Robinson over Warner. But after the Seventh District congressman declined, "the pragmatic thing to do was to turn to Warner," according to Godwin.[179]

At Atoka, the discussion was friendly, subdued, and serious. Peachee and Durrette explained the appeals that had been made to Godwin and Robinson and the continuing resistance of many Obenshain backers to Warner's prospective candidacy. Russell described the status of the Obenshain campaign's finances, including the existence of an $80,000 debt, which prompted Warner to comment that alleviating the shortfall was the responsibility of everyone in the party (obviously including himself). At one point, Judy Peachee and Elizabeth Taylor Warner talked privately about the impact of the tragedy on the Obenshain family; Mrs. Warner recalled the pain she had experienced when a previous husband, Michael Todd, was killed in an airplane crash, and Peachee described plans to create a trust fund for the Obenshain children's education. But the most important conversation during the visit concerned the possible Warner candidacy. It was clear that Obenshain loyalists controlled the GOP central committee, but the visitors emphasized that Warner also would need the enthusiastic support of the Obenshain people—not only the leadership but also the grass-roots Republican regulars—in order to win in November. The trio made it clear that they were in no position to guarantee Warner such support, but they warned that he would forfeit any chance of winning the conservatives' backing if he jumped into the race prematurely and thereby appeared to preclude bids by Godwin or Robinson. Warner insisted that he had made no decision about running and agreed to defer any declaration of candidacy for several days. He requested that a meeting be arranged so that he could face the Obenshain followers.

On Monday, August 7, McMath announced that the central committee would meet the following Saturday to choose Obenshain's successor. Newspaper accounts played up talk of an impending Warner nomination, but also noted that a number of alternative candidates were being discussed, including Godwin, Robinson, Nathan Miller, Wyatt Durrette, George McMath, and Sixth District Congressman Caldwell Butler. The next day proved decisive for Warner. He traveled to Richmond early Tuesday morning for a meeting with Governor Dalton, who stressed the need for an immediate infusion of campaign cash because of the imminence of the election and urged Warner to proceed with plans to run. Dalton then called Butler to explain his support for Warner, and a short time later Butler told reporters that he would not be a candidate. Durrette, who had been urged by a number of Obenshain lieutenants to seek the nomination, judged that campaign funding was an insurmountable obstacle, and announced that he would not run. After receiving a briefing from Peachee and Durrette, Miller reached the same conclusion.

---

[179]Godwin interview.

Finally, Robinson and Godwin publicly affirmed their decisions not to accept the nomination.

It was after the dinner hour on Tuesday when approximately 40 key Obenshain supporters assembled in a meeting room at the Hotel John Marshall in Richmond to caucus and hear from Warner. Most options other than a bid by Warner now had been eliminated, but the attitude of those present ranged from grudging acceptance of the former Navy secretary to defiant resistance. Before Warner's arrival, Judy Peachee began the meeting by summarizing the events of the preceding days. The refusals by Godwin and Robinson, the disclaimers by other potential candidates, the severe financial constraints, the discussions with Warner at Atoka, and other important considerations all were laid before the "heirs of the Obenshain legacy," as Warner later would describe them.[180] No conclusion concerning a continuing role for Peachee or other members of the Obenshain campaign staff had been reached in the discussions with Warner, Peachee stated in response to a question. And then, John Warner entered. The presumptive nominee sat at a table at the front of the room and spoke briefly and deferentially; he acknowledged the pain of loss that Obenshain's closest friends still were experiencing; and, he said he had made no decision about running for the Senate. He would not run, Warner declared to the Obenshain partisans, unless he believed that he could count on their support.

What followed was a grilling that could only be described as brutal. Would Warner adhere to conservative principles in the Senate? Would he work hard, rather than spending his time on the Washington social circuit? How would he vote on this key issue, or that one? What assurance was there that his "controversial wife" would not embarrass the state? "We don't trust you, and we really don't like you," a staunch conservative told him at one point, obviously seeking to provoke a reaction; "What can you tell us that will change our minds about you?" Through it all, Warner conducted himself calmly and impressively. And he made a number of specific assurances. In response to one query, he pledged that he would not attempt to control the state GOP or exert leadership in party affairs—a vow that he would keep to the letter in ensuing years. To another questioner, he replied that he wanted the Obenshain campaign staff to remain in place, and then he interjected—to the surprise and consternation of many listeners—that Judy Peachee already had agreed to be his campaign manager. At one point, besieged by questions about what position he would take on this or that issue, the candidate simply shrugged and demurred: "Just tell me what you want me to do." As Warner was ushered out of the room by his friend and sponsor, Joel Broyhill, the former congressman quietly advised, "Don't run,

---

[180]Warner interview.

John. These people will never support you."[181] It had been a very rough meeting.

"The meeting included some of those rather doctrinaire members of [Obenshain's] following. And, despite reports to the contrary, it was a very cordial exchange of viewpoints," recalled Warner in 1980.

[There was] a feeling of doubt. After all, I had no track record in the sense of aligning myself with the philosophical approach to politics. Mind you, when you're Secretary of the Navy you are not in partisan politics, and I'd had eight years of federal experience where I had to be out of politics. . . . And therefore there was a legitimate and justified measure of doubt on behalf of the strong Obenshain supporters.

. . . I was absolutely candid with them. I did not agree with everything they said, [and] I would not commit to everything they asked. But I think they measured the man and sort of said to themselves, "Well, let's take a risk." And a risk they took. And I don't think, if I may say so, that they've been disappointed—except in their hearts I know their sadness for Dick. I don't mean it in a cocky way, but my voting record up here [in the Senate] has been as good as anyone could have expected.[182]

Some would challenge that assertion later—after, among other things, Warner in 1987 sided with Senator Edward M. Kennedy and Democratic liberals in rejecting President Reagan's nomination of renowned jurist Robert Bork to succeed retiring Virginian Lewis F. Powell, Jr., on the U.S. Supreme Court. But Warner reassured many Republican conservatives during that August 8 encounter, and the long-sought Senate nomination was now within his reach.

One comment that Warner made at the meeting set tongues wagging, however. Judy Peachee had agreed to be his campaign manager, Warner had said. But, only moments earlier, Peachee had told the group that her plans and the future of the Obenshain campaign staff had not been determined. Could it be that the hard-charging and ambitious national committeewoman had independently made an arrangement with Warner? Was she acting as honest agent for the Obenshain insiders, or was she merely attempting to manipulate the group on Warner's behalf? The most unflattering of the possible interpretations would be adopted by some of the conservatives present at the Hotel John Marshall that evening, especially those who were least anxious to do the pragmatic thing and embrace Warner. "It was the opinion of many that Judy was reaching for power, that she was trying to create her own political base, to be the spokesman for the conservative wing of the party," said John Alderson of Botetourt County.[183] Peachee later insisted that she was as surprised as the

---

[181]The comment was overheard by conservative GOP activist Morton Blackwell of Arlington. Morton C. Blackwell interview, February 22, 1990.

[182]Warner interview.

[183]Alderson interview.

others by Warner's comment; at Atoka two days earlier she had emphasized to Warner the importance of keeping the statewide Obenshain organization intact, and Warner had acknowledged the wisdom of that, but the discussion had stopped there.[184] Nevertheless, Peachee's conduct and motives now were being questioned, and in the emotionally charged aftermath of Obenshain's death the trust necessary for further cooperative effort among his top lieutenants was dissipating rapidly.

On Wednesday, August 9, Warner declared his candidacy, and the next day he came to Richmond to receive Governor Dalton's public endorsement. After the Tuesday night meeting, there had been general acceptance of Warner's inevitability among the Obenshain backers, though some conservative hard-liners, especially Alderson and a number of conservative northern Virginians, continued to fume. The fallen candidate's widow, Helen, gave fleeting consideration to a bid of her own at the behest of Smith Ferebee, who promised to raise the funds that would be needed. But, fearing the impact of a campaign and possible defeat on the family's young children, the deceased Obenshain's father counseled strongly against such a move, and Helen Obenshain heeded his advice.

The GOP central committee, its members purposeful and dignified, assembled at the Hotel John Marshall on Saturday, August 12, to make Warner the Senate candidate by acclamation. After adopting a resolution of tribute to Obenshain, the committee heard Governor Dalton nominate Warner to replace him. Invoking the conservative-coalition strategy for which Obenshain generally was credited, the governor stressed the need to obtain "the help of others outside the regular Republican Party" in order to retain the Senate seat.[185] Warner's nomination was seconded by persons who had supported his opponents at the June convention, among them Jade West of Arlington, a fervent Obenshain conservative who gave the seconding speech only after a personal plea from the late candidate's widow.

"The committee's action," reported The Washington Post, "capped an unprecedented 10-day struggle within the state party as Obenshain's supporters sought to reconcile their late standard-bearer's conservative principles with the personal flamboyance and largely untested political philosophy of Warner and his actress wife."[186] If Warner's nomination was compelled by political exigencies, acceptance of it by Obenshain's grief-stricken followers ultimately was a product of Helen Obenshain's leadership. Her appearance at the central committee meeting on August 12 had not been announced in advance. As she stepped forward to speak following Warner's nomination, the

---

[184]Peachee, Durrette interviews; Robert E. Russell interview, March 11, 1991. Years later, Warner was unable to resolve the inconsistency. He told Peachee prior to the August 8 meeting that she was his first choice for campaign manager, Warner recalled, but he had no specific recollection as to whether she accepted the post prior to the meeting. Warner interview.

[185]The Washington Post, August 13, 1978.

[186]Ibid.

pent-up emotions of dozens of Obenshain followers no longer could be restrained. To a hushed and tearful audience, the poised widow spoke quietly of her husband's steadfast devotion to "the principles of limited government and individual freedom," of the victories that the Virginia GOP had won in reliance upon those principles, and of the need to win again in November.[187] "All must do their part. I intend to help John in every way I can. Let's go forward united to victory," she declared, as her inspiring presence dominated a platform shared by John Warner, Elizabeth Taylor, Governor Dalton, and Dalton's wife, Eddy.[188]

The succeeding days were awkward but productive for Warner and the Obenshain leadership, as former foes endeavored to become fast friends. With only 87 days remaining until the election, Warner hardly could have assembled a new campaign staff and organization even if he had been so disposed. And, having been defeated at the convention through their efforts, the new nominee had little trouble accepting that the Obenshain operatives comprised an exceptionally experienced and capable campaign team. But Warner's request that the Obenshain personnel stay on with his campaign met with initial reluctance. "It was a difficult time for everyone; emotions were running so high. But in the end what mattered most was making sure we won Dick's Senate seat," recalled manager Peachee.[189] Helen Obenshain's plea for unity and her courageous example convinced most of the staff members to remain at their posts, and the hope that Warner would be influenced by their conservatism provided further motivation.

For Warner, too, there was unease. A proud man, he was placing his fortunes in the hands of activists whose loyalty had been to another. But it eventually worked out well, as the candidate recalled:

> One of the attributes of Dick Obenshain was that he inspired tremendous personal loyalty, and a warmth and dedication and friendship. He was running that campaign on a shoestring; he was in debt. And these people [on his campaign staff] were nine-tenths operating on motivation and one-tenth operating on money. They had to pick themselves up, respectfully bury their leader, and go to work the next morning. And that takes a lot of personal courage. I am grateful to them. . . . They were a grand group. We made our peace among ourselves, and we had a challenge, and we met it.[190]

"It was a real tribute to [Obenshain] that his staff and forces continued to work," observed GOP Chairman McMath, adding that Warner's victory three months later would not have been possible without them.[191]

[187]Ibid.

[188]*Richmond Times-Dispatch*, August 13, 1978.

[189]Peachee interview.

[190]Warner interview.

[191]McMath interview.

While Peachee and the majority of Obenshain backers enlisted in the Warner cause, a number of the fallen candidate's most conservative followers sat on their hands in dismay. Several top Obenshain lieutenants were never reconciled to Warner's nomination, and others who saw the wisdom of the convention runner-up's selection nonetheless believed that Peachee and her allies had engaged in a self-serving power play by signing on with Warner. Shortly after Warner's nomination, dissatisfied conservatives led by John Alderson began to caucus independently and excluded from their meetings those Obenshain allies who were thought to be too closely aligned with Peachee. What began as a misunderstanding in the hectic, emotionally charged aftermath of Obenshain's tragic death was well on its way to becoming an enduring rift among the fallen conservative leader's closest friends and allies. But if the choice of a new Senate nominee had not occasioned the division within the conservative faction, some other dispute probably would have. The acknowledged leader was gone; there had been no second-in-command who now could step forward and exert control; and, Obenshain's strong-willed lieutenants had ambitions of their own. "It really was a case of who was to succeed the king," recalled Judy Peachee, "and all of the knights had their own ideas."[192]

"We lost more in that crash than just Dick," commented Kenneth Klinge, reflecting several years later on the division in the ranks of Obenshain's followers.[193] Obenshain's leadership had given the GOP direction in the '70s, and his realignment strategy had produced a Republican winning streak in Virginia unrivaled by any state party in the country. The strategy remained after him, of course, as John Warner's eventual election would attest. But Obenshain's dynamic personality, his profound convictions, and his seemingly boundless potential as a candidate and conservative spokesman had supplied the glue that bonded his loyalists. Though he above all others had stressed ideas as the *sine qua non* in politics, the truth was that Obenshain himself—the person—had become the cause for many of his followers. "We felt when he won [the senatorial nomination] that we had grasped the brass ring," recalled Donald Huffman.[194] "[It] was such a sweet victory," added Alderson,

"Here was Obenshain, the father of the modern-day Republican Party, leading us to victory after victory, a leader who had charisma and wisdom and foresight, who was philosophically acceptable, and who believed in building a broad and enduring coalition of conservative Republicans and independents. And the future was ours. . . . With Obenshain in the Senate and with the vast army of supporters that he had across the state, we really believed we were well on the way to achieving majority status for this

---

[192]Peachee interview.

[193]*The Washington Times*, August 2, 1983.

[194]Donald W. Huffman interview, August 20, 1984.

party. And when his death came almost two months to the day after that sweet victory, it absolutely crushed his people.[195]

With Obenshain gone, the cause lost much of its luster for his partisans. There would be no one who would measure up to his standard, no one who could follow in his footsteps. For some of the Obenshain lieutenants, it seemed that everything noble about politics was lost on August 2; all that remained were the more base aspects of the political power game.

The split in the Virginia GOP's dominant conservative faction would have far-reaching implications for the party and for Virginia politics generally in the decade that would follow. If Obenshain had lived and had taken his seat in the Senate, he likely would have been a party leader without parallel since the senior Senator Byrd. Obenshain, the political strategist and technician, would have been a hands-on manager of party affairs, with the clout necessary to make his decisions stick. In his absence, however, there was no one to fill that role. "Nobody could fill the void for all the conservatives," commented Judy Peachee.

> With the growth of the Republican Party, nobody else could bring everybody together. With Dick as leader, he would have dominated party activities. Dick's endorsement would have carried a lot of weight, [and we] could have gone through nominating without all the divisiveness. . . . He would have been an activist leader; he didn't mind taking the heat for making a decision. John Warner and Paul Trible (GOP senators in the '80s) are neutral before nominations. Obenshain would have taken positions. . . . He had the power base to be secure in doing it. There would have been an Obenshain organization.[196]

A Senator Obenshain would have been a powerful agent for unifying the GOP, consummating realignment, and consolidating the Republican gains of the 1970s. But that was not to be. Like the death of Democratic Lieutenant Governor J. Sargeant Reynolds in 1971, Obenshain's sudden departure changed the course of Virginia political history. In the '80s, realignment and the Republican renaissance would abruptly cease, in large measure because of a series of divisive and debilitating GOP nomination battles that might have been avoided through the sort of unifying leadership that Obenshain had been determined to provide.

What, then, is the legacy of the man who in his own time was acknowledged as the architect of the modern Virginia GOP? If the legacy is measured solely by the electoral outcomes in his wake, the ensuing decade of Republican defeats and Democratic sweeps in statewide contests attests to the illusory, or at most transitory, nature of his contributions. If it is measured by the progress of realignment since his death, there, too, is evidence that Obenshain's impact was fleeting. The opportunities for a more complete party realignment in

---

[195]Alderson interview.
[196]Tilley, p. 20.

Virginia ended with the emergence of the dominant center-left Democratic coalition that elected Chuck Robb and his two gubernatorial successors in the 1980s. What can be said, however, is that Obenshain's vision of a realigned political environment hastened the arrival of real two-party competition in Virginia—competition that continued and intensified at every level during the '80s even though the outcomes in statewide contests yielded a Democratic winning streak as impressive as the record compiled by the Virginia GOP a decade earlier.

It is sadly ironic that Obenshain did not live to see the triumph during the two-term Reagan Presidency of so many of the principles that he championed. Before Reagan's 1980 victory, unabashed conservatives like Obenshain had to endure pessimistic and disparaging claims that they were, like the paradigmatic Goldwater, "unelectable." But Reagan's election vindicated them all. Two years after Obenshain targeted normally Democratic Virginia voters with the populist appeal of an economic growth-producing, across-the-board tax cut and attacks on excessive governmental regulation, Ronald Reagan mobilized the so-called "Reagan Democrats"—low-income, blue-collar white voters who formerly voted reliably Democratic—to form a significantly broadened national Republican majority coalition. It was not Obenshain's lot to witness that development, or to see Reaganism work a rapid realignment and Republican renaissance throughout the South in the '80s. And, though he was one of freedom's most passionate advocates, it was not his gift to observe the subsequent triumph of free markets over planned economies, or of democracy over dictatorship, on the world stage. But principles were what mattered to Obenshain, and that his convictions had consequences never was demonstrated more dramatically than during the Presidency of Ronald Reagan, whom he supported vociferously. The success of the "Reagan Revolution" was a product of principles and policies popularized over several decades through the efforts of people like Richard Obenshain.

What was Obenshain's legacy? Six years after his hard-fought victory over John Warner at the 1978 state GOP convention, the deceased candidate's son, Mark, would stand before the assembled Republican delegates to second Warner's nomination for re-election to the Senate. Then a college graduate and former chairman of the state's College Republican federation, Mark Obenshain would discard the speech that campaign officials had prepared for him and speak from the heart:

> Six years ago, I watched as my father received [the Senate nomination as] the Republican Party stood united behind him and the philosophy he lived and died for. Six years ago this August, I watched my mother stand before the State Central Committee . . . with more courage than one usually sees in a lifetime and place John Warner's name in nomination to pick up the fallen banner and resume the tragic race for the United States

Senate. It is with that same sense of philosophical resolve that I stand here today six years later, to second the nomination of John W. Warner. . .[197] If there is a single great legacy of Richard Obenshain, it is "that same sense of philosophical resolve" that he instilled in so many Virginians who watched and listened and embraced his ideals.

---

[197]*The Richmond News Leader*, June 4, 1984.

Chapter 33
The Country Catches Up

"We have been for 10 years where the country is now. It's like New York fashions—it takes them 10 years to get to Richmond. In politics, it's the other way around."[198]

Judy F. Peachee, January 1981

For ten years, Republicans had been winning elections in Virginia. Though the issues, the personalities, and the composition of the successful coalitions varied from election to election, the GOP had won with remarkable—indeed unmatched—consistency. The victories came in spite of Watergate, in spite of recession, in spite of Jimmy Carter's regional appeal, and in spite of old Virginia's longstanding emotional and traditional ties to the Democratic Party. "How does Virginia fit the national pattern?" asked Larry Sabato in an article published two weeks before the 1978 election. "It doesn't really," he answered, and hasn't . . . for a decade. Elections in most of the other forty-nine states have been trending Democratic, while Virginia has been moving in precisely the other direction. In a few short years, the staid old Commonwealth has moved with surprising speed from a classification as one-party Democratic to a new label of two-party competitive, Republican leaning. The change, at base, is that the symbols of conservatism are now associated with the Republican party.[199]

In 1978, John Warner was the beneficiary of this remarkably swift transition. But the circumstances of his nomination and the abbreviated nature of the Senate campaign were major hurdles to overcome. Warner's entry into the race brought a desperately needed infusion of campaign cash; Warner himself loaned approximately $500,000. The new resources were used to expand the campaign staff, to finance telephone banks and other organizational efforts, and, most important, to pay for an extensive television advertising campaign. The Obenshain campaign debt was eliminated simultaneously through a direct-mail appeal signed by Governor Dalton and through sale of the former

---

[198]Garrett Epps, "As Virginia Goes . . .," *The Washington Post Magazine*, January 25, 1981, p. 8.

[199]Larry Sabato, "Where the Republican Dream Came True," *The Virginian-Pilot*, October 20, 1978, reprinted in Sabato, *Virginia Votes 1975–1978*, p. 1.

campaign's assets to the Warner enterprise. In the end, Warner's general election campaign spending of $1.2 million dwarfed Democrat Andrew Miller's $800,000, with Warner's personal wealth more than supplying the advantage. Miller charged late in the campaign that Warner was attempting to "buy" the election—he and fellow Democrats coupled that charge with the allegation that Warner had similarly secured his appointment as Navy secretary through large contributions to Richard Nixon's presidential campaign—but the issue appeared to have little impact on the race. Far more significant than the political fallout from his personal contributions was the distinct advantage in television advertising yielded by Warner's investment.

Funds raised by the Warner campaign from sources other than the candidate came almost exclusively from the conservative Richmond-based financial establishment. The majority of the "Main Street money" had been captured by Obenshain during the summer, and the Coalition leadership rallied behind Warner after he was chosen to pick up the mantle. A dinner for business leaders very similar to the one held for Obenshain in July was assembled in Warner's honor in September, and most of the original attendees returned. Continuing the tradition of past Coalition-backed GOP campaigns, a "Virginians for Warner" organization was established with Roy Smith and French Slaughter as co-chairmen, along with an important new addition in the person of Thomas T. "Tom" Byrd, son of independent Senator Harry F. Byrd, Jr. Warner probably would not have garnered such broad Coalition financial backing if he had gained the GOP nomination by defeating Obenshain at the June convention, but, after the August tragedy, he inherited nearly all of his former foe's support. "The Main Street people appreciated what John Warner did following the convention," recalled then-Governor Dalton. "He pitched in and was actively working for Dick Obenshain's election. You find that a lot of people who lose a convention go home and sulk, but John Warner didn't do that. And so when Dick was killed, those people were willing to work for him."[200]

In his two-month campaign against Obenshain, Andrew Miller had been bitterly disappointed by his failure to win support from key figures in the state's conservative independent business community. But against the more moderate Warner, he thought his chances would be better. He took a distinctly conservative tack, and less than three months after blasting Obenshain as a "right-wing extremist," the Democratic nominee urged Obenshain backers to abandon Warner and support him instead as "their best hope for the future."[201] Miller recruited John S. Battle, Jr., a prominent Richmond lawyer and son of the Byrd organization governor, to chair a "Virginians for Miller" group, and a handful of notable conservative stalwarts, including former Governor Colgate Darden, former Congressman Watkins Abbitt, and Virginia

---

[200]John Dalton interview.
[201]*Richmond Times-Dispatch*, June 11, 1978 and August 13, 1978.

Beach's Sidney Kellam, signed on. But most of Miller's "Virginians" were really inveterate Democratic loyalists, and the bulk of the Godwin-led Coalition fell in lockstep behind Warner.

With few policy differences separating the two Senate candidates, their exchanges during the abbreviated campaign were not especially illuminating. Warner stressed his Washington experience, while Miller emphasized his roots in the state and promised to take the "Virginia experience" to Washington. Much of the contenders' time was spent debating which of them was closer in philosophy to—and therefore was the secret choice of—Senator Harry Byrd, Jr. The presence of the senator's son in a Warner campaign leadership role gave the Republican a decided edge in the Byrd battle, and much of rural Virginia heard Mills Godwin and Tom Byrd tout John Warner's virtues in radio advertisements broadcast throughout the campaign. Godwin was especially vocal in challenging Miller's conservative credentials, and in the campaign's final fortnight he delivered a stinging attack on the Democrat at a "Virginians for Warner" luncheon in Richmond. "I've been in public life in Virginia for three decades," said the former governor sarcastically, and "I did not know until this campaign that Mr. Miller . . . agreed with our senior United States Senator on so many points. As a matter of fact, I have never heard anyone in Virginia allege that Mr. Miller was a conservative. . . ."[202] Godwin then recalled the Democrat's opposition to Harry Byrd, Jr.'s bids in the 1966 Democratic primary and 1970 and 1976 general elections.

After ten years of erosion in the Virginia Democratic Party's conservative base in state elections, Andrew Miller was determined to prevent Warner and the Republicans from polarizing the Commonwealth's conservative-leaning electorate against him in 1978. Black Democrats, organized labor, and other liberal-leaning partisans would not vote Republican, Miller and his strategists confidently assumed, and so they resolutely targeted the state's conservative voters. If paying homage almost daily to Harry Byrd, Jr., was the price of such a strategy, then Miller—whom *The Washington Post* once described as the "avenging son" of Byrd foe Francis Pickens Miller[203]—was willing to pay the tab. Miller's strategy was greatly assisted by two developments during the autumn campaign. The first was Byrd's vote in the Senate against the Kemp-Roth tax cut legislation, which Warner had endorsed and Miller had denounced as fiscally irresponsible. The second was the disclosure that Warner had contributed $1,000 to the campaign of GOP Senate nominee and Byrd foe Ray Garland in 1970. The latter was probably the more damaging development, because Warner had stated repeatedly that he had voted for Byrd in 1970 as well as 1976.

The contrast in the candidates' styles was stark and worked decisively in Warner's favor. The Republican struck the right pose and had a crisp delivery

---

[202]Copy of text on file with the author.

[203]*The Washington Post*, November 3, 1984.

on the stump, while the plodding Miller's rambling and complicated comments on the campaign trail frequently seemed evasive or overly cerebral. Warner proved to be a talented and almost tireless campaigner, and he seemed to hustle through extraordinarily long days with stamina to spare. Some of his time might have been better spent in resting and collecting his thoughts, however, for the Republican and his handlers frequently found themselves occupied with issuing corrections and clarifications, explaining away gaffes, and extricating the candidate and campaign from webs of inconsistent statements on a variety of subjects.[204]

A series of Warner missteps kept the GOP campaign off balance during the contest's crucial weeks. In mid-September, Warner suggested to a Washington television interviewer that he had attempted to slow the pace of Admiral Elmo Zumwalt's efforts to desegregate the United States Navy while Zumwalt was chief of naval operations and Warner was secretary of the Navy. What would have been a minor gaffe was made major a short time later when, at a campaign aide's suggestion, he sought in vain to gain the interviewer's cooperation in expunging the comment; the original remark and Warner's request to delete it were duly aired and prominently featured on the evening news broadcast. A few days later, with a campaign visit on his behalf by presidential candidate Ronald Reagan less than a week away, Warner publicly indicated that he preferred former President Ford—Reagan's rival—for the 1980 GOP presidential nomination. In early October, a Warner comment that he had not sought the AFL-CIO endorsement was directly refuted by union officials. And in mid-October, the revelation that he had contributed to Garland's campaign in 1970 seemed to rebut Warner's oft-repeated claims of fidelity to Byrd. Miller moved to capitalize on these and other misstatements and contradictions by declaring his foe's credibility to be the main issue in the campaign. Having supplied the ammunition, Warner sought to deflect Miller's attacks on his veracity by charging the Democrat with "taking the low road" and engaging in "personal attacks." Making the best of a bad situation, the Republican camp drew a link between Miller's criticisms and the shrill rhetoric employed by Henry Howell a year earlier. Late in the 1978 campaign, Warner's dubious claim to be the victim of personal attacks gained credibility when Miller's supporters lashed out at the Republican. One Democratic officeholder questioned Warner's "judgment" in marrying Elizabeth Taylor, and another charged that his former in-laws, the Mellons, had "bought him his [Nixon administration] job" with large campaign contributions.[205]

---

[204]Warner embraced most of Obenshain's policy positions, and two Obenshain advisers —former Delegate Wyatt Durrette and Obenshain campaign policy director Gary C. Byler—coached Warner on issues during the brief general election campaign. The task of explaining away Warner's misstatements fell to his campaign's capable press secretary, William Kling.

[205]*The Richmond News Leader*, November 2, 1978.

For Elizabeth Taylor Warner, the fall campaign was not particularly enjoyable, though she persevered with good humor. In mid-October, she was hospitalized after a chicken bone became lodged in her throat, and that took her off the campaign trail for several weeks. Before that, she campaigned energetically, though Warner's handlers worried continually about the impact she was having on their efforts to "decelebritize" her husband. In wrapping John Warner in the state's conservative tradition and surrounding him with icons like Godwin, Warner's team had more in mind than mobilizing the conservative vote. The Miller camp's not-so-subtle message was that their man was the "real Virginian" in the race and that Warner lacked the Commonwealth's traditional values. Identifying Warner with the state's venerated conservative symbols was an effective counter to that tactic. But every time the Warners appeared together it sent a contrary message. The GOP campaign thus determined to keep the couple apart in public as much as possible, and after the errant chicken bone supplied an excuse, Republican operatives saw to it that Mrs. Warner's hospital stay lasted well beyond the time necessary for a full recovery.

While the two major Richmond newspapers pilloried Miller editorially in the conservative Third District, the Republican nominee was hammered almost daily by *The Washington Post*, which gave extensive play in its news and editorial columns to each Warner misstep during the campaign.[206] In military-oriented Tidewater, Warner cashed in on his Navy connections and dissatisfaction with the Carter administration's defense policies and weapons cutbacks. In the rural, conservative Southside, a key battleground, the GOP candidate was boosted by the Godwin-Byrd radio messages and by Miller's surprising election-eve expression of support for pari-mutuel horse-race betting. The gambling referendum was on the November ballot, and conservative churches were active and organized in opposition to it in much of rural Virginia.

The favorite bogeyman used by Republican campaigns in the 1970s, Henry Howell, surfaced just long enough in 1978 to cause trouble for his arch-rival, Miller. Howell traveled to McLean for a highly publicized appearance at the home of liberal state Senator Clive DuVal, and his endorsement of Miller there was aired widely. In post-election assessments of the 1978 campaign, Miller faulted Howell for not "keeping a low profile,"[207] and he ventured that the Warner campaign's large-volume mailing linking the two Democratic antagonists had been the "decisive" factor in the contest.[208] In the mailing and

---

[206]Paul Edwards, a political reporter who left *The Washington Post* to join the Dalton administration as the governor's press secretary, recalled in a 1980 interview that his former newspaper's coverage of the campaign had decidedly favored the Democrat. Paul Edwards interview, June 3, 1980.

[207]Andrew Miller interview.

[208]*The Washington Post*, January 28, 1979.

in their frequent stump speeches for Warner, GOP leaders Dalton and Godwin harped on Miller's endorsement of Howell's candidacy in the autumn of 1977 and on Howell's reciprocal embrace of Miller a year later. To Miller's suggestion that he had been a fatal liability in 1978, Howell hooted before adding derisively, "I did whatever I could for him. But he couldn't even beat John Warner, who made more mistakes than any candidate I know of!"[209]

Interestingly, while Howell was making one of his final appearances as the GOP target-of-choice, the man who moderate Democrats would use to paint Republicans with the "extremist" brush in the '80s was emerging as a political force in the state. Most Virginians and most Americans in 1978 did not know of the Reverend Jerry Falwell; he and his Lynchburg-based "Moral Majority" organization would burst onto the national scene with their high-profile activities in the 1980 presidential election. But Falwell had endorsed John Dalton in 1977, and his large Thomas Road Baptist Church congregation and "Old Time Gospel Hour" television audience were big enough plums to attract both Senate candidates to the Lynchburg church on one mid-October Sunday during the 1978 campaign. The candidates eyed each other across the aisle and hoped for a Falwellian embrace until the introductions were made, and then it was Warner who received the blessing. The pastor introduced Miller as "the attorney general," and then referred to Warner as "a former secretary of the Navy" before adding, ". . . and my friend."[210] Within three years, Falwell would succeed Henry Howell as the state's premier political whipping boy; moderate Virginia Democrats would discover that suburban disdain for much of Moral Majority's conservative social agenda could be as politically powerful as suburban opposition to Howell-style liberalism on economic issues.

The Warner campaign's polls never showed their man in the lead, but the technological advantage owned by the Virginia Republican Party was enough to make the difference in a close contest. The GOP's sophisticated voter identification and turnout operation, spearheaded in 1978 by Warner organization director and veteran pol Robert Hausenfluck of Henrico, succeeded in getting a large percentage of the Republican's supporters out to the polls on election day, while Democrats were unable to wage a comparable effort on Miller's behalf. The Miller campaign suffered from frequent staff changes and evident disorganization throughout the contest—one political commentator termed the Democrat's campaign "a political disaster area"[211]—while the Obenshain-Warner operatives smoothly implemented their state-of-the-art campaign plan. In the end, the results were so close that any of numerous campaign activities and events could have made the difference. For example, the number of absentee ballots solicited from college students by Warner

---

[209]Howell interview.

[210]*Roanoke Times & World-News*, November 8, 1981.

[211]*The Radford Journal*, November 12, 1978.

youth organizer Robert Lauterberg and the state's College Republicans easily exceeded the razor-thin margin of victory. "The main difference [in the election]," reported Buster Carico in Roanoke, "was that the Republicans knew where to find their voters."[212]

On election night, Warner and his wife, Elizabeth, joined Governor and Mrs. Dalton at the executive mansion to await the results. The tally remained frightfully close all evening, and, trailing by about 10,000 votes as midnight approached, Warner huddled with the governor to prepare his concession remarks. The conversation quickly was interrupted, however, by a report of new totals that put Warner ahead by a few thousand votes. The GOP candidate's lead held; a recount petition filed by Miller was withdrawn in mid-December after a three-judge recount panel required a bond of $80,000 to cover the costs; and the official election canvass sent John Warner to the Senate by a margin of 4,721 votes. It was, to that time, the closest Virginia election in this century.[213]

Warner's victory was secured in the Hampton Roads and Richmond areas; in all other parts of the state his share of the vote was less than that in most other winning Republican campaigns of the 1970s. The two candidates each won five of the state's ten congressional districts, and Miller's majorities in both northern Virginia congressional districts were crucial to his strong showing. In the urban corridor, the race was nearly as close as in the state as a whole, and Warner's impressive 54 percent of the suburban vote gave him the edge. Despite his frequent praise for Harry Byrd and his long-running feud with Henry Howell, Miller amassed an estimated 93 percent of the black vote. The Democrat would have defeated Warner, however, if not for the significantly lower turnout among black voters in 1978. From 1977 to 1978, overall statewide turnout declined 2.3 percent, but among blacks the drop was 11.4 percent.[214]

As with most close elections, views varied as to whose performance had surpassed expectations. Newspaper columnist George Bowles found cause for Democratic satisfaction in the closeness of the results. "Arrayed against Miller," he noted,

> were the vast financial and organizational resources of the GOP, the fame of Elizabeth Taylor, the oratory of Mills Godwin, the editorial broadsides of the Richmond newspapers and the thinly veiled spiritual presence of Harry Byrd, Jr.[215]

Governor Dalton, however, saw the GOP victory as a "remarkable" feat in light of Miller's landslide re-election victory in 1973 and the fact that Warner's

---

[212]*Roanoke Times & World-News*, November 12, 1978.

[213]The vote totals were: Warner (R) – 613,232 (50.2%); Miller (D) – 608,511 (49.8%). Sabato, *Virginia Votes 1975–1978*, p. 93.

[214]Ibid., pp. 92–99.

[215]*The Radford Journal*, November 12, 1978.

campaign "really didn't get started until the first week of September."[216] Author Garrett Epps wrote that Warner's victory shattered some sacred Virginia taboos. Warner had been born out of state; he was a former official of the federal government; he was married to a movie star with scandal in her past, a woman who was not even an American citizen. Overcoming such handicaps against strong opposition was impressive enough; to have done so after a late—and devastatingly demoralizing—start was even more impressive. In the wake of Warner's election, Virginia's GOP reigned supreme.[217]

Incumbents of both parties, however, reigned supreme in the 1978 House of Representatives contests, as all ten House members from Virginia sought and won re-election.[218] With the exception of the two Democratic incumbents in competitive northern Virginia, none of Virginia's congressmen received less than 60 percent of the vote. The most junior member of the Virginia congressional delegation, hard-charging First District Representative Paul Trible, rolled up 72 percent in his race against Democrat Lewis B. Puller, and the most vulnerable Republican, Robert Daniel in the strongly Democratic Fourth District, faced no opposition. Republicans amassed a huge, 58.5 percent of the votes cast in the five major-party contested races.[219] In northern Virginia, Eighth District Congressman Herbert Harris narrowly survived a challenge from the GOP's John F. "Jack" Herrity, chairman of the Fairfax County Board of Supervisors, while Tenth District incumbent Joseph Fisher turned back Republican Frank Wolf by a more comfortable margin.[220]

Two years later, as Ronald Reagan completed his long march to the Presidency with a landslide victory over incumbent Jimmy Carter, Republicans in the Washington, D.C., suburbs and throughout Virginia surged to victory in congressional contests. The GOP gained three new seats and ensured solidarity in support of the new President's ambitious agenda among Virginia's congressional representatives. Frank Wolf built on the foundation laid during his 1978 bid and amassed a slim 5,000-vote victory margin in ousting the Tenth District's Fisher, while former Congressman Stanford E. "Stan" Parris won an Eighth District squeaker by outpolling Democrat Harris by 1,100 votes in a rematch of their 1974 battle. The GOP picked up a third new seat in 1980 with the retirement of Third District Democrat David Satterfield and the election

---

[216]Conversations with James Latimer, "A Different Dominion: The Republican Renaissance", WCVE-TV, 1986.

[217]Epps, "As Virginia Goes . . .," p. 11.

[218]For a comparison of the 1978 Virginia delegation in Congress with the state's delegations in the decade and a half after Harry Byrd, Sr.'s death, see Alexander J. Walker, "The Virginia Congressional Delegation Since 1965," *University of Virginia News Letter* (Charlottesville: Institute of Government, University of Virginia), October 1978.

[219]Sabato, *Virginia Votes 1975–1978*, pp. 101–105.

[220]The Eighth District vote totals were: Harris (D) – 56,137 (50.5%); Herrity (R) – 52,396 (47.1%); Charles E. Coe (I) – 2,632 (2.4%). Fisher polled 53.4 percent of the vote in his race with Wolf. Ibid., p. 102.

of Thomas J. Bliley, Jr., a former Democratic mayor of the city of Richmond, to succeed him. The easy re-election victories of the other six GOP congressional incumbents made Virginia's House delegation one of the most Republican in the country.[221] Only conservative Democrat W. C. "Dan" Daniel of the Fifth District prevented the GOP from making it unanimous, and he voted consistently with the congressional Republicans on most issues.

The GOP wins in populous northern Virginia and the popular Bliley's conversion to Republicanism gave realignment a major boost. With its orientation toward national rather than state politics, northern Virginia's choice of Republican congressional representation in 1980 reflected a growing alignment with the GOP in that crucial swing region—a trend that would continue in federal elections during the Reagan years. In Richmond, Bliley's party switch gave Republicans the benefit of a well-known local political figure with strong ties to the Main Street business community and also a reservoir of goodwill among black voters in the capital. Interestingly, several conservative GOP veterans, including 1962 congressional nominee Lewis Williams, Delegate George W. Jones, and Chesterfield attorney William Hurd, also were interested in the party's nod in 1980. But at a meeting hosted by Coalition leader FitzGerald Bemiss, they and their Third District GOP allies agreed to rally behind Bliley, thereby forging a beneficial marriage of Republican organization and Coalition money. After overcoming moderate Chesterfield Supervisor Joan Girone and former Satterfield aide Robert Lamb in an acrimonious GOP nomination contest, Bliley coasted to a lopsided victory over three foes in the general election.[222] He and campaign manager M. Boyd Marcus, Jr., an experienced Republican operative from Henrico County, thereafter embarked on an ambitious and remarkably successful decade-long effort to capture legislative and local government posts for the GOP in the conservative Third District.

Ronald Reagan's victory in Virginia was impressive, especially in light of the ambivalence toward his candidacy exhibited by the state's Republicans as 1980 opened. Many long-time Reagan admirers were reluctant to commit themselves early to support of the conservative warhorse's cause; at 69, he would be the oldest man ever elected President, and some worried that time had passed him by. Moreover, Texans George Bush and John Connally were the presidential favorites of the former Democrats and independent businessmen in the Coalition; Bush's long-time personal friend, FitzGerald Bemiss, actively promoted his candidacy, and former Governor Godwin, a Connally booster since their days as Democratic governors, lined up other Byrd organi-

---

[221]Of the 35 states with more than three members of the House of Representatives, Virginia had the highest percentage of Republican congressmen. See ibid., p. 29.

[222]The vote totals were: Bliley (R) – 96,524 (51.6%); John A. Mapp (D) – 60,962 (32.6%); Howard H. Carwile (I) – 19,549 (10.5%); James B. Turney (I) – 9,852 (5.3%). Larry Sabato, *Virginia Votes 1979–1982* (Charlottesville: Institute of Government, University of Virginia, 1983), p. 42.

zation alumni to back the former Texas Democrat. Most of the state's elected Republican leaders remained neutral during the early maneuvering and the initial round of GOP caucuses and primaries around the country. One exception was Congressman Paul Trible, who volunteered for a leadership role in the state Reagan effort. The ambitious First District lawmaker joined Helen Obenshain—who would succeed Judy Peachee as the party's new national committeewoman at the state GOP convention in June—in co-chairing Reagan's Virginia campaign. After Reagan's upset win in the New Hampshire primary, the conservative faithful in the Old Dominion rallied quickly to the Californian, and his forces dominated the Virginia delegation to the national convention in Detroit. A unified Republican Party and conservative establishment then helped the Reagan-Bush team roll to a lopsided Virginia victory in the fall.[223]

With Reagan's landslide, Republicans achieved a majority in the United States Senate for the first time in 26 years, and there was speculation in the election's wake that Virginia's Independent Senator Byrd might finally join the GOP. Byrd had broken his "golden silence" to endorse Reagan in October, but he declined to change his status after the Republican takeover. While pledging to work closely with the new President, Byrd declared, "I was elected as an Independent, and I want to pursue an independent course. I expect to vote as I have in the past—namely, Democratic on procedural matters and independently and conservatively on legislation."[224] In reacting to the senator's unwelcome decision, Congressman Trible gave a hint of what would come two years later when Byrd's term ended. "[T]he Republican Party is the dominant force in the state of Virginia today," Trible commented, "and I believe the Republican Party will field a candidate for the U.S. Senate in 1982."[225]

In the wake of the 1980 elections, Republican dominance in Virginia was apparent. The Commonwealth's Democrats had compiled by far the worst record of any state party in the country; they had not elected a candidate for governor or senator or a slate of presidential electors in 14 years.[226] Only the General Assembly remained a Democratic bastion, and, though Governor Dalton and the GOP fell short of their ambitious goals for the 1979 legislative races, Republicans nevertheless picked up a half-dozen seats to bring GOP representation in the 1980 General Assembly session to nine senators and 25 members of the House of Delegates—a twentieth-century high. The conservative tenets and the conservative coalition strategy long championed by Richard Obenshain were ascendant in Virginia, and, in Obenshain's absence,

---

[223]The vote totals were: Reagan (R) – 989,609 (53.0%); Carter (D) – 752,174 (40.3%); John Anderson (I) – 95,418 (5.1%); Barry Commoner (Citizens) – 14,024 (0.8%); Ed Clark (Libertarian) – 12,821 (0.7%). Ibid., p. 32.

[224]*Roanoke Times*, November 6, 1980.

[225]Ibid.

[226]Sabato, *Virginia Votes 1979–1982*, p. 29.

Governor Dalton labored to keep the true nature of their dizzying gains in focus for the GOP partisans. The 1980 results, he cautioned, were "not so much a vote for party, but for conservative principles."[227] There were other reminders, too, of Obenshain's leadership. In 1980, the GOP occupied its newly purchased headquarters building in downtown Richmond, which was named the "Richard D. Obenshain Center" in tribute to the party architect. Lauding his former rival at the headquarters dedication ceremony, Senator John Warner reflected on Reagan's nationwide landslide and observed that Obenshain's "wisdom guides not only Virginia, but the United States of America today."[228]

The months since Obenshain's death had seen the Virginia GOP perform impressively. Republicans had persevered in 1978 to win a major, if breathtakingly narrow, Senate victory; they had waged vigorous campaigns for the General Assembly in 1979 and had made important inroads at the local level; and, they had carried the state handily for the Reagan-Bush ticket and captured every congressional seat they sought in 1980. But the seeds of discontent and division in GOP ranks had been sown in Obenshain's absence, and they were soon to blossom. By 1980, there no longer was a single, dominant faction in the Republican Party, and there was no person or group in a position to lead by consensus. Some GOP conservatives looked to John Alderson, Reagan's 1980 Virginia coordinator, for leadership. Other Obenshain loyalists aligned themselves with Judy Peachee and with Governors Godwin and Dalton and the Richmond-based business community. And, the weakened remnants of the moderate mountain-valley GOP constituted a third major party faction. In addition to those divisions based on personal rivalries, past antagonisms, and philosophical differences, the emergence of Moral Majority as a formidable political force represented a new source of Republican Party strife. Popular party chairman George McMath had stepped aside in 1979, and his successor, conservative Culpeper physician and veteran GOP activist Alfred B. Cramer, III, was in the post less than a year before he was publicly warning GOP regulars to guard against takeovers of their local committees by conservative Christian activists aligned with Jerry Falwell. As Virginia Republicans triumphantly rang down the curtain on the '70s, few realized that the stage had been set for a decade of divisive internal fights, for which the price would be a lengthy string of Democratic victories in the Commonwealth.

Most Republicans and even most Democrats at decade's end viewed the Virginia GOP as the vanguard of a conservative movement that was sweeping the nation. "We have been for 10 years where the country is now," chortled Judy Peachee in reaction to the Reagan victory and election of a Republican majority in the United States Senate. "It's like New York fashions—it takes

---

[227]*The Richmond News Leader*, November 5, 1980.
[228]*Roanoke Times*, May 10, 1981.

them 10 years to get to Richmond. In politics, it's the other way around."[229] "It isn't that Virginia has caught up to the nation," agreed Jack Gravely, the liberal executive director of the Virginia NAACP. "It's that the rest of the nation caught up to Virginia on election day."[230] The Commonwealth's distinctly conservative and reliably Republican politics of the 1970s had foreshadowed the nationwide "Reagan Revolution" of the 1980s. But, true to her tradition of political independence, Virginia would not venture far into the '80s before she would again be out of step with, or perhaps ahead of, the national political trends. By decade's end, Virginia's Democrats would be touting their centrist winning formula to fellow partisans across the country, and two from the resurgent state Democratic Party would be counted among the national party's stable of prospective presidential candidates. But all that lay ahead, and in 1980, Republicanism ruled in the Old Dominion. Virginia was, by almost any measure, the most Republican state in America.

---

[229]Epps, "As Virginia Goes . . .," p. 8.
[230]Ibid.

Part Seven

Postscript to Realignment:
The Reagan and Robb Years

1981 - 1990

Chapter 34

About-Face:
The Democratic Decade in Review

"The great leap of faith Virginians made was not in electing a black . . . but in electing Robb [as governor] in 1981. For a decade Virginians had seen a Democratic Party run by liberals. . . . [Robb] reopened doors that had been shut to the business and money crowd; he firmly established the proposition that it was possible to be both fiscally responsible and socially enlightened. . . . [H]e redefined what it meant to be a Virginia Democrat."[1]

Dwayne Yancey, 1988

As Ronald Reagan stood on the west portico of the United States Capitol on January 20, 1981, to take the oath of office as the 39th President, the Virginia Republicans in the massive crowd were basking in the glow of their stunning string of successes. The autumn elections in the Old Dominion revealed a Virginia GOP at the peak of its power, and Republican partisans eyed the new year's statewide contests with the assurance of a tried and tested prizefighter poised to deliver a knockout punch. Pundits joined the partisans in portraying the 1981 contests as do-or-die for the state's Democrats. "If success eludes the Democratic Party again in 1981," warned inveterate commentator Larry Sabato, "Democrats may find themselves in the political wilderness indefinitely."[2] Reflecting the cockiness of many GOP activists who had begun to believe their flattering press clippings, Governor John Dalton's press secretary, Charles Davis, gloated that the only way a Republican could lose statewide in 1981 would be "if all the voting machines malfunctioned on election day."[3]

Nearly ten years later, with state Republicans gazing up blurry-eyed from the canvas after three successive knock-downs in gubernatorial races, few observers were able to fathom how the party's fortunes could have been so rapidly and completely reversed. Adding to the incomprehensibility was the fact that Virginians' apparent repudiation of Republicanism in state elections paralleled the remarkable Reagan-Bush decade in Washington, when nothing became so clear to most Americans as the rightness of the GOP's growth-

---

[1]Dwayne Yancey, *When Hell Froze Over* (Roanoke: Taylor Publishing Company, 1988), p. 373.

[2]*Richmond Times-Dispatch*, November 23, 1980.

[3]Epps, "As Virginia Goes . . .," p. 11.

oriented economic policies and the "peace through strength" strategy of the successive Republican national administrations. At a time of unprecedented national prosperity and foreign policy achievement under Republican presidential leadership, Virginians trimmed GOP representation in the state's congressional delegation back to 50 percent—at the close of the '80s, each party controlled one U. S. Senate and five House of Representatives seats—and gave the Old Dominion's Democrats a perfect record in the nine contests for top state government posts during the decade.

If the '80s were the "Reagan era" nationally, the decade has to be branded the "Robb era" in Virginia. Winning the governorship in 1981, Chuck Robb succeeded in forging a new majority coalition in the state—one that resembled the broad Democratic coalition that carried his father-in-law, Lyndon Johnson, to a presidential victory in the Commonwealth in 1964 and then elected Mills Godwin governor as a Democrat in 1965. Though Robb's fame stemmed (by marriage) from the Great Society, he was anything but a latter-day liberal. His moderate platform combined tenets of economic conservatism with racial progressivism, and these—along with his considerable wealth and deliberate, reassuring manner—supplied a formula for Democratic renewal among the prosperous, forward-looking young voters in Virginia's burgeoning suburbs. Swept into office with him in 1981 were a new Democratic lieutenant governor, former Portsmouth Mayor Richard J. "Dick" Davis, Jr., and a coattail-clasping member of the House of Delegates from Richmond named Gerald L. Baliles, who narrowly was elected attorney general. In the 1985 gubernatorial race, Democrat Baliles mimicked the popular governor so well and embraced his themes so thoroughly that reporters dubbed him "Robb II." And four years after that, Democratic gubernatorial candidate L. Douglas Wilder invested hundreds of thousands of dollars in television advertising to put his rival Robb on the airwaves singing his praises. The former governor himself went to the United States Senate in 1988, and from there Robb continued to trumpet his centrist strategy to a national Democratic Party that remained in the grip of avowed liberals.

The Robb-led Virginia Democrats achieved victory after victory, but, even so, it was possible to overstate Democratic strength in the state. The party's decade of successes in statewide races was accompanied by gradual erosion of its lopsided General Assembly majority and its domination of local offices. From 1979 to 1989, GOP representation climbed from 21 to 39 members in the House of Delegates, and from six to ten members of the State Senate.[4] More-

---

[4]Republicans' performance in legislative races was most impressive in 1989. In addition to gaining a net increase of four GOP seats in the House of Delegates, GOP candidates polled a century-high 44.8 percent of the aggregate vote in all House of Delegates districts. In the party-contested House races, Republicans collectively received 49.3 percent of the vote. See Larry J. Sabato, "The 1989 House of Delegates Contests," in *Virginia Government and Politics*, eds. Thomas R. Morris and Larry J. Sabato (Charlottesville: The Virginia Chamber of Commerce and the Center for Public Service, University of Virginia, 1990), pp. 181–189.

over, the Democratic statewide winning streak of the '80s, like the string of statewide GOP victories in the '70s, tended to mask the reality of spirited competition between the two Virginia parties—competition that had emerged and intensified following the turbulent, transforming 1964–1975 period. State Democrats were neither so weak in the '70s as was generally believed at the time, nor were Virginia Republicans so feeble in the following decade as their dismal won-loss record would suggest. If the very close Warner-Miller contest in 1978 was a source of encouragement for distraught Democrats, the razor-thin margin separating victory from defeat in the 1989 gubernatorial race served to reassure Republicans that either party could capture the prize in contemporary Virginia.

Unlike the dramatically shifting coalitions and fast-paced change that had animated Virginia politics for much of the period since the Second World War, especially the late '60s and early '70s, the 1980s brought more gradual evolution and the achievement of at least a semblance of stability. The rapid realignment process of the preceding decade gave way to a substantially dealigned political environment in which both parties vied for the decisive support of independent voters—a situation common across the nation. In examining Virginia politics during the '80s, therefore, it is beneficial to focus on the themes and trends that run through the decade as a whole. This chapter thus provides an overview of the decade's political developments, and the chapters that follow elaborate on two themes of primary importance in understanding the resuscitation of the Virginia Democratic Party and the success of its recent statewide candidates. The first of these chapters traces Republican Party division and the related fragmentation of the conservative coalition that dominated state politics after the demise of the Byrd organization. The second chapter focuses on the political influence of the state's fast-growing suburbs and the issues that pushed suburban voters into the Republican column in national elections and towards Democratic slates in state contests. It will become apparent that these factors played a substantial part in each of the three consecutive Democratic gubernatorial victories during the '80s.

The Art of Coalition Building

In the hotly competitive Commonwealth that emerged in the 1970s, coalition-building remained the name of the game as the major parties' fortunes ebbed and flowed. The primary thread running through Virginia politics after the demise of the Byrd organization was voters' penchant for partisan independence. Neither party possessed the loyalty of anything approaching a majority among the state's electorate, and opinion surveys regularly confirmed that the largest single group remained the body of unaffiliated voters who regarded themselves as independents. Indeed, even the major political benefactors in the state were, for the most part, free from party ties. Most in the business community reserved the prerogative to back candidates who were to their liking regardless of party label, and this remained true even as the contributor base's center-of-gravity shifted during the '80s from the traditional Richmond-based business and financial establishment to fast-growing northern Virginia and (to a lesser extent) the Hampton Roads area. With voters and donors roaming at large and generally choosing the person rather than the party, it was not remarkable that Virginians simultaneously embraced Robb-style Democratic leadership at the state level and Reagan Republicanism nationally.

The centrist Democratic coalition that made its debut in Virginia in the mid-'60s and then re-emerged to give Chuck Robb a crucial victory in 1981 contained widely divergent and sometimes antagonistic elements. In 1965, GOP gubernatorial nominee Linwood Holton had expressed amazement at the "incredible logic under which [Democrat Mills Godwin] was able to send . . . Armistead Boothe to Arlington to proclaim him a liberal in the finest tradition of the Great Society while he was also able. . . to send Bill Tuck to Danville to attest he was a conservative in the tradition of Harry Byrd."[5] In 1981, Republican Marshall Coleman could have used different names but almost identical words to describe his Democratic foe's feat. Touting Robb's candidacy simultaneously on the hustings that year—and playing clearly indispensable roles in the Democratic victory—were former Delegate W. Roy Smith, the erstwhile leader of the conservative Coalition, and State Senator Douglas Wilder of Richmond, then the lone black in the Assembly's upper chamber and a favorite of organized labor and liberals. The two men vouched for Robb's fidelity to various principles and policies deemed fundamental by their respective constituencies, which happened to be at opposite ends of the Virginia political spectrum. For more than a decade, the divergent views and discordant voices within the Democratic Party had thwarted the party's candidates for statewide office, but as the '80s unfolded, it was the GOP's conservative coalition that cracked and crumbled. Just as 1972 was the critical year in the formation of the winning Republican coalition, 1981 proved pivotal in its disintegration.

Long members of a distinctly minority party, state Republicans yearning for victories had submerged factional differences in the late '60s and '70s, and their unity of purpose had played a key role in producing a decade of electoral successes. But with that success eventually came over-confidence, organizational lethargy, personal rivalries, and a renewal of factional bickering. The sudden death of conservative leader Richard Obenshain in 1978 left his most prominent allies vying, often bitterly, for power and influence. That critical development coincided with the growth of the "New Right" or "Christian Right" elements within the party—religious fundamentalists, evangelicals, and others primarily motivated by morality-laden social issues such as opposition to legalized abortion. By 1981, the GOP's dominant conservative wing was hemorrhaging as differing policy agendas (e.g., emphasis of economic versus

---

[5]Hunter, p. 32.

moral issues), contending party-building strategies, and conflicting personal ambitions came to the fore. The new divisions did not supplant, but merely supplemented, the still-simmering dispute between the traditional Republicans to the west and the more conservative GOP partisans and Democratic converts east of the Blue Ridge.

The renewed GOP factionalism in 1981 was accompanied by the first major splintering of the Byrd organization remnants that comprised the Coalition. Since 1972, the bulk of the influential conservative independents had followed Mills Godwin's overt and Harry Byrd, Jr.'s veiled direction in supporting Republican candidates for statewide office. Republican activists, following the lead of Obenshain and Dalton, generally had cooperated by nominating candidates and constructing tickets that would appeal to the old-line Byrd Democrats. The result had been a winning conservative coalition that elected Republicans to statewide office and left conservative non-Republicans—such as Senator Harry F. Byrd, Jr., Congressmen David Satterfield and W.C. "Dan" Daniel, and numerous state legislators and local officials—politically unmolested. In 1977, the GOP leaders' ticket-building efforts were thwarted by rebellious delegates at the party's state convention, but the feared splintering of the Coalition in the general election never materialized because Henry Howell and the Democratic liberals deprived moderate former Attorney General Andrew Miller of the party's gubernatorial nod. Republicans were not so fortunate, however, in 1981. With neither the GOP's Coleman nor Democrat Robb regarded as distinctly more conservative than the other, the Coalition split almost evenly between them.

To the Republican Party division and the Coalition breach in 1981 was added a third key factor: Democratic Party unity. Sobered by their seemingly interminable hard times, Virginia Democrats had the "minority mentality"[6] necessary to forge a united front. To many in the once-proud party, winning the governorship in 1981 represented nothing less than a prerequisite for political survival, and that imperative ensured that internal party divisions would be quelled and factional interests would be subordinated. In Lieutenant Governor Chuck Robb, Democrats had a candidate equal to the challenge. A well-financed celebrity, gubernatorial in appearance and demeanor, cautious and traditional by nature, conservative in style, and moderate in opinion, the lieutenant governor had been one of only two Virginia Democrats since 1969 to amass a suburban majority in a statewide race.[7] He looked like a winner, and, if few Democrats were much excited by him, he had given fewer still reason to be hostile. Since his 1977 election, Robb's strategy had been to meet with and placate as many influential Democrats in as many quarters of the

---

[6]The phrase was coined by Professor Larry Sabato in his *Virginia Votes 1979–1982* (Charlottesville: Institute of Government, University of Virginia, 1983), p. 81.

[7]Robb's 1977 bid for lieutenant governor and Andrew Miller's landslide re-election victory in the 1973 campaign for attorney general were the only statewide Democratic efforts to garner a majority in the suburbs between 1969 and 1981.

diverse party as possible; rather than attempting to build a strongly loyal personal following, he purposely adopted the more modest goal of "[not having] enemies out there crusading against [him]."[8] For a Democratic Party desperate to win, little more was needed.

Robb also took steps to quell the feuding between the party's liberal Howell faction and its more moderate Miller element. "The personal animosity between [the Howell and Miller camps] was so strong," recalled Robb in 1984,

> that it took me two or three years of effort to bring the party back together so they wouldn't keep fighting that battle. It was very clear that they wanted to, and I had to move a number of people out of positions and a number of other people into them and keep some people very quiet in campaigns or we would have had those fights all over again.[9]

Shortly after becoming lieutenant governor, Robb asked former Senator William Spong to chair an informal commission tasked with recommending steps to revitalize the state Democratic Party. Among the commission's suggestions was a switch from the primary to the convention as the party's mechanism for nominating statewide candidates. As Robb intended, the Spong commission also concluded that the party needed new leadership. In January 1979, liberal Norfolk Senator Joseph T. Fitzpatrick resigned the Democratic state chairmanship, and the central committee tapped the Portsmouth mortgage banker and former mayor, Richard J. Davis, Jr., to succeed him. The change appeared to reflect a shift toward the center by Virginia Democrats—imagery that Robb desperately wanted. The new, more unified, and more moderate Democratic Party resolved to turn the page on the fiasco that was the '70s and directed its attention to eliminating the significant technological gap in fundraising and voter turnout programs favoring the state GOP. A string of successes followed.

Though the Democratic success story of the '80s initially centered around Robb, the decade saw another Democratic figure move from relative obscurity to the pinnacle of power in the Old Dominion and into forefront of the national political arena. L. Douglas Wilder was a "standard-brand liberal"[10] state senator from the city of Richmond—the highest elected black officeholder in the Commonwealth—when he helped mobilize black voters behind Robb's gubernatorial candidacy in 1981. In a formula that would be repeated throughout the decade, Wilder played a key role in keeping the Democratic black and liberal base intact while Robb and his emulators fashioned a moderate-conservative image attractive to suburban whites. Acknowledging "the conservative tone of the [Robb] campaign" and his own concerns about it,

---

[8]Robb interview.
[9]Ibid.
[10]Baker, p. 277.

Wilder wrote to his "Democratic Black Caucus of Virginia" constituents in 1981 that he had investigated Robb's stands and could attest to the gubernatorial candidate's commitment to various measures deemed important to blacks.[11] "I trust the man. . . . He has been consistent," Wilder wrote to the influential black political and community leaders, many of whom were wary of the conservative-sounding Democrat. Though Robb later played down the significance of Wilder's 1981 role[12]—the two feuded like jealous siblings for most of the '80s—Wilder played a crucial part in forming what Democrats soon were calling the "Robb coalition."

In stark contrast to the political stratagem of Jesse Jackson, who used his popularity among blacks as leverage to force the national Democratic Party and its presidential nominees to the left in the 1980s, Wilder made it possible for Democrats of a moderate-conservative stripe to run and win in Virginia with solid black and liberal support. In 1985 and 1989, it was the presence of a conservative-sounding Wilder himself on the statewide Democratic ticket —aided by Robb's imprimatur and black Virginians' determination to break the racial barrier by electing one of their own as governor—that kept the broad Democratic coalition intact and in power. By decade's end, the winning combination could more aptly be described as the "Robb-Wilder coalition," and the nation's first black governor[13] was stumping throughout the country, spreading the word about the formula that had worked so well for the Virginia Democrats even at the height of the "Reagan Revolution." In a telling bit of testimony about the depth and durability of Wilder's philosophical moorings, only a few years earlier he had denounced Robb's efforts to give the national Democratic Party a more centrist image; the Robb-led Democratic Leadership Council, Wilder derisively suggested in 1986, was comprised of "me-too-ists" who put on Reagan masks."[14] But, by 1990, a largely upstaged Robb was watching in frustration as the charismatic Wilder purloined his moderate message—Wilder tactician Paul Goldman dubbed it the "New Mainstream" in 1989[15]—and proceeded to capture the attention of Democratic partisans around the country. Not one, but two Virginia Democrats with presidential

---

[11]Ibid., p. 121.

[12]In his 1989 biography of Wilder, *Washington Post* reporter Donald P. Baker wrote,
How much help Wilder was to Robb in that campaign is a matter of debate. Robb didn't consider Wilder a key player in his campaign, although he said 'his embrace just before the convention helped alleviate some unrest in the black community.' He doesn't recall asking much of Wilder, or of him offering much.
Ibid., p. 120.

[13]Wilder actually was not the first black to serve as governor of an American state. P.B.S. Pinchback, whose mother was a slave and whose father was a slave owner, served as acting governor of Louisiana for five weeks during Reconstruction.

[14]See *The Washington Post*, March 12, 1989.

[15]See Margaret Edds, *Claiming the Dream: The Victorious Campaign of Douglas Wilder of Virginia* (Chapel Hill: Algonquin Books, 1990), pp. 181–183.

ambitions were touting their achievements in a state that a decade earlier had been deemed the most Republican in the country.

Federal Elections in Virginia

The invisible political pendulum swung as widely in the Democrats' direction in the '80s as it did toward the GOP in the '70s; Virginia Democrats registered gains at all governmental levels except locally and in state legislative races, where broadening two-party competition merely diminished their already huge numerical advantage. Nevertheless, it was apparent by the close of the decade that Republicans retained a competitive edge in federal contests (for President, senator and congressional representative), while Democrats had the upper hand in state elections (for governor, lieutenant governor, and attorney general). This two-tiered system was more than a historical remnant. It reflected somewhat the immense personal popularity of the decade's political giants—Reagan in Washington, Robb in Richmond—as well as the inevitable effects of incumbency. But it also paralleled a regional, and to a lesser extent a national, political trend. Virginians, like other Southerners, voted Republican in landslide proportions in the ideology-laden presidential races during the '80s, and GOP candidates generally benefited from the tendency of U.S. Senate contests and races for the House of Representatives to develop along conservative-versus-liberal lines. In the less ideological competition for the largely managerial state government posts, however, Democrats thrived not only in Virginia but throughout the South. As noted by Professors Earl and Merle Black in their seminal 1987 study, *Politics and Society in the South*, contests for federal office typically focused on national security, foreign policy, and economic and fiscal issues and thus provided GOP conservatives "with more targets and symbols to employ against their opponents than [did] the more mundane and practical agendas of state politics. . . . In state politics there [was] no reliable demand for an unadulterated conservative Republicanism."[16] To the extent that issues entered into state and local races, voters generally assessed candidates of both parties based on their practical approaches to such vexing concerns as education, transportation, public safety, and environmental protection. Also important in some state contests around the country were emotional social issues such as race relations and abortion policy, which tended to cut across traditional conservative-liberal alignments.

Virginia's enthusiasm for Reaganism never waned in the presidential contests of the '80s despite perfunctory attempts by the Robb Democrats to persuade state voters to the contrary. In the 1984 re-election campaign, the Reagan-Bush ticket amassed a 62-percent majority against the liberal Demo-

---

[16]Black and Black, pp. 315–316; see also Larry J. Sabato, *Virginia Votes 1983–1986* (Charlottesville: Institute of Government, University of Virginia, 1987), pp. 107–108.

cratic team of former Vice President Walter Mondale and Representative Geraldine Ferrarro of New York.[17] Defending his earlier embrace of Chuck Robb, conservative leader Roy Smith observed during the 1984 presidential contest that "Mills Godwin supported Lyndon Johnson openly in 1964—and, I think, with right much more fervor—than Robb has supported Mondale."[18] State Democrats initially were somewhat more enthusiastic about the prospects of Michael Dukakis in 1988, but the rosy outlook for the liberal Massachusetts governor and his moderate Texas runningmate, U.S. Senator Lloyd Bentsen, quickly faded in the Old Dominion, as it did in the rest of the nation. Earlier in the year, Vice President George Bush dominated the GOP preliminaries in the state despite the candidacy of Virginia Beach-based evangelist M. G. "Pat" Robertson, son of the late Democratic U.S. Senator, A. Willis Robertson. The other minister-turned-presidential candidate, Jesse Jackson, fared better in his party's Virginia competition; he garnered 45 percent of the vote to handily win the Virginia Democratic primary.[19] Bush and his runningmate, U.S. Senator Dan Quayle of Indiana, then coasted to a decisive victory in November, polling nearly 60 percent of the general election tally.[20]

Unlike the '70s, which had featured several lively contests for Virginia's two U.S. Senate seats, the '80s produced only one competitive Senate race—in 1982. In the Warner-Miller contest four years earlier, both party's nominees had vied unreservedly for association with Virginia's senior senator, popular Independent Harry F. Byrd, Jr. But after the GOP captured control of the Senate in the 1980 Reagan landslide, First District Congressman Paul S. Trible, Jr., began traveling throughout the state, seeking and obtaining assurances from Republicans and Independents that they would back him for the seat if Byrd chose to retire in 1982. In an artful use of carrot and stick, Trible publicly invited Byrd to join the GOP and to seek re-election as a Republican, but he and party chief Alfred Cramer also made it abundantly clear that they expected there to be a Republican nominee in 1982 regardless of Byrd's course.[21] Such implicit threats greatly annoyed Republican Governor John

---

[17]The vote totals were: Reagan (R) – 1,337,078 (62.3%); Mondale (D) – 796,250 (37.1%); Lyndon LaRouche (I) – 13,307 (0.6%). Sabato, *Virginia Votes 1983–1986*, p. 31.

[18]Smith interview.

[19]The vote totals for the four principal contenders were: Jackson – 164,709 (45.1%); Albert Gore, Jr. – 81,419 (22.3%); Michael S. Dukakis – 80,183 (22.0%); Richard Gephardt – 15,935 (4.4%). In the non-binding Virginia GOP primary, Bush polled 53.3 percent of the vote to Kansas Senator Robert Dole's 26.0 percent and Robertson's 13.7 percent. Larry J. Sabato, *Virginia Votes 1987–1990* (Charlottesville: Center for Public Service, University of Virginia, 1991), chapter 2 (forthcoming).

[20]The vote totals were: Bush (R) – 1,309,162 (59.7%); Dukakis (D) – 859,799 (39.2%); Lenora B. Fulani (I) – 14,312 (0.7%); Ron Paul (Libertarian) – 8,336 (0.4%). Sabato, *Virginia Votes 1987–1990*, chapter 3 (forthcoming).

[21]See *Roanoke Times*, March 9, 1981, and April 21, 1981.

Dalton, who was widely touted as a potential candidate for the seat but had no actual interest in the post. Privately, Coalition enthusiast Dalton brusquely admonished Trible that the GOP would not field a candidate if Byrd chose to seek re-election as an Independent; Trible, undaunted, responded that Republican regulars might well take a different view, and proceeded with his plans. When Byrd announced in November 1981 that he would not seek another term, Trible had the GOP nomination virtually sewn up. Though some Coalitionists and Republicans groused privately that the ambitious, 35-year-old congressman had elbowed Byrd out and should not be rewarded, only Eighth District Representative Stan Parris gave serious consideration to mounting a challenge. After quietly testing the water for several weeks, Parris found broad if somewhat tepid GOP support for Trible and made it known that he would run for re-election to his northern Virginia congressional seat. The Senate nomination was Trible's without a fight.

With Chuck Robb newly ensconced in the governor's mansion and the national economy in recession, Virginia Democrats had high hopes of capturing the Senate seat as 1982 opened. Several moderates were interested in the party's nod, but Virginia Beach Delegate Owen B. Pickett—who had succeeded Richard Davis as Democratic Party chairman a year earlier—emerged the favorite after Governor Robb and party leaders systematically rated and tallied the potential contenders' strengths and weaknesses. With the others stepping aside, Pickett quickly amassed the delegate support necessary to lock up the nomination. The bizarre developments that ensued would profoundly affect the course of state, and perhaps national, politics for many years to come. Angered by the defeat of several of his proposals during the 1982 General Assembly session, including legislation to honor Martin Luther King, Jr., with a state holiday, State Senator Wilder suddenly seized upon Pickett's conservative campaign pronouncements and benign praise of retiring Senator Byrd as justification for a threatened bid for the Senate himself. More significant, Wilder suggested that several of Pickett's statements were "anti-black,"[22] and he moved publicly toward a break with the party and an independent candidacy for the seat. Confronted with the disastrous loss of the Democrats' virtually monolithic support among blacks, Robb intervened and pressured Pickett to withdraw from the race upon Wilder's assurance that he would do likewise. The two would-be candidates stepped aside on May 4, 1982—both destined for better days—and Democratic partisans thereafter awarded their Senate nomination to a reluctant draftee, Lieutenant Governor Richard J. Davis, Jr.[23]

---

[22]*The Virginian-Pilot*, April 24, 1982.
[23]See generally Baker, pp. 124–149; Yancey, pp. 40–47.

Wilder's bold gambit consolidated and showcased his extraordinary clout within the state Democratic Party, and it guaranteed that he would face no opposition for his party's 1985 nomination for lieutenant governor—or four years after that when he sought its nod for governor.[24] Wrote *Roanoke Times & World-News* reporter Dwayne Yancey in 1988,

> Wilder was not simply black—he was brazen, and not afraid to shout "racism" whenever it suited him. This was where Wilder's showdown with Pickett became so valuable. All the "experts" had figured Wilder hurt himself by not being a team player in 1982. Instead, Wilder was now untouchable. Nobody wanted to make him mad.[25]

Though observers differed in their speculation over whether Wilder's challenge to Pickett had begun as a muscle-flexing power play, the triumphant state senator wasted no time after Pickett's retreat in citing it as a turning point in the way blacks (including himself) would be viewed and treated in the state Democratic Party. "I am certain that our cause will no longer be pooh-poohed and ignored the way [it was] before," he declared, adding that the "myth [that Democrats can automatically count on black votes] has been exploded."[26]

Nearly a decade later, *Richmond Times-Dispatch* political reporter Jeff E. Schapiro noted the increasingly bitter rivalry between Wilder and Chuck Robb and suggested that it could have been avoided:

> In 1982, when Wilder threatened to bolt the Democratic Party and seek the U.S. Senate as an independent, Robb should have held his ground and let Wilder run. Instead, Robb dumped his hand-picked candidate in a concession to Wilder. Sure, the Republicans probably would have still won the seat. But the Democrats, in general, would've been done with Wilder, and Robb, in particular, wouldn't have the self-imposed headache that lingers to this day.[27]

---

[24]Dwayne Yancey, whose *When Hell Froze Over* chronicled the 1985 campaign for lieutenant governor, wrote that Wilder

saw clearly the scenario he'd have to rely on to get the nomination [for lieutenant governor in 1985]: Do it my way or do without black votes in the fall. "I was convinced," [Wilder] says, "if I pushed it well enough and strong enough, whoever was seeking the nomination for governor would need my support and I hoped to neutralize them so they would not pick another candidate." It was essentially Wilder's 1982 Pickett strategy in reverse: Pre-empt the field for lieutenant governor, dare someone to challenge him, make him think if they opposed him they'd forever outrage black voters, then try to bargain with the gubernatorial candidates for a spot on the ticket in return for black support.

Yancey, p. 53. Similarly, "the memory of the 1982 Pickett affair hung over the quiet deliberations of Democrats as they looked toward 1989," according to Margaret Edds, whose book recounts Wilder's 1989 campaign for governor. "[I]f Wilder lost [a gubernatorial nomination contest with Attorney General Mary Sue Terry], the fear of another 1982—massive defections by alienated black voters—might preclude any hope of victory in the fall." Edds, p. 44. Ultimately, Terry and other potential Wilder rivals in the Democratic Party stepped aside in 1989, as would-be Wilder foes had done four years earlier.

[25]Yancey, p. 71.

[26]Baker, p. 144.

[27]*Richmond Times-Dispatch*, April 22, 1990.

Schapiro's retrospective view probably was correct, but it ignored the racially polarizing effect that a Wilder independent bid in 1982 would have had within the Democratic Party. "I will probably always have a black mark against me for not somehow making that right," Robb commented in a 1984 interview,

> and yet I always thought that the strongest single political act that I performed was to get both Pickett and Wilder out of the race. It required me to spend more of my political capital. I could have let that go, but I knew that I was the only one who could unhorse either of them. [A race including Pickett and Wilder] not only would have meant certain defeat; it would have permanently polarized not only the Democratic Party but the electorate because it was going to be on black-white issues. . . . I just could not let that happen.[28]

Had the Wilder-Pickett clash not been averted, the broad coalition that elected Robb in 1981 would have been demolished, and the ensuing Democratic division would have made the debilitating Howell-Miller schism of the '70s look like a minor squabble. Instead, the alliance among Democratic moderates, blacks, labor, and liberals held throughout the '80s, and Wilder soon joined Robb as a prime beneficiary of it.

The Trible-Davis duel for the U.S. Senate was set only after another unusual twist. In a move recalling the Godwin-led entreaty to the elder Senator Byrd in 1958, key backers of Senator Harry F. Byrd, Jr., in May 1982 publicly urged him to reconsider his decision to forego a re-election bid. Byrd toyed with the idea for several suspenseful days before reaffirming his retirement plans,[29] and the leaders of the drive to recruit him—Mills Godwin and Roy Smith—thereafter moved to quash any appearance of Coalition division by signing on as co-chairman of "Virginians for Trible." The autumn contest brought a barrage of negative salvos fired by the combatants and their respective supporters, and in its wake neither candidate was accused of waging a particularly uplifting, visionary, or technically proficient campaign. The close race ended with a narrow Trible victory, his advantage secured in the First District where he was intensely popular after representing the area in the House of Representatives for six years.[30]

In amassing 51 percent of the statewide vote against Davis, Trible had overcome the effects of a national recession, ebbing Reagan popularity, vigorous opposition from a new Democratic governor, and strong Democratic

---

[28]Robb interview.

[29]Byrd's reconsideration brought criticism from unexpected quarters. Long supportive of Byrd, Jr., and his father before him, *The Richmond News Leader* editorially assailed suggestions of a Byrd reprise and warned that Democrat Davis would be the unintended beneficiary. *The Richmond News Leader,* May 29, 1982.

[30]The vote totals were: Trible (R) – 724,571 (51.2%); Davis (D) – 690,839 (48.8%). Sabato, *Virginia Votes 1979-1982,* p. 106. Trible carried the First District by 28,375 votes, a net gain of approximately 40,000 votes over typical GOP performances in the district in statewide races. Ibid., p. 109.

campaigns in simultaneous contests for the U.S. House of Representatives and Virginia House of Delegates.[31] In a clear indication of the two-tiered nature of state politics and the pro-Republican tendencies of Virginia voters on national issues, Trible garnered 55 percent of the suburban vote against a popular Democrat who, just 12 months earlier in a state election, had led the Robb ticket in the suburbs by polling 52 percent of the vote there.[32] Trible and his campaign successfully portrayed Davis as a liberal and identified him with the failed economic and foreign policies of Jimmy Carter and the national Democratic Party. That tactic enabled the Republicans to capture the Senate seat owned by the Byrd family for nearly 50 years. But it also pinned the "liberal" and "loser" monikers on Davis, thereby diminishing his gubernatorial prospects and increasing the likelihood that the GOP in the 1985 race for governor would face the more moderate—and thus more formidable—Gerald Baliles.

The decade's other two Senate races—in 1984 and 1988—were monuments to political boredom. Incumbent John Warner, divorced from Elizabeth Taylor in 1982 and, by 1984, recognized as a hard-working, moderate lawmaker, coasted to re-election over a little-known liberal Democrat from Norfolk, former Delegate Edythe C. Harrison. Harrison's dismal showing in 1984—she polled less than 30 percent of the vote—was worse even than that recorded by Hazel Barger of Roanoke, the GOP nominee for lieutenant governor in 1961 and the only woman previously tapped by either Virginia party for a statewide race.[33] By 1990, Warner's invincibility was generally acknowledged, and prominent Democrats, from outgoing Governor Gerald Baliles on down, shied away from challenging him.[34] As the ranking Republican member on the Senate Armed Services Committee, Warner had seniority and influence in an area of tremendous importance to the Virginia economy—national defense. But the senior senator was probably more popular among the public at large than among Virginia Republican activists, as

---

[31]Pursuant to the order of a three-judge federal panel, which heard legal challenges to the 1981 Virginia House of Delegates reapportionment plan, special elections were held in newly drawn, single-member House districts on November 2, 1982. The delegates chosen in the 1982 voting, like those elected a year earlier in malapportioned districts, served judicially shortened terms of one year. The normal two-year cycle was restored in November 1983. For additional information regarding the issues in the redistricting litigation, see the author's "The Reapportionment Dilemma: Lessons from the Virginia Experience," 68 *Virginia Law Review* 541–570 (March 1982).

[32]Sabato, *Virginia Votes 1979–1982*, p. 110.

[33]The vote totals in the 1984 race were: Warner (R) – 1,404,194 (70.0%); Harrison (D) – 601,142 (29.9%). Sabato, *Virginia Votes 1983–1986*, p. 31. In 1961, Barger garnered 34 percent of the vote in losing to Mills Godwin, the Democratic nominee for lieutenant governor.

[34]In 1990, Warner garnered 80.9 percent of the vote in defeating Nancy Spannaus, an independent candidate linked to fringe political figure Lyndon LaRouche. The free pass given Warner by Democrats in 1990 represented the first time in the twentieth century that Virginia Democrats had foregone the opportunity to nominate a candidate for the U.S. Senate. Sabato, *Virginia Votes 1987–1990*, chapter 6 (forthcoming).

reflected in a May 1990 commentary by politician-turned-columnist Ray L. Garland:

When we last left him—and that was more than two years ago—John W. Warner flirted with the national spotlight in his last-minute declaration against Judge Robert Bork for the U.S. Supreme Court.

At that time we said, "It wasn't Warner's vote against Bork that conservatives should mind so much—the cause was lost in any case—it was the odiousness of the company he joined." We stand by that. Whenever the likes of Ted Kennedy, Joe Biden and Alan Cranston are singing in an unholy choir of moral indignation, decent people should run—not walk—to the nearest exit. . . .

While the general public has long forgotten Warner's vote against Bork, it has stuck in the craw of some Republicans. But more as a symptom of the senator's persistent refusal to be a point man for the conservative agenda. . . . Still, Warner is now the Republican Party's sole surviving statewide officeholder, and criticism of him has been carefully muted. Repeated helpings of disappointment have served to curb the appetite of the Virginia GOP for such rash adventures as pulling the rug out from under their few remaining sure bets.[35]

Warner's winning margin in 1984 was surpassed in a modern, party-contested race only by Chuck Robb's landslide win over Republican Maurice A. Dawkins in the 1988 race to succeed retiring Senator Paul Trible.[36] Plagued in 1987 and 1988 by revelations about his private life that belied his straight-laced public persona—including news accounts of raucous party-going and socializing while governor with members of a Virginia Beach cocaine ring[37]—Robb likely would have faced a tough fight and might have foregone the race entirely if Trible had decided to seek re-election. But the anxious Trible was frustrated by the legislative process and its demands on his family, saw Robb as a formidable obstacle, and opted instead to position himself for a possible 1989 gubernatorial bid. After former Representative Caldwell Butler turned aside suggestions that he seek the seat and all others

---

[35]*Chesterfield Gazette*, May 3, 1990.

[36]A more lopsided outcome in a major-party contest had not occurred since 1934, when Senator Harry F. Byrd, Sr., received 76 percent of the vote against a token Republican opponent.

[37]See *The Richmond Times-Dispatch*, May 3, 1987; *The Virginian-Pilot and The Ledger-Star*, August 28, 1988; *The Washington Post*, August 31, 1988; *The Washington Times*, October 7, 1988.

The more serious allegations against Robb, including drug use and sexual misconduct while serving as governor, were not widely circulated until 1991, when Billy Franklin, a Virginia Beach private investigator, published the findings of his three-year investigation of Robb. See Billy Franklin and Judy Tull, *Tough Enough: The Cocaine Investigation of United States Senator Chuck Robb* (Virginia Beach, Va.: Broad Bay Publishing Co., Inc., 1991). Franklin's investigative services were engaged in 1988 by Richmond physician Lewis H. Williams, a long-time GOP activist and candidate for Congress in 1962. *Richmond Times-Dispatch*, May 17, 1991. Franklin's book and related publicity triggered a chain of damaging disclosures that brought an abrupt end to Robb's political aspirations.

thought to have even a remote prospect of success declined to take on Robb, delegates to the 1988 Republican convention in Roanoke turned to the symbolic, spirit-lifting candidacy of Dawkins, a conservative black evangelist who captivated the assembled party faithful with a podium-thumping, stem-winding oration. The 67-year-old Dawkins had led Republican "outreach" efforts aimed at recruiting blacks to the state GOP, and, as the first black Senate candidate of either major Virginia party, he presented Republicans with an opportunity to "make history" a year ahead of Douglas Wilder's expected gubernatorial bid. But his nomination soon generated more cynicism than goodwill as disclosures about the hapless Dawkins's disorganized business and political affairs quickly undermined his candidacy and prompted Republican officeholders, fundraisers, and workers to distance themselves from his campaign. When voters went to the polls on election day, many of them no doubt already viewed Robb as the incumbent, and they awarded the Democrat 71 percent of the vote. Among black voters, Robb scored an even greater 84 percent.[38]

In the contests for election to the U.S. House of Representatives during the 1980s, Virginia Democrats posted a net gain of one seat and closed the decade with control of five of the state's ten seats—their best share since 1968, and the same number of Democrats elected in 1974 in the immediate aftermath of the Watergate scandal. When the decade opened, the Virginia House delegation had a six-to-four Republican majority. The 1980 Reagan landslide boosted the GOP advantage to nine-to-one, but with the 1982 economic recession Republican congressional gains receded as well. In the lively post–redistricting contests in 1982, Democrat Frederick C. Boucher narrowly toppled veteran Republican incumbent William Wampler in the Ninth District; the GOP's Robert Daniel fell to wealthy businessman and state legislator Norman Sisisky in the heavily Democratic Fourth District; Democrat James R. Olin edged Republican Kevin G. Miller to capture the seat of retiring Sixth District GOP incumbent Caldwell Butler; and the sole Democratic incumbent, conservative Fifth District Representative W. C. "Dan" Daniel, ran unopposed. Republicans retained seats in the six other districts, with Eighth District incumbent Stan Parris narrowly staving off another bitter challenge from two-time foe Herbert Harris, and State Senator Herbert H. Bateman easily claiming the First District seat being vacated by the state's new U.S. senator, Paul Trible.[39]

From 1982 until 1990, no Virginia incumbent who sought re-election failed to win. The Seventh District's revered GOP congressman, 14-year veteran J. Kenneth Robinson, retired in 1984, and Democrat-turned-Republican D. French Slaughter, Jr., of Culpeper handily won the fall contest to keep

---

[38]The vote totals were: Robb (D) – 1,474,086 (71.2%); Dawkins (R) – 593,652 (28.7%). Sabato, *Virginia Votes 1987–1990*, chapter 3 (forthcoming).

[39]See Sabato, *Virginia Votes 1983–1986*, pp. 122–132.

the seat in GOP hands.[40] Two years later, the immensely popular G. William Whitehurst, an 18-year Republican congressional veteran, stepped aside in the Second District; Democrats then posted a gain when Virginia Beach Delegate Owen B. Pickett overcame Republican State Senator Joe Canada in a rancorous struggle for the seat.[41] The death of conservative Congressman Dan Daniel in the Fifth District in 1988 occasioned a special election that year in addition to the regular fall contest, and resort owner Lewis F. Payne, Jr., of Nelson County kept the seat in Democratic hands with a pair of surprisingly easy wins over GOP foes. The stalwart Daniel's death marked the end of an era: he was the last of the conservative Byrd men to serve in Congress as a Democrat. Interestingly, however, three GOP congressional incumbents at the close of the decade—Slaughter, Bateman, and Third District Representative Thomas J. Bliley, Jr.—were former Democratic officeholders. The only lifelong Republicans in the House of Representatives were the two northern Virginians elected with Reagan in 1980: Frank Wolf and Stan Parris.

Republicans opened the 1990s with still another setback as Parris, the dean of the Virginia congressional delegation, lost his seat in a bruising battle with Alexandria Mayor James P. Moran, Jr.[42] Moran's win in November 1990 gave Democrats their first majority of the state's Virginia congressional delegation in a quarter-century. Voter dissatisfaction with budgetary stalemate in Washington and an economy sliding into recession were the principal problems for Parris, but the Virginia GOP compounded its difficulties by failing to field opponents for any of the five incumbent Democratic congressmen.[43] Not since the days when the Republican Party was a tiny western enclave— before the onset of realignment—had the Virginia GOP failed so miserably to fulfill its responsibility to offer voters a choice. The transformation was striking: Ten years earlier, the GOP had won in nine of ten congressional districts; in 1990, Republicans prevailed in only four.

---

[40]After remaining independent for much of the '70s, during which he was a key Coalition leader, Slaughter became a Republican in 1980.

[41]Pickett won election in 1984 with a 49.5-percent plurality of the vote, and two years later he topped 60 percent in his bid for re-election. Interestingly, Pickett won both races with backing from his 1982 rival, Douglas Wilder, and massive support from black voters. Pickett, whom Wilder had accused of making anti-black remarks in 1982, garnered more than 85 percent of the black vote in his 1988 re-election bid despite facing a black Republican opponent, retired Army General Jerry Curry. Sabato, *Virginia Votes 1987-1990*, chapter 3 (forthcoming); see also Sabato, *Virginia Votes 1983-1986*, pp. 131, 135, 139-140.

[42]The vote totals were: Moran (D) – 88,475 (51.7%); Parris (R) – 76,367 (44.6%); Robert T. Murphy (I) – 5,958 (3.5%). See Sabato, *Virginia Votes 1987-1990*, chapter 6 (forthcoming).

[43]Democrats challenged each of the Republican incumbents and narrowly failed to pick up a second congressional seat. First District Congressman Herbert H. Bateman barely survived an unexpectedly strong bid by Democrat Andrew H. "Andy" Fox, a former television reporter, who ran his campaign on a shoestring budget. Bateman's 51 percent of the vote was his smallest share in five successful congressional races. Statewide, Republican candidates polled only 35.6 percent of the vote in contests for the House of Representatives—a showing worse even than in 1974, when the Watergate scandal produced a wave of strong anti-Republican sentiment in Virginia and nationally. Ibid.

The Gubernatorial Contests

Though the Reagan and Bush landslides and rough partisan parity in the congressional delegation seemed to belie denomination of the 1980s as Virginia's "Democratic decade," the contests for governor, lieutenant governor, and attorney general from 1981 to 1989 left no doubt as to the accuracy of that label. After the ground-breaking sweep by the Robb-Davis-Baliles trio in 1981, Chuck Robb's coalition, record, and endorsement combined with the allure of a history-making ticket to catapult moderate Attorney General Gerald L. Baliles to the governorship in 1985. Elected on

1981–1989 State Election Results[44]

1981 Governor	Charles Robb (D)	750,367	53.5%
	Marshall Coleman (R)	659,398	46.4%
1981 Lt. Governor	Richard Davis (D)	750,743	55.4%
	Nathan Miller (R)	602,714	44.5%
1981 Atty. General	Gerald Baliles (D)	682,410	51.0%
	Wyatt Durrette (R)	656,284	49.0%
1985 Governor	Gerald Baliles (D)	741,438	55.2%
	Wyatt Durrette (R)	601,652	44.8%
1985 Lt. Governor	Douglas Wilder (D)	685,329	51.8%
	John Chichester (R)	636,695	48.2%
1985 Atty. General	Mary Sue Terry (D)	814,808	61.4%
	W. R. "Buster" O'Brien	512,269	38.6%
1989 Governor	Douglas Wilder (D)	896,936	50.1%
	Marshall Coleman (R)	890,195	49.8%
1989 Lt. Governor	Donald Beyer (D)	934,377	54.1%
	Edwina P. "Eddy" Dalton (R)	791,360	45.8%
1989 Atty. General	Mary Sue Terry (D)	1,096,095	63.2%
	Joseph Benedetti (R)	638,124	36.8%

Baliles's "New Dominion" ticket were the first black Virginian and the first Virginia woman to win statewide office—veteran State Senator Douglas Wilder as the new lieutenant governor, and Delegate Mary Sue Terry of Patrick County as attorney general. An anticipated Wilder-Terry slugfest for the 1989 gubernatorial nomination was averted in March 1988 when Terry announced that she would seek re-election, and the pair was joined on the 1989 statewide Democratic ticket by northern Virginia auto dealer, party

[44]Official Election Results (1981, 1985, 1989), Virginia State Board of Elections. The vote totals are also contained in Larry Sabato's *Virginia Votes 1979–1982*, p. 59 (1981 elections), *Virginia Votes 1983–1986*, p. 64 (1985 elections), and *Virginia Votes 1987–1990*, chapter 5 (forthcoming)(1989 elections).

benefactor, and political novice Donald S. Beyer, Jr., the candidate for lieutenant governor. In the closest Virginia gubernatorial election of the twentieth century, Wilder reached his goal with a bare 6,741 votes to spare, and his runningmates posted easier wins to complete the third consecutive Democratic sweep.

The defeated statewide GOP candidates at decade's end included some who had been among the party's most popular and promising political figures as the '80s opened—Attorney General J. Marshall Coleman, former Delegate Wyatt B. Durrette, Jr., First Lady Eddy Dalton, State Senator Nathan Miller, Delegate W. R. "Buster" O'Brien of Virginia Beach, State Senator John H. Chichester of Stafford County, and Richmond attorney (and later state senator) Joseph B. Benedetti. In terms of ability, experience, integrity, creativity, and vision, the cadre of Republican contestants, like the phalanx of Democrats who bested them, encompassed both strong and weak, exceptional and ordinary. With a different twist here or a slight turn of events there, these Republicans could have been tapped to steer the Commonwealth through the '80s, and they doubtless would have provided a brand of moderate-conservative leadership not markedly different in thrust or tone from that of the Robb Democrats. But the breaks and the voters went the other way, and so did the Republicans' opportunities to lead state government for a decade.

One unexpected event with profound political repercussions was the death of former Governor John N. Dalton in July 1986, the victim of lung cancer that, after a period of remission, recurred suddenly in late 1985. Dalton was the last in a trio of GOP governors in the 1970s and easily the most broadly popular of the three in the 1980s. The son of Virginia's premier "Mr. Republican," Dalton was similarly esteemed by many GOP partisans of his own generation. As governor, he had emphasized party-building and had made the Virginia Republican Party synonymous with business-like, fiscally responsible management. "I tried to slow down the growth of government in those four years and to leave government . . . with the people having a higher percentage of their tax dollars than they had when I took office," the former governor recalled in a conversation with reporter James Latimer shortly before his death,

> and we were able to do that. We were also able to cut down the number of people employed by government as it relates to the total population of the state. I want to be remembered for those things.[45]

At a time when economic issues dominated political discourse, Dalton helped fashion a Republican image with broad appeal to the state's conservative-minded suburban voters.

Though Dalton as governor had presided over a Virginia GOP at the peak of its success, he was deeply disappointed by his failure to accomplish the elec-

---

[45]Conversations with James Latimer, "A Different Dominion: The Republican Renaissance," WCVE-TV, 1986.

tion of a Republican successor in 1981. He worked feverishly that year to reassemble the winning conservative coalition of the '70s, only to be thwarted by a surge of GOP factionalism and conservative defections. In 1985, with the campaign of Republican gubernatorial nominee Wyatt Durrette flagging in the contest's waning days, the former governor took to the hustings and tried gamely to reverse the momentum with sharp attacks on Democrat Gerald L. Baliles and his platform calling for new social spending. In the wake of the 1981 and 1985 Democratic sweeps, Dalton seemed to sense that he alone could rescue his strife-torn party. With close associates, he discussed leaving the comfortable and lucrative confines of his high-powered Richmond legal practice and returning to public life for a second bid for the governorship in 1989. But the recurrence of his illness in late 1985 suddenly gave Dalton's life a more urgent focus. With his untimely death, like Richard Obenshain's eight years earlier, and J. Sargeant Reynolds' seven years before that, the course of Virginia politics and the fortunes of the state's political parties took another unanticipated turn.[46] "Dalton had unique standing—as a feisty party-builder and as a statesman who played the peacemaker," wrote veteran political reporter Margie Fisher in a 1988 article canvassing the GOP's continuing woes. "No Republican has emerged to fill the leadership void left by [his] death."[47]

The Republican statewide losing streak in the 1980s cannot, however, be attributed to unkind dispensations of fate or inexplicable misfortune. Illuminated in hindsight, the tapestry of the Democratic decade is neither seamless nor patternless, but rather appears as the product of discernible threads woven—sometimes purposely and skillfully, sometimes haphazardly and ineptly—across the unique fabric that is political Virginia. As with any garment, the threads were connected and interrelated. There was the factional strife and internal disarray that crippled the Virginia GOP despite its seemingly ascendant position as the decade opened. There was state Republicans' inability to consummate and capitalize fully on the party realignment process, as reflected in the existence and eventual splintering of the Byrd organization remnant known euphemistically as the Coalition. There was the persistent cohesiveness of the Robb-Wilder coalition throughout the decade despite the intense centrifugal pressures applied to it by ideological differences, racial polarization, personal animosity, and conflicting ambitions. And, there was the Democrats' rapid acquisition in the '80s of financial backing and campaign technology comparable to the GOP's.

Behind these developments lurked demographic, economic, and social trends with major implications for Virginia politics. The continuing accelera-

---

[46]For a discussion of the similarities of Richard Obenshain and John Dalton and their contributions to Republican victories in the '70s, see the author's "Dalton Taught State GOP How to Win," *The Richmond News Leader*, September 19, 1986.

[47]*Roanoke Times & World-News*, June 10, 1988.

tion of the state's already rapid suburban growth—and the attendant increase in the proportion of younger, upper-middle class voters in the Virginia electorate—worked a subtle shift in voter attitudes and political focus during the '80s. The typical suburban voter held conservative views on economics and foreign policy, and tended to credit the Reagan administration for the notable advances made in those areas during the decade. Ironically, however, the sustained prosperity enjoyed nationally and in Virginia after 1982 advantaged the Robb Democrats in state elections; with disposable income rising steadily in the suburbs, and with state government inundated with new revenue, the preoccupying economic concerns of the '70s gave way to widespread satisfaction in the '80s. As the party of incumbency at the state level, Virginia's Democrats reaped the harvest of this general contentment and, with few exceptions, carefully avoided saying or doing anything that would conjure up recollections of Democratic tax-and-spend liberalism. Rather, as per capita income soared in Virginia in the '80s, Robb and his successors claimed it as their legacy. With the strong economy, Democrats had the best of both worlds—they touted Virginia's fiscal integrity and economic dynamism before conservative suburban audiences while dramatically increasing state spending to the applause of traditional Democratic constituency groups. In this way, the long-running Reagan recovery provided glue that helped hold the diverse Robb-Wilder coalition together. "Unfortunately for the Republicans," chortled Delegate Richard Cranwell, a Roanoke County Democrat and key legislative leader, "their President [did] too good a job."[48]

With suburban concerns about the administration of state fiscal affairs largely alleviated in the '80s, Democrats were free to concentrate on other issues and, specifically, to emphasize topics that would aggravate the tensions within the conservative coalition that had elected Republicans statewide in the '70s. There were, of course, a host of campaign issues—education, transportation, public safety, the environment—that were deemed important by suburban and other voters. But in two contexts especially—race relations and abortion policy—the attitudes of the younger voters in the suburbs tended to diverge markedly from those held by other pro-Reagan, pro-Republican voting blocs. The individualistic, libertarian impulse in the suburbs ran counter to the morality-driven majoritarianism of the GOP's New Right, and the progressive suburban sentiments on civil rights bore little resemblance to the rigid racial codes that echoed from the Byrd era and resonated from its surviving symbols in the Coalition. These issues, coupled with the youth-oriented themes of change and progress, were skillfully exploited by state Democrats to varying degrees in all three gubernatorial elections of the '80s. Their suburban strategy was a page out of the Ronald Reagan playbook: seize the future thematically; identify with the optimism of the young and the upwardly mobile; run against the "failed policies of the past." For the Reagan Republicans, the

---

[48]Yancey, p. 367.

key issues were economic growth and national security, and the foils were Jimmy Carter and the "evil empire."[49] For the Robb Democrats, the favorite topics were race and abortion, and the negative symbols were massive resistance and Moral Majority. As discussed more fully in Chapter 36, these issues largely accounted for the suburban tendency, most evident in northern Virginia, to back Republicans for national office and Democrats for statewide office during the '80s.

The explosive economic and population growth in northern Virginia, and to a lesser extent in Tidewater, worked a major shift in political influence—votes, campaign contributions, and issues—away from the traditional power centers of rural Virginia and the Richmond area during the 1980s. The state's population grew by more than 500,000 during the decade, and roughly half of the new voters in northern and southeastern Virginia were immigrants from other states. In addition, new campaign contributors—wealthy real estate developers, home and office builders, and high-tech businessmen—emerged to give those regions dramatically increased political clout. Though both parties by decade's end had recognized the magnitude of the change and were responding to it, Democrats managed to discern and capitalize on these trends throughout the '80s. Northern Virginia and Hampton Roads became the mainstays of Democratic campaign financing and electoral majorities in statewide contests from 1981 to 1989, notwithstanding the regions' growing prosperity and increasingly Republican orientation in national and state legislative elections. As these vote-rich suburban areas swung back and forth between Reagan-Bush Republicanism in Washington and Robb-Wilder Democracy in Richmond, it was apparent that state Democrats had captured the alluring themes and symbols that swayed the "new" Virginia. Especially in the Washington, D.C., suburbs, where voters rarely followed Virginia statehouse developments between elections and received most of their campaign images through the liberal lens of *The Washington Post*, the Democratic themes were reinforced throughout the '80s by sympathetic campaign news coverage.

These and lesser factors combined with the vagaries of electoral politics and the ephemeral impact of personalities to produce a decade of election outcomes in the Old Dominion lopsidedly favoring the Democrats. But there was more to it than that. Virginia did not change precipitously between 1980 and 1990; most of the notable demographic and economic trends had been underway for several decades. Nor was the state—contrary to the superficial suggestions of observers beyond the Commonwealth's borders—suddenly transformed with the ground-breaking election of Governor Douglas Wilder in 1989. The election of the first black and first female statewide officeholders

---

[49]Early in his administration, President Reagan branded the Soviet Union an "evil empire," and the label became a slogan for Reagan's dogged—and ultimately fruitful—rhetorical and geopolitical campaign against international communism.

in the '80s, like the election of the first Republican governor in 1969, were reflections of Virginia's gradual evolution from the monolithic politics of the all-white, all-male, all-Democratic Byrd organization to a more competitive and pluralistic political culture.

That dynamic culture made Virginia a national political pacesetter in the late twentieth century. The Commonwealth entered the 1980s in the vanguard of a conservative Republican reform movement that would sweep the nation and usher in an era of striking economic expansion and global democratization. Reaganism brought to national preeminence a libertarian conservative philosophy rooted in Jefferson's Virginia, defended through New Deal and Cold War by conservative stalwarts like Harry F. Byrd, Sr., and championed in recent times by none more fervently than Virginia's Richard Obenshain. Where the historic American experiment in freedom began in the eighteenth century, some of its most passionate and persistent advocates were found in the late twentieth century, and thus there was an undeniable link between the Commonwealth's contemporary conservatism and those most heartening and historic of spectacles around the globe in 1989: Jefferson's truths quoted in the shadow of Lenin, throughout Eastern Europe, and on the hallowed pavement of Tiananmen Square.[50]

As Virginia exited the decade, there was evidence of still more leadership, more history proceeding from the cradle of democracy. One of Jefferson's truths too often denied or neglected by his heirs—the principle of equality before the law—was being writ large before the quizzical gaze of a watchful nation. That Douglas Wilder's circuitous path to prominence featured an unusual number of ethical detours and philosophical wanderings was undeniable, but his success stood nevertheless as a testament to tenacity, temerity, the power of personality in politics, and, most of all, the triumph of individual attainment over group-based prejudgment. More than the breaking of a barrier, however, it was the mainstream message of the nation's first black governor that seemed to portend a historic achievement. For, if Douglas Wilder could match his intrepidity with integrity and proceed from symbolism to substance, his moderate-conservative call could sound the death knell of monolithic Democratic liberalism among black voters and thus signal the long overdue racial integration of American politics.

Those high hopes, like Wilder's nascent presidential ambitions, were quickly damaged, however, by his fiscally troubled governorship—he inherited

---

[50]The close of the 1980s brought historic changes in Eastern Europe, where communism quickly collapsed, and in the Soviet Union, where communism's economic premises were thoroughly refuted. Democratic reforms were adopted in much of Eastern Europe, and even the Soviet Union moved haltingly toward popular sovereignty. In China, totalitarianism and communism remained dominant only through a bloody crackdown on student-led dissent in Beijing's Tiananmen Square in June 1989. During this seemingly sudden triumph of American ideals in the communist bloc, it became commonplace for new political leaders throughout Eastern Europe and the Soviet Union—and revolutionaries in China—to invoke the writings and ideas of the American Founders, most notably Virginians Jefferson, Madison, and Mason.

a budget shortfall that snowballed to $2.1 billion during his first year in office— and by his highly destructive internecine conflict with Senator Chuck Robb, which gained national notoriety in mid-1991. Wilder also damaged his political standing by opposing the Persian Gulf War effort in December 1990, and by embracing federal civil rights legislation denounced by President George Bush as calculated to promote racial hiring quotas. With a 32-percent approval rating after only 18 months in office,[51] Wilder had earned the unfortunate distinction of being perhaps the least popular Virginia governor since Lord Dunmore fled to England in 1775. For a brief, shining moment at the turn of the decade, however, the grandson of slaves stood as a self-proclaimed "son of Virginia," his hand raised to take the oath as the Commonwealth's governor, and the political horizon seemingly open wide before him.

Though the shifting fortunes of the political parties in post-realignment Virginia occupied the attention of participants, analysts, reporters, and historians, such developments mattered little to the state's independent-minded voters. Indeed, it seemed at times that Virginians in general were less than enthused about the more predictable brand of politics that followed the tumultuous late '60s and early '70s. It was a distressing by-product of America's democratic experiment that, even in Virginia, satisfied citizens exercised at best casually and sporadically a franchise desperately sought over the centuries by peoples in every part of the world. And yet, for those who troubled themselves to look, there were more than slogans, slick advertisements and ambitious personalities hawking their wares to lethargic consumers. Behind the numbing ordinariness of politics in Virginia lurked the power of extraordinary ideas.

---

[51]*The Virginian-Pilot* and *The Ledger-Star,* June 18, 1991.

Chapter 35

Republican Strife and the Collapse of the Conservative Coalition

"We blew that election at the convention."[52]

Former Governor John N. Dalton,
referring to the 1981 GOP convention and
gubernatorial election

The race that would set the course for the '80s—the 1981 campaign for governor—effectively began on election night in 1977, when Chuck Robb and Marshall Coleman celebrated their victories and instantly became favorites for their respective party nominations for governor the next time around. Four years later, after Robb prevailed in what had been a close race throughout, aghast Republicans immediately placed the full burden of the loss on the shoulders of their defeated gubernatorial standard-bearer. Indeed, Coleman, the upstart who had stunned the establishment in 1977 by becoming the first GOP attorney general in Virginia history, was blamed not only for losing the governorship, but also for a Democratic sweep that unexpectedly overwhelmed favored Wyatt B. Durrette, Jr., in the race for attorney general. As the first unsuccessful Republican gubernatorial candidate in 16 years, Coleman could hardly have been surprised by the negative reaction, nor could he have hoped to avoid a share of responsibility for the loss. But the reasons for the stunning Democratic victories and GOP defeats in 1981 were far more complicated than most Virginia Republicans wished to acknowledge. And the simplistic GOP appraisals of the causes of the 1981 setbacks, with the facile indictment of Coleman, set the stage for repetition of many of the same mistakes throughout the 1980s.

A principal factor in the Republican losses in 1981 and thereafter was the party's failure to consolidate and institutionalize its gains of the 1970s. Even as the GOP was compiling an unsurpassed winning streak in state elections, it was failing to convert its financial supporters in the business community and the influential pillars of the state's conservative establishment into Republican Party loyalists who would be committed to building a durable political organization and to fighting their struggles from within. The conservative coalition that dominated Virginia politics from 1972 until 1980 depended in

---

[52]*Richmond Times-Dispatch*, May 27, 1984.

each election upon the galvanizing presence of a threat from the Left. In the staunch liberalism of the national Democratic Party and the menacing populism of Henry Howell were ample incentives for conservative coalescence, but, when Virginia Democrats offered the reasonable and attractive Robb, the glue was gone. Without a long-term, institutional commitment to the GOP as their political vehicle, many of the older conservatives who comprised the Coalition fell back upon their traditional Democratic Party predilections and their network of Democratic friends and associates in the courthouses and legislature. Others made their electoral choices from year to year based upon the personality of the candidates, their own perceived political or business interests, non-ideological policy goals, and other factors specific to individual contests. Party loyalty was the farthest thing from their minds.

The realignment process of the '70s left Virginia with a Republican Party anchored to the right of center and a Democratic Party grounded to the left—an alignment consistent with the national political arrangement. For the Republicans, that development was good news, because Virginia was and remains a conservative-leaning state. The bad news was that, because so many conservative leaders, contributors, and voters staked out an independent position and refrained from Republican affiliation and identification, Virginia Democrats retained a marked advantage in any statewide race in which philosophical differences between the candidates were not pronounced. In this substantially dealigned environment, a Democratic candidate whose base among blacks, labor, and liberals was secure, and who could retain traditional Democratic backing in rural Virginia, needed to garner only a respectable share—not even a majority—of the suburban vote in order to gain election. In 1981, Chuck Robb was well positioned to accomplish exactly that.

Republicans had several options for responding to such a situation, though none guaranteed success. They could continue to pursue the conservative coalition strategy, and attempt to give each race an ideological focus by emphasizing Virginia Democrats' ties to their liberal national party and by developing issues that would motivate conservatives. Or, they could adopt an approach similar to Coleman's successful 1977 strategy, which enabled him to hold the Republican base and to offset Democratic inroads among rural and suburban independents by targeting specific Democratic constituency groups, such as blacks and organized labor. A third option—one that combined elements of the other two and paved a middle course between them—was to take a moderate-conservative tack overall and to direct an innovative, issue-oriented appeal to the suburbs emphasizing largely non-ideological concerns such as transportation, education, and public safety.

Not surprisingly, Marshall Coleman's moderate Republican supporters hoped that he would adopt one of the latter two courses in his race against Chuck Robb. Commenting in 1980, former Governor Linwood Holton observed that the Robb-led Democrats "are going to have a strong ticket next year," and added, "We're going to have to appeal pretty broadly to win, and I suspect that Marshall Coleman will. There we will get a chance to see not just the Obenshain elements of the [Republican] coalition, but the Obenshain *and Holton* elements of that coalition."[53] Coleman's campaign manager and trusted adviser, Anson Franklin, concurred in the need for a broad-based campaign, but one that would emphasize his candidate's appealing, conservative stands on fiscal and criminal justice issues. "Every campaign is a battle for the middle," Franklin noted in 1980.

> I think you always need to retain the capability of appealing to a broad base of people. This is a conservative state, so you are not exactly talking about going off into left field to appeal to a majority of voters. If you look at Dick Obenshain's [Senate campaign after he won the nomination], you will find that, while he had a campaign based on conservative principle, he realized that you have to appeal to a lot of people who may not be as conservative as some others.[54]

A moderate-conservative campaign stressing practical problem-solving—particularly on issues of importance in the state's fast-growing metropolitan areas—was the course with which Coleman himself was most comfortable. "There are terrific responsibilities the state has," he told political writer Garrett Epps in summarizing his goals for the governorship. "[State government is] the natural protector[ ] of the people against violence. We need to educate the young people, maintain a transportation system. All these things are not war-and-peace issues, but they're extremely important—and I think they are going to be where the action is in the '80s."[55]

With the GOP having won elections in Virginia for a decade by mobilizing conservatives, however, there was broad agreement in Republican ranks that assembling a conservative coalition was again the way to win in 1981. Robb had to be painted as a liberal, or at least as an expedient and unreliable captive of the liberal interests dominant in his party; Coleman had to tout his conservative views and connections and again unite the Right. No one was more fully committed to that strategy than the man who became Coleman's mentor, Governor John Dalton. Though generally regarded as more moderate in outlook than Obenshain, Godwin, and the Coalitionists, the thoroughly Republican chief executive shared the widespread view that GOP candidates won in Virginia by being perceived as more conservative than their Democratic foes. Successfully running to the right meant making common cause with the influential conservative Democratic and independent political and business leaders who generally took their cues from ex-Democrats Godwin and Byrd. The strategy had worked before, and most in the GOP understandably assumed that it would work again.

---

[53]Holton interview.
[54]Anson Franklin interview, June 4, 1980, and September 17, 1984.
[55]Epps, "As Virginia Goes . . .," p. 13.

Moreover, Dalton and the Republican leadership—including Coleman—recognized that the liberal and black votes garnered by Linwood Holton in his 1969 gubernatorial bid and by Coleman in his successful 1977 campaign were primarily protest votes cast *against* the Democratic candidates in those races. In 1969, disappointed Howell backers had bolted the party to "nail the coffin shut" on the Byrd organization.[56] In 1977, liberal defections were produced mainly by recollections of Democrat Edward Lane's support, however ancient and perfunctory, for massive resistance. No comparable circumstances beneficial to the Republicans existed in 1981. In a race against Robb, the Great Society scion and nominee of a Virginia Democratic Party united for survival, a Republican would have little prospect of siphoning enough left-leaning Democratic votes to make a difference. Though Robb actually thought himself to be most vulnerable to a Coleman strategy designed to challenge him on his left flank,[57] the GOP consensus was that the route to an electoral majority was to Robb's right.

There was only one major problem with the conservative coalition strategy in 1981: it called for convincing voters that Coleman was significantly more conservative than Robb, and a lot of Coalitionists and more than a few Republican regulars simply did not believe this was true. Coleman's legislative record had been generally conservative, but his support for civil rights, consumer measures, and environmental initiatives had rankled General Assembly hard-liners. Even more important, his aggressive style and biting, often taunting, partisan rhetoric had infuriated Democratic legislators, especially senior members like Senate kingpin Edward E. Willey of Richmond. A product of Waynesboro and Staunton, Coleman's roots in the traditionally moderate and anti-Byrd Republicanism of the western region also engendered suspicion. But his biggest liabilities had accrued in 1977, when he overcame the Obenshain faction's Durrette to win the GOP nomination for attorney general and then outflanked Coalition favorite Lane in the general election.

To Coleman and his campaign manager, the candidate's conservative credentials were authentic, and impressions to the contrary were products of misfortune and misperception. "I felt strongly that Marshall was a victim of circumstances," offered Anson Franklin.

He ran against the Obenshain wing, and Wyatt [Durrette] automatically was anointed as the conservative candidate irrespective of issues. [And many concluded] that Marshall could not be as conservative as Durrette because he was not endorsed by the Obenshain group. Then he ran against Ed Lane; he beat Main Street's boy. . . . And so there has been a sort of word-of-mouth campaign in the business community that he is [not

---

[56]Eisenberg, "Two-Party Politics," p. 79.
[57]Robb interview.

conservative enough]. It is not so much Marshall's positions on issues, but it is the image he's gotten by virtue of whom he has run against.[58] Coleman's critics countered that, though the choice of opponents was not within his control, his choice of tactics certainly was. In his campaigns against both Durrette and Lane, they charged, Coleman had assailed his foes unfairly.

"One of the substantial difficulties that Coleman ran into [in 1981] was the kind of campaign that he had run against Ed Lane," recalled former Governor Godwin, a Lane backer.

Ed Lane had been a staunch [Byrd] organization man; he had supported the organization in season and out. And Coleman saw fit to attack him rather bitterly about his involvement in the [massive resistance] legislation during the integration crisis, which had long passed. Most of our friends felt that it was not an issue and should not be an issue. I think a lot of conservative voters who were not Republicans felt that it was an unfair tactic . . ., and that Coleman did it for the purpose of attracting to his candidacy the more liberal elements of the voting patterns in Virginia.[59]

"When Marshall decided on his strategy for attorney general and sought the endorsement of the [Virginia Education Association] and the Crusade [for Voters] and said that they should support him because Ed Lane had been for massive resistance . . ., he was really attacking Mills Godwin and Roy Smith just as much as Ed Lane," observed Governor Dalton. "They were part of it, and I can't help but think that as the years went by people who were associated with that back in the '50s felt that Marshall in effect was attacking them, too."[60]

The ill feeling toward Coleman among the elder Coalition members was compounded by several developments that occurred after he took office as attorney general in 1978. With Coleman's encouragement, Governor Dalton agreed to a settlement of the state's dispute with the federal Department of Health, Education and Welfare (HEW) over the desegregation of Virginia's public institutions of higher education. Governor Godwin had taken a firm stand against the Carter administration's insistence upon inclusion of numerical mixing goals that he deemed tantamount to racial quotas, and Dalton had endorsed his predecessor's position on numerous occasions during the 1977 gubernatorial campaign. But, early in the new governor's term, Coleman and state Education Secretary Wade Gilley negotiated a compromise that averted protracted litigation and, while containing significant new ameliorative language, nevertheless included race-based numerical enrollment goals. Dalton's embrace of the settlement appeared to be a Coleman-engineered reversal of a solemn campaign pledge, and it greatly annoyed Godwin, former Delegate Roy Smith, and other prominent Coalition figures.

---

[58]Franklin interview.

[59]Godwin interview.

[60]John Dalton interview.

In the view of both Coleman and Dalton, avoiding further court battles over integration was important for the images of the state and the GOP. The settlement, as one commentator noted in 1981, "moved the [Republican] party away from Old South racial intransigence into a posture that stresses economics instead of race. The effect may be the same, but the emotional content is far different—and Dalton's conservatism is more palatable to the suburbanites who increasingly form the party's base."[61] To key Coalitionists, however, the compromise with HEW was just one more indication that Marshall Coleman was not their kind of conservative.

As if he had not already antagonized the old Byrd establishment sufficiently, Coleman as attorney general took an administrative step early in his term that also had profoundly negative, though apparently unintended, consequences within the Coalition. The first attorney general of his party in the state's history, Coleman more or less perfunctorily replaced most of the private practitioners with whom his office previously had contracted for legal services related to highway condemnation proceedings, and he awarded the lucrative work to suitable Republican attorneys around the state. The dismissed Democrats and independents included numerous members of the courthouse cliques that comprised the Coalition, and among them were backers of Dalton's gubernatorial bid and several friends, allies, and even a former law partner of Mills Godwin. Judy Peachee, a frequent GOP intermediary to Godwin and the Coalitionists in earlier campaigns, described the repercussions of the Coleman move:

> The Coalition really is two parts. There's the financial part that is epitomized by Smith Ferebee and the [Main Street] people. And then there is the grass-roots part . . ., those people who are the community leaders who pass the word on the local level and actually produce the votes. In replacing those attorneys in counties and cities around Virginia, Marshall went to the infrastructure [of the Coalition]. And so when the infrastructure started feeding back to the finance people that they were not going to go along with Marshall—that they did not like him because of what he had done on the grass-roots level—then the money people started splitting.[62]

Had Coleman realized the adverse reaction that his action would cause, he likely would have refrained; with Governor Dalton's help and encouragement, he was intent upon repairing his strained relations with the Main Street financiers and Coalition leaders. But Coleman the outsider really did not understand how the nebulous Coalition functioned, nor was he aware of the important network of personal relationships that would be affected by his decision. He was, he thought, merely dispensing patronage in the manner of any good partisan. And, having learned from the patronage-related mistakes of the first Virginia GOP governor in modern times, the first Republican

---

[61]Epps, "As Virginia Goes . . .," p. 9.
[62]Peachee interview.

attorney general did not intend to disappoint his supporters or give his party cause for complaint by failing to bestow the spoils of office on the deserving. The primary effect of the action, however, was to reinforce the perception of Coleman as a fiercely partisan Republican. "There was certainly nothing wrong with him being that way if he chose to," remarked Godwin, "but it did not endear him to those people who were not Republicans. It had a very negative impact" on the attitudes of conservative Democrats and independents around the state.[63] It also contributed to an early realization by Godwin that "the Coalition as we had known it in years previous to that was just not going to come together in a united manner" behind Marshall Coleman in 1981. To Governor Dalton, Godwin issued the pointed warning in late 1978 that a collapse of the GOP's winning conservative coalition loomed unless decisive action was taken.[64]

Dalton and Coleman labored mightily in 1979 and 1980 to turn the situation around. Numerous personal visits to key business leaders on Richmond's Main Street and a series of private conclaves involving Coleman, Dalton, and a group of 30–40 top Coalitionists from around the state produced limited success. Some key Republican-leaning conservatives, such as prominent benefactor Lawrence Lewis, Jr., were persuaded to back the conciliatory young attorney general, but others remained skeptical. As the inevitability of a Coalition split over the Coleman-Robb choice became increasingly apparent, Godwin and others began to explore options for a viable alternative candidate for governor—either a different Republican who could capture the party's nod, or someone who could mount a successful bid as an Independent in a three-way race. Meanwhile, in Republican Party circles, doubts among GOP conservatives regarding Coleman's political philosophy, lingering resentment over his 1977 campaign against Durrette, and concern about a splintering of the Coalition also produced talk of possible rival candidates for the gubernatorial nomination.

The potential alternatives to Coleman were numerous. High on the recruiters' wish list was Seventh District Congressman J. Kenneth Robinson and his predecessor, John O. Marsh, Jr., the Democrat who had switched parties and served as a cabinet-level advisor to President Ford. Both were earnestly and repeatedly entreated by prominent Republicans and Coalitionists, and both politely but firmly declined. Other Republicans whose names were bandied about by gubernatorial candidate-seekers at various times between 1978 and 1980 included party chief George McMath, Sixth District Congressman Caldwell Butler, First District Congressman Paul Trible, State Senator Herbert Bateman of Newport News, former Fairfax Delegate Durrette, recent GOP convert Thomas T. "Tom" Byrd, Hampden-Sydney

---

[63]Godwin interview.
[64]Ibid.

College President Josiah Bunting, former Congressman Stan Parris, and Delegate Raymond R. "Andy" Guest of Front Royal. Though several entertained fleeting thoughts of taking on the challenge, all ultimately came to the same conclusion: defeating Coleman at a GOP convention would be exceedingly difficult if not impossible.

While some conservative Republicans and GOP-leaning Coalitionists scoured the landscape in search of a candidate who could derail Coleman's prospective nomination, other independents and Democrat-leaning Coalition figures pondered possibilities for recruiting a Democrat to run for governor as an Independent. Though infinitely more appealing to this group than Henry Howell, Chuck Robb was hardly a favorite of the Byrd Democrats. He had actively courted the Main Street givers and especially the conservatives in the Democratic courthouses during his tenure as lieutenant governor, but, as with Coleman's overtures, Robb's efforts had generated little genuine enthusiasm for his candidacy. Except for the long-shot prospect that Harry F. Byrd, Jr., could be enticed into entering the race, the Democrat-leaning Coalitionists pinned their hopes mostly on conservative State Senator Elmon Gray of Waverly. In January 1981, veteran political reporter James Latimer disclosed the behind-the-scenes maneuvering for a Gray bid and provided this insight from an unnamed Coalition pol:

> Some people feel that Coleman and Robb are two peas in a pod, very much alike—that, as George Wallace used to say, there's not a dime's worth of difference between them. Elmon offers a distinct alternative that makes him attractive to a lot of us—more of us, in fact, than I had expected.[65]

A few weeks after Latimer's article appeared, however, Gray announced that he would not enter the race. Unmentioned but certainly factors in his decision were the results of a private poll showing him far behind Coleman and Robb, and concerns that Henry Howell might jump into the fray and make it a foursome if Gray moved to make it a three-way race.

Except for Gray's possible independent bid, there never was much of a chance that the 1981 gubernatorial contest would feature anyone other than Coleman and Robb. In fending off rivals within the GOP, Coleman had numerous advantages, including his well-known skills as a candidate, an intensely loyal personal following among Republicans, and his status as the presumptive nominee by virtue of his statewide post. But Coleman's biggest advantage came in the person of Governor Dalton. "John Dalton made it clear from the very first day of his administration that his candidate for the gubernatorial nomination in 1981 was Marshall Coleman," recalled Stan Parris. "Marshall had worked very hard at going around and solidifying the support

---

[65]*Richmond Times-Dispatch*, January 4, 1981.

that he had, and John Dalton was his campaign manager. That was a pretty tough combination."[66] Dalton later explained:

There were some people who did not want Marshall Coleman to be the candidate, but you look back at the history of Virginia politics and you find that most of the people who have been governor had either been lieutenant governor or attorney general. Those had been the stepping stones, and very seldom had a party denied the nomination to someone who had been in one of those roles. I became convinced that, with Marshall Coleman having been the only Republican ever to win an attorney general's race, the party was not going to say to Marshall in 1981, "You won—you've been one of only two people in the twentieth century who got elected to one of the two [lesser statewide offices]—but we're going to deny you the nomination for governor." It just wasn't in the cards. So then the question was, how do you go about bringing [the Coalition] to the table?[67]

Dalton understood that uniting the Coalition behind Coleman would require more than courting its key leaders and emphasizing conservative policy positions of importance to them, though both of these steps were necessary. The GOP had to construct a ticket on which the former Byrd Democrats had representation. The Coalition elders were not and probably never would be fond of Marshall Coleman, but Dalton and other GOP leaders were betting that most of the independent-minded conservatives would grin and bear Coleman's candidacy for governor if they had reason for enthusiasm about the Republican nominees for lieutenant governor and attorney general. "[The Coalition] might be willing to tolerate four years of Coleman," ventured Judy Peachee in 1980, "if they think they can get eight good years after that."[68] Wyatt Durrette, the consensus Republican candidate for attorney general, was held in high regard by Mills Godwin, Roy Smith, and other key Coalition leaders. And, until late 1980, it appeared that Tom Byrd, the senator's son, had a good shot at winning the party's nod for lieutenant governor. A Coleman-Byrd-Durrette ticket would pull together the mountain-valley Republicans, Byrd Democrats and GOP conservatives, thus reassembling the conservative coalition that had elected three Republican governors in a row.

The Coleman-Byrd-Durrette trio seemed like a dream ticket to many Republicans and was much discussed in 1979 and 1980. The youthful Byrd—he was 32 years old when Senator John Warner presented him to the GOP central committee as a Republican convert in 1979—would be a first-time candidate, but his familial and political ties made him invaluable to Coleman, and the party's coalition-minded leaders, including Dalton, Godwin, and party chief Cramer, were ready to back him for lieutenant governor. The 1977 GOP

---

[66]Parris interview.

[67]John Dalton interview.

[68]Peachee interview.

convention had shown, however, that Republican regulars would not follow the party leadership blindly. By 1980, it was clear that substantial segments of the Virginia Republican Party again had ideas of their own. State Senator Nathan Miller of Bridgewater made known his intention to seek the second spot on the ticket, and former Delegate Guy O. Farley, Jr., a Warrenton lawyer and ex-Democrat with ties to Jerry Falwell and Moral Majority, was making thinly veiled moves in that direction. A three-way split—one that would expose the party's treacherous factional fault lines—lay ahead.

Miller's candidacy for lieutenant governor had been expected for some time. His underdog bid for the U.S. Senate nomination in 1978 had been widely interpreted as the precursor of a more serious statewide effort, probably in 1981. But the 1978 venture—and specifically Miller's refusal to withdraw from that contest for five ballots—had badly damaged his relations with the party's dominant Obenshain faction. He therefore positioned himself in 1981 as the moderate, mountain-valley prospect for the lieutenant governor nomination. Not since Linwood Holton's hand-picked contender, George Shafran, received the nod for lieutenant governor in 1971 had a candidate presented himself unabashedly as the moderate alternative and prevailed at a GOP convention. But Miller's base was in the western region; he had inadvertently forfeited much of his conservative backing at the 1978 convention; and his only hope was to be the beneficiary of a conservative split.

In contrast to Miller's long-expected bid, Farley's candidacy for lieutenant governor would have been totally unpredictable as late as 1979. A three-term Democratic member of the House of Delegates in the '60s and an unsuccessful candidate for that party's nomination for attorney general in 1969, Farley had dropped out of sight politically for almost a decade. He attended the 1978 GOP convention as an Obenshain delegate, and in 1980 he became a prominent spokesman for the Reagan campaign in Virginia. A passionate foe of abortion and the Equal Rights Amendment (ERA), Farley's sharp-edged rhetoric stressed moral values and the conservative social agenda championed by the New Right. Though he was not a member of Moral Majority, Farley's religious ardor and political agenda resembled that organization's, and its leadership included many of his friends and associates. Those ties earned him both support and intense opposition among Republican regulars. Most important, however, Farley had the backing of Ronald Reagan's Virginia coordinator, John Alderson, who used the presidential campaign to position the former Fairfax delegate for a run for lieutenant governor.

Since the death of Richard Obenshain, Alderson had been a key player in the infighting that divided the once-dominant and cohesive Obenshain faction. Aligned with him were some of the party's most resolute conservatives, including GOP National Committeeman William Stanhagen, Vice Chairman Hugh Mulligan, and a number of Virginia Republicans with ties to the various northern Virginia-based, nationally oriented conservative political action committees that supplied the New Right's fundraising and organizational muscle. A veteran party operative with a keen mind, a stern gaze, and a penchant for assigning ideological import to his personal view on almost any issue, Alderson made little effort to mask his contempt for those in the old Obenshain group who had made peace with John Warner and in other ways had permitted malignant "pragmatism" to divert the GOP from its conservative mission. A number of prominent party activists felt similarly, and many other conservatives around the state rallied behind Alderson's leadership out of a shared resentment towards the influential Republicans in the Richmond area and their apparent leader, Judy Peachee.

Peachee's influence stemmed not only from her prominence in the Third District GOP, which regularly delivered large and often decisive margins for Republican statewide candidates, but also from her ties to Governor Godwin, fundraiser Smith Ferebee, and—through them—the Coalition and its financial base along Richmond's Main Street. As John Dalton came to identify increasingly with the Richmond-based business community, he, too, found himself working closely with the energetic national committeewoman. As a key managerial figure in the campaigns of Godwin, Dalton, Obenshain, and Warner, Peachee's credentials were more than adequate to qualify her as a top party leader, and she seldom missed an opportunity to parlay her positions and Coalition connections into ever-greater political clout. Her effectiveness won her admirers in Republican circles around the state, but her often manipulative methods and domineering demeanor produced at least an equal number of critics. No one in the latter category was more adamant, nor more intent upon breaking her grip on the GOP, than Alderson.

When it came time for the Reagan campaign to organize in Virginia for the 1980 election, the former California governor's operatives turned again to the Obenshain group, which had produced a Virginia delegation majority for Reagan in 1976. They found Helen Obenshain and a handful of others supportive, but many from the 1976 team, including Peachee, were unwilling to commit themselves during the early going. As an aide to Senator Warner, Peachee had in Warner's neutrality a ready excuse for her similar public posture, and, with Godwin, Dalton, and Main Street divided on the presidential race, she was not eager to take sides. Alderson, however, was not reluctant, and he was tapped early to coordinate the Reagan campaign in Virginia. The assignment provided the Botetourt County GOP veteran with the vehicle he needed to build his own conservative political organization in the state—one that could challenge the party power structure centered in Richmond.

Guy Farley, who volunteered in 1979 to travel around the state at his own expense as a spokesman for Reagan, had designs on public office that dovetailed nicely with Alderson's ambitions for party power. Alderson designated him as a "Special Coordinator" for the Reagan campaign, gave him choice speaking assignments, and saw to it that the Warrenton lawyer had the opportunity to play a prominent role in the drafting of the party platform at the national GOP convention in Detroit. Once the 1980 election was behind, Alderson's Reagan staff and much of the statewide Reagan organization appointed by him immediately switched hats and began work on Farley's campaign for lieutenant governor.

The stage thus was set in November 1980 for a fractious nomination battle featuring the party's three contending factions and their favored candidates: Nathan Miller for the party's traditional, moderate wing; Guy Farley for the New Right and the conservative forces aligned with Alderson; and Tom Byrd for the party's Richmond-based leadership, the Godwin-led Coalition, and the Main Street financial establishment. Shortly after the November election, however, the youthful Byrd stunned his supporters and rivals alike with the announcement that he would forego the race for a variety of unspecified personal and political reasons. There was immediate speculation, never confirmed, that the sudden withdrawal was prompted by Senator Harry Byrd, Jr., and motivated by continuing unease among Byrd's followers over Coleman's candidacy for governor. Some surmised that the Coalition was preparing to mount an independent gubernatorial effort in support of State Senator Gray. Regardless of the reason, the younger Byrd's bombshell left Dalton, Coleman, Peachee, and other senior party strategists in a quandary; neither Farley nor Miller enjoyed particular favor in the Coalition grass-roots or in the business community where Coleman needed help.

For a short while it appeared that Byrd's exit would leave Farley as the lone candidate for lieutenant governor from the party's conservative wing. Indeed, many fence-sitting conservative GOP activists signed on in support of Farley once Byrd dropped out, assuming—erroneously—that he and Miller would be the only contenders. But Farley's New Right agenda and emphasis on recruiting religious fundamentalists and evangelicals into the GOP were sources of consternation among many Republican regulars, Coalition members, and business leaders. Conservative in their views on economic, fiscal, business, and labor policy and national issues such as defense and foreign affairs, many of these partisans and independents had little interest in promoting a conservative social agenda emphasizing matters of morality such as abortion restrictions. There were also tactical concerns that such an agenda would adversely affect GOP fortunes in the vote-rich suburbs, where younger voters tended to be more libertarian in their outlooks. By 1981, polls showed that Jerry Falwell and his Moral Majority organization were extremely unpopular among the suburban voters who comprised a crucial element of the Republican base. The inherent tension between the principal precepts of the Reagan Revolution—cultural conservatism and anti-government libertarianism—was evident in the Virginia GOP, and it combined with personal rivalries to ensure division among Republican conservatives in 1981.

The most likely new entrant in the race for the lieutenant governor nomination after Byrd's withdrawal was State Senator Herbert H. Bateman, a former Democrat and Godwin ally who had switched parties in 1976 and was widely touted as a potential statewide candidate. Recognizing this, Alderson and other Farley backers made a last-ditch effort to persuade Bateman to challenge Coleman for the gubernatorial nomination; such a decision would gain them an entry in the governor's race, remove the imperative of a Coalition favorite for lieutenant governor, and give Farley an easy one-on-one contest against Miller for the second spot on the ticket. Bateman entertained the suggestion and publicly acknowledged in December 1980 that he was being urged to run for governor, but he concluded after little more than a week's deliberation that such a late-blooming challenge to Coleman would be futile. With encouragement from Governor Dalton and others eager to enhance the Coleman ticket's appeal to the Coalition, Bateman then announced in mid-January that he would enter the contest for lieutenant governor.

What ensued was an exceedingly bitter fray dominated by Bateman and Farley, with Miller avoiding most of the acrimony while his clever operatives privately egged on the conservative antagonists. As hotly contested mass meetings were held in cities and counties across the state, partisans of the rival conservative candidates and their feuding factions engaged in the political equivalent of no-holds-barred guerrilla warfare. The Bateman camp seized upon Farley's ties to the fundamentalist and evangelical Christian community and stoked party regulars' fears of a "Moral Majority takeover" of the state GOP, while the Farley forces cultivated grass-roots Republican resentment toward Bateman as the hand-picked candidate of the overbearing Richmond-based party leadership—"Main Street, the Third District, the Coalition, those anointed from On High to direct the unwashed masses," as Alderson sarcastically described them.[69] While their respective operatives were busy sullying each other, Bateman and Farley managed to stress a few positive themes. Positioned somewhere between his two opponents on the GOP's narrow philosophical spectrum, the Newport News senator emphasized his mainstream conservatism and the geographical balance that would be supplied by his inclusion on the ticket. With a head-start and an organizational edge, frontrunner Farley played up his leadership role in the Reagan campaign and his desire to be the point man for reform-minded conservatism at the state level.

Nathan Miller was in a strange position. Much of his support had been soft—motivated by fear of Farley, Falwell, and the New Right more than enthusiasm for his own candidacy—and Bateman's last-minute entry into the race produced immediate erosion. Not only was Governor Dalton quietly encouraging Republicans to back Bateman, but no less inveterate a Valley moderate than Sixth District Congressman Caldwell Butler also signed on with the Coalition favorite. Moreover, the GOP moderates who stayed with Miller were generally understood to prefer Bateman as their second choice over the more caustically conservative Farley. Nevertheless, as the competition played itself out during the spring months, Miller, Farley, and their

---

[69] Alderson interview.

respective campaign staffs found themselves increasingly pushed toward an alliance. "The thing that began to develop," recalled John Alderson, "was Farley and Miller against Bateman, Farley and Miller against Main Street, Farley and Miller against the party hierarchy, Farley and Miller against massa in the manor house."[70] Long antagonistic toward Mills Godwin and the Byrd Democrats who had wielded immense clout in the GOP for nearly a decade, Republican moderates now discovered that some of the most hard-core conservatives in the party shared their resentment. The stage was set for a very peculiar state convention and what reporter Buster Carico would later describe as the "Saturday Night Massacre" of the party leadership.[71]

When the Republican convention delegates gathered in Virginia Beach on June 5, Marshall Coleman and Wyatt Durrette knew that their spots at the top and bottom of the party's ticket would be awarded without contest, and, while publicly neutral, both hoped that Herbert Bateman would be joining them when the proceedings were concluded. Guy Farley arrived at the conclave with the support of a plurality of delegates and with barely concealed fury at Bateman and the party establishment for thwarting his efforts to convert that plurality into a majority. The Bateman and Miller camps both claimed second-place status, but, as the first ballot tally would confirm, it was the Bateman operatives who had the more credible vote count.

The proceedings included a symbolic display of unity that momentarily masked the most bitterly divisive assemblage of Republicans in Virginia history. Following the unanimous selection of Coleman as the party's gubernatorial nominee, the standard-bearer was joined on stage by the trio of Republicans who had borne the banner before him—Holton, Godwin, and Dalton. The significance of the moment was inescapable; Mills Godwin's embrace of Coleman, however reluctant, was something many never expected to witness. But none present could have imagined then that John Dalton would not live long enough to see another Republican occupy the governor's mansion, or that Linwood Holton would not support another Republican nominee for governor for at least a decade. The show of unity was merely a welcome respite from the fighting and seeming confirmation that the party would soon reunite its warring factions and win again.

The balloting in the contest for lieutenant governor began—and almost ended—as the pro-Bateman party leadership had hoped. With 1,690 delegate votes needed to win the nomination, Farley led narrowly on the first ballot with 1,195; Bateman was next with 1,162; and Miller had 993. The frontrunner's momentum was sapped by Bateman's strong second-place showing, and on the next two ballots, Miller's total declined as several hundred of the moderate's backers shifted into the Bateman camp. The Newport News senator garnered 1,461 votes on the third ballot; Farley's total inched upward to 1,236; and

---

[70]Ibid.
[71]*Roanoke Times*, June 8, 1981.

Miller, his collapse accelerating, dropped to 652. The trend was clear, and as the balloting got underway for the fourth time, it was apparent that Bateman's nomination was imminent. It was for that reason that many of Bateman's supporters, including Governor Godwin, were delighted to hear convention chairman Joe Canada interrupt the proceedings and recognize Guy Farley for the purpose of making a concession and withdrawal statement.

Farley, bowing to the inevitable, did indeed withdraw. But instead of moving that Bateman be crowned the nominee by acclamation, as many in the hall expected, he urged his delegates to vote according to the dictates of their consciences. The rancor between the Bateman and Farley camps was known to all, and it took no translation to discern what Farley meant. As stunned Bateman operatives watched helplessly, Nathan Miller's previously wavering delegates promptly reverted to his camp, and the Valley candidate's supporters went to work consoling impassioned Farley delegates and supplying them with Miller lapel stickers and posters. Whole blocs of Farley supporters soon were switching to the Bridgewater senator, their intense disappointment now turned to angry defiance of the party elders. Having breached proper procedure by interrupting the fourth ballot to permit Farley to speak, convention chairman Canada next compounded the error by instructing that the balloting be started anew. "It astounded me that Joe Canada stopped the ballot and then said that we had to start all over when most of the delegations had already voted," recalled Dalton. "He should have kept calling the roll, and if he had done that Bateman would have been the nominee."[72] However innocent, Canada's action proved decisive in the convention's outcome. The votes cast prior to Farley's exodus were voided; the fourth ballot proceeded afresh over the irate but futile objections of the now-outnumbered Bateman backers; and Miller won the nomination. The final tally at approximately 9:00 p.m. on Saturday evening gave Miller 1,744 votes to Bateman's 1,541 and Farley's 30.

Farley's controversial withdrawal came despite the adamant objections of his campaign chief, John Alderson, and it embarrassed prominent GOP conservatives like National Committeewoman Helen Obenshain and Committeeman William Stanhagen, who had lent him their endorsement but strongly preferred Bateman over Miller. Though charges of a "deal" between Farley and Miller and/or their respective campaign operatives abounded after the balloting, the sketchy allegation was never supported.[73] Nevertheless, the Warrenton Republican's motives were unmistakable. Farley withdrew "believing that such a withdrawal would in fact benefit Miller," Alderson said flatly, adding that his candidate "had an uncanny grasp of the psychology and person-

---

[72]John Dalton interview.

[73]Charles Lihn interview, September 28, 1984. Lihn, who with campaign chief Randolf Hinaman masterminded Bateman's nearly successful bid, expressed confidence that the shift of Farley delegates to Miller was driven by emotion rather than instruction.

ality of that convention."[74] A majority of Farley delegates switched to Miller on the fourth ballot because of "a stupid resentment at Bateman for being so strong," commented an angry former Congressman Joel Broyhill, himself a Farley supporter. "To burn down the whole barn because you do not get your way is no way to build a party. . . . It was one of the most distasteful things I had witnessed in the party in many years."[75] In helping Miller forge what one reporter on the scene described as a "raucous, anti-establishment coalition of party moderates, Reaganite conservatives and Christian fundamentalists,"[76] Farley had paid back Bateman, Dalton, Godwin and the GOP leadership for what he viewed—not without some justification—as an unprecedented and often mean-spirited campaign to stop him.

When the dust settled after the tumultuous Virginia Beach battle, several developments with lasting implications for the GOP were discernible, and none of them were conducive to winning elections. Confronted by the first significant influx of conservative Christian activists into state Republican Party processes, GOP regulars had given the newcomers the kind of greeting normally reserved for lepers. Worse still, the pro-Bateman forces had exaggerated and exploited fears of a party-wrecking Moral Majority epidemic in order to rally the faithful against Farley. To be sure, the ambitious—and, to some, ominous—pronouncements of Falwell and his Moral Majority officials during the previous year had contributed to takeover concerns. But the exceedingly hostile reception accorded the many well-meaning, conservative-thinking novices who had been attracted to Republican activism by Ronald Reagan's social agenda hardly foreshadowed harmonious assimilation and GOP growth in the years to follow.

A second consequence of the acrimonious 1981 nomination battle was creation of an enduring and extremely counterproductive factional breach within the state GOP. What had begun as resentment and rivalry among Obenshain's top lieutenants following his death became, after the Bateman-Farley contest, a deep and personal antagonism. The hostility would constitute a nearly insurmountable impediment to party consensus and unity for years to come. Long-time friends and allies had been forced to choose sides in the fight over the lieutenant governor nomination, and two intractable factions had been created where there had been a single dominant conservative group only a few years before. Though each camp had a cluster of influential activists rather than a single leader, one faction generally followed John Alderson's cue, while the other tended to look to Judy Peachee for direction. The former aligned itself with the New Right and the newly energized conservative Christian activists; the latter identified and cooperated with the Coalition and the Main Street business community. The former touted the grass-roots

---

[74]Alderson interview.
[75]Broyhill interview.
[76]Dale Eisman, *Richmond Times-Dispatch*, June 7, 1981.

political organization assembled during the Reagan campaign as its indispensable contribution to the Republican cause at election time; the latter cited its
business community ties and ability to fill campaign money coffers as justification for its clout in party affairs. Neither conservative faction commanded a
majority of votes on the GOP central committee, and thus neither could
control or direct party affairs without backing from some other quarter.

This circumstance in turn gave rise to a third major development: the
emergence of the party's long-declining moderate wing as an influential and
potentially decisive arbiter of disputes between the two more conservative
factions. For a time it appeared that Republican moderates' disdain for the
New Right agenda and their fears of a Moral Majority takeover would force
the mountain-valley partisans into an alliance with the Richmond-based
conservative establishment. Indeed, Congressman Caldwell Butler's embrace
of Bateman and the drift of Miller delegates to the Newport News legislator at
the Virginia Beach convention indicated such an alignment. But Miller's eventual nomination with the support of a large bloc of Farley's New Right followers suggested another possible combination for GOP hegemony: an
anti-Richmond, anti-Byrd, anti-Main Street coalition. The ambitious
Alderson had just such a pragmatic arrangement in mind when he commented
in 1984 that his conservative allies in the GOP stood to gain from cooperation
with "the disaffected moderates who have always had a suspicion of Richmond
and those with the plantation owner's mentality that they know what is best for
the party."[77] "There are some who believe," added a grinning Alderson, that
such an alignment could be "the way of the future."

Using the independent-minded Coalition and wealthy Richmond-based
business community as whipping boys to rally resentful Republican regulars
may well have been a way to power and influence for Alderson and frustrated
GOP moderates, but it was not a strategy calculated to help finance Republican campaigns or to forge winning right-of-center coalitions in statewide elections. Of all the adverse implications of the 1981 convention fight, none was
more damaging than the message that the developments in Virginia Beach
sent to the conservative non-Republicans around the state who had been an
indispensable component of GOP wins in the '70s. "We blew [the 1981 guber-
natorial] election at the convention," declared John Dalton in a 1984 interview, contending that Bateman had been the key to Coalition support for the
Coleman ticket. He explained:

> There was no question in my mind that [the former Democrats'] main
> interest was in Herb Bateman. But this is what the average old-line
> Republican doesn't realize, some of them still don't—that you've got to
> have that [Coalition] element. That element has made a significant move;
> they've left the Democratic Party, come into the Republican Party and
> brought people with them, and they like to be represented. Their main

---

[77]Alderson interview.

interest in that convention was Herb Bateman, who was one of them. And we in effect said to them: "We don't need you; we'll do it alone."[78] Agreed Ninth District Congressman William C. Wampler: "That was the beginning of the demise right there—the feeling caused by the convention among those who were necessary to put together the kind of coalition that could win that election."[79]

Not only had the GOP nominated a ticket that included three lifelong Republicans, two of whom were from the Shenandoah Valley and the Holton wing of the Republican Party, but the convention delegates had expressly, and angrily, repudiated the party leadership's coalition-building strategy. In a mailing to the delegates a few weeks before the June convention, Nathan Miller had moved to capitalize on Republican regulars' ill will toward the Godwin-led Coalition and Main Street financial establishment. He wrote:

> While some former Democrats have joined our party, other wealthy ones choose to remain Democrats but act as "power brokers" and exercise anointment, or at least veto power, in selecting the Republican statewide candidates. . . . The power brokers want to use the Republican Party for their own purposes—to endorse occasionally, refuse to endorse at other times, and use the threat of lack of endorsement as a whip to keep us all in line.
>
> That is what this race is about. If I am the nominee I intend to try to build the party, *from within*, free of deals and solely responsible to its members . . .[80]

Former Governor Holton echoed the theme in his nominating speech for Miller at the convention; the Bridgewater senator deserved the delegates' support, he intoned, because Miller was the only "real Republican" in the race. Alderson and other Farley backers similarly incited Republican regulars with sharp attacks on the alleged "plantation owner's mentality" of Godwin and the part-time party loyalty of the Main Street benefactors who, they charged, were forever trying to impose their will on the GOP. For a Virginia Republican Party that had reconciled itself only grudgingly to the practical imperative of cooperation with the Byrd Democrats in the '70s, such emotional appeals fell on fertile ground. It was unsurprising, then, that when the votes were tallied and Bateman had been rejected in an orgy of resentment, Mills Godwin strode out of the Virginia Beach Pavilion, got into his car, and drove home. He could take a hint, and so could his Coalition friends.

Godwin had pledged before the convention that he would back the GOP ticket, and he proceeded to support Coleman, Miller, and Durrette despite his ambivalence about the gubernatorial nominee and his dismay over the convention developments. Interestingly, when Miller was beset later in the

---

[78]*Richmond Times-Dispatch*, May 27, 1984.

[79]Wampler interview.

[80]Copy on file with the author (emphasis in original).

summer by charges that he had violated legislative conflict-of-interest strictures, the former governor was among the first who publicly came to his
defense. And, when Coleman was locked in an apparently close duel with
Robb in October, Godwin heeded a request from President Reagan and delivered a much-publicized Richmond speech designed to rally conservatives
behind the Republican nominee. But, such displays of loyalty aside, there was
no concealing the lack of enthusiasm and intensity on the part of the former
governor and the Coalitionists who stuck with the GOP ticket. The best argument for Coalition solidarity behind Coleman and his runningmates was that,
over the long term, Virginia would benefit from a continuing realignment of
conservatives with the GOP. But the inescapable message from Virginia Beach
was that the cocky, partisan Republicans no longer were interested in sharing
power with the ex-Byrd men.

During the competition for the second position on the Coleman ticket,
the Farley and Miller camps had scoffed at assertions by Dalton and others
that the GOP needed to nominate Bateman in order to win in November. The
Coalition, argued Bateman's detractors, was little more than a political dino-
saur slipping into irrelevance and destined for extinction. The influence of the
aging Byrdites was on the wane, they contended; the Virginia electorate had
become reliably Republican in its political attachments, and the presence of
Reagan in the White House would assure realignment's continued advance.
There was, of course, more than a little truth in the contention that the Byrd
alumni and their followers were increasing in age and declining in influence as
a new generation of voters, immigrants from other states, and residents of the
Commonwealth's swelling suburbs came to comprise a larger share of the
electorate. But, in the context of the 1981 elections, the Coalition was as
important as ever—probably more so—and the GOP faithful's failure to
understand that fact sealed the ignominious fate of the party's ticket.

Having privately decided to back Robb over Coleman, Coalition leader
Roy Smith was spurred to even greater levels of activity by the turn of events at
the GOP convention. He organized a "Virginians for Robb" organization that
was far more visible and active than the corresponding Coalition effort on
Coleman's behalf, and during the fall campaign he played a critical role in
bolstering Robb's conservative credentials and impugning Coleman's. Though
Smith denied that Bateman's presence on the Republican ticket would have
changed his course in the governor's race, Dalton was convinced otherwise,
and Godwin asserted that Smith likely would have assumed a much less prominent role in the Robb effort out of concern for the ancillary impact his activities might have on the campaigns of Bateman and Durrette, whom he
favored.[81] "Roy was a catalyst for the rallying of the Coalition toward Robb,"
Godwin explained. The GOP's failure to nominate Bateman "enabled [Smith]

---

[81]Smith, John Dalton, Godwin interviews.

and a whole lot of people, particularly in eastern Virginia, to become active for Robb who might not have been so active."[82]

Smith and the conservative "Virginians for Robb" were indispensable to Chuck Robb in 1981, not only in raising campaign money in the business community, but also in providing a cloak of conservative authenticity, vouching for his fiscal responsibility, and confirming the outsider's fitness for acceptance into polite Virginia society. Only a few years into his gubernatorial term, virtually all suspicion that Robb was secretly a carpetbagging liberal had been dispelled, but in 1981 he labored with the considerable political handicaps of being Lyndon Johnson's son-in-law, a member of Jimmy Carter's political party, and, perhaps most damaging of all, the successor to Henry Howell. "The very fact that Roy Smith and a number of other very credible people in the establishment community would support me," explained Robb later, "relieved me of the burden of Henry Howell."[83] Once committed to the Democrat, the indubitably conservative former House Appropriations Committee chairman from Petersburg accepted and ably executed the task of convincing Virginians that Robb would not tax and spend the Commonwealth into a Massachusetts-style mess.

Moreover, Smith and his "Virginians" group were ideally positioned to cast doubt on the sincerity of Coleman's conservative pitch. They had supplied nearly uninterrupted and seemingly automatic support to Republican candidates in Virginia for nearly a decade; consequently, when they refused to back Coleman, voters naturally inferred that something was wrong with the GOP nominee. "While Robb stayed comfortably above the hatchet work, and behaved becomingly gubernatorial," wrote Roanoke's Ray Garland,

> his campaign apparatus brilliantly kept Coleman off-balance and on the defensive throughout. Building on nervousness and uncertainty over Coleman within the GOP hierarchy itself, the Robbites skillfully planted seeds of doubt as to his general character and fitness for high office among those Virginians susceptible to such subtle messages. The point man in this process of demolition was none other than the redoubtable W. Roy Smith of Petersburg—the High Sachem of Southside and co-chairman of "Virginians for Robb."[84]

An unrelenting barrage of Smith-led attacks on the Republican standard-bearer throughout the fall helped to drive home the impression that Coleman was not the conservative that he and his promoters claimed.

Predictably, Coleman and the GOP spent much of the fall campaign endeavoring to counter the Democratic and "Virginians for Robb" assaults with conservative pronouncements and pledges of fidelity to Ronald Reagan. But, the more the Republican camp protested, the more doubts seemed to

---

[82]Godwin interview.

[83]Robb interview.

[84]*Roanoke Times & World-News*, July 25, 1985.

grow. Worse still, the raging battle on Coleman's sagging right flank gave Robb a largely uncontested field in seeking votes on the left and in the middle. Preoccupied with reinforcing the candidate's base among conservative Republicans and independents, the Coleman campaign never succeeded in penetrating the less ideological suburban consciousness with a positive message about what a new Republican administration would do to combat crime, enhance education, and alleviate mounting transportation pressures. With Roy Smith and his followers successfully foiling the conservative coalition strategy on which the GOP campaign had pinned all of its hopes, the outcome of the contest was scarcely in doubt. "In retrospect," commented Mills Godwin in 1984, "Marshall Coleman really never did have a chance to win that election because he just could not corral enough support outside of the Republican Party to do it."[85]

The Coalition split in the Coleman-Robb race was a watershed in Virginia's political realignment. Until then, the Coalition generally had been viewed by both political analysts and participants as a transition mechanism—a convenient stopover on the way to eventual moderate-conservative solidarity within an expanded Virginia Republican Party. But, with the split in 1981, the realignment process was derailed for the first time since the mid-1970s. Many business leaders who during the '70s had doubted that they ever would support another Democratic statewide candidate found themselves regularly backing Robb and other Democratic moderates in the '80s. The state's once-influential conservative symbols—pillars of the Byrd establishment like Godwin, Smith, and Harry Byrd, Jr.—saw the gradual diminution of their political clout quicken as their grass-roots constituency splintered. After 1981, candidates of both parties ritually drafted and distributed lists of respected "Virginians," but the impact of such public relations gestures had become slight. Emulating Robb's winning formula, Democrats continued to position themselves in the moderate-conservative Virginia mainstream. And, with voters alternately endorsing Reaganism at the national level and Robbism in Richmond, the electorate's tendency to shun partisan ties and ignore partisan cues was regularly reinforced.

The factional divisions that had thwarted Republican coalition-building efforts in 1981 continued to debilitate the party for most of the decade. In 1982, Paul Trible's Senate campaign was almost doomed by widespread discontent among conservative party regulars after he broke with his allies in the Alderson faction and, in a bid to solidify Coalition support, tapped Judy Peachee to manage his campaign. At the 1984 GOP convention, party factions warred over the choice of a successor to retiring Republican National Committeewoman Helen Obenshain, and over William Stanhagen's bid for an unprecedented fourth term as national committeeman. In a series of contests during the decade for open seats in Republican-leaning congressional districts,

---

[85]Godwin interview.

wounded GOP candidates emerged from acrimonious nomination battles to achieve only mixed success in general election races against centrist Democratic rivals. In 1980, former Democrat Thomas J. Bliley, Jr., won a spirited contest for the Republican nomination in the Third District and coasted to victory in the fall; and, in the 1984 race to succeed retiring Seventh District Congressman J. Kenneth Robinson, Coalition favorite D. French Slaughter, Jr., won a similarly impressive November victory after overcoming Guy Farley in a rancorous nomination fight. In the Sixth District, however, a bitter contest for the Republican nod followed Congressman Caldwell Butler's 1982 retirement decision, and Democrat James R. Olin capitalized on the division to win the general election. Similarly, in 1988, Democrat L. F. Payne, Jr., won the race for the seat of deceased Fifth District incumbent Dan Daniel after a fractious Republican nomination struggle. In local party affairs, too, the factional infighting frequently damaged GOP fortunes. In two of the largest and most heavily Republican units in the state—Fairfax County and Chesterfield County—a near-perpetual state of factional combat existed during the '80s. All of that friction and infighting paled, however, in comparison to the strife that afflicted the GOP and its gubernatorial ticket in 1985.

Having excluded the Godwin-led Byrd faction from their 1981 ticket, Republicans proceeded to err at the opposite extreme four years later by fielding a ticket that appeared hand-picked by Mills Godwin and Roy Smith from top to bottom. Completely without representation on the 1985 slate headed by former Delegate Wyatt Durrette, newly of Chesterfield County, was any candidate with ties to the moderate mountain-valley faction of the Republican Party. With early public endorsements from Godwin and Smith, Durrette successfully quashed a gubernatorial boomlet in the Richmond-based business community for Roanoke's Caldwell Butler. Then, in the contest for the second spot on the 1985 ticket, forces aligned with Durrette overcame a comeback-minded Marshall Coleman and, in another bitterly contested convention fight, gave the nomination to State Senator John Chichester of Fredericksburg. Chichester, a former Democrat with ties to Godwin, won the nomination for lieutenant governor on the fourth ballot by besting a field that included—besides Coleman—New Right fundraiser Richard Viguerie of Arlington, Staunton Delegate and former House Minority Leader A. R. "Pete" Giesen, and the inspirational black evangelist, Maurice Dawkins. Rounding out the Republican trio as the candidate for attorney general was W. R. "Buster" O'Brien, a former football star for the University of Richmond and a popular member of the House of Delegates from Virginia Beach.

Tailor-made to satisfy the Coalitionists, the 1985 Republican ticket excluded not only the party's western moderates, but also the Alderson-led New Right conservative faction. Fresh off another organization-building stint as chairman of Ronald Reagan's 1984 re-election campaign in Virginia, Alderson and GOP National Committeeman William Stanhagen had hoped to repeat Nathan Miller's 1981 feat by forging another anti-Richmond coalition—this time behind the gubernatorial candidacy of Eighth District Congressman Stan Parris. Durrette's 1983 relocation of residence from Fairfax to Chesterfield, his very visible backing from former Governor Godwin, and his close political ties to the controversial Judy Peachee all supplied reason to think the Alderson-Stanhagen plan could work. Moreover, Durrette's back-to-back losses in 1977 and 1981 had dimmed the glow of his once-brilliant star, and Parris had financial supporters in prosperous northern Virginia who were prepared to bankroll an all-out bid for the gubernatorial nod. But the popular Durrette's long labors and broad personal following in the GOP enabled him to surmount the party's factional lines, and his record as an anti-abortion legislative leader as far back as the early '70s enabled him to garner significant support in the nomination contest from the increasingly influential conservative churches across the state. Once again, the Virginia GOP in the spring of 1985 was the scene of bruising, hand-to-hand combat as the Durrette and Parris forces met in a long-running series of vitriolic mass meetings and district conventions. The simultaneous sparring in the race for lieutenant governor only served to multiply the infighting and magnify the intrigue.

In early May, Parris appraised his delegate count, conceded defeat, and withdrew from the race. His once-promising effort had never recovered the credibility it lost in a bizarre February incident, when his campaign staff gave the news media a copy of a letter purportedly written by Durrette finance chairman Smith Ferebee. In the letter, later established to be a forgery, the irascible Coalition fundraiser made it clear to business leaders that the conservative Christian activists assisting Durrette's nomination campaign would have no influence in a Durrette administration. For those familiar with Ferebee, the letter had a ring of plausibility, and to Parris's handlers it seemed the perfect device to drive a wedge between Durrette's business community backers and New Right supporters. The only flaw was that Ferebee never wrote it, and, being renowned for nothing so much as candor, protested his innocence convincingly. The Machiavellian hand that penned the phony missive was never publicly confirmed. And, though the letter had been released to the news media by Parris's staff and consultants in contravention of the candidate's instructions, Parris neither apologized nor took disciplinary action against any of his workers.

If the 1981 nomination contests gave birth to a new generation of GOP factionalism, the 1985 clashes saw the disharmony reach devastating maturity. When the Durrette-Chichester-O'Brien team emerged from the party's tumultuous Norfolk convention and turned its attention to the fall contest, it quickly began to reap the harvest sown in the spring as dissatisfaction and division turned to highly publicized discord and disloyalty. Assuming incorrectly that Durrette's immense personal popularity and a near-universal Republican desire to recapture the governor's mansion would mend the tears in party unity, the nominee's handlers—chief among them Judy Peachee—declined to

extend an olive branch to the vanquished partisans. Even with the most conciliatory of overtures, however, it is unlikely that the consuming, cresting desire
for retribution would have been quelled.

It was a cruel twist of fate that the faction-ridden GOP should sink to its
modern nadir with Wyatt Durrette at the helm. A staunch Republican loyalist,
intelligent and articulate, ever reluctant to return the blows of his GOP foes,
philosophically motivated, reform-minded, and bent on broadening the party's
base by adding converts, Durrette deserved better than he received in 1985.
More than any other person, he was, by temperament, conviction, and
capacity, the natural successor to the deceased Obenshain as Republican
leader. But for a handful of votes at the 1977 GOP state convention, he would
have been the party's nominee for attorney general that year and its heir-
apparent for governor in 1981. And, but for the strange turn of events at the
1981 GOP convention, which sent a debilitated Republican ticket into the fall
campaign, he likely would have been elected attorney general that year and
would have been well-positioned for a gubernatorial bid in 1985. But those
opportunities had eluded him, and in 1985 the twice-defeated Durrette
entered the contest as the nominee of a pathetic party riddled with internecine
conflict. From without his campaign and even from within, Republican friends
and foes alike placed personal agendas and old scores ahead of the electoral
objective.

In the first open breach of party loyalty in a decade, Parris campaign policy
chief Joel W. Harris led a small group of angry GOP dissidents in announcing
formation of a "Republicans for Baliles" organization. Though few partisans
followed the controversial operative's lead, Harris complemented his public
relations ploy with subterranean assistance to the Democratic camp in the
form of "opposition research"—services deemed sufficiently important to
earn the ex-Republican a subsequent appointment as Lieutenant Governor
Douglas Wilder's counselor and de facto chief of staff. While others in the
Parris camp did not openly repudiate Durrette and his ticket, newspaper
reports regularly featured anonymous Republican sniping at the GOP
campaign and leaks of important Durrette data, including crucial polling,
financial, and media advertising information. On several occasions, the staff of
Democrat Gerald Baliles was so well informed about planned Durrette
thrusts that it was able to issue rebuttals and to unleash counterattacks almost
simultaneously with the Republican's volleys. A key Baliles decision to invest
all available funds in a late August advertising blitz apparently was made after
leaks revealed that the GOP campaign lacked the financial resources to
respond quickly. As the contest drew to a close, even the most sensitive deliberations and debates within the inner councils of the Durrette campaign were
being replayed in the newspapers, as top advisors Judy Peachee and Edward
DeBolt waged an increasingly bitter and public duel over campaign strategy.
The anonymous criticism and leaks were so numerous and so varied—
campaign officials even had a private investigative firm search for electronic

listening devices—that attempts to isolate the sources were futile, and the compromising disclosures virtually immobilized the Durrette campaign.

Though Harris's "Republicans for Baliles" group was the only open breach of party loyalty, even more damaging to the GOP cause in 1985 was the deafening silence and threatened defection of former Governor Linwood Holton, the brooding personification of mountain-valley Republicanism. Long keenly interested in the progress of race relations in Virginia, Holton hoped for a Democratic victory in Douglas Wilder's ground-breaking contest for lieutenant governor, and he suspected that Mills Godwin and the Byrd men would mount a racially tinged campaign to thwart Wilder's bid. For that reason, he declined to support the Republican ticket and went even a step further—threatening privately to endorse the Democrats if the GOP campaign included racial appeals. A racial moderate himself, Durrette made it clear to Holton that he would brook no such tactic. Moreover, Holton's presumptuous injunction overlooked the fact that the Durrette camp already had ample incentive to avoid any real or seeming play on racial passions because of the immense negative reaction that such a ploy inevitably would provoke among the younger, suburban voters who were the key to the election. Indeed, it was the desire to give the Durrette ticket a more progressive hue and broader appeal that motivated the persistent GOP efforts to enlist Holton's active and visible support. But the former governor steadfastly refused to help, thereby exacerbating the estrangement of party moderates and the perception of the GOP ticket as a Byrd-era relic.

Ironically, Holton's price for assisting Durrette—he offered to break his silence and back the GOP standard-bearer if Durrette would issue a public remonstration of Godwin and the Byrd organization[86]—was stiffer than Holton himself had been willing to pay in 1969, when the Big Stone Gap native managed to overcome his moral reservations and accept indispensable campaign funding from the Byrd establishment. In 1985, Holton obviously relished his self-ascribed role as guardian of Republican virtue on matters racial, and he thus put the racially progressive Durrette to a Hobson's Choice. That fact was not lost on most party regulars or members of the news media, who generally saw Holton's non-support of the GOP ticket less as a stand on principle than as an act of revenge against those who had undermined his position as Republican leader a decade earlier. Twenty years after his gubernatorial duel with then-Democrat Mills Godwin, an embittered Linwood Holton was still fighting his old crusade against the Byrd organization. Even his life-long commitment to a two-party system in Virginia was sacrificed to settling that old score.

After the acrimonious and divisive GOP conventions in 1977, 1981, and 1985, and the back-to-back Democratic statewide sweeps in the first half of the '80s, a number of prominent Republican activists concluded that the party

---

[86]Holton interview.

might fare better in 1989 if it nominated its statewide slate by primary election rather than convention. It had been four decades since the Virginia GOP last experimented with a gubernatorial primary, and fewer had gone to the polls in that 1949 contest than had attended the party's 1978 and 1985 state conventions as delegates and alternates. Moreover, Democrats had experienced a reversal of their sagging fortunes in Virginia after abandoning primaries in favor of conventions in the late '70s. Nevertheless, the sentiment for change among Republicans was strong, and it was reinforced by the political interests of two candidates for the 1989 GOP nomination for governor, former Senator Paul Trible and Congressman Stan Parris. Both Trible and Parris believed their prospects for nomination would be enhanced in a primary because the third candidate in the field, former Attorney General Marshall Coleman, enjoyed broad and deep support among the activists likely to decide the nomination in a convention setting.[87] In opposing the primary, Coleman's backers and a few others on the party's central committee argued accurately, though unsuccessfully, that a primary contest would damage the party's general election prospects by draining precious campaign funds from GOP benefactors and applying them toward television ads critical of the party's eventual nominee.

Though Coleman and his supporters did not prevail when the GOP central committee selected the gubernatorial nominating method in December 1988, the former attorney general scored a stunning upset victory in the June 13 primary.[88] Coleman's aggressive primary campaign stressed his detailed policy initiatives, especially proposals to combat crime and illegal drugs, and his extensive state government experience. As reporter Margaret Edds explained, "Through a discouraging decade for the state GOP, [Coleman] had been the party's vigilant intellectual voice,"[89] and many Republicans came to believe that his knowledge of state issues and his debating skills would be the best match for Wilder's. Coleman also capitalized on doubts about his opponents stemming principally from Trible's abrupt retirement from the Senate and Parris's seeming preoccupation with federal rather than state issues— Coleman's television ads attacking the frontrunning Trible were particularly scathing and effective. Perhaps most important, the primary victor's campaign featured a sophisticated voter identification and turnout program that maximized his ballot total on election day.

---

[87]The nomination struggle began as a four-way contest, but Delegate Andy Guest of Front Royal, the Republican leader in the House of Delegates, dropped out in March, some three months before the June 13 primary. The lesser-known Guest had favored nomination by convention because of his belief that the convention delegates might turn to him as a compromise choice.

[88]The vote totals were: Coleman – 147,941 (36.8%); Trible – 141,120 (35.1%); Parris – 112,826 (28.1%). Larry J. Sabato, "Virginia Governor's Race, 1989 (Part 1: The Nomination Stage)," *University of Virginia News Letter* (Charlottesville: Center for Public Service, University of Virginia), July 1989, p. 76.

[89]Edds, p. 64.

While the outcome surprised most observers, the primary otherwise bore out the predictions of both its advocates and its opponents. Though the GOP trio waged an intense struggle over many months, the battle was fought mostly over the airwaves and through the mail, and it produced little of the bitter personal animosity generated among Republican regulars during the rough-and-tumble 1977, 1981, and 1985 convention fights. Yet, the primary contest also produced many of the damaging side-effects that convention proponents had feared. Coleman spent $3.4 million to secure his victory—the three contestants together spent $10 million—and the Republican nominee entered the general election campaign against the well-funded Douglas Wilder with a $900,000 deficit. Moreover, while Wilder had been carefully crafting a positive, upbeat image as the standard-bearer of a united Democratic Party, Coleman had been tarnished by the heated spring exchanges. The costly three-way battle for the 1989 GOP nomination prompted inevitable comparisons to the Democrats' divisive 1969 primary and runoff, which set the stage for the election of Virginia's first Republican governor since Reconstruction. Without the fierce spring 1989 clash for the GOP nomination, it is doubtful that Wilder would have eked out his narrow, history-making victory in November.

Riddled with multifarious factional divisions throughout the '80s, the Republican Party was held together during much of the decade by its state chairman, Roanoke attorney Donald W. Huffman. A conservative Republican veteran, Huffman had been active in the Virginia GOP since he left the Democratic Party to join the Goldwater movement in 1964. During the early 1970s, he led conservative insurgents in the Sixth District in challenging the moderate party leadership of Linwood Holton, and strongly backed Richard Obenshain's successful bid for the GOP state chairmanship in 1972. Though he was no favorite of the party's mountain-valley wing, Huffman had refrained from taking sides when the dominant Obenshain group split in the early '80s, and he thus enjoyed the respect and confidence of the party's two warring conservative factions. As a result, when Alfred Cramer resigned the party chairmanship in 1983 under fire because of the party's impoverished condition, the affable Roanoke lawyer was drafted as a non-factional, compromise choice to succeed him. Huffman was re-elected to the post in 1984 and again in 1988, with party combatants urging him to stay on each time in order to avoid a debilitating factional battle on the eve of a gubernatorial election.

Though Huffman's tenure brought electoral gains only in the state legislature, his long-running chairmanship—and the determined efforts of his hand-picked executive director, veteran Ohio GOP operative Joe Elton—produced significant enhancement of the party's fundraising and get-out-the-vote capabilities. During the early '80s, the party's widely touted technological and organizational expertise had slipped, and financial woes had combined with political setbacks to accelerate the decline. In 1985, Huffman and Elton acted to regain the lost resources and momentum by establishing the party's first permanent telephone marketing center. In the ensuing five years, the telemarketing program increased the number of party donors from 8,000 to 56,000, and facilitated identification of party and candidate preferences among potential voters, thus aiding efforts to get GOP sympathizers to the polls on election day. Coupled with enhanced in-house computer capacity and applications, the program enabled the state GOP to provide crucial services to Republican candidates and local party committees.

Marshall Coleman's primary and general election campaigns in 1989 also pushed GOP campaign technology and organization to a new level of proficiency. Under the direction of Michael E. Thomas of Chesterfield, the Coleman campaign's organizational wizard, more than 520,000 voters favoring Coleman were identified during the general election campaign, and more than 200,000 favorable and undecided households received follow-up communications by telephone or by mail during the autumn contest. Even with his narrow defeat, Coleman's vote total on November 7 approached one million and dwarfed previous statewide GOP performances. Ironically, despite a string of statewide electoral reverses, the Virginia Republican Party by decade's end was among the most technically advanced political organizations in the country.

It also was apparent at the close of the decade that the Republican Party's ruinous factionalism had significantly subsided. While the 1989 GOP primary contest hardly had a unifying effect, the allegiances it generated did not correspond to the factional divisions that had hampered the party for much of the '80s. Trible, Coleman, and Parris each sought and received varying degrees of support from Republican suburbanites, conservative Christian activists, the New Right, the GOP's mountain-valley wing, and partisans previously aligned with Main Street and the Coalition. Reflecting the growing political influence of northern Virginia and Hampton Roads, each candidate raised substantial funds from real estate developers and other business interests outside the Richmond area. A salutary effect of the new, cross-cutting alignments produced in 1989 was to render the old factional divisions largely obsolete. That development—coupled with a growing recognition among chastened GOP regulars that the party's statewide candidates in the '80s had been hobbled by acrimonious nomination fights—created strong grass-roots sentiment for party unity.

Nevertheless, the Virginia GOP exited the '80s in much the same way it entered them: without a clear sense of direction or a leadership consensus. Throughout the decade, Party Chairman Donald Huffman played an indispensable role as honest broker for the feuding GOP camps, but he seldom mustered the clout to provide direction to the troubled party. By 1990, successive electoral defeats and financial mismanagement at the state Republican headquarters had shaken confidence even in Huffman, though he clung to the chairmanship for want of an acceptable successor. Senator John Warner, the GOP's sole surviving statewide officeholder, remained detached from the party apparatus. A conciliator first and foremost, Warner campaigned frequently for GOP candidates but made little attempt to mask his disdain for partisan politics and for philosophical conservatism. Among the growing contingent of Republicans in the General Assembly, there seemed to be many competent lawmakers but no spiritual leader had emerged to unite his fellow GOP legislators, let alone to rally the Republican faithful. Among the activists who manned the GOP central committee and other party panels, there were many would-be chiefs but few real warriors. As in the days before realignment, many holding party office seemed to place a higher priority on preserving their sphere of influence in the party organization than on formulating a principled political message and winning elections. Twelve years after the death of Richard Obenshain, the Virginia Republican Party in 1990 was still searching for a leader or leaders capable of forging and sustaining a consensus about the party's mission. Party realignment and the once-powerful conservative coalition were victims of the GOP malaise.

"There is a tide in the affairs of men," as Shakespeare's Brutus observed,[90] and the ebb and flow of partisan fortunes nowhere was more apparent than in post-realignment Virginia. Though too early to discern a trend, there were indications early in the 1990s that the political tide was about to turn again in the dynamic Old Dominion. As this book went to press, it was the Democrats—not Republicans—who were aggressively airing their disagreements in public, placing personal rivalries and animosities ahead of common political objectives, and indulging the luxury of infighting in the blithe expectation of continued electoral success. An outbreak of fierce conflict between rivals Chuck Robb and Douglas Wilder in mid-1991 combined with the effects of decennial redistricting and recession-bred state budgetary problems to produce cracks in the diverse Democratic coalition that had dominated state politics since 1981. For the first time in well over a decade, Republicans in 1991 gained a prominent Democratic convert in the person of Delegate Edgar C. Eck of Richmond, and further party switches were rumored. The developments fueled Republican optimism; after years on the electoral rocks, many GOP partisans sensed a full sea of opportunity. But it remained to be seen whether the strife-torn Republicans could set aside their differences, reinvigorate their conservative coalition, and reclaim a prominent role in Virginia's governance.

---

[90]*Julius Caesar,* IV, iii.

Chapter 36

The Swinging Suburbs: Making Money and Making History

"Three years ago, Doug Wilder ran for lieutenant governor of Virginia. Many told him he could not win. He politely ignored them . . . . He talked not of the past, but of the future. And, he won.

"Now, Doug Wilder has his sights on a new office. . . . Again, he will address the future. And, again he will have a chance to make history in Virginia.

"Perhaps more to the point, Virginia will have the chance to make history [and to] establish[ ] that Virginia does not have time to waste on the old fears, the old habits, and the old divisions."[91]

Governor Gerald L. Baliles
May 15, 1988

Virginia during the 1980s was a portrait of mainstream America. Economically, the Commonwealth was diverse and dynamic; traditional manufacturing industries and agricultural enterprises, while generally prosperous, represented a declining portion of the state's overall economy, and were fast being eclipsed by the explosive high-technology and service-oriented business sectors. For two decades before 1980, the Commonwealth's policy-makers had cultivated a social and legal climate conducive to business and industrial development, and the Virginia economy had remained relatively strong while the nation experienced recession and stagnation during the '70s. With the sustained nationwide recovery in the '80s, the state enjoyed unprecedented economic growth. Particularly significant was the major boost that the Reagan administration's defense build-up gave to the economies of northern Virginia and the Hampton Roads area.

The corresponding population trends were away from the rural areas and central cities and toward the suburbs. The share of the statewide vote turned in by the suburbs grew from 39 percent in 1977 to 49 percent in 1989.[92] The urban corridor extending from northern Virginia through the Richmond metropolitan area to the Tidewater cities in the southeastern corner of the state was the locus of much of the suburban sprawl, with the fastest growth

---

[91]Baker, p. 56.

[92]See Sabato, *Virginia Votes 1983-1986*, p. 83; Larry J. Sabato, "Virginia Governor's Race, 1989 (Part 2: The General Election)," *University of Virginia News Letter* (Charlottesville: Center for Public Service, University of Virginia), January 1990, p. 4.

occurring at opposite ends of the corridor. It was in these vote-rich suburban areas that the prosperous baby-boomers—young, upwardly mobile, white professionals and business men and women—comprised the dominant population group and voting bloc. Also notable was the steady expansion of the suburban black middle class, an inevitable product of anti-discrimination measures and social and economic integration. While generalizations remained hazardous, a decade of polling data and social literature confirmed that the overriding concern of the upscale voters, white and black, was economic advancement. For most Americans and most Virginians, the decade of the 1980s was a very good time to make money—per capita income in the state rose sharply—and making money made for some very good times. It was a period when the pursuit of material wealth tended to obscure more fundamental measures of worth. "Reaganomics"—the sweeping tax reduction initiative championed early by Republican conservatives such as Virginia's Richard Obenshain and branded a "nightmare" by Democratic liberals such as Virginia's Douglas Wilder[93]—was, by decade's end, synonymous with the unparalleled prosperity. While federal government budget deficits remained an ominous cloud on the horizon, the prosperous (and those who aspired to join them) were generally content with the handling of economic affairs, and few wanted to risk a return to the discredited national policies of the 1970s.

Though tax restraint and growth-oriented economic policies supplied common ground for the younger voters in the suburbs and the Byrd-era conservatives throughout the state, the two groups' interests and social outlooks otherwise diverged markedly. The rapid growth of the suburbs, coupled with the influx of women into the workforce there, brought to the fore a host of special concerns—transportation improvements, child-care services, waste management and other environmental needs, land-use planning and regulation of development, educational and recreational facilities—that were widely viewed by suburbanites as governmental responsibilities. To such suburban voters, stand-pat Republican conservatism seemed as outdated and out-of-touch as dogmatic Democratic liberalism. Moreover, the suburban perspective was characterized by youthful optimism, prosperity-fueled expectations of progress, and general ignorance or nonchalance concerning evidence of cultural decline. Having come of age in the turbulent '60s, many suburban dwellers retained individualistic, libertarian attitudes on social issues even as they exuberantly adopted their elders' passion for the fruits of capitalism. In contrast, the outlook of older conservatives tended to be more culturally focused, tradition-oriented, and less sensitive to unfulfilled aspirations and social barriers to personal opportunity. The dramatic shift of political clout to the suburbs in the '80s thus was accompanied by a precipitous decline in the influence of the aging conservative symbols of the rural-based Coalition.

---

[93]*The Richmond News Leader*, May 5, 1982.

Virginia Republicans generally were slow to recognize that change, but GOP strategist Judy Peachee anticipated it in a 1980 interview:

I think [support from the Coalition] is a diminishing factor. The younger crowd that is coming along does not use the same yardstick to measure the candidate. The litmus test is changing, and our party has to be very sensitive to the evolution that is taking place. . . . The candidates that we nominate have to represent traditional principles of conservative government, but they also have to have a vision for the future; they have to have new ideas. The newer crowd is measuring by the future and not by the past. The "Coalition," as we know it, is measuring by known quantities; the younger crowd uses those quantities as a bedrock, but they've added on to it what they want for the future. So I think you are dealing with a changing conservative base . . .[94]

Unfortunately for the Virginia GOP, the only lesson many partisans seemed to glean from Chuck Robb's victory in 1981 was that the Republican Party had to act in concert with the Coalition in order to win. While that was largely true in the watershed Coleman-Robb race, it became markedly less so in the political climate that developed in that election's wake. Nevertheless, in the aftermath of 1981, Republican preoccupation with recapturing solid Coalition backing for GOP candidates almost completely obscured the imperative of fashioning a forward-looking message for younger, moderate suburban voters. The situation bore striking similarities to the plight of the Byrd organization in the '50s and '60s; because the aging Byrd leadership then had failed to accommodate state policies to the reality of urban growth, the organization had lost the loyalty of many of its metropolitan adherents. Somewhat ironically, it was Democratic Governor Mills Godwin who broke with tradition in the mid-1960s and supplied the leadership that enabled the state to address—albeit belatedly—an array of pressing urban needs. But by the 1980s, the pace of change had accelerated, and many suburban voters came to view Godwin and the Coalition as anachronistic symbols of an unflatteringly caricatured and unappreciated Virginia past.

Once in power with Robb's election as governor in 1981, Virginia Democrats were positioned to capitalize on the economic prosperity and the widespread contentment of voters throughout the decade. The Democratic demon of tax-and-spend liberalism was exorcised, not by spending restraint—the Robb-Baliles years saw state spending soar at an unprecedented inflation-adjusted rate[95]—but by the effects of economic growth, which consis-

---

[94]Peachee interview.

[95]The state budget nearly doubled during the back-to-back Robb-Baliles administrations. The inflation-adjusted growth rate was approximately four times that under the Democrats' two GOP predecessors, and the state budget increases were sharply higher than the federal budget growth during the same period. The rate of spending increase easily outpaced the rate of population growth and the rise in per capita income during the period. In taxation levels, the state climbed from 37th among the states to 22nd; the state and local tax burden rose faster in only seven other states.

tently filled state coffers and yielded steady increases in the disposable incomes of most voters. The Robb Democrats also distanced themselves from the party's prior liberal stands on key business and labor issues, such as repeal of the Right to Work Law and support for public employee collective bargaining. Republican candidates attempted throughout the decade to make campaign hay out of Democratic fiscal policies, but the general economic satisfaction in the suburbs and the absence of a unified stance on taxes and spending among General Assembly Republicans thwarted the attempts. GOP statewide contenders during the '80s thus faced a frightful dilemma: the issues that had been principally relied upon to forge winning conservative Republican coalitions in the '70s—taxing, spending, and labor policies—were generally unavailing; and, the more GOP candidates assailed the Robb-Baliles fiscal policies in an effort to reassemble that coalition, the more they opened themselves up to Democratic charges that they were mired in the past and opposed to worthwhile public investments in education, transportation, and other "forward-looking" programs with suburban as well as central-city appeal.

The problem, at bottom, was that most Virginia Republicans did not have a clear idea of what their party's agenda should be at the state level. The GOP's attraction to the Commonwealth's conservative-leaning electorate in the '60s and '70s—and the driving motivation for the ardently conservative activists who had propelled the party since the 1964 Goldwater campaign—had been the great national debates: free markets versus government planning as the way to prosperity; private institutions versus the welfare state as the engine of social improvement; individual liberty and moral responsibility versus paternalistic government as the means of virtue; military strength versus unilateral disarmament as the path to peace; state prerogatives versus federal mandates in governmental policy-making; judicial restraint versus judicial activism in applying the law; assertiveness versus passivity in promoting capitalism over communism and democracy over dictatorship on the world stage. That a clear majority of Virginians preferred the conservative Republican vision to the liberal Democratic view on these issues was apparent from the GOP's presidential victories, which continued uninterrupted with a single exception through the four decades after Eisenhower carried the state in 1952. But, with the exception of the 1970s, when the Henry Howell-led state Democrats embraced their national party's most liberal nostrums, those issues rarely differentiated the parties at the state and local levels. As in the heyday of the Byrd organization, the state's system of holding state and local elections in odd-numbered years—rather than in tandem with national and congressional contests in the even-numbered years—helped Virginia Democrats avoid an undesired association with their liberal national party's stands and candidates.

To many Virginia voters in the '80s, especially in the suburbs, the state Republican Party and its candidates seemed bereft of useful ideas for addressing the practical problems confronting the state. After 1981, the Democratic Party possessed the advantages of incumbency in the Commonwealth in times that were notable nationally for their hospitability to incumbents. Democratic candidates generally could boast of superior experience and clout in state government as well as an emerging record of economic prosperity, increased funding for education and transportation, and advances in environmental protection and international trade under Democratic governors. Republican politicians often offered creative proposals only to have the suggestions appropriated by their Democratic rivals who, by virtue of their ties to the party in power, were better situated to bring about the desired changes. Where the dominant Democrats failed to take significant action (such as in addressing mounting public safety problems and drug-related crime), and where their self-laudatory rhetoric was belied by the record (as in their claims of fiscal conservatism), Republicans proved ineffectual in calling the incumbents to account.

In the wake of the 1985 Democratic sweep, introspective GOP partisans agreed with Professor Larry Sabato that a major shortcoming during the Robb administration had been the absence of a vocal Republican "loyal opposition" pointing out flaws in and suggesting alternatives to the Democratic governor's policies.[96] Party Chairman Donald Huffman responded by creating a Republican Policy Committee that was chaired by one of his predecessors, former Delegate George McMath, and was charged with formulating Republican policy positions on major state issues. GOP legislative leaders, however, generally saw the initiative as an encroachment upon their policymaking prerogative and lent little support. Though the committee's efforts continued, any thought that Republicans actually might form a united front on major policy questions was quickly eliminated in the fall of 1986, when numerous GOP legislators rushed to give at least partial support to a $10 billion package of transportation-related tax increases advocated by Governor Gerald Baliles.

Less than a year earlier, GOP gubernatorial nominee Wyatt Durrette had made Baliles's lavish proposals for new state spending—and the attendant inevitability of higher taxes—a central campaign theme. Former Governor John Dalton had bitterly assailed Baliles for not being "man enough to admit" that the Democrat's spending proposals would necessitate tax hikes,[97] and former Delegate W. Roy Smith, who served as chairman of Governor Robb's council of economic advisers, had publicly offered a similar assessment. Baliles had responded to these charges through television advertisements and campaign pronouncements in which he gave increasingly firm, and eventually rock-solid, assurances that his administration would not propose any tax hikes. "I will not seek a tax increase to accomplish what I have set out as goals—period," Baliles declared impatiently during one mid-October campaign

---

[96]See Sabato, *Virginia Votes 1983–1986*, p. 109.
[97]Text of remarks on file with the author.

debate.[98] "If Jerry Baliles says he isn't going to raise taxes, you can bank on it," vouched outgoing Governor Robb, whose popularity in the state surpassed even that of President Reagan.[99] But, instead of capitalizing on the Democrat's broken promise when Baliles unveiled his large tax hike proposals only a few months after taking office, the GOP legislative caucus splintered and supplied enough votes to guarantee passage of the new levies. The Republicans' performance was in marked contrast to that of Democratic Lieutenant Governor Douglas Wilder, who recognized the political perils of association with a taxing governor and publicly repudiated the major funding element of the Baliles plan, a half-cent increase in the state sales tax. This was the first of several episodes in which Wilder beat the GOP to the punch by staking out conservative ground at the expense of his former runningmate, Governor Baliles. When the 1989 gubernatorial campaign rolled around, Wilder could credibly claim to have been a more reliable foe of higher taxes than the Republican contingent in the General Assembly.

Despite the improving GOP numbers in the Virginia General Assembly during the 1980s, the Republican legislative caucus remained largely unwilling or unable to develop and then unite behind innovative proposals—such as significant anti-drug and anti-crime measures, education reforms, environmental programs, stronger public ethics strictures, taxing and spending limitations, or regional transportation initiatives—that might serve to contrast the loyal opposition with the party in power and thereby give voters a *partisan* reason to oust Democrats and install Republicans. Only in 1991, for example— with the state in the throes of recession and a deepening fiscal crisis—did the Republican lawmakers galvanize in opposition to a Democrat-sponsored budget bill.[100] The GOP legislators' ineffectiveness was the product of several factors, including their differing local constituencies, their passive acceptance of gross partisan underrepresentation on influential legislative committees, and the Democratic majority's venerated practice of torpedoing meritorious Republican-patroned bills, retooling them as Democrat-sponsored legislation, and then floating them through in succeeding sessions. Ultimately, however, it was the lack of cohesiveness in the GOP's own legislative ranks that undermined the Republicans' ability to perform the loyal-opposition role, and

---

[98]This and other Baliles campaign statements foreswearing tax hikes are recalled in Kent Jenkins, Jr., "Baliles Contradicts No-Tax Pledge," *The Virginian-Pilot and The Ledger-Star*, September 14, 1986.

[99]*The Washington Post*, November 1, 1985.

[100]Beginning in 1988, Delegate Frank D. Hargrove and Senator Joseph B. Benedetti alternately chaired and co-chaired the GOP caucus; former Roanoke newspaper reporter Stephen D. Haner served as executive director. In addition to their efforts, development of a united Republican position on fiscal issues in 1990 and 1991 was assisted significantly by Richmond lawyer Patrick M. McSweeney, who took over as chairman of the Republican Policy Committee in 1988, and by James C. Miller, III, of McLean, who served as director of the Office of Management and Budget under President Reagan. Within the Republican caucus, Delegate Clinton Miller of Shenandoah County was instrumental in gaining support in 1991 for a set of GOP proposals to reform the budget process.

in that the fractious Republican legislative caucus mirrored the faction-ridden state GOP as a whole.

The lawmakers' failure to delineate the differences between the parties in the intervals between elections deprived Republican candidates of potentially powerful issues in statewide campaigns. Unlike the aggressive agitation by congressional Republicans that preceded Ronald Reagan's transforming election in 1980, for example, no case for change had been made at the legislative level in Virginia. When GOP candidates sought to spell out new ideas and major policy initiatives, such as those contained in the *Agenda for the 90's* issued by gubernatorial nominee Marshall Coleman in 1989, they were usually writing on a *tabula rasa*. Democratic candidates were free to embrace the GOP suggestions without fear of contradicting their own or other Democrats' prior legislative positions. In those cases where a legislative history did exist, the GOP campaign pronouncements often could be discredited by pointing out that they actually were inconsistent with stands taken by the party's General Assembly members.

It was against this adverse backdrop of Democratic incumbency, economic contentment, and Republican malaise that GOP candidates endeavored, ultimately without success, to break into the winning column in state elections during the '80s. In a phenomenon that was not limited to Virginia, the liberal-conservative dichotomy that made GOP victories in presidential elections largely predictable was effectively erased in state elections. "[T]he common denominator of the New South generation of Democratic nominees has been their refusal to present themselves unambiguously as either national liberal Democrats or unreconstructed southern Democrats," wrote Professors Earl and Merle Black in 1987:

> Most victorious southern Democrats have waged campaigns that skillfully intertwine conservative postures (budgetary restraint, opposition to increased taxation, enthusiasm for school prayer and the death penalty) with progressive themes (support for equal opportunities, educational advancement, environmental protection). . . . By deliberately blurring distinctions between conservatism and progressivism [Southern] Democratic politicians have been able to appeal on different grounds to black (and liberal white) Democrats and to moderate and conservative white Democrats.[101]

In Virginia, where Republicans for a decade had forged winning coalitions around conservative precepts, blurring the ideological differences between the parties was the chief prerequisite for Democratic success in the '80s. Once it was apparent that Virginia Democrats were not going to do anything to prevent upwardly mobile suburban voters from making money, the way was clear for Democrats to focus on other concerns that would satisfy the suburban appetite for progress and salve the suburban social conscience. Aided by the

---

[101]Black and Black, p. 287.

paucity of major policy differences between the parties in state contests, Democratic candidates successfully directed suburban voters' attention to the hot-button issues of race relations and abortion policy, and to the corresponding pejorative symbols of massive resistance and Moral Majority. Those were the topics with which Democratic tacticians constructed the thematic paradigm that repeatedly moved suburban voters into the Democratic column in the '80s: the GOP as the intolerant, divisive party of the past; Democrats as the inclusive, unifying force for the future.

Probably the most accurate description of the prevailing political philosophy in the Virginia suburbs—and within the expanding Southern middle class generally—was supplied by the professors Black, who termed it "entrepreneurial individualism."[102] Shared entrepreneurial aims and economic outlooks linked the suburbs to more traditional conservative elements of society and the electorate, but in important respects the ethic of individualism separated suburban voters from traditionalists. No topics more dramatically divided younger suburban voters from older conservatives throughout the state than race relations and civil rights. Ironically, both Marshall Coleman and Wyatt Durrette, the decade's two GOP gubernatorial standard-bearers, were racial moderates whose conservative credo of individual liberty embodied the conviction that every person should be accorded opportunity based on individual worth rather than the happenstance of racial identity. In that belief, they were in harmony with the progressive sentiments of suburbanites. But, as they tried to forge conservative coalitions in the '80s using the Byrd-era symbols that had so aided the realignment effort in the '70s, they repeatedly found that the specter of past racial discrimination hung like a cloud over the state's politics. Partly through Republican fumbling, and partly as a result of skillful Democratic manipulation, the GOP's ties to the remnants of the Byrd organization were repeatedly used to link Republican candidates to the broadly discredited racial codes and massive resistance policies of Virginia's past. Wilder's presence on the 1985 and 1989 Democratic tickets guaranteed that the issue of race relations would remain front-and-center throughout the decade. But, more than that, his candidacy gave voters a concrete opportunity to signal their repudiation of Virginia's legacy of discrimination, to purge their racial guilt, and to "make history" in a way that would capture both the attention and admiration of the nation.

If race was the Scylla upon which Democrats dashed GOP hopes, abortion by decade's end had become the Charybdis that drew Republicans into a perilous debate they rarely won before suburban audiences. Even before the U.S. Supreme Court's July 1989 Webster[103] decision energized advocates of

---

[102]Ibid., pp. 296–316.

[103]Webster v. Reproductive Health Services, 109 S.Ct. 3040 (1989). In the controversial ruling, the Supreme Court opened the way for some state-imposed restrictions on access to abortions.

legalized abortion and thrust the issue to the fore, GOP candidates suffered in the suburbs from identification with the conservative social agenda of the New Right and, particularly, with Jerry Falwell and his Moral Majority movement. Of course, the morality-laden issues emphasized by the politically active conservative Christian community touched a receptive chord among many Virginia voters. School prayer, restrictions on pornography, parental rights in education, even opposition to abortion, were policy positions that attracted large numbers of non-Republicans to GOP candidates and campaigns, especially in rural areas. But suburban voters—who were more numerous in Virginia—generally reacted negatively, and their reaction typically focused not on the particular issues but on the perceived moral imperiousness of televangelists like Falwell and on the merger of an intolerant-sounding religious absolutism with political action. The libertarian brand of conservatism prevalent in the suburbs and among younger voters throughout Virginia was fundamentally inconsistent with the majoritarian methods of the culturally conservative New Right, and the disagreement represented another major fault line in the conservative coalition that had elected Republicans in the '70s. Though the specific issue of abortion found Virginians ambivalent and rather evenly divided throughout the '80s, identification with the Religious Right and leaders like Falwell and 1988 presidential candidate Pat Robertson proved to be a major liability for GOP candidates among younger and suburban voters.

While the dynamics were markedly different in each of the gubernatorial elections in the '80s, these social issues played critical roles in the outcomes of all three contests. As he looked to the 1981 gubernatorial race, for example, Marshall Coleman worried little about appearing too conservative on social issues for the tastes of suburban voters. Republican strategists instead were chiefly concerned with shoring up Coleman's suspect conservative credentials among the independents who took their cues from the ex-Byrd men in the Coalition. With a record that included support for civil rights measures as a state legislator and a successful appeal for the votes of blacks in his 1977 campaign for attorney general, Coleman could hardly be portrayed as reactionary on race. Similarly, while fundamentalist congregations thought well of his efforts as attorney general to exempt church-run child care facilities from state licensing requirements, Coleman had neither taken a position on abortion nor emphasized other issues that might link him with Moral Majority. Guy Farley's strong bid for lieutenant governor had threatened to draw a very direct connection between Jerry Falwell and the GOP ticket, but it was precisely that possibility that led many partisans to strenuously, and successfully, resist Farley's nomination at the June Republican convention. Nevertheless, last-minute developments in the fall campaign prompted political analyst Larry Sabato to opine that race and Falwell were among the principal reasons that an exceedingly close Coleman-Robb race was converted at the eleventh hour into a comfortable Democratic win.[104]

---

[104]See Sabato, *Virginia Votes 1979-1982*, pp. 83–84.

Coleman's difficulties on race in 1981 could be traced to his and his party's decision to pursue a conservative coalition strategy. Aware of Coleman's problems among the Coalitionists and fearing a split by the Byrd men in the impending governor's race, Governor Dalton in March 1981 had acceded to insistence from that quarter, and had vetoed legislation to create a state holiday honoring Martin Luther King, Jr. Coleman privately opposed the veto but was obliged to support the Republican governor's action publicly, and in so doing he doused whatever flickering hope he entertained of garnering meaningful black support in his forthcoming race against Robb. Thus committed to the conservative coalition strategy under Dalton's tutelage, Coleman needed a former Democrat, such as Senator Byrd's son, Tom, or State Senator Herbert Bateman, to join his ticket and solidify the Coalitionists' support. Bateman would have been an especially attractive choice because he was a Coalition favorite with a record of opposition to massive resistance and an urban (Tidewater) political base. But the Newport News senator's bid for lieutenant governor was rejected at the party's Virginia Beach convention, and that development—widely seen as a rebuff of the Coalition by GOP regulars—made Coleman's problems on the right even more acute. By late October, Republican strategists were desperately looking for a way to counter the anti-Coleman drumbeat by the "Virginians for Robb" and to summon independent conservatives into the GOP camp. That need set the stage for a crucial late-October visit to Richmond by Ronald Reagan and Mills Godwin.

By the close of the '80s, Democrat Douglas Wilder would be expressing opposition to, or at least distancing himself from, such favorite black and liberal political causes as statehood for the District of Columbia, racial quotas and preferences, and post-card voting registration. But in 1981, these were the main issues he raised in a widely disseminated letter urging black leaders to support Chuck Robb for governor over Marshall Coleman. A few days later they were also among the issues Mills Godwin zeroed in on as he entreated conservatives to back Coleman over Robb. At the President's request, Godwin appeared with Reagan and the GOP ticket at a Richmond rally on October 27, 1981, and there delivered his first major campaign speech in support of Coleman. Both Reagan—whom Coleman had strained to embrace throughout the campaign—and Godwin were immensely unpopular figures in the black political community, and Wilder later reported that the former governor's remarks had "galvanized" previously apathetic blacks behind Robb's candidacy.[105]

Though the Godwin speech was not necessarily the one that the Coleman campaign would have preferred—Coleman and his staff had no advance notice of its content—the issues raised were plainly legitimate and were among the few identifiable policy differences between the two similar-sounding gubernatorial contenders. Indeed, Robb's strategists had been so deter-

---

[105]Baker, p. 122.

mined to minimize the perceived policy differences between their candidate and Coleman that they recoiled in horror when they learned that Wilder had raised such a controversial topic as post-card registration in his missive to blacks.[106] Nevertheless, Godwin's message was immediately controversial because of the messenger. Journalists rushed to report that the ex-champion of massive resistance had given a "racially tinged" speech on Coleman's behalf. To the lore of Virginia politics were added two legends that would be regurgitated with destructive simplicity in news articles throughout the decade. One was that Mills Godwin had injected race into the 1981 gubernatorial campaign (and presumably would be constantly searching for opportunities to do so again). The other was that Coleman would do anything to win, even to the point of countenancing a racial appeal in his behalf.[107] As with the information that Wilder, not Godwin, had first raised the "racially tinged" issues, the detail that Coleman and his campaign played no part in the content of the Godwin speech went overlooked.

A last-minute, unsolicited endorsement by Rev. Jerry Falwell also hurt Coleman in 1981. After their high-profile efforts on Ronald Reagan's behalf during the 1980 presidential campaign, prominent conservative evangelists and fundamentalists were looking for other opportunities to flex their newly found political muscle. Shortly after the 1980 Reagan landslide, Falwell declared that the "tremendous avalanche [of conservative Christian votes for Reagan] has given us the credibility we need to launch headlong into the real matters that concern us most, and that would be the moral issues."[108] Though opinion polls showed that Falwell and Moral Majority were decidedly unpopular in Virginia—a September 1981 survey found that the minister's endorsement would have an adverse impact on six people for every one that it influenced favorably[109]—the gubernatorial race in Falwell's own home state was too big a plum to pass up. If the conservative preacher failed to express himself on the Coleman-Robb contest, his silence would be taken as a tacit admission that his vaunted endorsement was more liability than asset. Falwell thus made his preference for Coleman known the weekend before the election—just as the large bloc of undecided suburban voters was preparing to make its choice. The endorsement hardly aided the GOP cause.

Four years later, Wyatt Durrette's bid for governor ran into similar problems in the general election campaign after he capitalized on support from fundamentalist congregations to win the nomination contest. The GOP candidate's anti-abortion views were seized upon by Democratic foe Baliles in the pair's first debate, and were discussed frequently during the campaign. Even more damaging, however, was a Durrette statement that he favored mandat-

[106]Ibid., pp. 121–122.

[107]Edds, p. 141.

[108]*The Richmond News Leader*, November 5, 1980.

[109]*Roanoke Times*, November 8, 1981.

ing instruction on creationism in public school curricula; the early October declaration, wrote Dwayne Yancey, made the GOP gubernatorial candidate "a laughingstock, especially among suburban voters."[110] Another unsolicited endorsement—this one from Virginia Beach-based television evangelist Pat Robertson—further linked Durrette with the conservative religionists. In his acceptance speech at the June Democratic convention, Baliles had signalled his intention to capitalize on suburban Republican disdain for the New Right when he declared:

> Our opponents offer a narrow and negative vision that looks backward and to the far right. . . . In this campaign, we will invite the refugees from the Mountain-Valley and the suburbs into our Party. We belong to no single group—whether it is the new right or any other narrow interest. We are beholden to no single issue. We will set no litmus test and we will reject the illusion that labels can solve problems. We are in the mainstream. . . . The Republican Party [is a party] of closed minds and closed doors. . . .[111]

Though the Democratic plan to isolate Durrette on the extreme right was obvious, the GOP campaign never found a way to project a broader appeal. Moreover, as Durrette's handlers responded to the Democratic strategy by attempting to downplay their candidate's conservative social agenda, they only managed to dampen the enthusiasm and sap the motivation of the Republican's pro-life (i.e., anti-abortion) and conservative Christian supporters.

Race, however, proved to be the most detrimental factor for the GOP in 1985. The Durrette campaign strategy was simple and sensible. Though Baliles generally was perceived as a moderate in the Chuck Robb mold, the little-known attorney general had allied himself with the liberal Douglas Wilder in order to overcome Lieutenant Governor Richard Davis in the Democratic gubernatorial nomination battle. Republicans planned to impugn Baliles's conservative credentials in the fall campaign by airing Wilder's liberal record on such key topics as law enforcement, labor policy, and taxes, and by then challenging Baliles to declare himself either in defense of, or in opposition to, his runningmate's stands. If Baliles opted for the former course, he would forfeit normally Democratic conservative votes, and, if he chose the latter path, he would enrage Democratic blacks. Either way, the Robb coalition would be rent, and the GOP campaign would be in a position to pick up the pieces. Republican strategists knew, however, that the attack on Wilder had to be completely devoid of racial content or it would trigger a backlash among youthful, suburban, and moderate white voters.

Durrette's handlers thought that their candidate's reputation as a racial progressive, coupled with efforts to keep Godwin and other Byrd organization figures mum on Wilder, would protect the GOP campaign against charges that its airing of Wilder's liberal record was a subtle appeal to racist sentiment

---

[110]Yancey, p. 279.
[111]Text of speech on file with the author.

among voters. Well before Wilder's place on the Democratic ticket was assured, Durrette had been cultivating personal ties in the black community, especially among the growing black middle class and the upwardly mobile black entrepreneurs who were less involved in Democratic Party activism than the entrenched black political and religious power structure. With his base among party conservatives and Coalitionists firm, Durrette and his advisers reasoned that he was well positioned to reach out to independent-minded blacks with an appeal based on personal trust and opportunity-oriented issues such as economic development, anti-discrimination enforcement, education reform, and an all-out attack on urban crime. Such minority outreach efforts promised multiple benefits: broadening the Republican Party base by recruiting like-minded blacks; fortifying the GOP gubernatorial nominee's racially progressive image in a way that would enhance his standing among suburban whites (and preclude the portrayal of attacks on Wilder's record as racially motivated); and positioning Durrette to harvest black disaffection if and when Baliles moved to distance himself from Wilder. To implement the plan, Durrette's campaign staff hired several operatives with political connections in the black community and scheduled a series of private meetings and public appearances before minority organizations. The efforts bore fruit as the GOP candidate won notable endorsements from prominent black businessmen, conservative black ministers, and the usually Democratic Newport News Crusade for Voters. Durrette even received one out of every four votes cast at the state Crusade for Voters endorsement meeting—an impressive showing for any conservative Republican, but especially for one whose Democratic opponent was a moderate with a black runningmate. Ultimately, however, none of those inroads mattered.

Three developments proved critical in the ultimate failure of the GOP plan. The first came in early May when Durrette casually referred to Wilder as one of the most liberal candidates ever to seek statewide office in Virginia. It seemed like an innocuous enough statement; the "liberal" moniker had been routinely placed on Wilder by politicians, journalists, and just about everyone else who had observed the Richmond senator's 16-year political career. But Wilder and his campaign manager, Paul Goldman, immediately charged that Durrette had used "liberal" as a racial code word. The charge brought a vitriolic rejoinder from the GOP camp, an outpouring of editorial criticism directed at the Democrat, and private expressions of chagrin from many of Wilder's fellow partisans. To Democrats from Governor Robb on down, wrote Dwayne Yancey in his 1985 campaign chronicle, it seemed that their "worst fears were being realized—Wilder careening out of control, pointing his finger and shouting racism at the top of his lungs."[112] But, as Goldman later acknowledged, the code-word charge was a calculated move to use Wilder's race as a shield against attacks on his legislative record. "Everybody was

---

[112]Yancey, p. 150.

nervous because it was race," the Democratic strategist recalled; "[i]t was like a brush-back pitch. It looked like we were out of control, but we knew exactly where we were throwing it."[113] As he had done frequently during his remarkable political and professional career, Wilder was playing the game by his own set of rules.

"It is difficult to overstate the impact Wilder's attack had," Yancey wrote. "Wilder came out the loser in the short run. But incredibly, with one simple news conference, he made it virtually impossible for Republicans to do what Republicans do best—accuse Democrats of being liberals."[114] He explained:

> Wilder's unexpected outburst terrified Virginia Republicans. The foul stench of being called racists—even when it was clearly untrue—was too much for Republicans to bear. Instead of holding their noses and flailing away at Wilder's voting record, from then on they went out of their way to avoid upsetting Wilder so he wouldn't call them that awful name.

Durrette was not the first, nor would he be the last, political figure pilloried by Wilder for alleged racial animus. Democrat Owen Pickett had been humiliated in 1982 for his supposed racial insensitivity, and when an exasperated Chuck Robb accused Wilder of dishonesty in two lengthy personal letters released to the public in 1986, the then-lieutenant governor suggested that Robb's criticism had racial overtones as well.[115] But the charge seemed particularly odious when applied to Wyatt Durrette. The father of eight children—including an Asian girl and, later, a biracial boy adopted as an infant—Durrette had practiced what many others merely preached about racial fairness and color-blindness. If Wilder could accuse him of racism and not be buried in an avalanche of political, press, and public indignation, there was not a Republican alive who was outside the reach of the Democrat's damning epithet.

Republicans backed off after Wilder's code-word allegation, in part because of the intended intimidation and in part because so many of them, like political observers generally, facilely believed that Wilder could not win the general election. In the Durrette camp, however, the desire to see Wilder's record challenged had little to do with concern about the contest for lieutenant governor; it was the cornerstone of the campaign's strategy for the gubernatorial race. Baliles could not be linked to and held accountable for Wilder's liberal record unless someone first held Wilder accountable for it. That duty necessarily would rest principally upon the shoulders of Wilder's Republican opponent.

As the June GOP convention approached, many of Durrette's top advisers and backers believed that State Senator John Chichester of Fredericksburg was up to the task of illuminating Wilder's past. From its begin-

---

[113]Ibid.
[114]Ibid., p. 151.
[115]Baker, p. 247.

ning, however, the contest for the second spot on the GOP ticket had as much to do with settling old scores as setting up a winning slate. To the extent that partisans did examine the merits, Chichester's apparent advantages over his chief rival, Marshall Coleman, were that he seemed non-controversial, he had not previously lost a statewide race (unlike Durrette and Coleman), and he was acceptable to the Coalition, which many GOP strategists believed Durrette needed in order to defeat the moderate Baliles. With the help of Durrette's lieutenants, Chichester overcame Coleman and gained a nomination that many mistakenly assumed was tantamount to election.

Chichester's nomination was the second crucial development that undermined the GOP gubernatorial strategy. The jovial Chichester proved constitutionally incapable of playing the aggressor's role, and his match-up with the nimble, intimidating Wilder proved to be a particularly glaring mismatch. Moreover, as a former Democrat backed by Mills Godwin, Chichester's nomination served principally to fortify the feeling that the Durrette ticket was a latter-day Byrd organization slate from top to bottom. One principal Durrette advisor who dissented from the pro-Chichester sentiment in the gubernatorial nominee's upper echelon was consultant Edward DeBolt, a former campaign aide to Godwin, Senator Harry F. Byrd, Jr., and Governor John Dalton. "I know what a race-baiting person Doug Wilder can be," DeBolt explained. "The last person you want to run against someone as adept as that is someone who is seen as part of the Byrd Machine."[116] Democrats also understood that Republican division again had helped their cause. "If the Republicans had nominated Marshall Coleman . . . they might have beaten us," conceded Wilder strategist Goldman.[117]

That Wilder and his handlers hoped to make the lieutenant governor's race a referendum on the racial codes of the Byrd era versus the egalitarian promise of the Democrats' "New Dominion" should have been apparent when Wilder began his campaign in the State Capitol beneath a portrait of Senator Harry F. Byrd, Sr. But it certainly was clear when the Democrats assembled for their convention shortly after the GOP trio was nominated. "Our candidate for lieutenant governor is not going to be a lackey for the overseer from Chuckatuck," declared an exuberant State Senator Virgil Goode of Rocky Mount to the enthusiastic Democratic delegates, making the first of several race-related references to former Governor Godwin at the party conclave.[118] Though some saw the Democratic rhetoric merely as an attempt to inoculate against anticipated racially motivated attacks on Wilder, the tactic was anything but defensive. "One thing [Wilder confidant and Senate Clerk J. T. "Jay"] Shropshire always had in mind," reported Yancey, "was trying to bait former Gov. Mills Godwin into the campaign with some sort of racial state-

---

[116]Yancey, p. 154.
[117]Ibid., p. 16.
[118]Ibid., p. 154.

ment that would help put the election in the stark contrast of the past vs. the future."[119] The Democratic dream came true, and the worst GOP fears were realized, on September 18 at Hampden-Sydney College in Prince Edward County in the heart of Harry Byrd's Southside, when Mills Godwin spoke, ever so fleetingly, of the state song.

Written by a black, James Bland, in 1875, "Carry Me Back to Ole Virginny" recalled the halcyon days of antebellum plantation life and slavery. As traditions go, the state song was much revered by older whites, but many black Virginians of the twentieth century did not yearn to be carried back even imaginatively to the days of the peculiar institution and understandably resented the notion that such offensive sentiments should be embodied in the Commonwealth's official anthem. In 1970, Wilder as a state senator had been among those blacks harboring such resentment, and he offered a bill in an unsuccessful attempt to remedy the situation during his first month in the legislature. The episode had been little discussed since then and was not a subject of campaign comment until that sunny September day in 1985. Having dutifully refrained, at the Durrette campaign's urging, from broaching the subject of Wilder during a day-long swing through Southside, Godwin strayed from his script only briefly during his final stop at conservative Hampden-Sydney. Unfortunately, the impromptu remarks concerned the state song, and therefore—inexplicitly but inescapably—the subject of race. "I have a hard time seeing how Jerry Baliles could . . . espouse the record of this man (Wilder)," Godwin declared. "Why, he actually introduced a bill to repeal the state song."[120] The words were few, but they echoed off the sleepy college campus like an atomic bomb.

The news media reaction was swift and severe. Godwin's speech at the close of the campaign four years earlier had received little attention, but it was now recounted in myriad news articles, along with the former governor's prominent role in Virginia's massive resistance during the '50s. In this context, the state song comment appeared not as an isolated, unfortunate reference to a sore subject, but rather as a calculated ploy to aid the GOP ticket by arousing racial passions. The reality, of course, was that the Democratic candidates were the only ones who could benefit from the remark, and that was immediately confirmed in campaign polling: Durrette's statewide standing slipped nine points virtually overnight, and the drop was even more precipitous in northern Virginia. Though newspapers across the state "jumped on the state song controversy and rode it for days,"[121] *The Washington Post* appeared to give special emphasis to the details of Godwin's segregationist past. Moreover, the newspaper's numerous stories on the subject uniformly failed to describe the 20-year interval between massive resistance and the Wilder-for-lieuten-

---

[119]Ibid., p. 226.
[120]Baker, pp. 208–209.
[121]Yancey, p. 266.

ant-governor campaign when Godwin had compiled a record as a two-term governor that led scholars of all stripes to rank him among the Commonwealth's most accomplished—and progressive—chief executives. The *Post* simultaneously declined to give any coverage to the endorsement of Durrette—several days *after* Godwin's state song comment—by the black Newport News Crusade for Voters. Republicans watched the devastating developments with a mixture of anger at their own misstep and furious incredulity at the news media's treatment of the subject. Only former Governor Linwood Holton seemed pleased; he had been under pressure to campaign on behalf of the GOP ticket, and the state song episode now "gave [him] an out."[122] It also gave the Democrats what they had been hoping for: from then on, wrote Dwayne Yancey, "the 1985 campaign would be increasingly viewed as a contest between the past and the future."[123]

As the election approached, Democrats used the race issue to full advantage. No one had known, when it all started, how Virginians really would react to a black statewide candidate. It was widely assumed that Wilder was seriously disadvantaged because of his race, but most made no effort to distinguish the liabilities that were Wilder's because of his liberal record from those that accrued by virtue of his race. In both Republican and Democratic camps, astute tacticians recognized that race would aid Wilder's candidacy in two crucial related respects—one positive, the other negative. The positive side of the equation was the appealing opportunity to "make history" by electing the first black statewide official. Despite his frequent protestations that race was irrelevant, Wilder's own campaign slogan—"Let's Make History"—made it clear that he thought his race not only was relevant, but indeed was among the most compelling arguments for his election. The alluring appeal to history benefited not only Wilder himself, but also the gray eminence positioned atop the Democratic ticket. An anesthetizing technocrat at his most animated and inspirational, Gerald Baliles found that his ground-breaking "New Dominion" ticket supplied the element of excitement that his candidacy and campaign otherwise lacked. At one rally late in the contest, the Democratic gubernatorial candidate proudly declared that his ticket was "part of Virginia's renaissance," and exclaimed, "I don't just read history, I make it."[124] Baliles' remarkable immodesty tended to obscure the more significant reality that the case for his election as governor rested largely on the attributes of others—namely, the achievements of his immensely popular predecessor, Chuck Robb,[125] and the "history-making" appeal of his eventual successor, Douglas Wilder.

---

[122]Ibid., p. 269.

[123]Ibid., p. 267.

[124]Ibid., p. 332.

[125]In response to exit polling in 1985, fully 48 percent of voters favoring Baliles cited satisfaction with Robb's performance in office as the primary reason for their choice. Sabato, *Virginia Votes 1983–1986*, p. 103.

At least as potent as the call to "make history" was the negative flip-side of that appeal—the challenge to reject Virginia's racially tinged past and "expurgate the stain of massive resistance."[126] From the beginning, Democratic strategists hoped that campaign events would make the election a referendum on racial tolerance, with voters presented a choice between a racially divisive past symbolized by the Republicans and a racially enlightened future represented by the Democrats. While members of the news media were expected to assist—wittingly or not—in that portrayal, few Democrats could have imagined how inept the Republicans would prove to be in resisting the damning characterization. The GOP not only failed to illuminate Wilder's liberal record, thereby foreclosing their main avenue for forging another winning moderate-conservative statewide coalition; they made matters incalculably worse by allowing an issue with racial connotations—the state song—to dominate the discourse. Since most voters were never informed of Wilder's conventionally liberal stands on law enforcement, labor, and fiscal issues, many no doubt suspected that criticism of him was motivated primarily by racial prejudice, a suspicion that seemed warranted after the state song controversy. In suburban Virginia, and especially in populous and cosmopolitan northern Virginia, upscale white voters—many of them originally from the North and West—eschewed any association with the distasteful attitudes of the massive resistance era, and voted Democratic in November less for policy reasons than because it had become the only socially acceptable thing to do. Indeed, northern Virginia was the one area of the state in which Wilder's percentage of the vote often exceeded Baliles's.

Once elected in 1985, Douglas Wilder had four years as lieutenant governor during which to complete his metamorphosis from liberal voice-in-the-wilderness to centrist insider. He used the time wisely. His speeches as lieutenant governor embraced Republican-sounding anti-tax and anti-crime themes, and, despite his frequent public and private feuding with Robb and Baliles between 1985 and 1988, Wilder presented himself in the 1989 gubernatorial campaign as their logical heir, a force for continuity and cautious progress. The fiscal storms that would become the chief legacy of the Baliles administration and the chief headache of the Wilder administration were but distant thunder in November 1989, hardly cause for concern in an otherwise sunny climate. Republican Marshall Coleman endeavored to focus attention on the Baliles administration's tax and spending hikes and the evidence that a state fiscal crisis loomed, but the extent of the mounting budgetary problems was successfully shielded from public view until after the election. Baliles himself dismissed Coleman's dire—though prescient—fiscal predictions as the politically motivated rhetoric of one who "knows very little about the budget process."[127] As in other statewide campaigns in the prosperous '80s, economic issues took a back seat to more immediate, emotional, and

---

[126]Yancey, p. 368.

[127]*The Virginian-Pilot*, October 24, 1989.

captivating topics. A decade of Democratic gains among younger and suburban state voters reached its peak in 1989 as developments conspired to make race and abortion the central topics in a nationally scrutinized Virginia gubernatorial campaign.

The Wilder stratagem in 1989 was not markedly different from his 1985 plan. The Democrat would seek to capture a sufficient share of the suburban swing vote by running to the right of center thematically and by minimizing policy differences with his GOP foe except on social issues. Racial pride and the novelty of Wilder's candidacy would be relied upon to keep black and liberal Democrats on board, and Wilder's legislative record and reassuring winks would keep organized labor's foot soldiers marching in his parade. The key to success, however, would be re-creating the past-versus-future dichotomy that had worked so well in the suburbs in 1981 and 1985. And the key to that, inevitably, was race. Governor Baliles set the theme early when, in a May 1988 speech widely credited with squelching Democratic opposition to Wilder's nomination, he declared:

Three years ago, Doug Wilder ran for lieutenant governor of Virginia. Many told him he could not win. He politely ignored them. . . . He talked not of the past, but of the future. And, he won.

Now, Doug Wilder has his sights on a new office . . . . Again, he will address the future. And, again he will have a chance to make history in Virginia.

Perhaps more to the point, Virginia will have the chance to make history [and to] establish[ ] that Virginia does not have time to waste on the old fears, the old habits, and the old divisions."[128]

Baliles's remarks reflected the confidence in Democratic circles that Wilder's race would be a net benefit in the coming campaign. As Margaret Edds observed in her account of the 1989 contest, "Whatever else it might become, the 1989 race for governor would also be a referendum on racial tolerance. History to the contrary, Wilder and his strategists believed that was a winning proposition."[129]

Wilder's unique status as a potential first elected black governor guaranteed immense favorable publicity for his "historic" candidacy; the symbolic importance of his potential achievement, when broadly advertised in the local and national news media, made his race a distinct political asset. Had the perceived racial barrier been broken before 1989, it may be safely ventured that Wilder's cause, like that of 1990 Georgia gubernatorial candidate Andrew Young,[130] would have attracted far less attention; in such a circumstance it is entirely possible (though by no means certain) that white votes forfeited

---

[128]Baker, p. 56.

[129]Edds, p. 14.

[130]Young, a protégé of Dr. Martin Luther King, Jr., had served as United Nations ambassador during the administration of President Jimmy Carter and later as mayor of Atlanta. Despite predictions that he would mount a formidable bid, Young was soundly defeated in the Georgia Democratic gubernatorial primary in 1990.

because of racial bigotry might have outnumbered those gained through positive racial imagery. But that was not the case in Virginia in 1989.

Most of the literally hundreds of national and international reporters who streamed to the erstwhile capital of the Confederacy to report on the Wilder-Coleman campaign were on the lookout for a racial incident—some dramatic confirmation of the widespread assumption that race remained a talisman to the Virginia electorate. News accounts typically portrayed the contest as a test of Virginians' integrity on matters racial; if Wilder won, the state's suspect citizenry would earn a passing grade, while a Republican victory would be taken as proof that the old attitudes persisted. Among the in-state news media there was much of the same. The State Capitol press corps had been the target of nonpartisan allegations of pro-Wilder bias four years earlier—"the most imbalanced and unfair picture of an election I've ever seen," Larry Sabato had charged[131]—and before the 1989 election a number of front-line state political reporters talked openly of subjecting Wilder's candidacy, record, and statements to close scrutiny in his campaign for governor. As the contest unfolded, however, there was little evidence of increased journalistic aggressiveness, and, in the critical weeks immediately preceding the election, major news outlets in the state echoed many of the race-related themes beneficial to Wilder that permeated the national coverage. The fact that three of the five daily newspapers most widely read in the state—those in Washington, Hampton Roads, and Roanoke—had reporters covering the campaign who were simultaneously writing, researching, or reaping financial rewards from books about Wilder hardly assuaged concerns of slanted coverage.[132]

Republican strategists assumed that Wilder's campaign for governor would feature a reprise of his 1985 "Let's Make History" theme. Indeed, his bid for the top spot in state government promised to make that message even more compelling, and there was no sign that the theme would be examined critically in the news media. But one thing was certain to be different in 1989: Republicans this time were not going to let Wilder's race deter them from call-

---

[131]Yancey, p. 312.

[132]Dwayne Yancey, whose *When Hell Froze Over* chronicled the 1985 Wilder campaign, was among the reporters covering the 1989 campaign for the *Roanoke Times & World-News*. The Yancey book was updated and reprinted after Wilder's 1989 win. Donald P. Baker, chief of the *Washington Post*'s Richmond bureau, published a biography entitled *Wilder: Hold Fast to Dreams* in September 1989. Margaret Edds researched *Claiming the Dream: The Victorious Campaign of Douglas Wilder of Virginia* while covering the 1989 gubernatorial campaign for the Norfolk *Virginian-Pilot and Ledger-Star*.

The three books were actually quite insightful and reasonably balanced, but concerns about biased campaign news coverage arose from the fact that the author-reporters were covering the gubernatorial contest notwithstanding their apparent financial stake in its outcome. As reporter Jeff Schapiro observed in a review of Edds's book, a Wilder victory would be counted upon to increase interest in, and thus sales of, books about the Democratic candidate. *Richmond Times-Dispatch*, June 10, 1990.

ing attention to his controversial past. In addition to his liberal legislative record, Wilder's professional, business, and political wake was strewn with ethical debris—a state Supreme Court reprimand in 1978 for unprofessional conduct as a lawyer, a serious legislative conflict-of-interest scrape in 1979, successive citations for building code violations, insistence upon honoraria for speeches to constituents while lieutenant governor, deficient financial disclosures, and, perhaps most damaging politically, two published letters from the popular Chuck Robb directly indicting his integrity. Wilder had explanations and excuses for some of these problems, to be sure, but the reality was that the problems themselves had not been aired in any systematic way before 1989. Marshall Coleman served notice at the start of his campaign that the gloves would come off; while stating firmly that he would tolerate no subtle or overt racial appeals on his behalf, Coleman also declared that he would "not be intimidated or deterred by groundless charges that my discussion of Mr. Wilder's record and views is racially inspired."[133] Republicans would challenge Virginians to vote for the best person regardless of race, convinced that if the real Wilder were exposed he could not win.

Coleman gained the GOP nomination only after he and rival Stan Parris unleashed a withering, multi-million-dollar attack on frontrunner Paul Trible. But, in the primary campaign's wake, commentators noted that the former attorney general in many ways seemed tailor-made to take on Wilder.[134] A racial moderate, Coleman's politically debilitating past clashes with the ex-Byrd men in his party now became something of an asset, freeing him to challenge Wilder's record without risking a repeat of the "racial code word" rejoinder from the Democratic camp. Moreover, Coleman had never shied away from robust exchanges with political opponents—former foes considered him a "vicious campaigner," according to Edds[135]—and the belief that he would carry the fight unrelentingly to Wilder had much to do with his upset primary victory. The GOP nominee also, of course, had extensive experience in public life, a thorough-going knowledge of state government, and an ambitious, reform-minded agenda for the new Republican administration he hoped to lead. But it was universally apparent to strategists in the Republican camp that the GOP would have to illuminate Wilder's record or face a third consecutive gubernatorial defeat. With the state economy seemingly strong, and with

---

[133]Marshall Coleman, *Agenda for the '90s: Fulfilling Virginia's Promise*, November 1988, p. 26. Copy on file with the author.

[134]See Larry J. Sabato, "Virginia Governor's Race, 1989 (Part 3: General Election Issues)," *University of Virginia News Letter* (Charlottesville: Center for Public Service, University of Virginia), February 1990, p. 7.

[135]Edds, p. 72.

Robb and Baliles ostensibly in his corner,[136] Wilder had all the advantages of pseudo-incumbency. At the same time, his unique candidacy satisfied the electorate's appetite for excitement, change, and the perception of progress. There was the powerful pull of "making history," the opportunity to signal a new era of racial harmony, and—as Virginians were repeatedly reminded by national news accounts during the campaign—the chance to impress the nation with Virginia's surprising progressivism. Either Coleman and the GOP would convince Virginians that Wilder was a soft-on-crime liberal[137] and an ethical disaster-area, or the Democrat would glide into office on a wave of good feeling. It seemed that simple—and it was.

As it turned out, Wilder's way to the governorship was no glide; but he did manage the narrowest of wins, and his success derived ultimately from two issues that ran interference for him throughout the fall campaign, successfully blocking Coleman's thrusts while keeping the GOP team off balance during much of the contest. The first was the "negative campaign" label. Coleman emerged in mid-June from a primary campaign in which he had played the aggressor, so, when he turned his sights on Wilder in the fall, he was particularly susceptible to the charge that he was too negative in his campaign tactics. Wilder's media consultants craftily exploited the Republican's vulnerability with ads that, according to Larry Sabato, "[f]requently [were] every bit as negative as Coleman's," but which artfully "blamed the Republican for practicing negative politics, thereby reinforcing Coleman's poor image while hurling charges of their own."[138] Correctly anticipating a Coleman campaign fusillade on Wilder's ethical misadventures, the Democratic missives coupled a sweeping denial of the GOP charges with the preemptive declaration that "you just can't trust Marshall Coleman." By October, newspaper polls indicated that voters were disproportionately blaming the Republican candidate for what

---

[136]Wilder had sparred with Robb and Baliles intermittently since his election as lieutenant governor in 1985, and he would flail both fellow Democrats with undisguised glee after assuming the governorship in 1990. During the 1989 campaign, however, Wilder benefited from the ostensible goodwill of Robb and Baliles, and portrayed himself as their natural successor. The popular Robb was especially helpful to Wilder: He supplied a televised endorsement that became the mainstay of the Wilder media campaign, and he sent word privately to the Coleman camp that he would intervene further on Wilder's behalf if the GOP sought to make campaign hay out of two highly critical letters that Robb had sent to Wilder in 1985–86 and then had made public.

[137]Though some observers argued after the election that Republicans had erred in not targeting Wilder's record on fiscal issues in their media advertising blitz, Coleman campaign polling data revealed that drugs and crime were far greater concerns of voters than taxes and spending. The economic hard times and budgetary crisis that suddenly emerged in Virginia in 1990 were not yet on the horizon. Moreover, Wilder had distanced himself from the Baliles administration's tax hikes. In contrast, Wilder's legislative record on criminal justice issues was particularly liberal—an apparent product of his extensive criminal defense work as a practicing attorney. In 1985, Wilder had gained crucial conservative credentials by winning the endorsement of the statewide Fraternal Order of Police (FOP); in 1989, Coleman's emphasis on Wilder's previous opposition to the death penalty and votes against other anti-crime measures enabled Coleman to capture the FOP nod.

[138]Sabato, "Virginia's Governor's Race, 1989 (Part 3)," p. 7.

they believed to be excessive campaign mud-slinging. "Coleman was hurt by a peculiar circumstance," ventured Sabato; "he was forced to run two negative campaigns back to back in the same year. That was probably one too many."[139]

The two Coleman campaigns in 1989 also exposed the Republican to another charge: that he was a "right-wing extremist" by virtue of his strong stance against legalized abortion. If, as Democratic Delegate Richard Cranwell once noted, Republicans suffered in Virginia because President Ronald Reagan fared too well in managing the national economy, the same could be said of the President's judicial appointments. Until the U.S. Supreme Court dominated by Reagan appointees signalled greater deference to state-legislated restrictions on abortion in its July 3, 1989 *Webster* decision, the preponderance of political energy and capital stemming from abortion-related activism was on the pro-life side. But the threatened rescission of abortion rights created in the Court's 16-year-old *Roe* v. *Wade* [140] ruling suddenly energized the pro-choice activists in the summer of 1989, thereby transforming the dynamics of the Virginia campaign for governor. Coleman, like GOP foes Trible and Parris, had staked out firm anti-abortion ground in vying for the Republican Party's gubernatorial nomination during the spring, and that turf proved exceedingly treacherous in the post-*Webster* general election campaign.

As a result of the *Webster* decision, Wilder never had to answer for his controversial record. While the "negative campaign" charge helped shield the Democrat from incoming Coleman missiles, the abortion issue supplied ammunition for a devastating Wilder counterattack. The Democratic camp responded to mid-September GOP blasts citing Wilder's prior opposition to capital punishment with advertisements assailing Coleman's abortion stance. And, when Coleman's handlers a month later launched the expected barrage focusing on Wilder's ethical lapses, the Democrat's handlers fired off another round of abortion ads. The Wilder missives were targeted to the youthful, GOP-leaning, libertarian audience in the suburbs; against a backdrop of the flag and Jefferson's Monticello, they stressed "keep[ing] the politicians out of your personal life," and warned that Coleman would "take us back" to the days of back-alley abortions when the procedure was illegal. The theme resembled that used in the unprecedented national media campaign against Supreme Court nominee Robert Bork two years earlier—indeed, some Wilder advisers actually were veterans of that battle[141]—and it was just as effective.

In what would become the most frequently second-guessed tactical decision of the fall campaign, Coleman's handlers responded to Wilder's

---

[139]Ibid., p. 6.

[140]*Roe* v. *Wade*, 410 U.S. 113 (1973).

[141]Michael Donilon and David Petts, who were polling and strategy consultants for the Wilder campaign, provided polling services to the anti-Bork coalition in 1987. They crafted a strategy for turning Southern senators against Bork's confirmation by emphasizing race relations and privacy rights.

September media blitz on abortion, not with an abortion-related rejoinder, but with further attacks on the Democratic nominee's criminal justice record. Wilder had raised abortion as an issue in order to stem the erosion in his support resulting from the GOP's sharp attacks on his death penalty stance, and Republicans were loathe to let him change the subject before they pressed the point home. Reading the polls, the Coleman team concluded that abortion would be distinctly inhospitable—and expensive—ground on which to join an electronic battle with Wilder. Rather, they would keep the heat on the Democrat with attacks on his criminal justice record, including a controversial Wilder-patroned bill that would have subjected young rape victims to courtroom interrogation about their past sexual conduct; then, in the campaign's closing weeks, they would zero in on the so-called character issues on which Wilder was deemed most vulnerable. The Republicans would simply duck and let the abortion wave pass over, convinced—incorrectly—that voters would tire of the issue and focus on other concerns by the time the November election rolled around.

While post-election analyses frequently faulted Coleman for not directly countering the abortion assault, retrospective observers generally overlooked the fact that Coleman's simultaneous crime-related attacks held Wilder to negligible abortion-related gains during the September exchange. Indeed, several commentators, including the University of Virginia's Sabato, ventured the opinion in early October that Wilder's most potent issue—abortion—had been exhausted with minimal impact, while Coleman had several sharp arrows remaining in his quiver.[142] It was only a few days later—when Coleman's handlers shifted to positive, image-oriented media messages in reaction to surveys that showed their man was bearing the brunt of voter displeasure with the negative tone of the contest—that Wilder's relentless abortion attacks produced deep and sudden gains. Even so, most of the lost ground was restored when the Coleman camp detected the erosion and went back on the offensive, this time with a provocative, emotionally charged television ad that featured a rape victim dissolving under cross-examination as an announcer recalled Wilder's legislative proposals. By mid-October, the candidates were again locked in an extremely close struggle. But that was good news mainly for Wilder, who now had arrived safely at the brink of "history," and whose single-issue campaign on abortion had completed his capture of national news media attention.

Much-ballyhooed events as far-flung as a special abortion-related state legislative session in Florida and the abortion-dominated gubernatorial contest in New Jersey guaranteed that voter interest in the controversial issue would not subside in the crucial closing weeks of the Virginia contest. To an electorate increasingly disgusted with negative campaigning, Coleman's long-awaited series of blasts on Wilder's ethics seemed not only shrill but

---

[142]See Margie Fisher, "Abortion Debate Fizzles," *Roanoke Times & World-News*, October 1, 1989.

impertinent, while the Democrat's no-less-persistent but more artful pounding on abortion fit nicely with the national political focus on that emotional topic. Months after the election, it would become "quite clear," according to a prominent journalist who covered the campaign, that abortion had been "debated to the exclusion of other important campaign issues."[143] But there was no changing the subject in late October. It was then that Coleman and his handlers began to wish that they had answered Wilder's abortion charges sooner—while they still had time to frame the issue in more favorable terms.

How much better Coleman ultimately might have fared if he had diverted precious media advertising resources to an abortion exchange with Wilder in September is a debatable question. Though the Democrat had dropped his opposition to broadly favored legislation requiring parental consent for teenage abortions, he remained vulnerable to GOP charges that he supported abortion-on-demand, abortion as a routine method of birth control, and abortion for the purpose of sex selection—all unpopular with voters. Wilder's July switch from a more moderate pro-choice stance under public pressure from National Organization for Women President Molly Yard, who derided him as "wimpy,"[144] opened up another possible line of attack for the Republicans. Any of those options would have had one notable advantage: by addressing the abortion issue squarely and aggressively, Coleman would have seemed decisive rather than appearing evasive and vacillating as a consequence of attempts to avoid discussion of the topic.

The Coleman campaign shied away, however, from all such approaches (and from the subject of abortion generally) out of concern that Wilder had at his disposal a show-stopping rejoinder: that Coleman would seek to outlaw abortions even in cases of pregnancy resulting from rape or incest. Like his rivals in the GOP primary, Coleman during the spring contest had routinely espoused support for restrictions on abortions except when necessary to save the life of the mother, thus admitting of no exceptions for rape and incest. Though he protested in the fall that legislation banning abortion in those statistically negligible cases would never pass in Virginia, and that he would never propose such a measure, Coleman was hamstrung by the more sweeping anti-abortion declarations he had made during the competition for the GOP nod. Polls typically showed that a ban on abortions in cases involving rape and incest was disfavored by a nine-to-one majority of Virginians.

In the final analysis, Coleman's ultimate tack on abortion—playing down the issue and reassuring voters that he would not seek limitations on rape and incest abortions—may have served him as well as any of the other alternatives in the unique circumstances of the 1989 contest. Of those voters who told exit

---

[143]Jeff E. Schapiro, "Story Details Historic Contest for Governor," *Richmond Times-Dispatch*, June 10, 1990.

[144]Yard used the derisive term after Wilder indicated in July 1989 that he favored some limitations on abortion rights. After a period of confusion in the immediate wake of the *Webster* decision, Wilder switched to a firm pro-choice stance. Edds, p. 149.

pollsters that abortion was their main concern, 55 percent favored Wilder to 45 percent for Coleman—a split not out of line with pre-campaign polls of Virginians' attitudes on the volatile issue.[145] Had Coleman abandoned his pro-life stance under campaign duress, he likely would have suffered a fate similar to that of unsuccessful New Jersey GOP gubernatorial candidate James Courter, who received only 32 percent of the votes cast by persons basing their preference on abortion.[146] On the other hand, if Coleman had more aggressively trumpeted his anti-abortion position, and had debated the subject more fully with Wilder, a post-election study by the Eagleton Institute suggests that his deficit would have increased as voters became better informed of the two candidates' stances.[147]

Two things seemed to emerge with clarity from the conflicting evidence of voter attitudes in the charged Virginia political atmosphere that followed the *Webster* decision. First, it became apparent that Coleman could have largely negated Wilder's abortion attacks by pointing to unpopular aspects of the Democrat's rigidly pro-choice posture if the Republican had not been hobbled by the emotional rape and incest issue produced by the GOP's nomination battle. Second, it was clear in the election's wake that the abortion issue had consumed the attention of Virginia voters and drowned out the other issues—crime, drugs, taxes, and ethics—on which Coleman and his handlers had pinned hopes of surmounting Wilder's substantial advantages as the "history-making" standard-bearer of the party in power.

Coleman and the Republicans were more successful in coping with the race issue, or so they believed. Throughout the contest, they had painstakingly—and successfully—endeavored to forestall any incident or appeal that could be construed as racially motivated and could thereby assist Democrats in portraying the election as a choice between a racially intolerant past and a racially progressive future. Though, for example, Wilder as a state senator had vehemently opposed popular "workfare" reforms, the Coleman camp refrained from emphasizing that issue out of concern that it might be interpreted as a subtle attempt to exploit an unfortunate racial stereotype. The GOP campaign similarly declined to air revelations that the state employment commission during the Baliles administration had been applying a racially preferential weighting system for minority job applicant test scores. And, when racial violence erupted in Virginia Beach during the Labor Day "Greekfest" celebration, Coleman and campaign manager Boyd Marcus rejected the advice of Senator John Warner, who suggested that the GOP candidate go to the resort city for a high-profile tour of looted commercial establishments.

---

[145]Sabato, "Virginia Governor's Race, 1989 (Part 3)," p. 2.

[146]Ibid. New Jersey and Virginia were the only states to hold gubernatorial elections in 1989. Democrats prevailed in both contests.

[147]Debra L. Dodson and Laura D. Burnbauer, *Election 1989: The Abortion Issue in New Jersey and Virginia* (Eagleton Institute of Politics, Rutgers, The State University of New Jersey, 1990), p. 95.

Despite such caution on racial matters, however, Democrats successfully invoked the desired past-versus-future imagery under the guise of discussing abortion rights and, to a lesser extent, the economic expansion and educational investment of the Robb-Baliles years. The Democratic rallying cry, "Don't let Marshall Coleman take us back," was not tied explicitly to race, but a reference to Virginia's segregationist past was clearly implied. "You were saying it, but you weren't saying it," chortled J. T. Shropshire, the Wilder intimate who later became his chief of staff.[148]

Having gone the extra mile to purge race from the gubernatorial campaign discourse, a frustrated Marshall Coleman watched in disbelief as news coverage in the closing weeks of the campaign seemed to romanticize Wilder's impending "history-making" achievement while giving short shrift to serious questions about the Democrat's integrity. Coleman found especially galling *The Washington Post*'s treatment on November 2 of revelations, confirmed in a tape recording disclosed by the National Right to Work Committee, that Wilder had secretly promised striking coal miners in southwest Virginia that he would assist efforts to weaken the state's venerated Right to Work Law. Though Coleman's television advertisements had indicted Wilder's trustworthiness, the Right to Work Committee's tape seemed to provide dramatic independent corroboration of the GOP's charge, and newspapers around the state gave the story devastating (for Wilder) front-page play. "Yet the *Post*," recounted Larry Sabato,

> buried the [tape] story on page A37, choosing to showcase on page A1 a positive Wilder piece and a very accusatory commentary about one of Coleman's "negative" phone bank operations—an article that even now appears to the lay reader to be utterly devoid of significant hard news.[149]

Ironically, *Post* reporter Donald Baker should have been among the quickest to recognize the import of Wilder's recorded suggestion that the miners should "get the camel's head in the tent" by eroding Right to Work protections gradually rather than moving directly to repeal the law.[150] Baker's election-year biography of the Democratic nominee quoted Wilder as using the very same analogy in describing the process through which he eventually succeeded in getting a state holiday honoring Dr. Martin Luther King, Jr., adopted in conservative Virginia.[151]

In a November 2 news conference, Coleman lashed out at the *Post*, and at the alleged news media bias generally, charging that reporters were applying a

---

[148]Edds, p. 125.

[149]Sabato, "Virginia Governor's Race, 1989 (Part 3)," p. 5. The article concerning Coleman's phone banks was written by political reporter Robert Melton. "Poll Firm That Irked Voters Paid By Coleman: Research Group Used Leading Questions on Wilder in Phone Calls," *The Washington Post*, November 2, 1989.

[150]*The Richmond News Leader*, October 31, 1989; *Roanoke Times & World-News*, November 1, 1989; *Richmond Times-Dispatch*, November 1, 1989.

[151]Baker, p. 109.

"double standard" to the gubernatorial candidates. It was, according to author Margaret Edds, the Republican's most "controversial performance" of the campaign.[152] Coleman had in mind several reasons for the alleged bias, with the two most salient and emotive issues of the campaign—race and abortion[153]—obviously high on the list; but he refrained from explicitly identifying any particular motive for the perceived unfairness. News accounts in the wake of the Coleman allegation varied sharply. *The Washington Post*, apparently chastened by the criticism, juggled the reporters it had assigned to cover the campaign, with the result that its coverage during the final days of the contest became noticeably less hostile in tone to Coleman. The Norfolk-based *Virginian-Pilot*, however, blistered the GOP candidate in a front-page story that depicted his "double standard" remark as a flagrant appeal to racial resentment among whites;[154] the newspaper followed up two days later in its Sunday edition with another page-one article reporting that a desperate Coleman had "played the explosive wild card in his deck: the color of his opponent's skin."[155] By contrast, the *Richmond Times-Dispatch*'s report on Coleman's news conference and bias plaints did not even hint at the possibility that the candidate had intended a racial appeal.

The divergent treatment of Coleman's eleventh-hour news conference demonstrated the volatility of race in the campaign and the sensitivity of the news media to allegations of bias, racial or otherwise. To the extent that Coleman was referring to a racial double standard, his focus was the positive publicity accorded Wilder because of the history-making nature of his candidacy and campaign—publicity that tended to overshadow questions about the Democratic nominee's ethics. "I for one am not going to stand by and watch a person who is unfit . . . glide into office with a 'feel good, make history' message," Coleman had defiantly declared to the assembled reporters.[156] An angry and aggrieved Wilder, who judged himself to be the "most ventilated candidate in Virginia history," heeded his advisers' advice and resisted the temptation to respond.[157] But his press secretary, Laura Dillard, saw an opening and unreservedly seized it. "[Coleman] is bumping up against a [racial] line that we in the Wilder campaign have assiduously avoided," she

---

[152]Edds, p. 224.

[153]Coleman campaign officials attributed pro-Wilder bias in in-state news coverage primarily to the pro-choice sentiments of most reporters on the high-profile abortion issue. A similar view was expressed by Larry Sabato, whose analysis of the gubernatorial contest highlighted the "clear pro-choice tilt" of the news media. See Sabato, "Virginia Governor's Race, 1989 (Part 3)," p. 3.

[154]Bill Byrd, "Coleman Blasts Racial 'Double Standard'," *The Virginian-Pilot*, November 3, 1989.

[155]Warren Fiske, "Wilder Looks Unscathed as Smoke Clears," *The Virginian-Pilot & The Ledger-Star*, November 5, 1989.

[156]Text of remarks on file with the author.

[157]Edds, p. 254.

protested,[158] apparently oblivious to the fact that, even then, more than a half-million dollars in unreported organized-labor contributions were being funneled through the state Democratic Party for, among other things, a last-minute direct-mail appeal for Wilder which arrived in an envelope bearing the exclamation, "You can help make history!"[159] "If tapping racial sentiment was [Coleman's] intent, he had done so in a sophisticated, New South way," commented Margaret Edds, whose account suggested that Coleman's "double-standard" charge may have been designed to capitalize on white resentment of affirmative action programs.[160] Yet, even the even-handed Edds seemed to miss the plain point of Coleman's news conference; a few days after the GOP candidate's protest, her *Virginian-Pilot* report began: "Forty-eight hours away from a possible rendezvous with history, Democrat L. Douglas Wilder . . ."[161]

Though news organizations and reporters are frequent, and easy, targets of criticism by political partisans, journalistic objectivity became a serious issue in the wake of the 1989 Virginia elections. *The Washington Post* received the lion's share of the attention—and unsurprisingly so, since its own ombudsman, Richard Harwood, joined in the criticism. Harwood recited a string of actions by the *Post*'s news department that were, in his considered judgment, "enough to raise non-paranoid questions about the disinterested nature of the coverage."[162] Professor Sabato agreed, observing in his analysis of the gubernatorial contest that the *Post* was among those who could take "credit (or blame, depending on one's viewpoint) for Coleman's defeat" in the close contest.[163] Coleman carried 73 counties to Wilder's 22, and 19 cities to the Democrat's 22, but he was decimated in vote-rich northern Virginia where the *Post* was the principal source of voter information, and he fared unusually poorly as well in the Hampton Roads area where the *Virginian-Pilot*'s coverage throughout the general election campaign was consistently critical. Though attributing election outcomes to particular news stories or campaign developments is a

---

[158]*The Virginian-Pilot*, November 3, 1989.

[159]Edds, p. 254; *Richmond Times-Dispatch,* May 16, 1990.

[160]Edds, p. 225. Although Coleman did not emphasize affirmative action as a campaign issue, the subject figured prominently in campaign discourse a year later in North Carolina and California, where Republican candidates did raise the issue and appeared to benefit from it. In North Carolina, incumbent Senator Jesse Helms won re-election by a comfortable margin after charging that his black opponent, former Democratic Mayor Harvey Gantt of Charlotte, favored employment quotas based on race and sex. In California, Senator Pete Wilson stressed his opposition to race and gender quotas in his successful gubernatorial contest with former Democratic Mayor Dianne Feinstein of San Francisco. The issue was brought to the fore by President Bush's veto of the Civil Rights Act of 1990 on the ground that it would impel companies to adopt quota systems for employment. Bush's veto was criticized sharply by Governor Wilder, who spent much of his first year as governor stumping across the country, discussing national issues, and bidding for a spot on the 1992 Democratic national ticket.

[161]*The Virginian-Pilot*, November 6, 1989.

[162]Richard Harwood, "Tilt! Tilt!," *The Washington Post*, November 19, 1989.

[163]Sabato, "Virginia Governor's Race, 1989 (Part 3)," p. 4.

dubious exercise, it requires no great leap of imagination to suppose that Coleman could have more than made up his razor-thin, 6,741-vote deficit on election day if the *Post*'s reporting on the Right to Work tape recording or the *Virginian-Pilot*'s coverage of the "double-standard" news conference had more closely resembled the treatment of those significant eleventh-hour events by other major news organizations around the state.

The most devastating developments in the decisive northern Virginia region, however, were those completely within the control of *The Washington Post*: the newspaper's in-house voter opinion surveys. For GOP partisans, it was like a quadrennially recurring nightmare. In 1985, the *Post* had published two polls that dramatically eroded the GOP ticket's standing in northern Virginia in the crucial weeks before the voting. The first, released on October 9, showed gubernatorial nominee Durrette trailing Democrat Baliles by 19 points, and overshadowed that day's appearance by President Reagan on the Republican's behalf. The second, coming less than 48 hours before the election, again showed a 19-point Baliles advantage, and put Wilder ahead of the GOP's Chichester by 24 points in the contest for lieutenant governor. Both *Post* surveys produced grossly inflated Democratic margins in comparison with other published surveys and the election day results.[164] Nevertheless, the effects of the *Post* surveys were palpable; especially in northern Virginia, GOP workers saw further effort as futile, and many Republican voters did not trouble themselves to go to the polls. The *Post*'s errant sampling, recounted Dwayne Yancey, supplied "a powerful cue [for] Northern Virginia voters, who may have had no real feel for how ridiculous the poll seemed downstate."[165]

Republicans assured themselves four years later that it could not happen again; after all, the *Post* had its reputation to protect, and the newspaper hardly had enhanced its credibility in the polling trade by forecasting a 1985 Wilder margin that was overstated by a factor of six. But on Sunday, October 29, 1989, it did indeed happen again. Northern Virginians awakened to survey results that showed Wilder sporting a 15-point lead little more than a week before the election. Though the *Post*'s survey was greeted with widespread skepticism among political and journalistic insiders—it had Wilder leading by a margin far greater than that suggested in any other poll during the campaign—the tone of news coverage around the state nevertheless changed perceptibly in the wake of its release. After that, wrote Sabato, "[v]irtually no story on Coleman was written without the obligatory, deflating qualifier, 'trailing badly in the latest *Post* poll,' with much of the prose that followed suggesting desperation and impending doom."[166] Another survey published six days later by the *Post*—this one showing a daunting 11-point Coleman deficit just 72 hours before the elec-

---

[164]In the actual voting, Baliles outpolled Durrette by ten percent, and Wilder's winning margin was four percent.

[165]Yancey, p. 297.

[166]Sabato, *Virginia Votes 1987-1990*, chapter 5 (forthcoming).

tion—compounded the damage to the Republican's cause. The ominous 1989 polls, like those four years earlier, debilitated the GOP's volunteer organization and depressed turnout by Coleman supporters on election day. The impact, though not objectively verifiable, likely exceeded Wilder's winning statewide margin. In Fairfax County alone, Wilder trounced Coleman by 27,000 votes, a figure nearly four times the Democrat's cumulative statewide advantage.

There were multiple explanations for the avalanche of Wilder votes in pivotal northern Virginia. Among them were Coleman's failure to successfully capture the potent transportation and tax issues in the region, his anti-abortion stance, fall-out from "negative" Republican media advertising, large financial contributions to the GOP campaign by developers which were targeted in Wilder television ads, and the enthralling appeal of the Democrat's history-making, guilt-purging candidacy among the area's cosmopolitan suburban voters. But Republican strategists came away from the 1985 and 1989 campaigns convinced that their most formidable obstacle in the politically powerful region was not the Democrats, but *The Washington Post*. With television advertising prohibitively expensive in the Washington, D.C., area, the widely read *Post* owned a virtual monopoly on campaign information. The experiences of the '80s suggested to Republicans that whenever the *Post* failed to restrain its "liberal intellectual predisposition," as Richard Harwood bluntly termed it,[167] GOP statewide candidates would have great difficulty winning elections. With the newspaper's own ombudsman joining in the criticism, it was untenable to dismiss the bias charges as the paranoid ravings of disappointed partisans.

Both the Democratic and Republican campaigns, of course, had their complaints with particular journalists, just as reporters had grievances of their own with campaign operatives who endeavored relentlessly to "spin" them with dubious contentions and partial truths. Who got the better of it in 1989, as in the other campaigns during the 1980s, is ultimately in the eye of the beholder, and political beholders are rarely objective. The larger political truths of the 1980s, however, are to be seen not in isolated or occasional events, but in the sweeping trends and recurring themes. Once in power, Democrats benefited throughout the decade from a prosperous national and state economy. Virginia voters seized opportunities in the '80s to make a symbolic statement about racial fairness; and, if unfairness to particular candidates was an unfortunate by-product of that exercise, at least it arose out of the most laudable of intentions. By decade's end, controversial social issues—most notably abortion—produced cross-cutting coalitions that reinforced the contemporary tendency toward partisan dealignment. And, from Reagan to Wilder, personality remained an intangible but often compelling force that bid

---

[167]*The Washington Post*, November 19, 1989.

fair to upset the most carefully laid of political plans. In retrospect, it is not a difficult decade to understand.

The voters in Virginia's burgeoning suburbs have been a catalyst for change in the Old Dominion for a generation now. When their demands for increased public services went unheeded, these voters rang down the curtain on the Byrd organization in the '50s and early '60s. By contrast, their conservative predilections on economic and foreign policy issues enabled Virginia Republicans to dominate federal and statewide elections in the '70s. In the '80s, Virginians' individualistic, libertarian attitudes on race and personal "privacy" issues helped bring state Democrats back to power. Even with these seemingly dramatic partisan swings, the mounting political competition in suburban Virginia steadily boosted Republican representation in the General Assembly, and created the not-so-remote possibility that redistricting and a round or two of legislative elections in the 1990s could yield a GOP majority in one or both houses.

The twists and turns of postwar Virginia politics are naturally puzzling, and further surprises no doubt lie ahead. The Commonwealth remains a dynamic place, full of the same promise, peril, and unpredictability that pervades the vibrant nation that is her enduring legacy. A half-century of partisan realignment in Virginia is now at an end—finished though not complete—and both state and nation are poised to move briskly in as-yet-uncertain political directions as a new millennium approaches, new social and economic challenges arise, and a new world order emerges. Though, as political journalist Jeff Schapiro observed, "making history—right up there with sausage-making and law-making—is not a pretty sight,"[168] Virginians seem to have the stomach for it. More than in any other place, politics in the Old Dominion remains a perennial if often tedious pastime, with each successive election campaign effectively beginning before the voting machines are rolled away after the preceding one. Perhaps it is the sport of it, or the tradition, or both. But somewhere, deep in the Virginia psyche, also lies a conviction best captured in the admonition of the preeminent Virginian and American, George Washington:

> The preservation of the sacred fire of liberty, and the destiny of the republican model of government, are justly considered as deeply, perhaps as finally staked, on the experiment entrusted to the hands of the American people.[169]

A man with a clear sense of his and his people's place in history, Washington was neither the first nor last Virginian to take his politics quite seriously.

---

[168]*Richmond Times-Dispatch*, June 10, 1990.
[169]First Inaugural Address, April 30, 1789.

Epilogue
"Why Stand We Here Idle?"

Passions are running high in Virginia as a much-ballyhooed election approaches. The contest features two men who ultimately will reach the White House. Now, however, they find themselves locked in a dramatic struggle for political dominance in the Old Dominion.

One contestant—widely regarded as the favorite—is a ground-breaking politician who has earned national acclaim for his artful coalition-building. He also has recently navigated the treacherous shoals of Virginia politics to achieve legislative success at the state capital. His unpredictable moves, however, have irked some supporters and infuriated influential colleagues in the Commonwealth. In particular, he is bedeviled by the vindictive manipulations of an embittered former governor whom he once counted as an ally.

The opposing candidate also is a man of substantial accomplishment and renown. Having first gained notoriety in uniform, the challenger has established a reputation as an appealing and capable public servant. As the campaign draws to a close, he has the momentum and is gaining fast.

With the outcome suddenly in doubt, the nimble frontrunner acts to avert an upset by switching his stance on a major civil rights issue. The move, regarded as cynical and expedient by some, nevertheless regains for him the support of an influential minority group that he had mistakenly taken for granted. With that critical backing, the early favorite becomes the final victor in one of the most lively political contests ever in Virginia.

The scenario above will strike the typical political observer as unexceptional. Self-serving shifts of position and no-holds-barred political conflict are hardly unfamiliar today. Before the political self-immolation of arch-rivals Chuck Robb and Douglas Wilder in 1991, the passage might even have been construed as a prophesy of electoral Armageddon for the three contentious men who were Democratic governors of Virginia in the 1980s. In reality, however, the scenario is neither a commentary on the state of contemporary politics nor an attempt at prognostication. Rather, the contest described above is one that actually occurred two centuries ago—in February 1789, during the election of the First Congress pursuant to the newly ratified United States Constitution. The favorite was the scholarly and diminutive James Madison; his attractive rival was Colonel James Monroe of Fredericksburg; and the behind-the-scenes manipulator was former Governor Patrick Henry. The source of Henry's hostility was Madison's new constitution, which Virginia had ratified—over Henry's adamant and formidable opposition—the preceding summer. That was the emotional topic on which hinged the outcome of the hard-fought 1789 congressional election in Virginia's Piedmont.

Students of the Constitution know the story well. Henry, George Mason, and other opponents of ratification were chiefly concerned about the strong central government created under the new constitution, and they objected to (among other things) the constitutional convention's failure to incorporate a bill of rights that would serve to restrain the central government's power. For his part, Madison was wary of the interpretive perils associated with enumerating certain personal rights while omitting others, and he regarded his elaborate structural scheme of governmental checks and balances as a more efficacious safeguard of liberty than mere "parchment barriers," such as a recital of rights.[1] By January 1789, however, Madison was locked in a struggle for his own political survival, and his desire for conciliation with his impassioned foes combined with campaign-related exigencies to produce a change of position. To Baptists in his congressional district, who desperately wanted an explicit constitutional guarantee of religious liberty, Madison pledged to work in Congress for the adoption of constitutional amendments embodying a bill of rights. With that vocal minority's support, he gained election to the First Congress. And, though Federalists pressured him to renege or procrastinate, Madison honored his pledge and secured the controversial amendments' adoption in Congress during the ensuing autumn.[2]

This early lesson in Virginia politics is instructive for several reasons. It is a reminder, first, that profound political consequences can flow from unpredictable and seemingly benign developments. If, for example, a misappraisal of the political climate—or even the vagaries of eighteenth-century travel—had prevented Madison from hurrying home to Orange County in time to affect the February 1789 balloting, the course of American history might have been altered dramatically. For two centuries, the Bill of Rights has been at the center of our great national political debates as the American people have wrestled with the dilemma inherent in the republican form of government: how to strike the proper balance between the imperatives of liberty and order . . . personal freedom and governmental restraint . . . individual autonomy and majority will. The pitched contemporary debates over abortion

---

[1]See *The Federalist No. 48* (J. Madison).

[2]See Robert Allen Rutland, *James Madison: The Founding Father* (New York: MacMillan Publishing Company, 1987).

and affirmative action are but two of the most recent manifestations of this ongoing struggle. That the adoption of the immensely important Bill of Rights depended upon a last-minute campaign conversion by the influential Madison highlights the extent to which Americans have placed their future at risk by entrusting it to popular whim and caprice.

A second, more reassuring insight to be gleaned from the 1789 congressional race is the recognition that the great leaders of the eighteenth century were politicians as well as statesmen. Virginia is renowned for her history, and there is a modern tendency to view the Revolutionary era as a period when Virginians were given to uncommon insights—a time when profound ideas about personal liberty and social organization flowed effortlessly from ingenious minds through quill pens onto enduring parchment vessels. Men such as Washington, Jefferson, Madison, Henry, Mason, and Marshall appear larger than life—as images, indeed icons, rather than the very human politicians and statesmen that they were. It is well to appreciate that the American Revolution and the Republic's founding were signal moments in mankind's quest for freedom, that prominent Virginians played pivotal roles in that grand enterprise, and that the principles those statesmen wove into the fabric of our law and society are among our nation's greatest gifts. But those uniquely gifted men also were politicians, and politics today is—or should be—but a continuation of the enterprise they began.

Although not every successful politician is a statesman, every successful statesman in our history has been a politician. Indeed, it would be cause for despair if ever that maxim were contradicted, for ideas have consequences in a free society only when they are manifested in effective political action. Virginia politics has been, and ever will be, a mixture of contending personalities as well as colliding principles, of self-serving aims as well as more noble motivations, and of mundane issues as well as extraordinary ideas. Matters of fundamental import invariably will be placed on the political agenda alongside subjects of momentary significance; historic tides will flow from seemingly isolated events; and, occasions will present themselves when one person can make a profound difference for good or for ill. Virginia politics in the latter half of the twentieth century is not different in basic character from that which preceded it by two centuries. And, rather than gazing back resignedly at the Old Dominion's "Golden Age" gone by, the challenge for current and future generations of Virginians is to understand their political heritage, to discern the fundamental principles that guided their forebears, and to apply those enduring principles sensibly, creatively, and with integrity to the resolution of contemporary public problems.

Another historical anecdote may reinforce the point. Just as James Madison's remarkable constitutional architecture has obscured his less inspiring political meandering, so, too, is Patrick Henry remembered for his enduring contributions rather than his connivances. Long before he embarked upon his vendetta against Madison, Henry had earned a place in the hearts of his heirs with his impassioned plea in 1775 for resolute defiance of the British Crown. Contrary to today's popular impression, however, neither the politicians nor the citizenry in 1775 were widely committed to the idea of revolution. Generations of Virginia school children have studied Henry's famed speech at St. John's Church in Richmond precisely because it was the spark that ignited the Virginia colony and aroused its people to risk everything in a fight for freedom. Then, as at all times since, there was a prospect that principle would fall victim to widespread apathy, hesitancy, and expediency. People had other, more pressing concerns and goals. But Henry awakened them from their resignation and indifference by presenting the issue squarely and declaring that, for him, death was preferable to life without liberty.

The simple yet evocative question that Henry directed to the conscience of his colleagues—"Why stand we here idle?"—has been posed by ensuing generations of Virginia leaders who, guided by principle, have confronted the imperative of change. Initiative, not passivity, was the course chosen by Virginians, for example, when the nation was plunged into civil war in 1860. It was the path taken by a youthful Governor Harry Byrd when progressive strides were desperately needed in the state in the 1920s. And, when the federal response to the Great Depression in the 1930s wrought a fundamental and destructive transformation in the division of power between the state and federal governments, it was the course of Virginia's influential leaders in Congress.

In the nearly half-century since the Second World War, as the pace of social, economic, and political change in the Commonwealth quickened, Virginia's leaders were moved with increasing frequency to pose Henry's question to their colleagues and constituents. Rarely was there unanimity; more often, change came only after dogged resistance and heated debate. But, rather than standing idle, Virginians opted to address the growing need for investment in education. They dismantled barriers to equal opportunity in society for racial minorities and women. They created abundant new economic opportunities and enhanced social mobility through a rapid transition from an agricultural to a more diverse economy. They opened wide the doors to political participation and ushered in an era of free-wheeling, two-party competition even as political parties were becoming weaker nationwide. On the great national political issues, too, there was a clearly identifiable Virginia position, as reflected in the ballots cast in federal election contests and the votes of the state's delegation in Congress. Virginians in the second half of the twentieth century resolutely resisted calls for retreat and unilateral disarmament in the face of communist expansionism. They championed free-market economic policies and conservative fiscal approaches conducive to economic growth and opportunity. And, they labored to stem the erosion of state and local prerogatives through the accretion of power by the federal bureaucracy and courts.

Political Parties in Competitive Virginia:
A Checkered Record

Though tracing a political party's lineage is at best a dubious enterprise given the extent of the realignment that has occurred since the Second World War, Virginia's Republicans can plausibly claim a legacy of leadership in promoting beneficial postwar change. Much of the progress in making state government responsive to the needs of its citizens can be traced to Ted Dalton's innovative agenda of reform in the 1950s and to the bold initiatives implemented by Mills Godwin (while a Democratic governor) a decade later. The aristocracy of merit that displaced the divisive, demeaning, and wasteful racial codes of Virginia's past is an enduring legacy of the first Republican governor since Reconstruction, Linwood Holton. The Commonwealth's traditions of fiscal stability and public integrity—values to which few states have adhered so unwaveringly—are happy vestiges of the Byrd era, to which, since realignment, Republicans have claimed relation by "marriage." And, the state's realigned, two-party competitive political system—with the resultant increase in governmental accountability and responsiveness—is a contribution principally of Richard Obenshain and John Dalton. These two preeminent Republican leaders of the 1970s did more, however, than forge a winning conservative coalition around a revitalized GOP. Each made his own indispensable contribution to the identity of the Virginia Republican Party and the political code of the Commonwealth: Obenshain, as the impassioned apostle of individual liberty, and Dalton, as the skillful practitioner of frugal, efficient, business-like government.

The modern Virginia GOP has often seemed an odd mixture of the conservative and the progressive, an attribute it has shared with its contemporary Democratic counterpart, and with the Commonwealth generally. Today's dynamic Virginia is neither "old" nor "new" in any conventional sense; rather, it is a conspicuous blend of the traditional and the progressive, the conservative, the libertarian, and occasionally even the liberal. Its people eschew political extremism, whether of the Right or the Left, and seek consensus. Yet, one hopes that on matters of principle they remain capable of—indeed, inclined toward—a Henry-like stand. "Even the mountains are moderate," Guy Friddell once observed of the state's geography and, implicitly, its politics.[3] It is an apt analogy, for, like the mountains, Virginia's leaders traditionally have adapted resiliently to changing conditions even as they have remained fundamentally unyielding.

This seeming contradiction disappears under the penetrating microscope of Russell Kirk, the scholar whose thoughts and writings have animated the modern conservative political movement in America. "Both the impulse to

---

[3]Friddell, p. 4.

improve and the impulse to conserve are necessary to the healthy functioning of any society," wrote Kirk.

Whether we join our energies to the party of progress or the party of permanence must depend upon the circumstances of the time. Of rapid change, healthy or unhealthy, we seem sure to experience more than enough in the concluding years of this century. [The question is w]hether the conservative impulse within modern society can suffice to prevent the disintegration of the moral order and the civil order by the vertiginous speed of alteration . . .[4]

If the measure of good governance is, as Kirk implies, the preservation and application of first principles in changing circumstances, then neither Virginia political party in the late twentieth century has met the test of leadership or lived up to its legacy. Republicans, who spent most of the 1980s honing their ability to cope with electoral failure, frequently were faulted—often justifiably—for lacking a policy agenda. In the absence of any unifying personality or organizing principle, the post-Obenshain GOP became synonymous in the public mind with intransigence and little else.

The Robb-Baliles Democrats, flushed with success, spent less time than the Republicans engaged in introspection, but they were scarcely more creative. Although the pace of change accelerated in the '80s, Virginia's government generally failed to respond to the challenges and opportunities the change presented. The dominant Democrats reaped the harvest of economic gains cultivated mostly by others, and—having defined "progress" primarily by the level of social spending—were generally content to appropriate vast public sums for education, transportation, and social services without any notable effort to achieve meaningful reform in those areas. Business-as-usual during the decade produced meager results in terms of improved educational offerings or performance, reduction of traffic gridlock, increased public safety, or enhanced opportunity for the less fortunate; indeed, many of the trends in these areas were adverse during the 1980s. But the cost of government soared, setting the stage for fiscal calamity and retrenchment at decade's end.

For all their unbridled power during the '80s—Democrats controlled both political branches of state government during most of the decade—the ruling party's leaders were hard-pressed to point to achievements that transcended symbolism. Virginia gained the national limelight with Douglas Wilder's narrow, ground-breaking election as governor in 1989, and the event represented a milestone in the state's march away from massive resistance to full participation for racial minorities. Even that symbolic achievement, however, was attributable less to the vision and beneficence of Democratic Party captains than to Wilder's own gutsy and savvy political gamesmanship. Wilder

---

[4]Russell Kirk, *The Conservative Mind* (Chicago, Washington, D.C.: Regnery Gateway, Inc., 1987), pp. viii–ix.

followed his own counsel: he got the "camel's head in the tent"[5] in 1982 by demonstrating that he could exercise veto power over Democratic statewide nominations, and he parlayed that clout into a place atop his party's statewide ticket in 1989.

Once nominated, Wilder's success in the gubernatorial election depended upon his convincingly embracing the record, coalition, and future-oriented imagery of Governors Robb and Baliles. Ironically, however, after he gained office, Wilder seemed intent upon dismantling much of what his popular Democratic predecessors had erected—especially in the fields of trade, transportation, and education. He unabashedly blamed the state's fiscal misery in 1990 and 1991 on the spending proclivities of his Democratic predecessor and, by implication, the General Assembly long dominated by his fellow Democratic partisans. Thus, while Virginia's Republicans were the ones who suffered from an identity crisis throughout the 1980s, Democrats opened the 1990s with their gubernatorial leader aggressively revising the party's decade-old agenda. More often than not, it seemed that Wilder's revisions served his own presidential ambitions far better than the interests of Virginia's Democrats, whose future success depended upon preserving an often-tenuous center-left coalition.

If Wilder's departures from Democratic orthodoxy threatened to destabilize the Virginia political environment in the 1990s, the same could be said of President George Bush's occasional retreats from Reaganism's key tenets in Washington. Support for a strong national defense and for reduced taxing, spending, and regulation by the federal government were the pillars of Reagan administration policy from 1981 to 1989. With the diminution of the international communist threat at the close of the decade, much of the glue that had held together the Republican coalition in presidential elections for four decades was gone. Though Bush's canny efforts to mobilize an international coalition and forcibly expel Iraq from Kuwait in 1990 and early 1991 left the President with an enormous reserve of personal popularity, it seemed doubtful that the successful Persian Gulf War effort would translate into sustained partisan advantage. On the domestic front, Bush's decision in 1990 to scuttle the GOP's no-tax-increase plank served to blur the key difference between the two parties in most voters' perception, and threatened to compound the adverse economic impact of new regulatory measures adopted in the first two years of his administration.

To anticipate the direction of Republican fortunes in the absence of polarizing foreign policy and economic issues, one may need to look no farther than Virginia and her statewide elections in the 1980s. By embracing traditionally

---

[5]Wilder used the analogy to describe the indirection that he successfully employed in order to secure adoption of a state holiday honoring Dr. Martin Luther King, Jr. Baker, p. 109. He repeated the phrase in 1989 when he confidentially advised striking coal miners that gradual changes were the only way to erode the protections of Virginia's Right to Work Law. *Richmond Times-Dispatch*, November 1, 1989.

conservative fiscal and foreign policy stances, Virginia's moderate Democrats checked GOP charges of liberalism. They then used issues that cut across conventional philosophical lines—principally race and abortion, but also education and environmental protection—to split the once-dominant Republican conservative coalition. Unless the Bush-led national GOP can develop a new way to attract simultaneously blue-collar "Reagan Democrats" and young, suburban professionals, Republicans may well suffer a reversal in federal elections as sudden and unexpected as the shift of party fortunes in Virginia's statewide elections from the 1970s to the 1980s.

In recent times, the Commonwealth's politics have eerily foreshadowed the nation's by about a decade. After Democratic moderates, led by a progress-minded Governor Mills Godwin and U.S. Senator William Spong, forged a new majority coalition in Virginia in the mid-1960s, a "New South" Democrat named Jimmy Carter achieved the Presidency in the mid-1970s. After Virginia Republicans assembled a conservative coalition and compiled an impressive winning streak in the 1970s, Ronald Reagan mobilized a similar constituency and dominated American politics throughout the 1980s. Whether the "New Mainstream" charted by Chuck Robb and skillfully navigated by Douglas Wilder in the 1980s will alter the national landscape in the 1990s remains, of course, to be seen. Though disabled from presidential politics by their own brawling and other controversies, Robb and Wilder appear to have provided a blueprint for Democratic renewal nationally by successfully reversing a decade-long trend toward the Republicans in conservative Virginia. But if Democrats do eventually manage to regain the initiative nationally, and if the recent pattern holds, Virginia Republicans also can expect a resurgence during the 1990s. For much of the period since the Second World War—and especially since the rapid realignment of the early 1970s—the party in power in Washington has not fared well in statewide elections in Virginia.

Out of the Crucible of Competition: An Agenda of Principled Reform

More than any mystical pattern, the choices made by leaders and activists in the two parties will determine the course of Virginia politics in the future. To reverse their sagging statewide fortunes, Republicans must overcome their self-defeating penchant for infighting and factionalism, reinvigorate their grass-roots organization, delineate their philosophical differences with the dominant Democrats, nominate urbane and telegenic candidates, and direct a forward-looking, issue-oriented appeal to the vote-laden suburbs. To remain on top, Democrats must develop new stratagems for holding together the divergent elements of their winning coalition, resist the tendency toward factionalism that shadows partisan success and conflicting personal ambitions, avoid symbolic association with the long-dominant liberal faction of the national Democratic Party, and craft a message with simultaneous appeal in the suburbs and central cities.

For the foreseeable future, neither political party in Virginia is likely to be successful if it and its candidates fail to sustain in working coalition their respective interest-group and single-issue constituencies. Yet, it is also true that neither party can expect to succeed without projecting an appeal to the broad, moderate-conservative, independent middle of the Virginia electorate. Because of these competing priorities, party leadership—and, through it, consensus—will be a critical commodity. Neither party can well afford hard-fought nominating contests that bruise feelings, deplete coffers, and pull candidates toward ideological extremes where they are rendered vulnerable to better-positioned general election foes.

If the Commonwealth's competitive system works well in the 1990s, it will yield at least one party of genuine reform—Republican or Democratic—whose mission will be to apply Virginia's traditional values innovatively to the state's rapidly changing and ever more complex conditions. For Republicans, the challenge will be to promote principled reform rather than lapsing into reflexive resistance to change; for Democrats, the challenge will be to temper change with tested values rather than blithely promoting the indiscriminate displacement of tradition. Neither the passive sentimentality of the conservative Old Dominion nor the aggressive technocracy of the Balilesian "New Dominion" offers real promise for resolving the great social and political dilemma of our time: how to realize the potential of this dynamic new age while preserving the character, culture, shared values, and sense of community among our people.

The values that have long characterized the Virginia polity are captured in familiar phrases: among them, individual freedom (embodying notions of both personal liberty and moral responsibility); limited, frugal government; constitutionalism; free markets and free enterprise; security of person and property against unwarranted intrusion; freedom of conscience; an ethic of initiative and self-reliance; a sense of civic duty (reflected in public service and private charity); devotion to the ideal of an educated citizenry; and commitment to the wise stewardship of natural resources. Such values or principles appear as abstractions on the printed page. But, without them—or some fundamental concept—as a compass, politicians inevitably find themselves adrift in a sea of choices with only the shifting, swirling currents of public opinion and political self-interest to guide them. Such untethered pragmatism is as inconsistent with and destructive of Virginia's political traditions as is ideological rigidity.

The Commonwealth's enduring political philosophy is rooted ultimately in a particular view of human nature—of its potential, its inherent limits, and its dependence upon Divine intercession—from which flow certain premises and expectations about the propriety and effectiveness of public policies. The contrasting conception of human capacity as ultimately limitless—constrained only by failures in application of intellect and reason—often yields contrary policy conclusions and choices. This fundamental philosophical cleavage remains a central feature of American politics, and is as relevant to political discourse and competition in Virginia today as at any time in the state's history.

Though past-versus-future imagery and symbolic candidacies frequently were decisive in Virginia elections in the 1980s, such superficial considerations are less likely to impress voters in the decade ahead. There are signs of a growing unease in the electorate about the character of modern society—its impersonal nature, moral uncertainty, and tendency toward cultural decline. Politicians who fail to appreciate and respond to this widespread, though seldom well-articulated, concern about erosion of traditional values will increasingly seem impertinent to voters. Similarly, the economic trials of the early 1990s are likely to deplete rapidly the reservoir of voter patience with politicians who measure creativity by the number of new ways conceived to spend taxpayers' dollars. As public resources become more scarce, awareness of unmet needs will increase, and so, too, will demands for new and better approaches.

In such challenging circumstances will be great opportunity as well as peril: the opportunity, born of necessity, to look for the essence of things, and the peril that the essence may be incorrectly discerned. A political transformation of enormous dimension is possible. Because both parties generally have failed to offer a distinctive vision worthy of the Commonwealth's heritage and potential, Virginia voters in the 1990s will seek reform-minded leaders— Republican or Democratic—who advocate creative approaches grounded in proven principles and common sense. Virginians appear poised to respond again to the summons, "Why stand we here idle?" and the illumination of a better way.

While it is beyond the scope of this volume to say what should constitute Virginia's agenda of principled reform, it is possible to identify a number of critical questions that are likely to confront policy-makers in the years ahead.

Why, for example, do Virginians stand idle today when the hope of young and old alike rests on an educational system that remains mired in mediocrity? Though these are times when people around the globe are discovering anew that competition and free choice foster excellence, Virginia's political leaders cling to an education orthodoxy discredited by virtually every objective measure of performance. Rather than taking the lead in reform, the Commonwealth's contemporary policy-makers generally have submitted to the demands of those with a vested interest in the education status quo—bureaucrats, employees, and their unions—and have left it to those with vision in other states to implement programs that empower parents and students as education consumers, create incentives for excellence through performance-based compensation, and bring the demonstrable benefits of competition and choice to the educational mission. A heritage of leadership in education dating to Jefferson has been abdicated in Virginia even as public expenditures have risen rapidly.

Similarly fundamental questions may be asked about the Commonwealth's approach to pressing law enforcement problems, especially the epidemic of illegal drug use and drug-related crime. Why, for example, does Virginia not hold drug *users* accountable for the consequences of their self-indulgence? Opinion polls confirm that the vast majority of Virginians are prepared to confront the drug crisis by forcefully reasserting a simple, traditional value: that people should assume, or be made to bear, responsibility for the harm their actions cause to others. It is inescapable that the persistent appetite for illegal substances is the immediate cause of the violent and increasingly destructive drug trade. Stiff penalties for drug users, such as large fines and community service obligations, would signal societal disapproval and deter widespread "casual" drug use without overburdening the hard-pressed Virginia corrections system. Yet, the state's political leadership has stood idle, choosing to engage mostly in hollow public-relations gestures rather than decisive action.

Virginians should also ask why their leaders have failed to respond to the tragedy of large numbers of disadvantaged citizens locked in a cycle of hopelessness and dependence on government assistance. It seems hardly a coincidence that a quarter-century after the federal government launched its celebrated "war" on poverty, opportunity is more elusive than ever for most urban poor, and young black males now have a greater likelihood of going to prison than to college. A wealth of social literature has illuminated the devastating psychological and economic consequences of well-intentioned "welfare" programs that supply the means for maintenance but do nothing to foster an achievement ethic or to create meaningful new opportunities. Yet, Virginia has trod that very self-defeating path behind the lead of the federal government. Merely to increase the level of resources expended in such demonstrably failed efforts is hardly more compassionate than a policy of outright neglect, and neither approach is consistent with Virginia's traditions of generosity and self-reliance. An agenda of principled reform would eschew dependency as well as indifference, and promote initiatives that measure success in terms of values inculcated, skills taught, and self-esteem, independence, and opportunity enhanced. Such initiatives eventually would free up more scarce public and private dollars to aid those who truly have no alternative but reliance upon the compassion and generosity of others.

Passive persistence in existing approaches also will not suffice to address the multifaceted challenges presented by population and economic growth. Virginia's population grew by 16 percent in the 1980s, and the expansion—following a pattern several decades old—was centered in the burgeoning suburbs that comprise the urban corridor from northern Virginia through the Richmond metropolitan area to Hampton Roads. The growing pains were felt most acutely at each end of the corridor. Indeed, Henry's historic query has become a familiar refrain in northern Virginia and Tidewater as frustrated commuters demand to know why they are forced to stand idle daily in seemingly interminable traffic jams. The price of new economic opportunity has been paid not only in traffic tie-ups, but through the loss of much of Virginia's once-charming countryside to miles of pavement and flickering neon. The Commonwealth's bountiful and beautiful natural heritage has been placed in jeopardy in many areas by helter-skelter commercial and residential development, and by the dirty, sometimes dangerous side-effects of production and "progress." Perhaps the most alarming consequence of suburban sprawl has been the loss of neighborhood identity and community spirit that have long been such a vital part of life in the Old Dominion.

If ever there was a problem that cried out for new thinking and creative new approaches, it is that complex of thorny issues comprised in the term "growth management." As residents of gargantuan Fairfax County were discovering anew as the 1980s closed, "no-growth" policies are no answer to the problems that attend economic and population growth; the effects of the supposed cure are far worse than the disease. But, if Virginians cannot forsake economic progress, neither can they realistically hope that unbridled expansion somehow will serendipitously relieve its own deleterious side-effects. Local governments and regional bodies must be given the tools to innovate, to develop necessary resources, and to implement new approaches that accommodate the variety of economic, environmental, and civic interests and needs that characterize Virginia's dynamic communities. The creative capacities of the Commonwealth's best minds must be focused urgently upon the development of growth-management strategies that are best calculated to yield vibrant, prosperous, livable communities—not mere population and commercial centers, but "communities" in the fullest traditional sense of that word. With population growth proceeding apace, Virginia's political leaders will find it increasingly difficult to explain continued inaction to their frustrated constituents.

Another form of growth—the rapid growth in the size of state and local government—also is likely to be on the minds of Virginia voters in the years ahead. Though economic exigencies (perhaps intermingled with national political ambitions) were prompting Governor Douglas Wilder to exercise fiscal restraint as the 1990s opened,[6] there was little evidence that state or local policymakers were undertaking the sort of elemental reappraisal of governmental functions, priorities, and performance that the times demand. It is axiomatic that, if a particular governmental program or activity is not strengthening the community and enhancing the condition of the citizenry, it

---

[6]In a stunning display of political acrobatics, Wilder unabashedly stumped across the country in 1990 and 1991 portraying Virginia's handling of its fiscal crisis as a model for the nation. Wilder's self-serving proclamations were belied by the reality that Virginia's whopping $2.1 billion budget shortfall was proportionally the highest in the country—an outgrowth of spending policies implemented while Wilder was lieutenant governor and a key leader of the party in power in Virginia. Robert F. Black, et al., "Rating the States," U.S. News & World Report, February 18, 1991.

is undermining both. Governmental initiatives, by their very nature, are accomplished only through the confiscation of private resources and the constriction of personal freedom; unless the good achieved through the governmental activity outweighs this cost, the activity is not only ineffective but harmful. Despite this inescapable reality, many government programs assume a life of their own once enacted, and are rarely fine-tuned, let alone seriously reexamined. After nearly three decades of fast-paced governmental growth in Virginia—which soared at an unprecedented rate during the Baliles administration from 1986-1990—the need for a comprehensive reassessment of public expenditures is plain. Until that occurs, no increase in taxation or spending levels can be justified. If the Commonwealth's policy-makers stand idle, trimming here and there but otherwise leaving the spending leviathan unmolested, the result may well be a drastic, long-term diminution of the economic vitality and fiscal stability that Virginia has enjoyed in the dynamic decades since the Second World War.

Not only the scope of government, but also its organization, seem overdue for reexamination. As Virginia has evolved in the latter half of the twentieth century from a mostly rural state to a largely urban one, the nature and scope of public policy challenges also have changed. While successful business enterprises regularly tailor their organization and services to meet changes in consumer demand, governments are rarely so introspective or sensitive to the need for structural adjustments. The matter is complicated by the existence of multiple governmental levels—municipal, county, state, and federal—as well as complicated structures at each level. Increasingly, for example, infrastructure needs (i.e., transportation, water, sewer, emergency services, corrections, etc.) require metropolitan or regional approaches unshackled by restrictions imposed at the state level and more comprehensive than plans pieced together by local governments. Though it is seldom a subject of widespread public concern, the task of determining the most efficacious allocation of functions and authority among governmental levels and units—with an appropriate, corresponding redistribution of revenue sources—will be among the most important challenges facing policy-makers in Virginia as a new century approaches.

More than considerations of efficiency must be factored into this reorganizational equation. Another consequence of Virginia's population growth has been the increasing remoteness of citizens from their state government. In 1940, the average member of the House of Delegates represented 27,000 Virginians; in 1992, each delegate will have approximately 62,000 constituents. This trend, coupled with the long-running transfer of governmental prerogatives from state capitals to Washington, D.C., has left many citizens with a sense that the important policy decisions are made by inaccessible politicians and faceless bureaucrats with little interest in the wisdom or wishes of their grass-roots constituents. The need for government "closer to the people" is more than a cliché; participatory democracy is an illusion where the great majority of people perceive individual participation to be futile. In the 1980s, the Reagan administration labored with mixed success to reinvigorate federalism by returning responsibility and revenue to state governments, and the Bush administration has resolved to continue and expand that initiative. Similar reform is needed in Virginia. Curtailment of state-imposed (and unfunded) mandates on local governments—an essential first step—should be followed by efforts to transfer significant policy-making authority from Richmond to municipal, county, and regional bodies, where the efficacy of citizen participation will be enhanced.

While some disillusionment with the political process will be relieved by placing more governmental authority within the reach of ordinary citizens, renewed emphasis on ethics in government also is essential. Among the most beneficial aspects of the Byrd organization's administration of public affairs in Virginia from the 1920s to the 1960s was adherence to a rigid code of public integrity. By comparison with many other states, the Commonwealth still seems a paragon of public virtue. But the principle of scrupulous public service is less remarked today than in the Byrd era, and the penchant for secrecy among prominent government officials in Virginia is a source of increasing consternation for many citizens. It may not be important for the general public to know where state officials such as the governor travel at state expense, or whom they call on the telephone at public expense, or how they dispose of excess campaign funds, honoraria, and funds raised through semi-official events such as inaugural festivities. The average citizen may not need to know how candidates, campaign committees, party organizations, labor unions, and political action committees raise and distribute their resources in pursuing political aims. Nor may public knowledge of the deliberations at key policy-making meetings during General Assembly sessions be essential. But efforts to avoid such disclosures typically have the appearance of concealment, and inevitably fuel speculation about improper conduct. The effect is to undermine public confidence in the integrity of government officials.

One of the state's most thoughtful political scholars and commentators, Professor Thomas R. Morris of the University of Richmond, has commented that the "pre-Watergate mentality" evinced by Governor Wilder and other Virginia officeholders is both a cause and effect of the Commonwealth's failure to enact a comprehensive government ethics statute with teeth—one that would spell out specific standards of conduct and also provide for their effective enforcement.[7] Even before disclosures of illegal eavesdropping by associates of Senator Chuck Robb[8] and allegations of politically motivated

---

[7]Thomas R. Morris interview, February 14, 1991.

[8]Evidence of illegal eavesdropping through the interception of cellular telephone calls first became public on June 7, 1991, when it was revealed that Robb's Senate office had received, and for more than two years had retained, a recording of a controversial 1988 telephone conversation by then-Lt. Governor Douglas Wilder. Additional information concerning the source and scope of the eavesdropping and the involvement of Robb and his aides was emerging as this book went to press, as were details of Robb's recreational activities at Virginia Beach while governor.

activity by the state police rocked the Virginia political establishment in summer 1991, Dr. Morris observed that the time was fast approaching when ethics in government would become a major focus of political debate in Virginia. As in the aftermath of the Watergate scandal in 1974, the controversies that enveloped the Commonwealth's top elected officials in 1991 are certain to trigger citizen demands for new safeguards to ensure the integrity of public institutions and new measures to police the conduct of public officials. A return to Virginia's traditionally high standard of governmental integrity is a foremost priority, because the trust and confidence of the citizenry is a prerequisite for any effective government action.

Such challenging public problems as education, law enforcement, social services, transportation, economic development, environmental protection, government administration, and government ethics necessarily will occupy the attention of political leaders in coming years and decades. But Virginia politics in the 1990s and beyond also is likely to dwell on the vexing moral questions about life, liberty, and equality that have emerged and re-emerged, with changes mostly in form and context, since Jefferson penned the Declaration of Independence and Mason crafted the Virginia Declaration of Rights. Affirmative action, as noted previously, is one contemporary issue that poses such fundamental questions; abortion is another—and both seem certain to be subjects of intense political debate in the years ahead. The arguments for and against affirmative action reflect a conflict between contrasting visions of liberty and equality. The abortion issue, at bottom, involves conflicting moral views about life and liberty, and about which of those values should prevail when they collide. Perhaps because they involve such profound choices, both are sensitive subjects that many voters and politicians would like to avoid.[9]

With public and private use of racial preferences now commonplace in Virginia, the subject of affirmative action promises to loom large in the political discourse of the 1990s. Support for special treatment favoring traditionally victimized groups crept into American law and politics as a remedial notion—a temporary expedient designed to undo the effects of once-pervasive racial, ethnic, and gender discrimination. Though invidious discrimination is still with us, the array of legal tools to combat it today is formidable. And, as the period of enforced segregation and widespread discrimination has receded farther into the past, the remedial rationale for affirmative action has become progressively less plausible. Then, too, there are the destructive side-effects noted by Supreme Court Justice Lewis F. Powell, Jr.: "[P]referential programs may only reinforce common stereotypes holding that certain groups are unable to achieve success without special protection based on a factor having

---

[9]Political strategists have more practical reasons for concern about these issues. The abortion issue in recent years has tended to split the Republicans' moderate-conservative coalition; affirmative action tends to drive a wedge between moderate and liberal elements of the Democrats' center-left coalition.

no relationship to individual worth."[10] Increasingly, well-meaning citizens of both races are spotting the flaw inherent in the affirmative action concept: that our values and fundamental law accord primacy to the *individual* and recognize individual rights, not group entitlements. Any form of discrimination based on race is repugnant to the principle of individual liberty and thus detrimental to the ideal of equal opportunity.

Quotas and other preferential policies based on race do have their advocates, though such persons usually endeavor to mask rather than defend the policies. For those who favor preferential affirmative-action programs, equality is properly measured not in terms of individual opportunity, but in relation to the achievement of equal or proportional results for racial groups. So viewed, minority preferences are not a perversion of the ennobling, liberating purposes of the civil rights movement, but a logical extension of that struggle. As this debate is joined in the years ahead, each side will try to lay claim to the moral high ground, and each will seek to invoke the powerful symbolism of the civil rights movement. Notwithstanding their own painful history on matters racial, Virginians are unlikely to stand idle as this important chapter in the struggle for liberty and equality is written—nor should they. Least of all should Governor Wilder seek to side-step the issue, for, as the nation's highest-ranking black elected official, he is uniquely positioned to frame this debate in Virginia and across the country.

The debate over abortion policy also promises to remain an important part of the political discourse. Given the immense implications of the abortion question from a variety of moral, religious, social, scientific, and personal privacy perspectives, it is hardly surprising that strong opinions, emotional expressions, and divisive exchanges attend the debate. Though candidates of both political parties in Virginia—of late, Democrats—have benefited from the abortion controversy in various ways, no statewide officeholder in the Commonwealth has placed the issue atop his policy agenda. Indeed, few topics other than the weather have been discussed more and legislated less. The majority of Virginians remain ambivalent on the subject, and thus appear uncomfortable with both the strongly pro-life and pro-choice positions. If the U.S. Supreme Court gives the states greater leeway in fashioning abortion policy, it is probable that Virginia will move gradually from its current, quite liberal abortion law to a more centrist—and thus somewhat more restrictive—policy. Already, for example, a proposed legal requirement that parental consent be obtained before a minor may undergo an abortion procedure appears to enjoy broad public support. Pro-life politicians who eschew incremental legal changes and insist instead on a sweeping abortion ban are likely to repel many moderate voters, just as pro-choice politicians who insist upon preserving unfettered abortion prerogatives will risk being branded abortion-on-demand liberals. The political climate will counsel moderation even

---

[10]*University of California Regents* v. *Bakke*, 438 U.S. 265, 298 (1978).

as the battle for the hearts and minds of Virginians rages on the underlying moral and scientific question of when life begins.

Of moral issues, there will never be a shortage in politics; most law ultimately is a reflection of someone's view of morality. Nevertheless, the expression of political positions through moralistic rhetoric is risky business. In the 1980s, for example, large numbers of younger voters, especially in the swollen Virginia suburbs, reacted negatively to what they perceived as holier-than-thou preachments emanating from the evangelical and fundamentalist Right. A similar reaction can be expected in the future. That is not to say, however, that these suburban voters do not share the growing concern over the evident disintegration of moral consensus in modern society. Many children of the 1960s and 1970s are now parents striving to mold the characters and secure the futures of their own children. And, though these parents' libertarian impulses may be strong, such impulses do not render them immune from concerns about the values instilled in classrooms, or the impact of pop culture, or the easy availability of illegal drugs, or the undermining of key institutions that traditionally have inculcated values, such as churches, families, schools, and other cohesive communities.

The daunting task, even dilemma, facing political leaders is to give voice to these morally based concerns without seeming to moralize, and to promote a constructive response to the underlying problems without treading upon widely accepted notions of personal freedom. While statecraft may necessarily constitute "soulcraft," as philosopher-commentator George Will has argued,[11] the predominant Virginia view of the proper relation between religion and politics is perhaps best captured in a seldom-sung verse from a favorite patriotic anthem: "... America! America! God mend thine every flaw. Confirm thy soul in self-control; Thy liberty in law." If it is to be successful, Virginia's response to the pressing moral problems of the day must be fashioned principally in the hearts of its citizens, rather than in legislative halls.

Far from entering a "post-philosophical" era, as some pundits have predicted with the demise of communism, politics in the nation and in Virginia will continue to reflect the conflicting visions and values that have characterized the first two centuries of American self-governance. Notions of individualism and egalitarianism will coexist uneasily and collide often, as will the values of autonomy and community. The promise of "life, liberty and the pursuit of happiness" will mean starkly different things to different people. Though the death knell of communism represents a momentous victory for American ideals over a crude and hostile ideology, that historic development will serve to recast more than resolve the underlying debate. In America and around the world, the champions of opportunity, choice, and competitive

---

[11]See George F. Will, *Statecraft as Soulcraft* (New York: Simon and Schuster, 1983).

selection undoubtedly will continue to clash with the advocates of entitlement, conformity, and collective assurance. If the issues are clearly drawn—and that is no small "if"—there can be little doubt that Virginians will place themselves in the former camp.

Through 45 years of dramatic change in the Old Dominion, much has remained the same. From the New Deal to the Reagan Revolution, from the Byrd organization to the Robb coalition, from Ted Dalton to Richard Obenshain, and Governor Tuck to Governor Wilder, the Commonwealth's sudden, often surprising, political twists and turns have masked a more gradual and logical political, social, and economic evolution. A substantial partisan realignment has occurred, an era of vigorous two-party competition has arrived, and, through it all, many of the tenets that guide political behavior in the Commonwealth have emerged intact.

Most important, there remains even after this dynamic period an abiding conviction among Virginians that their Commonwealth possesses something unique, something of value, something worth preserving. In his Second Inaugural Address, Governor Godwin—the leader whose own reluctant and painful transfer of party allegiance epitomizes the historic political realignment that has occurred in Virginia—placed responsibility for the Commonwealth's future where it inevitably must lie. "Let us abandon the hunt for someone or something we can blame for whatever offends or aggrieves us," he declared. "Where the people govern, no citizen can hold himself completely blameless if government be found wanting."[12]

As a new generation of Virginians struggles to preserve the Commonwealth's distinctive heritage while adapting to the brisk winds of change, the challenges no doubt will be formidable. Political conflict, partisan and otherwise, will be sharp. But in this process the venerated tenets of individual freedom and responsibility, limited government, free enterprise, equal opportunity, public integrity, and private charity will find new expression. And, Virginians will affirm again the timeless wisdom of their state Constitution: "That no free government, nor the blessings of liberty, can be preserved to any people, but . . . by frequent recurrence to fundamental principles . . . ."[13]

---

[12]*Leadership in Crisis: Selected Statements and Speech Excerpts of The Honorable Mills E. Godwin, Jr., Governor of Virginia, 1974–1978*, p. vii.

[13]Constitution of Virginia, Art. I, §15.

Bibliography

Books and Articles

Abramowitz, Alan, McGlennon, John, and Rapoport, Ronald. "Voting in the Democratic Primary: The 1977 Virginia Gubernatorial Race," *Party Politics in the South*. New York: Praeger, 1981.

Abramowitz, Alan, McGlennon, John, and Rapoport, Ronald. *Party Activists in Virginia: A Study of Delegates to the 1978 Senatorial Nominating Conventions*. Charlottesville: Institute of Government, University of Virginia, 1981.

Atkinson, Frank B. "Dalton Taught State GOP How to Win," *The Richmond News Leader*, September 19, 1986.

Atkinson, Frank B. "The Reapportionment Dilemma: Lessons from the Virginia Experience," 68 *Virginia Law Review* 541-570, March 1982.

Baker, Donald P. *Wilder: Hold Fast to Dreams*. Cabin John, Maryland: Seven Locks Press, 1989.

Barkley, Numan V., and Graham, Hugh D. *Southern Politics and the Second Reconstruction*. Baltimore and London: The Johns Hopkins University Press, 1975.

Bass, Jack, and DeVries, Walter. *The Transformation of Southern Politics*. New York: Basic Books, Inc., 1976.

Beagle, Ben, and Osborne, Ozzie. *J. Lindsay Almond: Virginia's Reluctant Rebel*. Roanoke: Full Court Press, Inc., 1984.

Black, Earl, and Black, Merle. *Politics and Society in the South*. Cambridge, Mass.: Harvard University Press, 1987.

Black, Robert F., et al. "Rating the States," *U.S. News & World Report*, February 18, 1991.

Bugg, James L., Jr. "Mills Edwin Godwin, Jr.," *The Governors of Virginia 1860-1978*. Charlottesville: The University Press of Virginia, 1982.

Buni, Andrew. *The Negro in Virginia Politics, 1902-1965*. Charlottesville: The University Press of Virginia, 1967.

Butler, M. Caldwell, "A Republican Looks at the 1966 Virginia General Assembly," *University of Virginia News Letter*. Charlottesville: Institute of Government, University of Virginia, August 25, 1966.

Coleman, Marshall J. *Agenda for the '90s: Fulfilling Virginia's Promise.* Richmond: Coleman for Governor Campaign, 1988.

Cooper, Weldon, and Morris, Thomas R. *Virginia Government and Politics: Readings and Comments.* Charlottesville: The University Press of Virginia, 1976.

Crawley, William Bryan, Jr. *Bill Tuck: A Political Life in Harry Byrd's Virginia.* Charlottesville: The University Press of Virginia, 1978.

Crawley, William Bryan, Jr. *The Governorship of William M. Tuck, 1946–1950: Virginia Politics in the Golden Age of the Byrd Organization.* Unpublished Dissertation, University of Virginia, 1974.

Dabney, Virginius. *Virginia: The New Dominion.* New York: Doubleday and Company, 1971.

Darden, Colgate W., Jr. "Virginia's Indirect Debt," *University of Virginia News Letter.* Charlottesville: Institute of Government, University of Virginia, February 15, 1963.

Dent, Harry S. *The Prodigal South Returns to Power.* New York: John Wiley & Sons, 1978.

Dodson, Debra L., and Burnbauer, Laura D. *Election 1989: The Abortion Issue in New Jersey and Virginia.* Eagleton Institute of Politics, Rutgers, The State University of New Jersey, 1990.

Edds, Margaret. *Claiming the Dream: The Victorious Campaign of Douglas Wilder of Virginia.* Chapel Hill: Algonquin Books, 1990.

Eisenberg, Ralph. "Gubernatorial Politics in Virginia: The Experience of 1965," *University of Virginia News Letter.* Charlottesville: Institute of Government, University of Virginia, March 15, 1969.

Eisenberg, Ralph. "The Emergence of Two-Party Politics," *The Changing Politics of the South.* Baton Rouge: Louisiana State University Press, 1972.

Eisenberg, Ralph. "The Presidential Election in Virginia: A Political Omen?" *University of Virginia News Letter.* Charlottesville: Institute of Government, University of Virginia, April 15, 1965.

Eisenberg, Ralph. "1966 Politics in Virginia: The Elections for U.S. Senators," *University of Virginia News Letter.* Charlottesville: Institute of Government, University of Virginia, May 15, 1967.

Eisenberg, Ralph. "1966 Politics in Virginia: The Elections for U.S. House of Representatives," *University of Virginia News Letter.* Charlottesville: Institute of Government, University of Virginia, June 15, 1967.

Eisenberg, Ralph. "1969 Politics in Virginia: The Democratic Party Primary," *University of Virginia News Letter.* Charlottesville: Institute of Government, University of Virginia, February 15, 1970.

Eisenberg, Ralph. "1969 Politics in Virginia: The General Election," *University of Virginia News Letter.* Charlottesville: Institute of Government University of Virginia, May 15, 1970.

Eisenberg, Ralph. *Virginia Votes 1924–1968.* Charlottesville: The University Press of Virginia, 1971.

Ely, James W., Jr. "J. Lindsay Almond, Jr.," *The Governors of Virginia 1860–1978.* Charlottesville: The University Press of Virginia, 1982.

Ely, James W., Jr. *The Campaign for Massive Resistance: Virginia's Gubernatorial Election of 1957.* Unpublished Thesis, University of Virginia, 1968.

Ely, James W., Jr. *The Crisis of Conservative Virginia.* Knoxville: The University of Tennessee Press, 1976.

Epps, Garrett. "As Virginia Goes . . .," *The Washington Post Magazine,* January 25, 1981.

Franklin, Billy, and Tull, Judy. *Tough Enough: The Cocaine Investigation of United States Senator Chuck Robb.* Virginia Beach, Va.: Broad Bay Publishing Co., Inc., 1991.

Friddell, Guy. *Colgate Darden: Conversations with Guy Friddell.* Charlottesville: The University Press of Virginia, 1978.

Friddell, Guy. *What Is It About Virginia?* Richmond: The Dietz Press, Inc., 1983.

Goldwater, Barry M. *Goldwater.* New York: Doubleday, 1988.

Hall-Sizemore, Richard W. "Money in Politics: Financing the 1977 Statewide Elections in Virginia," *University of Virginia News Letter.* Charlottesville: Institute of Government, University of Virginia, August 1980.

Harwood, Richard. "Tilt! Tilt!," *The Washington Post,* November 19, 1989.

Hatch, Alden. *The Byrds of Virginia.* New York: Holt, Rinehart and Winston, 1969.

Havard, William C. (ed.). *The Changing Politics of the South.* Baton Rouge: Louisiana State University Press, 1972.

Henriques, Peter R. *John S. Battle and Virginia Politics: 1948–1953.* Unpublished Dissertation, University of Virginia, 1971.

Hershman, James Howard, Jr. *A Rumbling in the Museum: The Opponents of Virginia's Massive Resistance.* Unpublished Dissertation, University of Virginia, 1978.

Hunter, Jack R. *Linwood Holton's Long Quest for the Governorship of Virginia and its Impact on the Growth of the Republican Party.* Unpublished Thesis, University of Richmond, 1972.

Johnson, Steven Daniel. *Charles S. Robb and the Reserved Governorship.* Unpublished Dissertation, University of Virginia, 1990.

Kelley, George M. "The Changing Style of Virginia Politics," *University of Virginia News Letter.* Charlottesville: Institute of Government, University of Virginia, February 15, 1966.

Key, V.O., Jr. *Southern Politics in State and Nation.* New York: Alfred A. Knopf, Inc., 1949.

Kirk, Russell. *The Conservative Mind.* Chicago, Washington, D.C.: Regnery Gateway, Inc., 1987.

Latimer, James. "A Different Dominion: The Republican Renaissance," WCVE-TV, 1986 (videotape).

Latimer, James. "Living History Makers (Parts I and II)," WCVE-TV, 1975 (videotape).

Latimer, James. "Living History Makers, Part III: Harrison, Godwin and the 1960s," WCVE-TV, 1982 (videotape).

Latimer, James. *Virginia Politics 1950–1960.* Unpublished Manuscript, 1961.

Madison, James. *The Federalist* No. 48 (Chadwick ed.). Springfield, Va.: Global Affairs Publishing Company, 1987.

McDowell, Charles. "Notes from the Mountains and Valleys of Virginia on the Resurrection of the Grand Old Party and the Ambitions of Linwood Holton," *The Washingtonian*, September 1969.

Meiburg, Charles O. "The Average Virginian as Seen by the Census," *University of Virginia News Letter.* Charlottesville: Institute of Government, University of Virginia, February 15, 1973.

Miller, Francis Pickens. *Man from the Valley.* Chapel Hill: University of North Carolina Press, 1971.

Moger, Allen W. *Virginia: Bourbonism to Byrd, 1870–1925.* Charlottesville: The University Press of Virginia, 1968.

Morris, Thomas R. "The Office of Attorney General in Virginia," *University of Virginia News Letter.* Charlottesville: Institute of Government, University of Virginia, April 1980.

Morris, Thomas R. *The Virginia Supreme Court: An Institutional and Political Analysis.* Charlottesville: The University Press of Virginia, 1975.

Morris, Thomas R., and Sabato, Larry J. *Virginia Government and Politics.* Charlottesville: The Virginia Chamber of Commerce and the Center for Public Service, University of Virginia, 1990.

Muse, Benjamin. *Virginia's Massive Resistance.* Gloucester, Mass.: Peter Smith, 1969.

Peirce, Neal R. *The Border South States.* New York: W.W. Norton and Company, 1975.

Roebuck, James Randolph, Jr. *Virginia in the Election of 1948.* Unpublished Thesis, University of Virginia, 1969.

Roland, Charles P. *The Improbable Era: The South Since World War II.* Lexington, Ky.: The University Press of Kentucky, 1976.

Rubin, Louis D., Jr. *Virginia: A History.* New York: W.W. Norton and Company, 1977.

Rutland, Robert Allen. *James Madison: The Founding Father.* New York: MacMillan Publishing Company, 1987.

Sabato, Larry J. *Aftermath of "Armageddon": An Analysis of the 1973 Gubernatorial Election.* Charlottesville: Institute of Government, University of Virginia, 1975.

Sabato, Larry J. *PAC Power: Inside the World of Political Action Committees.* New York and London: W.W. Norton & Company, 1984.

Sabato, Larry J. *The Democratic Party Primary in Virginia: Tantamount to Election No Longer.* Charlottesville: The University Press of Virginia, 1977.

Sabato, Larry J. *The Rise of Political Consultants*. New York: Basic Books, Inc., Publishers, 1981.

Sabato, Larry J. "The 1989 House of Delegates Contests," *Virginia Government and Politics*. Charlottesville: The Virginia Chamber of Commerce and the Center for Public Service, University of Virginia, 1990.

Sabato, Larry J. "Virginia Governor's Race, 1989; Part 1: The Nomination Stage," *University of Virginia News Letter*. Charlottesville: Center for Public Service, University of Virginia, July 1989.

Sabato, Larry J. "Virginia Governor's Race, 1989; Part 2: The General Election," *University of Virginia News Letter*. Charlottesville: Center for Public Service, University of Virginia, January 1990.

Sabato, Larry J. "Virginia Governor's Race, 1989; Part 3: General Election Issues," *University of Virginia News Letter*. Charlottesville: Center for Public Service, University of Virginia, February 1990.

Sabato, Larry J. *Virginia Votes 1969–1974*. Charlottesville: Institute of Government, University of Virginia, 1976.

Sabato, Larry J. *Virginia Votes 1975–1978*. Charlottesville: Institute of Government, University of Virginia, 1979.

Sabato, Larry J. *Virginia Votes 1979–1982*. Charlottesville: Institute of Government, University of Virginia, 1983.

Sabato, Larry J. *Virginia Votes 1983–1986*. Charlottesville: Institute of Government, University of Virginia, 1987.

Sabato, Larry J. *Virginia Votes 1987–1990*. Charlottesville: Center for Public Service, University of Virginia, 1991 (forthcoming).

Seagull, Louis M. *Southern Republicanism*. Cambridge, Mass.: Schenkman Publishing Co., Inc., 1975.

Serow, William J. "Population Change in Virginia, 1960–1970," *University of Virginia News Letter*. Charlottesville: Institute of Government, University of Virginia, May 15, 1971.

Serow, William J. and Meiburg, Charles O. "The Average Virginian as Seen by the Census," *University of Virginia News Letter*. Charlottesville: Institute of Government, University of Virginia, February 15, 1973.

Steed, Robert, Moreland, Laurence W., and Baker, Tod (eds.). *Party Politics in the South*. New York: Praeger, 1981.

Strong, Donald S. *Urban Republicanism in the South*. Birmingham: Birmingham Printing Co., 1960.

Taylor, Elizabeth. *Elizabeth Takes Off*. New York: The Berkley Publishing Group, 1987.

Tilley, B. Scott. *Richard Obenshain: Visionary and Engineer of the Rise of the Republican Party in Virginia*. Unpublished Paper, University of Virginia, 1988.

Turk, James C. "A Republican Looks at the 1970 Virginia General Assembly," *University of Virginia News Letter*. Charlottesville: Institute of Government, University of Virginia, August 15, 1970.

Virkler, John Stanley. *Richard Obenshain: Architect of the Republican Triumph in Virginia.* Unpublished Thesis, Auburn University, 1987.

Vogt, George L. *The Development of Virginia's Republican Party.* Unpublished Dissertation, University of Virginia, 1978.

Walker, Alexander J. "The Virginia Congressional Delegation Since 1965," *University of Virginia News Letter.* Charlottesville: Institute of Government, University of Virginia, October 1978.

Whitehurst, G. William. *Diary of a Congressman.* Norfolk: The Donning Company, 1983.

Wilhoit, Francis M. *The Politics of Massive Resistance.* New York: George Braziller, Inc., 1973.

Wilkinson, J. Harvie, III. *Harry Byrd and the Changing Face of Virginia Politics, 1945–1966.* Charlottesville: The University Press of Virginia, 1968.

Wilkinson, J. Harvie, III. "Linwood Holton," *The Governors of Virginia 1860–1978.* Charlottesville: The University Press of Virginia, 1982.

Will, George F. *Statecraft as Soulcraft.* New York: Simon and Schuster, 1983.

Wood, Deborah L. *Summary of Interview with D. Dortch Warriner.* Unpublished Paper, Republican Party of Virginia Archives, 1979.

Wood, Deborah L. *Summary of Interview with Glen Williams.* Unpublished Paper, Republican Party of Virginia Archives, 1979.

Wood, Deborah L. *Summary of Interview with I. Lee Potter.* Unpublished Paper, Republican Party of Virginia Archives, 1979.

Wood, Deborah L. *Summary of Interview with Linwood Holton.* Unpublished Paper, Republican Party of Virginia Archives, 1979.

Yancey, Dwayne. *When Hell Froze Over.* Roanoke: Taylor Publishing Company, 1988.

Younger, Edward, and Moore, James Tice (eds.). *The Governors of Virginia 1860–1978.* Charlottesville: The University Press of Virginia, 1982.

Government Publications

Leadership in Crisis: Selected Statements and Speech Excerpts of The Honorable Mills E. Godwin, Jr., Governor of Virginia, 1974–1978. Richmond: Commonwealth of Virginia.

Official Election Results. Richmond: Virginia State Board of Elections, 1977.

Official Election Results. Richmond: Virginia State Board of Elections, 1981.

Official Election Results. Richmond: Virginia State Board of Elections, 1985.

Official Election Results. Richmond: Virginia State Board of Elections, 1989.

Selected Speeches of The Honorable Mills E. Godwin, Jr., Governor of Virginia, 1966–1970. Richmond: Commonwealth of Virginia.

Votes Cast for Governor, Lieutenant Governor and Attorney General, General Election, November 7, 1961. Richmond: Division of Purchase and Printing, Commonwealth of Virginia, 1962.

Votes Cast for Governor, Lieutenant Governor and Attorney General, General Election, November 2, 1965. Richmond: Division of Purchase and Printing, Commonwealth of Virginia, 1966.

Judicial Decisions

Reynolds v. *Sims*, 377 U.S. 533 (1964).
Roe v. *Wade*, 410 U.S. 113 (1973).
University of California Regents v. *Bakke*, 438 U.S. 265 (1978).
Webster v. *Reproductive Health Services*, 109 S.Ct. 3040 (1989).

Newspapers

The Chesterfield Gazette.
Danville Register.
Norfolk Journal and Guide.
The Radford Journal.
Richmond Times-Dispatch.
Roanoke Times & World-News.
The Daily Press.
The Richmond News Leader.
The Virginian-Pilot and The Ledger-Star.
The Washington Post.
The Washington Times.
Washington Star.

Interviews

Abbitt, Watkins M., June 13, 1980.
Alderson, John E., Jr., September 24, 1984.
Bateman, Herbert H., June 11, 1980, and September 18, 1984.
Battle, William C., November 4, 1988.
Bayliss, William, June 20, 1980.
Bemiss, FitzGerald, June 5, 1980.
Bliley, Thomas J., Jr., September 18, 1984.
Boushall, Thomas C., June 6, 1980.
Brinkley, Arthur S., Jr., July 1, 1980.
Broyhill, Joel T., April 11, 1984.
Butler, M. Caldwell, April 5, 1984.
Byrd, Harry F., Jr., March 12, 1984, and February 1, 1989.
Byrd, Thomas T., February 1, 1989.
Callahan, Vincent F., Jr., May 29, 1980.
Canada, A. Joe, Jr., June 12, 1980.
Carico, Melville "Buster", June 16, 1980.
Coleman, J. Marshall, June 4, 1980, and September 17, 1984.

Corber, Robert J. "Jack", May 27, 1980.

Craigie, Walter W., Jr., September 19, 1984.

Cramer, Alfred B., III, June 19, 1980, and September 27, 1984.

Curtis, Carl, February 10, 1989.

Dabney, Virginius, June 23, 1980.

Dalton, John N., July 1, 1980, and September 10, 1984.

Dalton, Theodore Roosevelt "Ted", June 17, 1980.

Davis, Jack, July 24, 1980.

Dawbarn, H. Dunlop "Buz", June 21, 1980.

DeBolt, Edward S., June 18, 1985.

Dent, Harry S., October 26, 1988.

Dovel, I. Randolph, June 20, 1980.

Durrette, Wyatt B., Jr., June 26, 1980, and September 28, 1984.

Echols, M. Patton, Jr. May 30, 1980.

Edwards, Paul, June 3, 1980.

Farley, Guy O., Jr., May 29, 1980, and September 17, 1984.

Ferebee, J. Smith, June 4, 1980, and August 30, 1984.

Franklin, Anson, June 4, 1980, and September 17, 1984.

French, Warren, June 18, 1980.

Gambill, Walter, June 2, 1980.

Garland, Ray L., June 17, 1980.

Giesen, Arthur R. "Pete", June 19, 1980.

Godwin, Mills E., Jr., September 9, 1979, September 18, 1984, and May 8, 1990.

Gravely, Jack, June 3, 1980.

Green, George Mason, Jr., May 28, 1980.

Gregson, Jeff, September 28, 1984.

Harrison, Albertis S., June 13, 1980.

Helms, Jesse, January 31, 1989.

Henderson, Horace E. "Hunk", June 12, 1980.

Hoffman, Walter E., June 3, 1980.

Holton, A. Linwood, May 28, 1980, and April 19, 1990.

Howell, Henry E., June 12, 1980.

Huffman, Donald W., August 20, 1984.

Hurd, William H., May 4, 1989.

Kellam, Sidney, June 10, 1980.

Klinge, J. Kenneth, May 27, 1980, and August 30, 1984.

Lampe, Virginia "Ginny", July 2, 1980.

Lane, Edward E., June 3, 1980.

Lewis, Lawrence, Jr., November 2, 1988.

Lihn, Charles, September 28, 1984.

Lowance, Carter O., June 11, 1980.

Loyacono, Joe, September 21, 1984.

Mackenzie, Ross, June 23, 1980

McDowell, Charles, Jr., July 3, 1980.

McMath, George N., August 19, 1980.

Miller, Andrew P., July 24, 1980.

Miller, Bruce C., July 2, 1980.

Miller, J. Clifford, Jr., June 2, 1980.

Miller, Nathan H., June 19, 1980, and September 20, 1984.

Morris, Thomas R., February 14, 1991.

Mulligan, Hugh, January 10, 1991.

Newman, Cynthia, July 2, 1980.

Obenshain, Mrs. Richard D. "Helen", June 30, 1980.

Parris, Stanford E., September 26, 1984.

Peachee, Judy F., September 14, 1979, August 30, 1984, and September 20, 1984.

Pearson, H. Clyde, June 17, 1980.

Perper, Martin, June 25, 1980.

Pickett, Owen B., September 19, 1984.

Poage, Richard C., June 24, 1980.

Poff, Richard H., April 12, 1984.

Pollard, Fred G., June 4, 1980.

Potter, I. Lee, May 28, 1980.

Rains, Alan T., Jr., July 3, 1980.

Ritchie, John, June 30, 1980.

Robb, Charles S., October 5, 1984.

Robinson, J. Kenneth, September 26, 1984.

Rolfe, Shelley, June 5, 1980.

Royall, William A., June 5, 1980.

Russell, Robert E., August 30, 1984, and March 11, 1991.

Scott, William L., May 28, 1980.

Shafran, George, May 27, 1980.

Short, Richard T., June 10, 1980, and August 26, 1988.

Shull, Edd, May 27, 1980.

Slaughter, D. French, Jr., June 18, 1980.

Smith, W. Roy, July 21, 1980, and October 8, 1984.

Spong, William B., Jr., September 23, 1985.

Stanhagen, William, September 27, 1984.

Thornton, William S., June 3, 1980.

Thurmond, J. Strom, January 31, 1989.

Trible, Paul S., Jr., September 17, 1984.

Wampler, William C., February 22, 1984.

Warner, John W., June 27, 1980, and May 17, 1990.
Warriner, D. Dortch, October 26, 1979, and August 30, 1984.
Wessells, John, July 15, 1980.
Wheat, James C., Jr., June 24, 1980.
Wilkinson, J. Harvie, III, March 10, 1980.
Willey, Edward E., Jr., June 6, 1980.
Williams, Lewis H., June 4, 1980, and August 30, 1984.

Index